MANAGEMENT
Concepts and Controversies

MANAGEMENT
Concepts and Controversies

EDITED BY
Joseph A. Litterer
UNIVERSITY OF MASSACHUSETTS

John Wiley & Sons
SANTA BARBARA • NEW YORK • CHICHESTER • BRISBANE • TORONTO
A Wiley/Hamilton Publication

Library of Congress Cataloging in Publication Data
Main entry under title:

Management: concepts and controversies.

   "A Wiley/Hamilton publication."
   1.   Management—Addresses, essays, lectures.
2.   Organization—Addresses, essays, lectures.
I.   Litterer, Joseph August, 1926–
HD31.M29177   658.4   77-20031
ISBN 0-471-03611-0

Printed in the United States of America
10 9 8 7 6 5 4 3 2 1

About the Author

Joseph A. Litterer is professor of management at the University of Massachusetts, Amherst. Before coming to Amherst, Professor Litterer was professor of business administration at the University of Illinois, Urbana.

Dr. Litterer's work has as its focus, management practices and organizations. He is the author of a number of books including *The Analysis of Organizations; Organizations: Structure and Behavior; Organizations: Systems, Adaptation, and Growth; Managing for Organizational Effectiveness;* and *An Introduction to Management. Analysis of Organizations* received the Organization Development Council Medal for the best book in 1965.

Dr. Litterer has been President of the Academy of Management and Chairman of the College on Organizations of the Institute of Management Science.

Preface

Books of readings in management are usually intended to supplement available textbooks. So too with this set of readings (i.e., *An Introduction to Management* Litterer, Wiley/Hamilton, 1978). Books of readings in management are usually intended to supplement either by providing additional material for deeper exploration of topics or to permit coverage of topics not conveniently included in texts. Neither of these is true of this set of readings.

The intent of this anthology, quite simply, is to provoke, stimulate, and challenge. The ultimate objectives are not to frustrate or to be an academic gadfly, but rather to create interest and to keep the study of management in a healthy perspective. Any text, because of the need for coherency in writing and because of the fact that the contents are strained through one person's mind is bound to homogenize material and to blur issues. This may be necessary when first studying a topic to avoid confusion. Later, however, this needs to be altered to develop a more mature understanding of the subject. Our knowledge of management is not homogenous, the subject matter is not fully integrated. This is frustrating, but it is also a fact. Management is too complex and is growing and changing rapidly for a coherent subject matter to be possible.

This anthology deliberately focuses on those areas of management where issues are not clear but where answers to vital questions are vigorously sought. The objective is to help the reader become aware of the breadth of problems that faces management and that there are sound, thoughtful but nonetheless conflicting positions on many issues. There is no authority to turn to for an answer. Each person must make up his own mind.

What are the major concepts and controversies that should be included in an anthology such as this? There are many answers and, in fact, this editor has several sets of answers himself. There are so many matters to be dealt with there is no hope of being representative or complete. I do think all matters included here are important and that the articles are both solid in content and well written. They will, I believe, give the reader an appreciation of how challenging and vital the issues are that face practicing managers.

Papers included in this anthology are organized by concept and controversy (for example Part IV, People in Organizations includes an article on sex and race discrimination in business). Usually there is one article on each side of the argument, but occasionally we find a three-way discussion.

The anthology then, is an invitation to join a vital dialogue with some of the best thinkers in management, the social sciences, business and public affairs on some of the most pressing issues facing management and our society today.

December, 1977

Joseph A. Litterer

Introduction

One risks being a bore to observe that our world is becoming more complex. We have all thought or been told that too many times for this to be a fresh and exciting observation. What is exciting are the challenges and demands, the problems and the opportunities this increasingly complex world brings us.

With the possible exception of people in political office it is hard to think of any group of people who deal more directly and extensively with this increasing social complexity than managers. At one time, perhaps, a business could operate as a fairly self-contained entity producing its products and hopefully making a profit with few constraints but the availability of resources, the extent of the market and the native capabilities of the managers and/or owners. Commodore Vanderbilt is reputed to have said, "The public be damned." No longer. Firms today are required both by law and social pressure to be concerned with the effects of their actions on customers, employees, the environment, and even their competitors. Firms are being required to take actions to support overall goals and objectives of our society. They are increasingly being required to develop affirmative action plans to change the racial, sexual, and ethnic composition of their work force. They are urged and encouraged through tax and other incentives to build plants in urban areas, when they might otherwise have located them in more remote, rural areas.

But these matters, of direct impact on businesses, are but the tip of the iceberg when compared to the wide array of more subtle factors managers today must take into account. A short war between Israel and some of its Arab neighbors can upset the whole world's economic and energy situation. Firms that operate overseas find they can be severely criticized in this country for following what are accepted as normal business practices in the host country. The list is endless.

To have any understanding of management today it is necessary to understand not only what management does and how it goes about its work, but also the complex problems and challenges it faces.

This book brings together some of the issues and conflicts that face management. These questions are complex. What is to be done is not at all clear. In fact, in many instances not even the nature of the problem is clear. The writers presented here offer diverse viewpoints on these complex problems. Serious thought has been given to them. We may not find agreed-upon solutions in their writings, but through their disagreement we can come to a better understanding of the issues involved.

Some of the writers in this book are addressing one side or another of a conflict. Others are addressing issues that need attention. All are concerned with matters of immediate or long run importance to managers. Together they give a picture of the diversity and complexity of issues confronting modern managers.

Contents

INTRODUCTION

I MANAGEMENT—WHOM DOES IT SERVE?
  Lilienthal, David E., *Management Leadership as a*
    Humanist Art   3
  Hart, David K. and Scott, William G.,
    The Organizational Imperative   15

II ORGANIZATIONS
  A. *Are There Organization Men?*
    Whyte, William H., *Selections from* The Organization Man
      The Pipe Line   37
      The "Well-rounded" Man   54
    Porter, Lyman, *Where Is the Organization Man?*   62

  B. *Are Organizations Healthy for People?*
    Argyris, Chris, *Personality vs Organization*   79
    Strauss, George, *The Personality vs Organization*
      Hypothesis   97
  C. *Is Bureaucracy Disappearing?*
    Bennis, Warren G., *The Coming Death of Bureaucracy*   109
    Miewald, Robert D., *The Greatly Exaggerated*
      Death of Bureaucracy   120

III MANAGERS MANAGING
  A. *Perspective on Management*
    Carlisle, Arthur Elliot, *MacGregor*   133
    Wilson, Charles R., *Turf vs Systems:*
      Two Management Styles   148
    Lazarus, Ralph, *The Case of the Oriental Rug*   154
    Burns, Thomas S., *Line and Staff at ITT*   162

   B. *Managers and Management Science*
      Grayson, Jackson C., *Management Science and*
         Business Practice   171
      Zeleny, Milan, *Managers Without Management Science*   183
   C. *Managers Approaching Their Work*
      Jay, Antony, *Who Knows What Primitive Instincts Lurk*
         in the Heart of Modern Corporation Man?   193
      Leavitt, Harold, *Beyond the Analytic Manager: Part I*   207
      Hellriegel, Don and Slocum, John W. Jr.,
         Managerial Problem Solving Styles   220
   D. *Careers in Management*
      Webber, Ross, *Career Problems of Young Managers*   233
      Shetty, Y. K., and Peery, Newman S. Jr.,
         Are Top Executives Transferable Across Companies?   257

IV PEOPLE IN ORGANIZATIONS
   A. *Motivating and Developing Personnel*
      Albrook, Robert C., *Participative Management:*
         Time for a Second Look   267
      Lakin, Martin, *Some Ethical Issues in*
         Sensitivity Training   282
   B. *The Strategy of Job Enlargement*
      Ford, Robert N., *Job Enrichment Lessons from AT&T*   292
      Sayles, Leonard R., *Job Enrichment:*
         Little that's New—and Right for the Wrong Reasons   309
   C. *Sex and Race Discrimination in Business Management*
      Silberman, Charles E., *Black Economic Gains—*
         Impressive but Precarious   318
      Still More Room at the Top   324

V MANAGERS AND SOCIAL ISSUES
   A. *What Should Management's Social Responsibilities Be?*
      Petit, Thomas A., *The Doctrine of Socially*
         Responsible Management   331
      Phillips, Charles F. Jr., *What is Wrong with*
         Profit Maximization?   339
      Lodge, George C., *Business and The Changing Society*   351
   B. Social Values for Business
      Cassell, Frank, *The Corporation and Community:*
         Realities and Myths   371
      Nehemkis, Peter, *Business Payoffs Abroad:*
         Rhetoric and Reality   385

VI MANAGEMENT IN OTHER CULTURES
   Burck, Gilbert, *A Socialist Enterprise That Acts*
      Like a Fierce Capitalist Competitor   413
   Diebold, John, *Management Can Learn From Japan*   429
   Kraar, Louis, *I Have Seen China—and They Work*   434

VII LOOKING AHEAD

Drucker, Peter, *New Needs and New Approaches*   447
Perrow, Charles, *Is Business Really Changing?*   458
Murthy, K. R. Srinivasa and Salter, Malcolm S.,
    Should CEO Pay Be Linked To Results   475
Burgen, Carl G., *The Scenario for Tomorrow's Executive*   486
Ross-Skinner, Jean, *European Executives: Union Now*   491
Leavitt, Harold, *Beyond the Analytic Manager: Part II*   498

Index   515

I | MANAGEMENT–WHOM DOES IT SERVE?

Managers are seen quite differently in different parts of the world. In Japan they are seen as a highly respected professional group. In other places they are looked upon as rapacious pirates—to be tolerated, but of low social standing. In the United States, seen everywhere as the home of the modern manager, the stature of and respect for the manager has slipped considerably from its once high position. Today for many reasons many people feel that U.S. managers are indifferent to the needs of society as a whole, and that they serve only their own interests, or perhaps at best, those of the organizations that employ them.

In the first selection, David Lilienthal, one of the most successful managers of our times, talks about management leadership as a humanistic art. He is looking at the roles managers can play in the broad social issues of our times. As the original head of the TVA, Lilienthal guided its development into one of the most extensive and successful public service corporations of all time. He later directed private business organizations, and most recently has been applying his own managerial expertise and that of others to a host of complex social problems around the world. He speaks to us thoughtfully from a wealth of experience.

In the second selection, Hart and Scott look at managers both as the creators and operators of organizations, and thus both as their masters and their servants. From some basic observations, they carefully conclude the manager can have no other logical or legitimate role than to serve the needs of the organization. They would seem to argue that management is not a humanistic art but an organizational art.

What do you think?

DAVID E. LILIENTHAL

Management Leadership as a Humanist Art

The central motif of these three lectures is an effort to redefine the role and function of the modern manager. The manager's function, basically, is to get things done, to make things happen. But to make things happen by virtue of his special human qualities: his capacity to lead and inspire and move other men to act. In the opening lecture, I proposed such a redefinition, calling it the highest form of the managerial function and suggesting that that function be regarded as a humanist rather than merely a technical skill.

The highest and truest managerial function is leadership in the crisis areas of human life today, areas in which the decisive need is for those human qualities which managerial talent at its best exhibits: the capacity to get things done by an understanding of people and a capacity to persuade and to move them. In this lecture I pursue this theme further, and will also seek to apply this redefinition to some of the acute issues in our own country, such as water and air pollution, urban elephantiasis, and other pressing American issues.

The importance of the manager's function is not something new, not something arising out of the coming of modern industry and government. The nature of the function changes, sometimes radically, as the society of which it is a central fact changes. I suggest that it is worth our while to take a look at the history of the managerial

Source: David E. Lilienthal, *Management: A Humanistic Art*, Pittsburgh, Carnegie Institute of Technology, 1967, pp. 26-40. Copyright © Carnegie-Mellon University Press.

function, to give us a better perspective on the present and the future. So I shall divert your attention momentarily for a quick glance at that history.

I spoke of the necessity for perspective. But obtaining perspective is not an easy thing. I had a lesson in perspective from a little old lady in the mountains of western North Carolina, the wife of the keeper of a rather primitive ferry across a stream in that part of the country. A group of engineers and I from the TVA were on our way one evening to the site of a new dam; we knew that we had a stream to cross in that ferry. But we got to talking and didn't pay much attention, and the first thing we knew we'd driven our car right smack in the middle of this river; it took quite a while to get it pulled out. I was delegated to go up to the ferry keeper's house and tell him what we thought of him. So I knocked on the door and a sweet little old lady said, "What's the matter?" And I said, "What's the matter? We just drove into the river. You keep a ferry here. Why don't you put up a big sign, 'River Ahead,' so a fellow would know." And she said, "God a-mighty, mister, if you couldn't see the river, you couldn't see the sign."

Beginning about ten years ago the management company which I head has been deeply involved in a vast area of the Mesopotamian plains in Persia—or Iran, as it's often called—the eastern part of the Fertile Crescent of ancient days; the land that in the Old Testament is called Elam. There we have been responsible for devising a program for the restoration of a very large region, including responsibility for the design and erection of one of the world's highest dams, of irrigation canals, the working out of new land cropping patterns, the training of Persian farmers in agriculture and in health, to restore the land's productivity and the people's health; and also concerned with electric power in large quantities, so as to bring that region into the industrialized 20th Century. In this huge enterprise the modern manager's function is a central part of the task. But the point I wish to make now is that thousands of years ago, in this very area where civilization is said to have had its beginnings, it was managers who made that beginning of civilization a reality.

In a recent scholarly work, Professor McNeill of the University of Chicago refers to the very beginnings of organized agriculture and community life on this planet, which occurred, he and other scholars say, in Mesopotamia thousands of years ago. Then he has this to say about the role of the manager in that dawn of civilization (I am now quoting from Professor McNeill's book, *The Rise of the West*): "Irrigation was vital to early civilization because it put the production of a regular agricultural surplus easily within the reach of primitive farmers." I think if Professor McNeill had been working with primitive farmers, as I have, he would have stricken the word "easily"; but it certainly put it within the reach of farmers. "Even more important," he goes on to say, "by requiring very massive coordination of social effort, irrigation facilitated the creation of a social engine for the concentration of surplus foods *in the hands of a managerial group*. And once the body of managers had established its right to collect a part of the farmers' surplus crops, growing numbers of men could be employed not only to dig canals, but also to elaborate the cult of the god, to undertake military enterprises, and to specialize as craftsmen, artists, or musicians: to create, in short, a civilization. . . . Without the necessity of organized large-scale collective effort on canals and dikes," Dr. McNeill continues, "a managerial group could not establish control over whatever surplus may have been available."* (My italics)

So I think it can be said that the managerial function has indeed remote historic antecedents. But in some parts of the world, that role is now outmoded. Only ten years ago, when our company first began work in Persia on the Mesopotamian plains of which Professor McNeill writes, the managerial group, the large landowners, were exercising essentially an autocratic managerial function and authority over the people on the land and the fruits of their labor. The peasants, many of them, were still using methods less productive than those in the days of Hammurabi, centuries and centuries ago. In the past ten years, the beginning of a new kind of managerial role has come to that ancient beginning point of civilization. A very different concept of the manager is emerging in Persia, taking the place of the landowner as manager.

In our own country, and within the memory of many of my generation, the manager's function was also essentially an autocratic one. That function in the early decades of this century in America was generally not leadership by persuasion or inspiration or participation, but by authority and by command. It is worthwhile to remind ourselves of this older concept of the manager's function to help give perspective to the new.

As a youth I lived for a time in Gary, Indiana, where only a few years before the United States Steel Corporation had established a great steel complex on the shores of Lake Michigan. A new city, Gary, was created essentially by the decision of one strong and very able man, Judge Elbert Gary. The hours of labor—seven days a week and twelve hours a day—the rate of pay and the conditions of living of the labor force were matters the manager's group decided. As I learned at firsthand two or three years later, as a cub reporter on a Gary newspaper,

*W.H. McNeill, *The Rise of the West.* Mentor edition (1965), pp. 80, 81.

the political life of Gary also was largely determined by the managerial group of U.S. Steel. There was no need to get the approval of anyone, whether the question was conditions of safety or health in the mills, or the educational system provided for the city of Gary—which incidentally was an unusually good one.

Gary and its new mills represented the usual pattern of the managerial role of those days. All over America, at that time, it was this power to decide, often benevolently, often ruthlessly, but always without having to consult its work force, or to heed public opinion, or seek to persuade or consult any public authority, that wrought a kind of physical miracle in our land: the creation of America's industrial sinews. And just as the managerial group of ancient Mesopotamia made possible the development of a higher standard of living, of cultivation of the arts, and the capacity to defend against enemies, so those early days in our own history have made possible the kind of developed and developing country we have become, and will increasingly become.

But times have changed since the early decades of this century, and with time the very nature of the managerial function has changed. Contrast Gary and the establishment of that steel mill more than 50 years ago with the decision of the Bethlehem Steel Co. to erect a steel complex at Burns Creek on Lake Michigan, not far from Gary. The function of the Bethlehem managers in the 1960's was not simply to decide, but to persuade, to lead and move the minds of many people, at every step, on almost every conceivable subject. For example, some people thought that the Bethlehem mills at Burns Harbour would destroy an important scenic and recreational resource, the sand dunes that in Judge Gary's day were considered by most people as simply wasteland, their use of no possible concern to anyone but U.S. Steel. The impairment of a scenic resource is wholly unrelated to the economics and the technical aspects of steel making. Yet it became a major public issue in recent years, widely debated in Congress and in the press, and before the Bethlehem mill could be built many people had to be persuaded on this issue.

Or take water and air pollution: When I was a young man in Gary the ovens and furnaces poured great wastes into the atmosphere. Lake Michigan's waters were used, in huge quantities, in steel making with scant thought by the managerial group of the effect on the purity of Lake Michigan for water supply and recreation. Judge Gary, I daresay, would have been aghast at the notion that health officials or the general public must be consulted about how that mill was run. Yet today Bethlehem (and U.S. Steel also, I'm sure) has invested large sums to minimize pollution of the air and water, and they are proud enough of their public outlook to advertise this fact widely. Keeping air and water pollution at minimum levels has become a part of the modern concept of the manager's function, and persuading the public and the health authorities that its efforts are effective is no longer considered an outrageous invasion of the function of the manager. This change in outlook is a revolution in managerial concepts.

But there are other parts of the world—notably in the underdeveloped countries, and in some parts of Europe as well—where the manager's function is still that of dictation, and where the manager is typically not a leader but an order-er. This we sometimes forget as a changed America struggles with the problems of communicating with and understanding and doing business with some of these countries that are still living in that world we have left behind.

The nature of the manager's job in the days of Judge Gary was different because the society was different. What constituted a successful "job of doing," i.e., of management, was utterly different than it is today. Driving the job through, regardless, was the test of the manager.

The modern manager in our American society is a quite different kind of man because the society is so changed it is hardly recognizable. Now the modern manager must and usually does take the broad public interest and public opinion into account. The successful manager of today needs a range of understanding, of stamina and above all ability to lead and persuade and motivate and induce agreement beyond anything ever laid on the shoulders of any manager in all history. What the manager, particularly in what I've called the risk areas, the crisis areas, must know, has become all encompassing. The specialist and the expert must know some things intimately; the new manager that I am describing, to perform well, must know almost everything well.

The manager must have knowledge of technical and scientific developments of many kinds. If he is engaged in industry, he must consult and persuade labor organizations. If his responsibilities reach overseas—and with the internationalization of business they are likely to—he must have a grasp of foreign affairs, be aware of the culture and the sensibilities of those in the countries in which his managerial function is exercised. If he takes on foreign partners, as is becoming increasingly true in large enterprises, he must have knowledge of business conditions and business ethics, or public opinion and cultures in those countries too. And here at home, such intense social and human issues as providing economic opportunities for Negroes become part of the range of understanding he must somehow have at his command.

But far more than broad knowledge or great skills in harmonizing divergent interests is demanded in my concept of the new manager. To be a mediator or conciliator between people or interests is not the heart of the new managerial function. For the manager, in the great and urgent tasks of manhood, is a man responsible *for making things happen* in the areas of venture, of social entrepreneurship. He is dealing, under the pressure of events, with other human beings. And, therefore, whatever the particular subject matter, he must possess the personal, emotional, and imaginative qualities that move other people, that enable him to motivate and induce them not only to agreement *but to action.*

In the past fifteen years or so, a great deal of emphasis has been put on surveys, on great masses of "facts," on feasibility studies, and prefeasibility studies and studies of studies, on systems analysis and analysis of systems analysis, on "Plans" (with a capital "P"). Clearly there is a great value in such studies, if done with good sense. But the degree of confidence some people tend to put in their magic is misplaced. This intense preoccupation with survey-itis grows, I think in some cases, out of a lack of awareness that it is action by people, by individuals, that is central to the management function. And to move and motivate people, the manager must be a man who has a good understanding of them. This kind of leadership calls for a human capacity to interpret the desires and emotions of others, and to convey a realistic picture of these desires to others.

Recently Secretary Gardner, former head of the Carnegie Corporation (a foundation devoted to education), and now the head of a very sprawling department of our government, Health, Education and Welfare, referred to what he called the "new twists" being added to the modern art of what he called "how to reach decisions without really deciding," the devising of "elaborate statistical systems, cost-account systems, information-processing systems, hoping that out of them will come unassailable support for one course of action or another." We must beware lest we breed a narrow stratum of people who are smart and facile—and insensitive to the springs of action within human beings; insensitive to human emotion.

If I were asked what I have learned, or what I think I have learned, about the managerial process over the past thirty years and about the dynamics of change with which the managerial life must deal, I would put it this way:

The greatest of all resources, the indispensable ones, are the energies of individuals. Therefore, it is a key task of managerial leadership to recognize the existence of these often unused or partially used human talents, energies, and imagination. In short, the full release of human energy is the central purpose and function of the manager at all levels, in private as well as civic enterprises.

With this concept of what the managerial process is all about, at its core and center, naturally I look with the greatest of skepticism at efforts to eliminate or minimize elements of human diversity—the difference between people—to eliminate this from economic life or political life. And, therefore, I look with reservations upon those instances I have observed, and it seems to me they're increasing, of an uncritical or euphoric effort to use mathematical techniques and models for the broader aspects of the management process. Or, I may add, to use them in military strategy. Indeed, my reservations are even greater about some of the newly risen priesthood, the civilian professional military strategist who confidently applies various forms of impersonal mathematics of systems analysis to the basically human problem we call warfare, or the equally human and essentially non-technical issue of disarmament.*

The raising to a new level of excitement and acuteness of spiritual energies is the ultimate goal of leadership. It was this that glorified the pages of the history of Elizabethan England; it was this that marked the great era of the Spanish and Portuguese explorations and adventures; it was this that built great cathedrals and immortal works of art. It is this same magic of human personality that the new concept of the managerial function brings to the urgent crisis areas of our life today. The farther leadership is separated from the problem of stirring and inspiring and enlarging the capacity of individuals, the farther it wanders from what I believe to be the heart of leadership. It is no wonder that efforts are made in this direction, for this kind of leadership of people is a highly subtle thing; too great preoccupation in some quarters with computers, with electronic data processing, the glamourizing of what are at best tools, and very good tools, seems to be an understandable effort to escape from the necessity for sensitivity to emotional and political factors, to escape from the diverse qualities of individuals and the demands of human judgments.

I was reading last night the first volume of the memoirs of Harold Macmillan, former Prime Minister of England. He referred to an instance that illustrates this point. At the close of World War I, Britain

*Note the comment of a distinguished British scientist and strategist, Dr. P.M.S. Blackett: "If it is difficult to find legitimate military reasons for the vast number of U.S. nuclear weapons and delivery vehicles, it is clear that military arguments alone are not likely to be dominant in U.S. discussion of a possible drastic first step toward nuclear disarmament. This is widely admitted in the U.S., where the impediments to disarmament are *being seen more and more as economic, political and emotional in origin* rather than as based on operational military considerations." (My italics) Essay on "Steps toward Disarmament" in *The Strategy of World Order*, ed. Falk and Mendlovitz. World Law Fund, 1966.

had the problem of demobilizing one of the most heroic civilian armies that had ever been assembled to protect that island. And the job of an orderly demobilization of these men, who wanted to get home and out of the Army, as civilians who are soldiers do, was turned over to planners. And they came up with a plan which Macmillan said had everything to be said for it—in terms of logic. But anyone with any sensitivity about people would have recognized that this plan would be regarded as unfair, and "unfair" in the United Kingdom is a very ugly word; unfair to individuals. The plan had to be junked, and Winston Churchill, who did have a sense of what's fair and what isn't fair, threw it out and devised a simpler one that appealed to the fairness of the average Briton in the Army. So serious was this reaction to the logic of this plan that the historic Brigade of Grenadiers almost had a mutiny. This is what happens when one carries rationality too far, overriding the nature of the human being.

If our purpose is to lead, and stimulate, and stir, and release the full scope of their latent talents, computerizing human beings will not work. One can manipulate human beings in great mobs and crowds— they can be manipulated by force. But this is not leadership and it is not good management any more than it is good political philosophy or economic philosophy.

The manager in the area of great events is capable by the nature of his function and his personality to see what others aren't in a position to see. He sees qualities and capacities in other people that they themselves cannot see, is able to interpret other people to themselves. These qualities constitute a force, a stimulus that moves others to action, action that is understood and comprehended by those who are acting.

One man sees in a block of stone an inert piece of rock. A sculptor sees in that stone a figure that he can shape from the stone, into what may become an immortal object. The sculptor's act is creative. No less an act of creation is that of the manager, who sees in human desires, loves, hates, aspirations, the materials from which to create something that did not exist before, whether it is in the development of a community, the increase in food, or the alleviation of tensions. These human materials are more complex, volatile, changeable, difficult to deal with, than anything that even the artist faces. And the results fully as creative, and fully as consequential. The full beauty of the creative process in managerial life appears when people say, "Yes, that's the way it is, or that's the way it could be," just as people instinctively recognize truths which artists project through painting, through poetry, through music.

But what distinguishes the manager as leader from other kinds of leadership is this: that it is the manager's function to get things done, sometimes "impossible" things, urgent, critical things. And this he must do under the gun of necessity, sometimes under the gun almost literally; for of some of the problems of the world the alternative to a measure of success is violence, bloodshed, and revolution, or in some parts of the world, the shadow of famine.

I reserve for my concluding lecture a statement of my views on the art of getting things done overseas, in the deteriorating picture of economic development in the poorer countries. For the remaining portion of this lecture, I turn, primarily, to contemporary cases in our own country that illustrate the nature of the manager-leader role.

I put at the top of a list of such cases of need for a managerial leadership, the need to open wider the doors of human and economic opportunity to our Negro citizens; this may indeed prove to be the most explosive, the most urgent, and the most difficult of all, and in which the broad gauge comprehension of the manager-leader may prove decisive.

The progressive physical congestion and deterioration of the *quality* of life that men can lead in our great urban centers should certainly be on such a list.

Air pollution has reached the point in many cities where it can no longer be ignored, or treated as a mere sporadic nuisance. Nor is the poisoning of the atmosphere any longer a problem of certain big cities; it has become, in many places, a regional problem or great magnitude. Nor will the mere passing of legislation, a common American way of sweeping a problem under the bed, be enough. Human managerial leadership is the essential ingredient.

This point, I think, is well illustrated by an article in a recent (September 27, 1966) issue of the *New York Times*. A report from Los Angeles began in this way:

> "In a large city in the Middle West a few weeks back, a nationally respected air pollution official concluded a disquisition on the nation's mounting smog problem by abruptly sweeping aside his sliderule, charts and tabulations and exclaiming:
> " 'That's the official story. Now do you want to hear the truth?
> " 'The truth is that the critical ingredient in smog simply is politics. By that I mean people and their instruments of government, and their attitudes about a community problem.
> " 'We know how to cure smog. It's not unduly difficult or expensive. The problem is getting the people in the community to support a cleanup program.' "

In some of the vast arid regions of the earth with which, because of my work, I am familiar, water has for centuries been the difference between life and death. Not so in America, with its abundance—or so we thought. But no longer is this quite true. Hanging over much of America is the spectre of diminishing supplies and unbelievably filthy pollution of many of our greatest rivers and bodies of water: the Hudson, the Potomac, the Delaware, Lake Erie, Lake Michigan, and so on.

I suggest we spend a few minutes examining the question of water supply and pollution, as a way of illustrating the points I have tried to make earlier about the strategic and essential role of the human factor in getting things done, in this case, water supply and purity.

What are the main obstacles?

Clearly not the absence of a broad concept. We've had a broad concept dealing with the waters of America since Theodore Roosevelt's commission almost fifty years ago, and then these were set out with great literary skill and compelling technical support in the Morris L. Cooke Report of 1950. We did have a concept and we had technology. But nothing *happened*, and it is *what can be made to happen* that is the manager's chief concern. The pollution of rivers and the improvident use of our water resources continued on its way, reports or no reports. Technology and manufacturing facilities to purify polluted water were not lacking in this period. Yet the pollution continued and increased, and increases today.

Suddenly, as if the danger were something quite new, localities and the nation have become aroused, emotionally at least, sufficiently to pass legislation and appropriate very large sums of money. Industries have taken the problem with the greatest seriousness.

Will anything substantial happen now; will those things get done we know how to do but have not done before?

The answer will depend, I suggest, not principally upon technology or finance, although obviously both are involved, but upon that area of affairs which is within the scope of the manager-leader's special ability. In short, the conquering of water pollution is primarily a problem of human response and human agreement, within the communities, within industries, throughout the nation.

A great many people and many communities must see pollution as the result of the action of many industries and many municipalities throughout an entire watershed. To pick out a scapegoat here or there will not solve the problem. To clean up a stream at city A or industry B by technical means long since at our disposal will not suffice. The watershed is the smallest practical unit.

Now, to get joint action through an entire watershed requires creation of the awareness of the nature of the problem and a widespread conviction of the need for particular action. It requires the creation and manning of new institutions, participated in by many units in that watershed. Such awareness of the nature of the problem, such a conviction, must be shared by many people and by many institutions, public and private, local and region-wide. Moreover, how the cost is to be paid for, and particularly how the total costs are to be allocated among industries, cities, regions, is a complex question full of the certainty of conflict of opinions and interests. If not resolved by the talents of manager-leaders, experienced and wise in just such matters, the issues could produce a decade of delay and acrimony—and more pollution. Only when we realize the human problems in this area will the dimensions of the managerial task become fully apparent. People generally—and not just their Congressmen or Governors—will have to be persuaded in graphic ways that water pollution does have a very high priority; they will have to be persuaded that the high costs are justified, and, not the least prickly, that those costs are fairly and reasonably shared.

None of this will happen just by passing laws or setting up commissions or appropriating money. It will be the function, I think, of the new manager-leader to evoke a human response, to get others to see those problems as he sees them, and to stimulate the beginnings of a community of excitement about the possibilities that lie in action in this huge task. The foundations will have to be laid not in Washington but within the communities, among civic leaders in private life, in private business and in education. I need only refer to what I said last Thursday about the way in which Pittsburgh and Boston and Philadelphia have shown the way in which civic leaders and civic leadership can make changes which without that kind of leadership are quite impossible. The same thing will be true, I think, with the other problems that communities throughout the country are facing.

How does the manager approach such challenges to social entrepreneurship? On this, let me make one general observation or two.

First, the manager must have a sense of timing, a sense of what can be done *when*; he must be able to recognize when a situation has reached a point where people are ready to act. Water resources is certainly such a case. In 1950, at the time of the distinguished Cooke Report, the answers were technically clear. But it came at a time when little could be done; and little was done. By 1966 conditions had so worsened that action was possible; it became a time when the manager has a chance to be effective. Action came within the range of the feasible.

Let me divert for a moment from the United States to another part of our Hemisphere. We can see this same sense of timing that marks the manager-leader in the great impetus now being given to a concept long cherished in Latin America, that of economic integration of that vast region of 200 million people. Some of the younger modern leaders of Latin America have been able to create a mood of looking forward to the great things that can come as a result of economic integration. A community of confidence and optimism is coming into being. Without this the manager-leader knows no action can be taken; but with that mood, action can at least come within the range of the feasible. One after another of the new business and political leaders of much of Latin America show clearly—and as a part of my current work in Latin America I see this at first hand—that they begin to sense that the timing is right. This sense of timing is one of the marks of how the broad-gauged manager-leader goes about his function.

Let me repeat what I have said earlier: I am *not* asking that we wait for a new race of supermen, a self-anointed elite, an elite alone capable of filling the high role of leadership I have been trying to describe. My own experience persuades me that there already exists an enormous potential resource of this quality in the primitive villages of Persia or Colombia, or in the small towns of the Tennessee Valley or the Middle West, with which I'm familiar, as well as in large business or governmental organizations. An enormous potential of humanist managerial capacity does exist, and not just at the level of presidents of corporations or generals or great political leaders, but what one can only call natural leaders; men in the neighborhoods and towns and even in the remote villages overseas. My thesis is that this latent capability be more fully recognized, motivated, and liberated.

DAVID K. HART
WILLIAM G. SCOTT

The Organizational Imperative

American values have undergone a massive change. The pluralistic
forces that shaped our national character have withered away and the
collective strivings of our society have been consolidated into a single
social invention: modern organizations. They are *vast, complex, technologically based administrative systems which synthesize clusters of resources into rationally functioning wholes.* In contemporary America,
the needs of organization overwhelm all other considerations, whether
those of family, religion, art, science, law, or the individual. This has
had a shattering impact on us, for it has caused us to become a different
people than we thought we would be. However, that value change
is by now a fait accompli, and the dominant force behind that change
has been "the organizational imperative." Why has this happened?

Basically, it has been because modern organizations have been so
immensely successful. They seemed to advance the material welfare
of both individuals and the nation quite automatically. Such organizations, under the guidance of administrative elites, turned our enormous potentials—physical and human—into an unprecedented material
abundance. This job was done so well and so unobtrusively that the
automatism of material progress became an article of faith for Americans. We accepted what we had gained neither gratefully nor un-
gratefully, but as a simple and just inevitability.

Source: "The Organizational Imperative," by William G. Scott and David K. Hart is reprinted from *Administration
& Society* Vol. 7 No. 3 (November 1975) pp. 259-285 by permission of the publisher, Sage Publications, Inc.

However, in order to accomplish such material miracles, we had to become a different people from what we had historically hoped and dreamed for ourselves. The abundance created by modern organizations required a shift away from the values of the American tradition, even though we have continued to profess a pathetic loyalty to the lost values of our national youth. Thus, no small part of our present national malaise is the result of an increasingly obvious disparity between what we had idealized and what we have become. When we look closely at what we made for ourselves, we recoil, for we see American values that are suitable for the efficient performance of organizations, but painfully inadequate for man himself.

However, the situation is even more complicated. There is a dawning realization that the earth cannot sustain our automatic progress into that good future. Even worse, we are beginning to comprehend that affluence has not brought a marked increase in personal happiness. The question now being asked is how we have managed to drift into this appalling situation. We have written this essay in partial response to that question. Our main contention is that a new value *paradigm* (Kuhn, 1970) has displaced the old paradigm, and that the organizational imperative is both the cause and the center of the new order.

THE ORGANIZATIONAL IMPERATIVE

The organizational imperative consists of two a priori propositions and three rules for behavior. The imperative is founded on a primary proposition, which is absolute: *whatever is good for man can only be achieved through modern organization.* The question of what is "good" for man is left open; what must be beyond question is the conviction that the only way to achieve that good is through modern organization. The secondary proposition derives from the first: *therefore, all behavior must enhance the health of such modern organizations.*

From the primary and secondary propositions come three rules for organizationally healthy behavior, which define, guide, and evaluate all administrative performance. They apply to every administrator in every organization in modern society. The behavioral rules require that the administrator be rational, a good steward, and pragmatic. Since the concepts of rationality, stewardship, and pragmatism carry heavy burdens of numerous interpretations, it is necessary to specify their exact meaning as part of the organizational imperative.

Rationality. The rule of rationality provides the common denominator for all scientifically conditioned, technologically oriented organizations in advanced industrial nations: administrators must be rational. This does not refer to the philosophic tradition of rationalism, but to that form of rationality central to scientific method, which requires the economizing of means to achieve ends.

Drawing on its heritage of science, engineering, and economics, administration has made rationality indistinguishable from efficiency— the ratio of E = O/I. The task of administration, guided by this operational formula, is to increase the value of E by adjusting the relative values of outputs over inputs. While we may argue over definitional refinements, this formulation must be accepted, along with its behavioral implications, because there is no other way to account for what managers do in modern organizations.

Stewardship. The organizational imperative requires stewardship behavior from administrators. Ultimately, an administrator is a steward of the a priori propositions, but practically he must manage the more immediate affairs of the organizations in the interest of "others." It does not make a particle of difference who the others are: the public at large, stockholders of corporations, members of consumer cooperatives, members of labor unions, and the like. The rule of stewardship applies with equal force in all cases. For one thing, it legitimizes a necessary hierarchy. If the administrator as a steward is to fulfill this behavioral commitment, those who work for him must be obedient to his commands and he becomes steward for the combined destinies of his subordinates.

Additionally, stewardship requires the administrator to husband organizational resources. Thus administrators are socially and legally responsible to their clients outside the organization for their behavior as stewards; if the stewardship rule is successfully executed, the health and wealth of the organization is protected and increased, the welfare of the people dependent on the organization is improved, and the fortunes of its administrators are advanced. Just as with rationality, contrary ideas about the nature of stewardship are unthinkable within the framework of administrative theory and practice that has developed during the last 75 years.

Pragmatism. Pragmatic behavior enables the organization to survive in good health in changing environments, since practical circumstances continually impose different necessities on administrators. The rule of administrative pragmatism simply requires expedient behavior, guided by the a priori propositions. Beyond this, the rule for pragmatic behavior has *no other moral content.*

The organizational world of administration is one where complex problems of short-term duration must be dealt with expediently. Pragmatism demands that administrators direct their energies and talents to finding solutions for practical, existing problems within an immediate time frame. The language, reward systems, and activities of administration demonstrate this concern for the present and indicate the devotion that administrators have to securing an orderly, purposeful world composed of endlessly fascinating, narrow puzzles to be solved. This pragmatic puzzle world unburdens administrators of the need for moralistic reflection. Successful, expedient solutions to administrative puzzles are rewarded, and little honor goes to those whose efforts do not have immediate payoffs in terms of organizational performance (Scott and Hart, 1973).

Each of these behavioral rules entails the others. They exist in a web of interrelationships within the imperative, with the primary purpose of strengthening the a priori propositions of the imperative.

Thus, the organizational imperative is the sine qua non of administrative theory and practice. It cuts across all jurisdictional boundaries and applies to all organizations: public, private, educational, religious, or whatever. It changes slowly, if at all. It is not affected tangibly by political and social turmoil, or even war—in fact, the imperative might even be strengthened by them. The imperative is, so to speak, the metaphysic of administration: absolute, immutable, and unchanging. It is *persuasive* (it alters values in order to alter behavior), it is *universal* (it governs through the a priori propositions all collective efforts for achieving major social and individual objectives), and it is *durable* (it is the one source of stability and continuity in a turbulent world). For these and other reasons, the organizational imperative has become the dominant moral force in our society.

ADMINISTRATIVE NORMS

Administration does the vital job of linking organizations (which are the most elaborate of abstractions) with the institutional infrastructure of society at large. Organizations are run by administrators who must make decisions about goals, policies, and strategies of action that influence human values and behaviors, both within and outside the organizations. Administrators respond with varying sensitivity and accuracy to the needs and interests of the different groups affected by their decisions. But their loyalties are seldom given to those they touch most profoundly, and certainly they are neither trained nor encouraged to speculate about the moral worth and moral impact of their decisions.

Conventional wisdom has it that an administrator's primary loyalty should be to those who own his organization: the stockholders (if it is a private company) or the citizens (if it is a public organization). While this wisdom may have been correct once, it is certainly not now. The overriding concern of the adminstrator is to keep the organization healthy. This mission of organizational health is best accomplished by the administrator's total allegiance to the organizational imperative. To advance this mission, the values of *all* people who influence the organization—whether from within or from without—must be modified so that they are supportive of the organizational imperative. The administrator, therefore, must discipline himself, his subordinates, and his relevant clients to arrange their values, expectations, and practical affairs so that the organizational imperative is served.

The result of such modification has been the conversion of almost all social values into administrative norms. Administrative norms serve as the guidelines for organizationally useful behavior and are the links between the organizational imperative and social values—partaking of both, but with the advantage going to the organizational imperative. It is important to understand why these norms came to be in this central location, and how they influence the direction of value change.

Traditional American values have always been rooted in the dream that a good life was available to everyone, and no small part of that dream has been the possibility of a relatively high degree of material well-being. Americans believed that this dream could be realized through individual efforts, working directly on the natural environment. Historically optimistic, blessed by the natural advantages of a geographically and geologically favored land, and fired by a work ethic, Americans saw material affluence as a realizable goal—if not for themselves, then at least for their children.

Out of this dream grew the belief that material *growth* was absolutely essential to the vitality of national life and that the material *abundance* obtained from such growth was limitless. These were the necessary preconditions for the good life. Whatever else Americans sought could be found by them, as individuals, in the consumption of products and services. Material well-being was, to an appreciable extent, the basis of a major consensus in the social order.

There has not been much difference between how Americans defined their individual aims and what administrators tried to accomplish within organizations. *Administrative norms generally have been consistent with the expectations of Americans at large, since successful administrative practices were thought to be translatable into individual welfare.* As technology was carried by modern organization into nearly every corner of society, a new—and extremely important—premise was added to the concept for a good life. This premise did not eradicate customary assumptions about individual happiness. Rather, it converted them into organizational terms. The most important change it wrought was to create popular acceptance of the thesis that the dream of individual welfare could be realized *only* by the preeminence of modern organization and its administrative apparatus.

The traditional social values survived, but their connotation changed. Thus, growth was a good, but the most important growth was organizational. Abundance was a good, but it was an organizationally produced abundance. Consensus was a good, but the crucial consensus was among potentially conflicting interest groups within organizations. For the most part these organizationally derived goods did benefit individuals. By managing organizational resources efficiently, growth resulted in material abundance that, when distributed in a reasonably equitable way, promoted positive attitudes about the utility of organization, the legitimacy of administration, and the general community of interest in expanding productivity. Thus the norms of growth, abundance, and consensus were the "guidelines of administrative practice"—administrative norms that resulted from the reconciliation of the organizational imperative with extant social values.

But, as we said in the introduction, we have had to become a different people from what we idealized for ourselves in order to accomplish the great achievements made possible by the modern organization. Traditional American values had been significantly battered about in the process of our industrial maturation, creating major social and psychological displacements—value lags separating what we thought we were from what we were forced to be as citizens within an organizational society. As technology, organization, and administration penetrated the social order, collisions of increasing severity could hardly be avoided between the values of our past and the new value requirements of the organizational imperative.

The major American value change, nearly completed at present, was largely unanticipated even a decade ago. However, warnings were sounded by perceptive observers such as William H. Whyte, Jr. His book *The Organization Man* enjoyed great success in the 1950s because it was a sensitive, accurate, and timely appraisal of some extraordinarily important events. Whyte argued that America was shifting from an individualistic ethic to a social ethic—but that the latter was not then articulated. His contention was that organizations, through their administrative systems, had imposed their imperative on all they contacted, in nearly every human situation imaginable.

> People grow restive with a mythology that is too distant from the way things actually are, and as more and more lives have been encompassed by the organization way of life, the pressures for an accompanying ideological shift have been mounting. The pressures of the group, the frustrations of individual creativity, the anonymity of achievement: are these defects to struggle against—or are they virtues in disguise? The organization man seeks a redefinition of his place on earth—a faith that will satisfy him that what he must endure has a deeper meaning than appears

on the surface. He needs, in short, something that will do for him what the Protestant Ethic did once. And slowly, almost imperceptibly, a body of thought has been coalescing that does that [Whyte, 1956: 6].

Unfortunately, most people misunderstood that message and read the book simply as a nonfiction version of the popular novel *The Man in the Gray Flannel Suit*, which had appeared a year earlier in 1955. The theme of conformity was blown all out of proportion, and the essential meaning of Whyte's book, pertaining to the organizational imperative behind the value change, was almost completely overlooked.

Somewhere in the turmoil of the last decade, Whyte's warnings were forgotten. But in spite of campus riots, civil rights demonstrations, militant peace movements, and all of the other distractions of that era, the organizational imperative continued to work, and to work well indeed. As America drifted inexorably into an organization-dominated society, the contemptible organization man of the 1950s turned into a laudable model of administrative obedience. Further, in order to bring coherence and security into his life, he constantly exerted pressures to bring social values into a harmonious and reinforcing relationship with the organizational imperative, to which he had given total allegiance.

So, contrary to popular assumptions, the "ideal" man of the 1960s was *not* the "with-it" hippie, the peace activist, the committed and articulate university student, or the humanist psychologist. Rather, he was the superbly trained, functionally amoral administrator—the "best and the brightest" among us. They were we, and most of us became they—if not in actuality, then at least in spirit. The irony of it all was that we presumed we were following another path: John F. Kennedy set a style and proclaimed the doctrine of an accelerated national performance in 1960. But we did not become like him—we became like those he hired. Whyte's prophecy was fulfilled with barely the slightest public acknowledgment of what was happening.

The new faith of which Whyte wrote emerged as a public acceptance of the organizational imperative—that large-scale, technologically based administrative systems are the optimal mode of social organization. From commitment to this belief, all else follows, including the fact that the organizational imperative must go on unremittingly even if American values change. Administrators can serve the imperative regardless of whether society is faced with scarcity or an abundance of resources; whether the economy is expanding or contracting; or whether conservation or exploitation of the environment is the order of the day. The point is that through the intermediating process of administration, social values have become either actually or potentially reinforcing to the organizational imperative. In defense of this contention, in the next few pages we compare some of the displaced values of our past with some of the present, organizationally determined values that serve as administrative norms.

CULTURAL VALUES AS ADMINISTRATIVE NORMS

The new order of organizational dominion fired by the human instrumentality of administration requires specific cultural value commitments if it is to survive. To illustrate, we discuss five sets of paired values: the first indicating a value of our tradition, and the second indicating the value now dominant. The pairings are: from individuality to obedience; from indispensability to dispensability; from community to specialization; from spontaneity to planning; from voluntarism to paternalism. The pairings are not exhaustive—they do not describe "either-or" situations, nor are they complete. However, they do delineate the major changes in the fundamental American value paradigm.

From Individuality to Obedience

De Tocqueville, among others, correctly observed that Americans have ranged, with marvelous inconsistence, from individuality to conformity. Nevertheless, individuality held a unique and dominant place in our tradition, no matter how badly we abused it. It has been interpreted many ways, but central to them all was the confidence the individual knew (or could know) what was best for himself. As Mill (1950: 178) wrote: "with respect to his own feelings and circumstances, the ordinary man or woman has means of knowledge immeasurably surpassing those that can be possessed by any one else." Thus, legitimacy was conferred on social, economic, and political values to the extent that they conformed with the individual's perception of the right. Granted, this was an ideal, but nonetheless it was an ideal we tried to practice. The most significant justifications for action came from the individual, and the satisfactions derived from such personal actions were infinitely superior to those that came from obedience to collectivities. All of that has now changed.

Poignantly, we still proclaim the importance of individuality on public occasions—knowing all along that very little of importance gets done without modern organization. Given that reality, we have shifted our allegiance from individuality to obedience to the organizational imperative and that obedience must be total. The belief is now that superior satisfactions are to be obtained from such obedience. In short, it is good to be obedient.

There are many things that should be said about obedience, for it is the cornerstone of the organizational edifice. However, it would take a book to develop these and related ideas in the detail they deserve (Milgram, 1974; Janis, 1972). We will limit the discussion herein to some observations about two features of obedience that are particularly important.

First, we have become an obedient people, as distinguished from a conformist people. Milgram (1974: 113) distinguishes between the two as follows:

> *Conformity* . . . [is] . . . the action of a subject when he goes along with his peers, people of his own status, who have no special right to direct his behavior. *Obedience* . . . [is] . . . the action of the subject who complies with authority.

To say that Americans have become an obedient people is to say that we have accepted the premise of the organizational imperative. In that way, we have become all the same, not because we are conformists—looking to significant others in search of security—but because we have *individually* committed ourselves to a single ultimate value. By all accepting (most often implicitly) the organizational imperative and by agreeing to abide by the administrative norms derived therefrom, we become, de facto, homogenous. This is different from conformity—we have not become a herd. The traditional value of individuality was NOT abolished—rather it was converted into an individual commitment to obedience to the demands of the organizational imperative. This makes us homogenous.

Second, a widely accepted administrative truism for modern organizations is the disruptiveness of individual goals that are not congruent with organizations' goals. Obviously, individual idiosyncrasies cannot be allowed to impede the effective functioning of the organization. Hence, the desired moral stance for individuals vis-à-vis the organization is functional amorality—the willingness to substitute organizational valuations for personal valuations. In order to be maximally useful to a modern organization, an individual must be personally amoral and organizationally moral. That is, he must willingly internalize the goals of the organization as his goals, without qualm. Notice, we do not say that the individual must be immoral—just that he must be ethically malleable. If the goals of his organization are socially approved, then he will be adjudged a worthy man by his society. The reverse is also true. However, the comparative goodness or badness of organizational goals, in and of themselves, is not the central issue. The key issue is the nearly unanimous acceptance, in administrative theory and practice, of the ethical superiority of the organizational imperative over individual ethical commitments. The reader may argue that he is not required to do such things, nor would he, even if management insisted. Perhaps. But obedience to authority is so deeply in-grained by now that it takes a formidable personality to be disobedient.

We are not talking about a new phenomenon altogether. Human his-tory is filled with accounts of "true believers"—individuals who obtained meaning for their lives by committing themselves totally to mass move-ments. What is new is that the organizational imperative does not re-quire the fanaticism so common to mass movements. Indeed, the orga-nizational way of life is scarcely a mass movement at all. But the central feature of mass movements is present: the substitution of the collective absolute for personal values.

Certainly, this is *not* the age of the individual; heroes are in short supply, and individual moral virtue, while often extolled, is seldom separated from organizational needs. Thus, individual values are usually implicit, not clearly understood and, hence, weakly defended. When confronted with the clarity and force of the organizational imper-ative, conflicting individual values are easily converted into organi-zationally relevant values. By adopting the organizational imperative as the foundation of personal values, the individual articulating his moral commitments removes his agonies, and purpose is returned to private lives.

This situation is strongly reinforced by the fact that the conversion is usually painless, materially rewarding, and brings with it the distinc-tion of being "a professional." The hallmark of professional administra-tive education is the emphasis it places on loyalty to the organizational imperative and the resultant administrative norms. The moral rule that emerges from this—which is nearly universal throughout our institu-tions—is that efficiency in the service of organizational goals equals morality. Thus, we condition ourselves for functional amorality.

To summarize, because of the successes of modern organizations, organizational values are given precedence over individual values. The individual is invariably rewarded for such value substitution. This ne-cessitates a belief in man's moral malleability—that he can make value substitutions whenever and as often as required. Once that malleability is accepted, there is no "reason" why people should hold values other than those that are organizationally useful (Scott and Hart, 1971; Hart and Scott, 1972). Thus the burden of individual responsibility for iden-tifying a personal value system is removed. The organizational impera-tive is now sufficient.

From Indispensability to Dispensability

An important value in the American tradition has been the right of individuals to feel indispensable to the groups, organizations, and communities of which they are a part. An honorable man could feel confident that his loss would have a profound effect on those who surrounded him. For beyond sorrow was the fact that their world would be less without him. The reader may protest, arguing that throughout history—including our own—men have dispensed with one another in callous and brutal ways. It is also safe to assume that most people have never really felt indispensable. Be that as it may, the *ideal* of personal indispensability has been central to our tradition as one of the important rewards earned through good effort. Simply, it was the sense of being necessary to one's world.

Presently, the organizational imperative demands that nothing be indispensable and that, indeed, dispensability is a prized commodity. The modern American economy is built on the dispensability of things. Obsolescence serves the major purpose in enriching organizations. Our lives are spent in surroundings of constant material replacement, because our technology and our economy have made it more efficient to dispose of things rather than to reuse them.

All of this is well known. What is less well understood is how an individual within a society that exalts dispensability might eventually come to view himself. Alternatively, how does a society which demands that nothing be indispensable come to value the individual? The answer is obvious. The organizational imperative requires that each person understand he is dispensable and, further, that this is a good thing.

Modern organizations cannot allow individuals to become indispensable. If they did, the organization then would become dependent on those individuals. That prospect is anathema to administrative theory and practice. Allow us to illustrate with the metaphor of the organization as machine. It assumes that in the organization, as in the machine, each part is linked as efficiently as possible with all other parts. Each performs its specific tasks in a productive rhythm with all of the others. If there is an ample supply of spares, any part of the machine is dispensable, even though some parts are more expensive to replace than others. The primary mission of the engineer is not only to keep the machine running, but also to ensure an adequate supply of spare parts.

So it is with the people in an organization, *at all levels and in all capacities.* Personnel must be instantly replaceable by others with similar abilities, with a minimal loss of efficiency during the substitution. If there are enough human spares, then there need never be any major upheavals with the turnover of personnel. Like the engineer, one of the primary responsibilities of the administrator is to ensure that an adequate supply of spare parts is immediately available, including his own. Indeed, how often do we hear the incantation, "Train your own replacement!"? The difficulty, of course, is that while no machine part needs to be convinced of its dispensability, a human being does.

This educational task is central to all schools of administration. Books, articles, and teachers hammer away at the theme that the individual has no *right* to expect to become indispensable, nor should he attempt to. It is stressed (as a "fact of life" in the "real world") that the dream of personal indispensability is childish and, even worse, organizationally bad. The point was well made by one of our graduate students, who observed that he was like a sausage being prepared for consumption by a large organization. He argued that nothing should be stuffed into him that would give his prospective organization "indigestion." This may be a bit blunt, but some variant of this evaluation is drilled into our students as an essential part of the administrative "attitude" they will take with them onto the job.

But the process does not stop at the boundaries of the employing organization. As the organizational imperative has touched more and more social values, this attitude has been extended into all areas of our lives. Thus, there is a pervasive belief in our society that indispensability is an illusion, nowhere to be found. As a final defense, the reader might argue that he is indispensable to his family. Perhaps. But, given the condition of the American family, the unfortunate truth is that the economic role played by the father could be more efficiently performed by an organization. Certainly this theme is constantly stressed by the advertising of our large financial institutions. Thus, a lethal blow is thrown at the last area where personal indispensability might be found. If man has an innate need to be necessary in his world, then this particular value transition is quite destructive. People convinced of their personal dispensability suffer many consequences, from alienation to existential fear. To avoid these conditions, most of us flee more deeply into the organization, searching for security. Ironically, we find there that we are the most dispensable commodity of all.

From Community to Specialization

Part of the American's magnificent inconsistency has been a stubborn commitment to the seemingly contradictory values of individuality and community (Nisbet, 1969; McWilliams, 1973; Stein, 1972). However, the values of community and indispensability went hand in hand, for one who was valued for his personal qualities contributed something unique to the warm, supporting, and persisting nature of the community. When he was gone, the quality of the communal relationships could never be reexperienced in quite the same manner.

The organizational imperative has diminished and transformed the value of community. In this instance, the organizational imperative requires that the individual's dedication be primarily to a specialty that is harmonious with and contributory to the ultimate success of an organization. Clearly, specialization does not exist for its own sake. For specialization to have any meaning, it must have *utility* for the organization, whether one is a vice-president or a foreman. The stewardship of one's responsibility is measured by its contribution to the total organization. Loyalty must not be given, therefore, to the work group, to the place, or to some abstract ideals of honor, hospitality, or obligation; rather, loyalty must be to the specialized function the successful performance of which adds to the whole organizational effort. In short, the organization has evolved as an inadequate surrogate for community.

It is important to note that the criteria on which individual worth is evaluated in a community are quite different from the criteria by which individual utility is assessed in an organization. An individual's worth, in organizational terms, is not measured affectively in the quality of his relationships with others. When has friendship ever been considered as a standard in wage and salary administration? Worth is measured quantitatively, wherever possible, by the level of one's specialized performance relative to the achievement of organizational goals.

Finally, specialization and dispensability are comfortable—even necessary—partners. Specialty has always been treated as depersonalized in administrative theory and practice. The most efficient way to meet the obligations of stewardship is to objectify, as far as possible, what people do in organizations and to assign quantitative standards in order to judge performance. These standards allow little room for affective considerations, other than those that might have organizational utility. There is no room for community, in the best sense of the word, within modern organizations, since in order to thrive it must have stability and continuity of human relationships. The loss of meaning in one's life because of the absence of community cannot be replaced easily by the rewards that come from specialization.

From Spontaneity to Planning

Another value central to the American tradition has been spontaneity. It was interpreted in a number of ways. In its more dramatic form, it was believed that people should be willing to abandon the security of the known in order to venture into the unknown, taking risks for the sake of personal gain. But in its most significant form, it was believed that the really urgent problems most often would be solved by individuals through spontaneous, creative action. While such spontaneity was unanticipatable in detail, it was assumed that it would somehow occur, in mysterious ways and at appropriate times, to the benefit of society in general or to specific organizations in particular. The spontaneous, creative, enterprising individual would work wonders in all areas, from farming to industry, and even to the political system. The results of such actions would be more efficacious ways of doing things, producing more jobs, goods, and services.

Thus, spontaneity became an integral part of the American entrepreneurial ethic, defined as ingenuity or "Yankee know-how." The moral lesson in the Horatio Alger and Frank Meriwell stories was simply that a young man with "pluck and luck" could move inexorably ahead in business, finance, or whatever. The essence of the American value of spontaneity is found in this pluck-and-luck theme. Pluck meant the motivation to act creatively (even impulsively), in unforeseen circumstances, to solve problems. Luck pertained to the element of risk that a plucky person had to assume if he was to make his way successfully through life. The interesting twist in these stories was that if a person took action from an instinctive knowledge of what was right, Lady Luck would bend in his favor. So individual, spontaneous action was prized because it was believed that it brought favorable outcomes for all concerned, especially when guided by a sense of moral rectitude. This gave Americans an additional reason to be optimistic about the future. The uncertainties of the future were not to be feared, for they were the breeding ground of opportunity.

However, this has been changed by the administrative needs of modern organization. As we have said, the world of administration is concerned with complex, short-term problems. Nevertheless, the future must obviously be taken into account in order to set goals, to map strategies, to make budgets, to establish policies, to allocate resources, and so on. Administrators must plan, and there is no way they can plan for spontaneity. Thus, the organizational imperative not only reduces the premium formerly placed on spontaneity, the imperative makes spontaneity dysfunctional. Planning has replaced spontaneity as the primary means of handling the uncertainties of the future. It requires speculation about events that are anticipated but as yet unrealized. So planning is, in some ways, incompatible with the rule of pragmatism. But the needs of modern organizations have forced a reconciliation between the two, and this reconciliation has caused the change in the way spontaneity is perceived and valued.

As more investment capital is committed to plant and equipment, as the time span between the beginning and end of tasks or projects lengthens, as more specialized manpower is hired, and as the flexibility of an organization diminishes in relation to its increased fixed resources, long-ranged planning activities expand dramatically. The problem is how to adjust the planning function to the rule of pragmatism. Certain planning practices have evolved to this end. First, guesswork must be eliminated. This necessitates the development and application of a technology of forecasting. Second, as many external "variables" as possible must be controlled. They influence the future direction of the organization in uncertain ways. By controlling these variables, today's forecasts are made into tomorrow's self-fulfilling prophecies. Third, the possibilities that aberrant individual behavior will unpredictably alter the course of planned future events must be eradicated. This practice has two subconditions. Behavior in the planning *process* itself must be controlled. This means that planning ideally should be a collective process, because group performance is more visible and predictable than individual performance. Then, the implementation of plans must be controlled by means that are visible and understandable to all involved.

Control, therefore, is the way that planning and pragmatism are reconciled. That control and planning are conceptual counterparts is a frequently cited, but poorly understood, administrative adage. However, it is a certainty that as planning grows, controlling also grows, if for no other reason than to prevent random or aberrant events from confounding plans. This explains why spontaneity is by now a less valued, even dangerous behavior. It is unpredictable, and therefore uncontrollable. So, while the organization may lose some advantage from spontaneously creative acts, this loss is offset by the more easily controlled behavior that arises from collective planning processes.

From Voluntarism to Paternalism

In the past, when individuals desired concerted action to achieve common aims, it was assumed that they would combine in voluntary interest groups and that their resultant efforts would be sufficient to accomplish their goals. Associations of freely participating individuals were so much a part of the American way of doing things that the traditional political theory of pluralism and the economic theory of countervailing power rested in substantial degree on the efficacy of voluntarism. This principle molded the familiar American ideals of industrial democracy, collective self-determination, federalism, decentralization, government by consent, and so on.

We have traditionally believed that social phenomena are the result of deliberate decisions traceable to individual acts. This belief implied autonomy, free will, individual responsibility and accountability, and generalized social norms that guided the conduct of individuals in making choices. However, it is also true that we believed in the usefulness of collective action, especially when the leverage of power was required to advance one's own interests in the face of opposing collective interests. So voluntarism allowed a person to retain the rights and obligations of individualism, but it also permitted him to take advantage of the power of concerted action, within a self-governing organizational framework. The principle of voluntarism was accepted through American society. Laborers, farmers, accountants, consumers, doctors, professors, engineers, businessmen, lawyers, and many others have formed voluntary associations at different times in our history, with varying degrees of success. The point is that voluntarism reflected a compromise between individualism and collectivism, presenting us with an ingenious amalgamation of these polarities.

Voluntarism was an effective but fragile compromise. It was always under assault—both from the side of individualism and from the side of collectivism. For example, even the most conservative craft unions still are damned in some quarters because they allegedly curtail individual autonomy. Political lobbyists are portrayed as greedy power merchants whose interests are opposed to those of individual citizens. The argument used against the unionization of university professors is that individual freedom, for many the sine qua non of scholarly excellence, will be destroyed. Yet, at present, the most devastating attacks on voluntarism are not coming from those who advocate individualism. Rather, the strongest assault is coming from those who advocate collectivism, and it has taken form as organizational paternalism.

It is not as if paternalism—the benevolent concern of management for the welfare of their employee "children"—is something new on the organizational scene. The spirit of business welfarism has been prevalent in Great Britain and in the United States for a long time. This spirit initially grew out of the social doctrines of Calvinism, which imposed on the "elect" the responsibility for the collective spiritual welfare of their charges. Following the industrial revolution in England such responsibilities were reflected in the rules of work and worship that were widely circulated and applied in factory towns. Regardless of how primitive, convoluted, and cynical this early paternalistic thinking may seem to us now, it was justified as following Christian teachings.

As social change swept through Great Britain and America, it produced major transformations in paternalistic doctrines. First, society became secularized, so that the religious justification for paternalism became irrelevant. Second, organizational economic benefits became the dominant rationale. As Carnegie (1902: V) put it: "The employer who helps his workmen through education, recreation, and social uplift, helps himself." Third, responding to the challenge of unionism in the

1920s, management adopted the paternalistic "American plan" as a counterstrategy.

Paternalism was used by management for the practical purposes of either fighting unions or raising worker productivity. While the focus of paternalism shifted from the spiritual to the temporal, it remained basically a collective undertaking, ideologically justified as the means of promoting general employee welfare. In any event, there was nothing in paternalism that allowed for any tolerance of the voluntaristic principle of self-determination.

With the rise of sophisticated professional management in the 1930s another shift occurred in the doctrine of paternalism that can be traced directly to the rule of stewardship. This new aspect of the doctrine is, in some respects, the most effective attack on voluntarism yet mounted. It is the result of some fundamental value changes, directly attributable to the growing dominance of organizations in our society and to a concomitant influence of the behavioral sciences over social policy-making. While the first assault of paternalism on voluntarism was spiritual in origin and the second was clearly secular, the third and most recent assault is therapeutic.

As we explained earlier, professional administration from its inception has been guided by the rule of stewardship. The separation of corporate ownership from control gave managers virtual sovereign power to dispose of the resources of the organization in ways that would most satisfy the interests of its clientele. When stewardship and the separation of ownership and control were being examined analytically for the first time (Berle and Means, 1933), emphasis was on the management of material resources, particularly financial resources. However, it did not take long for the grasp of managerial stewardship to extend to the human resources of an organization as well. How were they to deal with them?

Managers of modern organizations quickly succumbed to the utility of behavioral science therapy values. The lessons of the various humanistic movements were learned and put into practice by administrators. These lessons contain the following premises. First, "normal" people behave dysfunctionally in organizations if they do not accept the imperatives of obedient behavior. Second, the administrative elite of the organization has sovereign power to impress the norms of the organization on the people in it, for their own welfare. Third, organizationally "deviant" behavior (and values) should be "cured" by applying behavioral science techniques rather than punishment.

Paternalism has traveled the entire route, starting with spiritual welfare, moving through physical welfare, and ending with the mental welfare of employees. The last is the most insidious, since in our age the best way to ensure obedience is to create a state of psychological dependency. This is exactly what the new form of paternalism does—it defines self-determination, autonomy, and the other conditions of individualism as illness. Clearly, voluntarism as well is a principle that therapeutic paternalism cannot abide. Thus we have completed the circle, returning to where we began this discussion of changing values—to Milgram's analysis of "obedience to authority." There is no more despotic authority than the "father" righteously legislating the terms of mental health for his children, and equipped with the means for enforcing these terms.

CONCLUSION

The organizational imperative is the core of our well-entrenched value paradigm, which has displaced the values of our tradition. The period of transition was marked by feelings of alienation and dislocation among large numbers of people as those traditional values were found inappropriate to the demands of the present. Regardless, the organizational imperative prevailed and has assumed its final shape. Not all people are committed to the organizational imperative. There are still some few who live in the ignored corners of our society who have little to do with it. Nonetheless, the organizational imperative is the dominant article of faith for all administrators of the innumerable, overlapping, and inescapable organizations that make up contemporary society. Theirs is the significant involvement. But this is also true of workers who must conform to the rules of modern organization and those others whose lives are inextricably involved as clients of modern organizations. In short, *all* must embrace the values of the organizational imperative if they want to obtain the great rewards promised by modern organization.

This promise seemed about to be fulfilled in the decade of the 1950s. The unanticipated turmoil of the 1960s seemed but a temporary setback. During this time the deep-rooted sense of American optimism persisted. We believed that our leaders, public and private, would somehow assert themselves and get us successfully through the heavy weather. Our optimism has not been justified.

The 1970s have brought considerable national peril, exacerbated by the war in Vietnam, festering domestic inequalities, government venality, incivility in our major cities, shortages of basic commodities, serious economic inflation, and a major recession. The dreary list could be multiplied, but, what is even worse, we know that the future will be filled with even greater perils. Somehow, the promise of the leadership of the best and the brightest has turned sour, and the people are increasingly aware of it.

There is evidence of growing public doubt that our expectations for continuous growth and affluence are realizable. Conditions point toward a nongrowth, stable-state economy. Yet politicians, public administrators, and business executives resist policies of economic stabilization, reduction of agency services, or the leveling of sales volume and corporate earnings. Even more, schools of administration will have nothing to do with such topics. Who, for instance, has ever taken a course in an administrative curriculum on "How to Shrink a Business"? Articles and books are seldom found in the professional literature of administration advocating models of nongrowth, although there are some notable exceptions. Such things do not happen, because they are *seemingly* foreign to the organizational imperative, and hence to the norms of administrative theory and practice.

But modern organizations can exist in such an environment. Further, public attitudes about these matters can be conveniently changed and with little disruption (Ellul, 1965). The organizational imperative will *easily* survive. It has the power and the flexibility to ride out these crises without having to change its essential features. In fact, the a priori propositions and their rules will be strengthened in the process of responding to those crises. The major casualty will be the individual. Is there any doubt that modern organizations, public or private, will arrive in that unprecedented future in much better shape than the individual?

Thus, we can anticipate the strengthening of the organizational imperative as large-scale organizations restructure themselves to meet the future challenges. This will require, of course, an intensification of mass loyalty to the organizational imperative. However, that can be accomplished once those in the significant positions in society understand what is needed.

Given this situation, we cannot just sit tight and "muddle through," on the anticipation that everything will turn out well. We are confronted with the problems right now, and administrators have begun to solve those problems Now, if this new paradigm is not harmful to man qua man, then these "soft" normative issues can be dismissed and we can get down to the "hard" work of making organizations more effective. But, if one believes that the paradigm is destructive to man, then corrections must be made immediately.

Thus, the most fundamental task of our time is to provide an answer to the ancient and persistent question, *What is man that these things should or should not be done to him?* Is there anything innate in man that is offended, and perhaps even destroyed, by the values of the new paradigm? Unless that question is answered first, there is really no reason to resist the organizational imperative. In fact, resistance is counterproductive, for it just slows down the fight for organizational survival in times of great peril.

Further, the question cannot be resolved by empirical means, for by its very nature, it transcends empiricism. It will require moral discourse of a high order and a *deliberate* selection of new values that enhance that which is morally innate in man, if indeed there is such a thing. To choose values deliberately is unprecedented in human history, but it must be done (Gorney, 1972: 8-9).

REFERENCES

Berle, A.A., Jr. and G. S. Means (1933) The Modern Corporation and Private Property. New York: Macmillan.

Carnegie, A. (1902) The Empire of Business. New York: Doubleday, Page.

Ellul, J. (1965) Propaganda. New York: Alfred A. Knopf.

Gorney, R. (1972) The Human Agenda. New York: Simon & Schuster.

Hart, D. K. and W. G. Scott (1972) "The optimal image of man for systems theory." Academy of Management J. 15 (December): 531-540.

Janis, I. L. (1972) Victims of Groupthink. Boston: Houghton Mifflin.

Kuhn, T. S. (1970) The Structure of Scientific Revolutions. Chicago: Univ. of Chicago Press.

McWilliams, W. C. (1973) The Idea of Fraternity in America. Berkeley: Univ. of California Press.

Milgram, S. (1974) Obedience to Authority. New York: Harper & Row.

Mill, J. S. (1950) Utilitarianism, Liberty, and Representative Government. New York: Dutton.

Nisbet, R. A. (1969) The Quest for Community. New York: Oxford Univ. Press.

Scott, W. G. and D. K. Hart (1971) "The moral nature of man in organizations." Academy of Management J. 14 (June): 241-255.

——— (1973) "Administrative crisis: the neglect of metaphysical speculation." Public Administration Rev. 33 (September/October): 415-422.

Stein, M. R. (1972) The Eclipse of Community. Princeton: Princeton Univ. Press.

Whyte, W. H., Jr. (1956) The Organization Man. Garden City, N.Y.: Anchor.

II | ORGANIZATIONS

Managers create and control organizations; and as we have seen argued by some, managers are also controlled by organizations. Business organizations, government organizations, social agency organizations, social and fraternal organizations—we are inundated by them throughout our lives. Future historians may well call ours "the Organizational Society."

What being in an organization means for people has been the subject of repeated inquiry. The answers, however, are hardly clear.

One of the most widely known studies of people in organizations is William Whyte's *Organization Man.* He argues that experiences in organizations convert intelligent, ambitious, hardworking individuals into passive members of the organization who give up their individual goals and self direction. Instead they accept the goals and direction of the organization on how they should behave and even think. It is a chilling and persuasive account.

Lyman Porter, however, cannot find the organization man. Instead of the cautious, conforming, security conscious manager Whyte describes, Porter finds managers who are decisive, forceful, imaginative and independent.

What are we to make of the differences? Is one right and the other wrong? Is each to some degree both right and wrong? Can they both be right?

Parallel to Whyte's thesis is another, best expressed by Chris Argyris, that traditionally constructed organizations are unhealthy, emotionally and perhaps even physically, for people in them. His basic point is that the conditions organizations create run counter to the conditions that adult human beings need. This leads people to become alienated and antagonistic toward the organizations they are in.

"The Personality-versus-Organization Hypothesis" examines this point carefully. George Strauss claims that it is neither totally right nor totally wrong. He argues that people may find disadvantages being in organizations, but they also find important advantages. What is one person's disadvantage may be another's advantage. People are just too different for one to make blanket statements about them. One can easily imagine Argyris replying, "Since we cannot construct a separate organization for each individual, how are you going to avoid having some people have more disadvantages than advantages by being in organizations? What do you intend to do about *that?* What can managers do?"

The most widely recognized form of organization is the bureaucracy. Originally thought of as a form of governmental organization, it is now recognized anywhere that there are explicit positions and relationships among them, rules and procedures for doing work, permanent employment in the organization, etc. Bennis, for one, argues in "The Coming Death of Bureaucracy" that the ties and conditions that encouraged and supported this form of organization are passing, and that it too will pass, to be replaced with other forms of organizations. Miewald, however, looks at some of the new organizational roots that Bennis points to and claims that they will be inadequate for the newer "post-bureaucratic" world Bennis looks for. Miewald concludes, therefore, that bureaucracy is likely to be around for some time yet, since we need something that apparently only this form of organization can presently provide.

Do you think bureaucracy will pass away? Do you want it to?

WILLIAM H. WHYTE JR.

Selections from The Organization Man

The Pipe Line

Before we follow the senior into the corporation's postgraduate training schools, we must pause a moment longer on the campus. For it is here, in one important respect, that these new schools are being shaped. They are a projection of what the senior wants, and more than corporations care to admit, what the senior wants these days has a lot to do with what he gets. Corporation people talk much about the intensive screening by which they have sifted out of the common ruck such a superlative group of recruits for their particular organization. The blunt fact, however, is that these days it is the college senior who does most of the screening. With more job vacancies than there are graduates, the attractive senior will usually have some eight or nine offers to choose from. He does not throw the advantage away.

What he wants, above all, is the guarantee of a training program. Almost every recruiter implies to him that he will find security, happiness, and perpetual advancement if he chooses Ajax, but he is apt to remain visibly unimpressed unless the recruiter can back up the promise with a training program—and a formal, highly organized one too. Seniors don't leave it at that either. Having narrowed the choice to companies whose brochures promise training ("individual development program tailored to your particular needs" ... "no dead-end jobs" ... "no ceiling"), the senior starts applying other yardsticks. How

long is the training program? Is it a real training program or just afterhours indoctrination about the company? Will he be exposed to
many different operations of the company or will he be pigeonholed
in a specialty? How will he be rated? Is the program geared to a fixed
salary increase schedule?

What he wants is a continuation. He is used to formal training and
he is wary of stepping out into the arena without a good deal more.
This is one of the reasons he does not incline to the smaller firm;
it may offer opportunity, but it offers it too soon. By contrast, big
business's reassuringly institutionalized schools—sometimes complete
with classrooms, dormitories, and graduating classes—is an ideal next
step. It will defer opportunity until he is ready for it, For the same
reason, it offers him far more security; the more the company spends
on him, goes a popular line of thought, the less likely is it to let its
investment in him lapse. The training program, in short, promises to
obviate the necessity of premature decision, and to those concerned
because they don't yet know what kind of subspecialty they want to
follow, enrollment in the formal program is a sedative. "We tell them,
in effect, 'You don't have to make up your mind,' " says one executive.
" 'Come with us and you will find out while you're in training.' "

The companies which deliver best on this promise, as a consequence,
are the ones that get the most applicants. Students are not easily fooled;
by spring they are connoisseurs of placement interviewing, and their
information network is quick to pass along the word about specific
company situations. If the placement director is energetic he will have
checked up with recent alumni as to how well the companies have
done by them. If the company welched by taking on more trainees
than it would promote, or otherwise exploited them, the placement
director then warns his men away from it—though, as we will see later,
there are exceptions to the rule

The placement director is in a seller's market, and half the fun of
the game for him is to get a most-favored-college position with the
companies that do best by trainees. He schools his men in the way
to deport themselves with particular recruiters, the weighting of the
personality profile each is looking for, the right answers to the curved-
ball questions. In some colleges, regular courses have been set up foɪ
the task, and seniors can't enter the placement competition until they've
taken them. The Carnation Company's Wallace Jamie, one of the leaders in the field of corporate recruiting, tells of an experience at Indiana
University: "I began to notice that every applicant wore a dark-blue
suit and a conservative tie and had ready and right answers for most
of my questions." As he had suspected, it turned out that the students
had trained for the interview in a special class. Like other recruiters,
who have similar experiences, he rather admires their sophistication.

The eager beaver of today, he points out, knows the value of not being too eager, and only the company with the first-rate training program can command his attention.*

But corporations have not been setting up training schools simply because seniors want them to. Corporations started experimenting with such programs many years ago, and while the predilections of the young men have been a powerful prod, in time many corporations would have made the shift anyway. For the training schools are not simply a sugar-coating, a more attractively packaged indoctrination; they are a manifestation of a deep change in the organization's own view of what *kind* of man it wishes to achieve.

There are two divergent conceptions, and the question of which is to become dominant is still at issue. On the surface the trainee programs of most big corporations would seem very much alike. Beneath such new standardized trappings as testing, automatic rating, rotation, and the like, however, is a fundamental difference in policy.

One type of program sticks to what has been more or less the historic approach. The young man is hired to do a specific job; his orientation is usually brief in duration, and for many years what subsequent after-hours training he will get will be directed at his particular job. If he proves himself executive material he may be enrolled in a management development course, but this is not likely to happen until he is in his mid-thirties.

The newer type of program is more than an intensification of the old. The company hires the young man as a potential manager and from the start he is given to thinking of himself as such. He and the other candidates are put together in a central pool, and they are not farmed out to regular jobs until they have been exposed, through a series of dry-run tasks, to the managerial view. The schooling may last as long as two years and occasionally as long as four or five.

At the risk of oversimplification, the difference can be described as that between the Protestant Ethic and the Social Ethic. In one type of program we will see that the primary emphasis is on work and on competition; in the other, on managing *others'* work and on co-operation. Needless to say, there are few pure examples of either approach; whichever way they incline, the majority of training programs

*In their own way, English undergraduates are becoming connoisseurs too. The London *Sunday Times* (March 18, 1956) writes of the way business executives are haunting the provincial universities in search of bright young men. There is now such a shortage, the *Sunday Times* writer reports, that "one young physicist I know has spent every weekend since he came down from the university voyaging up and down the country in first-class compartments to interviews, lodging at four-star hotels, dining with directors, and drinking more than is good for him. He has no intention of taking any of the posts he is offered, since he is very well placed already, thank you. But these weekly outings have become a hobby with him."

have elements of both approaches, and some companies try to straddle directly over the fence. But an inclination there is, and the new training program may prove the best of introductions to the "professional manager" of the future.

To sharpen the fundamental differences, I am going to contrast two outstanding trainee programs. For an example of the first type, I am going to take the training program of the Vick Chemical Company as it was in the late thirties. There are several reasons for the choice. First, it has been one of the best-known programs in the whole personnel field. Second, though it has often been cited as a pioneer example of modern practice, it was in its fundamentals the essence of the Protestant Ethic and so undefiled by change that there was nothing in it which Henry Clews would take exception to. Third, I happen to have gone through it myself. If I grow unduly garrulous in these next pages, I bespeak the reader's indulgence; I have often pondered this odd experience, and since it furnishes so apt an illustration of certain principles of indoctrination, I would like to dwell on it at some length.

It was a school—the Vick School of Applied Merchandising, they called it. The idea, as it was presented to job-hunting seniors at the time, was that those who were chosen were not going off to a job, but to a postgraduate training institution set up by a farsighted management. In September, some thirty graduates would gather from different colleges to start a year's study in modern merchandising. There would be a spell of classroom work in New York, a continuing course in advertising, and, most important, eleven months of field study under the supervision of veteran students of merchandising and distribution. Theoretically, we should be charged a tuition, for though we understood we would do some work in connection with our studies, the company explained that its expenses far outweighed what incidental services we would perform. This notwithstanding, it was going to give us a salary of $75 a month and all traveling expenses. It would also, for reasons I was later to learn were substantial, give us an extra $25 a month to be held in escrow until the end of the course.

Let me now point out the first distinction between the Vick program and the more current type. It was not executive training or even junior-executive training. Vick's did argue that the program would help produce the leaders of tomorrow, and prominent on the walls of the office was a framed picture of a captain at the wheel, with a statement by the president that the greatest duty of management was to bring along younger men. This notwithstanding, the question of whether or not any of us would one day be executives was considered a matter that could very easily be deferred. The training was directed almost entirely to the immediate job. The only exception was an International Correspondence Schools course in advertising, one of the main virtues of which, I always felt, was to keep us so occupied during the week ends that we wouldn't have time to think about our situation.

The formal schooling we got was of the briefest character. During our four weeks in New York, we learned of Richardson's discovery of VapoRub, spent a day watching the VapoRub being mixed, and went through a battery of tests the company was fooling around with to find the Vick's type. Most of the time we spent in memorizing list prices, sales spiels, counters to objections, and the prices and techniques of Plough, Inc., whose Penetro line was one of Vick's most troublesome competitors. There was no talk about the social responsibilities of business or the broad view that I can remember, and I'm quite sure the phrase *human relations* never came up at all.

What management philosophy we did get was brief and to the point. Shortly before we were to set out from New York, the president, Mr. H. S. Richardson, took us up to the Cloud Club atop the Chrysler Building. The symbolism did not escape us. As we looked from this executive eyrie down on the skyscraper spires below, Golconda stretched out before us. One day, we gathered, some of us would be coming back up again—and not as temporary guests either. Some would not. The race would be to the swiftest.

Over coffee Mr. Richardson drove home to us the kind of philosophy that would get us back up. He posed a hypothetical problem. Suppose, he said, that you are a manufacturer and for years a small firm has been making paper cartons for your product. He has specialized so much to service you, as a matter of fact, that that's all he does make. He is utterly dependent on your business. For years the relationship has continued to be eminently satisfactory to both parties. But then one day another man walks in and says he will make the boxes for you cheaper. What do you do?

He bade each one of us in turn to answer.

But *how much* cheaper? we asked. How much time could we give the old supplier to match the new bid? Mr. Richardson became impatient. There was only one decision. Either you were a businessman or you were not a businessman. The new man, obviously, should get the contract. Mr. Richardson, who had strong views on the necessity of holding to the old American virtues, advised us emphatically against letting sentimentality obscure fundamentals. Business was survival of the fittest, he indicated, and we would soon learn the fact.

He was as good as his word. The Vick curriculum was just that—survival of the fittest. In the newer type of programs, companies will indeed fire incompetents, but a man joins with the idea that the company intends to keep him, and this is the company's wish also. The Vick School, however, was frankly based on the principle of elimination. It wouldn't make any difference how wonderful all of us might turn out to be; of the thirty-eight who sat there in the Cloud Club, the rules of the game dictated that only six or seven of us would be asked to stay with Vick. The rest would graduate to make way for the next batch of students.

Another difference between Vick's approach and that now more characteristic became very evident as soon as we arrived in the field. While the work, as the company said, was educational, it was in no sense make-work. Within a few days of our session at the Cloud Club, we were dispatched to the hinterland—in my case, the hill country of eastern Kentucky. Each of us was given a panel delivery truck, a full supply of signs, a ladder, a stock of samples, and an order pad. After several days under the eye of a senior salesman, we were each assigned a string of counties and left to shift for ourselves.

The merchandising was nothing if not applied. To take a typical day of any one of us, we would rise at 6:00 or 6:30 in some bleak boarding house or run-down hotel and after a greasy breakfast set off to squeeze in some advertising practice before the first call. This consisted of bostitching a quota of large fiber signs on barns and clamping smaller metal ones to telephone poles and trees by hog rings. By eight, we would have arrived at a general store for our exercise in merchandising. Our assignment was to persuade the dealer to take a year's supply all at once, or, preferably, more than a year's supply, so that he would have no money or shelf space left for other brands. After the sale, or no-sale, we would turn to market research and note down the amount sold him by "chiseling" competitors (i.e., competitors; there was no acknowledgment on our report blanks of any other kind).

Next we did some sampling work: "Tilt your head back, Mr. Jones," we would suddenly say to the dealer. For a brief second he would obey and we would quickly shoot a whopping dropperful of Vatronol up his nose. His eyes smarting from the sting, the dealer would smile with simple pleasure. Turning to the loungers by the stove, he would tell them to let the drummer fella give them some of that stuff. After the messy job was done, we plastered the place with cardboard signs, and left. Then, some more signposting in barnyards, and ten or twelve miles of mud road to the next call. So, on through the day, the routine was repeated until at length, long after dark, we would get back to our lodgings in time for dinner—and two hours' work on our report forms.

The acquisition of a proper frame of mind toward all this was a slow process. The faded yellow second sheets of our daily report book tell the story. At first, utter demoralization. Day after day, the number of calls would be a skimpy eight or nine, and the number of sales sometimes zero. But it was never our fault. In the large space left for explanations, we would affect a cheerful humor—the gay adventurer in the provinces—but this pathetic bravado could not mask a recurrent note of despair.*

To all these bids for sympathy, the home office was adamantine. The weekly letter written to each trainee would start with some perfunctory remarks that it was too bad about the clutch breaking down, the cut knee, and so on. But this spurious sympathy did not conceal a strong preoccupation with results, and lest we miss the point we were told of comrades who would no longer be with us. We too are sorry about those absent dealers, the office would say. Perhaps if you got up earlier in the morning?

As the office sensed quite correctly from my daily reports, I was growing sorry for myself. I used to read timetables at night, and often in the evening I would somehow find myself by the C & O tracks when the George Washington swept by, its steamy windows a reminder of civilization left behind. I was also sorry for many of the storekeepers, most of whom existed on a precarious credit relationship with wholesalers, and as a consequence I sold them very little of anything.

The company sent its head training supervisor to see if anything could be salvaged. After several days with me, this old veteran of the road told me he knew what was the matter. It wasn't so much my routine, wretched as this was. It was my state of mind. "Fella," he told me, "you will never sell anybody anything until you learn one simple thing. The man on the other side of the counter is the *enemy*."

It was a gladiators' school we were in. Selling may be no less competitive now, but in the Vick program, strife was honored far more openly than today's climate would permit. Combat was the ideal—combat with the dealer, combat with the "chiseling competitors," and combat with each other. There was some talk about "the team," but it was highly abstract. Our success depended entirely on beating our fellow students, and while we got along when we met for occasional sales meetings the camaraderie was quite extracurricular.

Slowly, as our sales-to-calls ratios crept up, we gained in rapacity. Somewhere along the line, by accident or skill, each of us finally manipulated a person into doing what we wanted him to do. Innocence was lost, and by the end of six months, with the pack down to about twenty-three men, we were fairly ravening for the home stretch back to the

---

*I quote some entries from my own daily report forms: "They use 'dry' creek beds for roads in this country. 'Dry!' Ha! Ha! ... Sorry about making only four calls today, but I had to go over to Ervine to pick up a drop shipment of ¾ tins and my clutch broke down. ... Everybody's on WPA in this county. Met only one dealer who sold more than a couple dozen VR a year. Ah, well, it's all in the game! ... Bostitched my left thumb to a barn this morning and couldn't pick up my first call until after lunch. ... The local brick plant here is shut down and nobody's buying anything. ... Five, count 'em, *five* absent dealers in a row. ... Sorry about the $20.85 but the clutch broke down again. ..."

Cloud Club. At this point, the company took us off general store and grocery work and turned us loose in the rich drugstore territory.

The advice of the old salesman now became invaluable. While he had a distaste for any kind of dealer, with druggists he was implacably combative. He was one of the most decent and kindly men I have ever met, but when he gave us pep talks about this enemy ahead of us, he spoke with great intensity. Some druggists were good enough fellows, he told us (i.e., successful ones who bought big deals), but the tough ones were a mean, servile crew; they would insult you, keep you waiting while they pretended to fill prescriptions, lie to you about their inventory, whine at anything less than a 300 per cent markup, and switch their customers to chiseling competitors.

The old salesman would bring us together in batches for several days of demonstration. It was a tremendous experience for us, for though he seemed outwardly a phlegmatic man, we knew him for the artist he was. Outside of the store he was jumpy and sometimes perspired, but once inside, he was composed to the point of apparent boredom. He rarely smiled, almost never opened with a joke. His demeanor seemed to say, I am a busy man and you are damned lucky I have stopped by your miserable store. Sometimes, if the druggist was unusually insolent, he would blow cigar smoke at his face, "Can't sell it if you don't have it," he would say contemptuously, and then, rather pleased with himself, glance back at us, loitering in the wings, to see if we had marked that.

Only old pros like himself could get away with that, he told us in the post-mortem sessions, but there were lots of little tricks we could pick up. As we gathered around him, like Fagin's brood, he would demonstrate how to watch for the victim's shoulders to relax before throwing the clincher; how to pick up the one-size jar of a competitive line that had an especially thick glass bottom and chuckle knowingly; how to feign suppressed worry that maybe the deal was too big for "the smaller druggist like yourself" to take; how to disarm the nervous druggist by fumbling and dropping a pencil. No mercy, he would tell us; give the devils no mercy.

We couldn't either. As the acid test of our gall the company now challenged us to see how many drugstores we could desecrate with "flange" signs. By all the standards of the trade this signposting should have been an impossible task. Almost every "chiseling competitor" would give the druggist at least five dollars to let him put up a sign; we could not offer the druggist a nickel. Our signs, furthermore, were not the usual cardboard kind the druggist could throw away after we had left. They were of metal, they were hideous, and they were to be screwed to the druggists' cherished oak cabinets.

The trick was in the timing. When we were in peak form the procedure went like this: Just after the druggist had signed the order, his shoulders would subside, and this would signal a fleeting period of mutual bonhomie. "New fella, aren't you?" the druggist was likely to say, relaxing. This was his mistake. As soon as we judged the good will to be at full flood, we would ask him if he had a ladder. (There was a ladder out in the car, but the fuss of fetching it would have broken the mood.) The druggist's train of thought would not at that moment connect the request with what was to follow, and he would good-naturedly dispatch someone to bring out a ladder. After another moment of chatter, we would make way for the waiting customer who would engage the druggist's attention. Then, forthrightly, we would slap the ladder up against a spot we had previously reconnoitered. "Just going to get this sign up for you," we would say, as if doing him the greatest favor in the world. He would nod absent-mindedly. Then up the ladder we would go; a few quick turns of the awl, place the bracket in position, and then, the automatic screwdriver. Bang! bang! Down went the sign. (If the druggist had been unusually mean, we could break the thread of the screw for good measure.) Then down with the ladder, shift it over to the second spot, and up again.

About this time the druggist would start looking up a little unhappily, but the good will, while ebbing, was still enough to inhibit him from action. *He* felt sorry for us. Imagine that young man thinking those signs are good looking! Just as he would be about to mumble something about one sign being enough, we would hold up the second one. It had a picture on it of a woman squirting nose drops up her nostrils. We would leer fatuously at it. "Just going to lay this blonde on the top of the cabinet for you, Mr. Jones," we would say, winking. We were giants in those days.

I suppose I should be ashamed, but I must confess I'm really not, and to this day when I enter a drugstore I sometimes fancy the sound of the awl biting irretrievably into the druggist's limed oak. I think the reader will understand, of course, that I am not holding up the Vick School of Applied Merchandising as an ideal model, yet I must add, in all fairness to Vick, that most of us were grateful for the experience. When we get together periodically (we have an informal alumni association), we wallow in talk about how they really separated the men from the boys then, etc. It was truly an experience, and if we shudder to recall the things we did, we must admit that as a cram course in reality it was extraordinarily efficient.

The General Electric program to which I now turn was in full force in the thirties and is actually an older one than the Vick's program. Where the latter was a late flowering of a philosophy already in the descendant, however, GE's was a harbinger of things to come. Even today, it is still somewhat ahead of its time; at this moment there are not many corporation training programs which come near General Electric's either in the size or elaborateness of facilities or, more importantly, in consistency of principles. Yet I believe that as we take up these principal features of the General Electric program, we will be seeing what in a decade or so hence may be the middle of the road.*

The most immediately apparent thing about the General Electric program is the fact that it *is* a school. While the plants serve as part of the campus, the company maintains a full-time staff of 250 instructors and an educational plant complete to such details as company-published textbooks, examinations, classrooms, and alumni publications. In direct operating costs alone the company spends over five million dollars annually—a budget larger than many a medium-sized college.

The program is highly centralized. To keep this plant running, GE's corps of recruiters each year delivers between 1,000 and 1,500 college graduates, mostly engineers, to the company's Schenectady headquarters. There the trainees enter what is for them a continuation of college life. Like fraternity brothers, they live together in boarding houses and attend classes in groups. For afterhours recreation, they have the privileges of the Edison Club where, along with other GE employees with college degrees, they can meet after classes to play golf, bridge, and enjoy a planned series of parties and dances. (GE employees who haven't gone to college are eligible to join if they have achieved a supervisory rating.)

The curriculum is arranged in much the same manner as a university's. The trainee enters under one of several courses, such as engineering and accounting. All these courses will have much in common, however, for the trainee's first eighteen months are regarded as the basic part of his training. At the end of this time he will then go on to a "major." If he has been in the manufacturing training course, for example, he can elect as a major factory operations, manufacturing engineering, production and purchasing, or plant engineering.

The work the trainee does during this training is not, like Vick's applied merchandising, considered an end in itself. From time to time the trainee will work at specific jobs, but these jobs, while not mere

---

*Even Vick has moved considerably in this direction. The heroic years are over; now it is "The Vick Executive Development Program," and though there has been no basic shift in underlying philosophy (Mr. Richardson is still at the helm), Vick now offers many of the material features of the GE program. Security is reasonably guaranteed; no longer are trainees "graduated"—of the roughly one hundred seniors taken in each year, all but a handful can remain as permanent employees. They are exposed to many more aspects of management and they don't have to do things like putting up flange signs.

make-work, are outside the regular cost-accounted operations of the company. The company considers them vehicles for training, and it rotates students from one to another on a regular schedule.

The most noteworthy feature of the General Electric approach is the emphasis on the "professional" manager. As in all training programs, the bulk of the instruction is on specifics. Unlike most, however, there is considerable study in subjects that cut across every kind of job. Trainees study personnel philosophy, labor relations, law, and, most important, the managerial viewpoint.*

Only a minority or the trainees will ever become managers; in ten years 1,500 to 2,000 executive slots will open up, and this means that most of the thousands of young men trained during this time will never get further than middle management. Nevertheless, it is these future executive slots that the company is thinking of, and it makes its concern plain to the trainee. On the report card form for trainees, there is a space for an evaluation as to whether the trainee is suited "for individual contribution" or whether, instead, he is suited "to manage the work of others." The company tells the trainees that it is perfectly all right for them to aim at "individual contribution," which is to say, a specialty. It would be a dull trainee, however, who did not pause before consigning himself to such a role. In one of GE's textbooks there is a picture of a man looking at two ladders. One leads up to a specialty, the other to general managing. The question before the young man, the textbook states, is: "Will I specialize in a particular field?"—or "Will I become broad-gauge, capable of effort in many fields?"

Who wants to be narrow-gauge? Trainees do not have to read too strenuously between the lines to see that one should aim to manage; as a matter of fact, they are predisposed to read a good bit more between the lines than many of their elders would like them to. Which brings us to an important point. In gauging the impact of the curriculum on the young man, his predispositions are as important as the weighting of the courses. Elders at General Electric can demonstrate that the actual amount of time devoted to the abstract arts of management is far less than the time devoted to specific skills. But the managerial part is what the trainees want to hear—and they want to hear it so much that one hour's exposure to the managerial view can be as four or five hours of something else in proportion to its effect on impressionable minds. Trainees are interested, to be sure, in how turbines are made, in the techniques of the accounting department and

*Among other things, the trainees take HOBSO. This is the course in How Our Business System Operates, originally developed by Du Pont to inoculate blue-collar employees against creeping socialism. Though GE has no reason to fear its trainees are ideologically unsound, it explains that the course will help them "detect any bad guidance they receive from union and political leaders, and even from educational and spiritual leaders."

such, but they do not want to be *too* interested. It would make them unbalanced.

They regard specific work very much as many educators view "subject matter" courses: narrowing. As trainees play back the lesson, they see a distinction, sometimes a downright antithesis, between the qualities of the broad-gauge executive and the qualities that one must have to do a superlative piece of concrete work. Not work itself but the managing of other people's work is the skill that they aspire to. As they describe it, the manager is a man in charge of people getting along together, and his *expertise* is relatively independent of who or what is being managed. Or why.

Not surprisingly, the part of the curriculum for which they have the greatest affinity is the human-relations instruction. They are particularly enthusiastic about the "Effective Presentation" course worked up by the sales-training department. They can hardly be blamed. "You can always get anybody to do what you wish," the textbook proclaims. To this end the students spend four months eagerly studying a battery of communication techniques and psychological principles which General Electric tells them will help them to be good managers. (Sample principle: "Never say anything controversial.")

There is nothing novel about teaching people how to manipulate other people, and GE's scientific psychological techniques bear a strong resemblance to the how-to-be-a-success precepts standard in the U.S. for decades. What is different about them is their justification. They are not presented on the grounds that they will help make people do what you want them to do so that you can make money. GE trainees see it in much more eleemosynary terms. They do like the part about selling yourself to others so you can get ahead, for they think a lot about this. But they don't abide the thought of enemies on the other side of the counter; they see the manipulative skills as something that in the long run will make other people *happy*. When in years to come the trainees are charged with the destiny of subordinates—a possibility most take remarkably much for granted—they will be able to achieve a stable, well-adjusted work group. They won't drive subordinates, they explain. They will motivate them.

Trainees are also predisposed to emphasis on co-operation rather than competition, and this they get too. The emphasis is built into the structure of the school. For one thing, the student is given a high measure of security from the beginning, and while there may be promotion of the fittest there can be survival for all. There are exceptions, but one must be a very odd ball to be one. For the first two years the trainee is part of a system in which his salary raises will be automatic, and while later on he will be more on his own there will be no planned elimination as there was at Vick, nor an up-or-out policy such as the Navy's.

To get ahead, or course, one must compete—but not too much, and certainly not too obviously. While overt ambition is a bad posture for the ambitious anywhere, the GE system has especial sanctions for the rate-buster. The trainee is, first of all, a member of a group, and the group is entrusted to a surprising degree with the resolution of his future. How well, the company wants to know, does he fit in? His fellow trainees provide the answer, and in the "case study" group discussions the eager beaver or the deviant is quickly exposed. And brought to heel. Trainees speak frequently of the way close fraternity life atmosphere is valuable in ironing out some trainees' aberrant tendencies. It may be tough on him, they concede, but better now than later. In a few years the trainee will be released from this close association and the social character that he has perfected will be a fundamental necessity; he will be moving from one company branch to another, and he must be able to fit into the same kind of integrated social system.

The company officially recognizes the disciplining of the group. In its periodic rating of the man, the company frequently calls on his comrades to participate in the rating. If a man is liked especially well not only by his superiors but by his peers, he may be given the job of guiding about eight or ten of his fellow trainees. He is now a "sign-up," and if he keeps on maturing he may become a "head-of-tests," the seven "sign-ups" reporting to him. Since the opinions of one's peers are so integral to advancement, this system virtually insures that the overzealous or the "knocker" type of man will not get ahead—or, at the very least, that he will successfully remold himself to the managerial image.

The fact that the trainee must spend so much time thinking of what other people think of him does not oppress him. Quite the opposite, the constant surveillance is one of the things the average trainee talks about most enthusiastically. The rating system is highly standardized, he explains; it is the product of *many* people rather than one, and this denominator of judgments frees him from the harshness or caprice that might result from the traditional boss-employee relationship. He is also freed from being ignored; the system insures that other people must be thinking about him quite as much as he is thinking about them, and for this reason he won't get pigeonholed. At General Electric, as one trainee remarked, not only can't you get lost, you can't even hide.

Needless to say, ambition still pulses, and I am not trying to suggest that the General Electric man is any less set on the main chance than my Vick comrades. It is quite obvious, nevertheless, that he must pursue the main chance in a much more delicate fashion. To get ahead, he must co-operate with the others—but co-operate *better* than they do.

The rules of the game do permit a few lapses, but these lapses, characteristically, are the display of personality. Somewhere along the line the trainees must get themselves hired into a regular job, and to do this they must attract the attention of superiors. There is a tacit understanding among trainees that it is perfectly all right to make a bald play to get on a first name-basis with superiors that might do one some good. "As soon as you know your way around a new department you start telephoning," one trainee explains, tapping the inter-communication telephone directory. "Believe me, this little green book here is a man's best friend." The company encourages superiors to encourage this kind of contact. "I or anybody else," another trainee says, "can walk into a manager's office just as easily as we can each other's. By ten o'clock of the day I hit the New York office I was calling everybody by his first name."

In contrasting the General Electric type program with the old Vick's program, I have been contrasting extremes. The dividing line they illustrate, however, is one that more and more companies are having to recognize. For a long time businessmen have been rather carelessly talking about the coming of the "professional manager" as if this development was merely a further refinement of the mixture as before. When executives began expanding trainee programs right after the war, management literature on the subject gave no evidence that there were any policy issues involved, and the matters discussed were mainly those of the length of time men should be trained, the frequency of their rotation, and the like.

As time has gone on, however, excutives have found that the trainee programs are forcing them to think a lot more than they wanted to about questions more fundamental. Was not the trainee program itself producing a rather definable type? Was this what the company wanted? And what was the company "character," anyway? For a long time executives have sensed that organizations tend to select and fashion a certain type, and while they cannot actually put their finger on it they know that, say, a Union Carbide man is somehow different from a W. R. Grace man. But they would like to leave it at that—in the realm of mystique. Now they have to analyze it.

Eventually, they would have to ponder the compatibility of the "professional manager" with the company spirit whether they put in a centralized training program or not. Times are moving fast, and from the great proselyting centers of the business schools the new man will be going forth to leave his mark on every kind of organization, traditional or otherwise. In the centralized training program, however, he does it ahead of time. It is the ideal culture for him, and though it is a case of evolution rather than revolution, the suddenness of his growth has been rather unsettling to many executives. Here, all at once, is an advance view of the man of the future, and for many a management it has proved too advanced to assimilate.

What the programs have done is accentuate the difference between generations. Ordinarily, this shift in outlook is so gradual as to be imperceptible, except in retrospect, and the company ideology can be revised without pain, or, for that matter, without anyone's knowing it's been revised at all. But not now. More consciously than other age groups before them, today's trainees see themselves as a new breed, and when you talk to them you cannot help but feel a certain premature condescension on their part for the present managers. One of the points younger men frequently make in praising their advanced training is its value to *older* men. "It brings them out of their shells," one twenty-three-year-old engineer explains. "It teaches them that there is an outside world and that there are good ideas and procedures around that the company has not come up with yet." The trainees make the same point about human-relations teaching; even if they don't need to be converted, they explain, the teaching does percolate up to the older, less progressive levels of management. "It's sad," one trainee said, "that you have to teach people how to be human in business. But the brass do need it."

Thanks to a misadventure of the Ford Motor Company, there exists a case study of what happens when this advanced view is introduced without a comparable change in the company spirit. For many reasons, including, perhaps, a certain sensitivity to charges that it was old-fashioned, shortly after the war Ford introduced an ambitious "field training program" for college graduates. Somewhat like the General Electric program, it was a centralized observation-orientation program through which incoming recruits were taken on a grand tour of the company which lasted some two years.

Ford executives now grimace at the memory of it. While no one planned it that way, the program created a cadre of "crown princes" that did not jibe at all well with the organization. As older hands were quick to remark, the trainees had gotten such a broad view of things that they had become quite confused as to what, specifically, they wanted to do in the way of actual work. Eventually they were placed in regular jobs, but to do it personnel people had to peddle them around and use a good bit of persuasion. Today the recruit gets a physical examination, a one-day orientation, and then is put to work. He is not encouraged to call the brass by their first names, and his advancement depends on what his line superior happens to think of his work.

The basic collision has been a philosophical one. Quite perceptibly, the schooling in the broad view produced a definite attitude toward work, and in Ford's case, an attitude 180 degrees away from what the company was used to. In companies like Ford—and this would include General Motors and du Pont—the emphasis on a specific task as an end in itself shows quite readily in the way people talk about their jobs. Talk to a non-program Ford man or a du Pont or a GM man and he will rarely dwell on abstractions that cut across the organization, but instead will talk on the concrete work he's connected with, like designing transmissions or opening new markets for paint. He may accuse himself of being too narrow, but he really doesn't worry about it—at that time, anyway—and even the highly ambitious will tend to leave to the president and the executive committee the chore of pondering the big picture. Where at General Electric a young man is likely to talk about managing, in short, at Ford he will talk about cars.

This identification with work was long regarded as the natural order of things, and it has been with some surprise that executives have found it necessary to make the reasons for it explicit. Looking back on the training program, one Ford executive summed up his complaint this way: "I always felt that human relations and getting along with people was all very important. But these trainees made me do a lot of thinking. At Ford we judge a man by results. I mean, what he gets accomplished. And I think this is the way it should be. Sure, human relations is important, but it should be subsidiary to results. Look at it this way: if the girls in a steno pool run away when a man comes around to give dictation on account of his manners, or other people hold out information on him, his results will be bad. I think that the colleges that send these men to us ought to put more emphasis on *doing things*. A lot of the young fellows I talk to think that most engineering problems are all solved and that it's just a question of human engineering. That's just not right."

Interestingly, it is management people in the thirty-five to forty-five age range who are most sensitive to the difference of viewpoint stimulated by centralized programs. Not only do they see more of the trainees than the older executives do, they expect less difference between their generation and the younger one and are surprised to find how much difference there is. Common to almost all of their criticisms is the charge that the younger men are much more sanguine than they had ever been and that the great expectations should be chastened rather than stimulated. Robert C. Landon, Industrial Relations Manager of

Rohm & Haas, puts it this way: "Since the time they entered kindergarten they have spent sixteen years during which the world has been presented to them in study courses to be absorbed in an atmosphere of security. To extend this kind of thing when they reach the corporation—except for a well-founded research program—is a dangerous concept." Executives of this persuasion feel that present-day organizations are benevolent enough already. "We should let the wheel of fortune turn," one says. "It's all right for a young man to develop himself, but he shouldn't *be* developed."

I do not wish to overdraw the present distinctions. The first-rate General Electric trainee would not find it insuperable adjusting to the climate at Ford, and a first-rate Ford trainee could adapt to General Electric. Neither do I wish to suggest that a gulf is yawning between two kinds of companies. There has always been more diversity within the business creed than the nonbusinessman suspects and there always will be. But there is a problem of weighting common to all organizations, and this is my reason for dwelling on the "social character" developed by the training programs; exaggerated somewhat, here is the most likely alternative to the past. In these terms no one would choose, certainly not businessmen. The choice will be made through a multitude of day-to-day decisions which at the time will seem squarely poised over the middle way. But a shift there will be for all that.

WILLIAM H. WHYTE JR.

Selections from The Organization Man

The "Well-rounded" Man

Let's examine first the model as younger men see him. They are in remarkable agreement on the matter. There are dissenters, precious few that they may be, and no generalization can do justice to all the different shadings in the majority's view. On the fundamental premise of the new model executive, however, the young men who hope to be that vary little, and from company to company, region to region, you hear a litany increasingly standard. It goes something like this:

Be loyal to the company and the company will be loyal to you. After all, if you do a good job for the organization, it is only good sense for the organization to be good to you, because that will be best for everybody. There are a bunch of real people around here. Tell them what you think and they will respect you for it. They don't want a man to fret and stew about his work. It won't happen to me. A man who gets ulcers probably shouldn't be in business anyway.

This is more than the wishful thinking normal of youth. Wishful it may be, but it is founded on a well-articulated premise—and one that not so many years ago would have been regarded by the then young men with considerable skepticism. The premise is, simply, that the goals of the individual and the goals of the organization will work out to be one and the same. The young men have no cynicism about the "system," and very little skepticism—they don't see it as something to be bucked, but as something to be co-operated with.

This view is more optimistic than fatalistic. If you were to draft an organization chart based on some junior-executive bull sessions, the chart wouldn't look too much like the usual hierarchical structure.

Instead of converging toward a narrow apex, the lines on the chart would rise parallel, eventually disappearing into a sort of mist before they reach any embarrassing turning points.

The prosperity of recent years has had a lot to do with the rosiness of the view. Corporations have been expanding at a great rate, and the effect has been a large-scale deferral of dead ends and pigeonholes for thousands of organization men. With so many new departments, divisions, and plants being opened up, many a young man of average ability has been propelled upward so early—and so pleasantly—that he can hardly be blamed if he thinks the momentum is a constant.

The unity they see between themselves and The Organization has deeper roots, however, than current expediency. Let's take the matter of ambition as further illustration. They do not lack ambition. They seem to, but that is only because the nature of it has changed. It has become a *passive* ambition. Not so many years ago it was permissible for the ambitious young man to talk of setting his cap for a specific goal—like becoming president of a corporation, building a bridge, or making a million dollars. Today it is a very rare young man who will allow himself to talk in such a way, let alone think that way. He can argue, with good grounds, that if it was unrealistic in the past it is even more so today. The life that he looks ahead to will be a life in which he is only one of hundreds of similarly able people and in which they will all be moved hither and yon and subject to so many forces outside their control—not to mention the Bomb—that only a fool would expect to hew to a set course.

But they see nothing wrong with this fluidity. They have an implicit faith that The Organization will be as interested in making use of their best qualities as they are themselves, and thus, with equanimity, they can entrust the resolution of their destiny to The Organization. No specific goal, then, is necessary to give them a sense of continuity. For the short term, perhaps—it would be nice to be head of the electronics branch. But after that, who knows? The young executive does not wish to get stuck in a particular field. The more he is shifted, the more broad-gauge will he become, and the more broad-gauge, the more successful.

But not *too* successful. Somewhat inconsistently, trainees hope to rise high and hope just as much not to suffer the personal load of doing so. Frequently they talk of finding a sort of plateau—a position well enough up to be interesting but not so far up as to have one's neck outstretched for others to chop at. It figures, the young man can explain. Why knock yourself out when the extra salary won't bring home much more actual pay? You can make a very good living in the middle levels—well, not exactly middle, a little higher than that—and the work, furthermore, can be just as fulfilling. If The Organization is good and big, to put it another way, there will be success without tears.

For the executive of the future, trainees say, the problem of company loyalty shouldn't be a problem at all. Almost every older executive you talk to has some private qualifications about his fealty to the company; in contrast, the average young man cherishes the idea that his relationship with The Organization is to be for keeps. Sometimes he doesn't even concede that the point need ever come to test.

Their attitude toward another aspect of organization shows the same bias. What of the "group life," the loss of individualism? Once upon a time it was conventional for young men to view the group life of the big corporation as one of its principal disadvantages. Today, they see it as a positive boon. Working with others, they believe, will *reduce* the frustrations of work, and they often endow the accompanying suppression of ego with strong spiritual overtones. They will concede that there is often a good bit of wasted time in the committee way of life and that the handling of human relations involves much suffering of fools gladly. But this sort of thing, they say, is the heart of the organization man's job, not merely the disadvantages of it. "Any man who feels frustrated by these things," one young trainee with face unlined said to me, "can never be an executive."

On the matter of overwork they are particularly stern. They want to work hard, but not too hard; the good, equable life is paramount and they see no conflict between enjoying it and getting ahead. The usual top executive, they believe, works much too hard, and there are few subjects upon which they will discourse more emphatically than the folly of elders who have a single-minded devotion to work. Is it, they ask, really necessary any more? Or, for that matter, moral?

Tom Rath, hero of *The Man in the Gray Flannel Suit*, puts the thought well. He has just been offered a very stimulating, challenging, and perhaps too-demanding job by his dynamic boss. As the dust jacket says, Rath is a true product of his times. He turns the job down. "I don't want to give up the time," he tells the boss. "I'm trying to be honest about this. I want the money. Nobody likes money better than I do. But I'm just not the kind of guy who can work evenings and week ends and all the rest of it forever. I guess there's even more to it than that. I'm not the kind of person who can get all wrapped up in a job—I can't get myself convinced that my work is the most important thing in the world. I've been through one war. Maybe another one's coming. If one is, I want to be able to look back and figure I spent the time between the wars with my family, the way it should have been spent."

The boss should be damn well ashamed of himself. As Rath implies so strongly, when the younger men say they don't want to work too hard, they feel that they are making a positive moral contribution as well. In this self-ennobling hedonism, furthermore, they don't see why they shouldn't have the good life and good money both. There doesn't have to be any choice between the two.*

Which brings us to the best part of all. Younger men don't believe there has to be a choice because they believe organizations have been coming around to their own way of thinking. It's just plain good sense for The Organization, they argue, not to have people getting too involved in their jobs. Overwork may have been necessary once, they say, and perhaps you still need a few, very few, dynamic types, but business now sees that the full man is the model. What it needs is not the hard driver but the man who is so rested, so at peace with his environment, so broadened by suburban life, that he is able to handle human relations with poise and understanding.

So they believe, and because they believe this they see the organization life of the future as one in which tensions will be lessening. Again, it figures. The people who will be moving into the key slots then will be people like themselves, and as the last, unreconstructed drivers disappear there will be less trouble for everyone. Out of necessity, then, as well as natural desire, the wise young man is going to enjoy himself—plenty of time with the kids, some good hobbies, and later on he'll certainly go in for more reading and music and stuff like that. He will, in sum, be the apotheosis of the well-rounded man: obtrusive in no particular, excessive in no zeal. He will be the man in the middle.

A young man's idle dream? It is a playback only mildly exaggerated of a vision of the future that is becoming stronger and stronger among personnel executives and the business-school people who intellectualize for business. And their influence should not be underrated. The personnel men are of the staff, rather than the line, but it is they who choose the trainees and administer the schools that affect trainees in their formative years with the corporations.†

What personnel men have in mind as the manager of the future is more of a departure than is generally recognized. Personnel executives don't care to insult the company's brass and, except in the privacy

---

*Tom Rath, incidentally, found he wasn't making any sacrifice at all. After his speech he asked the boss if he still wanted him to work for him. "Of course," the boss says. "There are plenty of good positions where it's not necessary for a man to put in an unusual amount of work. Now it's just a matter of finding the right spot for you."

†The number of personnel people, compared to other employees, has been rising at a rapid rate. A study made by Dale Yoder and Mona L. Walz of the University of Minnesota's Industrial Relations Center indicates that by 1955 there were 8 personnel people per 1,000 employees—a jump of 15 per cent over the 7 per 1,000 in 1954.

of the conferences and workshops endemic to the field, they manage to muffle the criticism of the top executives their new model implies. For another thing, most definitions of executive traits are so encompassing that no matter how radical or conservative one's views of the future executive, there will be comfort in almost any of the usual all-purpose definitions. The executive, everyone agrees, must be forceful, patient, able to get along with other people, foresighted, imaginative, decisive, and of sound views.

But what, among these contradictions, is to be emphasized? To draw personnel people and executives out on the matter I tried an experiment. Out of the usual inventory of executive qualities I drew out two antithetical definitions. One description of the ideal executive hewed fairly close to the Protestant Ethic; the other to the Social Ethic. I then wrote to 150 personnel directors and asked them to say which one they inclined toward. At the same time, I sent an identical letter to 150 corporation presidents.

If they *had* to choose, I asked them, which of the following schools of thought would they favor:

a.   "Because the rough-and-tumble days of corporation growth are over, what the corporation needs most is the *adaptable* administrator, schooled in managerial skills and concerned primarily with human relations and the techniques of making the corporation a smooth-working team."

b.   "Because the challenge of change demands new ideas to keep the corporation from rigidifying, what the corporation needs most is the man with strong personal convictions who is not shy about making unorthodox decisions that will unsettle tested procedures—and his colleagues."

The response was spirited. Many of the hundred who answered jumped on me for asking such a question, but most of them did choose one way or the other and, more importantly, they went into their reasons at length.* The vote: presidents voted 50 per cent in favor of the administrator, 50 per cent in favor of the other type; personnel men: 70 per cent for the administrator.

In the wording of their letters the personnel men showed an inclination to the administrator even stronger than the vote indicated. Presidents who favored the administrator generally noted that the individualist had his place too; personnel men quite often not only

---

*We had expected that the type of industry the executive was in and the size of the company would have a great deal to do with the way he answered. This did not turn out to be the case. No matter how we tried to correlate the answers, by type of company, age, etc., no pattern manifested itself; the choice, evidently, was primarily a reflection of the executive's own personal outlook.

failed to make such a qualification but went on to infer that the individualist should be carefully segregated out of harm's way if he should be tolerated at all. They were, furthermore, strikingly unanimous in their explanations: among the 70 per cent voting for the administrators the explanations offered so complemented one another as to produce a quite cohesive philosophy. Here, in paraphrase, is the gist of it:

The rough-and-tumble days are over. Since the job is to keep things going, more than pioneering, the leader must be the professional manager, "the man who knows how to elicit participative consultation, how to motivate groups and individuals, how to enhance job satisfactions ... how to conduct problem-solving meetings." He will be a generalist who will not think in terms of specific work but in the science of making other people work.

In the old sense of work, he does not work; he encourages others to work. He does not create; he moderates and adjusts those who do create. "Primarily he is the balance wheel on the tendency of the professional-type individual to wander into new, unexplored, and perhaps dangerous territory."

Unorthodoxy can be dangerous to The Organization. The pro-administrators sometimes conceded that the administrator could have unconventional ideas himself at times. But, they were in haste to add, he ought to be rather sober about it, and it was on the dangers rather than on the advantages of such unorthodox thinking that they dwelled.*

Unorthodoxy is dangerous to The Organization. Some personnel men didn't simply omit mention of inner qualities such as "drive" and "imagination"; they went out of their way to warn against them. "Any progressive employer," said one personnel director, "would look askance at the individualist and would be reluctant to instill such thinking in the minds of trainees." Another personnel man put it in more direct terms: "Men of strong personal convictions, willing to make unorthodox decisions, are more frequently given to the characteristics of 'drive' *rather than* 'leadership.' " (Italics mine.) This invidious pairing of qualities once thought congenial with each other was not restricted entirely to personnel men. "We used to look primarily for brilliance," said one president. "Now that much-abused word 'character' has become very

*When we checked the words which recurred most often in letters, we found that among presidents the most frequent were "imagination," "vigor," "judgment," "dynamic," and "aggressive." Except for those personnel men who voted for the individualist (and in fairness it should be noted that some were as strong as presidents on this score), personnel men tended to use words like "harmonious," "co-operative," etc.

important. We don't care if you're a Phi Beta Kappa or a Tau Beta Phi. We want a well-rounded person who can handle well-rounded people."

Ideas come from the group, not from the individual. The well-rounded man is one who does not think up ideas himself but mediates other people's ideas, and so democratically that he never lets his own judgment override the decisions of the group. "The decisions should be made by the group," says a personnel director, "and agreement reached after discussion and consultation prior to action." "The leader must be attentive and receptive to the ideas of his followers," says another personnel man, "and he must adjust his ideas accordingly."

If the corporation concentrates on getting people who will process other people's ideas, where will it get the other people—that is, the people with ideas? Some of the pro-administrators did concede that a question was left begging. Where would the spark come from? How could a corporation ever change to new ways if the top man was so concerned with equilibrium? They submitted a solution:

Creative leadership is a staff function. Organizations need new ideas from time to time. But the leader is not the man for this; he hires staff people to think up the ideas. While the captive screwball thinks about the major problems of the corporation, the leader—a sort of nonpartisan mediator—will be able to attend to the techniques of solving the problem rather than the problem itself. "He will be able to accomplish change without upsetting relationships," explains one, "because he has been trained to think about *how* the change should be accomplished quite as much as to think about what the change should be." His job is not to look ahead himself but to check the excesses of the kind of people who do look ahead. He does not unbalance himself by enthusiasm for a particular plan by getting involved with the basic engine. He is the governor.

In part, this vision of the new management can be explained away as rationalization. For the trainee it masks the conflicts ahead; for the personnel man it affords a function and status for what is still a highly ambiguous field of work. "From where we sit in the company," says one of the best personnel men in the country, "we have to look at only the aspects of work that cut across all sorts of jobs—administration and human relations. Now these are aspects of work, abstractions, but it's easy for personnel people to get so hipped on their importance that they look on the specific tasks of making things and selling them as secondary. It's heresy, but I swear I am not so sure human relations are really any better than they were twenty years ago. We just talk about them more, and the muddy-headed way so many of us do gives young men a very bum steer."

But even if the "well-rounded" ideal were no more than rationalization, the concept would still be powerful. It is self-proving. As an example of one very practical consequence we have only to note that in many large corporations the junior executives help out on the interviewing and selecting necessary to restock the cadres. As the trainees go back to the campus to search for their own image, they go back strengthened more than ever in their anti-intellectualism, and in a great Mendelian selection process well-rounded men who were chosen by well-rounded men in turn chose more well-rounded men.

It is possible that a genius, supposing he wanted to join the company in the first place, could so feign the role of the well-adjusted extrovert as to hoodwink a trainee into giving him a job. But he'd have to be skillful about it. A group of GE trainees were asked what they would do if a brilliant person like Steinmetz were to apply to them for a job. After some thought, a few trainees said they thought maybe he could work out; because of the fraternity-like life of the training program, they "could iron out his rough spots." Others disagreed; the man would be too hopelessly anti-social to remold. "I don't think we would put up with a fellow like that now," one said. (Fortunately for GE's research division, as we will see later, it does not use trainees as recruiters.)

From company to company, trainees express the same impatience. All the great ideas, they explain, have already been discovered and not only in physics and chemistry but in practical fields like engineering. The basic creative work is done, so the man you need—for every kind of job—is a practical, team-player fellow who will do a good shirt-sleeves job. "I would sacrifice brilliance," one trainee said, "for human understanding every time."

And they do, too.

LYMAN W. PORTER

Where Is the Organization Man?

Large companies seem to be fair game these days for critics of the U.S. business scene. The slings and arrows hurled at "bigness" are many and varied. Since the target is large, figuratively and literally, undoubtedly many of these shots have hit the mark in the past and will continue to do so in the future.

It is not my purpose to defend big business on all fronts. Rather, I wish to address myself to one particular type of criticism that has been raised with increasing frequency in recent years. I refer to the claim that the big company is the home of the cautious, conforming, security-conscious middle manager—that the very size of large organizations compels managers to behave in this mold. It is this aspect of the size problem that I shall discuss; the various additional "faults" of big business I leave to others. For the reader wishing a bird's-eye view of this study, here are my main points and conclusions:

- The popular assumption that bigness encourages the "organization man" has not been adequately supported in the literature to date. Either the criticism reflects only one man's or one company's experience, or it is based on findings that fail to take some crucial comparisons into account.

- Judging from the responses of more than 1,700 managers in companies of all sizes, administrative jobs in large firms are generally seen as being

Source: *Harvard Business Review*, Nov.-Dec. 1963, pp. 53-61. Copyright © 1963 by the President and Fellows of Harvard College; all rights reserved.

more challenging, more difficult, and more competitive than jobs in small firms.

- The personality traits of the so-called "organization man" are seen as being in greater demand in small than in large companies.

- Large companies seem to satisfy as wide a variety of managers' psychological needs as do smaller firms.

- In large and small organizations alike, managers' attitudes vary significantly with two factors: (1) level of position, and (2) whether the position is described as line or staff.

THE CASE AGAINST BIGNESS

The case against large corporations—in terms of the type of behavior they supposedly force on their managers—has been made by a number of writers, both within and outside the business community. In addition, various studies have been made that, to some observers, seem to reinforce the criticism of bigness.

Dark View From Whyte

Probably the most influential, and perhaps the most eloquent, condemnation of the inhibiting effects of large organizations on those who work in them was made several years ago by William H. Whyte, Jr., in *The Organization Man.*[1] Of course, it is true that Whyte never says, in so many words, that the "organization man" resides *only* in large companies. However, reading through the book one is certainly left with the impression that Whyte feels a disproportionate number of organization men are to be found in large rather than small companies. A very tenable assumption is that most of the legion of readers of *The Organization Man* finish the book picturing a strong link between the organization man and the big company.

In his book, Whyte makes two major points regarding the big corporation:

1. Large organizations recruit the type of individual who fits the prototype of the organization man. These recruiting efforts are reflected in the type of college senior who prefers to join the large company versus the type who wants to go into a small business. According to Whyte, "In turning their back on the Protestant Ethic they [the college seniors who prefer big business] do not cherish venture. . . ."[2]

2. A more serious charge is that the big organization promotes, encourages, and nourishes the organization-man type of behavior. In other words,

regardless of what kind of a person goes into a large company—and big companies do make "mistakes" sometimes and hire the nonconforming, non-organization man—the chances are that the organization will mold and shape his personality so that it is more conforming and more subservient to the group and the organization than it was before he joined.

I should hasten to point out that Whyte is by no means the only critic to make these points. For instance:

> A very persuasive book about what life can be like in the large company, a book that provides an actual case history to back up the types of contentions put forward by Whyte, is *Life in the Crystal Palace*, by Alan Harrington.[3] Of course, he was only one individual out of 34,000 who worked in the company in question, and the company is only one of a number of large firms, so there are certain problems in generalizing from his experiences. Nevertheless, what his book does show in graphic detail is that such things as Whyte alleges can and do happen in large companies.

The key questions are these:

- Does the big company foster organization-man behavior more often or more extensively than does the small company?
- Are the "faults" of the large company in this respect more severe than those of the small firm?

It is the *comparative* disadvantages (and advantages) of large and small companies that have not been brought out in books such as *The Organization Man* and *Life in the Crystal Palace*. While many people feel they know the answer to the comparative question, the arguments they put forward about the relative disadvantages of large companies are based simply on personal opinion and observation, rather than on any objective, verifiable evidence.

Size-ups of Size

What do the more scholarly studies show? A brief review of their findings will allow the new findings that I shall present later to be put into a more meaningful context.

Actually, size, as a variable affecting job attitudes, has been studied with some frequency in the past. Most often, these studies have been concerned with the relationship between company size and morale or job satisfaction. A review of these studies shows that the majority of them come to the same general conclusion, namely, that smaller size *is* associated with higher morale and job satisfaction. For example:

In a widely cited series of articles on organization structure and morale, James Worthy has stated, "Our researches demonstrate that mere size is unquestionably one of the most important factors in determining the quality of employee relationships: the smaller the work unit, the higher the morale and vice versa."[4] Since Worthy, at the time of this statement, was a high-level executive for a very large organization, Sears, Roebuck and Co., it might appear that his comments amount to heresy against the kind of organization in which he worked. However, close examination of his summary statement will show that Worthy is talking about the size of "work units" and not about the total size of organizations.

In other words. Worthy's findings, just as almost all of the other studies on the relation of size to morale, are applicable to *intra*-organization, not *inter*-organization comparisons. That is, the evidence does seem fairly clear-cut that smaller work units within a given organization do have higher morale than larger units in that same organization. This finding has been confirmed in one form or another in almost every study dealing with the question in the past 20 or 30 years. Granted this, what are the limitations of the studies? What key questions do they leave unanswered? Two points must be stressed.

Sub-organizations vs. Separate Organizations. The previous studies have not demonstrated whether small organizations *as entities* have higher morale or more satisfied employees than large organizations. There are good reasons why one might expect different—though not necessarily opposite—results for *inter*-organization size comparisons in contrast to *intra*-organization comparisons. Most companies try to apply the same personnel policies to all parts of the organization, regardless of size of work group; and, even though a "larger" organization unit may be twice as large as a "smaller" unit, it will probably constitute only a relatively small per cent of the total work force (especially if the company itself is large). Therefore, larger units within an organization would not be able to provide any special advantages for their members, even though members might *expect* special advantages as a result of the units' potentially greater power.

Now, contrast the situation if large organizations are compared with *separate* small organizations. The picture may be considerably different from that described above for *intra*-organization comparisons. Where separate organizations of different size are compared with each other, the comparisons may indeed allow for some of the potential advantages of large size to appear. Thus:

- Large companies presumably have more resources—technical, financial, and personnel—than do small companies, which may result in greater material benefits for employees.

- Since large companies generally have more community and national prestige than smaller companies, employees of larger organizations who identify with the company could conceivably have as great or greater feelings of self-esteem than those in smaller companies.

- Even in the areas of ego and self-fulfillment needs, the larger company may offer greater advantages than the smaller company, especially for those individuals who reach the middle and upper levels of management. This is because the manager in the big company influences more people and had command over more resources than his counterpart in the small company.

Work Level. A second critical variable that has not been taken into account in previous research on size is the organizational level of the employee. Virtually without exception, previous studies in this area have been carried out on the nonmanagement worker or, in a few cases, the first-level supervisor. Almost no studies have been concerned with attitude comparisons of *managers* from large companies or units and from small companies or units.

There are, again, some good reasons why one might expect organization level to have an effect on the relation of size to job satisfaction. Employees at the bottom levels of large companies have a much greater superstructure of organization levels and of sheer numbers of people above them than do similarly situated employees in small companies. In effect, at a low organization level— for instance, at the hourly paid level—a worker in a small organization has fewer bosses above him and more absolute influence on his work environment than does a worker in a large company. However, at high levels of the hierarchy the picture should change. An upper-level manager in a large company controls or "bosses" more people—in absolute numbers—than a similar upper-level manager in a small company. Hence, the large-company manager should have more absolute influence than the small-company manager.

There is one further thing to note about previous research on the effects of size on job attitudes. Almost the only kind of attitude that has been studied in the past has been in the area of job satisfaction. There have been very few studies, if any, that have related company size to other kinds of attitudes, especially those that would have any implications for the question of where the organization-man type of behavior is most likely to be found.

SCOPE OF NEW STUDY

In order to try to answer these questions about the comparative effect of large and small companies on the attitudes of managers, we have recently completed, at the University of California, a large-scale, nationwide job attitude study of over 1,700 managers from a great variety of types and sizes of companies. This was a questionnaire study carried out with the cooperation of the American Foundation for Management Research, an affiliate of the American Management Association. The sample of respondents was obtained by taking a random sample of members of the association and one of a similar number of nonmembers whose names were on mailing lists available to the association. The method of distribution of the questionnaire ensured against the possibility of any single company being represented by more than a few managers (except by chance) in the total sample. Thus, the results obtained are not due to the particular set of conditions or circumstances existing in a specific company.

In order to study the relationship of size to certain job attitudes, respondents in the study were classified as belonging to small, medium, or large companies on the basis of the total number of company employees they reported:

- Respondents who indicated that the total size of their company was from 1–499 employees (both management and nonmanagement) were placed in the small-company category.

- Those who said that the size of the company for which they worked was between 500 and 4,999 employees were classified as belonging to medium-size companies.

- Managers who said that their company employed more than 5,000 people were put in the large-company category.

Exhibit I presents the number of respondents from each of the three company size categories and the median size of the company represented in each category. As can be seen from this chart, the typical size for small companies is 240 employees, the typical or median size for medium-size companies is 2,160 employees, and for large companies it is 20,000. Thus, medium-size companies in our sample are about nine times the size of small companies, and the large companies are nine times as big as the medium-size companies and 81 times as big as the small companies. Clearly, our two extreme size groups—small and

SIZE CATEGORY	RANGE OF COMPANY SIZES	MEDIAN SIZE OF COMPANY	NUMBER OF RESPONDENTS
	(NO. OF EMPLOYEES)		
SMALL	1-499	240	329
MEDIUM	500-4,999	2,160	720
LARGE	5,000 or more	20,000	652

Exhibit I. Characteristics of sample by company size

large companies—differ substantially in their over-all size. Thus, if size is a factor in what affects the job attitudes we studied, our separation by size should be great enough to allow the factor to operate.

For purposes of the present article, respondents were cross-classified by level of management position as well as by size of company in order to ensure that results attributed to the size variable were not contaminated by the level factor. Thus, the data to be presented in Exhibits II, III, and IV are based on the average values for vice presidents, upper-middle managers, and lower-middle managers for the three company sizes. The level of a respondent's position was classified on the basis of (a) how many levels were above it, and (b) how many levels in total existed in the organization. For instance, if the respondent reported two levels above his and five altogether, he was classified as upper middle management.

We studied (and I shall report on) three major types of attitudes:

1. How managers rate and describe their jobs, including the perceived challenge, complexity, interest, and other qualities of the job.
2. The kinds of personality traits managers think are necessary for people to perform successfully in their particular administrative jobs. This second area specifically focuses on organization-man and non-organization-man types of traits.
3. The degrees of need fulfillment that are obtainable in managerial jobs.

REACTIONS TO JOBS

How do managers in large and small companies describe their jobs? The answers to this part of the study will surprise many people. Before reporting the findings, however, let me comment on our methodology:

In the first section of the questionnaire managers were asked to describe their current positions by checking 20 adjective scales. Each scale was marked at each end by a pair of opposite adjectives (e.g., *good–bad*) and respondents indicated not only which adjective was more descriptive of their job but also to what degree that choice was true. Thus, by this means, it was possible to see the relative description applied by each group of respondents from different size companies. For example, on the *good–bad* scale all three size groups reported that their jobs were more accurately described by *good* rather than *bad*, but it was also possible to determine that managers from large companies felt this even more strongly than did those from medium-size companies, and the latter in turn described their jobs as closer to the *good* end of the scale than did the small-company managers.

In Exhibit II those scales which show consistently similar trends from large to medium to small companies are presented in white bands, and those scales which show no consistent trends are shown in gray bands. The latter scales are included in the exhibit on the theory that it is as instructive to know what effects size does not have as it is to know the effects that it does have. For the scales with the consistent trends, the adjective trait at the left of each scale is more intensively applied by managers from large companies. In each of these instances, with one minor exception, the answers by respondents from medium-size companies fall between those from large- and small-company respondents. This means that for each of the white bands the trend runs directly in relation to size. Thus, in the case of the *difficult–easy* scale (ranging from 1 to 7) the mean value for large-company executives is 2.80; for medium-size company executives, 2.92; for small-company executives, 3.17.

Larger Size, More Challenge

The interesting thing about the nine scales in Exhibit II that show trends is not the size of the trends; rather, the key point of interest is the total picture one gets of the differences in the way that large-company managers describe their jobs compared to small-company managers. Managers from large companies are more apt to use the terms *good, interesting, difficult, intense, complex, profound, challenging,* and *competitive* in describing their jobs than are the managers from small companies. The picture is hardly consistent with that painted

SCALES SHOWING TRENDS	(white)
SCALES SHOWING NO TRENDS	(shaded)

STABLE	CHANGEABLE
INTERESTING	BORING
GOOD	BAD
HIGH	LOW
DIFFICULT	EASY
INTENSE	RELAXED
IMPORTANT	UNIMPORTANT
UNUSUAL	USUAL
TANGIBLE	INTANGIBLE
COMPLEX	SIMPLE
ROUTINE	VARIED
FORMAL	INFORMAL
PROFOUND	SUPERFICIAL
BROAD	NARROW
INDEPENDENT	DEPENDENT
CHALLENGING	NOT CHALLENGING
PRECISE	VAGUE
WEAK	POWERFUL
ACTIVE	PASSIVE
COMPETITIVE	COOPERATIVE

Exhibit II. How managers' job descriptions in large companies compare with descriptions in smaller companies

in *The Organization Man, Life in the Crystal Palace,* and other books and articles.

If accepted at face value, these comparative job descriptions certainly seem to point to the large, not the small, company as offering the more challenging, the more difficult and competitive job. In fact, of all 20 scales investigated, the one showing the greatest trend was *challenging–not challenging;* the larger the organization, the greater the challenge in the job! Of the nine scales showing trends, only the *formal–informal* scale is probably in accord with common conceptions of the differences in management jobs between large and small companies.

PERSONALITY TRAITS

What personality traits do executives consider important for managerial success? To answer this question we asked managers, in the second part of the questionnaire, to rank a set of 10 personality traits in the "order of their importance for success in your management position." Note that the managers were not asked to describe themselves, but rather to indicate which traits were most necessary for a person to be successful if he occupied the manager's position. The 10 traits that were ranked by the managers were so chosen that there would be 5 traits representative of organization-man type of behavior, or what sociologist David Riesman calls "other-directed" behavior, and 5 traits representative of non-organization man, or "inner-directed" behavior. These 10 traits were:

"Organization-man" ("other-directed") traits

Adaptable	Cooperative
Agreeable	Tactful
Cautious	

"Non-organization-man" ("inner-directed") traits

Decisive	Self-confident
Forceful	Independent
Imaginative	

By means of the ranks that the managers gave to these 10 traits it was possible to see which size-of-company group placed relatively more emphasis on other-directed or organization-man type of behavior as a necessity for job success.

The results for this part of the questionnaire can be seen in Exhibit III. Of the 10 traits studied, 6 showed no clearly discernible increasing or decreasing trends from smaller to larger companies. However, there

TRAITS SHOWING TRENDS	TRAITS SHOWING NO TRENDS
FORCEFUL*	DECISIVE
IMAGINATIVE*	INDEPENDENT
CAUTIOUS †	SELF-CONFIDENT
TACTFUL†	ADAPTABLE
	AGREEABLE
	COOPERATIVE

* Seen as relatively more necessary in large companies
† Seen as relatively more necessary in small companies

Exhibit III. Personality traits necessary for job success

were 4 traits—2 other-directed traits and 2 inner-directed traits—that did show definite trends. These 4 traits are listed in the left-hand column of Exhibit III. Large-company managers placed relatively more emphasis on the traits *forceful* and *imaginative* as being necessary for success in their jobs than did small-company managers, and the small-company managers attached relatively more importance to being *cautious* and *tactful* than did the large-company managers.

Taken together, what do these results show? They indicate that there is more demand for organization-man or other-directed behavior in the *small* than in the large company. This is, again, exactly the opposite picture from that described by Whyte and many other observers.

NEED FULFILLMENT

A third and final portion of the questionnaire consisted of a series of items designed to measure degrees of fulfillment of various types of psychological needs. The managers were asked to indicate the amount of fulfillment of each need that they felt they were obtaining in their particular job situation. To do this, they rated the degree of fulfillment on a scale running from 1 (low) to 7 (high).

The types of needs that were investigated are based on a theory of motivation developed by A. H. Maslow, a psychologist:

> Briefly, Maslow's theory says that there is a hierarchy of motives that individuals seek to fulfull, starting with the very basic and prepotent requirements for the necessary elements of life such as food and water,

and then followed by security needs, social needs, esteem needs, and, finally, needs for autonomy and self-realization. The last two needs are regarded as less basic and prepotent since the individual tries to fulfill them only after he has achieved a reasonable degree of fulfillment of those that are more directly concerned with his physical well-being.

In our study, we looked at five types of needs: all of the needs mentioned above with the exception of the needs for the basic elements of life. Thus, of those we studied, security needs were most basic, and self-realization needs (i.e., self-development, growth, accomplishment, and so on) least basic.

Many writers have maintained that large companies do a better job than small companies do of satisfying relatively basic needs, such as those for security; however, they maintain that higher order needs, such as those for independence and self-realization, are better met in small companies where there is supposedly greater individual freedom and more concern for the employees as individuals.

What do our results show? They are summarized in Exhibit IV, where we have indicated that for four of the five types of needs we studied—for all but *security*—fulfillment is greatest in large companies. These differences are, though, quite small when averaged across the middle levels of management. Moreover, if the size comparisons on this part of the questionnaire are looked at separately for each management level, the findings indicate that at the lowest levels of management *small*-company managers are more satisfied, whereas at higher levels the picture reverses and *large*-company managers report definitely greater fulfillment.

As for *security*, fulfillment is rated greatest in medium-size companies, next greatest in large companies, and least in small companies—a result that checks with the general notion that big companies provide plenty of security for their managers.

The over-all results from this part of the questionnaire indicate that large-company managers feel they receive at least as much or more fulfillment of *all* types of needs than do small-company managers. There does not seem to be, therefore, any superiority of the small company in providing need fulfillment in any particular area, as some observers have supposed.

IS SIZE THE PROBLEM?

It is obviously unwise to generalize to too great an extent from a single research study, even this one where the sample is large, nationwide, and quite heterogeneous with respect to sizes and types of companies. Nevertheless, the results described in the preceding sec-

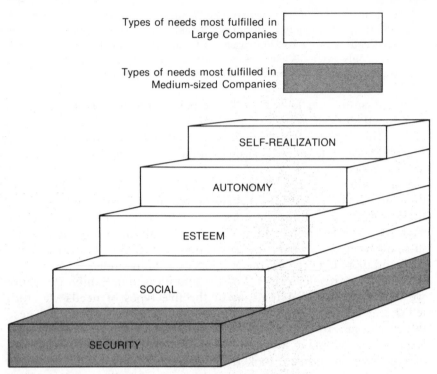

Exhibit IV. How managers view the fulfillment of psychological needs

tions represent some of the first concrete objective data available concerning the effects of different-size organizations on job attitudes, *especially at managerial levels.* Therefore, at the very least, these results can be used to evaluate many of the speculations that have been put forth concerning some of the possible deleterious effects of large size. Where they differ from widely held opinions, they indicate that we need additional facts before we decide to accept conclusions based on individual observations.

Taken together, our findings on this sample of some 1,700 managers and executives definitely do *not* support the contentions of Whyte and others that the really challenging jobs in today's business world lie in the small company, and that the small company is the final holdout against the encroachment of the organization man into our business and industrial firms. If anything, our results point in the opposite direction. None of the various trends reported earlier in the article are strong in themselves, but, considered as a total collection, they indicate that in the minds of managers, at least, the more challenging job, the job requiring *less* organization-man type of behavior, is to be found more typically in the large than in the small company. The facts, based on our data, seem incontrovertible.

Should we be surprised at these findings? It is my contention that we should not. If we look at the question of the possible effects of organization size on managerial job challenges from the standpoint of logic, it is possible to see why our findings are plausible.

New Job Challenge

Many years ago, in the late nineteenth century and the earlier years of this century, a young man's big challenge in the business world was to strike out independently and start his own company. The heroes of business in those days were the individuals who could not only found a company but also make it grow into a going concern. Certainly there is still a real challenge for a young person to leave the security of an organization (of any size), or never join one in the first place, and undertake to start his own company. So, even in present times, this type of challenge is there waiting for the ambitious young man to take advantage of it.

However, there is another type of challenge today which was rarely present in the business world of 50 or 70 years ago. This is the challenge of leading and administering a large organization. Remember that 50 years ago there were very few big companies in this country. Today there are more than 400 industrial firms (not counting banks, insurance companies, transportation companies, and utilities) that employ 5,000 or more people.

I would argue that the jobs of upper and top managers who help to run one of these large organizations are at least as great a challenge as starting one's own small business. And, even more to the point, being at the top or toward the top in a large company should offer as many or more challenges as being near the top of a small company. The upper-level, or even middle-level, executive of a big company probably has command of, and responsibility for, more resources—human, technical, and financial—than his counterpart in the small company who is at an equivalent position in the vertical hierarchy of his organization.

Doesn't this explain why the managers from large companies in our sample report greater challenge in their management jobs compared to the managers from small companies? For the *unambitious* individual a large organization apparently does provide the maximum in security and the minimum in personal risk. At the same time, for the *ambitious* manager the large company may also provide the maximum in job challenge.

Even at lower or beginning levels of management one can make a strong argument that the greater challenges exist in large rather than small companies. Here I am referring to the challenge of working one's way up to the top of the organization, or at least to upper levels where there is great responsibility. In mountain climbing the most challenging mountains are, generally speaking, the taller mountains. While difficulty in reaching the top of a mountain and the height of the mountain are not perfectly correlated, who would deny that Everest, K2, Annapurna, and other peaks of similar magnitude offer the supreme challenge for mountain climbers? Analogously, it is the large organizations that should offer the maximum in challenge to the organization climber who is just embarking on his managerial career. The risks are probably greater, but so are the potential feelings of personal accomplishment.

From the type of data used in our study it is not possible to determine whether large companies *cause* jobs to be more challenging and competitive or whether they *attract* men who are more likely to see these characteristics. I suspect that our findings are the result of both conditions.

Differences Overlooked

What about the question of conformity? As pointed out at the beginning, many people suppose that conforming, sheep-like behavior is more often and more strongly required of the employee of the big company than of one who is working for a small company. The inference is that it is sheer size that forces the large organization to act this way. What some of the commentators seem to forget is that small companies can often be severely tradition-bound, and that the chief executive of a small company can sometimes be an extreme autocrat who requires strict adherence to his own idiosyncratic ways of doing things. It is certainly possible, therefore, that small companies can require at least as great a degree of conformity as large organizations.

Also, it should be pointed out that although big companies can often be frustratingly ponderous in terms of such functions as communications and speed of decision making, they are frequently quite progressive in terms of personnel policies such as management training. In many management training courses not only are the big companies more likely (on a per-capita basis) to send more managers for training, but those managers tend—in my own experience, at least—to be more responsive to the content than are some of the managers from the small companies. Where this is the case it can often be attributed to the large-company trainee's expectation that the ideas taught will be received favorably in his home organization.

Level and Kind of Job

Now I want to mention one other important finding of our study: the level of a manager's position in an organization and its characteristic as a line or staff job seem to have an even stronger effect on the man's attitudes than does size. Staff managers report less challenge in their jobs and greater necessity for organization-man type of behavior than do line managers. And lower-level managers, regardless of the size of the company for which they work, describe their jobs in much less favorable terms than higher-level managers, and they also report that it is necessary to behave in a much more organization-man or other-directed fashion than do higher-level managers.

The significance of the existence of stronger trends for these level-of-position and line-staff factors, especially the former, is this: sheer size does *not* seem to be the only real problem in whatever harmful effects an organization may have on those who work in it. If management wants to understand the attitudes of executives and supervisors toward their work, it may well learn more by examining factors inherent in the construction of the organization itself—i.e., the formation of horizontal layers into a hierarchy and the vertical line-staff division.

CONCLUSION

Our study does not show that large organizations are always the ones that provide greater challenges and require less conforming behavior than small organizations. Rather, it demonstrates that large companies can produce at least as favorable management attitudes as small companies, in terms of job challenges and the kind of behavior seen as necessary for job success.

We cannot ignore the near unanimity of the previous findings on the relation of work-group size to employee morale. As mentioned earlier, those studies have found larger size work groups (of nonmanagement employees) to have significantly lower morale. If we couple the findings on work-group size with our findings concerning the total size of organizations, one important implication would seem to be this: an increase in the total size of an organization—with the consequent technological advantages of large-scale operation—will not necessarily reduce the morale and job satisfaction of employees as long as intra-organization work units are kept small. At least this is a hypothesis worth investigating in future research on the relation of company size to employee morale.

If we are to be concerned with the effects of organizations on individuals, we should direct our attention to the internal structure of organizations rather than to their sheer external size. Our findings indicate that big companies need not be apologetic either for their bigness or for their effects on their managers.

NOTES

1. New York, Simon and Schuster, Inc., 1956.
2. *Ibid.*, p. 70.
3. New York, Alfred A. Knopf, Inc., 1959.
4. "Organization Structure and Employee Morale," *American Sociological Review*, April 1950, p. 172.

CHRIS ARGYRIS

Personality vs. Organization

Approximately every seven years we develop the itch to review the relevant literature and research in personality and organization theory, to compare our own evolving theory and research with those of our peers—an exercise salutary, we trust, in confirmation and also confrontation. We're particularly concerned to measure our own explicit model of man with the complementary or conflicting models advanced by other thinkers. Without an explicit normative model, personality and organization theory (P. and O. theory) tends to settle for a generalized description of behavior as it is observed in existing institutions—at best, a process that embalms the status quo; at worst, a process that exalts it. Current behavior becomes the prescription for future actions.

By contrast, I contend that behavioral science research should be normative, that it is the mission of the behavioral scientist to intervene selectively in the organization whenever there seems a reasonable chance of improving the quality of life within the organization without imperiling its viability. Before surveying the P. and O. landscape, however, let's review the basic models of man and formal organization.

FUNDAMENTALS OF MAN AND ORGANIZATION

The following steps indicate how the worlds of man and formal organization have developed:

1. Organizations emerge when the goals they seek to achieve are too complex for any one man. The actions necessary to achieve the

Source: Reprinted by permission of the publisher from *Organizational Dynamics* (Vol. 3, No. 2: Autumn 1974) © (1974) by AMACOM, a division of American Management Associations.

goals are divided into units manageable by individuals—the more complex the goals, other things being equal, the more people are required to meet them.

2. Individuals themselves are complex organizations with diverse needs. They contribute constructively to the organization only if *on balance*, the organization fulfills these needs and their sense of what is just.

3. What are the needs that individuals seek to fulfill? Each expert has his own list and no two lists duplicate priorities. We have tried to bypass this intellectual morass by focussing on some relatively reliable predispositions that remain valid irrespective of the situation. Under any circumstances individuals seek to fulfill these predispositions; at the same time, their exact nature, potency, and the degree to which they must be fulfilled are influenced by the organizational context—for example, the nature of the job. In their attempt to live, to grow in competence, and to achieve self-acceptance, men and women tend to program themselves along the lines of the continua depicted in Figure 1.

Together, these continua represent a developmental logic that people ignore or suppress with difficulty, the degree of difficulty depending on the culture and the context, as well as the individual's interactions with the key figures in his or her life. The model assumes that the thrust of this developmental program is from left to right, but nothing is assumed about the location of any given individuals along these continua.

A central theme of P. and O. theory has been the range of differences between individuals and how it is both necessary and possible to arrange a match between the particular set of needs an individual brings to the job situation and the requirements—technical and psychological—of the job itself, as well as the overall organizational climate.

We have written four studies that highlighted an individual's interrelationship with the work context. In each study, a separate analysis was made of each participant that included (1) the predispositions that he or she desired to express, (2) the potency of each predisposition, (3) the inferred probability that each would be expressed, and (4) a final score that indicated the degree to which the individual was able to express his or her predispositions.

A personal expression score enabled us to make specific predictions as to how individuals would react to the organization. We had expected individuals with low scores, for example, to state that they were frustrated and to have poorer attendance records and a higher quit rate—expectations that also showed how individual differences in predispositions were differentially rewarded in different types of departments.

Figure 1. Developmental continua

Infants begin as	Adults strive toward
(1) being dependent and submissive to parents (or other significant adult)	(1) relative independence, autonomy, relative control over their immediate world
(2) having few abilities	(2) developing many abilities
(3) having skin-surfaced or shallow abilities	(3) developing a few abilities in depth
(4) having a short time perspective	(4) developing a longer time perspective

Bank employees with a need to distrust and control others, for example, instinctively opted for positions in the internal audit department of the bank.

So much for the model of man. Now to organizations, which have a life of their own, in the sense that they have goals that unfortunately may be independent of or antagonistic to individual needs. The next step was to determine if there was a genetic logic according to which organizations were programmed.

Observation and reading combined to suggest that most organizations had pyramided structures of different sizes. The logic behind each of these pyramids—great or small—was first, to centralize information and power at the upper levels of the structure; second, to specialize work. According to this logic, enunciated most clearly by Frederick Winslow Taylor and Max Weber, management should be high on the six organizational activities summarized in Figure 2.

This model assumed that the closer an organization approached the right ends of the continua, the closer it approached the ideal of formal organization. The model assumed nothing, however, about where any given organization would be pinpointed along these continua.

PERSONALITY VS. ORGANIZATION

Given the dimensions of the two models, the possibilities of interaction are inevitable and varied; so is the likelihood of conflict between the needs of individuals and the structured configuration of the formal organization. The nature of the interaction between the individual and the organization and the probability of conflict vary according to the conditions depicted in Figure 3.

From this model, we can hypothesize that the more the organization approaches the model of the formal organization, the more individuals

Figure 2. Continua of organizational activities

Designing specialized and fractionalized work	
low	high

Designing production rates and controlling speed of work	
low	high

Giving orders	
low	high

Evaluating performance	
low	high

Rewarding and punishing	
low	high

Perpetuating membership	
low	high

Figure 3. Conditions of interaction

If the individual aspired toward	And the organization (through its jobs, technology, controls, leadership, and so forth) required that the individual aspire toward
(1) adulthood dimensions	(1) infancy dimensions
(2) infancy dimensions	(2) adulthood dimensions
(3) adulthood dimensions	(3) adulthood dimensions
(4) infancy dimensions	(4) infancy dimensions

will be forced to behave at the infant ends of the continua. What if—still operating at the level of an intellectual exercise—the individuals aspired toward the adult end of the continua? What would the consequences be? Wherever there is an incongruence between the needs of individuals and the requirements of a formal organization, individuals will tend to experience frustration, psychological failure, short-time perspective, and conflict.

What factors determine the extent of the incongruence? The chief factors are: first, the lower the employee is positioned in the hierarchy, the less control he has over his working conditions and the less he is able to employ his abilities; second, the more directive the leadership, the more dependent the employee; and last, the more unilateral the managerial controls, the more dependent the employee will feel.

We have said that individuals find these needs difficult to ignore or suppress, and if they are suppressed, frustration and conflict result. These feelings, in turn, are experienced in several ways:

- The employee fights the organization and tries to gain more control—for example, he may join a union.
- The employee leaves the organization, temporarily or permanently.
- The employee leaves it psychologically, becoming a half-worker, uninvolved, apathetic, indifferent.
- The employee downgrades the intrinsic importance of work and substitutes higher pay as the reward for meaningless work. Barnard observed almost 40 years ago that organizations emphasized financial satisfactions because they were the easiest to provide. He had a point—then and now.

We want to emphasize several aspects about these propositions. The personality model provides the base for predictions as to the impact of any organizational variable upon the individual, such as organizational structure, job content, leadership style, group norms, and so on. The literature has concentrated on employee frustration expressed in fighting the organization, because it's the commonest form of response, but we shouldn't ignore the other three responses.

In a study of two organizations in which technology, job content, leadership, and managerial controls confined lower-skilled employees to the infancy end of the continua, their response was condition three— no union, almost no turnover or absenteeism, but also apathy and indifference.

Last, we believe that the model holds regardless of differences in culture and political ideology. The fundamental relationships between individuals and organizations are the same in the United States, England, Sweden, Yugoslavia, Russia, or Cuba. A drastic statement but, we think, a true one.

RESEARCH THAT TESTS THE MODEL

Several studies in the past six years designed specifically to test the validity of the model all bore it out, to a greater or lesser extent. One study involved a questionnaire that measured self-expression as defined by our model. In a random sample of 332 U.S. salaried managers, hourly-paid workers, and self-employed businessmen, it was found that the lower the self-actualization, the more likely employees were to exhibit the following behavior: To day-dream, to have aggressive feelings toward their superiors, to have aggressive feelings toward their co-workers, to restrict output or make avoidable errors, to postpone difficult tasks or decisions, to emphasize money as the reward for service, and to be dissatisfied with their current jobs and think about another job.

A study in a different culture—Brazil—dealt with 189 employees in 13 banks. It revealed that 86 percent of the employees registered a discrepancy between their own felt needs and the formal goals of the organization. All agreed that the organizational goals were important, but only the top managers felt an absence of conflict between their own needs and the goals of the organization.

A second U.S. study involving 329 respondents—104 businessmen, 105 managers, and 120 workers—confirmed the model, but not in most cases to a degree that was statistically significant. On balance, however, the respondents supported the proposition that employees who perceive their work situations as highly bureaucratic feel more isolated, alienated, and powerless.

RESEARCH THAT SUPPORTS THE MODEL

Additional studies with no formal relationship to the model nevertheless tend to underwrite it. A national sample of 1,533 employees in 1972, for example, showed that among all age groups interesting work was more important than money in providing job satisfaction.

Bertil Gardell, a Swedish psychologist, examined four plants in mass production and process industries, seeking to relate production technology to alienation and mental health. Among his findings were these:

- The more skilled the task and the more control the individual feels over how he performs it, the more independence and the less stress he experiences.

- There is a big discrepancy between people as to which jobs they deem interesting; some employees, for example, describe jobs with low discretion as interesting—this is a contradiction of our model, but they account for only 8 percent of the employees surveyed.

- Income is not a factor in determining alienation. A high-income employee with little control over his job feels just as alienated as the man laboring for a pittance.

Gardell concluded:

> Severe restrictions in worker freedom and control and in skill level required are found to be related to increased work alienation and lowered level of mental health even after control is made for age, sex, income,

type of leadership, and satisfaction with pay. The relation between task organization and mental health is valid, however, only after allowance is made for work alienation. In both industries certain people regard jobs of low discretion and skill level as interesting and free from constraint, but these groups amount to only 8 percent in each industry and are strongly overrepresented as to workers above 50 years of age.

Within the mass-production industry, restrictions in discretion and skill level are found to go together with increased feelings of psychological stress and social isolation. People working under piece rate systems—compared with hourly paid workers—find their work more monotonous, constrained, and socially isolating, as well as having lower social status. . . .

High self-determination and job involvement are found to be related to high demands for increased worker influence on work and company decisions in the process industries, while in the mass production industries demand for increased worker influence is greatest among those who feel their work to be monotonous and constrained. Perceptions of strong worker influence by collective arrangements are accompanied by increased demands for individual decision-power as well as increased job satisfaction and decreased alienation.

A batch of studies reaffirmed the relationship between job specialization and feelings of powerlessness on the job and of frustration and alienation. One that compared craftsmen, monitors, and assemblers found that job satisfaction varied dramatically according to the degree of specialization: Job satisfaction was lowest among the assemblers—14 percent; next were the monitors—52 percent; and last were the craftsmen—87 percent. The same study found a strong relationship between job specialization and powerlessness on the job. Thus, 93 percent of the assemblers and 57 percent of the monitors, but only 19 percent of the craftsmen, experienced a lack of freedom and control.

Still other studies related job levels to the degree of dissatisfaction with the jobs. A comparison of 15 managers with 26 supervisors and 44 workers showed that the degree of satisfaction paralleled their position in the hierarchy, with managers the most satisfied and workers the least satisfied.

Frederick Herzberg reported a study of 2,665 Leningrad workers under 30 that again correlated job level with job satisfaction. Researchers who have concentrated on the higher levels of the organization typically have found a systematic tendency—the higher the positions held by the individuals in the organization, the more positive their attitudes tended to be.

An unusual study by Allan Wicker compared undermanned situations in which participants assumed more responsibility and performed larger tasks with overmanned situations in which the tasks were small and the responsibilities minute. Not surprisingly, in the overmanned situations employees reported less meaningful tasks and less sense of responsibility.

Can we reduce powerlessness at work, a factor closely linked to job alienation? One suggestive article points up three possibilities: Employees should allocate their own tasks; crews should be allowed to select themselves through sociometric procedures; the members of the group should select the group leaders.

Finally, research throws light on the question of whether time is the great reconciler. How long do dissatisfaction and frustration with the job persist? The answer appears to be—indefinitely. An interesting comparision of an old and a new assembly plant found that after 14 years the presumably acclimated employees were more dissatisfied and less involved with the product and the company than the new employees. Familiarity breeds frustration, alienation, and contempt.

RESEARCH RESULTS EXPLAINED BY THE MODEL

If employees are predisposed toward greater autonomy and formal organizations are designed to minimize autonomy, at least at the lower levels, we would expect to find a significant correlation between job status and job satisfaction—the lower the job, the less the job satisfaction. This has been found in a number of studies. Harold Wilensky, for example, reported in one of his studies the proportion of satisfied employees ranged from 90 percent for professors and mathematicians to 16 percent for unskilled auto workers. Furthermore, he found that the percentage of people who would go into similar work if they could start over again varied systematically with the degree of autonomy, control, and the chance to use their abilities that they experienced in their current jobs.

Several studies focused on the relationship between control and job satisfaction. An analysis of 200 geographically separate systems that were parts of larger organizations—for example, automotive dealers, clerical operations, manufacturing plants, and power plants in the same company—revealed that the greatest discrepancy between actual and ideal control occurred at the level of the rank-and-file employee. Ninety-nine percent of the work groups wanted more control over their immediate work area. Still another study found that employees became more dissatisfied after moving to a new, more efficient plant because of the reduction of their control over work. These studies were in the United States. Similar research in Yugoslavia and Norway further buttressed the point that employees want to enlarge the degree of their control over their immediate work world.

What about the impact of control upon turnover? The logic of the model leads us to predict that employees would be more likely to quit an organization when they experienced too much control by the organization or its representatives. Once again, research supports the hypothesis. One study found that the authoritarian foreman was a major factor in labor turnover; a second showed that there was a close relationship between the supervisor's inequitable treatment—he could not be influenced, did not support his subordinates, and did not attempt to redress employee grievances—and the turnover rate. Employees, in short, fled from unfair treatment.

One assemblage of studies would appear at first glance to contradict the model. We refer to those studies that show that lower-skilled workers appear to be more interested in how much money they make than they are in how interesting their jobs are. As John Goldthorpe and others demonstrate, however, they are merely being realists. Goldthorpe, in particular, points out repeatedly and documents in detail the fact that workers do desire intrinsically satisfying jobs, but find such aspirations to be unrealistic. In the long run, however great the reluctance and the pain, they adapt.

His research dealt with British workers but a number of studies in the United States replicate his findings. As you move up the job hierarchy, employees consistently assign a higher value to job characteristics that potentially fulfill growth needs. Medium- and high-status white-collar workers, for example, placed primary emphasis on work-content factors as a source of job satisfaction, while low-status white-collar workers and blue-collar workers tended to play them down. As our model would predict, employees seek out job satisfactions they feel are second rate, because higher-level satisfactions are unattainable—certainly in their current jobs.

In summary, this research demonstrates first, that the overall impact of the formal organization on the individual is to decrease his control over his immediate work area, decrease his chance to use his abilities, and increase his dependence and submissiveness; second, that to the extent to which the individual seeks to be autonomous and function as an adult he adapts by reactions ranging from withdrawal and noninterest, to aggression, or perhaps to the substitution of instrumental money rewards for intrinsic rewards. The weight of the deprivations and the degree of adaptation increase as we descend the hierarchy. Formal organizations, alas, are unintentionally designed to discourage the autonomous and involved worker.

JOB ENLARGEMENT OR ENRICHMENT

Job enlargement in the true sense, not the multiplication of meaningless tasks, but quite literally the enrichment of the job either by adding tasks that provide intrinsic satisfactions or increasing the worker's control over the tasks he already performs, obviously conforms to our models. And we would expect that employees whose jobs were enriched would be more satisfied with their jobs and less likely to manifest their dissatisfaction in ways that undermine the organization. Looking at the other side of the coin, we also would expect that more positive attitudes would be accompanied by increased productivity.

And we would not be disappointed. No fewer than eight studies testify that designing jobs that permit more self-regulation, self-evaluation, self-adjustment, and participation in goal-setting both improved attitudes and increased productivity.

Of particular importance is a study by Hackman and Lawler that correlated the core dimensions of jobs—variety, autonomy, task identity, and feedback—with motivation, satisfaction, performance, and attendance. The principal findings of their study are these:

- The higher the jobs are on core dimensions, the higher the employees are rated by their supervisors as doing better quality work and being more effective performers.

- When jobs rank high on the core dimensions, employees report feeling more intrinsically motivated to perform well.

- Core dimensions are strongly and positively related to job satisfaction and involvement.

- The job satisfaction items that strongly correlate with the job core dimension are related to control over one's own work, feeling of worthwhile accomplishment, and self-esteem.

- The strength of the relationships described above increases with those employees who seek to meet higher-order needs. This finding is significant because research seldom examines individual differences in this way.

Hackman and Lawler differentiate between horizontal enlargement—increasing the number of things an employee does—and vertical enlargement—increasing the degree to which an employee is responsible for making most major decisions about his work. They would argue and we would concur that a combination of both types of enlargement—what we have earlier called role enlargement—is optimal.

What about practice? The concept of job enrichment isn't new. A study of IBM published in 1948 included an assessment of job enrichment and its benefits.

We would expect a concept so fulfilling, so helpful in meeting the goals of both the employee and the organization to be widely adopted. And we would be disappointed. A recent survey of 300 of the top 1,000 *Fortune* industrials showed that only 4 percent had made any formal, systematic attempt to enrich jobs. And even they had enriched only a very small percentage of their total jobs.

What accounts for the lag in adopting job enrichment? Two factors seem to be at work and to reinforce each other. First, most managements are convinced that job enrichment doesn't pay off economically. This belief, in turn, leads them to exhibit signs of the ostrich syndrome—they ignore the accumulating body of evidence as to the substantial psychic dividends that employees derive from job enrichment.

Let me quote from just two of the voluminous reasearch studies that demonstrate the efficiency of job enrichment. The first is the ambitious and significant attempt by the Gaines dog food division of General Foods to design an entire plant using horizontal and vertical enlargement of work. The key features of the design are the following:

1. Autonomous work groups that develop their own production schedules, manage production problems, screen and select new members, maintain self-policing activities, and decide questions such as who gets time off and who fills which work station.

2. Integrated support functions. Each work team performs its own maintenance, quality control and industrial engineering functions—plus challenging job assignments.

3. Job mobility and rewards for learning. People are paid not on the basis of the job they are doing, but on the basis of the number of jobs that they are prepared to do.

4. Self-government for the plant community.

The transition from a work environment on the infant ends of our continua to the adult ends was not easy for the people involved. Drastic change never is, even when the participants benefit from the change. The results to date, however, are impressive. A similar plant, organized along traditional lines, would require 110 employees; this one was manned by 70. The plant has met or exceeded production goals. Employees reported greater opportunities for learning and self-actualization. And team leaders and plant managers were more involved in community affairs than foremen and managers of comparable plants.

A second significant experiment in job enlargement is taking place at Volvo's new auto assembly plant in Kalmar, Sweden. Volvo faced serious problems—wildcat strikes, absenteeism, and turnover that were getting out of hand. Turnover in the old car assembly plant was over

40 percent annually. Absenteeism was running 20 to 25 percent. Now, assembly has been divided among teams of 15 to 25 workers, who will decide how to distribute the job of car assembly among themselves. Each team determines its own work pace, subject to meeting production standards that are set for them. Each team selects its own boss, and deselects him if it's unhappy with him.

The new plant cost approximately 10 percent more than it would have if it had been constructed along traditional lines. Will the benefits justify the extra expense? Time alone will tell—the plant has been on stream for only a matter of months—but Pehr Gyllenhammar, the managing director of Volvo, hopes that it will realize both his economic and social objectives: "A way must be found to create a workplace that meets the needs of the modern working man for a sense of purpose and satisfaction in his daily work. A way must be found of attaining this goal without an adverse effect on productivity."

THE MODEL OF MAN AND THE DESIGN OF ORGANIZATION

Organizations depend on people. Thus, many organizational variables are designed around an explicit or implicit model of man. Taylor's molecularized jobs, for example, took a one-dimensional view of man and assumed that one could hire a hand; by contrast, the champions of vertical and horizontal job enrichment assume that one hires a whole human being.

Then there are the theorists who take the sociological viewpoint and impoverish their theories by ignoring the psychological element and treating man as a black box.

In each case the complexity of organizational reality leads them into contradictions, the significance of which they either play down or ignore altogether. Crozier, for example, although lacking an explicit model of man, also concluded that his data did not confirm the inhumanity of organizations toward individuals—but how can one define inhumanity without a concept of man? Nevertheless, in the same work he stated that monotonous and repetitive work produces nervous tension in workers, that apathy and social isolation are great, and that work loads produce pressure.

Charles Perrow is a technological determinist who argues that the structure of organization depends on the requirements of the technology. An electronics plant making components should have a different structure from one making inertial guidance system components because of differences in the kind of research required by their technology, unanalyzable versus analyzable, or the number of exceptions it requires—few or many. Perrow's insight, valid but partial, is an inadequate concept to explain the total relationship between man and organization, an inadequacy that Perrow himself is coming to recognize. He concedes that "personality factors can have a great deal of influence upon the relations between coordination and subordinate power," that Robert McNamara, for example, was the key factor in changes in the Defense Department.

To elevate any one as *the* defining characteristic of organizations as Perrow did with technology and make all other characteristics dependent variables only leads to poor theory and inadequate and incomplete explanations of behavior in organizations. An error of equal magnitude is to ignore either the sociological or the psychological view in studying organizations.

We need a synthesis of the sociological and psychological views in studying man and a recognition that there are no fewer than four sets of independent but interacting characteristics that determine the behavior of any organization—structure and technology, leadership and interpersonal relations, administrative controls and regulations, and human controls. The strength of each of the four will vary from organization to organization, vary within different parts of the same organization, and vary over time within the same parts of each organization. However, any major change in an organization's structure is doomed to failure unless major changes take place in all four characteristics.

RATIONAL MAN DECISION THEORISTS

In addition to those with no explicit model of man we have the rational man decision theorists such as Simon, Cyert, and March, whose partial view of man focuses on the concept of man as a finite information processing system striving to be rational and to "satisfice" in his decision making. What this model neglects are the issues stressed by P. and O. theory, such as dependence, submissiveness, the need for psychological success, confirmation, and feelings of essentiality. As we have written elsewhere, "Simon saw management's task as designing organizational structures and mechanisms of organization influence which ingrained into the nervous system of every member what the organization required him to do. Intendedly, rational man was expected to follow authority, but he was also given appropriate and indirect inducements to produce."

Cyert and March retain the basic perspectives of the pyramidal structure—specialization of tasks and centralization of power and information—but they add elements of reality and sophistication. By cranking into their models the concepts of people as members of coalitions politicking against each other for scarce resources and settling for the quasi-reduction of conflicts between them, they were able to predict more accurately how the organization was going to behave, for example, in setting prices.

That the rational man thinkers have indeed helped managers to make more effective decisions in some situations—those in which the factors involved corresponded to their model—shouldn't lead us to ignore the more frequent situations in which the rational man theories were either a poor predictive tool or acted themselves to exacerbate the situation. Recent research suggest that managers may resist the management information systems designed by the rational man theorists precisely because they work well—for example, accomplish the desired objective of reducing uncertainty. What accounts for the apparent paradox? Man is not primarily rational, or rather he reacts in response to what we like to call the rationality of feelings. He dislikes being dependent and submissive toward others; he recognizes the increased probability that when management information systems work best he will tend to experience psychological failure. The organization's goals are being met at the expense of his own. Management information systems, in consequence, have become to managers at many levels what time-study people were to the rank and file years ago—an object of fear commingled with hatred and aggression.

Another trend that totally escapes the rational man theorists is the increasing hostility of an increasing number of young people toward the idea that organizations should be able to buy off people to be primarily rational, to submit to the mechanisms of organizational influence, and to suppress their feelings.

A third trend flows from the combined impact of the first two. Given the inability to predict the relationship of emotionality versus rationality in any particular context, and the reaction against rational man and organizational mechanisms of influence, add to these elements the largely unintended support of the status quo, and the use of "satisficing" to rationalize incompetence, and we end up with an interaction of forces that makes change in organizations seem almost impossible.

Hard to follow or accept? The line of argument is as follows:

1. To the degree that man accepts inducements to behave rationally, he acts passively in relation to the way power, information, and work are designed in the organization.

2. Over time, such individuals sterilize their self-actualizing tendencies by any one or a combination of approaches: They suppress them, deny them, or distort them. Eventually, they come to see their legitimate role in the organization—at least, as it bears on the design of power, information, and tasks—as pawns rather than as initiators.

3. A little further down the road, individuals come to view being passive and controlled as good, natural, and necessary. Eventually, they may define responsibility and maturity in these terms.

4. Individuals soon create managerial cultures—some have already done so—in which the discussion of self-actualizing possibilities is viewed as inappropriate.

5. The youth who because of the very success of the system are able to focus more on the self-actualizing needs will attempt to change things. They will come up, however, against facts one to four and end up terribly frustrated.

6. The frustration will tend to lead to regression, with two probable polarized consequences—withdrawal into communes or militancy.

7. Because we know very little about how to integrate self-actualizing activities with rational activities, older people will resent the hostility of youth or look upon their withdrawal as a cop-out.

The last and most important point is that the rational man theory, unlike P. and O. theory, could not predict the single most important trend about public and private organizations—their increasing internal deterioration and lack of effectiveness in producing services or products. As citizen, consumer, and presumably an organization man, you either feel it or you don't. We do feel strongly on this score. And we cite that while 25 years ago 75 percent of the respondents in a national survey felt that public and private organizations performed well, only 25 percent had the same opinion in 1972. How many believe that the percentage would be higher today?

THE CASE FOR NORMATIVE RESEARCH

Most of the research that we have reviewed has been descriptive research that contents itself with describing, understanding, and predicting human behavior within organizations. In our research the emphasis is normative and based upon the potentialities of man. We're interested in studying man in terms of what he is capable of, not merely how he currently behaves within organizations.

Looked at from this normative viewpoint, the most striking fact about most organizations is the limited opportunities they afford most employees to fulfill their potential. We can show empirically that the interpersonal world of most people in ongoing organizations is characterized by much more distrust, conformity, and closedness than trust, individuality, and openness. This world—we call it Pattern A—fits with, if indeed it isn't derived from, the values about effective human behavior endemic in the pyramidal structure or in what Simon calls the mechanisms of organizational influence. Thus, findings based on descriptive research will tend to opt for the status quo.

Moreover, unless we conduct research on new worlds, scholars will tend to use data obtained in the present world as evidence that people do not want to change. Many of them are doing so already. What they forget is how human beings can desire or even contemplate worlds that they have learned from experience to view as unrealistic.

Take a recent publication by Ernest Gross in which he suggests that concepts like individual dignity and self-development probably reflect academic values instead of employee desires, because employees rarely report the need to express such values. The question still remains whether this state of affairs implies that people should accept them and should be trained to adapt to them. Gross appears to think so. He stated that there is little one can do by way of providing opportunities for self-actualization and, if it were possible, providing them would frighten some people. Furthermore, he noted that assembly-line jobs didn't require a worker to demonstrate initiative or to desire variety. "One wants him (the worker) simply to work according to an established pace. Creativity, then, is not always desirable."

Note the logic. Gross starts by asserting that the P. and O. theorists cannot state that one *should* (his italics) provide workers with more challenge or autonomy in accordance with their values because to do so would be to rest their case not on a scientific theory, but on a program for organizations. Then he suggests that no one has proved how harmful dissatisfaction, anxiety, dependency, and conformity are to the individual—which is probably correct. He goes on to argue that these conditions are, to a degree, both unavoidable and helpful, although offering no empirical data to support his assertion. Then he concludes that employees should be educated to live within this world:

> Perhaps the most general conclusion we can draw is that since organizations appear to be inevitable . . . a major type of socialization of the young ought to include methods for dealing with the organization. . . . [For example] an important consideration in the preparation of individuals for work should include training for the handling of or adjustment to authority.

At this point Gross has taken a normative position, but one with which I vigorously dissent.

I am very concerned about those who hold that job enrichment may not be necessary because workers in an automobile factory have about the same attitude toward their jobs as do workers in jobs with greater freedom and job variety. But what is the meaning of the response to a question such as "How satisfied would you say you are with your present job?" if the man is working under conditions of relative deprivation? We think that what it means is that workers recognize that they are boxed in, that few opportunities are available to them for better-paid or more interesting work; in consequence, they become satisfied with the jobs they have because the jobs they want are unobtainable. It is frequently observed that the greatest dissatisfaction on a routine job occurs during the first years. After three to five years, the individual adapts to the job and feels satisfied. On the other hand, Neil Herrick in a recent book with the catchy title *Where Have All the Robots Gone?* reported that for the first time, there was a major drop in the number of Americans expressing job satisfaction.

That most jobs as currently designed are routine and provide few opportunities for self-actualization, that the social norms and the political actions that support these norms tend to produce mostly individuals who simultaneously value and fear growth and who strive for security and safety, tell only part of the unfortunate tale of the present industrial conditions. Employees perceive—and the perception is accurate—that few men at the top want to increase their opportunities for self-actualization; even fewer men at the top are competent to do the job.

Make no mistake—employees are conservative on this issue. They have no interest in seeing their physiological and security needs frustrated or denied because their organization collapsed while trying to increase their chances for self-actualization. And the possibility of such a collapse is a real one. Our own experience and the published research combine to suggest that there now does not exist a top-management group so competent in meeting the requirements of the new ethic that they do not lose their competence under stress. With expert help and heavy emphasis on top-management education, one such group was still encountering great difficulties after five years of attempting to raise the quality of life within its organization.

If the ethic, as employees themselves recognize, is so difficult to realize in practice, is the effort worthwhile? Is a game with so many incompetent players worth the playing?

On two counts we feel strongly that it is: First, on normative grounds we feel that social science research has an obligation to help design a better world. Second, we feel that the game is worth the playing because eventually some people and some organizations can be helped to play it effectively. Take the case of job enrichment. Let us assume that all jobs can be enriched. The assumption is probably unrealistic; many jobs in fact, can never be enriched. If we opt for the world that is psychologically richer, however, we will induce employees at every level into developing whatever opportunities for enrichment exist in each job situation.

I believe with Maslow in taking the behavior that characterizes rare peak experiences and making it the behavior toward which all employees should aspire. The skeptic argues that such behavior is so rare that it is useless to try to achieve it. I agree that the behavior is rare, but go on to plead for systematic research that will tell us how the behavior may be made more frequent. Twenty years ago no one had pole-vaulted higher than 16 feet. Yet no one took this as a given. Today the 16-foot mark is broken continually because people refused to view the status quo as the last word and focused on enhancing the potentiality of man. Over time, a similar focus on enhancing the potentiality of man-on-the-job should produce similar breakthroughs.

GEORGE STRAUSS

The Personality-Versus -Organization Hypothesis

Over the years, out of the contributions of individuals such as Argyris (1957), Herzberg (1960), Maier (1955), Maslow (1954), and McGregor (1960) has come a consistent view of human motivation in industry.[1] With due credit to Chris Argyris, I would like to call it the "personality versus organization" hypothesis. I will state this hypothesis briefly first and then criticize it.

1. Human behavior in regard to work is motivated by a hierarchy of needs, in ascending order: physical, safety, social, egoistic, and self-actualization. By "hierarchy" is meant that a higher, less basic need does not provide motivation unless all lower, more basic needs are satisfied, and that, once a basic need is satisfied, it no longer motivates.

Physical needs are the most fundamental, but once a reasonable (satisficing, as Simon would put it) level of physical-need satisfaction is obtained (largely through pay), individuals become relatively more concerned with other needs. First they seek to satisfy their security needs (through seniority, fringe benefits, and so forth). When these, too, are reasonably satisfied, social needs (friendship, group support, and so forth) take first priority. And so forth. Thus, for example, hungry men have little interest in whether or not they belong to strong social

Source: George Strauss, "The Personality-Versus-Organization Hypothesis," in *The Social Science of Organizations: Four Perspectives*, by Harold J. Leavitt, editor, © 1963, pp. 45-57. Reprinted by permission of Prentice-Hall, Inc., Englewood Cliffs, New Jersey.

groups; relatively well-off individuals are more anxious for good human relations.

Only when most of the less pressing needs are satisfied will individuals turn to the ultimate form of satisfaction, self-actualization, which is described by Maslow (1943) as "the desire to become more and more what one is, to become everything that one is capable of becoming. . . . A musician must make music, an artist must paint, a poet must write, if he is to be ultimately happy. What a man *can* be, he *must* be." (p. 372.)

2. Healthy individuals desire to mature, to satisfy increasingly higher levels of needs. This, in practice, means that they want more and more opportunity to form strong social groups, to be independent, creative, to exercise autonomy and discretion, and to develop and express their unique personality with freedom.

3. The organization, on the other hand, seeks to program individual behavior and reduce discretion. It demands conformity, obedience, dependence, and immature behavior. The assembly-line worker, the engineer, and the executive are all subject to strong pressures to behave in a programmed, conformist fashion.[2] As a consequence, many individuals feel alienated from their work.

4. Subordinates react to these pressures in a number of ways, most of which are dysfunctional to the organization. Individuals may fight back through union activity, sabotage, output restriction, and other forms of rational or irrational (aggressive) behavior. Or they may withdraw and engage in regression, sublimation, childish behavior, or failure to contribute creative ideas or to produce more than a minimum of work. In any case, employees struggle not to conform (at least at first). To keep these employees in line, management must impose still more restrictions and force still more immature behavior. Thus, a vicious cycle begins.

5. Management pressures often lead to excessive competition and splintering of work groups and the consequent loss of cooperation and social satisfaction. Or work groups may become even stronger, but their norms may now be anti-management, those of protecting individuals against pressures from above.

6. A subtle management, which provides high wages, liberal employee benefits, "hygienic," "decent" supervision, and not too much pressure to work, may well induce employees to *think* they are happy and not *dissatisfied*.[3] But they are not (or should not be) truly *satisfied*; they are apathetic and have settled for a low level of aspiration. They do as little work as they can get away with and still hold their job. This is an unhealthy situation which is wasteful both to the individual and to the organization.

7. There seem to be some differences in emphasis among authorities as to whether the behavior of the typical subordinate under these circumstances will be rational (reality-oriented) or irrational (frustration-oriented). In any case, organizational pressures, particularly being subjected to programmed work, may lead to serious personality disturbances and mental illness.[4] Thus, traditional organizational techniques not only prevent the organization from operating at maximum efficiency, but, in terms of their impact on individual adjustment, they are also very expensive to society as a whole.

8. The only healthy solution is for management to adopt policies which promote intrinsic job satisfaction, individual development, and creativity, according to which people will willingly and voluntarily work toward organizational objectives because they enjoy their work and feel that it is important to do a good job.[5] More specifically, management should promote job enlargement, general supervision, strong cohesive work groups, and decentralization. In a nutshell, management should adopt "power-equalization techniques."

CRITICISM

The above is, in a sense, a hypothesis as to human behavior in organizations. But it is more than a coldly objective hypothesis: it is a prescription for management behavior, and implicit in it are strong value judgments.[6] With its strong emphasis on individual dignity, creative freedom, and self-development, this hypothesis bears all the earmarks of its academic origin.

Professors place high value on autonomy, inner direction, and the quest for maximum self-development. As much as any other group in society, their existence is work-oriented; for them, creative achievement is an end in itself and requires no further justification. Most professors are strongly convinced of the righteousness of their Protestant ethic of hard work and see little incongruity in imposing it upon the less fortunate.

And yet there are many misguided individuals (perhaps the bulk of the population) who do not share the professor's values and would not be happy in the professor's job. Further, the technical requirements of many lines of work are very different from those of academia. Academic work is best accomplished by those with academic values, but it is questionable whether these values are equally functional in other lines of work—where creativity is not required to get the job done, but only the ability to follow orders.

In the pages which follow, I shall seek to re-evaluate the personality-versus-organization hypothesis. I shall suggest, first, that it contains many debatable value judgments, and, second, that it ignores what Harold Leavitt has called "organizational economics." I shall conclude that a broad range of people do not seek self-actualization on the job—and that this may be a fortunate thing because it might be prohibitively expensive to redesign some jobs to permit self-actualization.

VALUE JUDGMENTS

It seems to me that the hypothesis, as often stated, overemphasizes (1) the uniqueness of the personality-organization conflict to large-scale industry, (2) the universality of the desire to achieve self-actualization, and (3) the importance of the job (as opposed to the community or the home) as a source of need satisfaction. Thus, too little attention is given to economic motivation.[7]

The Uniqueness of the Problem

At least some authors seem to over-dramatize the personality-organization conflict as something unique to large-scale organization (particularly to mass-production industry). But this conflict is merely one aspect of what has been variously characterized as the conflict between individual and society, individual and environment, desire and reality, id and superego. "Thus the formal organization ... is not truly the real villain; rather any kind of organized activity, from the most democratic to the most authoritarian contains within itself the necessary conditions for conflict."[8]

Similarly, the impact of the industrial revolution on work satisfaction can be overemphasized. Much is made of "alienation" (dictionary meaning: turning away) from work. Comparisons are constantly made between the old-time craftsman who did the entire job and the mass-production worker of today. But I doubt whether the medieval serf or the Egyptian slave enjoyed much sense of autonomy or creativity (although one might perhaps argue that he had more of a sense of identification and less of a feeling of anomie than does his better-fed modern counterpart). Perhaps there is less job satisfaction today than there was 100 years ago. Obviously, there are no objective ways of measuring this, but my surmise is that the "turning away" has been less dramatic than some have suggested. There have been boring, programmed jobs throughout history.

Others are as skeptical as I am regarding the theory of increased alienation. In his conclusion to a survey of job-satisfaction studies, Robert Blauner (1960) questions "the prevailing thesis that most workers in modern society are alienated and estranged. There is a remarkable consistency in the findings that the vast majority of workers, in virtually all occupations and industries, are moderately or highly satisfied, rather than dissatisfied with their jobs.... The real character of the [pre-mass production] craftsman's work has been romanticized by the prevalent tendency to idealize the past...." (pp. 352–353). And J. A. C. Brown (1954) asserts "that in modern society there is far greater scope of skill and craftsmanship than in any previous society, and that far more people are in a position to use such skills" (p. 207).

The Universality of the Desire for Self-actualization

The basic hypothesis implies a strong moral judgment that people should want freedom and self-actualization,[9] that it is somehow morally wrong for people to be lazy, unproductive, and uncreative. It seems to me that the hypothesis overemphasizes individuals' desire for freedom and underemphasizes their desire for security. It can even be argued that some of the personality-versus-organization writing has a fairly antisocial, even nihilistic flavor; it seems to emphasize individual freedom and self-development as the all-important values. Yet "mature" behavior does not mean freedom from all restrictions; it means successful adjustment to them.

As Eric Fromm has suggested, most people do not want complete freedom. They want to know the limits within which they can act (and this is true both on and off the job). To put it another way: most people are willing to tolerate and may even be anxious for a few areas of their life which are unpredictable and exciting, but they insist that, in a majority of areas, events occur as expected. The research scientist, for example, may relish the novelty and uncertainty of laboratory work, but he insists that his secretary be always on call, that his technician give predictable responses, and that his car start with complete regularity.

True, some people seek much broader limits than do others, and some are not too upset if the limits are fuzzy. However, there are many who feel most comfortable if they work in a highly defined situation. For them, freedom is a burden; they want firm, secure leadership. And there are many more who, if not fully happy with programmed work, find it rather easy to accommodate themselves to it.

Argyris, for example, might reply that such individuals are immature personalities who have adjusted to organizational restrictions by becoming apathetic and dependent. Were the organizational environment healthy, these individuals would react differently. But in many cases, the restrictions which made these people this way occurred in childhood or are present in the culture. Such individuals may be "too far gone" to react well to power equalization, and their attitude is not likely to be changed short of intensive psychotherapy. Indeed, many people may have internalized and made part of their self-concept a low level of aspiration regarding their on-the-job responsibilities and their ability to handle these. What psychologists call the *theory of dissonance* suggests that sudden attempts to increase their sense of autonomy and self-determination might be quite disturbing.

Impressive evidence of the need for self-actualization is provided by the preliminary results of the mental health studies, which suggest that poor mental health is correlated with holding low-skilled jobs. And yet the evidence is still not complete. Apparently, not everyone suffers equally from unskilled work, and some adjust more easily than others. (Perhaps these studies will help us to improve the prediction process, so that we can do a better job of selecting and even training people for this kind of work.)

Further, it is far from clear whether this lower mental health is caused primarily by the intrinsic nature of unskilled work or by the fact that such work pays poorly and has low status both off and on the job.[10] Insofar as mental disturbances are caused by economic and social pressures at home, higher wages may be a better solution than improved human relations on the job or a rearrangement of work assignments.

A hasty glance at the research in this field, as summarized in two reviews (Kasl and French, 1962; Vroom and Maier, 1960; see also Guerin, *et al.*, 1960), makes it abundantly clear that unskilled workers are not the only ones to suffer from poor mental health. Depending on which study one looks at or what mental health index is used, one can conclude that executives, clerical personnel, salespeople, and lower-level supervisors *all* suffer from below-average mental health. The evidence makes one sympathize with the old Quaker, "All the world is queer save me and thee; and sometimes I think thee is a little queer."

The Job as the Primary Source of Satisfaction

There is an additional value judgment in the basic hypothesis that the *job* should be a primary form of need satisfaction for everyone (as it is for professors). But the central focus of many peoples' lives is not the job (which is merely a "way of getting a living"), but the home or the community. Many people find a full measure of challenge, creativity, and autonomy in raising a family, pursuing a hobby, or taking part in community affairs. As Robert Dubin (1959) puts it:

> Work, for probably a majority of workers, and even extending into the ranks of management, may represent an institutional setting that is not the central life interest of the participants. The consequence of

this is that while participating in work a general attitude of apathy and indifference prevails. . . . Thus, the industrial worker does not feel imposed upon by the tyranny of Organizations, company, or union (p. 161).[11]

In my own interviewing experience in factories, I often ran across women who repeated variants of, "I like this job because it gets me away from all the kids and pressures at home." One girl even told me, "The job is good because it gives me a chance to think about God." Such individuals may feel little need for power equalization.

In any case, as Kerr, Dunlap, Harbison, and Myers (1960) predict, work, in the future, will doubtless be increasingly programmed and will provide fewer and fewer opportunities for creativity and discretion on the job. On the other hand, the hours will grow shorter and there will be a "new bohemianism" off the job. All this suggests the irreverent notion that *perhaps* the best use of our resources is to accelerate automation, shorten the work week just as fast as possible, forget about on-the-job satisfactions, and concentrate our energies on making leisure more meaningful.

Underemphasis on Economic Rewards

Since the hypothesis overemphasizes the job as a source of need satisfaction, it also underemphasizes the role of money as means of motivation. The hypothesis says that, once employees obtain a satisficing level of economic reward, they go on to other needs and, presumably, are less concerned with money. However, the level of reward which is *satisficing* can rise rapidly over time. Further, money is a means of satisfying higher needs, for example, the individual who (perhaps misguidedly) seeks to live his life off the job engaging in "creative" consumption. True, employees expect much better physical, psychological, and social conditions on the job today than they did fifty years ago. But they also expect more money. There is little evidence that money has ceased to be a prime motivator.

"ORGANIZATIONAL ECONOMICS"

Perhaps the most fundamental criticisms of the personality-organization hypothesis is that it ignores (or at least misapplies) "organizational economics"; that is, it fails to balance carefully the costs and gains of power equalization. To be sure, most power-equalization advocates point out the hidden costs of autocracy: apathetic and resentful employees, turnover, absenteeism, sabotage, resistance to change, and all the rest. Traditional forms of supervison may be expensive in terms of the lost motivation and energy which might have been turned to organizational ends; they are even more expensive in terms of mental health. Yet some writers, in their moments of wilder enthusiasm, tend to overestimate the gain to be derived from eliminating autocracy and to underestimate the costs of power equalization.

The Gains from Eliminating Autocracy

Carried to excess, anxiety and aggression are undoubtedly harmful to both the organization and the individual. But many psychological studies suggest that dissatisfaction and anxiety (and even aggression, depending on how it is defined) spur individuals to work harder—particularly in simple, highly programmed tasks. Autocratic, work-oriented bosses very often get out high production; on occasion, their subordinates even develop high morale and cohesive work groups.[12]

Still, beyond certain limits, dissatisfaction, anxiety, and aggression are not in the organization's interests. There is much more doubt about apathy and conformity. It is often argued that an apathetic worker who is subject to "hygienic" supervision will only work enough so as not to get fired, that he will never exercise creativity or imagination or put out an outstanding performance.

On many jobs, however, management has no use for outstanding performance. What is outstanding performance on the part of an assembly-line worker? That he works faster than the line? That he shows creativity and imagination on the job? Management wants none of these. *Adequate* performance is all that can be used on the assembly line and probably on a growing number (I know no figures) of other jobs in our society. Here the conformist, dependent worker may well be the best.[13] As Leavitt and Whisler (1958) put it, "The issue of morale versus productivity that now worries us may pale as programming moves in. The morale of programmed personnel may be of less central concern because less (or at least a different sort of) productivity will be demanded of them" (p. 46).

Even at the management level, there may be an increasing need for conforming, unimaginative types of "organization men" if Leavitt and Whisler's prediction comes true that "jobs at today's middle-management levels will become highly structured. Much more of the work will be programmed, i.e., covered by sets of operating rules governing the day-to-day decisions that are made" (p. 41). Despite the *organization man*, it might be argued that nonconformity will be useful to the organization only in increasing limited doses.

The Costs of Power-equalization

On the other hand, power-equalization can be quite costly to the organization. To make general supervision or participative management work, many of the old-line autocratic supervisors must be retrained or replaced; this is an expensive process which may result in the demoralization or elimination of the organization's most technically competent individuals. Since it is extremely difficult to develop internalized motivation on many routine jobs, once the traditional, external sanctions (monetary rewards, fear of discharge, and so forth) are removed, *net* motivation may fall on balance. And it is fairly meaningless to talk of permitting exercise of discretion to assembly-line workers or girls on a punch-card operation; the very nature of the technology requires that all essential decisions be centrally programmed.

"But if the nature of the job makes power-equalization techniques impractical," some may argue, "change the nature of the job." Rensis Likert (1961) puts this well:

> To be highly motivated, each member of the organization must feel that the organization's objectives are of significance and that his own particular task contributes in an indispensable manner to the organization's achievement of its objectives. He should see his role as difficult, important, and meaningful. This is necessary if the individual is to achieve and maintain a sense of personal worth and importance. *When jobs do not meet this specification they should be reorganized so that they do* [p. 103, my emphasis].

True, there are many opportunities to redesign jobs and workflows[14] so as to increase various forms of job satisfaction such as autonomy and achievement. But whether such changes should be made is a matter for organizational economics.

In many instances these changes, when accompanied by appropriate forms of supervision and proper selection of personnel, may result in substantial increases of productivity. (Purely technological losses in efficiency may be more than offset by increased motivation, less workflow friction, and so forth.) Obviously, in such instances organizational economics would dictate that the changes should be introduced.

But there are other areas where technological changes can be made only at a substantial cost in terms of productivity—and the impact of automation and information technology seems to be increasing the number of jobs where this may be true. Should we scrap the advances of technology in these areas in order to foster good human relations? Or should we say, "Thank God for the number of people who have made an apparent adjustment to routine jobs. Would that there were more." Perhaps—as has been suggested earlier—it would be best to devote our resources to ever-shortening the work week and helping people to enjoy their leisure more fully.

There seems to be considerable evidence (Argyris, 1960, Chap. 5) that a relatively stable situation can exist in which workers perform relatively routine, programmed jobs under hygienic supervision. Although these workers may not be satisfied (in the Hertzberg sense) and may be immature, apathetic, and dependent (in the Argyris sense), they are not actively dissatisfied, they do not feel a need for additional responsibility, and they seek meaning in life from their home and community rather than from their jobs. To be sure, these individuals are maximizing neither their productive efforts nor their possible job satisfaction. But both management and employees find the situation satisficing (in the Simon sense). Barring sudden change, it is stable. It may well be the best we are likely to get in many situations without costly changes in technology, child upbringing, and so forth.

THE PERSONALITY-ORGANIZATION HYPOTHESIS SUMMARIZED

My concern in this section has been with the personality-versus-organization hypothesis. I have tried to demonstrate:

1. Although many individuals find relatively little satisfaction in their work, this may not be as much of a deprivation as the hypothesis would suggest, since many of these same individuals center their lives off the job and find most of their satisfactions in the community and the home. With these individuals, power-equalization may not liberate much energy.

2. Individuals are not motivated solely to obtain autonomy, self-actualization, and so forth. With various degrees of emphasis, individuals also want security and to know what is expected of them. Power-equalization may certainly stir up a good deal of anxiety among those who are not prepared for it, and at least some individuals may be reluctant to assume the responsibility that it throws upon them.

3. Power-equalization techniques are not too meaningful when management needs no more than an "adequate" level of production, as is often the case when work is highly programmed. Under such circumstances, the costs entailed by modification in job design and supervisory techniques may be greater than the gains obtained from increased motivation to work.

All of the above does not mean either that the personality-organization hypothesis is meaningless or that power-equalization techniques are not useful. Quite the contrary. What it does mean is that many individuals can accommodate themselves to the demands of the organization without too much psychological loss, and for them the personality-organization conflict is not particularly frustrating. Similarly, in many circumstances the gains to the organization from power-equalization may be moderate and more than offset by its costs.

For other individuals (for example, scientists working in large companies), the personality-organization conflict may be felt quite acutely. For the most part, these are the very individuals whose work cannot be programmed and from whom management wants more than merely "adequate" production.

All this re-emphasizes the often-made point that no single style of leadership can be universally appropriate. The techniques which work on the assembly line will almost certainly fail with research scientists. Indeed, it is fair to predict that, over time, the differences among supervisory styles may increase. Perhaps, in the future, we shall have at one extreme research scientists and others doing creative work who will be putting in a 40-hour or longer work week under conditions of relative power-equalization. At the other extreme may be those who submit to close supervision on highly programmed jobs, but for only 20 hours or so. Shades of *Brave New World:* the alphas and the gammas!

NOTES

1. For an excellent summary of this hypothesis and its application, see Clark (1960-61). Somewhat the same position is taken by Merton (1957) and Selznick (1949); both suggest that organizational attempts to obtain conformity lead to unanticipated consequences, such as lack of innovation and even rebellion.
2. These three groups are discussed in Walker and Guest (1952); Shepard (1960); and Whyte (1956).
3. Herzberg, Mausner, and Snyderman (1960) distinguish between dissatisfiers (basically, the absence of "hygienic" factors such as good "supervision, interpersonal relations, physical working conditions, salary, company policies, and administrative practices, benefits and job security") (p. 113) and motivators (basically challenge, autonomy, and interesting work). Similar conclusions are reached by Guerin, Vernoff, and Feld (1960). The Herzberg, Mausner, and Snyderman analysis is criticized by Vroom and Maier (1960).
4. Recent evidence suggests that unskilled workers are significantly more likely to suffer from personality disturbances and psychosomatic illnesses than are skilled workers, and that these differences become manifest only after the individuals take up their work. (In other words, once individuals land in unskilled jobs, they tend to become more maladjusted.) (Kornhauser, 1962; French, Kahn, and Mann, 1962.)
5. Perhaps the most general statement of this position is McGregor's Theory Y. See McGregor (1960.)
6. There seems to be a certain amount of confusion as to whether prescriptions for power-equalization are written from the point of view of organizational efficiency or that of mental health (and possibly the degree of confusion has increased since the primary source of research funds in this area has shifted from the military to the National Institute of Mental Health). There are those who claim that what

is good for the individual will, in the long run, be good for the organization, and vice versa. Regardless, it is useful to keep one's criteria explicit.

7. I must confess that many of these criticisms apply to my own writing. See Strauss and Sayles (1960), especially Chapters 4-8 and 12, chapters for which I was responsible. See the review by Brayfield (1962).

8. Bennis (1959, p. 281). Ironically, some of those most concerned with the tyranny of the organization would substitute for it the tyranny of the participative group.

9. Though the concept of self-actualization is insightful, I tend to agree with Bennis (1959) that it "is, at best, an ill-defined concept . . . [and that] self-actualized man seems to be more myth than reality" (p. 279).

10. Both the Wayne State and the Michigan studies emphasize that no single factor explains the relationship. Kornhauser (1962) concludes: "Both on rational grounds and from empirical evidence, I see no reason to think that it is useful to single out one or a few of the job-related characteristics as distinctly important . . . If we are to understand why mental health is poorer in less skilled, more routine factory jobs, we must look at the entire pattern of work and life conditions of people in these occupations—not just at single variables." (p. 46).

11. Maslow (1954) himself suggests that self-actualization can be obtained off the job, as "an ideal mother [or] . . . athletically" (p. 373). Dubin's point may also be exaggerated. I would guess that for the most part those who participate actively (seek self-actualization) off the job also seek to participate actively on the job, in the community and at home.

12. For a list of the conditions under which "authoritarian leadership might be as effective as its alternatives," see Wilensky (1975). Interestingly, the personality-organization hypothesis is strongly influenced by Freud. Yet Freud postulated that "productive work is partially a function of the expression of hostility to the leader" (Bennis, 1959, p. 292).

13. For an outstanding example, see Goode and Fowler (1949).

14. See, for example, Davis and Werling (1906); Friedmann (1955); Chapple and Sayles (1961); Strauss and Sayles (1960), Chapters 2 and 16.

WARREN G. BENNIS

The Coming Death of Bureaucracy

Not far from the new Government Center in downtown Boston, a foreign visitor walked up to a sailor and asked why American ships were built to last only a short time. According to the tourist, "The sailor answered without hesitation that the art of navigation is making such rapid progress that the finest ship would become obsolete if it lasted beyond a few years. In these words which fell accidentally from an uneducated man, I began to recognize the general and systematic idea upon which your great people direct all their concerns."

The foreign visitor was that shrewd observer of American morals and manners, Alexis de Tocqueville, and the year was 1835. He would not recognize Scollay Square today. But he had caught the central theme of our country: its preoccupation, its *obsession* with change. One thing is, however, new since de Tocqueville's time: the *acceleration* of newness, the changing scale and scope of change itself. As Dr. Robert Oppenheimer said, ". . . the world alters as we walk in it, so that the years of man's life measure not some small growth or rearrangement or moderation of what was learned in childhood, but a great upheaval."

How will these accelerating changes in our society influence human organizations?

A short while ago, I predicted that we would, in the next 25 to 50 years, participate in the end of bureaucracy as we know it and in the

Source: Reprinted by permission from THINK Magazine, published by IBM, copyright © 1966 by International Business Machines Corporation.

rise of new social systems better suited to the twentieth-century demands of industrialization. This forecast was based on the evolutionary principle that every age develops an organizational form appropriate to its genius, and that the prevailing form, known by sociologists as bureaucracy and by most businessmen as "damn bureaucracy," was out of joint with contemporary realities. I realize now that my distant prophecy is already a distinct reality so that prediction is already foreshadowed by practice.

I should like to make clear that by bureaucracy I mean a chain of command structured on the lines of a pyramid—the typical structure which coordinates the business of almost every human organization we know of: industrial, governmental, of universities and research and development laboratories, military, religious, voluntary. I do not have in mind those fantasies so often dreamed up to describe complex organizations. These fantasies can be summarized in two grotesque stereotypes. The first I call "Organization as Inkblot"—an actor steals around an uncharted wasteland, growing more restive and paranoid by the hour, while he awaits orders that never come. The other specter is "Organization as Big Daddy"—the actors are square people plugged into square holes by some omniscient and omnipotent genius who can cradle in his arms the entire destiny of man by way of computer and TV. Whatever the first image owes to Kafka, the second owes to George Orwell's 1984.

Bureaucracy, as I refer to it here, is a useful social invention that was perfected during the industrial revolution to organize and direct the activities of a business firm. Most students of organizations would say that its anatomy consists of the following components:

1. A well-defined chain of command.
2. A system of procedures and rules for dealing with all contingencies relating to work activities.
3. A division of labor based on specialization.
4. Promotion and selection based on technical competence.
5. Impersonality in human relations.

It is the pyramid arrangement we see on most organizational charts.

The bureaucratic "machine model" was developed as a reaction against the personal subjugation, nepotism and cruelty, and the capricious and subjective judgements which passed for managerial practices during the early days of the industrial revolution. Bureaucracy emerged out of the organizations' need for order and precision and the workers' demands for impartial treatment. It was an organization ideally suited to the values and demands of the Victorian era. And just as bureaucracy emerged as a creative response to a radically new age, so today new organizational shapes are surfacing before our eyes.

First I shall try to show why the conditions of our modern industrialized world will bring about the death of bureaucracy. In the second part of this article I will suggest a rough model of the organization of the future.

FOUR THREATS

There are at least four relevant threats to bureaucracy:

1. Rapid and unexpected change.
2. Growth in size where the volume of an organization's traditional activities is not enough to sustain growth. (A number of factors are included here, among them: bureaucratic overhead; tighter controls and impersonality due to bureaucratic sprawls; outmoded rules and organizational structures.)
3. Complexity of modern technology where integration between activities and persons of very diverse, highly specialized competence is required.
4. A basically psychological threat springing from a change in managerial behavior.

It might be useful to examine the extent to which these conditions exist *right now:*

Rapid and unexpected change. Bureaucracy's strength is its capacity to efficiently manage the routine and predictable in human affairs. It is almost enough to cite the knowledge and population explosion to raise doubts about its contemporary viability. More revealing, however, are the statistics which demonstrate these overworked phrases:

a. Our productivity output per man hour may now be doubling almost every 20 years rather than every 40 years, as it did before World War II.
b. The Federal Government alone spent $16 billion in research and development activities in 1965; it will spend $35 billion by 1980.
c. The time lag between a technical discovery and recognition of its commercial uses was: 30 years before World War I, 16 years between the Wars, and only 9 years since World War II.
d. In 1946, only 42 cities in the world had populations of more than one million. Today there are 90. In 1930, there were 40 people for each square

mile of the earth's land surface. Today there are 63. By 2000, it is expected, the figure will have soared to 142.

Bureaucracy, with its nicely defined chain of command, its rules and its rigidities, is ill-adapted to the rapid change the environment now demands.

Growth in size. While, in theory, there may be no natural limit to the height of a bureaucratic pyramid, in practice the element of complexity is almost invariably introduced with great size. International operation, to cite one significant new element, is the rule rather than exception for most of our biggest corporations. Firms like Standard Oil Company (New Jersey) with over 100 foreign affiliates, Mobil Oil Corporation, The National Cash Register Company, Singer Company, Burroughs Corporation and Colgate-Palmolive Company derive more than half their income or earnings from foreign sales. Many others—such as Eastman Kodak Company, Chas. Pfizer & Company, Inc., Caterpillar Tractor Company, International Harvester Company, Corn Products Company and Minnesota Mining & Manufacturing Company—make from 30 to 50 percent of their sales abroad. General Motors Corporation sales are not only nine times those of Volkswagen, they are also bigger than the Gross National Product of the Netherlands and well over the GNP of a hundred other countries. If we have seen the sun set on the British Empire, we may never see it set on the empires of General Motors, ITT, Shell and Unilever.

LABOR BOOM

Increasing diversity. *Today's activities require persons of very diverse, highly specialized competence.*

Numerous dramatic examples can be drawn from studies of labor markets and job mobility. At some point during the past decade, the U.S. became the first nation in the world ever to employ more people in service occupations than in the production of tangible goods. Examples of this trend:

a. In the field of education, the *increase* in employment between 1950 and 1960 was greater than the total number employed in the steel, copper and aluminum industries.

b. In the field of health, the *increase* in employment between 1950 and 1960 was greater than the total number employed in automobile manufacturing in either year.

c. In financial firms, the *increase* in employment between 1950 and 1960 was greater than total employment in mining in 1960.

These changes, plus many more that are harder to demonstrate statistically, break down the old, industrial trend toward more and more people doing either simple or undifferentiated chores.

Hurried growth, rapid change and increase in specialization—pit these three factors against the five components of the pyramid structure described on page 110, and we should expect the pyramid of bureaucracy to begin crumbling.

Change in managerial behavior. There is, I believe, a subtle but perceptible change in the philosophy underlying management behavior. Its magnitude, nature and antecedents, however, are shadowy because of the difficulty of assigning numbers. (Whatever else statistics do for us, they most certainly provide a welcome illusion of certainty.) Nevertheless, real change seems underway because of:

a. A new concept of *man*, based on increased knowledge of his complex and shifting needs, which replaces an over simplified, innocent, push-button idea of man.
b. A new concept of *power*, based on collaboration and reason, which replaces a model of power based on coercion and threat.
c. A new concept of *organizational values*, based on humanistic-democratic ideals, which replaces the depersonalized mechanistic value system of bureaucracy.

The primary cause of this shift in management philosophy stems not from the bookshelf but from the manager himself. Many of the behavioral scientists, like Douglas McGregor or Rensis Likert, have clarified and articulated—even legitimized—what managers have only half registered to themselves. I am convinced, for example, that the popularity of McGregor's book, *The Human Side of Enterprise*, was based on his rare empathy for a vast audience of managers who are wistful for an alternative to the mechanistic concept of authority, i.e., that he outlined a vivid utopia of more authentic human relationships than most organizational practices today allow. Furthermore, I suspect that the desire for relationships in business has little to do with a profit motive per se, though it is often rationalized as doing so. The real push for these changes stems from the need, not only to humanize the organization, but to use it as a crucible of personal growth and the development of self-realization.[1]

The core problems confronting any organization fall, I believe, into five major categories. First, let us consider the problems, then let us see how our twentieth-century conditions of constant change have made the bureaucratic approach to these problems obsolete.

Integration. The problem is how to integrate individual needs and management goals. In other words, it is the inescapable conflict between individual needs (like "spending time with the family") and organizational demands (like meeting deadlines).

Under twentieth-century conditions of constant change there has been an emergence of human sciences and a deeper understanding of man's complexity. Today, integration encompasses the entire range of issues concerned with incentives, rewards and motivations of the individual, and how the organization succeeds or fails in adjusting to these issues. In our society, where personal attachments play an important role, the individual is appreciated, and there is genuine concern for his well-being, not just in a veterinary-hygiene sense, but as a moral, integrated personality.

PARADOXICAL TWINS

The problem of integration, like most human problems, has a venerable past. The modern version goes back at least 160 years and was precipitated by an historical paradox: the twin births of modern individualism and modern industrialism. The former brought about a deep concern for and a passionate interest in the individual and his personal rights. The latter brought about increased mechanization of organized activity. Competition between the two has intensified as each decade promises more freedom and hope for man and more stunning achievements for technology. I believe that our society *has* opted for more humanistic and democratic values, however unfulfilled they may be in practice. It will "buy" these values even at loss in efficiency because it feels it can now afford the loss.

Social influence. This problem is essentially one of power and how power is distributed. It is a complex issue and alive with controversy, partly because studies of leadership and power distribution can be interpreted in many ways, and almost always in ways which coincide with one's biases (including a cultural leaning toward democracy).

The problem of power has to be seriously reconsidered because of dramatic situational changes which make the possibility of one-man rule not necessarily "bad" but impractical. I refer to changes in top management's role.

Peter Drucker, over 12 years ago, listed 41 major responsibilities of the chief executive and declared that "90 percent of the trouble we are having with the chief executive's job is rooted in our superstition of the one-man chief." Many factors make one-man control obsolete, among them: the broadening product base of industry; impact of new technology; the scope of international operation; the separation of management from ownership; the rise of trade unions and general education. The real power of the "chief" has been eroding in most organizations even though both he and the organization cling to the older concept.

Collaboration. This is the problem of managing and resolving conflicts. Bureaucratically, it grows out of the very same process of conflict and stereotyping that has divided nations and communities. As organizations become more complex, they fragment and divide, building tribal patterns and symbolic codes which often work to exclude others (secrets and jargon, for example) and on occasion to exploit differences for inward (and always fragile) harmony.

Recent research is shedding new light on the problem of conflict. Psychologist Robert R. Blake in his stunning experiments has shown how simple it is to induce conflict, how difficult to arrest it. Take two groups of people who have never before been together, and give them a task which will be judged by an impartial jury. In less than an hour, each group devolves into a tightly-knit band with all the symptoms of an "in group." They regard their product as a "master-work" and the other group's as "commonplace" at best. "Other" becomes "enemy." "We are good, they are bad; we are right, they are wrong."

RABBIE'S REDS AND GREENS

Jaap Rabbie, conducting experiments on intergroup conflict at the University of Utrecht, has been amazed by the ease with which conflict and stereotype develop. He brings into an experimental room two groups and distributes green name tags and pens to one group, red pens and tags to the other. The two groups do not compete; they do not even interact. They are only in sight of each other while they silently complete a questionnaire. Only ten minutes are needed to activate defensiveness and fear, reflected in the hostile and irrational perceptions of both "reds" and "greens."

Adaptation. This problem is caused by our turbulent environment. The pyramid structure of bureaucracy, where power is concentrated at the top, seems the perfect way to "run a railroad." And for the

routine tasks of the nineteenth and early twentieth centuries, bureaucracy was (in some respects it still is) a suitable social arrangement.
However, rather than a placid and predictable environment, what
predominates today is a dynamic and uncertain one where there is
deepening interdependence among economic, scientific, educational,
social and political factors in the society.

Revitalization. This is the problem of growth and decay. As Alfred
North Whitehead has said: "The art of free society consists first in
the maintenance of the symbolic code, and secondly, in the fearlessness
of revision . . . Those societies which cannot combine reverence to their
symbols with freedom of revision must ultimately decay . . . "

Growth and decay emerge as the penultimate conditions of contemporary society. Organizations, as well as societies, must be concerned
with those social structures that engender buoyancy, resilience and
a "fearlessness of revision."

I introduce the term "revitalization" to embrace all the social mechanisms that stagnate and regenerate, as well as the process of this
cycle. The elements of revitalization are:

1. An ability to learn from experience and to codify, store and retrieve the
    relevant knowledge.

2. An ability to "learn how to learn," that is, to develop methods for improv-
    ing the learning process.

3. An ability to acquire and use feed-back mechanisms on performance,
    in short, to be self-analytical.

4. An ability to direct one's own destiny.

These qualities have a good deal in common with what John Gardner
calls "self-renewal." For the organization, it means conscious attention
to its own evolution. Without a planned methodology and explicit direction, the enterprise will not realize its potential.

Integration, distribution of power, collaboration, adaptation and *revitalization*—these are the major human problems of the next 25 years.
How organizations cope with and manage these tasks will undoubtedly
determine the viability of the enterprise.

Against this background I should like to set forth some of the conditions that will dictate organization life in the next two or three decades.

The environment. Rapid technological change and diversification
will lead to more and more partnerships between government and
business. It will be a truly mixed economy. Because of the immensity

and expense of the projects, there will be fewer identical units competing in the same markets and organizations will become more interdependent.

The four main features of this environment are:

a.   Interdependence rather than competition.

b.   Turbulence and uncertainty rather than readiness and certainty.

c.   Large-scale rather than small-scale enterprises.

d.   Complex and multinational rather than simple national enterprises.

"NICE"—AND NECESSARY

Population characteristics. The most distinctive characteristic of our society is education. It will become even more so. Within 15 years, two-thirds of our population living in metropolitan areas will have attended college. Adult education is growing even faster, probably because of the rate of professional obsolescence. The Killian report showed that the average engineer required further education only ten years after getting his degree. It will be almost routine for the experienced physician, engineer and executive to go back to school for advanced training every two or three years. All of this education is not just "nice." It is necessary.

One other characteristic of the population which will aid our understanding of organizations of the future is increasing job mobility. The ease of transportation, coupled with the needs of a dynamic environment, change drastically the idea of "owning" a job—or "having roots." Already 20 percent of our population change their mailing address at least once a year.

Work values. The increased level of education and mobility will change the values we place on work. People will be more intellectually committed to their jobs and will probably require more involvement, participation and autonomy.

Also, people will be more "other-oriented," taking cues for their norms and values from their immediate environment rather than tradition.

Tasks and goals. The tasks of the organization will be more technical, complicated and unprogrammed. They will rely on intellect instead of muscle. And they will be too complicated for one person to comprehend, to say nothing of control. Essentially, they will call for the collaboration of specialists in a project or a team-form of organization.

There will be a complication of goals. Business will increasingly concern itself with its adaptive or innovative-creative capacity. In addition, supragoals will have to be articulated, goals which shape and provide the foundation for the goal structure. For example, one might be a system for detecting new and changing goals; another could be a system for deciding priorities among goals.

Finally, there will be more conflict and contradiction among diverse standards for organizational effectiveness. This is because professionals tend to identify more with the goals of their profession than with those of their immediate employer. University professors can be used as a case in point. Their inside work may be a conflict between teaching and research, while more of their income is derived from outside sources, such as foundations and consultant work. They tend not to be good "company men" because they divide their loyalty between their professional values and organizational goals.

KEY WORD: "TEMPORARY"

Organization. The social structure of organizations of the future will have some unique characteristics. The key word will be "temporary." There will be adaptive, rapidly changing *temporary* systems. These will be task forces organized around problems to be solved by groups of relative strangers with diverse professional skills. The groups will be arranged on an organic rather than mechanical model; they will evolve in response to a problem rather than to programmed role expectations. The executive thus becomes a coordinator or "linking pin" between various task forces. He must be a man who can speak the polyglot jargon of research, with skills to relay information and to mediate between groups. People will be evaluated not vertically according to rank and status, but flexibly and functionally according to skill and professional training. Organizational charts will consist of project groups rather than stratified functional groups. (This trend is already visible in the aerospace and construction industries, as well as many professional and consulting firms.)

Adaptive, problem-solving, temporary systems of diverse specialists, linked together by coordinating and task-evaluating executive specialists in an organic flux—this is the organization form that will gradually replace bureaucracy as we know it. As no catchy phrase comes to mind, I call this an organic-adaptive structure. Organizational arrangements of this sort may not only reduce the intergroup conflicts mentioned earlier; it may also induce honest-to-goodness creative collaboration.

Motivation. The organic-adaptive structure should increase motivation and thereby effectiveness, because it enhances satisfactions intrinsic to the task. There is a harmony between the educated individual's need for tasks that are meaningful, satisfactory and creative and a flexible organizational structure.

I think that the future I describe is not necessarily a "happy" one. Coping with rapid change, living in temporary work systems, developing meaningful relations and then breaking them—all augur social strains and psychological tensions. Teaching how to live with ambiguity, to identify with the adaptive process, to make a virtue out of contingency, and to be self-directing—these will be the tasks of education, the goals of maturity, and the achievement of the successful individual.

NO DELIGHTFUL MARRIAGES

In these new organizations of the future, participants will be called upon to use their minds more than at any other time in history. Fantasy, imagination and creativity will be legitimate in ways that today seem strange. Social structures will no longer be instruments of psychic repression but will increasingly promote play and freedom on behalf of curiosity and thought.

One final word: While I forecast the structure and value coordinates for organizations of the future and contend that they are inevitable, this should not bar any of us from giving the inevitable a little push. The French moralist may be right in saying that there are no delightful marriages, just good ones. It is possible that if managers and scientists continue to get their heads together in organizational revitalization, they *might* develop delightful organizations—just possibly.

I started with a quote from de Tocqueville and I think it would be fitting to end with one: "I am tempted to believe that what we call necessary institutions are often no more than institutions to which we have grown accustomed. In matters of social constitution, the field of possibilities is much more extensive than men living in their various societies are ready to imagine."

NOTES

1. Let me propose an hypothesis to explain this tendency. It rests on the assumption that man has a basic need for transcendental experiences, somewhat like the psychological rewards which William James claimed religion provided— "an assurance of safety and a temper of peace, and, in relation to others, a preponderance of living affections." Can it be that as religion has become secularized, less transcendental, men search for substitutes such as close interpersonal relationships, psychoanalysis— even the release provided by drugs such as LSD?

ROBERT D. MIEWALD

The Greatly Exaggerated Death of Bureaucracy

The inevitable revolution in the conditions of life within the organization is heralded by experts in administrative theory. Warren Bennis, in particular, seems to have caught the fancy of many by describing this coming breakthrough in terms of some exciting predictions about the death of bureaucracy and the evolution of a "post-bureaucratic" managerial system.[1] Certainly there can be no doubt that the organization is changing, but will the change in direction leave the specter of bureaucracy far behind? Quite the contrary, it can be argued that the forces of bureaucratization were never in finer fettle and, indeed, that the very same theorists who are singing the dirge have had much to do with the rejuvenation of bureaucracy.

The perspective of all modern scholars on the subject of bureaucracy is probably conditioned by the extent of their exposure to the pioneering work of Max Weber. If it is assumed that all there is to bureaucracy is the collection of features, primarily structural, identified by Weber in his famous essay,[2] then there is little doubt that we have solved the problem. But surely the transformation of this highly abstract ideal type into an easily demolished straw man can be of little comfort to the millions who today dread the implications of bureaucratization. Genius though he was, Weber was not prescient; he could not have

Source: Copyright © 1970 by The Regents of The University of California. Reprinted from *California Management Review*, Vol. 13, no. 2, 65-69 by permission of The Regents.

foreseen all the many forms that the essence of bureaucracy could take. His formulation of the concept of bureaucracy has provided an invaluable tool for the analysis of organization. However, rather than making the superficial assumption that "postindustrial" means "post-bureaucratic," it might be wiser for today's students to inquire whether bureaucracy can adjust to the new age which, so the sociologists and economists insist, we have recently entered. Bennis, for example, believes that the transition in administrative thought from mechanical to organic models will be fatal to bureaucracy.[3] But is bureaucracy restricted to the mechanical? In many cases it would appear that external bureaucratic constraints have simply been replaced by more subtle influences on the individual. The end result in either case is the same: a high degree of predictability about human behavior within the large, complex organization.

In other words, when Weber stated that "der Bürokratisierung gehört die Zukunft," he was surely not suggesting that the thoroughly Teutonic version he had captured within his ideal type was the universal, eternal terminus of history.[4] When he deplored the direction of Western civilization, he was not so upset with the actual work of the bureaucracy as he was with the worship by modern man of the "Scheuerteufel," of the fanatic for neatness and order.[5] For Weber, any historical bureaucracy was merely a concrete manifestation of the inexorable process of "demystification," which was conquering the world. This process is independent of specific forms; the true essence of bureaucratization feeds upon that which will make the affairs of men more amenable to rational calculation. Given the administrative technology of the nineteenth century and his familiarity with the authoritarian tendencies of the Germans, it is little wonder that Weber described the bureaucratic instrument as he did. He would hardly have been surprised, however, to learn that more sophisticated means of controlling behavior had been invented.

Weber's main scholarly concern, then, was with the progressive rationalization of the world and its impact on human relationships. A scientifically derived concept of efficiency governs our economic activity, and the more energetically we participate in what Polanyi calls the One Big Market, the more we must adapt our lives to the abstract "fictions" which serve to harmonize the industrial-technological complex.[6] As the spooks and spirits are exorcised from society, the individual must consciously construct a life strategy from the "facts" provided by Western empirical science. The behavior pattern characteristic of industrial man, therefore, is dependent upon a social environment that is so stable that the opportunities for precise calculation are available.

In Weber's view modern man had subdued his environment, but not simply because of the refinement of bureaucratic decision-making systems; such systems only represent a mode of thought which holds that both nature and society are subject to ascertainable regularities. That is, the individuals who shaped the industrial development of the West were not so much scientists as they were firm believers in the efficacy of science. As Weber often stressed, their actual comprehension of the secrets of the universe is secondary to their deep faith that the world can be controlled according to rational calculation. In contrast to the "savage," the civilized man is distinguished by accepting the idea that his activity and the activity of those who come within his sphere of interest are as predictable as any mechanical process.[7] Knowledge in such a society is power. At the peak of its influence that classical bureaucratic form was the most efficient means for applying rationality to the natural and human environment. Of all social institutions it promised the maximization of scientifically correct decision-making.

Bureaucracy, in the Weberian scheme of things, is only "the most rational offspring" of the social phenomenon called discipline.[8] This neutral, impersonal force permitted large numbers of people to be coordinated in efforts aimed at the methodical accomplishment of formal goals. If the worker can be indoctrinated to accept the discipline of the organization, then his behavior can be calculated, along with nonhuman production factors, in a formula for optimum productivity. As Weber noted, it was the recognition of the need for such calculation in terms of the human resources which accounted for the success of the American brand of management.[9] A rational discipline, in short, is the underlying strength of the bureaucratic structure.

POSTBUREAUCRATIC SYSTEM

And now we may ask, how does the so-called postbureaucratic situation differ from the administrative style which one might reasonably expect in a completely demystified milieu? Of course, as most laymen can testify, it does not differ at all in any significant sense, and one might go on to argue that, in the most critical areas, the postbureaucratic system is nothing more than the Weberian model with all the most sophisticated modifications. Despite all the agonized contortions which management specialists have put themselves through in the twentieth century, the remarkable fact remains that there has been no substantial change in their basic premises. The guiding belief is still that those regularities exist which, on one level or another, may be learned and acted upon. Whether the knowledge is embodied in the "bounded rationality" of a formal bureaucratic structure or in the professional's internalized determinants of behavior, administration is nothing more than the pursuit of a limited concept of rational discipline.

In reviewing the literature of a half-century of management science, one comes to the conclusion that bureaucracy is not dead, but rather that the most controversial element of the Weberian model is gradually being replaced by a less artificial and more effective variation. This troublesome element is the nature of authority in an organization based on knowledge. Management science, at whatever stage in its growth, has not been concerned with eliminating bureaucracy, but instead with improving it by finding a way around the dilemma of knowledge and authority in an organization with a unilinear definition of rationality. The language used by several generations of theorists retains the same flavor.

LAW OF THE SITUATION

Advocates of "scientific management" as well as behaviorally oriented schools of management research have claimed for their own folk heroes the honor of demanding the replacement of the impersonal bureaucrat with an even more impersonal Goddess of Reason. A former managing director of the Taylor Society argued that it was the father of scientific management who first pointed out that the dysfunctional consequences of an arbitrary bureaucrat could be eliminated by getting all members of the organization to accept as their clue to action the immutable requirements of specific situations. Because of the "relative fixity of nonhuman elements in a managerial situation," there was only one course of action which managers and operatives alike could take.[10] At about the same time a similar kind of technological determinism was stressed in Mary Parker Follett's dictum about "the law of the situation."[11] According to Follett, the submission of boss and employee to the law of the situation would eliminate friction by depersonalizing the operation of the organization to the greatest degree. For both schools of management thought, in other words, rationality itself and not human actors would be in command.

Today, some forty years after the pioneers of management theory proposed their alternative to bureaucratic authority, the charm of the law of the situation remains undiminished. In his latest book Peter Drucker argues quite persuasively that, in our "knowledge society," the members of the organization must be free from formal structures in order to pursue the logic of the situation.[12] The modern knowledge worker, the highly trained specialist, must be independent of boss-centered authority if he is to maintain his status as a professional.

Moreover, as do many recent theorists, Drucker insinuates that the problems of maintaining a rational discipline will shift from the organization to the individual; the employee will find his freedom in submitting to the demands of his particular field of knowledge.[13]

A durable theme in administrative theory is this belief that the discipline needed for large-scale cooperative effort will be voluntarily contributed, if only the workers have been educated to see the one true way. Or, in Weber's terms, the rational discipline needed to hold together several specialties has been internalized through the professionalization of the great majority of employees. The "team concept" of management, for example, implies that all members of the team are divided in their attack on a common problem only by their specialized view of that problem. They are doing collectively what a rational individual would do, if he had the intellectual capacity to grasp the total complexity of the mission. In short, because the members of the knowledge society have been educated in a single perception of reality, they will be able to replace arbitrary bureaucratic regimentation with a form of self-regimentation.

Is this new self-regimentation a cause for celebration, even if it does not actually mean the end of bureaucracy? To be sure, there is some advantage in ridding the world of the crabbed personalities who flourish under a rigid bureaucratic structure. The martinets, the autocrats, the compulsives who find security in stable rules and regulations will be missed only by fiction writers. However, it does not seem likely that the transformation of bureaucracy as described above will have any significant impact on the problems of modern society. For many, from old conservatives to young radicals, the supposedly innovative trends in management theory represent a hateful transmogrification, enabling bureaucracy better to carry out its sinister business.

For one thing, it is evident that the projected changes will do nothing to improve the control of any bureaucracy by members of the public outside the organization. If anything, the self-disciplined professionals will behave more irresponsibly than before. With the growth of professionalism, as Robert Lane pointed out in his discussion of the "knowledgeable society," there will be "a change of venue for political maneuvering"; policy-making, formerly a matter of general public concern, becomes the prerogative of the inhabitants of definite "knowledge domains."[14] Such freedom from outside interference stems naturally from the professional's whole reason for being, and each aspirant to that station longs to be told, "you're the doctor." And as society becomes more dependent upon the close coordination of several specialties, the expectation of deference can be enforced by the withholding of participation by organized professions. The substitution of the arrogance of high office with the arrogance of high training is a hollow—even dangerous—triumph, since there now exist no institutional means for the public to control professionals.

A CURABLE ILLNESS

Political irresponsibility, however, has always been a curable illness. The indictment of postbureaucratic society can be quashed only by truly finding a social form above and beyond the bureaucratic. If we are moving toward an age in which the law of the situation has replaced formal structure, we must then ask, what is the nature of that law? For those who find themselves persuaded by Jacques Ellul's bleak appraisal of the technological society, there can be no doubt about which law the modern organization must follow.[15] Bureaucracy through self-discipline can only lead to the perfection of a completely autonomous technology in which the human is a slave and not a master. It promises only a pursuit of what is technically feasible to the bitter end: an antiseptic world in which spontaneity is a gross crime. Even Orwell's *1984* would be a romantic idyll compared to a society of, by, and for technocrats.

Yet such apprehensions about a dehumanized future, whether brought about by bureaucratic or postbureaucratic means, are at the root of the malaise which afflicts so many in Western society. In the eyes of one poet, it is the cause of the Great American Frustration; it is the source of the uneasy feeling that, for all our material progress, we have somehow lost control of events.[16] As Archibald MacLeish asked, how is it that men can seriously ask, "where is technology taking us?" rather than determining, in light of a wide range of human values, where will we go with our technology? What else could account for the instant elevation of such an opaque philosopher as Herbert Marcuse to the status of guru, except that he hints that one might somehow refuse to march obediently along a one-dimensional path of history.

The entire ritual of "dropping out" is the most articulate rejection of the mentality which conditions modern administrative thought. For today's college student, there is little difference between a Kafkaesque bureaucrat and the proudest product of our graduate schools of business administration; both bear the mark of the System and of the System's definition of rationality. Whether the means is a flogging or an invitation to group encounter, they know that the organization expects the same type of behavior. So it is not surprising that the subculture of the young is a confusing combination of several alternatives to the dominant metaphysics. The "drug scene" is one example; the curiosity about Eastern philosophy is another. Perhaps the most surprising outbreak of discontent with our organizational society is the mystical counter-revolution. As Arnold Gehlen predicted a decade ago, the pressure of rationalization can drive people to search for a "new scientific picture of the world," such as astrology.[17]

WEBERIAN OUTLOOK

It must be emphasized that Weber himself would not have been relieved by the claims of those who say the struggle against bureaucracy is over. In his brilliant analysis of his political sociology, Wolfgang Mommsen argues that Weber attached the highest priority to the free development of the individual personality.[18] He was, of course, too much a product of his culture to endorse the glorification of the irrational, but he did regard the conclusions which arose from his many sociological studies with despair; the universal rationalization of life was depriving the personality of its grand role as the final arbiter of values. In more familiar Weberian terminology, the process of demystification was robbing the charismatic impulse of its vitality, of its creative force in society. During his lifetime, Weber's personal preference for a dynamic society in which the individual retains the largest possible number of options was being made obsolete by the irresistible drive toward greater predictability of behavior.

It is not too much to say, then, that Weber would conclude that bureaucracy is still alive and well. And this is the essential point which students of administration must come to realize if they are going to attack effectively the multiple crises of our era. To find specific elements of Weber's model of bureaucracy poorly adjusted to our times is a reasonable concession to the fact that conditions do change. But this is not the same as eliminating bureaucracy, for, in the most profound sense, bureaucracy will be with us as long as men insist that there is only one perception of reality by which rationality can be measured.

NOTES

1. Warren Bennis, "Beyond Bureaucracy," *Trans-Action 2* (1965): 31-35; "Organizational Revitalization," *California Management Review* 7 (1966): 41-55; "The Coming Death of Bureaucracy," *Management Review* 56 (1967): 19-24; "Post-Bureaucratic Leadership," *Trans-Action 6* (1969): 44-52.
2. Max Weber, "Bureaucracy," in H. Gerth and C.W. Mills, eds., *From Max Weber* (New York: Oxford University Press, 1946).
3. Bennis, "Post-Bureaucratic Leadership," *Trans-Action*, p. 45.
4. Max Weber, *Staatssoziologie* (Berlin: Duncker and Humbolt, 1966), p. 46.

5. Max Weber, "Debattereden auf der Tagung des Vereins für Sozial-politik in Wien 1909 zu den Verhandlungen über 'Die wirtschaftlichen Unternehmungen der Gemeinden,' " in Weber, *Gesammelte Aufsätze zur Soziologie und Sozialpolitik* (Tubingen: Mohr, 1924), p. 414.

6. Karl Polanyi, *The Great Transformation* (Boston: Beacon Press, 1957), p. 72.

7. Max Weber, "Ueber einige Kategorien der verstehenden Soziologie," in Weber, *Gesammelte Aufsätze zur Wissenschaftslehre* (Tübingen: Mohr, 1922), pp. 449-50.

8. Max Weber, "The Meaning of Discipline," in Gerth and Mills, *From Max Weber*, pp. 253-64.

9. Ibid., p. 261.

10. Harlow Person, "The New Attitude toward Management," in Person, ed., *Scientific Management in American Industry* (New York: Harper, 1929), p. 18.

11. Mary Follett, "The Giving of Orders," in Henry Metcalfe and L. Urwick, eds., *Dynamic Administration* (New York: Harper, 1940), pp. 58-64.

12. Peter Drucker, *The Age of Discontinuity* (New York: Harper and Row, 1968), p. 290.

13. Ibid., pp. 259-60.

14. Robert Lane, "The Decline of Politics and Ideology in Knowledgeable Society," *American Sociological Review* 31 (1966): 657.

15. Jacques Ellul, *The Technological Society* (New York: Alfred A. Knopf, 1964).

16. Archibald MacLeish, "The Great American Frustration," *Saturday Review* (July 13, 1968): 13-16.

17. Arnold Gehlen, *Die Seele im technischem Zeitalter* (Hamburg: Rowohlt, 1957), p. 15.

18. Wolfgang Mommsen, "Max Weber's Political Sociology and His Philosophy of World History," *International Social Science Journal* 27 (1965): 23-45.

III | MANAGERS MANAGING

What is it managers are about when they manage organizations? What are they doing? What are they trying to do? What do they have to work with? In this part we take a look at some aspects of managers at work.

The first set of readings gives us several different perspectives on managers and how they work. Carlisle introduces us to MacGregor, a manager who has thought through what is needed to manage his large refinery and has delegated to his subordinate managers most of the work of managing. He has, however, kept some crucial things to himself. It looks simple—but more careful reading brings out how skilled a manager MacGregor is, and how successful he is in training and developing other managers.

While we get some glimpse of the specifics of how MacGregor manages, the basic thing we learn of his way of managing is that it rests more on his outlook or approach than on specific techniques or methods. MacGregor also reveals his outlook on other, particularly subordinate, managers. Charles Wilson in "Turf vs. Systems: Two Management Styles," examines two basic orientations managers can have toward their jobs and what the outcomes for the organizations will be from these outlooks. Lazarus and Burns each describe different outlooks superior managers have had toward their subordinate managers.

The next two sets of readings examine techniques managers can use in doing their work. A major development in management since World War II has been the growth of Management Science. Aided by the electronic computers Management Science has generated an extensive array of analytical tools intended to aid managers in decision making. But do they? In "Management Science and Business Practice," C. Jackson Grayson claims that while he was in the federal government serving as Chairman of the Price Commission during the early 1970's, he was able to use *none* of the Management Science tools in his decision making. What makes this comment particularly telling is that not only was Mr. Grayson the Dean of the Business School at SMU before and after his Washington service, but that prior to becoming Dean he was a leading developer of the field of Management Science.

Needless to say, Mr. Grayson's comments were promptly challenged. Milan Zeleny argues that, if we do not use science, logic, and tested concepts, we are left with only intuition, experience, hunches and that elusive thing called genius to make decisions. He goes on to say that today problems are too complex, too difficult, and too important to be left to such elusive properties as hunches and intuition. This debate has long raged in the halls of academe. Grayson and Zeleny bring it out to where we all can see it and join in, as we should; for in one way or another we all have a stake in the fundamental issues involved.

Sometimes it helps in understanding how people approach life, their work, and each other to shift our perspective; that is, to look at the same events through someone else's glasses. This is in effect what Antony Jay does. In his piece, "Who Knows What Primitive Instincts Lurk in the Heart of the Modern Corporation Man?" Jay examines the business manager much as an anthropologist would examine a primitive and presents us with a witty spoof of the modern manager—or is it a spoof? Are there things other than rational, objective thought influencing the actions and decisions of managers?

The debate between Grayson and Zeleny introduced the issue of whether managers do or should rely on objective, rational processes or experience, intuition, and feelings. The matter is taken further by Leavitt in the first section of his two-part article, "Beyond the Analytical Manager." Here, he probes further into the promise and problems of the manager as a rational analyst. Hellriegel and Slocum stand back a bit from the whole debate and ask whether there are not several decision making or problem solving styles that managers may use, depending upon their own personalities and upon the situation they face. As an interesting beginning to an answer, they describe a model which sorts the different decision styles available to managers.

In the last section of Part III on Managers Managing, we look at two aspects of having a career in management. Ross Webber examines some of the problems people commonly face when beginning a management career. The transition—from a non-managerial to a managerial role, commonly, of moving from a university to a corporation—often involves a wrenching shift in many aspects of a person's life. The very least is likely to be a change in physical location. Far more trying are matters of loyalty, values, self-image and dealing with a complex, imperfect world. There is no way to eliminate the strains and discomforts of the transition into a managerial career. But more accurate information about what is possible can ease and shorten the adjustment process.

After successfully entering the ranks of management, what then? Advancement upward? Hopefully and probably. Often, however, careers might be advanced more rapidly by moving to another organization. How likely is that prospect? One answer is to look at what intercompany moves can mean for the firms involved. Shetty and Peery do this in their paper, "Are Top Executives Transferable Across Companies?"

ARTHUR ELLIOTT CARLISLE

MacGregor

No question about it—some managers are better organized than others, but how often have you run into a really well organized manager—I mean *really* well organized? Not too often, I bet! In the course of my work I run into hundreds of managers a year, yet I can think of only one who managed to be superorganized—to the point where he had time to play an enormous amount of golf. As further proof of his organization, consider this: About two years after I ran into MacGregor, which incidentally is *not* his real name, he was promoted to the post of chief of operations at the corporate level—a fact I discovered when I saw his face looking out at me from the financial section of my newspaper above the announcement of his new executive assignment.

My encounter with MacGregor came about during the course of a study of the extent to which operating managers actually *use* participative management techniques in their dealings with subordinates. The problem with an inquiry of this nature is that nearly every manager either says that he uses a participative approach (because isn't that what every good manager does?) or maybe honestly believes that this is his preferred *modus operandi;* in any event, what I was interested in was information about behavior, not about beliefs (pious or otherwise). So I had to develop an indirect approach for use with the managers being interviewed and follow it up with some questions directed

Source: Reprinted by permission of the publisher from *Organizational Dynamics,* (Vol. 5, No. 1: Summer 1976), pp. 50-62. © 1976 by AMACOM, a division of American Management Associations.

at the subordinates they supervised. Accordingly, I developed a questionnaire that I used in interviewing more than 100 managers in ten major U.S. and Canadian firms. The first item on the questionnaire asked whether the interviewee held regular meetings with his subordinates; if so, how often; and what was the nature of the matters discussed. Finally, it tried to determine whether subordinates were offered the opportunity to initiate discussion and actively participate in the decision-making process or were merely afforded the opportunity to hear about decisions the boss had made.

MacGregor, who at the time was manager of one of the largest refineries in the country, was the last of more than 100 managers I interviewed in the course of the study. Although the interview had been scheduled in advance, the exact time had been left open; I was to call MacGregor at his office early in the week that I would be in the vicinity and set up a specific date and time.

Here's how that phone call went: The switchboard operator answered with the name of the refinery. When I asked for MacGregor's office, a male voice almost instantly said, "Hello." I then asked for MacGregor, whereupon the voice responded, "This is he." I should have recognized at once that this was no ordinary manager; he answered his own phone instantly, as though he had been waiting for it to ring. To my question about when it would be convenient for me to come see him, he replied, "Anytime." I said, "Would today be all right?" His response was, "Today, tomorrow, or Wednesday would be O.K.; or you could come Thursday, except don't come between 10:00 A.M. and noon; or you could come Friday or next week—anytime." I replied feebly, "I just want to fit in with your plans." Then he said, "You are just not getting the message; it makes no difference to me when you come. I have nothing on the books except to play golf and see you. Come in anytime—I don't have to be notified in advance, so I'll be seeing you one of these days," and he then hung up. I was dumbfounded. Here was a highly placed executive with apparently nothing to do except play golf and talk to visitors.

I took MacGregor at his word and drove over immediately to see him without any further announcement of my visit. MacGregor's office, in a small building at one corner of the refinery, adjoined that of his secretary—who, when I arrived, was knitting busily and, without dropping a stitch, said to me, "You must be Mr. Carlisle; he's in there," indicating MacGregor's office with a glance at a connecting door.

MacGregor's office was large and had a big window overlooking the refinery, a conference table with eight chairs arranged around it (one of which, at the head, was more comfortable and imposing than the rest), an engineer's file cabinet with a series of wide drawers, two easy chairs, a sofa, a coffee table with a phone on it, and a desk. The desk had been shoved all the way into a corner; there was no way a chair could be slipped in behind it, and it was covered with technical journals. A lamp stood on the desk, but its plug was not connected to an outlet. There was no phone on the desk. MacGregor, a tall, slender man with a tanned face, stood by the window peering absently into space. He turned slowly when I entered his office and said, "You must be Carlisle. The head office told me you wanted to talk to me about the way we run things here. Sit down on the sofa and fire away."

MACGREGOR'S MODUS OPERANDI

"Do you hold regular meetings with your subordinates?" I asked.

"Yes, I do," he replied.

"How often?" I asked.

"Once a week, on Thursdays, between 10:00 A.M. and noon; that's why I couldn't see you then," was his response.

"What sorts of things do you discuss?" I queried, following my interview guide.

"My subordinates tell me about the decisions they've made during the past week," he explained.

"Then you believe in participative decision making," I commented.

"No—as a matter of fact, I don't," said MacGregor.

"Then why hold the meetings?" I asked. "Why not just tell your people about the operating decisions you've made and let them know how to carry them out?"

"Oh, I don't make their decisions for them and I just don't believe in participating in the decisions they should be making, either; we hold the weekly meeting so that I can keep informed on what they're doing and how. The meeting also gives me a chance to appraise their technical and managerial abilities," he explained. "I used to make all the operating decisions myself; but I quit doing that a few years ago when I discovered my golf game was going to hell because I didn't have enough time to practice. Now that I've quit making other people's decisions, my game is back where it should be."

"You don't make operating decisions any more?" I asked in astonishment.

"No," he replied. Sensing my incredulity, he added, "Obviously you don't believe me. Why not ask one of my subordinates? Which one do you want to talk to?"

"I haven't any idea; I don't even know how many subordinates you have, let alone their names. You choose one," I suggested.

"No, I wouldn't do that—for two reasons. First, I don't make decisions, and second, when my subordinate confirms that I don't make decisions, you'll say that it's a put-up job, so here is a list of my eight immediate subordinates, the people who report directly to me. Choose one name from it and I'll call him and you can talk to him," said MacGregor.

"OK—Johnson, then. I'll talk to him if he's free," said I.

"I'm sure he's able to talk to you. I'll call him and tell him you're on the way over." Reaching for the phone, he determined that Johnson wasn't doing anything, either, and would be happy to have someone to talk to.

SUBORDINATES' VIEWS OF MACGREGOR

I walked over to Johnson's unit and found him to be in his early thirties. After a couple of minutes of casual conversation, I discovered that MacGregor and all eight of his subordinates were chemical engineers. Johnson said, "I suppose MacGregor gave you that bit about his not making decisions, didn't he? That man is a gas."

"It isn't true though, is it? He does make decisions, doesn't he?" I asked.

"No, he doesn't; everything he told you is true. He simply decided not to get involved in decisions that his subordinates are being paid to make. So he stopped making them, and they tell me he plays a lot of golf in the time he saves," said Johnson.

Then I asked Johnson whether he tried to get MacGregor to make a decision and his response was:

"Only once. I had been on the job for only about a week when I ran into an operating problem I couldn't solve, so I phoned MacGregor. He answered the phone with that sleepy 'Hello' of his. I told him who I was and that I had a problem. His response was instantaneous: 'Good, that's what you're being paid to do, solve problems,' and then he hung up. I was dumbfounded. I didn't really know any of the people I was working with, so because I didn't think I had any other alternative, I called him back, got the same sleepy 'Hello,' and again identified myself. He replied sharply, 'I thought I told you that you were paid to solve problems. Do you think that I should do your job as well as my own?' When I insisted on seeing him about my problem, he answered, 'I don't know how you expect me to help you. You have a technical problem and I don't go into the refinery any more; I used to, but my shirts kept getting dirty from the visits and my wife doesn't like washing all the grime out of them, so I pretty much stick in my office. Ask one of the other men. They're all in touch with what goes on out there.'

"I didn't know which one to consult, so I insisted again on seeing him. He finally agreed—grudgingly—to see me right away, so I went over to his office and there he was in his characteristic look-ing-out-the-window posture. When I sat down, he started the dirty-shirt routine—but when he saw that I was determined to involve him in my problems, he sat down on the sofa in front of his coffee table and, pen in hand, prepared to write on a pad of paper. He asked me to state precisely what the problem was and he wrote down exactly what I said. Then he asked what the conditions for its solution were. I replied that I didn't know what he meant by that question. His response was, 'If you don't know what conditions have to be satisfied for a solution to be reached, how do you know when you've solved the problem?' I told him I'd never thought of approaching a problem that way and he replied, 'Then you'd better start. I'll work through this one with you *this* time, but don't expect me to do your problem solving for you because that's *your* job, not mine.'

"I stumbled through the conditions that would have to be satisfied by the solution. Then he asked me what alternative approaches I could think of. I gave him the first one I could think of—let's call it *X*—and he wrote it down and asked me what would happen if I did *X*. I replied with my answer—let's call it *A*. Then he asked me how *A* compared with the conditions I had established for the solution of the problem. I replied that it did not meet them. MacGregor told me that I'd have to think of another. I came up with *Y*, which I said would yield result *B*, and this still fell short of the solution conditions. After more prodding from MacGregor, I came up with *Z*, which I said would have *C* as a result; although this clearly came a lot closer to the conditions I had established for the solution than any of the others I'd suggested, it still did not satisfy all of them. MacGregor then asked me if I could combine any of the approaches I'd suggested. I replied I could do *X* and *Z* and then saw that the resultant *A* plus *C* would indeed satisfy all the solution conditions I had set up previously. When I thanked MacGregor, he replied, 'What for? Get the hell out of my office; you could have done that bit of problem solving perfectly well without wasting my time. Next time you really can't solve a problem on your own, ask the Thursday man and tell me about it at the Thursday meeting.' "

I asked Johnson about Mr. MacGregor's reference to the Thursday man.

"He's the guy who runs the Thursday meeting when MacGregor is away from the plant. I'm the Thursday man now. My predecessor left here about two months ago."

"Where did he go? Did he quit the company?" I asked.

"God, no. He got a refinery of his own. That's what happens to a lot of Thursday men. After the kind of experience we get coping with everyone's problems and MacGregor's refusal to do what he perceives as his subordinates' work, we don't need an operating superior any more and we're ready for our own refineries. Incidentally, most of the people at our level have adopted MacGregor's managerial method in dealing with the foremen who report to us and we are reaping the same kinds of benefits that he does. The foremen are a lot more self-reliant, and we don't have to do their work for them."

I went back to see MacGregor. His secretary was still knitting. The garment she was working on was considerably more advanced than it was on my first visit. She motioned me into MacGregor's office with her head, again not dropping a stitch. MacGregor was in his traditional office posture, looking vacantly out of the window. He turned and asked, "Well, now do you believe that I don't make any decisions?"

I said, "No, that could have been just a fluke." He suggested I see another subordinate and asked me to pick another name from the list. I picked Peterson who, when phoned to see whether he was available, said that he had nothing to do. So I went to Peterson's office.

Peterson was in his late twenties. He asked me what I thought of MacGregor. I said I found him most unusual. Peterson replied, "Yes, he's a gas." Peterson's story paralleled Johnson's. MacGregor refused to make decisions related to the work of his subordinates. When Peterson got into a situation he could not deal with, he said he called one of the other supervisors, usually Johnson, and together they worked it out. At the Thursday meetings, he reported on the decision and gave credit to his helper. "If I hadn't," he added, "I probably wouldn't get help from that quarter again."

In reply to a query on what the Thursday meetings were like, he said, "Well, we all sit around that big conference table in MacGregor's office. He sits at the head like a thinned-down Buddha, and we go around the table talking about the decisions we've made and, if we got help, who helped us. The other guys occasionally make comments—especially if the particular decision being discussed was like one they had had to make themselves at some point or if it had some direct effect on their own operations." MacGregor had said very little at these past few meetings, according to Peterson, but he did pass on any new developments that he heard about at the head office.

HEAD-OFFICE ASSESSMENT OF MACGREGOR

By the time I had finished with Johnson and Peterson, it was time for lunch. I decided I'd go downtown and stop in at the head office to try to find out their assessment of MacGregor and his operation. I visited the operations chief for the corporation. I had wanted to thank him for his willingness to go along with my study, anyway. When I told him I had met MacGregor, his immediate response was, "Isn't he a gas?" I muttered something about having heard that comment before and asked him about the efficiency of MacGregor's operation in comparison with that of other refineries in the corporation. His response was instantaneous, "Oh, MacGregor has by far the most efficient producing unit."

"Is that because he has the newest equipment?" I asked.

"No. As a matter of fact he has the oldest in the corporation. His was the first refinery we built."

"Does MacGregor have a lot of turnover among his subordinates?"

"A great deal," he replied.

Thinking I had found a chink in the MacGregor armor, I asked, "What happens to them; can't they take his system?"

"On the contrary," said the operations chief. "Most of them go on to assignments as refinery managers. After all, under MacGregor's method of supervision, they are used to working on their own."

MORE POINTERS ON MACGREGOR'S STYLE OF MANAGING

"How do they run their own operations—like MacGregor's?" I asked.

"You guessed it. More and more of our operations are using his system."

I went back to the refinery with a few last questions for MacGregor. His secretary had made considerable progress on her knitting and her boss had resumed his position by the refinery window.

"I understand you were downtown. What did they tell you about this place?"

"You know damn well what they said—that you have the most efficient operation in the corporation."

"Yup, it's true," he replied, with no pretense at false modesty. "Periodically, I get chances to go to work for another major oil company—but I've gotten things so well organized here that I really don't want to take on a job like the one I faced when I came here five years ago. I guess I'll hang on here until something better comes up."

"Let me ask you a couple of questions about the Thursday meeting," I continued. "First of all, I understand that when you are away, the 'Thursday man' takes over. How do you choose the individual to fill this slot?"

"Oh, that's simple. I just pick the man who is most often referred to as the one my subordinates turn to for help in dealing with their problems. Then I try him out in this assignment while I'm off. It's good training and, if he proves he can handle it, I know I have someone to propose for any vacancies that may occur at the refinery manager level. The head-office people always contact me for candidates. As a matter of fact, the Thursday-man assignment is sought after. My subordinates compete with each other in helping anyone with a problem because they know they'll get credit for their help at the Thursday meeting. You know, another development has been that jobs on the staff of this refinery are highly prized by young people who want to get ahead in the corporation; when junior management positions open up here, there are always so many candidates that I often have a tough time making a choice."

"Sounds logical," I said. "Now let me focus a bit more on your role as refinery manager. You say you don't make decisions. Suppose a subordinate told you at a Thursday meeting about a decision he'd made and you were convinced that it was a mistake. What would you do about it?"

"How much would the mistake cost me?"

"Oh, I don't know," I answered.

"Can't tell you, then. It would depend on how much it would cost."

"Say, $3,000," I suggested.

"That's easy; I'd let him make it," said MacGregor. I sensed I'd hit the upper limit before MacGregor either would have moved in himself or, more likely, would have suggested that the subordinate discuss it with the Thursday man and then report back to him on their joint decision.

"When was the last time you let a subordinate make a mistake of that magnitude?" I asked skeptically.

"About four weeks ago," said MacGregor.

"You let someone who works for you make such a serious mistake? Why did you do that?"

"Three reasons," said MacGregor. "First, I was only 99.44 percent sure it would be a mistake and if it hadn't turned out to be one, I'd have felt pretty foolish. Second, I thought that making a mistake like this one would be such a tremendous learning experience for him that he'd never make another like that one again. I felt it would do him more good than signing him up for most of the management-development courses that are available. Third, this is a profit center. It was early in the budget year and I felt that we could afford it."

"What was the result?" I asked.

"It *was* a mistake—and I heard about it in short order from the controller downtown by phone." (I realized suddenly that during the whole time I had been in the office, neither MacGregor's phone nor his secretary's had rung.)

"The controller said, 'MacGregor, how could you let a stupid mistake like that last one slip through?' "

"What did you say?"

"Well, I figured a good attack is the best defense. I asked him which refinery in the corporation was the most efficient. He replied, 'You know yours is. That has nothing to do with it.' I told him that it had everything to do with it. I added that my people learn from their mistakes and until the rest of the plants in the organization started operating at the same degree of efficiency as this one, I wasn't going to waste my time talking to clerks. Then I hung up."

"What happened?"

"Well, relations were a bit strained for a while—but they know I'm probably the best refinery manager in the business and I can get another job anytime, so it blew over pretty quickly," he said, not without a degree of self-satisfaction.

MACGREGOR'S CONTROL SYSTEMS

"Peterson told me you have quite a control system here. How does it work?" I asked.

"Very simply," said MacGregor. "On Wednesdays at 2:00 P.M., my subordinates and I get the printout from the computer, which shows the production men their output against quota and the maintenance superintendent his costs to date against the budget. If there is an unfavorable gap between the two, they call me about 3:00 P.M. and the conversation goes something like this: 'Mr. MacGregor, I know I have a problem and this is what I'm going to do about it.' If their solution will work, I tell them to go ahead. If not, I tell them so and then they go and work on it some more and then call back. If the new one will work, I tell them to go ahead with it. If not, I suggest they get in touch with one of the other men, work it out together, and then call me and tell me how they are going to deal with it. If that doesn't work, I refer them to the Thursday man. That way, I don't get involved in making operating decisions.

"I used to have a smaller refinery than this one where I found myself frantically busy all the time—answering the phone constantly and continually doing my subordinates' problem solving for them. They were always more than willing to let me do their work because it was easier than doing it themselves and also because, if the solution did not work out, then I was to blame. Can't fault them for trying that. But when I came here, I resolved to get myself out of that kind of rat race and set about designing this system. I worked out a computer-based production control system in conjunction with a set of quotas I negotiate each year with each of my operating people and a cost budget with the maintenance man. Then I arranged for Wednesday reports. Sometimes it takes a bit of time to renegotiate these quotas—and I've been known to use peer pressure to get them to a reasonable level—but these performance objectives really have to be accepted by the individual before they have any legitimacy or motivational value for him. I chose Wednesday because if a problem did develop, I'd still have time to act on my own if my subordinates couldn't come up with a solution. You see, our production week ends Saturday night. I don't want my head to fall in the basket because of their inability to make good decisions, so I minimized the risk this way.

"I can't even remember when I've had to get directly involved myself with their work. I do a lot of reading related to my work. That's why, when they call me with solutions, I can usually tell accurately whether or not their proposals are going to work out. That's my job as I see it—not doing subordinates' work but, rather, exercising supervision. A lot of managers feel that they have to keep proving to their people that they know more about their subordinates' jobs than the subordinates themselves by doing their work for them. I refuse to do that anymore."

"Is there anything else you do?" I asked.

"Well, I look after community relations. One more thing—I work on these." He stepped over to the engineer's file cabinet in the corner of his office. "In here are manning and equipment tables for this plant at five levels of production—at one-year, two-year, five-year, and ten-year intervals. If I get a phone call from the head office and they ask me what it would take to increase production by 20 percent, I ask over what period; if they say, for example, five years, I just read off the equipment and the personnel that would be needed. That's what I see as being an upper-level manager's job. As I recall, Peter Drucker once said that managers get paid for the futurity and irreversibility of the decisions they make. Well, these sorts of decisions are way in the future and are terribly difficult and expensive to reverse once they are embarked on. Too many managers say they have no time to plan—yet that's what they are being paid to do, not to do their subordinates' work. Not me. I plan, listen to Wednesday reports and Thursday decisions, and play golf."

"Do your subordinates help you make these planning decisions?" I asked.

"No," said MacGregor. "They gather some of the information and I show them how I go about making up the plans. They all know how to do it after they've been here a couple of years. The actual decisions, though, are made by me. If they are wrong, I have to take the blame— and if they are right," he said with a smile, "I take the credit. Now, I have a most important golf game scheduled. If you have any further questions, just come in any time except Thursday between 10:00 A.M. and noon. I don't have much to do except to talk to visitors."

As I drove back home, I started to think about the MacGregor approach to management. Did MacGregor use job enrichment? Yes, his men were motivated by their jobs themselves. Did MacGregor train his subordinates? Evidently, because they seem to be constantly in line for promotion. And there was certainly no doubt about the efficiency of his operation. No question about it: MacGregor was a well-organized manager who still had enough time to work on his golf game.

MACGREGOR EPILOGUE

It is clear that MacGregor had several things going for him that helped make his system effective. Not the least of these was that he had very precise measures of the output of each of his subordinates—barrels of product or performance against budget. It is also true that he was in charge of a profit center and that his own performance was appraised over a time span sufficiently long for him to offset short-term diminished performance with long-term results. Further, MacGregor's responsibilities were confined to production; he did not have to contend with marketing problems. His job was merely to deliver a line of products in the quantities called for at minimum cost, by means of production processes that had been well established and understood by those in charge of them. Certainly all these factors helped MacGregor run his operation the way he did and there is no doubt that as his reputation became established, his superiors gave him a freer hand. But to explain MacGregor in terms of a fit between his leadership style and the nature of his responsibilities is to deny what he tells us about how the really effective manager performs his functions.

MacGregor's overriding concern was with results: the results his subordinates achieved through methods they developed either by themselves or by working with their peers. He simply refused to do their work for them, even at the risk of incurring short-run costs. By refusing, he enabled them to grow in terms of their ability to make decisions even under conditions of uncertainty. MacGregor's contact with his subordinates centered on the negotiation of performance standards and the receipt of progress reports on the results they were achieving. When their performance fell short of these standards, he saw his role as one of reminding them that they had a problem and he was interested in hearing how they were going to deal with it. If they could not solve it themselves (and he was confident that he was technically able to assess the likelihood that their solution would be successful), he referred them to one of their peers. He would not permit them to become dependent on him as the ultimate problem solver—ever ready to prove his technical proficiency and perfectly willing to be

Big Daddy to subordinates in distress..For MacGregor, each problem encountered by his subordinates represented a self-teaching opportunity. He recognized that he was ultimately responsible for finding the right answer to the problem, but not for formulating its solution, and that for him to become involved in his subordinates' responsibilities was to assume part of the burden that was appropriately their own. Perhaps even more important, doing so would be to deny them the chance to develop their own problem-solving abilities. This refusal to involve himself in their activities afforded him the opportunity to fulfill the planning obligations inherent in higher-level management assignments.

Essential to MacGregor's system of management was a team of subordinates highly committed to their job objectives. This commitment was achieved by negotiation of the specific results each was to accomplish, and these negotiations continued until both sides were satisfied that they were realistic and attainable. When a subordinate suggested unrealistic objectives, on either the low or the high side, they were modified through open discussion with a willingness on both sides to adjust previously held positions. In all cases MacGregor left specifics on how agreed-upon results were to be achieved to the subordinates themselves. By insisting that he be informed on how decisions were actually made, including who helped in the process, MacGregor not only ensured that his subordinates helped each other, but also received the information that he needed to make valid judgments on how well each of them was developing in his job.

Because of the record his subordinates achieved in receiving promotions to the position of refinery manager, MacGregor had no trouble attracting highly capable candidates for managerial jobs in his refinery. Once on his staff, managers recognized that the way to become a Thursday man was through a combination of high performance and an ability to work with peers in a way that enabled them to solve their own problems and reach their own objectives.

Uniqueness of MacGregor

MacGregor was unique among the managers I interviewed in the course of my study. Presumably his approach was a distinct possibility for each of the nine refinery managers I talked to, and certainly with adaptions it could have been used by many of the 100 executives I interviewed—but it wasn't. He had taken management by objectives to its logical limits by concentrating his efforts on formulating and negotiating objectives and had divorced himself from direct involvement in solving problems his subordinates came upon in carrying out their responsibilities.

MacGregor's frequency of regularly scheduled meetings with his subordinates was typical of the managers interviewed in the study: 10 percent met less frequently and about 5 percent more often. But his focus on discussion of completed decisions was unique. Slightly less than three-quarters of the executives with whom I talked saw the purpose of their meetings as a combination of information communication and problem solving; the balance were split evenly between a primary focus on communication of information and a primary emphasis on problem solving. Interestingly, the majority of those who emphasized problem solving were refinery executives.

When describing the degree of reliance they placed on the contributions made by subordinates in the determination of final decisions, half of the managers felt that it was considerable, a quarter that it was heavy, and the balance that it was either not too significant or that it varied with the individuals involved. Only MacGregor left the actual decision making (except in rare circumstances) to the subordinates themselves.

All the managers, except MacGregor, either stated explicitly or made it clear during the course of the interviews that all important decisions arrived at in these meetings were made by themselves. They received suggestions, considered their sources, and either compared the proferred solutions with solutions they had developed on their own, or considered them carefully before reaching a final solution. In using this approach to group decision making, the managers were obviously manifesting their deeply held convictions that one of the key responsibilities of an upper-level executive is to act as chief decision maker for those who report to him. They believed that, after all, the superior is ultimately responsible for the quality of the decisions made in his organization and the only way to carry out this task is to become directly involved in the decision-making process itself.

Most of the managers I have encountered—both organizational superiors and outside managers involved in the studies I've conducted or the consulting assignments I've carried out—pride themselves on the extent to which they invite their subordinates to participate in organizational decision making; but their perceptions of this process and its organizational impact often differ sharply from those of the subordinates involved. For many of the latter, the participative management routine is just that—a routine acted out by the boss because it evidences his espousal of a technique that is supposed to increase the likelihood that subordinates will accept and commit themselves to decisions; he may even *believe* the decisions were jointly determined. However, most participative management is, in fact, a fiction. Under these conditions, participative management is seen by lower-level participants as, at worst, a manipulative device and at best an opportunity for them to avoid decision-making responsibility and assure that if a wrong solution is reached, the boss himself was a party to the decision.

MacGregor avoided this trap by refusing to give managers reporting to him the opportunity to second-guess the solution he would be most likely to choose. Although he allowed himself some margin in case emergency action on his part should become inevitable, he made it clear that he wanted to hear about problems only after they had been solved and about decisions only after they had been made.

Perspective on MacGregor's Use of Time

It is interesting to compare MacGregor's use of time, which perhaps better than any other index shows his priorities, with the findings reported by management researchers who have conducted detailed quantitative studies of the way managers perform their jobs. In two articles—"A New Look at the Chief Executive's Job," *Organizational Dynamics* (Winter 1973, pp. 20-30) and "The Manager's Job: Folklore and Fact," *Harvard Business Review* (July-August 1975, pp. 49-61)— Henry Mintzberg cites the work of Rosemary Stewart, Leonard Sayles, Robert Guest, and others on the work characteristics of managers and then develops ten roles of the chief executive, which he divides into three groupings: interpersonal, informational, and decisional. Under the *interpersonal* classification, Mintzberg includes such roles as figurehead, leader, and liaison; under *informational*, monitor, disseminator, and spokesman; and under *decisional*, entrepreneur (seeking to improve his unit and adapt it to changing conditions in the environment), disturbance handler, resource allocator, and negotiator.

The job of refinery manager falls between that of chief executive (responsibility for all aspects of the operation and profit accountability) and that of production manager (only indirect concern for the integration of such functions as finance, accounting, marketing, and so on). Mintzberg points out that production managers give greatest attention to decisional roles, especially those of disturbance handler and negotiator. MacGregor, by contrast, minimized his role as disturbance handler but did put a lot of time, energy, and effort into negotiating objectives with his subordinates rather than laying them on his people and then selling them on the reasonableness of his decisions. He also worked constantly to improve his unit, to adapt it to changing environmental conditions, and to allocate present and potential organizational resources for optimal present and future effectiveness. In his interpersonal role MacGregor was readily available for figurehead and liaison activities, and his program for subordinate self-development attracted enough attention within the corporation to ensure a supply of highly motivated subordinates.

In his informational role, MacGregor monitored the output of the management information system he had devised, but he did so after the same information had been reviewed by his subordinates. The dissemination function was partly achieved by the management information system and partly through the joint review of managerial decisions conducted at the Thursday morning meetings. As spokesman for his unit, he was easily accessible to individuals inside and outside the corporation.

What sets MacGregor apart from other managers is that he had consciously thought out his role as an upper-level administrator. He did not blindly adopt the methods of his predecessor; neither did he merely adapt the *modus operandi* he had previously found reasonably successful to the greater demands of running a larger unit. Rather, MacGregor reflected on what the key responsibilities of the executive in charge of a large operating facility really are and concluded that they involve being well informed on changes occurring in the environment that might have an impact on his operation and determining how best to adjust operations to benefit from these changes. At the same time, MacGregor recognized that profitable operations must be carried out in the here-and-now and that a supply of qualified subordinates must be developed for the future.

He concluded that his time was the scarce commodity and he threw himself into the design and implementation of a managerial system that had as its hallmarks self-development for his subordinates, an efficient operation for his employer, and time for himself to actively consider the impact of future developments on his unit. His wise investment of that scarce commodity, his own time, in designing an effective management system paid an extra dividend—surplus time for recreational pursuits.

CHARLES R. WILSON

Turf vs. Systems: Two Management Styles

TWO MODELS

Imagine a leader faced with many organizational problems or inadequacies ... what might be called a "mess" or a "can of worms." Let us call it organizational chaos. Using the word "chaos" will help us maintain some theological perspective. The job has to do with creating order, form or structure expressing meaning and purpose. So imagine this leader ... it could be an executive taking over a leadership position in some enterprise that has been torn with strife and demoralized ... a university perhaps. Or it could be you looking at your organization.

Let us also suppose that the leader is approaching the situation with a positive attitude. No doubt there are many "problems" to be solved in the corporate chaos in which he finds himself. But there are opportunities. In many situations it is merely a matter of individual perspective, but the person who "sees" opportunities instead of problems is already well on the way to getting the energies focused and to developing a swinging outfit.

So there is the picture, and a kind of attitude about it. Now let's see how the person is going to tackle the job at hand ...

The Homesteader

One model of action is the homesteader. A couple generations ago the homesteader faced thousands of square miles of undeveloped land. He scanned the horizon, picked out one little hundred and sixty acre

Source: Copyright 1971 by Charles R. Wilson of CRW Management Services, Lebanon, New Jersey.

piece and literally staked out its boundaries and registered his claim. Perhaps he even fenced it.

It was thus established, before the rest of the world, that this was indeed his place. He then proceeded to organize that which lay inside with little concern for that which was outside. He built a house, subdivided the land for grain, pasture, row crops and so on. Once organized, he could apply himself to a piece at a time; do what was required in each part season by season and thus manage his turf.

Let's underline a few key points about this model of management: There is a strong emphasis on defining boundaries; a clear sense of what is in and what is out. The manager is the "owner" . . . he is possessive . . . it is *his* claim. Finally, what he is managing is a place. There is a kind of *space-things* basic orientation to his whole style.

The Astronaut

Another model of action is the astronaut. Like the fish that is not preoccupied with water, the space man is not particularly concerned with space. What is important to him are centers of gravity: how much pull each center has and what else is circling around it. He orbits around one center for awhile, then kicks free of its gravity and swings into orbit around another.

(We can stretch the image a bit in order to develop our model.) Note the similarity of the space man to the person who wants to promote a cause. There is no need to define boundaries or build fences. Rather, the person with a cause looks for centers of ferment or of action or of disaffection. He psychs out the nature of each, sees what kind of stuff orbits around each; what kind of leadership there is. He then decides which centers to relate to, and sets about strengthening them. He provides for linkage between them, strives to make common cause with them and in this manner builds his network.

Now to underline some key points in this model of management: Instead of concern with boundaries there is a primary focus on centers, a search for handles. To the extent that there are boundaries, they are open. The manager is not possessive; ownership is not particularly important to him. Finally, he is watching the dynamic interconnectedness of events . . . sequences, movements, influences . . . what he is managing is a process. Basic to this style is a kind of time/purpose rather than space/things orientation.

THE TWO STYLES AND RESULTANT ORGANIZATIONS

We now return to our person confronted with chaos. The theme is creation. He intends, deliberately and systematically, to bring about structure, form, order and meaning. If he is basically a homesteader, he will approach it this way:

The Homesteader

"You don't do everything, so identify the boundaries of what you want to do, divide up what is inside and begin to assign responsibilities and resources to people for the parts."

As he gets the thing in shape, here is what it will look like:

It will be a closed system. You will probably see organization charts showing each person's turf, and the chain of command indicating how each person is to relate to those "above" or those "below." Lines of authority, chain of command, who administers which budget will all be matters of great importance.

Decisions will tend to get pushed "up" in the organization where there is more authority to decide. A person's job description will probably define his "box" on the organization chart, his place in the authority structure and the things he is supposed to do daily, weekly and/or monthly. Considerable loyalty to the organization is expected of him.

This man's organization will probably be pretty rigid. However, there are some advantages. For one thing, he does not have to organize the whole universe. He just carves out a small piece and gets it in shape. Things will probably look pretty neat and people who are a part of it probably have a pretty good idea of what is expected of them. The organization avoids what Tillich calls "the anxiety of annihilating openness" and the accompanying nightmares of falling endlessly through infinite, formless space.

The Spaceman

On the other hand, our man (confronted with chaos) might be something of a spaceman. If so, his approach will go like this:

"You can't do everything (but we are not really going to rule out the possibility) so wade into the mess looking for centers of power, activity or interest. See what is swinging around each. How can they be strengthened? What are the clusters or patterns of action? How can the range of influence of healthy action be increased? Where are the handles where one might take hold; what can be managed from each?"

As he gets things in shape, here is what the organization will look like:

It will be an open system with ideas, people and resources flowing in and out. You will probably see flow charts showing how things are processed through the system. There will be considerable lateral activity and information flow, and no great concern with the formalities of the chain of command.

Decisions will tend to get pushed "down" in the organization where there is more information on which to base decisions. A person's position description will register the areas in which he has agreed to apply himself and the results expected. It will be assumed that he is loyal to the cause and will keep faith with his own integrity, but loyalty to the organization as organization is no big deal. People will change hats frequently in this organization, getting involved in all kinds of ad hoc agendas and temporary assignments.

The organization will be flexible; difficult to conceptualize mechanistically (organization charts and clearly defined roles).

With this approach to organization, we have the advantage of not limiting the size or scope of the effort and our organization avoids what Tillich calls "the anxiety of annihilating narrowness" and the accompanying nightmares of being boxed in . . . trapped . . . no escape.

HOW PEOPLE FIT

So we have two organizational models drawn. Now let's take a look at the people who might want to be a part of them.

Two Kinds of Employees

First man:
"I want to sell some of my time (as little as possible) for some money, so I can use the rest of my time doing what I really want to do. Therefore, I am interested in salary, fringe benefits and job security. Also, it will help if the things that you want me to do are pretty clearly spelled out because I really don't want to bother thinking about your long-range aims and where I fit in. Oh yes, I'd like to work for a boss who is a nice guy."

Second man:
"There are some things I'd like to get done in this world and I want a chance to take a crack at them. Therefore, I'll use this organization as my base. I think there is sufficient compatibility between what the organization stands for and what I am after. I can probably help shape its goals and I am willing to have the organization influence mine . . . well, to some extent! I enter with my own agenda, values, outside contacts and even (perhaps) power base. I'll be loyal to our corporate effort but don't expect me to be pious about institutional loyalty, its mythology, or about values from on high. I'll recognize the authority of those with personal integrity and professional com-

petency but don't try to impress me with the chain of command
or titles. I need a salary and benefits if I'm going to be able to stay
here and such should be in line with my own self-esteem."

Obviously, the first man is looking for a job in a homestead; the
second for an opportunity in a space station. Both will probably find
what they are looking for. The questions are: (1) What kind of organization do *you* have? and (2) Which of these two men do you *want*
to attract?

My impression is that there are many organizations that would like
to function as a space station rather than a homestead but their personnel practices seem to assume that the first man described is really
the only kind of person available. The result is more chaos. The rhetoric
of the organization attracts some of the second type persons but the
practices encourage only the first type to stay. The others move on.

There are so many subtleties in this whole area. It is not easy to
develop an appropriate style in an organization. For example, there
is considerable talk among managers these days about how to keep
the innovative kind of person. He is unpredictable, a bit eccentric,
unimpressed with the organization's history or values . . . not that he
is against them . . . he just hasn't noticed them. So how do you keep
him and his idea generating capacity in your organization?

Let's see how the homestead type organization would approach him:
First of all it is asumed that money is power and that it can motivate
the man. So an attempt is made to buy his time. The organization
will try very hard to put up with his oddities and hope that the price
they pay will produce some ideas. "The basic reality is money, and
with money we can buy ideas and make more money."

In the space station type of organization it is assumed that ideas
have their own value and power. This organization will have quite a
different approach to the man and his cause. The idea is the more
basic reality. There is no shortage of capital if you have ideas, but
there *is* a shortage of ideas. So: "we can use the idea to generate capital
and then use the capital to develop the idea."

Again it is obvious that the innovator will feel relatively at home
in this type of organization. He will probably feel boxed in in the first.

Choosing a Style

Yet apart from what kind of organization you *want* to have, what
about this question: "What kind of people are more generally available?" In response to this, I feel that it is quite clear that we are living
in the space age. It is not just that we live in an age in which space

(incidentally) is beginning to get explored, but rather that we are the kind of people who have decided to explore space instead of (for example) the bottom of the sea. There is a deep psychological reality here. I believe, for instance, that the average modern man experiences more anxiety in the thought of being trapped in a wrecked submarine, never to return to the surface; than in the thought of being lost in a damaged space ship with no possibility of returning to earth.

He is just as dead in either case but, for modern man, "the anxiety of annihilating openness" is much more tolerable than "the anxiety of annihilating narrowness." We are space men not cave men.

With that my bias is clear. I feel that church organizations and probably most other organizations must be open systems deliberately designed to attract self-motivating people. So from this point on I shall assume that that is the kind of organization we want and forget the homestead.

RALPH LAZARUS*

The Case of the Oriental Rug

Just about a year ago a good friend of mine (I'll call him Joe) came to my home one weekend to tell me a sad but all-too-familiar story.

At age 42, he said, he had just been asked to resign from a vice-presidency in one of the nation's leading corporations. Worse, this was the third consecutive time, he confessed, that he had been forcibly separated from gainful employment. "What," he asked plaintively, "is the matter with me?"

Together we ran over the facts: Top graduate of a top business school. Good family background. Good appearance. Sound personal habits. No visible clue that could reasonably explain his failures.

A week or so later I met the president who had fired him.

"What happened to Joe?" I asked.

"Listen," the President replied, "Three years ago we thought Joe was a real find. I even visualized him as my successor. He knew how to smell out a problem. He knew how to get the facts. He knew how to make a decision. But we learned to our sorrow that that's all he knew. It never occurred to him that the best decision in the world is no good until somebody does something about it. He never learned that an executive has to be effective through other people—and that you make a decision not just on the facts but in terms of who will do what you think needs to be done."

Source: Reprinted by permission from the November, 1963 issue of the *Michigan Business Review*, published by the Graduate School of Business Administration, The University of Michigan.

*Ralph Lazarus, President of Federated Department Stores.

"PEOPLE-BLINDNESS"

Hidden in this single unhappy incident is, I believe, a fundamental truth about today's class of rising young executives. Many of them will fail to reach their goals. They will fail, not for lack of competence, but because they have a "people-blindness" that, time after time, traps them into making a technically good decision that just won't work in practice. They haven't learned that an executive succeeds or fails not so much because of what *he* does, but because of what he is able to get someone else to accomplish.

Graduates of our business schools, I regret to say, seem to me to be particularly susceptible to this malady—and in its most virulent form. That is true even though today's MBA's are, on average, the best-trained prospective employees that we have ever interviewed. Knowledgeable. Competent. Aggressive. The problem is that these graduates are frequently even more impressed with their qualifications than we are. They seem to feel that their teachers have taught them everything they need to know and that their classroom training assures them success. In short, their heads are full to overflowing with the knowledge from which good decisions spring. Their hearts, unhappily, have not yet developed that human sensibility that would permit them to understand that *what* should be done can often be learned as a classroom exercise, but *how* it should be done and getting it done involve people—and people experience is seldom to be had under campus or laboratory conditions.

TODAY'S "PRACTICAL EXPERIENCE"

Let me hasten to make this point that my objective here is to do more than to repeat that hoary, old executive cliche about the difference between "book learning" and "practical experience." I know that today's "book learning" is far superior to yesterday's. I know that today's student is harangued endlessly to "weigh the human factor." It is also true, however, that today's "practical experience" involves far more than was encompassed by the old saw about learning the business from "the bottom up."

Practical experience, by my definition, means these things:

1. A thorough understanding of how a particular organization works, what its principles are, how and why they were developed.

2. A thorough knowledge of and respect for the people who were smart enough to invent these principles and make them successful.

3. A realization that an individual can succeed in a particular organization only when he discovers how to contribute within a previously established

framework and only when he is writing a song that someone else must sing.

IDEAS AND IMPLEMENTATION

All this adds up to people-experience—the development of a set of antennae that will be sensitive to the intricate relationships of the modern corporation. And that's precisely where so many promising young men fall off the sled. Their educations have taught them to pick, in the abstract, an academically right answer. At that point, they think the job is done—never realizing that *what* you decide to do is dependent on *how* you plan to do it. And, beyond that, that you can only know the *how* when you have visualized it in terms of *who*. Bluntly stated, it all comes down to this: Good ideas are easier to come by than good implementation. A brilliant idea poorly implemented is almost always less successful than a mediocre idea enthusiastically executed. And when you use those polysyllables—implement and execute—you really mean who is going to do it and how will he get it done.

THE RUG BUYER

I had my first lesson on this subject many years ago when I was getting my lumps as a novice in our family store in Columbus, Ohio— F. & R. Lazarus & Company. We had a rug buyer there who became a legend—and for good reason.

Like all of our buyers, he prepared a written plan for the upcoming selling season prior to going to market to buy his merchandise. The plan, in the case I am describing, was approved by management. The only difficulty was that, when he returned from his buying trip, he had bought—not what he had outlined—but the biggest assortment of Oriental rugs that any of us had ever seen. Pressed for an explanation he said, "I liked them."

Now, management had a problem. A survey of customers would have proved, I feel sure, that there was no burning desire on the part of Columbus housewives to carpet their floors with the bounty of the East. The prices were far beyond the store's normal range. There was, in short, no conceivable reason why our store should put perhaps 75 percent of its floor-covering investment in a product that Columbus obviously did not want. No reason, that is, except the one that my father instantly understood.

That reason was the buyer himself. My father knew he was an enthusiast—a man who, if backed in his convictions, could translate an unsupportable idea into a cash-register success. We kept the rugs. The buyer sold them—using every wile in his considerable experience. Even today Columbus may be unique for at least one thing. It probably has more square feet of Oriental rugs than most cities twice its size. And all because the store was smart enough to look harder at the man than at the facts.

THE BRANCH STORE

There is modern counterpart of this same story. Not long ago we sat around the conference table in our Cincinnati headquarters discussing the question of opening a branch store for one of our twelve divisions. Our central office staff was on one side of the table, the divisional management on the other. We were agreed that the growth potential of the trading area served by this division justified branch expansion. The question was what kind of store should the new branch be. We had surveyed the area. We knew all about income levels, population trends, traffic patterns, shopping habits, customer preferences. The facts seemed to substantiate the central office position. The new branch should be a smaller version of the successful downtown store—catering, in price lines and assortments of merchandise, to the kind of people who already thought so well of us.

That's what *we thought*. The man who had the responsibility for the building and the profitable operation of the new branch had the exact opposite idea. He argued for a totally different store. He didn't want what we call an "image" branch; he wanted a convenience store stocked with major emphasis on budget merchandise. There were very few facts to support his position. He was asking us, in effect, to invest millions of dollars in a store that was in precise contradiction to his successful downtown operation. He really had only one argument on his side: He was convinced he could make *his* idea succeed. We were pretty sure that, feeling as he did, he could not summon the enthusiasm to make *our* idea pay out.

We built the store his way. I don't like it very well. Customers sometimes complain that it doesn't stack up with the downtown store. The hard fact is, however, that that branch store is one of the most profitable in our company.

ANOTHER BRANCH STORE

There is an encore to that incident that does not have so happy an ending. The basic facts are the same. Another division of our company likewise was in a position, in our opinion, to add a branch store. The difference was that that store management did not want to expand, even though admitting that the opportunity was clearly theirs. We debated the question endlessly. Finally, the store reluctantly agreed to build. The resulting branch was handsome in design, sound in policy, efficient in operation—and disappointing in results. It had everything but the enthusiastic backing of the people who didn't want to build it but now had to operate it. The right decision had produced the wrong result. People were the difference.

In reciting these stories I do not want to create the impression that I think that a good executive can be defined as a man who merely accepts other people's ideas because they happen to be enthusiastic about them. That would be nonsense. But it is equally true that you can't earn your keep in top management if all you can do is to bludgeon your subordinates into accepting your solutions—even when you're right. Perhaps I can illustrate the difference in terms of our business.

MANAGEMENT SUPERVISION

Our company, Federated Department Stores, Inc., consists of 12 divisions operating 61 department stores. These divisions are largely autonomous. Financial control is maintained at headquarters but, beyond that, each division is pretty much its own master and each is held accountable for its sales, growth, and profit performance.

We exercise management supervision through the device of twice-yearly planning meetings and irregular store visits where we learn to know the organization and see what they are doing on their home grounds. Prior to the planning meetings the central office makes a detailed study of the division's performance, its forecast of sales for the year ahead and for as much as ten years ahead. Our statistical analysis covers each of the some 250 departments in the store—men's wear, shoes, dresses, infant's wear, home furnishings, and so on. We compare the results of the preceding period and the plans for the future with those of our eleven other divisions. This preliminary analysis then goes to the division for comment and review. Together we agree on an agenda for the upcoming meeting. Before division and central office actually sit down to talk, we have drawn a kind of portrait of the problems and opportunities that we may have with that particular division. We can jointly see its strengths and weaknesses in relation to its trading area and in comparison to our other operating results against the well-defined framework of long-term objectives which we have together developed as the basis of operating policy.

MANAGING BY INFLUENCE

The simplest thing to do when we sit down with our store principals face-to-face would be to say, for example: "You're doing a lousy job in furniture. Go to division Z where the profits are four times yours.

Find out how they do it and run your store accordingly." That would be the easy way—the easy way to disaster.

The direct order approach wouldn't work in our business for a variety of reasons. Good as division Z's furniture idea is, it was designed for a different city and designed to be effective in the hands of a different organization. It wouldn't work in another division because it is human nature to resent being forced to accept another man's idea. Most important, it wouldn't work because we hold each division accountable for growth and profit. We can't make them accountable unless we also give them the freedom, the authority, to run the show as they see fit.

That does not mean that we ignore the problems—or leave them in limbo for a sometime solution. We don't. We wouldn't last long in the brutally competitive world of retailing if we did. It does mean that we have had to abandon authoritarianism as a management method—and we have had to learn how to manage by influence, by suasion, by example.

MANAGEMENT STRATEGY

What I am saying, of course, is simply this: Federated has a sales plan for each of its divisions. That plan, in every instance, is designed to isolate the essentials of success in the immediate future; it is tailored to fit the people who must implement it. But we also have a second plan—our own management strategy for convincing divisional executives that the objectives we have jointly agreed to are both desirable and attainable. We are deadly serious about our responsibility to persuade—so serious, in fact, that when our plans go awry, we charge the failure to *our* lack of salesmanship, not the division's lack of implementation.

Take, for instance, the case of the sickly furniture department. We would do these things. We would first discuss the problem generally—in terms of the kind of store we have agreed we want to run. We would suggest a half-dozen possible causes of that problem—such things as merchandise suitability to the market, physical presentation of the items for sale, capability of the buying and selling organization. We would name a store or stores which have solved the same problem. We would urge study of those successful stores. But there would be no table-thumping and no "you-do-it" directives.

Rather, we would probably wind up the discussion by saying something like this to our division president: "Obviously, you need to do something about furniture. But don't make the mistake of *adopting* anybody's idea, including ours. Look at the successful ideas and then *adapt* them to your situation. Just let us know what you're going to do, and when you're going to do it." In short, we would try to illuminate the problem—and give it a sense of urgency—but we would not dictate the solution.

THE GAINS FROM FREEDOM

While no principle is universally applicable, this kind of management works best for us—and for what seem to me to be obvious reasons. Our divisional chief executives are superior men. We want the full force of their superiority to be felt in our business. We want the flavor of their varied personalities, the flower of their individual creativeness reflected in our enterprise. It can be only if we give them freedom and authority to run their own shows.

And there's another thing. By guaranteeing to our top executives this kind of freedom and responsibility we encourage them to do likewise with their subordinates. The end result is that planning, decision-making, responsibility for profit are pushed farther and farther down in our organization. Down, for example, to the man who runs that ailing furniture department and who, ultimately, must make it work.

HUMAN WISDOM

Many a young man steeped in the right-and-wrong, black-and-white textbook method of problem-solving finds this kind of theory of management hard to take. He is the "computer-executive" who reads the tape and knows the answer to anything. Some others, by contrast, have the flexibility of mind and spirit, the intellectual humility to keep on learning. These men succeed. The tragedies are the Joes of the business world—men who spend their acknowledged brilliance devising ideal solutions which can be executed only by those ideal men who do not exist. The result is that today, in almost any company, you'll find at least one might-have-been president who has been quietly sealed off from further promotion because his people-blindness will not permit him to bend his own definition of a good decision to fit the people who have to execute it.

The fact is that the best top-executives today are the men who add the qualities of human wisdom and effective salesmanship to the findings of the slide rule. They know that it doesn't make much difference nowadays whether you produce shoes, steel, or toothpaste—or sell real estate or insurance. They know that we're all in the people business. We sell to people or buy from people. And as executives we look to people to do those things which make us succeed or fail.

THE EXECUTIVE'S EAR

There is an interesting corollary to this point. Not long ago, I spent an evening with a veteran magazine editor of national reputation. I asked him this question:

> "How can you possibly cram into your head all the things you need to know to judge the hundreds of different stories you publish each year? Politics. Atomic energy. Sports. Medicine. Taxes. Marriage. Foreign relations with Latin America, India, and the Common Market. Are you really expert in all those fields?"

His answer, in my opinion, might well be reproduced in our business textbooks. He grinned and said:

> "I'm a fraud. I appear to know so much and I really know so little. The complexities of the modern world are totally beyond the grasp of any single man. I don't just judge ideas. I try to fit those ideas into a total picture I have developed of the kind of magazine I want to edit. Most particularly, I judge the people who submit those ideas. Over the years, I've developed an ear that distinguishes the sound of truth from the sound of exaggeration and falsehood. In every issue that I publish I bet my job that my ear has told me right."

That editor is doing exactly what most chief executives have to do. Surrounded by experts on finance, law, research, real estate, and marketing—each a labyrinth of special knowledge—the boss must depend on his ear, too.

The ear that hears people, that hears what they feel as well as what they say—this is the key to success in any business today. It takes a lot of listening to develop that kind of ear. Listening to customers who do or don't buy what you have to sell. Listening to outrageous ideas that somebody believes in. Listening *to* gripes and listening *for* that sound of excitement that spells success.

This kind of sensitivity is what management is so earnestly seeking in the young men it hires today. Business can't use men at the top whose college training has made them rigid with scholastic arrogance. But there are big opportunities waiting for those who will bring us two things: The fine intellectual tool kits they have assembled in college; a modest acceptance of the fact that they still have to learn how to put them through other human hands.

THOMAS S. BURNS

Line and Staff at ITT

With the emergence of the business conglomerate in America in the early sixties came the reemergence of centralized authority and the supervisory staff system of management.

President Ralph Cordiner's decentralized management system, as researched and perfected by the General Electric Company, was in vogue in the fifties—cheered on by management consultants and business school deans. The staff system robbed management of its entrepreneurial prerogatives, they said. It might be satisfactory for slow, cumbersome, military-type organizations, but it was unwieldy and unresponsive in the dynamic arenas of business. All of the negative adjectives were applied to centralized management. Professor Peter Drucker was hailed as the apostle of the new decentralized, line-oriented philosophy, and the rush was on to reduce staffs to lean operating crews of specialists. Staff people of any stripe or skill were suspect.

Then along came the conglomerate—a management organization that operated like a central bank for both funds and talent. As the conglomerates gobbled up company after company and grew ever more profitable, opinions changed with respect to their management policies. Conglomerates assembled large, knowledgeable staffs to audit and control the acquisitions in many diverse business activities. Companies

Source: Thomas S. Burns, *Tales of ITT*, New York, Houghton Mifflin, 1974, pp. 59-68, 140-147. Copyright © 1974 by Thomas S. Burns. Reprinted by permission of Houghton Mifflin Company.

that thought they had reached a happy medium began to doubt their staff-line relationships. As the conglomerates surged ahead, the desire to look like Litton or LTV or ITT was great enough to start the pendulum swinging. Gradually the circles of power became heavy with staff specialists, and the centralization of business management was back.

In understanding the *Darkness at Noon* atmosphere of ITT, it is necessary to understand how the staffs influenced policy. They operated like a cross between the secret police and a kindly family doctor. To a degree the staff was supreme so long as it reported all of the facts. But it also was required to confess when it was technically incompetent for a particular assignment. So staff people apologized a lot and mitigated their advice. But top ITT management knew that there was no way to run the company on the formula devised by Harold Geneen, ITT chairman and chief executive officer, without heavy emphasis on the staff role.

ITT gradually developed a unique, efficient centralized operating system of line-staff management, both in organization and methods. In procedure it grew closer to the military general staff concept than any other major company, even to sporting an espionage organization and worldwide intelligence-gathering networks.

Unfortunately for Geneen's dreams and magnificent obsessions, ITT could never enjoy the leverage of General Motors or Dupont. It did not have the ability to dominate one or more major industries. The company seems destined to continue its piecemeal acquisition policies in diversified industries, ganging sales and profits to purchase the growth Geneen so dearly prizes. And with unrelated businesses in the assembly process at all times, management control problems become ever more complex, resulting in a tendency toward increased centralization and larger and more specialized staffs.

The ITT staffs were peppered with graduates of the management consulting profession, people who could appreciate the manipulation of power as almost an academic exercise. They seemed to have no psychic need for profit and loss responsibility and were the stuff great audit groups are made from. ITT claimed to run the largest and most efficient management consulting company in the world and continually proselytized some of the best talent away from the old-line management consulting houses.

"The only difference between a management consultant and an ITT staff man," a senior vice president said, "is that if you don't accept the consultant's advice, you leave." Another staff man said, "We get these MBAs from the Ivy League business schools all the time. But unless they learn our system, they don't last. We are taking the place of the Harvard Business School, so far as Geneen is concerned. He is proud of his Harvard tie, he lists the school's Advanced Management Program in his biography, but he balks at sending anyone back to the program. He believes that we are the trailblazers and the rest of the business world is 'sucking hind tit.' "

The staffs had taken over some functions to the point of completely emasculating company divisions management. Financial management and long-range planning were securely in staff hands. They also controlled the operations research, project management, and the market research and analysis which resulted in most of the company's acquisitions. Obviously, the staff chieftains reported directly to Geneen.

"To get to the top in this company you've got to go through one of the staffs," Frank Deighan said. He was a graduate of Booz, Allen & Hamilton, management consultants, and had been seasoned by two tours with ITT staff groups. "You may be operating well in the field, but it will only be a matter of time before they want you back in New York. If you're going to work on the top levels, the brass must be sure of your reactions, gut and otherwise. You've got to be able to hang tough—they have to be sure. In short, you must become a known quantity. I thought the guys at Booz were ruthless until I joined H.S.G. and company. But Booz guys were little old ladies with bleeding hearts compared to these ITT guys."

As was intended, the staff struck fear into the hearts of the line management. There was a staff man always looking over your shoulder, and he was outside your jurisdiction and the control of your operating management. In fact, sometimes the staff man was outside of any authority or jurisdiction except the office of the president. The staff men were routinely rotated in assignments to avoid any rapport being achieved between division management and the staff. They were the Ogres of Operations, and headquarters intended to keep them that way.

The staff titles changed with the vogues of management policy. A fashionable one in the early seventies was "product line manager." To read the product line manager's job description you would assume he was a general manager, marketing manager, and financial specialist all rolled into one. And functionally his assignment was impressive, including a number of companies, usually scattered worldwide, assembled by industry or product line. But in fact the PLMs were spies, pure and simple. Their responsibility was to carry back to top management, and particularly Geneen, information concerning division operations.

The failing of these staff courtesans was often a superiority complex which allowed the line operators of the business to build up subtle defenses. Since the staff man could not know all of the key factors in the operation of the business, he was always vulnerable to a techno-logical sandbag or conflicting expert opinion. Only if he reached some kind of peace with his line counterpart would he be fed "straight dope" insofar as the real problems were concerned. So often there developed an Alphonse and Gaston relationship not unlike the deals made between top management and labor leaders. When some controversy was inevitable, the scene was rehearsed by staff and line secretly before it got to the forum of a business plan or top management review. It was amusing to sit through such meetings, in which even the friction and dissent had been contrived.

On occasion the line and staff did battle without quarter. With so many people on both sides possessing a strong instinct for the jugular, such confrontations were usually mean, ugly, and counterproductive. But stimulated by top management interrogation, the staff had to make an occasional example of some errant or cocky division president.

"You watch your boss on the staff side and you get the signal," a North American staff manufacturing specialist said. "If Geneen and Executive Vice President Bennett start zeroing in on some guy, you had better be able to pull out the sheet of embarrassing questions from your little black notebook and join in. *Au contraire*, if H.S.G. is smiling, philosophizing, and telling stories about his old days in this or that industry, then we just clam up. No matter what we have on the division boss, we make some obvious comment concerning how brilliantly the division is being operated and suggest, *sotto voce*, some minor changes. This is a totalitarian government, buddy, and we don't ever forget it."

Criteria for selecting ITT staff men indicated, by nuance, the type of man that best fitted the role.

"Does he make recommendations based on a visibility of the situation not yet recognized by division management?"

"Does he keep cool, even during periods of violent disagreement with line managers?"

Other requirements ranged from technical grasp to social presence but came across as being much the same as those the CIA uses to select an agent.

The system of a staff man overseeing each major line function did not encourage an entrepreneurial business climate. But the staffs did provide direction and could marshal a number of diverse technical skills very quickly to solve a problem.

Geneen's concept of forcing the divisions to constantly run their businesses "on paper" was policed by the staffs. Reports submitted by each division monthly were examined in detail by the assigned staff man. A system of marginal notations was developed by the staffs which allowed top management to analyze the problems, opportunities, danger signals, and errors contained in the reports after only a cursory glance through the thick notebooks. More than a few "red flags" meant heavy going for the division managers involved.

The disadvantage, of course, was that such star-chamber procedures often eliminated the opportunity for line people to explain their business. It was a temptation for a line manager to accept the recommendations of the staff with mild reservations, even though he might feel strongly that they were in error. By carrying out the recommendations to illogical conclusions and requesting further staff direction as the losses mounted, the situation might become embarrassing enough to drive off the staff men and allow the manager to reap the rewards of setting things right.

"I gained a hell of a lot more respect for the staff after they fried us at the business plan review," a general manager said. "Mind you, not respect for their ability. Some of them don't know their ass from a hole in the ground. But let me tell you, they know how to play the game. They sat on the other side of the table with all the questions, while my managers sat over here and tried to come up with answers, poor bastards. I'm not fool enough to put us in that situation again, let me tell you!"

With the same clarity as they recall their first sexual experience, most managers remember their maiden voyage to New York for the annual business plan review. Mr. Geneen's "show and tell" parties take place for each and every division and company in the ITT fold once every year. The Europeans are reviewed in Europe, the North Americans are reviewed in New York, and other reviews are arranged at times and places convenient to Geneen. But everyone goes under the knife.

The ITT planning process, now famous among management consultants and business historians, began as a semiformal set of directives and guidelines accumulated over the years since the early days at ITT. Geneen took the system and honed it to a fine operating edge. His reverence for facts and figures was very much in evidence. The planning process was a no-nonsense philosophy of numbers. Every division or company president was responsible for preparing such an annual business plan—a book-length document of plans, graphs, financial exhibits, and analyses. The format was standardized for all, even to the preprinting of book covers and forms. The plan was conceived, written, and presented by division management—but it was approved successively by all levels of management between the division and Geneen before it was presented to him (personally, mind you) for final approval. The work of preparation was exhaustive; the requirements for planning specialists simply to keep the plan current was a financial burden for many of the smaller divisions. Most U.S. companies cannot or do not support such a planning function or take the time to assemble all the detailed information required in the Geneen system. And not surprisingly, this is exactly where Geneen sees ITT's competitive advantage. His managers know the down, the play, the score, and even the details of the referee's sex life in that grand game called business. By comparison, competitors seem to be standing in ticket lines or still suiting up while Geneen puts points on the board.

The performance put on by division management in front of Geneen during their once-a-year confrontation is the most important mark in their overall rating. He sees and hears them, and he knows whether or not they are good disciples of the Word. During the sessions—like a Pentagon briefing, advertising agency presentation, or political rally— the results of past actions and future projections are heavily colored by the personality and charisma of the actors on stage. So the production must be carefully planned and staged to achieve the maximum favorable exposure in the short time the division will have before the gathered New York staffs, ITT top management, and Geneen himself. The mighty have risen and fallen by the flickering lights of the slide projector and the whine of the microphone.

It was cold in New York in late December when our division's first business plan was finally scheduled for review. We had been twice delayed, confirming our suspicions that the staffs were saving their best chance at a massive humiliation to the last. There was black slush on the ground, and the sky was the color of old lead. We huddled in a mid-Manhattan Hamburger Heaven, catching a quick, pre-lunch meal, which we felt might be our last of the day. The division was scheduled to be "on" at four in the afternoon, so what with preparation, waiting in the wings, the presentation, and an interrogation, the day would be filled, with no time for the niceties of dining. Binks, the division controller recently elevated from the ranks, was shaken. "Have you ever done this before?" he asked Hayden Moore, the acting general manager.

"No," Moore said weakly. "Not alone. I've carried papers to a lot of the sessions."

"So have I," said Binks. "And given testimony and wrestled graphs and all that stuff. But this is different. Boy, just the three of us. And this goddam plan—it's full of holes. Maybe you guys don't know what can happen up there. I've watched guys get torn to pieces. I've seen Geneen scream at a general manager until I thought the guy was going to crawl under the table."

"Let's ask for a bye until next year," I said. "Plead nolo. Or why don't you have a seizure? No controller, no numbers."

The cab ride to headquarters had all the hardy camaraderie of a trip to the gallows. With our slides, graphs, and hats in hand we presented ourselves to the security guards on the meeting room floor and were duly identified and badged. We waited what seemed an interminable time in the lounge, then took our seats in the great chamber to watch the plans of other Defense Space Group companies unfold as we waited our turn.

Rumors drifted out from the business plan sessions in progress to the lounges and waiting rooms, alternately encouraging and discouraging.

"Geneen just said operations cash management is the most important consideration this year," a staff man announced. "Hope your operations cash management plan is sound." He nudged our controller with his elbow and cackled. Binks was now blanched and shaking. I began to wonder what we would do if he couldn't see it through. A year of planning only to pass out on the stage before Geneen. A tragic prospect: Binks lying there atop his forms and ledgers.

"No negative thinking. Forget about the goddam recession, that's the word," a friendly department manager said. "Rich Bennett doesn't want any 'can't do' shit. If you're looking for things to get worse, better tone it down."

Ushered successively closer to the podium, we watched the production with a partisan interest and awe. Geneen sat like an Oriental potentate, flanked by vice presidents in descending order of importance. The hierarchy was marvelously disciplined, speaking only when called on by Geneen or the interlocutor, Executive Vice President Rich Bennett. Bennett kept the harangue and monotonous division dialogues moving with questions, invitations for staff inquiries, and an occasional attempt at levity.

Finally, our turn came. As in the Mad Hatter's tea party, we had been moving our seats closer to the speaker's rostrum, and now we were there. Moving to stage center, the middle of the table, we now faced Geneen across the ten-yard expanse of green carpet. The *Caine* mutiny court-martial scene with Queeg on the wrong side of the green cloth.

We had been warned that everything would depend on Geneen's reactions. If he began serious questioning, the staff would be on us like a pack of hounds. We had tried to second-guess his curiosities— which areas to concentrate on and present with slide and story, where his chief interest might lie between the political and the practical. But it was impossible to cover all the holes and patches in the Cable Division program. If Geneen wanted our hides, he had only to delve a little.

Rich Bennett introduced us with a quip about leaving the good golf weather in San Diego to tell them all about our Silver Strand Plot. We were launched. Slowly, deliberately, we presented the plan. Geneen said nothing, nodding on occasion in agreement with some statement. Bennett asked a few questions of the product line managers on the staff responsible for cable and communications areas. They gave quick answers, referring to the piles of papers scattered over the table in front of them. As the last slide passed, our brevet general manager sat down, looking exhausted. His voice had cracked several times in the presentation, and the controller's replies to financial questions had been halting. But it was over, and we waited for the decision. Thumbs up or down.

Geneen rose and said, "These gentlemen are taking on some big people. This is probably the largest investment we've made in facilities in a long time." He turned to us. "Just get the goddam plant built and start turning out cable." He motioned to the staff. "These people will take care of the rest. Any questions?"

There were no questions.

"Watch those bastards from Western Electric in Washington," Geneen said to me, "and don't even have a cup of coffee with them. Or the other competition. No matter how well you know them. There can't be any smell of collusion. We may have some problems...." His voice trailed off. He waddled slowly across the expanse of carpet that separated the tables, followed by a gaggle of corporate vice presidents. He shook hands with the three of us in what we later learned was an unprecedented gesture of support. Soft-spoken and pleasant, he chatted for a few minutes while the assembled gathering sat in silence. He asked me about the markets, the prospects for government business, AT&T plans, and the program schedules.

"Good work," he said. "I'll be out to see that beachfront property sometime, too." Then he paraded out of the room, receiving nods and smiles as he trouped the line. The meeting was temporarily adjourned. Then tension lifted like a curtain. A few brave souls lit cigarettes on their way to the refreshment tables in the lounges.

"I feel as though I've just had a battlefield decoration pinned on," I said.

The controller looked at his hand. "I've been with this company 20 years, and this is the first time I've ever met the president. And I just shook hands with him."

"Fred will never wash that hand again," a staff assistant said. "Congratulations. You just had holy water sprinkled over you, and you will shortly be inundated with more cooperation than you can use."

After basking in the reflected glory of Geneen's approval in the lounge, we packed our exhibits and headed back to the Barclay Hotel. In the Gold Room we began a half-hearted victory celebration, but the emotional drain had been too much, and the evening went flat after two drinks.

"What won Geneen over, do you suppose?" the general manager asked, now out of shock.

"We showed a lot of confidence. That's important. You can't come on tentative with Geneen. He wants a team that is all for hard charging," Binks said, now high on Scotch and blessed relief.

"What a relief to have the bloody thing over," said Moore. "Here's how."

And he drained the last drink of our one and only victory celebration ever.

C. JACKSON GRAYSON, JR.

Management Science and Business Practice

"What we need to do is humanize the scientist and simonize the humanist." This dictum is a popularization of C.P. Snow's view of science and the humanities as two distinct cultures, and it is all too true when applied to management. Managers and management scientists are operating as two separate cultures, each with its own goals, languages, and methods. Effective cooperation—and even communication—between the two is just about minimal. And this is a shame.

Each has much to learn from the other, and much to teach the other. Yet, despite all kinds of efforts over the years, it seems to me that the cultural and operating gap which exists between the two is not being closed. Why?

I can offer some explanations, based on my years as an academician, consultant, businessman, and, most recently, head of an organization with control over a large part of our economy—the Price Commission. I can also suggest a way to build the bridge so badly needed between the two cultures and the people who make them up. This bridge must span the gap between two quite different types:

● *The management scientists.* As people, they want to help managers make decision making more explicit, more systematic, and *better* by using scientific methodology, principally mathematics and statistics. They can be found largely in universities and in staff operations of enterprises. They may belong to any of a number of professional associations, such as The Institute of Management Sciences (TIMS), Operations Research Society of America (ORSA), and the American Institute for Decision Sciences (AIDS).

- *The managers.* They make and implement decisions, largely by rough rules of thumb and intuition. They are the operating executives, found principally in the line.

The lines of distinction are never so pure, but most people, I believe, understand what I mean.

What I have to offer to the management scientists is a few bouquets and then a load of bricks. First, the bouquets:

- Management scientists have had *some* impact on real-world operations and managers.
- Some management science tools have been successfully applied in accounting, finance, production, distribution, and weapons systems.
- Managers do tend to give a little more conscious thought to their decision making than in previous years—but still precious little.
- By indicating how abysmal our knowledge is about decision making, management scientists have highlighted areas for further research.
- Both the faculty and the students at business schools have gained some added prestige in the business and academic communities for being more "scientific."

And now the bricks. The total impact of management science has been extremely small. Its contribution looks even smaller than it is if one compares it to the revolution promised for management offices in the early years. And the "wait-until-next-generation" theme is wearing thinner and thinner.

Let me quickly acknowledge that there are *some* management scientists who operate effectively in both cultures. But they are rare birds. Most management scientists are still thinking, writing, and operating in a world that is far removed from the real world in which most managers operate (and in which I personally have been operating). They often describe and structure nonexistent management problems, tackle relatively minor problems with overkill tools, omit real variables from messy problems, and build elegant models comprehensible to only their colleagues. And when managers seem confused or dissatisfied with the results of their activities and reject them, these scientists seem almost to take satisfaction in this confirmation of the crudity and inelegance of the managerial world.

Have I overdrawn the picture? Only very slightly.

WHY THE GULF?

I do not mean to say that management scientists have purposefully created this cultural gap. Most of them feel that much of what they are doing today is really helpful to managers. But I'm afraid it simply isn't so. Others argue that much of what they are doing is "pure research," which will be useful one day. I do not discount the value of pure research; some of it is needed. But the fact remains that only a small fraction of management science "results" are being used.

Those management scientists who do acknowledge a gap often excuse it by one of two reasons:

- "The manager doesn't understand the power of the tools."
- "He isn't sympathetic to systematic decision making and would rather fly by the seat of his pants because this is safer for his ego."

I myself am a counterexample to both these excuses. I have had some fairly good training in management science. I have done research in the area and written a book urging the use of more explicit decision tools in a specific industry—oil well drilling.[1] I have taught various courses in the area, for example, in statistics, management control systems, and quantitative analysis.

And yet, in the most challenging assignment of my life—putting together the Price Commision—I used absolutely *none* of the management science tools explicitly. One might think that in the task of developing an organization of 600 people (mostly professionals), creating a program to control prices in a trillion-dollar economy, and making decisions that involve costs, volume, prices, productivity, resource allocations, elasticities, multiple goals, trade-offs, predictions, politics, and risk values, an expert would have found ways to use his familiarity with management science to advantage. I did not.

A defender of the faith will quickly say that, although I did not use them explicitly, I probably used them *implicitly*, and that they helped to discipline my approach to decision making. I agree that this is probably true. But I nevertheless think it is a damning indictment that I can identify *no* incident of a conscious, explicit use of a single management science tool in my activities as head of the Price Commission.

Further, my conscience is clear. To my mind there are five very valid reasons for my rejecting the idea of using management science.

Shortage of Time

Although I thought about using management science tools on many occasions, I consistently decided against it because of the shortage of time. Management scientists simply do not sufficiently understand the constraint of time on decision making, and particularly on decisions that count; and the techniques they develop reflect that fact. They may write about time as a limitation. They may admonish managers for letting time push them into a "crisis" mode. They may recognize the constraint of time with a few words and comment on its influence. They may say that they, too, experience time constraints. But their techniques are so time consuming to use that managers pass them by.

Does this mean that all management science work ought to be thrown into shredders? No, it simply means that management scientists (a) need to get out of their relatively unpressured worlds and *experience* the impact of time on the decision-making process, and (b) need to build the time factor into models instead of leaving it as an exogenous variable.

Inaccessibility of Data

The second reason for ignoring management science in practice is related to the time problem. A manager will ordinarily use data or a management science tool only if both are conveniently, speedily accessible. If he is told that the needed data are buried in another part of the organization, or that they must be compiled, or that the model must be created, nine times out of ten he will say, "Skip it." I did, ten times out of ten.

True, many management scientists would say that I must have developed "trade-offs" in my mind, weighing the cost of obtaining data or building a model against the probable opportunity payoff, and that my mental calculator ground out negative responses on each occasion. This is perfectly plausible. Unconsciously I probably did build a number of such informal investment-payoff models.

But where does this leave us? It leaves us with management scientists continuing to construct models that call for substantial investments in design and data collection and managers discarding them. The statement is made ad nauseam that most data are not in the forms that most models call for, or that they are not complete; yet the management scientists go right on calling for inaccessible, nonexistent, or uncompiled data to suit "theoretically correct" models. And hence managers continue to say, "Skip it."

Instead of asking a manager to lie in the Procrustean bed of the theoretically correct model, why shouldn't the management scientist design a realistic model, or a realistic part of a model, or come up with a realistic data prescription? The result might be extremely crude; it might embarrass a theoretician; it might be shot down by the purist and the theoretician. But it just might be used.

Resistance to Change

The third reason that I did not use management science tools explicitly is that educating others in the organization who are not familiar with the tools, and who would resist using them if they were, is just too difficult a task. Management scientists typically regard this problem as outside the scope of their jobs—at most, they remark on the need to educate more people and to change organizations so they become more scientific. Or, if they *do* recognize the problem, they grossly underestimate the time and organizational effort needed to "educate and change." I suggest that management scientists do two things:

1. They should build into their models some explicit recognition of the financial and emotional cost of change of this kind and make explicit allowance for the drag of change resistance. I am quite aware that some change techniques are being used: sensitivity training, Esalen-type devices, management by objectives, quantitative analysis courses for managers, and so on. I have used them myself, and I know that they help. But the magnitude of time and energy required to install them is not generally appreciated—certainly not by management scientists—and their impact is highly overrated.

2. They should get themselves some education and direct experience in the power, politics, and change-resistance factors in the real world of management so they can better incorporate the imperfect human variables in their work.

Long Response Time

Fourth, few management science people are geared up to respond to significant management problems in "real time." Management science people in universities live largely by the school calendar, and if they receive a request for help, they are likely to respond in terms of next semester, next September, or after exams. And once again the manager is likely to say, "Skip it." Even most management science personnel in staff positions of live organizations operate in a time frame that is slower than that of the line managers. It is their nature to approach a problem in a methodical, thorough way, even when the required response time dictates that they come up with a "quick and dirty" solution.

Invalidating Simplifications

Fifth, and finally, it is standard operating procedure for most management science people to strip away so much of a real problem with "simplifying assumptions" that the remaining carcass of the problem and its attendant solution bear little resemblance to the reality with which the manager must deal. The time constraints, the data-availability questions, the people problems, the power structures, and the political pressures—all the important, nasty areas that lie close to the essence of management—are simplified out of existence so that a technically beautiful, and useless, resolution may be achieved.

This is somewhat paradoxical since management science originated in wartime Britain, when many interdisciplinary talents were forced into combination to grapple with the problems of total mobilization. That situation tolerated no fooling around. But in subsequent years management science has retreated from the immediate demands for workable results. It has increased its use of the hard sciences of mathematics and statistics, hardening itself with methodological complexity, weakening its own reliance on the softer sciences of psychology, sociology, and political science, and losing the plain, hardheaded pragmatism with which it started out.

Realizing this, many managers think it pointless to turn the really important problems over to management science. Their experience has shown them the impotence of emasculated solutions.

At the risk of repeating a tired joke, let me recall the story of the man who said he had a way to destroy all the enemy submarines in the Atlantic during World War II: "Boil the ocean." Asked next how he would do this, he replied, "That's your problem." Similarly, when managers ask management scientists how to solve a problem, they too often say, in effect, "Boil the company." They leave it to the manager to worry about shortages of time, inaccessibility of data, resistance to change, slow response times, and oversimplified solutions.

FIRING THE FURNACE

At the Price Commission we operated, I think fairly successfully, without getting the data we "should" have had, without using any explicit decision tools, without once formally consulting a management scientist, and without building models of our decision-making processes. I am not especially proud of these facts; I am a member, and an intellectually loyal member, of ORSA, TIMS, and AIDS. I believe in the general direction in which these organizations want to go. But I also have a personal dedication to action, a sense of the urgency and immediacy of real problems, and a disbelief in the genuine responsiveness of management science models to my managerial needs.

I have asked myself the question whether we might have done better by using some management science models, and my honest answer is *no*. Using models would have slowed decision making. It would have frustrated most of our personnel. Given the fact that most models omit the factors of time, data accessibility, people, power, and politics, they simply would not have provided sufficient predictive or prescriptive payoff for the required investment of energy.

Consider the severity of the demands that were made. Establishment of the Price Commission required fulfillment of seemingly impossible tasks and directives:

- Create and staff a fully competent organization.
- Work out regulations worthy to bear the force of law.
- Keep the program consistent with policies established in Phase I and the current state of the economy.
- Work in conjunction with the Pay Board, the Internal Revenue Service, and the Cost of Living Council.
- Control the prices of hundreds of millions of articles and commodities in the world's largest economy.
- Do not inhibit the recovery of the economy.
- Do not build a postcontrol bubble.
- Do all of this with a regulatory staff of 600.
- Have the entire operation functioning in 16 days.

A natural first reaction to such demands might well have been General McAuliffe's famous one-word response: "Nuts!" It would have been very easy to point out, for example, that:

- Nobody could begin to do the job of price control with 600 people, even with the services of 3,000 Internal Revenue Service agents to help with enforcement. It had taken 60,000 people to handle the assignment in World War II and 17,000 in the Korean War.
- To do the job right would require a thoroughgoing study of what was involved—the resources and kinds of personnel required, the most efficient way of actually controlling prices, the optimum method of working in concert with other federal agencies—as well as the accumulation of data about the economy and the testing of various models.

- The 16-day period was too short. There was not enough time to get the Price Commission appointed, let alone to build, organize, and house the right kind of staff, promulgate regulations, and get it all functioning.

I might have pointed out these things and many others. I did not. I simply started bringing in staff, renting quarters, creating an organization, framing regulations, and developing a modus operandi. In 16 days the organization was accepting requests for price increases from U.S. business; the staff was at work—in some cases eight to an office, four to a telephone, and a good many spending up to 20 hours a day on the job.

I cite this record not to boast. Our achievement did not grow out of extraordinary capability. It was simply a matter of orientation and intuition—orientation and intuition toward action. But just as managers incline toward intuition and action, management scientists incline toward reflective thinking. They tend to be scholarly, less action-oriented, and averse to taking risks—even risk of criticism from their peers. They dissect and analyze, they are individualistic, and they are prone to trace ideas much as one can trace power flows in a mechanical system, from gear to belt to gear. They have not cared much about firing the furnace that makes the steam that drives the gear in the first place.

The manager offers an almost complete contrast. He integrates and synthesizes; he sees situations as mosaics; his thoughts and decision processes are like electrical circuits so complex you can never be sure how much current is flowing where. At the core of his value system are depth and breadth of experience, which he may even permit to outweigh facts where the whole picture seems to justify it.

For his part, the management scientist tends to optimize the precision of a tool at the expense of the health and performance of the whole. He has faith in some day building ultimate tools and devising ultimate measurements, and this lies at the foundation of his values and beliefs.

The problem, then, boils down to two cultures—the managers' and the management scientists'—and not enough bridges between them. Somebody has to build the bridges.

WHO SHALL BUILD THE BRIDGES?

Closing any gap requires that one or both cultures change. It is my strong belief that the management scientist must move first, and most. *The end product is supposed to be management, after all, not management science.* Further, as a philosophical point, I think science has greater relevance to our world if it moves constantly toward art (in this case the management art) than the other way around. Then, instead of moving toward increased and separated specialization, both evolve toward a mature symbiosis, a working and dynamic unity of the kind found in successful marriages, détentes, and mergers.

The management scientist is not going to find it easy or comfortable to change, and yet it is he who must change most in attitude, action, and life style. He is going to have to think in terms of the *manager's* perceptions, the *manager's* needs, the *manager's* expectations, and the *manager's* pressures—that is, if he wants to have impact in the real world of the manager. If not, he will go on missing the mark.

What, concretely, can be done? Let me offer a few suggestions to the management science people and the managers they are supposed to be helping.

Inside Operating Organizations

First, top management should not isolate the management science people but sprinkle them throughout the organization in situations where they can really go to work. It should give them *line* responsibility for results. Their natural tendencies will cause them to flock together at night or on weekends to compare and refine tools, and that, again, is as it should be; but their prime responsibility should be to the line unit, not to a management science group. To put the matter another way: management should not think of having an operating person on a management science team—it should think of having a management scientist on an operating team.

Second, managers should demand implementation by management scientists; they should not tolerate "package" solutions that leave out the complicating factors. In that way, managers can avoid simplistic, unworkable solutions that ignore the factors of time, data accessibility, unwillingness of people to change, power, and so on.

Third, even when professional management scientists are brought into companies as consultants, they are often given the easy, old problems, for the reasons that I have named. This expectational cycle has to be broken.

At the University

The same general approach is valid within universities.

First, both management science faculty and students have to get out of the isolated, insulated world of academe. They must go beyond structured cases and lectures and become directly involved in real-world, real-time, live projects, not as a way of applying what they know, but as a way of learning.

It is a mistake to teach the student linear programming or decision theory and then search for a problem to which the tool can be applied. That creates the classic academic situation from which managers are revolting—the tool in search of a problem. Instead, tackle the *real* problem. This will be frustrating, but the frustration of trying to reach a *workable* solution can be used to teach the management scientist or student in a way that is useful both to him and to the business or government unit. The solutions thus derived may not be so elegant as they might be, but they may be used. The student who wants to reach for higher, more sophisticated theories should be treated as a special case, not the general case.

Second, management science people should stop tackling the neat, simple problems, or refining approaches to problems already solved. These projects may be easier, but working and reworking them will not help bridge the cultural gap I am talking about. Instead, tackle the *tough* problem. The management of time pressure and the use of the persuasion and negotiation required by a real, tough problem will give both the faculty member and the student some salutary discipline in convincing others to follow a strange idea, to cooperate, and to listen.

The best example of what I am describing occurred at Case Institute in the early days of Russell L. Ackoff, E.L. Arnoff, and C. West Churchman. There, faculty and student teams worked on real problems in real time in real business settings. That example does not seem to have caught on at other universities, partly because of the difficulty of doing it, and partly because it flies against the nature of the management science personality that I have described. The process is messy, people-populated, schedule-disrupting, time-demanding, and complicated by power and politics. That is exactly as it should be.

Third, faculty members should plan to get out of the university, physically and completely, for meaningful periods of time. They should plan their careers so that they schedule at least a year, periodically, in which they get direct, real-world experience in business, nonprofit organizations, or the government.

One helpful device with which I am familiar is the Presidential Personnel Interchange Program of the federal government, now in its third year. So far this year it has brought 60 business executives into government work and 18 federal government managers into business. These numbers should be expanded tremendously, and the organizations involved should include universities. The universities could well join in a three-way interchange or start their own program with business.

Finally, universities should bring in real managers and involve them directly in problem-solving and joint-learning sessions. Doctors expect to return to medical school as part of their normal development; so should managers. The universities can offer managers an update in science; corporate managers can offer universities an update in management.

These are some of the ways to build bridges. There are other ways to tear them down, or to maintain the gap. Jargon, for example, will drive away managers. So will intellectual snobbery toward "intuitive" decision making. Management scientists should dispense with both. Managers can maintain the gap by continuing to refer to past disillusionments and never allowing management science people to tackle executive-suite programs. Managers should recognize that. In fact, defensive behavior on the part of either group can block reconciliation and progress.

People *do* exist who effectively bridge the two cultures. Such people do not always bear an identifying brand; one cannot distinguish them by their degrees, university course credits, titles, experience, or even home base. But they do have one strong, overriding characteristic—they are *problem- and action-oriented*. They are essentially unicultural; they employ a healthy mix of science and intuition in their decision making.

WORDS TO THE WISE

I am not suggesting that the two specializations—management science and management—be destroyed. Primary bases and modes of operation can be preserved, provided that both groups are receptive to and understanding of the other's basic orientation, and that they work together in harmony, not in dissonance. And all should remember that the problem is the thing, not the methodology; the function, not the form.

My slings and arrows have been directed mostly toward management science—rightly so, I think. But managers must assist in the bridge-building process:

- They should stop recounting tales of how "they never laid a glove on me" in encounters with management scientists. They should make it a point of future pride to use management science.

- They should make available the real nasty, complicated decisions to management scientists.

- They should not expect a lot.

- They should not deride small gains.
- They should hold any management science approach or individual accountable for producing *results*, not recommendations.

The management science people must play their part, too:

- Get out of the monasteries, whether these are universities or staff departments.
- Submerge the paraphernalia (journal articles, computer programs, cookbooks) and rituals ("sounds like a linear programming program to me" or "we need to get the facts first").
- Put people, time, power, data accessibility, and response times into models and create crude, workable solutions.
- Learn to live with and in the real world of managers.

Again, I submit it is the management science people who will have to change most. They should take the first step toward closing the gap between the two cultures. The consequences can only be better for managers, for management science, and for the problem itself.

NOTES

1. *Decisions Under Uncertainty* (Boston, Division of Research, Harvard Business School, 1960).

MILAN ZELENY

Managers Without
Management Science?

Since scientific methods simply exhibit free intelligence operating in the
best manner available at a given time, the cultural waste, confusion,
and distortion that results from the failure to use these methods, in all
fields in connection with all problems, is incalculable.

John Dewey,
Logic, The Theory of Inquiry

INTRODUCTION

In a recent article C. Jackson Grayson, Jr. states that he used absolutely
none of the management science tools explicitly.[1] Yet, to the question
whether he might have done better by using *some* management science
models his answer is *no*. How does he know?

That question is the main subject of this note. Can a decision maker
do better without science, models, computers etc.? In other words, can
we rely exclusively on experience, intuition, expert judgment, hunch
or genius? The answer is *no*. Or, *more precisely*, it all depends on the
decision maker, the problem and the environment.

Source: Copyright © *Interfaces* (Vol. 5, No. 4: August, 1975), pp. 35-42, published by The Institute of Management
Sciences.

The arguments are structured according to the following sequence of problems:

- How reliable is human intuitive judgment in simple as well as complex decision situations?
- Can a scientific, mathematical, computerized model outperform human decision makers?
- How crucial is the quantity and the quality of information for intelligent decision making?
- What is intuition and counterintuition in a good decision?

TESTING THE EXPERTS

Most important business decisions occur under conditions of uncertainty, and thus the intuitive assessment of probability must be part of any judgment, implicitly or explicitly.

Amos Tversky and Daniel Kahneman[2] have conducted some interesting experiments on judgmental evaluations of probabilities. The results are not encouraging. Take for example *anchoring*.

Humans usually make estimates by starting from some initial value which is *then* adjusted to yield the final answer. In one experiment these initial values were determined by spinning a wheel of fortune in the subjects' presence. The subjects were instructed to indicate whether the value was too low or too high, and then they were asked to make their estimate by a proper adjustment. Different groups were given different initial values. These "roulette" values had a marked effect on the estimates—e.g. the percentages of African countries in the U.N. were estimated as 25% and 45% by groups which received 10% and 65% as initial values respectively. Even a monetary reward for accuracy did not reduce the anchoring effect!

Also, the researchers have shown that human decision makers demonstrate remarkable *insensitivity to prior probability* of outcomes. Subjects were shown brief personality descriptions of several individuals from a group of 100 professionals—engineers and lawyers. They were asked to assess, for each description, the probability that it belonged to an engineer rather than to a lawyer. One group was told that the sampled group consisted of 30 engineers and 70 lawyers and the other group was given reversed ratio. The subjects in the two different situations produced essentially the same probability judgments. Even when the personality description was intentionally made irrelevant to either engineers or lawyers!

In another experiment, subjects assigned the *same* probability of obtaining an average height greater than six feet for samples of 1000, 100, and 10 men. Moreover, subjects *failed to appreciate the role of sample size* even when it was emphasized in the formulation of the problem.

Another important conclusion of Tversky-Kahneman is quoted directly:

> Given input variables of stated validity, a prediction based on several such variables can achieve higher accuracy when the input variables are independent of each other than when they are redundant or correlated. Redundant input variables generally yield input patterns that appear internally consistent, whereas uncorrelated input variables often yield input patterns that appear inconsistent. The internal consistency of the pattern of input (e.g., a profile of scores) is one of the major determinants of representativeness, and hence of confidence in prediction. Consequently, people tend to have greater confidence in predictions based on redundant input variables than in predictions based on uncorrelated variables. Because redundancy among inputs usually decreases accuracy and increases confidence, *people tend to have most confidence in predictions that are very likely to be off the mark.*

This observation can have an enormous impact on our view of the value of information as we shall discuss later.

Consultants and other experts are often called upon to predict the future value of a stock, the demand for a commodity, the Dow-Jones average or future profit. These predictions have been shown to be insensitive to the *reliability of the information* used and to the *expected accuracy of the prediction.* For example, if the descriptions of various companies (favorable or unfavorable) are unrelated to their profits, the same value should be predicted for all companies. But in reality, very high profit will be estimated if the description is most favorable. Similarly, the prediction of a remote value (e.g. future profits) was found to be identical to the evaluations of the information on which the prediction was based (e.g. previous year profits).

Another phenomenon which usually escapes most decision makers is *regression toward the mean*, i.e., the successful performance is likely to be followed by a deterioration in performance and vice versa. Still, rewards are typically administered when performance is good and punishments are administered when performance is poor. Because of regression toward the mean, behavior is most likely to improve after punishment and most likely to deteriorate after reward. Therefore, one is most often rewarded for punishing others and most often punished for rewarding them!

We could go on describing the experiments of Tversky and Kahneman. Let us state their conclusions in a summary:

- Reliance on heuristics and the presence of common biases are general characteristics of intuitive judgment of *both* laymen *and* experts.

- It is astonishing that experts fail to infer from life-long experience such fundamental statistical rules as regression toward the mean or the effect of a sample size.

- Most judgmental errors are systematic and predictable. People do not usually detect them because events are not normally coded in terms crucial for grasping statistical rules.

"BOOTSTRAPPING"

Let us turn to the work of Robyn M. Dawes.[3] His main concern is what role the human judge *should* play in prediction and decision making. Let us state his main conclusion, based on extensive experimental work:

> If a reasonable sample of cases exists for which the output values are known, the best way to make the predictions is to derive rational weights for the input variables on the basis of multiple regression; *human judges should be ignored.*

Dawes goes even further. What if we do not have a reasonable sample from which to derive regression weights? Can anything be done which would still be superior to human judgment? His answer is yes.

Experiments have shown that many linear models did a better job of predicting the outcome the decision maker was trying to predict than did the decision maker himself. The paramorphic representation of a decision maker's behavior may be more predictive of the outcome than is the decision maker himself. This phenomenon is called *"bootstrapping."*

In general, linear models seem to be superior to human decision makers under certain conditions. Actually, linear models whose weights were randomly selected *on the average* outperformed the linear models whose weights were selected on the basis of experts' judgments!

Another researcher, Paul Slovic,[4] has supported most of Dawes' findings and demonstrated them on examples of stock market "decision makers." First, he discusses the finding that the decision maker's *length of professional training and experience* often showed little relationship to accuracy of judgments. Similarly, the amount of information available to the decision makers was not necessarily related to the accuracy of their inferences.

As for the weights entering linear regression models it has been found that the longer a broker had been in the business, the less accurate was his insight into his weighting policy. Slovic also suggests that the algebraic model captures the judge's weighting policy and applies it more consistently than the judge. Substitution of the model for the manager, under certain conditions, can produce decisions superior to those the manager made on his own.

It is implied that the current role of the human decision maker could be misplaced. Man simply cannot take proper account, simultaneously, of various multiple attributes (and their complex interactions) of existing alternatives. Essentially a man should "tell" the computer *how* he wants decisions made, and then let the machine make the decisions for him, i.e. a man decides which variables should be included in the input, performs elementary comparisons with respect to subjective attributes, decides what kind of information will be gathered and how much, but mainly is concerned with the criteria of decision, goals and objectives. These have to be defined and human judgment always will be essential here.

In an article by Yntema and Torgerson[5] one source of misunderstanding between managers and management science is identified:

> ... in business it is now common to use computer programs to calculate how to maximize some quantity or other; linear programming is the prime example. As the mathematics becomes more sophisticated and computers become more powerful, the success of these methods will depend less and less on the number of variables and the complexity of the relations that can be considered. Planners will find themselves paying even more attention than they do now to the precise definition of the quantity to be maximized.

We are still witnessing management scientists paying more attention to the problems of handling large numbers of variables and constraints and to the sophistication of algorithms and managers still refusing to use them. Both sides should concentrate on *what* and *why* rather than *how* to optimize.

Finally, some managers argue that they cannot use linear models because the reality is nonlinear. So they push for even more complex mathematical models (nonlinear) and thus encourage management science and the scientist to move further away from being useful to them. Would a manager accept the decision of a complex nonlinear model if he has rejected that of a simple linear model?

There is no sufficient evidence that nonlinear models are superior to linear models. Actually the opposite might be true. Linear models are usually extremely robust approximations to nonlinear monotone functions. Linear models are of great practical value in decision making. Dawes describes an experiment in which the linear model constructed of every single one of 80 judges did a better job than the judges themselves.

HOW MUCH INFORMATION IS ENOUGH?

It is probably safe to state that the current manager's view of a man-computer interaction is that a computer, with all of its mathematical models, is supposed to provide a sufficient amount of information on which a decision maker can base his decision. Another view of this interaction is the reverse, i.e. man should decide about the information and the criteria and let the model make the final decision.

Man is a bad processor of information generated by computer—he is a bad processor of information in general. Then why this craving for more information, for MIS, data banks, and other expensive tools believed to improve a decision maker's decision?

S. Oskamp[6] describes a study of 32 judges, including 8 professional clinicians, who were given background information about a patient's case. The information was divided into four sections. After reading each section of the case, the judges established their diagnoses. The correct diagnosis was known only to the investigator. Oskamp found that, as the amount of information about the case increased, accuracy remained at about the same level while the clinicians' confidence increased dramatically and became disproportionately great!

This finding supports the conclusions of Tversky and Kahneman, namely that people tend to have most confidence in predictions that are very likely to be off the mark.

The current boom in Management Information Systems (MIS) is directed toward obtaining as much information as possible. Additional information boosts managers' confidence and helps their decisions to be more forcefully implemented; it does not necessarily improve the quality of their decisions. Only some minimum threshold level of information is actually utilized in forming a decision—all the rest of this expensive information is used to increase the decision maker's confidence. Actually information in excessive doses is harmful since it increases confidence where caution and doubt should be exercised. But one doesn't make it as a manager by being cautious and modest. One must appear aggressive and confident. Therefore managers reject management science which is intended to improve their decisions but are inclined to accept management information systems which tend to increase their confidence, though the decisions might stay inferior.

Tversky and Kahneman found that people respond differently when given no information and when given *worthless information*. When no specific information is given people tend to employ statistical laws; when worthless information is given—they use it and ignore the laws!

It is not necessary to concur with "bootstrapping" and to advocate replacing decision makers by machines. But managers should realize what management science has to offer and that the managers should make necessary steps in bridging the gap between them and management scientists. This rather complex recommendation might appear to be counterintuitive.

INTUITION, COUNTERINTUITION AND ACCEPTABILITY

Complex systems tend to behave counter-intuitively and thus their models (if they are correct) tend to suggest counter-intuitive answers. Consequently, management science models are not likely to be accepted because they give different solutions from what an expert would expect intuitively.

We find again and again that acceptability is the ultimate criterion of a successful model (and of its creator). It does not really matter whether the model is correct or incorrect or whether the decision maker is right or wrong. In both cases the intuitive preconception must be satisfied as a necessary condition for acceptance. This is a very serious *dilemma:* A correct model (possibly counterintuitive) will probably be unacceptable because it does not support intuitive judgment. Yet, an incorrect model has a better chance of acceptance because it tends to be less counterintuitive and thus more appealing to intuition of top executives. It is therefore "useful."

C. West Churchman[7] supports the point that the acceptance by managers should be the ultimate test of management science. He says: "If the manager doesn't act as the model says he should, then something is wrong, and until the error is explained the model cannot be accepted." And later he concludes that: "... we *can* say that acceptance is an ultimate test of the validity of a model." In view of what has been stated about the reliability of intuitive judgments it looks as though management science models are utilized for what they are not designed: to support managers' intuition and to improve their confidence. Whether they provide correct or incorrect answers seems to be irrelevant.

Churchman actually knows the answer: "If we could accomplish a fuller understanding of the process of acceptance, we would create a very beautiful thing to behold. The manager and the scientist would 'work together' in a very intricate and elegant way." But he is quite skeptical about its feasibility because "... ignorance may be of value to the manager. The manager may want to be ignorant, i.e. to ignore knowledge." Although the manager's ignorance should be taken into account, management scientists should help to remove it.

As Peter Drucker[8] observes: "Managers, by and large, have failed to take managerial responsibility for management scientists and management sciences. They have left the management sciences unmanaged—and are therefore largely responsible for their degenerating into a bag of tricks, a 'management gadget bag' of answers to nonexisting questions in many cases."

Managers are responsible, responsibility is their profession. They should understand the limitations of intuitive expert judgments. They must understand what the management sciences can do, that they are the manager's tools, and not the tools of the management scientist. They have to realize the limitations of management science, caused by its origin and history. Management sciences (and scientists) can change but they must be stimulated and led in proper directions by managers. They must be managed.

CONCLUSIONS AND IMPLICATIONS

We have shown how unreliable managers' judgment could be in dealing with well-structured and well-defined problems of analytical nature. It is quite tempting to conclude that if human performance is inferior in dealing with simple problems, not much should be expected from its encounters with complex and messy problems.

There is a catch. Complex problems are not simple collections of simpler problems, they are not decomposable. We often confuse largeness with complexity. Large, combinatoric problems are usually well-structured, decomposable into simpler subproblems and thus can be entrusted to computers and models. They are not complex in the sense of being messy, fuzzy, ill-structured, qualitative, etc. Thus, the conclusions of judgmental psychologists are not transferable to all types of human problem solving. No experiments have yet been conducted to evaluate human performance in dealing with true complexity.

To find a product of, say 1000 numbers is a well-structured, although a large, problem. It is not complex but we can learn that finding the answer by intuition could be a misplaced effort. On the other hand, to find a solution to a traffic mess at a busy intersection should better be entrusted to the sure and fast functioning of the human mind. Even a model involving velocities and masses of all objects, probabilities of their trajectories, and expectations of subjects' states of mind, even such models could not compete with human grasp of totality, simultaneity, and gestalt of the situation.

There are essentially two modes of human problem solving: analytic and intuitive. Both these modes are the endpoints of the same continuum of thought. The analytic end can be characterized as having explicit, sequential, and recoverable attributes, while the intuitive end has implicit, nonsequential, and nonrecoverable attributes. Analytic thinking relies on logical sequences, symbolic structures, component-wise decomposition, and vertical reasoning. Intuitive thinking relies on holistic impressions, visual and spatial images, impulsive synthesis, and lateral reasoning.

As managerial concerns advance from simple, well-structured, static, and deterministic problems toward more complex, fuzzy, dynamic, and stochastic problems, the *optimal* working framework of the human mind changes from logical, rational, sequential and quantitative, to perceptive, intuitive, simultaneous and qualitative. To approach the problems of reality in their full complexity of an analytical-intuitive unity requires a conscious enhancement of both ends of this ever shifting continuum of thought.

Most problems of management are neither purely analytic, nor purely intuitive; rather, they combine both components in an intricate interaction. Information might be processed according to explicit rules, but the conclusions reached through such transformations are often checked, revised and even distorted by past experience, expert judgment and intuition. In this sense the problems are mixed or "messy" and cannot be effectively approached within either purely analytic or purely intuitive framework of thought.

Both modes of thinking are optimal, both are equally important. They are used interchangeably in dependency on the properties of a particular problem. To solve a well-structured problem by intuition is as suboptimal as to solve ill-defined problems by analytical simplification.

Management science has been successful where it enhanced man's analytical faculties in dealing with analytical problems. It has been less successful in trying to approach complex problems via analytical decomposition. It has not even tried to enhance man's intuitive faculties in dealing with intuitive problems.

The continuous refinement and sharpening of existing analytical tools helps to delegate an increasing number of human tasks to human contrivances such as computer models, decision rules, or automatic devices. The effect is that it allows more and more problems to be transferred from the realm of intuition into that of analysis. The outcome should be the development of new analytical tools permitting intuition to be set free to develop its capability to deal with additional problems.

Management science has neglected the intuitive factor of managerial decision making. It tends to replace intuition by analysis rather than to enhance intuition. Peter F. Drucker [9] offers the following view:

> Insight, understanding, ranking of priorities, and a "feel" for the complexity of an area are as important as precise, beautifully elegant mathematical models—and in fact usually infinitely more useful and indeed even more "scientific". They reflect the reality of the manager's universe and of his tasks.

NOTES

1. C. Jackson Grayson, Jr., "Management Science and Business Practice," *Harvard Business Review*, July-August 1973, pp. 41-48.
2. Amos Tversky and Daniel Kahneman, "Judgement Under Uncertainty: Heuristics and Biases," *Science*, 185, pp. 1124-1131.
3. Dawes, Robyn M., "Objective Optimization Under Multiple Subjective Functions," in: *Multiple Criteria Decision Making*, USC Press, 1973, pp. 9-17.
4. Slovic, P., "Psychological Study of Human Judgment: Implications for Investment Decision Making," Oregon Research Institute, Vol. 11, No. 1.
5. Yntema, D. B. and Torgerson, W. S., "Man-Computer Cooperation in Decisions Requiring Common Sense," *IRE Transactions on Human Factors in Electronics*, HEE 2 (1961), pp. 20-26.
6. Oskamp, S., "Overconfidence in Case-Study Judgments," *Journal of Consulting Psychology*, 1965, 29, 261-265.
7. Churchman, West C., "Reliability of Models in the Social Sciences," *Interfaces*, Vol. 4, No. 1, November 1973.
8. Drucker, P., *Management, Tasks, Responsibilities, Practices*, Harper & Row, New York, 1973, p. 513.
9. Op. cit., p. 516.

ANTONY JAY

Who Knows What Primitive Instincts Lurk in the Heart of Modern Corporation Man?

In front of my house there is a short semicircular drive which in a more gracious age allowed carriages to drive up to the door, set down the occupants, and continue on into the road again. In those days there were gates at each end; but they proved a nuisance in the age of the motorcar, so now there are two open gateways. A few months ago I looked out the window and saw three strange young men walking along the pavement. As they came level with the house they had the unbelievable audacity to turn off the pavement and in through the gateway, through my garden, past my front door, and back into the road again. The insolence of it! Who did they think. . . . As I watched them, the whole emotional range of the Enraged Householder syndrome welled up inside me, the same response that I myself used to provoke when as a small boy I climbed over suburban fences to get my ball back. But in this case it was different; I had just finished reading Konrad Lorenz's *On Aggression*, and recognized that my instinctive anger was not a private and personal quirk, but an ancient aggressive response to a territorial threat. The knowledge could not subdue my feelings, but at least it restrained my actions and prevented

Source: *New York Magazine*, Sept. 20, 1971. Copyright © 1971 by the NYM Corp. Reprinted with the permission of NEW YORK Magazine.

me from trying to pretend to myself that the resentment was an entirely rational and logical consequence of an act which in fact was only the most harmless of adolescent larks. This is the real fascination of the New Biology: not the data but the programs, not the facts it unearths but the new way of looking at the world that it gives you—above all, the new way of looking at yourself and your fellow-men. Perhaps the best way to express this is by the phrase "acceptance of the irrational."

The New Biology shows us how powerfully the irrational operates within us, and how much of our behavior is not the logical response of the intellect to the facts of the situation, but an emotional reflex set off by some primitive survival mechanism. I felt a surge of aggression toward those three young men because I belong to a species that for millions of years had to defend its territory to survive. Chance no doubt brought into the world many variants without any urge to defend their children or their caves; they could not continue their line, and they were selected out. I am here because there were some who fought tooth and nail against every intruder to protect their home and their young. It may be that in the orderly suburbs of the 1970s the sharpness of that reaction is no longer necessary. That is not the point: my instincts and emotions are governed not by current social supply and demand, but age-old genetic history. It is enough that an aggressive response to territorial aggression was a survival necessity once; and who is to say that it will not one day be a survival necessity again?

It is inevitable that within a generation the findings of the New Biology, as already interpreted by writers like Lorenz, Robert Ardrey and Desmond Morris, will work a revolution in our understanding of ourselves. The revolution will be more profound and more constructive than the one set off 80 years ago by Sigmund Freud, and it already looks as though it is encountering the same bitter resistance. But for me the New Biology, the biology of behavior, has a special significance, though it took quite a long time to dawn on me.

It is nine years now since I became fascinated by the way corporations organize themselves. It started when I realized that half the troubles of the corporation I worked for were the product of its own absurd internal structure of departments and divisions. I realized that if only we were organized right, something like a half of my time would be liberated from administrative machine maintenance and available for the real problems thrown up by the product and the customers. But what was "right"?

I started by looking in the management books, but they were not much help. They are fine on techniques and details, but as they approach the central problems their value is diminished almost to zero by their assumption that what cannot be measured does not exist. The consequence is that most management theory is like studying *Hamlet* by counting how many times each character enters and leaves the stage, by plotting a graph of how many players are on the stage at any given time, by analyzing how many lines each character speaks to the others (and to himself), and by comparing the number of verbal messages sent and delivered with the number of written ones. An interesting occupation for the academically underemployed, but no help if you want to write a great play.

Having drawn a blank in the management books, I might never have gotten any further. But then I had an extraordinary stroke of luck. As I was still pondering the problem I began reading Machiavelli's *The Prince*, and with every page it became clearer that one writer at least had been prepared to grapple with the central problem of how to run a big organization. Machiavelli was writing about princes and barons and courtiers, not about directors and executives and corporate officers, and yet time and again he hit on universal truths that corporation men are still having to learn privately and painfully every day. These insights and parallels led eventually to my writing a book, *Management and Machiavelli*, which came out in 1967. Its theme was that the modern corporation follows exactly the same pattern as the medieval or Renaissance state, with wars and treaties, baronial revolt, colonization and conquest translated into commercial competition and agreements, truculent heads of divisions refusing to disclose figures, expansion into new products and the acquisition of companies: and that this was not just an entertaining parallel, but the expression of a fundamental identity. They act the same because they are the same. The headquarters of today's giant corporations are the direct political descendants of the courts of Augustus and Charlemagne, Henry VIII and Louis XIV; Robert Townsend would be instantly at home in the corridors of seventeenth-century Versailles or sixteenth-century Hampton Court. He might miss the air conditioning and the dictaphones, but he would arrive knowing all the rules of the game.

Nevertheless, to point a parallel is not to discover a cause. It occurred to me even while I was writing the book that there must be, somewhere, a single root from which the state and the corporation had both grown, but I did not imagine that I or anyone else would ever dig down to it. Certainly I did not realize that even while I was writing, that root was actually being exposed. It took two or three more years for the truth to dawn on me—again, because I was looking in the wrong place. Why did it take so long? I can only explain it by recalling the answer I was once given by Francis Crick, the DNA Nobel Prize winner, when I asked him what it was that kept one scientist from making a breakthrough which another scientist made. He said that it was very rarely an absence of the necessary facts: you always kicked yourself if you were the one who had missed it, because all the facts were in front of you all the time. There were various obstacles he mentioned—for instance, a piece of experimental evidence that was wrong—but the one I chiefly remember was this: an assumption you are not aware you are making. I had unconsciously assumed that the key to corporate organization and corporate behavior was hidden somewhere in the shelves labeled "Political Theory," whereas all the time it lay in animal behavior.

At first sight the idea was preposterous, except as a metaphor or a joke: the corporation is not a jungle, and its employees are not animals, except in figures of speech. But with every page of Ardrey's *Territorial Imperative*, Lorenz's *On Aggression* and Morris' *The Naked Ape* I heard the same bells chiming that I heard when I read *The Prince*. Take status; in just about all species of animals who live in groups, you find a status hierarchy, and many of them have evolved precise conventions of behavior or display to indicate it. Among vervet monkeys, for instance, the status of adult males in the troop is demonstrated by the color of the scrotum—deepest indigo for Number One, shading down to the palest pastel blue for the monkey at the bottom of the heap. It means that a quick glance shows each member whether to push in front or stand back. Number One gets all the food and females and deference he wants, then Number Two gets his turn, and finally the last one gets the leftovers, if any—the females are not interested in him and all the males shove him out of the way. This observation was confirmed when an experimenter removed the lowest-status individual and painted his scrotum an even deeper indigo than Number One's and returned him to the troop. No human act could ever come closer to the magic of Cinderella's fairy godmother: suddenly all the males deferred to him, all the females clustered around him, and he had all the best food and as much of it as he wanted. The poor little chap suddenly found himself living out the wildest fantasy of every downtrodden underdog from Bottom the weaver to Charlie Chaplin. I have never found out what happened when the paint wore off.

It is impossible to work in a large corporation without realizing the living force of status displays every hour of the day. Not perhaps the exact convention adopted by vervets, but many others which are no less powerful for being less intimate. I remember the day I became head of a department, and exchanged the measly green windshield sticker which allowed me to use the general parking lot for the proud red badge of the senior executives' lot. I remember going to lunch for the first time in the senior executives' dining room, and the slightly exaggerated geniality of the welcome from colleagues I had known for many years and who would hardly have noticed my arrival in the bar of the club downstairs. I remember the official from the accommodation department who brought me a slide viewer with pictures of the new selection of office furnishings I was now entitled to. I also remember two moments of deep shame. One was when I found that my red leather chairs did not go with the carpet, and asked for blue ones instead, and the other was when I asked for a waitress to bring coffee to my office: on both occasions a junior official had to convey to me, in an agony of embarrassment, that blue chairs and waitresses were badges of a status higher than mine. Since one of the rules of status is that you can only allocate relative status to your subordinates, never to your superiors, I had violated a convention instead of competing within it, and so we both lost face.

Of course the prime status indicator in the corporation is the paycheck. Since salary is one of the simplest ways in which the corporation conventionally grades its staff, it is a quick and reliable guide. It is, however, often extremely hard to find out other people's salaries. Nevertheless, when it does emerge that a colleague you rank below yourself is being paid more, the discovery strikes at the very heart of your security, identity and self-respect. I have known some terrible corporate battles over money, but none of them have been motivated by the money as an absolute. If you are concerned over money as an absolute, you can—assuming you are underpaid—always leave and go to another company. You only fight if you want to stay, but have received an affront to your status. Always the cause of anger has been money relative to the money someone else was getting. This, however, cannot be openly stated, so the battle is fought in disguise, and the argument rages around the difficulty of the work, the time it consumes, the level of responsibility borne, and comparable salaries in other corporations (where they help the case).

But salary is not the only conventional prize in the status race. There is another of equal or even greater significance, which is perhaps even more damaging than salary when it becomes a source of status conflict. It is function, the actual job you are given: and the battlefield is the corporate or divisional or company organization chart. The organization chart causes more agonized exasperation than any other piece of paper, and for a very good reason: it is drawn up in good faith by men who are trying to arrange the most effective means of deploying the corporation staff for success in the survival battle, but everyone on the chart is looking at it as evidence of how the corporation judges his status, and every staff member sees the lines and boxes as conventional prizes for which he is invited to compete. Again the naked status argument has to be clothed: this time it wears the guise of operational theory. "If I have to go through the controller it will cause the most appalling delays." "If he reports direct to you instead of through me, we're going to get the most ghastly crossed lines." "Won't it simplify the lines of communication if all those twelve come under me—wouldn't that make your span of command more manageable?" Or more menacingly, "If I have to clear everything with him then the job can't be done, and that's that." The poor well-meaning fellow who drew up the chart does not know what hit him: he had no idea the corporation contained so many passionate experts on the theory of organizational structure. But every compromise he makes to soothe ruffled feathers is a compromise of operational efficiency; and after he has been through the performance once and got it over, he privately vows never to do it again. The existing organizational structure will have to serve unchanged for the rest of his career.

But salary and function are only two among many status indicators in large organizations. In fact, once you look around the great corporations you quickly discover a complex honor system with at least a dozen different orders and any number of grades within each order; not every corporation has all of them, but few are without some. There is the secretary, ranging from access to the pool through a secretary in your office, then a secretary in a separate office, to two secretaries, to finally an assistant with her own secretary. There are flowers, from zero when your secretary has to bring her own, through rubber plant and then flowering plant, up to fresh-cut flowers every day. Office area is another, from cupboard size to ballroom size, and office furnishings from light oak and linoleum through endless gradations to fitted Indian carpet, Sheraton or Chippendale furniture, and genuine Impressionist paintings. Then there is stationery, rising from thin printed to thicker embossed and culminating in something very much like cardboard, embossed with your own name. Drinks are another order, from the bar down the block through the executives' club, then the office cocktail cabinet, up to a bar with a waiter in a corner of your office suite.

The Order of the Bath, in the corporation, starts with sharing the general concrete-floored lavatory, progresses through various grades of more refined toilet facilities, until you have a key to the executives' washrooms and finally a complete suite with bath and shower in your own office. Tea and coffee start at the vending machine in the corridor and go through wagon service to room service, while the receptacles progress from thick canteen cups to fine bone china and a silver coffeepot brought in on a silver tray by a butler. Where you eat is another universal badge, with grades rising from a special table in the factory canteen through a range of more elegant and exclusive dining rooms, until a butler serves lunch in the dining area of your office suite. The make of company car provides a long series of different grades from a secondhand Chevy to this year's Cadillac, and the place you put it goes from the street through the company lot, then to the director's garage, until finally you do not have to know since the chauffeur always drives your Cadillac to the door and is always waiting there when you come out.

I have dwelt at some length on status displays because they are the most visible and obvious form of animal behavior. Territorial defense is less obvious, though anyone who has watched a departmental manager fight to preserve his department's functions and responsibilities under threat of reorganization, and then reads about troops of howling monkeys defending their territory with deafening shrieks and aggressive gestures, will not need anyone to make the point for him.

The instinct to defend the territory that is the source of your livelihood, the desire of status and the need to display it—these are part of that unmeasurable 95 percent of corporate behavior which the books have to ignore. But if we go a little further into animal behavior, they fit into place—though the picture they help compose is very different from the accepted theory of corporate identity; it is, however, a great deal closer to the real corporation which we encounter every day.

Status and territory are common to any number of animal species—insects, fish, birds and reptiles, as well as mammals. They do not explain the corporation, even though they explain many of the things that happen inside it. To understand Corporation Man we have to look back to the origin of our branch of the primate family. And the starting point is this: we are not, and never have been, a solitary species. However far you trace our history and prehistory, you find groups: not just the family group, but something larger. Moreover, this is true of all species of ape and monkey except the gibbon and the orang-utan. True, the apes are only collateral branches of our evolutionary line: but if you go back seventy million years to a direct ancestral species, the lemur, you still find a larger grouping than the family as the basic unit. This is now so deep in us that we have to accept it as immutable; wherever we live, whatever projects we undertake, whatever dangers we encounter, we will form a group if it is remotely possible.

This simple primate grouping, however, is only half the story. It is the other half, that which makes us different from all the other primates, that has the profound implications for the modern corporation.

Most of the scientists seem to agree that this difference began well over a million years ago—more likely five million and perhaps as long as fifteen million. Before then, we, or rather our ancestors, were vegetarians like the rest of the family. But then, at some point in the Pliocene or Miocene era, we turned from vegetarians into carnivores. Perhaps we started by catching or trapping the small mammals—monkeys and rats and rabbits; but as the ages rolled by a new meat supply opened up—meat on the hoof: the great herds of large grazing animals where a single kill could feed a community.

There was, however, a drawback to those large varieties of antelope and waterbuck and oryx: they were too large and too swift for any man, or emergent ape, to catch and kill on his own. But they were not too large for a group of them working together. Already we were a social species; we traveled around together, and banded together for defense, even if each one collected his fruit and vegetables for himself. Now we adapted the existing cooperative way of life to a purpose different from that of any other primate: the systematic hunting and killing of game. Begotten by opportunity out of necessity, millions of years ago, the hunting band was born. And it has taken one branch of the primate family down from the trees and up to the moon.

Of course, Corporation Man is a great deal more than a hunter: he can speak and write, he can compose music and poetry, he can learn and reason, he can experiment and invent with an ingenuity and adaptability that are unique in the animal world. But all these are additions to, not subtractions from, the hunting primate. The hunting band is still there, and when we deal with the corporation, we are dealing with a very recent adaptation of it. The board, the executive committee, the project team and all the thousands, maybe millions, of successful groups in industry, commerce, banking, government, and war—indeed every area of collective human enterprise—have not been forging a new weapon on the anvil of modern industrial civilization: they have picked up an ancient one and used it with only the smallest of modifications.

The primitive hunting band is the key to understanding the modern corporation. Survival no longer requires the hunting and killing of game, so this particular skill has been allowed to atrophy; it has been replaced by agriculture and mining and manufacturing, by the skills of devising, making, transporting and selling goods, by thousands of entirely new survival activities. But although the end product may have changed, it has changed very recently: the way we organized the hunting band, the method of operation, its communication system, its survival mechanisms, above all the instincts and emotions it calls forth—all these are still there, and we will begin to understand our human organizations in a new way if only we can see them; or rather, if only we can see them for what they are, since they have been staring us in the face all our lives.

To accept this means accepting that the instincts evolved for ancient hunting needs are still active inside us. I find this very easy to believe; if we accept that a mother's instinct to protect her young is the product of an evolutionary need, it is not hard to extend this to the defense of the home, to status, and to hunting activity. And if, as I have, you have ever worked in a successful, united corporation hunting band, you know it with a deep inner certainty. It is only because a farming interlude has separated corporation man from his hunting ancestry that we have not seen this before: but you have only to think about it to realize that ten thousand years of farming cannot possibly dissipate a genetic inheritance built up and handed down during five to fifteen million years of hunting. Indeed, if we go back a quarter of those ten thousand years we meet Plato and Sophocles and Aristophanes, whose intellects and emotions were so similar to ours today (and that is flattering ourselves) that it is impossible to think that the other three quarters can have had any noticeable genetic effect at all. The employees and the managers of the modern corporation, in their sprawling factories and towering office blocks, have been formed into what they are, not by three hundred generations down on the farm, but by half a million generations in the hunting band.

But we can do more than discover the ancient hunting band still at work in the modern corporation: we can find out its optimum size. Obviously there cannot be just one number which is the only possible one, and for a long time it did not occur to me that the question was worth asking. A group is a group is a group. If it works, then it's the right number. I had always believed that there was a truth in Parkinson's general rule that no board, council, cabinet or committee can ever function when membership rises above twenty, but on reflection even twenty seemed too large. The feeling in my bones told me that six or seven was comfortable, and ten perfectly reasonable; twelve could not be ruled out, but fifteen sounded a little improbable. If it was twenty, I would need a great deal of convincing that it could operate as a single team: if a meeting of twenty ever worked, it worked because several people were subordinates of others present, or specialists advising on particular topics, and though there were twenty faces around the table, there were only ten voices that mattered. All the same, this was completely personal and subjective.

Then I thought about the army. I had spent two years of military service as recruit, cadet and officer, and although I entered it with no enthusiasm for the military way of life, I emerged with considerable respect for the way it was run. So the army seemed to me a good place to look; the organization of an army is not a question of having fun with charts, it is a matter of life and death; its structure has been hammered out by the logic of survival over many centuries of bloody experience. And it was quite clear that in virtually any army the basic unit of survival, the group that stood or fell together, was the infantry section. There were platoons, companies, battalions and regiments, but all these were assemblies of smaller units; the section was a band of men, and the section was ten or eleven in number when at full strength. And this applies not only to the modern armies: the Roman army was based on units of ten, the squad who shared a tent; the army of Genghis Khan was based on units of ten; indeed almost every long-standing successful army, whatever larger formations it might adopt for battle, rested for its permanent organization on units of that sort of size.

And it is not just the army. When we play games together, the same size keeps cropping up. Basketball has five men and ice hockey has six; almost all other team games have teams of between eight and fifteen in number. Juries are twelve; the Jewish minyan is ten. Indeed, once you look around at human groups with the hunting band in mind, the number leaps out at you. Every practicing manager I have discussed the subject with agrees without question that ten is close to the maximum for a board or project team or work group, and if I had wanted any further corroboration of its application to industry, it was supplied by the paper on productivity bargaining that won the Institute of Management Consultants' Sandford Smith award for 1969. The author, Robert Spillman, says: "Whatever the formal organization, people develop an informal organization, which may or may not coincide with the formal organization, and within which certain of their needs are satisfied. The basic unit of informal organization is the work group; and this may consist of from three to eighteen persons carrying out a common task or engaged in linked operations. Each person in that group reacts or responds to the other persons in that group, and the result is that each group tends to act as a cell or unit with characteristics and needs of its own. Members of a social group will tend to subordinate their individual needs to the needs of the group as a whole; but in return the work group protects and shields its members."

By the time I had got this far, I was convinced. Since no one could go back to the Pliocene epoch and check up, I was sure that the only evidence we would ever have about the size of those hunting bands would have to be supplied by projecting back from Corporation Man or forward from the lemur, and as far as I was concerned they both pointed in the same direction. But I reckoned without the ingenuity of the paleozoologists. They approached the question like this: the hunting band would have to bring its kill back to the camp because of vultures and other scavengers, and it would normally have to return before nightfall for collective security against lions and leopards and to feed the women and children if stores were low. From this the scientists plotted the maximum hunting radius. Meanwhile, from other evidence, they discovered the density of game population in that part of Africa at that time. And they have worked out that within the human or emergent-ape radius there was about enough food to support a total population of forty, which would mean a male hunting band of something between nine and eleven.

This, it seems to me, is the key to the way we work in the modern corporation. The corporation is an association of hunting bands, of tightly knit groups of up to ten men who know that they succeed or fail together. Of course by no means every member of the corporation belongs to one of these ten-groups, but most of the really satisfied and really effective ones do. In fact the ancient need for this ten-group comradeship and activity is so strong that men who fail to find it at work seek it outside, in sports teams or social clubs or local government or community committees or labor unions.

I have stressed the importance of the ten-group because it is the driving force behind all creative corporate achievement. All the same, every member of a corporation hunting band is aware of a double loyalty. As well as the ten-group and its immediate task, there is the wider corporation whose long-term needs may restrict or conflict with the demands of the job at hand. This double loyalty has ancient origins too: as well as the hunting band of ten there was the camp of forty or so, the home-base. The hunt was the instrument of day-to-day survival, but the camp, the home base, was the instrument for preserving and continuing the species. The camp in the daytime was the place for the women, the children and the old men. There was work to do—collecting fruit and roots and berries and water, bringing up the children, some rudimentary attention to hygiene and comfort— but it did not have the dangers or rewards of the hunting band.

All the same, the species could die out just as easily by failure to keep the camp secure and free from disease and internal strife as it could by failure to kill the game. Consequently, the ancient primate society, which had long been used to living and wandering in small groups, must have preserved what it could of that form of organization while adapting to the compulsions of the hunting life. The hunt was a special, separate activity. When the hunters returned, they rejoined the older social organization. Communal defense against predators or other marauders of their own species, the prevention of lethal strife within the group, some means of making group decisions about which way to move on, some sort of social conventions and regulations—all these must have existed long before we turned carnivorous, and must have continued and developed over several hundred thousand generations to reach the refinement and complexity they show when we first encounter them in history.

Every modern corporation has its camp in addition to its hunting bands. It contains all those who are not actually devising, making, and selling the product that brings in the money. They may be physically only just across the corridor, but in all other ways they are in a different world. Many of them are women—secretaries and personnel assistants, cleaners and coffee ladies—but in the modern corporation many are men as well. They are in departments with names like finance, personnel, planning, public relations, administration, registry, welfare, and so on; and, however devoted their efforts, however valuable their contribution, the members of the hunting bands look on them as the "women and children" of the corporation. Any hunter who is sweating his guts out to meet a production or copy deadline or a sales target thinks of them as, to some extent, a burden that he and his fellows have to carry, and I suspect there is even a submerged feeling that it is women's work they are doing. Healthy, strong, active men ought to be sharing the exertions and perils of the hunt, not skulking in the warmth and safety of the camp all day. It is very difficult to say who in the corporation is in the camp and who is in the hunting band—but only if you are in the camp.

You then think of the importance of your contribution—the tax savings you have devised, the pressure under which you work, and how you go home absolutely drained an hour after everyone else—and you almost kid yourself that you are really one of the hunters. But the hunting bands know with absolute clarity who are the hunters and who are the passengers. Some of the passengers may in fact prove their usefulness so clearly, in the way they make the hunters' work easier and more effective, that they will be accepted and even respected; but that respect has to be earned from the hunting bands, not in the camp.

What the corporation's hunters find absolutely intolerable is the squaw-men in the camp starting to behave as if they were as important as, or more important than, the men who go out and kill the game. If this false importance is endorsed by the management, the contemptuous resentment is turned upward on them. Many industrial disputes are given an extra streak of bitterness when the men making the product that makes the money see their friends being laid off so as to support an army of smart young parasites in warm, carpeted offices.

The hunting band and the camp are two basic groupings which we have brought with us out of our dim prehistory to dominate the life of the modern corporation. But there is a third. For genetic reasons, the hunting band and its camp can never have been completely self-contained: they must have been part of a wider breeding population. But how large was that population? Here the paleozoologists cannot help us: if we are to find any clues, they must be lying about us now. And I suggest there are several, and that they all point in the same direction.

Try asking an experienced executive in industry what is the maximum size for a one-man firm, the sort that a dominating but managerially unsophisticated boss can run on his own. The answer almost always falls somewhere between three hundred fifty and seven hundred fifty. Of course this is unscientific: but when a large number of practical men reach the same conclusion independently, I tend to be impressed. Five hundred is the most common answer, and when you think about it, five hundred is a very interesting number. Somewhere around four hundred or five hundred or six hundred is about the normal size for a village. It is also what most headmasters and principals think of as the "right" size for a school or college: the size they would be very happy to run. And what about the army, where the logic of survival is at its strictest? A battalion in wartime was about six hundred; and the Romans—that most decimal of nations—had the squad of ten and the century, a company of approximately one hundred; yet the cohort, one of the ten divisions in a legion, was not the thousand that simple multiplication would suggest, but a variable of between three hundred and six hundred men.

But there is more evidence. Researchers studying marriage records in France discovered "breeding communities" (groups within which marriages were frequent, and between which they were rare) of about 1,100 in rural communities and, astonishingly, more like 900 in Paris. Furthermore, anthropologists have noted how aboriginal hunting communities in Australia form "dialectal tribes"—which are also breeding communities—of five hundred people who speak the same dialect. They sometimes grow to a thousand, but then they split and become two separate dialect-groups. And there is a fascinating instance in modern China. Mao Tse-tung's agricultural revolution was based on the concept of total mobility of labor within a commune of some seventy thousand people. Each man and woman would be told where to work each day, according to operational needs. The scheme proved impossible to organize. It was reconstituted with the village of a few hundred, and not the individual laborer, as the basic unit: each village was allocated its task for the day or the week. On that basis the plan worked and is still working. And five hundred is about the largest number you can reach with the unaided human voice in the open air.

All this, I am convinced, points to a human tribal size of about five hundred. It is still about the largest group within which everyone can know everyone else, where people will notice if you're not there, where every individual knows that the boss knows him. And that five hundred tribe—maximum a thousand—is still the largest unit the corporation can handle as a unit: if it tries to run two thousand as a single unit, trouble soon starts: disaffection, loss of identity, absence of that crucial sense of belonging to the corporation and being a part of it.

Can we really accept all this? Can we seriously look at our corporation as a clustering of animal communities with territorial jealousies, status displays, hunting bands, tribal assemblies and tribal rituals? There is not, and I suspect there will never be, objective scientific proof of this interpretation. It depends on you. Either you believe that modern civilized man has outgrown all his primitive tribal instincts and responds to all situations in the light of reason, experience and training, or you accept that underneath the civilized exterior the primitive hunting band is still alive and well and living in New York, or Dearborn or Seattle or Wilmington or Poughkeepsie. Speaking for myself, having once seen the modern corporation as a group of cooperative (or competitive) tribes of social hunting primates, I shall never be able to see it in any other way again.

HAROLD J. LEAVITT

Beyond the Analytic Manager: Part I

In recent years a certain disenchantment has arisen with the hard-nosed, number-oriented emphasis in managerial decision making. The promise of the computer-assisted management analyst, the operations researcher, and the long-range planner has not, in the eyes of many managers, come to fruition.

This essay argues that the disenchantment is healthy and partially correct; that there is something not so much wrong as limited and incomplete about the whole analytic style of thought that has pervaded Western management for the last hundred years; that the stereotypical modern management analyst (of whom the extreme caricature is the management-science-oriented M.B.A.) is one personification of those limitations; that the current wave of backlash against the analytic emphasis in management is understandable in the historical perspective of its development; and most important, that both in management and in other realms we may be moving into a period of search for alternatives and supplements to the analytical ways in which we have always thought that we were supposed to think.

This article, then, is intended to alert managers and perhaps to stimulate them to reconsider some implicit beliefs about what is or is not good managerial thinking, good problem solving, or a good mind. Part I examines the limits of the analytic method and Part II (see page 498) looks at alternatives, ranging from Zen to executive sabbaticals.

Source: © 1975 by the Regents of the University of California. Reprinted from *California Management Review*, Vol. 17, No. 3, pp. 5–12, by permission of the Regents.

PART I. A CRITIQUE OF THE ANALYST'S ROLE IN MANAGEMENT

The Rise of the Rational Analyst

Beginning in the early fifties (along with the emergence of the computer), modern quantitative analytic approaches to management rapidly gained strength both in business schools and in business. One catalyst was the studies of business education conducted by the Ford (1959) and Carnegie (1959) foundations. Even earlier, analytic approaches had developed considerable strength in government by demonstrating their utility in military planning.

In business schools econometricians, computer scientists, and quantitative analysts led the revolution away from the prevailing styles—a much more wisdom-oriented, experience-based case approach, and the nonempirical logical analysis of classical organization theory. They led management education toward systematic, empirical, quantitative analysis. These new analytic members of business school faculties rapidly began to be numbered among the academic stars.

A distinction must be made here between "analytic thinking" and "analytic techniques." In management education we have tried to nurture analytic thinking by developing and teaching analytic techniques. Sometimes all we have succeeded in producing is substantively rather empty, though skilled number pushers. By analytic thinking I mean more than a set of specific techniques; I mean a predominant style of thinking that is difficult to characterize completely but includes a preference for the language of numbers, a propensity to divide problems into components, to search for operational decision rules, and to search also for convergence—that is, for *an* answer. I shall not defend this rather loose definition further, but rather point out that a variety of psychologists and others have wrestled with what appears to be the same issue, setting up such dichotomies as tough- versus tender-minded, convergent versus divergent,[1] vertical versus lateral,[2] and logical-analytic versus intuitive-synthetic thinking.[3] Perhaps Wertheimer's list of the characteristics of "logical-analytic thinking" will help. This type of thinking, he asserts, is characterized by emphasis on generalizations, conceptual hierarchies, formation of class concepts, formation of syllogisms, and comparison processes—as opposed to intuitive-synthetic emphases on association, acquiring connections, trial-and-error behavior, and responding to the frequency and recency of stimuli.

In recent years, the emphasis on analytic thinking has taken a great leap forward in management because of the invention of a number of new analytic tools—such as operations research and systems analysis—which significantly increase the power of such thinking as applied to complex managerial problems.

There is a real danger, of course, of setting up unidimensional analysts. The complex human being can be analytic in his thinking style, use contemporary analytic tools, *and also* think imaginatively, or laterally, or divergently. So where I speak of "analysts" or "analytic thinkers," the modifier "predominantly" should be included. And by predominantly, I do not only mean strongly or capably, I mean predominantly *relative* to the imaginative-intuitive side.

In real-world organizations—business and governmental—this emerging set of newly equipped analysts has played more supporting than starring roles. They have become staff men, option producers for kings and princes—while the kings and princes themselves continue to be recruited from other varied sources. Perhaps the most dramatic example of the rise of the influential analyst in government was Robert McNamara, of the Department of Defense, in the early sixties, but the presidents whom McNamara served were not themselves notably analytic types. The political process does not seem selectively to breed, support, and reward dominantly analytic skills, perhaps because politics remains so human. But in governmental staff and administrative roles, particularly in ordering the complex and disorderly, the well-equipped, quantitatively analytic mind is most highly valued.

In industrial organizations the propensity to value the analyst appears to have been the same as in government, but with variations. Although in industry, too, the most highly skilled analysts are not typically found in key line leadership roles, they sometimes do appear there. McNamara became president of Ford Motor Company. Indeed, the Thornton group that planned for the U.S. Air Corps during World War II bred more than one industrial leader. That such types should achieve key line leadership and decision roles more frequently in industry than in government is understandable. In industry the process by which people are selected for those roles is much more restricted, more directly based on assessments made by a small number of members of the managerial club than in the political sphere. One does not have to appeal to a broad and heterogeneous set of constituencies to become a top manager in industry—not yet. Moreover, the model of what constitutes a good mind seems to be more uniformly shared, much more consensual, among those few who select others for positions of power in large industrial organizations than among members of society at large, or correspondingly, among members of Congress.

Perhaps a primary reason for the great but secondary influence of the analyst in organizations is the existence of a wide and long-standing (although implicit) consensus among educated and powerful men that analytic thinking is good thinking, even if they don't do it very well themselves. That, after all, is what most of our educations have taught us to believe. Indeed, analysis is what education has been mostly about.

Managers have valued such analytic thinking in themselves and others for a long time. One thing that seems new is the computer-assisted emergence of *context-free* analytic virtuosity as something to be valued in itself, largely independent of experience, wisdom, or deep knowledge about specific problems. Over the last decade the promise of great analytic skill has earned high starting salaries for M.B.A.'s and awe (along with hostility) from less skilled old-timers. What is relatively new is the emergence of rather large numbers of young managers who believe (and whose bosses believe) that they can successfully tackle any problem, anywhere, because they are equipped with modern analytic tools and skills. But as most managers have discovered, the hotshot young analyst does not always live up to his billing.

Some Social Problems Generated by the Rise of the Analyst in Organizations

Viewed socially and interpersonally, the successful rise of the skilled analyst has been accompanied by some rising dangers. Since the society surrounding the analyst has been generally supportive, granting high status to analytic thinking, it is easy for him to appear (and to feel) arrogantly superior to less effective or nonusers; it is easy for him to use his skills to win points in managerial games, to achieve power for himself and to criticize others. In face-to-face settings the skillful analyst can often outpoint less systematic opponents. He can do this because he is often right, but also, unfortunately, because the generally accepted rules of the game (as they have evolved in Western society) are precisely the rules that favor his kind of gaming.

"The Method"—the analytic method—is particularly exploitable in this last regard. It is easy to use cruelly, to put down others in person or in memoranda. There are few defenses, within the circles of organizational power, against an attack that says: "You don't have the facts, and I do," or "I've caught you in a logical inconsistency," or "All you're expressing is unsupported hunches and intuitions." At the risk of stereotyping, one of Halberstam's descriptions of Robert McNamara seems illustrative here:

> If the body was tense and driven, the mind was mathematical, analytical, bringing order and reason out of chaos. Always reason. And reason supported by facts, by statistics—he could prove his rationality with facts, intimidate others. He was marvelous with charts and statistics. Once,

sitting at CINCPAC for eight hours watching hundreds and hundreds of slides flashed across the screen showing what was in the pipe line to Vietnam and what was already there, he finally said, after seven hours, "Stop the projector. This slide, number 869, contradicts slide 11." Slide 11 was flashed back and he was right, they did contradict each other. Everyone was impressed, and many a little frightened. No wonder his reputation grew; others were in awe . . . [4]

Even now, if one were advising a bright young person about how to get ahead in business (or government or academia), I propose, reluctantly, that the following is sound: "Learn to use your analytic tools not only as instruments of truth but as instruments of power. See others as opponents, and demand of them 'What's the hard evidence?' Be tough-minded; never tender-minded. Emphasize method, not content." And these qualities, more than imagination or empathy, should lead you not only to excellence but also to high repute. Of course one must be good at using The Method to use it successfully for either purpose, truth or power. A second-rate analyst can be a sadly frustrated figure, and an even easier target for first-rate ones than are humanists or artists.

The implication of that advice sounds strongly antianalytic, but that is far from my full intent. For the analytic, the empirical, the systematic mind has long since proved itself a productive and effective mind in moving us from guess to knowledge, from uncertainty to control, from inefficient small organizations to efficient large ones. The gamey, power-oriented uses of The Method are mostly an unintended by-product. We must not throw out the discipline with its more troublesome disciples.

Thus, I will argue that the refereed academic journal (which many of my social scientific friends see as an archaic relic) is a good product of The Method, a good device for preventing charlatanism, for setting a piece of work up against an appropriate jury, and thus for moving us all toward higher truth. Some associated costs may be a certain amount of sterility and undue concern with method over substance and with purity over importance. But perhaps these are costs that must be borne, for the alternative would seem to be the unrefereed journal, with all its implications for declining standards and for other less savory forms of trying to get ahead.

How, after all, is one to distinguish the charlatan or the incompetent from the competent worker, if not by specifying, albeit implicitly, certain methods of thought that are within the rules and others that are not? One can tell an incompetent or a quack because his peers not only feel but can demonstrate that he has done an analytically inadequate job. They can "prove" its inadequacy if it violates the widely shared analytic norms of the profession; that is, if it is internally inconsistent, cannot be replicated, or is otherwise methodologically weak. By that screening process we have surely, though inadvertently, screened out a few oddball geniuses, some of whom were perhaps seeking alternatives to the analytic method. But these cases are not identifiable if we play within the existing rules. And most of us have assumed, until now at least, that their loss has been worth the price, especially since the most outspoken supporters of such oddballs are usually thought to be oddballs themselves.

There are other serious complaints about the hard-headed analyst in management. One is that he is "empty," which sometimes means that he is amoral and sometimes that his understanding is shallow. Some critics are disillusioned with the stereotype of the new M.B.A. for those reasons, and perhaps because he behaves the way many physical scientists used to behave, treating his professional skills as though they were socially neutral, and thus failing to accept responsibility for his recommendations; or because he seems shallow, lacking in wisdom and savvy, believing that method *is* substance, naively ready to attack any problem, anywhere, because he is armed with The Method.

Some of these criticisms seem to me to have a certain basis in fact, although they also reflect the distortions of prejudice. I suspect the valid portion results more from the way the analytic method has been taught than from any more basic amorality or shallowness. The fault is in the way we socialize the neophyte, inadvertently teaching (along with analysis itself) a quasi-religious faith in The Method, both for what problems it can solve and where it will get him in the hierarchial power struggle. For though The Method is itself coldly objective, its teachers (like the teachers in any other field) cannot avoid (or at least have not yet avoided) teaching its practitioners a strong emotional commitment along with it.

Education is, after all, a social and emotional as well as an analytic process. We not only learn our trade, we learn to love it. We learn to feel affinity for other users and to value membership in the club of users. We learn to be true believers in the same way that artists and priests and Eastern businessmen are socialized into their respective cultural communities.

In the case of analysis, the socialization process is probably helped along by the fact that its educational milieu (and the managerial one later) is very crowded. Students have to learn how to allocate their time, to minimize their costs, to be systematic in order to survive. They have five courses, four term papers, and three midterms to prepare

by next Thursday at 9 A.M., all of which provide secondary rein-
forcement for internalizing the analytic over other models. The analytic
model is self-reinforcing because it immediately helps its users to solve
on-site educational problems.

Moreover, a clever student can *see* The Method work. He can see
growth in his own capacity not only to solve problems he couldn't
solve before, but also in his capacity to outrun less well-trained competitors. The more The Method works, and the greater the feeling of membership in the users group, the more will alternative methods atrophy
and even be denigrated.

Which brings us to a familiar double bind. One of the analyst's rules
of thumb, *it is useful if it is measurable,* has broader implications.
Not only does the rule imply that the unmeasurable is not useful, but
also that if something is unmeasurable, one can't have useful ways
of thinking about it. So one must either ignore it or recast it into a
form in which one can think he is measuring it. Zealots of The Method
(like zealots in any field) are therefore more likely to reject inputs
from other less measurable worlds or to convert them into simply
measurable, but incomplete forms. Don't talk of hunches and gut feelings—not until you can index them.

A further danger emerges, as well. The analytic rules are the pervasive, generally agreed upon rules of the game; society accepts them.
So in the crunch, and over the long pull, the measured will surely
gain approval over the unmeasured. Even if one's gut feelings are right,
they are not serious competition in the power struggle. Knowledge or
conjecture not derived from The Method can easily be pigeonholed
as non-knowledge.

And nonusers—women, stereotypically, or artists and old-fashioned
scholars—can be easily pigeonholed as second-class thinkers, especially
by the "old boy" network, where analysts talk to one another or to the
appreciative power elite. Of course this in-group-out-group phenomenon is not limited to analysts. There are counterparts among artists
and "soft" social scientists that only serve to exacerbate the problem
of communication across intellectual cultures. But the power of these
other in-groups is more limited because, societally, they are out-groups.

Second-order Power, Implementation, and the Emotional Problems of the Analyst

One reason for some of the current concern about the limits of
analysis in management is that its major contribution to problem solving has been primarily in ordering alternatives. But if one thinks (as
many people have) of the broader problem-solving process as tripartite,

including *problem finding* and *solution implementing,* as well as the usual notion of *problem solving* (defining, and ordering alternatives), some of these issues may become clearer. The Method says a lot about how to solve a given problem, but not too much about the other two parts of the process. It says little about how to look for the problems that ought to be solved or how to implement choices.

At the extreme, on the implementation side, true believers in The Method seem almost to assume that the world will behave as rationally as the analyst thinks he does. Thus, given a set of options, the relevant segments of society will implement the best one. But of course the world doesn't behave that way. Even rational analysts know that the world out there, where implementation must take place, is largely peopled by nonanalysts—generals, salesmen, and politicians. And almost always these are the people who have to accept and run with the ball. But analytic training has not been much concerned with teaching skills for dealing with irrationality. So far-out analysts, at least, when they encounter trouble on the implementation end, are likely first to fall back on their best skill, analysis, and to treat implementation as a problem in rational communication—and fail. And then they will try either to be more rationally persuasive or to fall back to a more primitive alternative, power.

Both the training and the type of person predisposed toward analysis probably unwittingly exacerbate weakness on the implementation side. Our training tends not only to teach analysis but simultaneously to "unteach" emotionality. Yet implementation is a heavily emotional process. To worry about selling, persuading, and urging others to do what is obviously right is almost a violation of the analyst's implicit ethics. It is easier to denigrate and attack impulsiveness and emotionalism than to use one's own emotionality as a tool. It is very hard for a person trained to deny his or her own emotionality to appeal to spiritual standards, to lead the troops with trumpets blaring and flags waving, or even to cajole or backscratch. I suspect that the one set of emotional tools for implementation that may be tolerable to the stereotypical analyst is the power tools. The way to get irrational people to do what is so patently right is to club them into it. Clearly one role for the behavioral scientist in management has been to try to pick up this slack on the implementation side—with even more mixed results. But more of that later.

A related set of skills also seems important in the *problem-finding* process.[5] Questions such as "Is this a crisis?" or "What do we truly want to do?" are not typically emphasized in analytic seminaries. They are questions with strong imaginative, emotive, and value overtones. The analyst is happiest when the problem is a given; for instance, "We have a goal. Work out several alternative ways to achieve it." Then he can take off and do his analytic magic. In a similar vein, a colleague of mine has suggested that analytic training may produce better decomposers than designers.

But if analysts have concentrated on problem solving and behavioral types on implementing, who has been worrying about *problem finding?* Educationally speaking, the answer may be that no one has. (But that is what Part II of this article will be about.)

There is a third and perhaps even more serious emotional problem for the analyst. It lies in his relationship with those he serves. The dilemma of advising kings and still keeping one's head is not a new one and not limited to analytic-type advisors. But the advisor-advisee relationship is probably especially difficult for the analytic advisor serving a nonanalytic master. Even though the master may stand in awe of the analyst's skills, at least two things can go wrong: first, if the master does not himself understand those skills, he is likely to be unsympathetic about wrong answers or weak ones (though the analyst may know that the "wrong" part lay in implementation or in some other phase of the process, a phase for which he does not feel responsible). But the second and more serious psychological problem must lie within the analyst himself. How can a rational analyst feel unambiguously loyal and committed to a nonanalytic, politically expedient, perhaps emotionally intuitive master? Although the master may be impressed by him, how can he fail at some deep level to feel distant from or even contemptuous of the master?

The analyst's quest for survival and resolution in such a relationship will surely lead him once again to use his most powerful weapon, his analytic skill. If he can be clear and organized and right, perhaps he will survive by outclassing competitors; or perhaps he will also be driven to use those skills to block off competitors before they can get to the master. But can his analytic skill help him resolve the emotional dilemma of loyalty versus commitment?

Some Forces Toward Reconsideration of the Role of the Managerial Analyst

I have proposed that the great second-order power of the modern analyst seems due for reconsideration, and there is a danger that much of the reconsideration will be vengeful. Some of it will come from peer levels—a revolt not of the slaves, but of the bypassed. Many middle-level organization members have been hurt, ignominiously cut up, often publicly defeated by those whom they perceive to be the analysts of their organizations. The great masses of students and blacks and women may have triggered the revolt by setting off sharp social explosions, but those explosions have enabled smouldering others closer in to join the melee. It is in the higher ranks that the sharpest daggers are being unsheathed. From my clinical observations, it is the nonanalysts in management, perceiving themselves to have been wounded by the arrogant analysts, who are now on the attack.

But to return to the broader social explosions themselves: although the student revolt of the 1960s looked then like a revolt against the draft and Vietnam and the military-industrial complex, it can now sensibly be partially (by no means wholly) reinterpreted as a vague and groping search for alternatives to analytic thought. Gurus, touchy-feely encounter groups, drugs, astrology, attacks on the depersonalization of the university all can be partially regarded as searchings for other ways of thinking, of finding meaning, of identifying and solving the *big* problems. The students, one will recall, seemed especially hostile to the more analytic disciplines. The reasons they offered were that those disciplines, particularly the technological ones, were too materialistic, too tied in to the military-industrial complex. But such reasons (offered both by students and by the establishment) are themselves indicative of entrapment in the rules of The Method. One had to give hard-nosed reasons for what he was doing. One had to have clear objectives, clear purposes; perhaps less clear reasons lay underneath— ill-defined, undirected, unmeasured yearnings for new rules, indeed for a new ball game.

It is also possible partially to reinterpret the blacks' rebellion as a rebellion against the preeminence of analytic thought. Persons less educated, in formal terms, are also typically less skilled in analysis; it is in school, after all, that most analytic techniques are learned. Some black demands can be read as insistence that white society change its evaluation rules, that it upgrade *soul*. One example is the demand for a redefinition of the concept of intelligence, a concept traditionally defined largely in analytic terms.

It also seems a fair bet that the women's movement will soon begin to include a stronger cognitive emphasis. Until now women, like blacks earlier, have specified their goals mostly in terms of parity with men in a world of men's rules. They have argued that they can think as well as men, that they are capable of occupying the powerful and decision-making roles that have been denied them. Women also have tended to reject as a denigrating stereotype (which it has been) the "irrational" impulsiveness and intuitiveness ascribed to them. But like blacks, women may soon become "beautiful." Those irrational styles of thought may turn into mines of new possibilities for organizations. It is the male who may be seeking to add intuitiveness to his own repertoire rather than trying to train the female into the tough and orderly male way.

Not all of the disillusionment with the "empty analysts" emanates from those displaced by them in the power hierarchy or from broader, less direct social changes. Certainly books like Halberstam's *The Best and the Brightest* both reflect and generate disillusion with the analyst in public policy roles, particularly in relation to Vietnam.[6]

In industrial management there are also clear signs of reaction, particularly against the stereotypical new M.B.A., a product of the relatively new analytic business school. The analytic revolution in business education during the fifties was unequivocally successful if one measures success analytically; by measuring, for example, the change in status of the business school on the campus, the salaries commanded by new M.B.A.'s, the test scores of M.B.A. candidates as compared with medical or engineering students, or the spread of the American business school model to other countries. But there have always been groups who resented what they perceived as the arrogance, the aggressiveness, and even the naivete of this new-model M.B.A., and in recent years they have had a chance to counter-attack. During the recession of the late sixties there was almost as much crowing among non-M.B.A. businessmen about the difficulties M.B.A.'s were supposedly having in finding and keeping jobs (though in fact they were not having much trouble) as there was among European businessmen about the decline of American dominance.

It may be worth noting that these new reactions are arising mostly from the periphery of the in-group itself. Out-group reactions—from artists and humanists—have been around longer but have had relatively little impact on those in power.

We must remember, too, that the hard-nosed analysts have not been influential in industry or government for very long, so they are not quite solidly rooted. The predecessors of the analytic M.B.A. were representatives of still another alternative model. Roosevelt's, Truman's, and even Eisenhower's brain trusters tended to be the elders of the tribes, the Baruchs, the Cohens, the Lovetts.[7] They tended to be more wise, creative, and experienced than analytically tooled up.

Given their short history it is not surprising that the power of many technique-oriented analysts is rather tenuous. If one were to ask a typical company president, "How much have the computer, systems analysis, and model building influenced the way you do your job?" he would probably deny much influence.

Of course the president would probably be kidding himself if he were to argue that the analytic revolution has had little effect on his behavior. Let him look to the sources of the options he considers now and those he used to consider. This year much of what he is deciding has been laid before him by young analysts, not by old wise men. Even if the sages are still around to help, the young staff workers provide the map for the elders to ponder, and thereby constrain the elders' decisions.

In industry much of the new criticism of the analysts centers on their insensitivity to shades of gray, on what they have missed—the same sociopolitical elements that government analysts seem to have missed in relation to Vietnam. They didn't forecast changes in societal values, nor in worker attitudes, nor the student, the black, and the women's revolts, nor Ralph Nader and the consumer movement. Their intelligence about the environment was weak, in part because it stuck to the measurable, the countable; it missed less easily quantified moods, attitudes, and feelings. It saw what a stereotypical man might see, not what a stereotypical woman might see. Of course, nonanalysts did a lousy job, too, but perhaps the world expected less from them. Inside the organization, the analysts have been accused of setting up their own version of problems and solving those, rather than the problems that were really there.

And even if the ephemeral social and emotional issues had been sensed, analytic tools (at least as they existed then) were not very useful for doing much about them. One may believe in racial equality, but no analytic planner would have tried to bring it about by using Martin Luther King's techniques, let alone Eldridge Cleaver's.

Some analysts have argued that such weaknesses are transient, indicative only of the relatively new state of analytic techniques. More and better techniques can be developed for measuring moods and itches and adding those variables into our models. Perhaps if we had had a system of social indicators in the sixties it might have provided hard data that could have improved predictiveness. So one obvious correction for weaknesses in existing analytic methods is to strengthen The Method, to find new ways of measuring the heretofore unmeasurable. After all, tools need to be refined. A reasonable man can argue, rationally, that we must push further along the same path, especially since no very good alternatives appear to have been put forward.

That is one way to go. But another may be to explore and develop—for managerial purposes—some much neglected supplements and alternatives to analysis. Part II of this article is about this latter issue, the search for alternatives and supplements to analytic methods.

The author expresses his thanks to Gene Webb, Bill Ouchi, Fran Gordon, Lee Bach, and Mason Haire for their criticisms and suggestions.

NOTES

1. J. P. Guilford and R. R. Merrifield, *The Structure of Intellect Model: Its Uses and Implications* (Los Angeles: USC Press, 1960).
2. E. deBono, *Lateral Thinking: Creativity Step by Step* (New York: Harper & Row, 1970).
3. M. Wertheimer, *Productive Thinking* (New York: Harper & Row, 1959).
4. D. Halberstam, *The Best and the Brightest* (New York: Random House, 1969), p. 17.
5. W. F. Pounds, "The Process of Problem Finding," *Industrial Management Review* (Fall 1969).
6. Halberstam, op. cit.
7. T. E. Cronin and S. D. Greenberg, eds., *The Presidential Advisory System* (New York: Harper & Row, 1969).

DON HELLRIEGEL AND
JOHN W. SLOCUM, JR.

Managerial
Problem-solving Styles

What does your ideal organization look like? How do you go about solving problems? Is there really only one way to solve problems? Can your problem-solving style interact with different situational factors to increase or decrease the probability of effective decisions? If so, can you learn to modify your problem-solving style to fit certain basic situational requirements?

This article will explore different managerial problem-solving styles. Either consciously or subconsciously, managers are able to exercise somewhat different styles to cope with different situational requirements and personal needs, although they often have a natural tendency to use one problem-solving style more than the others. Personality may have a strong influence on the use of particular problem-solving styles, but differences in individual styles should not be synonymous with differences in personality. We do not attempt to discuss the numerous perspectives or conflicting positions existing within the field of personality theory. For our purposes, personality is defined as how a person affects others, how he understands and views himself, and his pattern of inner and outer measurable traits.

Our major objectives are the following: to present and explain a model for differentiating problem-solving styles of managers; to develop an understanding of some contingencies under which certain

Source: *Business Horizons*, December, 1975, pp. 29–37. Copyright © 1975 by The Foundation for the School of Business at Indiana University. Reprinted by permission.

problem-solving styles are likely to be more effective for managerial and organizational performance; to develop the ability to diagnose and recognize one's own and other's problem-solving styles; and to increase empathy and understanding of individual differences.

PERSONALITY THEORY

The theoretical and empirical basis for our discussion of managerial problem-solving styles was developed by Carl Jung.[1] We draw primarily upon this work for the orientation of personality, including extroversion or introversion, and the four basic psychological functions—thinking, feeling, sensing and intuiting. Before discussing some specific characteristics of Jung's personality theory, it should be useful to mention a few of his major themes.

First, Jung maintained that the individual's behavior is influenced by his past as well as by his goals and aspirations for the future. The individual is not simply a slave to the past, but can also be proactive in selecting goals and influencing his own destiny. Second, Jung's personality theory assumes an optimistic view of the individual's potential for growth and change, stating that constant creative development is possible. Third, Jung suggests an open systems view of personality. Personality consists of a number of differentiated but interacting subsystems. These subsystems can be receptive to inputs and exchanges between each other. Also, the personality as a whole, or one of its subsystems, can change as a result of inputs and interactions with the external environment, particularly through influences from other individuals. The subsystems within Jung's personality theory that we will consider include the ego, personal unconscious, basic attitudes (extroversion-introversion) and the psychological functions (thinking, feeling, sensing and intuiting).

The ego refers to the conscious mind. It consists of feelings, thoughts, perceptions and memories we are aware of and can articulate to others. The personal unconscious includes experiences and wishes which have been repressed (suppressed below the level of consciousness); feelings and thoughts that lie below conscious awareness but have never gone through the process of repression; and feelings and thoughts that have not yet reached consciousness, but which are the basis for certain forms of future consciousness such as creativity. The personal unconscious is often first expressed in the form of dreams and fantasies, and can change its content in coordination with the conscious mind.

The personal unconscious and conscious are often in a compensatory relationship to one another. Compensation is a key element in Jung's personality principles, and consists of the theory that for the normal personality, one subsystem may compensate for another subsystem. A period of intense, extroverted behavior may be followed by a period of introverted behavior. A manager who is characterized by the psychological functions of thinking and feeling in the conscious mind may emphasize the intuitive and sensation functions in the unconscious mind. Thus, contrasting types equalize, preventing the personality from becoming neurotically unbalanced.[2]

BASIC ATTITUDE-TYPES

According to Jungian theory, the two orientations of the personality are extroversion and introversion. Although these are opposing orientations, they are both present in our personality. One of them is usually dominant and exists in the conscious mind, and the other is subordinate and exists in the unconscious. The introvert attitude is "normally characterized by a hesitant, reflective, retiring nature that keeps to itself, shrinks from objects, is always slightly on the defensive and prefers to hide behind mistrustful scrutiny." The extrovert is "normally characterized by an outgoing, candid, and accommodating nature that adapts itself easily to a given situation, quickly forms attachments, and, setting aside any possible misgivings, will often venture forth with careless confidence into unknown situations."[3]

The introverted manager needs quiet for concentration, must work without interruptions, has problems communicating with co-workers and usually works best alone. Extroverts "like variety and action, are impatient with long, slow jobs, usually communicate well, like to have people around, and are good at greeting people."[4] Most of us can probably think of individuals that characterize the extremes of introversion and extroversion. However, most individuals vary by the degree to which they are extroverted, introverted or relatively balanced between the extremes.

The managerial occupation seems to be disproportionately represented by extroverts. Some research even suggests that extroversion is important to managerial success. Since the manager's role often involves identifying and solving problems with and through other individuals, a certain degree of extroversion is likely to be functional. However, an extreme extrovert can literally sacrifice himself to external conditions and demands. The manager who becomes totally immersed in his job at the cost of all other concerns is one example of this. His limitation is one of getting "sucked" into external objects or demands and completely losing himself in them.

At the other extreme is the introvert, who tends to be more concerned with personal factors than with external factors. As a consequence, the introvert may choose courses of action that do not readily fit the external situation. Jung emphasized that when external understanding is overvalued, the subjective or personal factor is repressed, thus causing a denial of self. Perception and cognition (in other words, knowledge and understanding) are not simply externally determined, but are also subjectively determined and conditioned. The world exists not merely in itself, but also as it appears to us.

PSYCHOLOGICAL FUNCTIONS

Although extroversion and introversion can be directly related to differences in managerial problem-solving styles, they can operate indirectly as well through the four psychological functions. We will first consider the basic relationships between these four functions. The thinking and feeling functions represent the two opposite types which managers may prefer for making decisions. As with introversion-extroversion, the feeling-thinking functions are paired opposites which should be thought of as ranging in intensity along a continuum, with feeling at one extreme and thinking at the other. These extremes of individual decision-making orientations influence evaluations and judgments of external facts and the fact world.

The psychological functions of sensation and intuition are also paired opposites, and may be thought of as ranging in intensity along a continuum. Sensation and intuition represent the extreme orientations to perceptions which may be preferred by managers. As used here, perception refers to the ways by which we become aware of people, things and situations.

Only one of the four functions is likely to dominate in each individual. But the dominant function is normally supported by one of the functions from the other set of paired opposites. For example, thinking may be backed by sensation, or sensation may be supported by thinking. These two combinations are regarded as most characteristic of modern man in Western industrialized societies. As a consequence, feeling and intuition are functions which are apparently disregarded, undeveloped or repressed. We will first consider each of the four psychological functions as a dominant type and then consider the two perceptual orientations (sensation and intuition) in combination with the two decision-making orientations (thinking and feeling).

Feeling-Thinking Orientations

Feeling types are "... aware of other people and their feelings, like harmony, need occasional praise, dislike telling people unpleasant things, tend to be sympathetic, and relate well to most people."[5] They are inclined to be comformists who accommodate themselves to others.

This type of manager tends to make decisions that will win the approval of his peers, subordinates and superiors, and tends to avoid problems that will result in disagreements. When avoidance or smoothing of differences is not possible, the feeling type is prone to change his position to one more acceptable to others. The establishment and maintenance of friendly relations may even supersede, and possibly interfere with, a concern for achievement, effectiveness and sound decision.[6] A feeling type manager may find it extremely difficult to suspend or discharge a subordinate for inadequate performance that is widely recognized by others, including the poor performer's own peers. In sum, the feeling type emphasizes affective and personal processes in decision making.

At the other extreme, thinking types are ". . . unemotional and uninterested in people's feelings, like analysis and putting things into logical order, are able to reprimand people or fire them when necessary, may seem hardhearted, and tend to relate well only to other thinking types."[7] This manager is constantly trying to make his activities and decisions dependent on intellectual processes, and has a tendency to fit problems and their solutions into standardized formulas. He applies external data and impersonal formulas to decisions, often forgetting to consider his own welfare. For the sake of some goal, this manager may neglect his health, finances, family or other interests. In terms of a problem-solving style, thinking managers are likely to

- make a plan and look for a method to solve the problem
- be extremely concerned with the approach they take to a problem
- define carefully the specific constraints in the problem
- proceed by increasingly refining their analysis
- search for additional information in a very orderly manner.[8]

There are many similarities between the thinking type, elements in the scientific method, and what our society often characterizes as rational problem solving. Our educational institutions have also been most concerned with developing the thinking type of function. The elements of this type are obviously crucial to any advanced industrialized society, but Jung's concern and ours is with the too frequent one-dimensional emphasis on thinking over feeling.

Sensation-Intuition Orientations

In terms of individual perceptual orientations, the sensation types of individuals ". . . dislike new problems unless there are standard ways to solve them, like an established routine, must usually work all the way through to reach a conclusion, show patience with routine details, and tend to be good at precise work."[9] The sensation type usually dislikes unstructured problems which contain considerable uncertainty that requires some degree of judgment. Sensation types are satisfied and are good performers as detail persons or bureaucrats. As used here, bureaucrat refers to a manager whose organizational life revolves primarily around the implementation and use of rules, regulations and standard operating procedures. Lower level managerial roles are often designed like this. Sensation types may adequately fill such roles because they have a minimal need to exercise discretion.

A sensation type manager may experience considerable anxiety over the uncertainties inherent in making decisions in gray areas because of his orientation to realism, external facts and concrete experiences. Along with his preference for concrete reality, this manager is not inclined toward personal reflection and introspection.

The routine and structured role enjoyed by a sensation type is likely to be performed poorly by an intuitive type. An intuitive type is one who ". . . likes solving new problems, dislikes doing the same things over and over again, jumps to conclusions, is impatient with routine details, and dislikes taking time for precision."[10] Whereas the sensation type tends to perceive the external environment in terms of details and parts, the intuitive type manager tends to perceive the whole or totality of the external environment. In terms of a problem-solving style, intuitives tend to:

- keep the total problem continuously in mind as the problem-solving process develops
- continuously redefine the problem as the process unfolds
- rely on hunches and unverbalized cues
- almost simultaneously consider a variety of alternatives and options
- jump around or back and forth in the elements or steps in the problem-solving process. After presumably defining a problem, identifying alternatives to the problem, and evaluating consequences of each alternative, the intuitive manager may suddenly jump back to a reassessment of whether the true problem has even been identified.
- very quickly consider and discard alternatives.[11]

Unlike the sensation type, the intuitive manager is suffocated by stable conditions and constantly seeks out and creates new possibilities. Intuitives are often found among business tycoons, politicians, speculators, entrepreneurs, stockbrokers and the like. The intuitive type can be extremely valuable to the economy and society as an initiator and promoter of new enterprises, services, concepts and innovations within organizations. If the intuitive is more people oriented than thing oriented, he may be exceptionally good at diagnosing the abilities and potentials of other individuals.

The discussion of problem-solving style to this point has focused on the four pure and dominant psychological functions for differentiating managers. As suggested earlier, each dominant type is likely to be supported by one of the other paired opposite types. Thus, the analysis for differentiating managerial problem-solving styles must be carried one step further. This will be accomplished by considering the four pure composite styles that might be derived when combining the two decision-making orientations with the two perceptual orientations.

COMPOSITE MODEL

Figure 1 presents a composite model of managerial problem-solving styles. This model is derived from the decision-making orientations of thinking and feeling and the perceptual orientations of sensation and intuition. Since we have already presented the nature of the four psychological functions when each is dominant in an extroverted individual, the following will briefly review the four pure combined types. Then, a profile of a specific manager who seems to approximate the attributes of the combined type is presented. Since the classification of these managers is based on secondary data, the reader should be more concerned with the behaviors described than whether the specific individuals are truly of a particular composite type.

SENSATION-FEELING TYPE

Managers in cell A of figure 1 rely primarily on sensation for purposes of perception and feeling for purposes of decision making. These managers are interested in facts that can be collected and verified directly by the senses. They approach these facts with personal and human concern because they are more interested in facts about people than about things. When asked to write a paragraph or two on their perception of the ideal organization, these individuals often describe an organization with a well-defined hierarchy and set of rules that exist for the benefit of members and society. The ideal organization would also satisfy member needs and enable them to communicate openly with one another.[12]

Stewart Rowlings Mott, multimillionaire liberal and philanthropist, seems to manifest a number of attributes of the sensation-feeling type.[13] Stewart Mott inherited his fortune from his father, who was one of

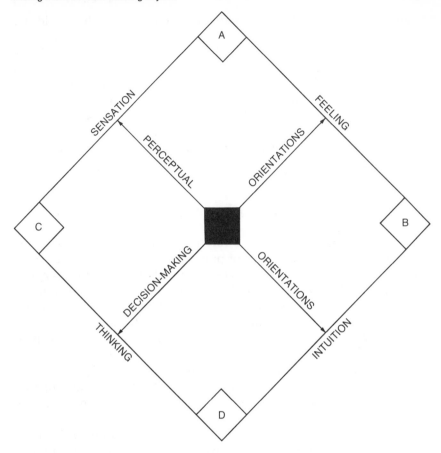

Figure 1. Composite model of managerial problem-solving styles

the biggest stockholders of General Motors. Through 1974, Mott's annual income ranged from $950,000 to $1.5 million. He greets individuals with a friendly and open smile and is quite willing to discuss any aspect of his life in an open and candid manner. His Park Avenue penthouse in New York serves as his office and home. Mott's main office is filled with piles of papers scattered around the room in an organized manner. He says, "I don't know how to throw things out—people, old newspapers or cigarette boxes." Details fascinate him. He works long hours, constantly reviewing reports and memoranda to keep informed on all the major and minor activities of the organizations he helps to support.

Mott contends that the two major problems facing the world are population control and arms control, and much of the $6 million he has donated between 1964 and 1974 has gone to charitable and political groups concerned with these two causes. Although Mott is an activist for people causes, he is not interested in taking the time for abstract reflection or considering global philosophies. Mott says, "I'm no ideologue. I feel uncomfortable when asked to explain in some cogent, complete, lucid way a blueprint of my political perceptions. I believe in chipping away at the defects in the present system without attempting to change the way it fundamentally works."

INTUITION-FEELING TYPE

Managers in cell B of figure 1 rely primarily on intuition for purposes of perception and feeling for purposes of decision making. These managers focus on new projects, new approaches, new truths, possible events and the like. They approach these possibilities in terms of meeting or serving the personal and social needs of people in general. Intuitive-feeling types avoid specifics, and focus instead on broad themes that revolve around the human purposes of organizations, such as serving mankind or the organization's clientele. The ideal organization for these individuals would be decentralized, with flexible and loosely defined lines of authority, and few required rules and standard operating procedures. Intuitive-feeling types emphasize long-term goals and desire organizations that are flexible and adaptive.

Our example of the intuitive-feeling type is Steve Carmichael, a project manager with nine subordinates who worked for a federally funded neighborhood youth corps. The following excerpt is from Studs Terkel's book, *Working*.[14] At the time of the interview, Steve was twenty-five years old, married and had one child.

Steve said, "They say I'm unrealistic. One of the fellas that works with me said, 'It's a dream to believe this program will take sixteen-, seventeen-year-old dropouts and make something of their lives.' This may well be true, but if I'm going to think that I can't believe my job has any worth. . . . We've got five or six young people who are burning to get into an automotive training program. Everybody says, 'It takes signatures, it takes time.' I follow up on these things because everybody else seems to forget there are people waiting. So I'll get that phone call, do some digging, find out nothing's happened, report that to my boss, and call back and make my apologies. . . . The most frustrating thing for me is to know that what I'm doing does not have a positive impact on others. I don't see this work as meaning anything. I now treat my job disdainfully. . . ."

SENSATION-THINKING TYPE

The sensation plus thinking type, in cell C of the accompanying figure, emphasizes external factual details and specifics of a problem. The facts of a problem are often analyzed through a logical step-by-step process of reasoning from cause to effect. This manager's problem-solving style tends to be practical and matter-of-fact. When asked to describe his ideal organization, this individual often describes an extreme form of bureaucracy, characterized by its extensive use of rules and regulations, a well-defined hierarchy, emphasis on high control, specificity and certainty, and its concern with realistic, limited and short-term goals. Although he is not an extreme sensation-thinking type, John deButts, chairman of the board of the American Telephone and Telegraph Company, revealed some attributes of this type in a published interview.[15] From this interview, he appears to focus on short-term problems, using standard operating procedures to solve problems, and keep the system under control.

DeButts stated that the quality of decisions depends on the quality of input, on how unvarnished information is after it has passed up the chain of command. "And I do get information of that quality," said DeButts. "The constant contacts I have with the key people at AT&T and the top people of our subsidiaries give me that quality. The organizational structure we have here helps provide quality information, too. . . . Every other week I meet with all the officers of AT&T; and practically every month I meet with all the presidents of our subsidiaries. In between I have many conversations with individuals in these groups. These contacts give me a lot of my input."

When asked if he ever finds himself unprepared for something, deButts responded, "Seldom is there a significant surprise. Naturally, details come up with which I am not familiar. That's why we have discussions. . . . The key, for me, has been to set up my broad objectives and then deal with the tasks within that framework. . . ."

Asked how he spends his time, deButts replied, "Usually, before I arrive at the office, I try to get into my mind the things I want to accomplish that day. I also jot down notes to myself. Today, for example, I've got several things I need to talk to people about. Then I'll try to take care of the mail. Incidentally, I read every letter that's addressed to me, either by name or by title. Nobody signs my name but me."

INTUITION-THINKING TYPE

The fourth pure composite type is shown in cell D. Intuitive-thinking managers tend to focus on possibilities, but approach them through impersonal analysis. Rather than dealing with the human element, they consider possibilities which are more often theoretical or technical. These managers are likely to enjoy positions which are loosely defined and require abstract skills, such as long-range planning, marketing research and searching for new goals. The ideal organization for these individuals would be impersonal and conceptual. Goals of the organization should be consistent with environmental needs (such as pure air, clear water and equal opportunity) and the needs of organizational members. However, these issues are considered in an abstract and impersonal frame of reference.

Our example of the intuitive-thinking type is Irving Shapiro, who at the age of fifty-seven, became chairman of the board and chief executive officer of E. I. duPont de Nemours and Company in 1974.[16] Others at duPont regard Shapiro as well qualified to deal with the wide ranging changes affecting duPont and all other multinational corporations. It is said that no one else in duPont's top management has his ability to analyze risks, comprehend complex issues of law and politics, and negotiate and devise solutions that the company—and those watching it—can accept. Shapiro holds strong opinions but listens carefully to others. He is cautious but willing, if the odds are right, to take big risks.

At the start of World War II, Shapiro went to work at the Office of Price Administration (OPA), where he helped set up rationing systems for sugar, automobiles and bicycles. After a while, bored with the OPA, Shapiro soon had a job in the criminal division of the Justice Department. Shapiro soon had a reputation as an outstanding writer of briefs, with the ability to grasp the critical issues in a case, clarify them, and argue in support of the government's position. The Justice Department at that time was divided into two factions, both of which considered Shapiro a member—he was smart enough to debate the intellectuals and practical enough to satisfy the activists. Soon after joining duPont in 1951, Shapiro became known as the "can do" lawyer. Instead of putting up legal roadblocks, he suggested ways by which duPont's management could accomplish their objectives legally. Shapiro's associates say that one of his greatest gifts is his ability to put complex and often emotional issues into simple, practical terms. One executive tells about a personnel problem he was unable to resolve. He phoned Shapiro at home one afternoon and was immediately invited over for a drink. The executive said he laid out three alternatives, and after talking for only fifteen minutes, the best alternative became obvious.

The validity and long-term utility of this model for considering differences in managerial problem-solving styles is still being developed. Previous research and our own applied research suggest it is worthy of recognition, discussion and consideration. The model presented is also consistent with a number of key assumptions and findings from other models of individual decision making. Among these assumptions and findings are:

- Individual differences in judgement reflect the characteristic styles in which individuals perceive, construe and organize their environment.
- These individual differences are reflected in differences in the weighting and combining of stimuli in the situation.
- Judgmental differences are themselves intervened by and functionally related to a wide variety of characteristics of individuals (which were not investigated in our model of problem-solving styles) such as intelligence and values.
- The dimensions of the stimuli in the environment as well as the individual need to be assessed.[17]

We have discussed four pure composite problem-solving styles, but do not mean to suggest that every manager can be characterized as one of the four pure types. A manager could exist any place along the grid shown in the figure. According to Jung, the developing individual tends to move toward a balance and integration of the four psychological functions. This balance would exist in the center of the figure. Since all individuals are so rich in variety and complex in nature, we need to be especially cautious of categorizing managers by inferring that they cannot adapt to situations that do not fit their preferred style. We hope this article has served to develop an empathy and understanding of differences between managers; help managers understand their characteristic style and how it might influence their actions and reactions to certain problems and provide a framework for possible forms of desired personal growth and development. No single composite style is inherently better than another. We have suggested that the requirements of certain organizational roles may be more natural to one style than another.

NOTES

1. Carl G. Jung, *Collected Works*, eds. Herbert Read, Michael Fordham and Gerhard Adler, vols. 7,8,9, Part I (Princeton, N.J.: Princeton University Press, 1953–).
2. Calvin S. Hall and Gardner Lindzey, *Theories of Personality* (New York: John Wiley, 1970), pp. 90-91.
3. Gerhard Wehr, *Portrait of Jung: An Illustrated Biography* (New York: Herder and Herder, 1971), pp. 64-65.
4. I. B. Myers and K. C. Briggs, *Myers-Briggs Type Indicator* (Princeton, N.J.: Educational Testing Service, 1962).

5. Myers and Briggs, *Type Indicator.*
6. R. E. Boyatzis, "The Need for Close Relationships and the Manager's Job," *Organizational Psychology: A Book of Readings*, eds. D. A. Kolb, I. M. Rubin and J. C. McIntyre (Englewood Cliffs, N.J.: Prentice-Hall, 1974), pp. 183-187.
7. Myers and Briggs, *Type Indicator.*
8. James L. McKenney and P. G. Keen, "How Managers' Minds Work," *Harvard Business Review* (May-June 1974), pp. 79-90.
9. Myers and Briggs, *Type Indicator.*
10. Myers and Briggs, *Type Indicator.*
11. McKenney and Keen, "How Managers' Minds Work."
12. Ralph H. Kilman and V. Taylor, "A Contingency Approach to Laboratory Learning: Psychological Types Versus Experiential Norms," *Human Relations* (December 1974), pp. 891-909.
    Ian Mitroff and Ralph H. Kilman, "On the Importance of Qualitative Analysis in Management Science: The Influence of Personality Variables on Organizational Decision-Making" (working paper, Graduate School of Business, University of Pittsburgh, 1974).
13. Irwin Ross, "The View from Stewart Mott's Penthouse," *Fortune* (March 1974), pp. 134-135.
14. Studs Terkel, *Working* (New York: Pantheon Books, 1974), pp. 341-343.
15. "An Interview: The Management Style of John deButts," *Harvard Business Review* (January-February 1974), pp. 34-42.
16. Peter Vanderwicken, "Irving Shapiro Takes Charge at duPont," *Fortune* (January 1974), 70-81.
17. Nancy Wiggins, "Individual Differences in Human Judgments: A Multivariate Approach," in *Human Judgment and Social Interactions*, eds. Leon Rappaport and David A. Summer (New York: Holt, Rinehart and Winston, 1973).
    R. N. Taylor and M. A. Dunnette, "Influence of Dogmatism, Risk-Taking Propensity, and Intelligence on Decision-Making Strategies for a Sample of Industrial Managers," *Journal of Applied Psychology* (August 1974), pp. 420-423.

ROSS A. WEBBER

Career Problems of Young Managers

Drawing on interviews with more than one hundred managers, discussions with several hundred more, and published literature, this article examines some of the common difficulties experienced by young specialists and managers and offers some advice on career management. Hopefully, no one is so unlucky as to confront them all, but knowledge forewarned is courage armed.

EARLY FRUSTRATION AND DISSATISFACTION

The early years of one's first permanent job can be difficult. The young college graduate's job expectations often exceed reality, eliciting feelings of underutilization that can result in departure.[1] The causes of this condition rest with the young person, organizational policy, and incompetent first supervisors.

Conflicting Expectations

Business school graduates often are trained through cases to think like managers and to solve top-level executive problems. If they enjoyed this perspective in college, they may expect real work to be similar and their actual authority to equal the synthetic authority in class. But this takes years to achieve, so they frequently experience difficulty in adapting to changed time horizons that accompany the transition from school to work. Many students have been accustomed to almost imme-

Source: © 1976 by the Regents of the University of California. Reprinted from *California Management Review*, Vol. 18, No. 4, pp. 19-33, by permission of the Regents.

diate gratification and to short time spans—this semester, next academic year, a few years to graduation. The passage of time and status changes are clearly signaled by changes in routine and frequent vacations.[2]

A permanent job is quite different. The time horizon is much longer, fewer events mark time passing, and it is a full year until a two-week vacation. Not surprisingly, some young employees attempt to perpetuate the school perspective by changing jobs frequently and taking off on unofficial vacations. However understandable the behavior, older managers perceive it as immature.

These older managers may also be at fault because they don't provide young specialists and managers with sufficient challenge. Large organizations tend to treat newly employed college graduates as all the same and to assign them to boring tasks that could be performed by people with less education. Management argues that young people's expectations are unrealistic and they must prove themselves before being assigned more important jobs.[3] But many young people detest being treated as "average" or as a member of a category like everyone else. They want to be considered unique, if not special, because their culture stresses the individual.[4] Corporate culture, however, emphasizes efficiency in handling large numbers of people identically until individuals have demonstrated their uniqueness. Paradoxically, management's attitudes and policies may promote the very "immature behavior" that is given as the reason for the policies in the first place. Obviously, patience and understanding are needed on both sides.

Before concluding that it is better to work for a small organization, one should realize that situations change. Beginning professional and managerial positions in small businesses are reported to be more challenging and satisfying than similar posts in large firms. Small companies can't afford to train young graduates on unproductive jobs, so they put them to work on important tasks immediately. Nonetheless, five to ten years into careers, the views reverse: middle managers in large organizations report their jobs as more challenging and rewarding than those in small firms, who mention frustration and pressure for conformity. In the large organizations, middle-level jobs apparently carry more autonomy and authority than do similar level positions in small firms where the top can dominate everything.[5]

Incompetent First Supervisor

A first boss plays a disproportionate role in a young person's career.[6] The impact of an incompetent first supervisor can be especially unfortunate because the early experience tends to be perpetuated. What operates is a kind of self-fulfilling prophecy. If a superior doesn't expect much of his young subordinates, he doesn't challenge them and many don't perform well.[7] Even worse, if the incompetent supervisor doesn't set high standards for himself, almost everyone's performance deteriorates.[8] The word spreads that other managers don't want people from the group; the young person can be stuck in a dead end.

Ambitious young specialists and managers want visibility and exposure—opportunity to show higher-level executives how well they can perform and to understand executive problems and objectives. A fearful intermediate supervisor, however, can block such opportunity by relaying all communications himself and not allowing his subordinates to see higher levels. Handing a report to your immediate boss with no opportunity to argue in its favor and never hearing what happens to it can be very disturbing (especially if you discover later that your name on the cover was replaced by your superior's).

Organizations should institute policies to ensure that young specialists and managers enjoy the opportunity to communicate with and be evaluated by several higher executives and not just by their immediate supervisors. And young managers should fight for the right to go along with reports.

Resignation may be the best answer to an untenable position under an incompetent supervisor, but short of this step, understanding the situation may allow an individual to set higher personal standards than the boss does. He or she may be able to perform better than others in a demoralized department—even only slightly better may bring the attention of other executives who are not blind to the difficulty of performing well in that setting. The organization, of course, would be better off if young graduates were assigned mainly to the best supervisors, and many firms do this.

INSENSITIVITY AND PASSIVITY

All human organizations are political. This is neither condemnation nor praise, merely fact. For an organization to be effective, its managers must engage in the politics by which power is directed to problems and solutions implemented. Unfortunately, many young managers are insensitive to or even resentful of the political aspects of organizations.[9] This hurts them personally because they are passive about their careers, and it hurts the organization because it hinders development of power coalitions necessary for effective results.

Insensitivity to Political Environment

Managers who climb hierarchies rapidly tend to be proteges of successful higher executives.[10] These sponsor-protege linkages move together because members come to respect and trust each other. They personalize organization life and make it more predictable. When a manager has a problem, he prefers to consult someone whom he knows, not just an anonymous occupant of a bureaucratic position. To be sure, the criteria for inclusion in the group are often arbitrary and undemocratic in devotion to old-school tie and proper religion, race, or sex, but they are important nonetheless.

The importance of political relationships to the organization is that they form the power coalitions necessary to make and implement decisions.[11] Very few organizations are autocratically ruled by one omnipotent person; even fewer are pure democracies where the majority dominates. Most require a skillful minority coalition able to lead the majority through competent argument and common action. Without strong coalitions, power remains fractionated, actions are divisive, and the organization drifts willy-nilly.

A common complaint about young business school graduates is that they overemphasize analytical tools and rational decision making to the detriment of human understanding.[12] In spite of their desire to be treated as unique individuals, some observers note, they treat others as objects to be manipulated. Thus, the new graduates apparently are more Machiavellian in their managerial attitudes and more willing to use coercion than are practicing managers.[13] As one corporation vice president puts it, "It takes us a couple of years to show our business school graduates that an organization is composed of people with whom they must develop personal relationships."

Personal Passivity

Insensitivity to political environment is frequently accompanied by personal passivity and inadequate probing of the world around the young manager.[14] Such a person fears what he may discover about himself or assumes that virtue guarantees reward, so that good intentions will ensure that people will think he is doing a fine job. One man's experience as committee chairman illustrates such a common career mishap. Dave Seymour was assistant administrative manager of a regional office of a large company. He reported to the regional administrative manager responsible for office operations. Shortly after Dave assumed the post, the regional vice president personally requested that he become chairman of a committee to find ways to improve office efficiency. The committee was composed of various junior managers whom the vice president appointed. Dave accepted the job with alacrity because he saw it as an opportunity to prove his managerial potential.

Unfortunately, two years passed and nothing happened except meetings and collection of hundreds of pages of data and recommendations.

None were implemented by district or regional managers. Dave hadn't known what to do: the vice president never inquired and Dave couldn't make up his mind to raise the issue with him. Dave had been flattered to be appointed chairman and figured it was an opportunity to distinguish himself. Months later he found that he had made no impact. Details differ, but the pattern is common.

Dave's first mistake was that he accepted the assignment without analyzing his political position and the attitudes toward change among the executives who would actually implement any improvements. Second, he did not clarify his personal power or the committee's authority. What were they to do? Issue orders directly to managers and try to persuade them to adopt the changes? Or just gather information in case anyone ever asked for it? The third mistake was that Dave did nothing to avoid his fate as time passed. He did not initiate action to modify the political environment or to better define his authority.

When accepting a delegated task, it is important that a subordinate try to clarify the nature of the delegation by asking certain questions.

- After I look into the problem, should I give you all the facts so that you can decide?

- Should I let you know the alternatives available with the advantages and disadvantages of each so you can decide which to select?

- Should I recommend a course of action for your approval?

- Should I select the alternative, let you know what I intend to do and wait for your approval?

- Should I take action, let you know what I did and keep you informed of results?

- Should I take action and communicate with you only if it is unsuccessful?

Dave did not ask these questions of his vice president. Worse, he didn't inform his superior that no changes were being made. No doubt this is one of the most difficult acts in management, but sometimes a subordinate must inform a superior that he (the subordinate) is powerless and that nothing will improve unless the superior acts. At times you must push your boss to make a decision.

It is often easier to drift with the times and hope things will work out for the best, but this is not a recipe for managerial success. The paradox is that the most promising young staff specialists may be the ones who find it easiest to drift. To be in demand is a mark of status and being busy gives a feeling of importance. Consequently, a good young person might allow himself to be dominated by other's desires, to be overcommitted to a narrow specialty, and to remain in a staff position too long. If you think of the organization as a cone, the staff tends to be on the outer surface, while line management is closer to the central power axis.[15] In his or her thirties, a young person may find himself making too much money to accept the pay of a lower line position, which is farther away from the top but has a more direct route to it. Young managers should take time to explore and probe the organizational environment and to understand people's attitudes, develop relationships, and clarify their own positions.

Ignorance of Real Evaluative Criteria

A central rule for managerial success is "please your boss." Unfortunately, what pleases him or her is not always clear so that insensitive and passive young managers don't know the real criteria by which performance is being evaluated. Business is often less structured and more ambiguous than the authoritarian stereotype that many young people bring with them. Of course, managers highly value good performance, as measured by profits, sales, productivity, and so on. Subordinates who occupy positions where results can be easily measured in these terms tend to report greater satisfaction and autonomy in their jobs than those in posts where performance cannot be evaluated quantitatively.[16] People in positions measured only by subjective evaluation tend to be less satisfied and to feel greater pressure for conformity in dress, thought, and action. In the absence of other criteria, these people may be measured by how closely they fit the superior's prejudices rather than by actual results.

Most people are biased by their own successes or failures in making judgments. We like others to be like ourselves, especially successful others because they verify our own correctness. Superiors tend to rate more highly those subordinates who are like them in appearance and managerial style.[17] Hence, hair length, speech habits, and clothes do affect how personnel are evaluated, with some superiors seeing mustaches and mod suits as signs of immaturity and radicalism while others perceive them as showing creativity and vitality.

The same is true for evaluation on the basis of managerial style. However, since the predominant style in the past has been authoritarian, many superiors more highly value subordinate managers who demonstrate authoritarian leadership. Even in the absence of corroborating performance data, authoritarian managers may be more highly rated than those who are participative or abdicative. One study indicated that a "permissive" manager whose division had good performance and much higher morale was rated as having no promotability, while a parallel authoritarian division manager with equal performance and lower morale was cited for excellent potential.[18]

A manager who desires to utilize a less directive style that is ill-suited to his superior's expectation is in a difficult position. If his boss is a hard-driving authoritarian manager, he may expect good subordinate managers to be similar to himself. By asking frequent questions and demanding reports, he makes it difficult for the subordinate to be anything but authoritarian.

A courageous, tough, and independent manager in the middle may serve as a buffer between his superior and his subordinates. By absorbing the pressure coming from above and not passing it on immediately to his people, he allows them enough autonomy to proceed collaboratively. Such leadership requires demonstrable success to survive.

Tension Between Older and Younger Managers

Tension between older and younger professionals and managers is very common. It may be exacerbated by individual personalities, but basically it stems from differences in life and career stages. A recently graduated specialist or manager understandably relies on what he or she knows best—academic knowledge. He or she is at least somewhat familiar with statistics, psychology, and economics, and these can be very valuable. Unfortunately, they can also hinder his working relationships with older managers.

Armed with an arsenal of analytical techniques, the young manager looks for problems to which they can be applied. But frequently the problems which the textbook solves are not the important ones. He may even talk to older personnel in the arcane vocabulary of "stochastic variables," "break-even points," and "self-actualizing opportunities." Such talk can be very threatening to an older person to whom it is unfamiliar. He may perceive the younger person as endeavoring to manipulate him.

In some cultures, older persons are automatically respected for age and assumed wisdom, but in the United States the young may respond to the older person's skepticism with veiled contempt. Because the older manager doesn't know the new techniques, the young specialist or manager erroneously infers that he is not as competent or important. But this can be a career-crippling mistake, because organizational contribution and influence have little to do with technical knowledge. An offended older executive can oppose the younger person's future advancement.

A young person should recognize that some older managers will see him or her as a threat (although the managers will deny it, even to themselves). The threat is not to position, but one of obsolescence and a reminder of human mortality.[19] Tension can arise even when the older person likes the younger. The young specialist should endeavor to show respect for the older, to frame his vocabulary appropriately, and to avoid condescension. As the young person comes to recognize the importance of political influence and intuitive judgment, he can develop the vertical coalitions helpful to both older and younger.

LOYALTY DILEMMAS

Loyalty is a popular but vague concept that is subject to both praise and scorn. There is little doubt, however, that most people in authority value subordinates' loyalty. But what is this quality? Some of the various unspoken views on loyalty that superiors expect of subordinates are: obey me; work hard; be successful whatever it takes; protect me and don't let me look bad; and tell me the truth. All of these concepts of loyalty are partially valid and contribute to organizational effectiveness. Unfortunately, all can also be distorted to the detriment of people and organization.

Loyalty As Obedience

The superior can equate loyalty with subordinates' doing what they are told. All managers have a right to expect general obedience, but excessive emphasis on it enshrines the "yes man" philosophy as organizational religion. It is understandable that a subordinate's willful disobedience would be construed as disloyalty, but equating loyalty and obedience assumes that authoritarian management is the only valid style while it ignores the possibility that loyalty may sometimes reside in not doing what the boss has ordered because disaster could follow.[20]

Loyalty As Effort

Young specialists and managers are rightly expected to work hard in the interest of the organization. Executives are skeptical of the intentions of young people who make a minimal commitment to their work. Yet when effort and hours worked are equated with loyalty, people will put in excessive hours without real effort or contribution. Consider the comments of some young managers in the home office of an insurance company:

> "The officers are the first here in the morning and the last to leave at night; they are always here Saturdays and many Sundays."
> "They set the pace and, at least implicitly, it is the pace we must accept and follow."

"If you want to get ahead this is the pattern you must accept. Contribution tends to be judged in terms of time spent in the office, not things accomplished."

"If you want to get ahead, you come in on Saturdays regardless of whether it is necessary or not. The cafeteria and offices are sometimes filled with people who just feel they can't afford not to come in on Saturday."

Thus, behavior can become a game to convince others that you are loyal even when it contributes nothing to organizational effectiveness.

Loyalty As Success

The superior can see loyalty as synonymous with reliability and successful performance whatever it takes (and don't bother him if it entails shady things he shouldn't know about). It is reasonable to expect honest effort, but this version of loyalty can be tough because it adds a moral criterion to judgment of competence. Thus, not all young managers who miss deadlines are disloyal. The task may simply be impossible within legal or ethical limits. A superior who judges all people and performance from a loyalty perspective will discourage honest communication and encourage illicit managerial practice.

Loyalty As Protection

The superior expects the subordinate to protect him and the organization from ridicule or adverse evaluation by others. Subordinates who only follow their superior's instructions to the exact letter *are* disloyal if they don't exercise common sense and fill obvious gaps. This version of loyalty has particular relevance where the superior is a generalist over specialist subordinates who know more than he does in their areas of expertise. In return for subordinate concern and protection, he implicitly promises to look out for their personal and political interests.

This loyalty concept sometimes includes an injunction to subordinates never to disagree with the superior in public when the boss's boss or outsiders are present. This makes sense, but it can become exaggerated when a sharp distinction is made between "us," to whom we owe loyalty, and "them," to whom we don't. The efforts of coalitions to conceal, contain, or cover up their mistakes reflect this view of loyalty. Violation through "leaks" and overly candid communication with outsiders is one of the most heinous organizational crimes because it threatens the security of the hierarchical system.[21] There is little that managers fear more than subordinates' trying to make them look bad in order to get their positions. Unfortunately, an insecure superior will sometimes attribute this motivation to a young manager when it really doesn't exist.

Loyalty As Honesty

This view of loyalty exults truth over harmony. The superior expects the subordinate to warn him of potential failure before the control system picks it up or others find out. This can be particularly hard on a young manager because it tells him to report his own mistakes. To do so is threatening because the bearer of bad tidings is sometimes confused with the tidings. The Turks have an old proverb that warns, "he who delivers bad news should have one foot in the stirrup." Most of us would prefer not to report impending failure in the hope that it will go away or that no news will be interpreted as good news. One of America's most dynamic companies fights this by pushing the dictum, "don't let us be surprised by unpleasant news." Not reporting failure before it produces adverse results is worse than the failure itself.

The Dilemma

The young manager's problem is that sometimes he doesn't know what version of loyalty is expected by the organization or superior. He may even discover that a boss entertains several simultaneously contradictory views: that he expects strict obedience, but will be angry if obedience leads to poor performance; or that he interprets mistakes as disloyalty but still expects advance warning of impending failure. Loyalty expectations may violate the young manager's personal values if there is no excuse for failure and the hierarchy must be protected at all costs. Under such unhappy circumstances, the role-conflict-resolution tactics possible include conformance to power or authority, selectively ignoring what he can get away with, attempting to modify the superior's expectations, or departure.

PERSONAL ANXIETY

With time, promotions, and increased rewards, job satisfaction improves for most managers. The daily task becomes more challenging, yet new concerns crop up for many young managers—anxiety about personal integrity, organizational commitment, and dependence on others.

Anxiety About Integrity and Commitment

People admire different qualities at different stages of life. High school students place high value on independence as they struggle to become adults; college students stress individuality as they endeavor to find their uniqueness; older executives admire decisiveness that would allow them to bear the burdens of high office more easily. Young middle managers especially admire conviction and integrity in the person who remains his own man but believes in what he or she is doing. As they are rewarded by the organization, many persons begin to question the fundamental value of their jobs.[22] As one young brand manager for a major food company put it, "I'm a success, I earn over $20,000 per year, and I get a big kick from my job and seeing the climbing sales chart, but sometimes I wonder if getting 'Colonel Zoom' cereal on every breakfast table is really that important!" (Especially since it is being attacked by nutritional experts as having little food value.)

This questioning can be difficult for a young manager to understand. After years of apprenticeship, he is reaping the rewards of effort—autonomy, discretionary authority, and opportunity to achieve. Job morale is high. But for some it is not enough, because questions nag. "Am I really selling out to the organization?" "Have I forgotten to ask the important question of what I'm contributing to society?" If he or she concludes that the answers are more affirmative than negative, the young manager is faced with a dilemma—what to do?

Open complaint about the organization's activities may cause others to view the complainer as disloyal, hindering present security and future promotability. Associates and superiors will subtly suggest to the displeased young manager that he keep quiet, work his way upward, and then change company policy if he desires to. This is not bad advice, but the young manager might find being an executive so satisfying that he forgets what it was that he wanted to change. He might alleviate his dissonance by changing his personal values to agree with the dominant view. This facilitates total commitment to the organization and promotes the certainty that most of us desire. Such a solution may work for the individual, but it may ultimately harm society.

No entirely satisfactory answer exists for this dilemma. If the organization's mission and policy are in violent disagreement with personal values, the best course is resignation and perhaps a new career.[23] But premature departure can also be a cop-out, a flight from difficult moral choices. If the decision is to stay, the young manager should strive to keep alive his values, to apply them to small matters which he controls, and to remember them when he has the power to affect policy.

Attitudes toward commitment are ambivalent. A sense of certainty about career is desired because it simplifies one's life and stills the restlessness about whether one is in the right place. Nonetheless, many young people also fear commitment because it means closing doors and giving up the pleasant illusion that they can still do anything they wish. Yet maturity means facing reality and deepening interest. Therefore, a central facet of all careers is balancing commitment to the organization with maintaining a sense of independence.[24] Pure rebellion which rejects all organizational values and norms can end only in departure; pure conformity which accepts everything means loss of self. Creative individualism accepts pivotal values and norms, but searches for ways to have individual impact.

The occasion for loss of integrity is often a person's first failure. After a history of success in school and work, a young manager with a weak sense of identity can be overwhelmed by destruction of his illusions that he cannot fail, that he is immune to career crisis, and that he enjoys widespread social support. The current generation of young people may be especially vulnerable in this area because they are the progeny of prosperity. Success has grown, unchecked by fear of economic deprivation.[25]

Anxiety About Dependence

One aspect of the struggle for maturity is to declare psychological independence of home and parental authority while identifying oneself as an individual. Dependence on others is difficult to handle shortly after successfully establishing one's independence. Thus, undergraduate students tend to dislike team projects in which their grades can be lowered by others' mistakes. Nonetheless, total independence is impossible in real organizations. Superiors are dependent on subordinates' performance, subordinates are dependent on their superior's judgment and effective representation, and middle managers are dependent in both directions.

All of this dependence can provoke anxiety. For example, many junior military officers have suffered from psychosomatic illness because they bear the responsibility for their unit's safety and performance when they don't have as much experience or technical knowledge as their senior enlisted personnel. They cannot solve their problems by denying their dependence, but these problems can be reduced by learning the technical details of subordinates' duties. In the long run, however, young supervisors must recognize interdependence and strive to facilitate subordinate performance while representing their interests upward.

Most young adults are aware of their fear of being dependent on others, but they usually are not conscious of anxiety about having others dependent on them.[26] As they acquire spouse, family, job status, and community position, they receive increasing demands to give financial, temporal, and emotional support to more and more people and organizations. This sense of others' dependency can be gratifying, but time and energy are limited. Independent and self-reliant managers are sometimes disturbed to discover that they feel dominated by the needs of people dependent on them. If and when the burden becomes too great, they must establish life priorities that balance demands of family, organization, and community in a way that may fully satisfy none, but allows relations to continue with all.[27]

ETHICAL DILEMMAS

Few young people begin their careers with the strategic intention of being unethical as a means to success. And few managers are unethical as a matter of policy. Yet the majority share a problem of determining what is ethical or unethical when faced with unexpected dilemmas.[28] Many people believe that ethical means "what my feelings tell me is right." Unfortunately, feelings are very subjective phenomena, so one person may think that misleading advertising is all right while another believes it is wrong.

Others argue that ethical means religious beliefs or the golden rule, law and common behavior, or what contributes to the most people. Clearly, no single view of ethics is always correct or incorrect. A manager should assess his decisions from a variety of useful perspectives.[29]

Ethics As Economic Self-interest

When a young manager in a high-technology firm was offered a position by a competitor, his employer sought a court injunction to prevent his moving. On the witness stand it was suggested that there was a matter of loyalty and ethics involved in leaving with the knowledge and expertise he had derived from his employment. The young man's response was, "Loyalty and ethics have their price; as far as I am concerned, my new employer is paying the price."[30]

It is easy to criticize this manager for his ethics and choice of language, but he is expressing faith in the free market system—that scarce resources such as he should flow to the buyer who can utilize them most and who is willing to pay the highest price. Ability to pay theoretically reflects market demand and social interest, so he could best serve society by changing employers for more money.[31] In addition, his position reflects the temporary nature of his demand. Like the athlete, his technical skills are subject to obsolescence and he owes it to himself to gain the most from them while they last. Under this ethic, his only responsibility to his present employer is to give him the opportunity to match the offer.

Not everyone shares this faith in the free market system, however, because ability to pay could reflect raw monopoly power and consumer wishes.[32] And even those who believe that the market should allocate resources in this way don't all agree that economic self-interest is a good criterion for ethical decisions at the individual level. Most people see no connection between "ethical" and "economic" or "self-interest."

Ethics As Law

When asked about kids' buying his pornographic magazines, a publisher and purveyor of "adult" material responded, "What's the matter, don't you like to look at pictures of naked pretty girls and boys? I keep within the law. My magazines aren't meant for kids, but I can't keep them from buying them. That's the government's problem."

For this businessman, law is the criterion for decision making. If society thinks what he is doing is unethical, it is government's responsibility to legislate. In the absence of prohibition, he does what is allowed. Certainly managers bear responsibility as citizens to obey the law.[33] The young marketing managers in the electrical equipment industry who secretly met to fix prices and allocate markets violated the law, and in their case the law was relatively clear.[34]

Sometimes the law is not clear, though. Even the managers in the electrical conspiracy argued that the law was vague because it required competition and prohibited collusion, yet they believed that cessation of "cooperation" would lead to dominance by the giant firms and decreased competition.

Most people feel that adherence to law is a necessary but insufficient basis for ethics. Behaving legally so you won't be punished is merely being prudent, not ethical. Law imposes demands from outside, while ethics should come from inside.[35] Besides, if law constituted the only behavior limits, government and law enforcement would swell to overwhelming proportions. Big Brother would be everywhere and freedom to do either wrong or right would disappear.

Ethics As Religion

If government law is not sufficient, what about higher law? One business executive suggests that there should be no problem knowing what is proper, "If a man follows the Gospel he can't go wrong. Too many managers have let basic religious truth out of their sight. That's our trouble."

Most religions maintain that there are universal moral principles that should guide human behavior[36]—that in almost all times and places, thou shalt not lie, steal, or murder, for example. Thus, advertisements that deceive customers and industrial espionage to discover a competitor's secrets are clearly proscribed by common religious principles. Nonetheless, only a minority of managers think such principles are the basic ethical criteria for their managerial decisions. The problem is that moral principles are often abstract and difficult to apply to specific cases.[37] To be sure, intentional lying is clearly wrong, but most businessmen sincerely believe they must hide information and distort public communication as protection against competitors or unions. And stealing seems wrong, but padding expense accounts or "borrowing" company tools doesn't seem so immoral when the employer knows and seemingly condones it (perhaps this is a form of supplemental compensation). Catholic theology holds that every employer has an obligation to pay at least a "living wage," but determining this is subject to debate. Perhaps it is just unrealistic to expect a guide to conduct developed in the Middle East 2000 years ago to have direct relevance to the complex conditions of modern managers.[38]

Pragmatists argue that religious teachings and the golden rule are not meant to apply to competitive business anyway, that management is more akin to a poker game than to the religious life.[39] If obfuscation and deception are part of the game and everyone knows it, then they are not sinful. Finally, many people subscribe to no religious beliefs and bitterly resent believers' attempts to impose their tenets on everyone. Clearly, religion as an ethical guide is helpful and good, but only to some people some of the time.

Ethics As Common Behavior

"But everyone does it" has been a popular guide and justification for behavior from time immemorial. Realists argue that if the majority engage in certain activity, then it must be all right, regardless of what parents or policemen say. The young manager could make his judgments based upon the characteristic behavior of his boss and his organization or industry, not universal rules. Thus, the garment salesman argues that he couldn't possibly follow the strict custom against booze and sex as aids to selling computers. His industry accepts such inducements and buyers expect them, so he feels he couldn't compete without them. Similarly, managers in fiercely competitive industries argue that they can't be as open about costs and policies as a monopoly such as telephone communications.

Every young manager will experience the pressure of others' behavior as determinant of his own.[40] Yet we have a paradox: most agree that others' behavior is not the most elevated criterion for individual decisions yet still maintain that their superior's behavior is the major reason they behave unethically. It is the top that sets the ethical tone in most organizations and this is one of the gravest obligations of high-level executives. Their behavior will be emulated and converted into institutionalized custom by lower managers.[41]

A young person caught in such an unhappy situation pursues one of several courses: he adjusts his personal beliefs and stays happily; he stays, but with a guilty conscience (hopefully to change things when he gains power), or he departs.

Ethics As Impact on People

Upon being asked about unethical managers, a former president of General Electric observed that unethical people are not the problem: "What we must fear is the honest businessman who doesn't know what he is doing." Thus, most companies that have polluted the air and despoiled the land did so out of ignorance, not immorality. Knowledge may assist managers in making decisions based upon what is best for the greatest number of people.

This is what schools of business administration and management have striven for—to make management a profession whose primary concern is social contribution, not narrow self-interest.[42] By teaching prospective managers how business, economy, society, and environment interact, the hope is that their graduates will take the broader picture into account when making decisions. No intelligent executive in the last quarter of the twentieth century can really believe that air and water are "free goods" to be used as he or she unilaterally deems most profitable for the firm. Even if the firm doesn't pay for them, his education should have shown him that society does.

No doubt ignorance has occasioned much apparently unethical behavior, and greater professional knowledge should be of great benefit to all. But unfortunately, some professionals who have taken the Hippocratic oath or sworn allegiance to the Constitution cheat clients, defraud the public, and rape the environment. It is naive to expect that education alone is a sufficient guide for ethical behavior. Besides, what contributes to the greatest number of people sometimes means exploitation of the few or even breaking laws. Some executives have violated various business laws in order to protect the jobs of employees on the grounds that no one is hurt by colluding with a competitor, but many would be out of work and collecting unemployment compensation if pure competition existed.

Beware of Cynicism

No single ethical criterion is sufficient. The young manager striving to be ethical should do more than depend on economic self-interest, obey the law, observe his religious principles, follow his superior, and obtain the greatest good for the most people. He will have to take all of these into account filtered through his subjective judgment of what is right. In making these judgments, however, he should guard against cynicism.

Many people attribute poorer motivation and more unethical behavior to others than themselves. Young people today seem to be very cynical about business ethics and managers. They tend to believe that practicing managers engage in more unethical behavior than they would and more than the managers themselves think they do. Thus, students attribute such activities as padding expense accounts, stealing trade secrets, and immoral cooperation to managers to a greater extent than the managers anonymously report that they do. Research suggests that the younger the person, the greater his cynicism about managers; the older the manager, however, the greater the optimism about others. Whether this reflects time or "the times" is unknown. Do people become less cynical as they become older and see that everyone isn't as unethical as they had once thought? If so, today's young people might become less cynical as they climb their organizational ladders. Or is today's cynicism actually justified because older managers forget what it is like at lower levels or delude themselves about actual practice?

Nonetheless, excessive cynicism encourages unethical behavior on the grounds that "I'd be a fool not to if everyone else is." Cynicism thus can be self-fulfilling prophecy. More likely, a younger manager who believes everyone does it will discover that they don't and that if he does, his career may be ruined.

ADVICE ON CAREER MANAGEMENT

Advising young people on how to manage their careers is a risky proposition. It depends upon the individual's objectives and his or her definition of success: Climbing to the top? Maintaining integrity? Keeping job and home separate? Happiness? These are not mutually exclusive goals, but they can be competitive.[43]

Assuming that a young manager's objective is to climb to higher managerial ranks, the following suggestions have been offered by various people:[44]

- Remember that good performance that pleases your superiors is the basic foundation of success, but recognize that not all good performance is easily measured. Determine the real criteria by which you are evaluated and be rigorously honest in evaluating your own performance against these criteria.

- Manage your career; be active in influencing decisions, because pure effort is not necessarily rewarded.

- Strive for positions that have high visibility and exposure where you can be a hero·observed by higher officials. Check to see that the organization has a formal system of keeping track of young people. Remember that high-risk line jobs tend to offer more visibility than staff positions like corporate planning or personnel, but also that visibility can sometimes be achieved by off-job community activities.

- Develop relations with a mobile senior executive who can be your sponsor. Become a complementary crucial subordinate with different skills than your superior.

- Learn your job as quickly as possible and train a replacement so you can be available to move and broaden your background in different functions.

- Nominate yourself for other positions; modesty is not necessarily a virtue. However, change jobs for more power and influence, not primarily for status or pay. The latter could be a substitute for real opportunity to make things happen.

- Before taking a position, rigorously assess your strengths and weaknesses, what you like and don't like. Don't accept a promotion if it draws on your weaknesses and entails mainly activities that you don't like.

- Leave at your convenience, but on good terms without parting criticism of the organization. Do not stay under an immobile superior who is not promoted in three to five years.

- Don't be trapped by formal, narrow job descriptions. Move outside them and probe the limits of your influence.

- Accept that responsibility will always somewhat exceed authority and that organizational politics are inevitable. Establish alliances and fight necessary battles, minimizing upward ones to very important issues.

- Get out of management if you can't stand being dependent on others and having them dependent on you.

- Recognize that you will face ethical dilemmas no matter how moral you try to be. No evidence exists that unethical managers are more successful than ethical ones, but it may well be that those who move faster are less socially conscious.[45] Therefore, from time to time you must examine your personal values and question how much you will sacrifice for the organization.

- Don't automatically accept all tales of managerial perversity that you hear. Attributing others' success to unethical behavior is often an excuse for one's own personal inadequacies. Most of all, don't commit an act which you know to be wrong in the hope that your superior will see it as loyalty and reward you for it. Sometimes he will, but he may also sacrifice you when the organization is criticized.

SUMMARY

Frustration and dissatisfaction in young graduates' early careers is widespread because of several factors: their job expectations are unrealistic; they find it difficult to change from school's short-range perspectives to work's long-range view; many employers assign them boring tasks that don't challenge them; and they may begin under an incompetent first supervisor. As a result, turnover from first positions is substantial.

Many young specialists and managers are insensitive to the organization's political aspects so that they needlessly offend older managers and fail to develop alliances necessary to concentrate power on important issues. To compound their problems, some are passive in not asking questions to clarify what is expected of them and what authority they possess. They let their careers drift under the control of others without even knowing the real criteria by which superiors evaluate their performance.

Loyalty presents one of the most difficult dilemmas for many young managers: everyone values it, but its meaning varies. For some superiors loyalty is subordinates doing exactly what they are told. For some it is subordinate success whatever the means. For still others it is subordinates who protect the executives and organization from looking bad. Finally, for a few it is subordinates who communicate honestly what is going on. All of these conceptions of loyalty are partially valid; an organization should value obedience, effectiveness, effort, reliability, and honesty, but all can distort behavior if carried to excess.

With time's passage and achievement, many still young managers experience anxiety about personal integrity, commitment, and dependence. They worry that they are losing track of their personal values while being rewarded for their contributions. They wonder if they are really doing something worthwhile that justifies the doors they have closed and the opportunities passed by. And some feel they are so interdependent with others that they are losing control of their lives.

The occasion for personal anxiety about integrity and commitment is when young managers are faced with ethical dilemmas. Most think they should be guided by personal feelings, but this is extremely subjective and other criteria should also be examined: economics and self-interest, regulations and laws, religious principles, others' customary behavior, and impact on people. All of these criteria can be helpful in making decisions, but none alone is sufficient all the time. In making decisions, however, be wary of cynicism that assumes the worst in everyone else. It can lead to improper and inappropriate behavior.

Career advice includes admonitions to perform well, be active in managing your career, strive for visibility and exposure, develop relations with senior sponsors, learn quickly and train a subordinate, nominate yourself for new positions, rigorously assess your strengths and weaknesses, don't be trapped by narrow job descriptions, recognize that organizational politics are inevitable, and be prepared for ethical dilemmas.

NOTES

1. Over 50 percent of all MBA's leave their first employer within five years. J. A. De Pasquale and R. A. Lange, "Job-Hopping and the MBA," *Harvard Business Review* (November-December 1971), p. 4ff. See also, J. A. De Pasquale, *The Young Executive: A Summary of the Career Paths of Young Executives in Business* (New York: MBA Enterprises, Inc., 1970); and G. F. Farris, "A Predictive Study of Turnover," *Personnel Psychology* (1971), pp. 311-328. When a young graduate joins an organization, a "psychological contract" is forged between individual and organization. If the organization doesn't live up to the individual's perception of the contract, he feels offended and leaves. Unfortunately, the specific terms of this implied contract are seldom discussed. J. P. Kotter, "The Psychological Contract: Managing the Joining-up Process," *California Management Review* (Spring 1973), pp. 91-99. The reasons why the relationship is initially vague lie in the implicit bargaining and selling that take place in the attraction and selection process. No one really wants to communicate "truth." See L. W. Porter, E. E. Lawler III, and J. R. Hackman, "Choice Processes: Individuals and Organizations Attracting and Selecting Each Other," in *Behavior in Organizations* (New York: McGraw-Hill, 1975), pp. 131-158.

2. Lawler argues that expectation of immediate gratification means that management should shorten periods between evaluation and award frequent small raises rather than yearly. E. E. Lawler, "Compensating the New Life-style Worker," *Personnel* (1971), pp. 19-25. See also, T. F. Stroh, *Managing the New Generation in Business* (New York: McGraw-Hill, 1971).

3. In general, the younger the managers, the higher the level they expect to reach in their careers. Thus, virtually all are disappointed at some time. M. L. Moore, E. Miller, and J. Fossum, "Predictors of Managerial Career Expectations," *Journal of Applied Psychology* (January 1974), pp. 90-92. Some executives are highly skeptical of MBA's in particular. Here is a portion of a letter written to the editors of *Columbia Journal of World Business* (May-June 1968), p. 5.

   "I can't agree completely with Mr. [T. Vincent] Learson's statement (Jan.-Feb. 1968) that the salvation of the business world is the 'scientifically trained man that comes from the ranks of the graduate schools.' I have found many of these people have no concept of the value of a dollar. They are theorists only and for the most part have no desire to learn the basic fundamentals of the business they are engaged in, but rather consider themselves above finding out the basic principles of the business by experience. They want everyone to hand them experience on a velvet pillow and are too concerned with taking over the presidency of an organization six months after they enter an organization. I do believe the scientifically trained graduate student does have his place in industry, but. . . ."

4. A. G. Athos, "Is the Corporation Next to Fall?" *Harvard Business Review* (January-February 1970), pp. 49-60. For more on characteristics and expectation of young managers and specialists, see J. Gooding, "The Accelerated Generation Moves into

Management," *Fortune* (March 1971), p. 101ff.; and L. B. Ward and A. G. Athos, *Student Expectations of Corporate Life* (Boston: Graduate School of Business Administration, Harvard University, 1972).

5. L. W. Porter, "Where is the Organization Man?" *Harvard Business Review* (November-December 1963), pp. 53-61.

6. J. A. Livingston, "Pygmalion in Management," *Harvard Business Review* (July-August 1969), pp. 81-89.

7. D. E. Berlow and D. T. Hall, "The Socialization of Managers: Effects of Expectations on Performance," *Administrative Science Quarterly* (September 1966), pp. 207-223.

8. In general, a superior's stringent personal standards are associated with higher subordinate performance than lower personal standards. The superior's personal standards also seem to exert more influence on subordinate performance than subordinate's personal standards. The best performance, however, is where both superior and subordinate have high personal standards. J. P. Campbell, M. D. Dunnette, E. E. Lawler, and K. E. Weick, *Managerial Behavior, Performance and Effectiveness* (New York: McGraw-Hill 1970), pp. 447-551.

9. For some case studies of sensitive and insensitive young managers, see W. R. Dill, T. L. Hilton, and W. R. Reitman, *The New Managers* (Englewood Cliffs, N. J.: Prentice-Hall, 1962).

10. E. E. Jennings, *The Mobile Manager: A Study of the New Generation of Top Executives* (Ann Arbor: Graduate School of Business Administration, University of Michigan, 1967). For examples of the critical importance of sponsors or mentors for ambitious females, see Gail Sheehy, *Passages: Predictable Crises of Adult Life* (New York: E.P. Dutton, 1976) and J. Thompson, "Patrons, Rabbis, Mentors—Whatever You Call Them, Women Need Them, Too" *MBA* (February 1976), p. 26.

11. On the importance of power, McMurry writes:
    "The most important and unyielding necessity of organizational life is not better communications, human relations or employee participation, but power. . . . Without power there can be no authority; without authority there can be no discipline; without discipline there can be difficulty in maintaining order, system and productivity. An executive without power is, therefore, all too often a figurehead or worse, headless. . . . If the executive owns the business, that fact may ensure his power. If he does not, and sometimes even when he does, his power must be acquired and held by means which are essentially political."—R. N. McMurry, "Power and the Ambitious Executive," *Harvard Business Review* (November-December 1973), p.140.

12. J. S. Livingston, "Myth of the Well-educated Manager," *Harvard Business Review* (January-February 1971), pp. 79-88. In general, Livingston argues that there is no relation between managerial success and school performance and that schools don't develop important attributes. That "wisdom" is the neglected attribute is maintained by L. Urwick, "What Have the Universities Done for Business Management?" *Management of Personnel Quarterly* (Summer 1967), pp. 35-40.

13. One survey indicates that MBA students express more authoritarian and Machiavellian views than do practicing managers, but that business school professors were more Machiavellian than either! J. P. Siegel, "Machiavellianism, MBA's and Managers: Leadership Correlates and Socialization Effects," *Academy of Management Journal* (September 1973), pp. 404-411. A similar finding is in R. J. Burke, "Effects of Organizational Experience on Managerial Attitudes and Beliefs: A Better Press for Managers," *Journal of Business Research* (Summer 1973), pp. 21-30.

14. D. Moment and D. Fisher, "Managerial Career Development and the Generational Confrontation," *California Management Review* (Spring 1973), pp. 46-55. See also, D. Moment and D. Fisher, *Autonomy in Organizational Life* (Cambridge: Schenkman, 1975).

15. Three-dimensional cone model of organization from E. H. Schein, "The Individual, The Organization and The Career. A Conceptual Scheme," in D. A. Kolb, I. M. Rubin and J. M. McIntyre, *Organizational Psychology: A Book of Readings* (Englewood Cliffs, N.J.: Prentice-Hall, 1971), pp. 301-316.

16. Porter, op. cit.
17. Campbell et al., op. cit.
18. The study compared three regional managers of different styles—"authoritarian," "permissive," and "recessive" (*laissez-faire*). Objective measurements indicated no difference in regional performance, but higher management consistently rated the authoritarian as most effective and promotable. J. H. Mullen, *Personality and Productivity in Management* (New York: Temple University Publications, Columbia University Press, 1966).
19. H. Levinson. "On Being a Middle-Aged Manager," *Harvard Business Review* (July-August 1969), pp. 51-60.
20. That not obeying may be loyalty is demonstrated by D. Wise in *The Politics of Lying* (New York: Random House, 1973). Newton Minow, appointed head of the Federal Communications Commission by President John F. Kennedy, is quoted as saying that in April 1962, after a story that was highly critical of the President was broadcast on the NBC "Huntley-Brinkley Report," Kennedy called Minow. As Minow recalls the conversation, it went like this:

    JFK: "Did you see that goddamn thing in 'Huntley-Brinkley'?"

    Minow: "Yes."

    JFK: "I thought they were supposed to be our friends. I want you to do something about that."

    Minow says he did not do anything, instead calling a Kennedy aide the next morning and asking him to tell the President he was lucky to have an FCC chairman who doesn't do what the President tells him.
21. For a disturbing example of the retribution heaped on a manager who reported his firm's shortcomings to the press, see K. Vandivier, "The Aircraft Brake Scandal," *Harper's Magazine* (April 1972), pp. 45-52.
22. On changing career identities, see D. T. Hall, "A Theoretical Model of Career Subidentity Development in Organizational Settings," *Organizational Behavior and Human Performance* (January 1972), pp. 50-76; and J. F. Veiga, "The Mobile Manager at Mid-Career," *Harvard Business Review* (January-February 1973), p. 115ff.
23. Hirschman suggests that economists will tend to exaggerate the power of leaving while political scientists and sociologists conversely underrate it. A. Hirschman, *Exit, Voice and Loyalty* (Cambridge, Mass.: Harvard University, 1970). On new careers see D. L. Hiestand, *Changing Careers After Thirty-Five* (New York: Columbia University Press, 1971). Conner and Fielder recommend that firms pay for the reeducation of unhappy managers who could then move on to other careers. S. T. Connor and J. S. Fielder, "Rx for Managerial Shelf Sitters," *Harvard Business Review* (November-December 1973), pp. 113-120. See also, R. F. Pearse and B. P. Pelzer, *Self-directed Change for the Mid-career Manager* (New York: Amacom, 1975).
24. A. Zaleznik, G. W. Dalton, L. B. Barnes, and P. Laurin, *Orientation and Conflict in Career* (Boston: Graduate School of Business Administration, Harvard University, 1970). The authors suggest that many people never reconcile this conflict between personal identity and organizational values, yet those in conflict may be more effective than those who are "oriented" toward the organization. See also, E. H. Schein, "Organizational Socialization and the Profession of Management," in Kolb et al., *Organizational Psychology: A Book of Readings*, pp. 1-16. Stoess reports a study indicating that managers are relatively more conforming than the general population. A. E. Stoess, "Conformity Behavior of Managers and Their Wives," *Academy of Management Journal* (September 1973), pp. 433-441.
25. E. E. Jennings, *Executive Success: Stresses, Problems and Adjustments* (New York: Appleton-Century-Crofts, 1967): and E. E. Jennings, *The Executive in Crisis* (East Lansing: Graduate School of Business Administration, Michigan State University, 1965).
26. E. Fromm, *The Art of Loving* (New York: Harper & Row, 1956).
27. J. Steiner, "What Price Success," *Harvard Business Review* (March-April 1972), pp. 69-74. For optimistic advice on how open communication between husbands and

wives can help to solve many of the conflicts at home caused by an executive's commitment to career, see E. J. Walker, " 'Til Business Us Do Part?" *Harvard Business Review* (January-February 1976). pp. 94-101.

28. The conceptions of ethics are from R. Baumhart, *Ethics in Business* (New York: Holt, Rinehart and Winston, 1968). See also S. H. Miller, "The Tangle of Ethics," *Harvard Business Review* (January-February 1960), pp. 59-62; J. W. Towle (ed.), *Ethics and Standards in American Business* (Boston: Houghton Mifflin, 1964); T. M. Garrett, *Business Ethics* (New York: Appleton-Century-Crofts, 1966); C. C. Walton, *Ethos and the Executive* (Englewood Cliffs, N.J.: Prentice-Hall, 1969).

29. G. F. F. Lombard, "Relativism in Organizations," *Harvard Business Review* (March-April 1971), pp. 55-65; J. F. Fletcher, *Situation Ethics* (Philadelphia: Westminster Press, 1966); J. F. Fletcher, *Moral Responsibility: Situation Ethics at Work* (Philadelphia: Westminster Press, 1967).

30. M.S. Baram, "Trade Secrets: What Price Loyalty," *Harvard Business Review* (November-December 1968), pp. 66-74. On various horror stories of managers who supposedly put profits over ethics, see F. J. Cook, *The Corrupted Land* (New York: Macmillan, 1966) and R. L. Heilbroner, et al., *In the Name of Profit* (Garden City, N. Y.: Doubleday, 1972).

31. M. Freedman, *Capitalism and Freedom* (Chicago: University of Chicago Press, 1962). Carr argues that it is dangerous to a manager's career to act purely upon personal beliefs, but he can help his organization if he can show how unethical policies actually harm economic performance. A. Z. Carr, "Can An Executive Afford a Conscience?" *Harvard Business Review* (July-August 1970), pp. 58-64. Thus, Carr is both pessimistic and optimistic—pessimistic that only economics guides business behavior, but optimistic that many dilemmas may be converted to economic terms where economics and public interest correspond. That good ethics is good economics and good business is argued by G. Gillman, "The Ethical Dimension in American Management," *California Management Review* (Fall 1964), pp. 45-52.

32. J. K. Galbraith, *The New Industrial State* (Boston: Houghton Mifflin, 1967).

33. A. Chayes, "The Modern Corporation and the Rule of Law," in E. S. Mason (ed.), *The Corporation in Modern Society* (Cambridge, Mass.: Harvard University Press, 1959), p. 25ff.

34. C. C. Walton and F. W. Cleveland, Jr., *Corporations on Trial: The Electrical Cases* (Belmont, Ca.: Wadsworth, 1967).

35. A former chairman of the Chase Manhattan Bank writes about ethical problems:
    "Government's response to the problem, characteristically, has been that 'there oughta be a law.' In the first session of this Congress, more than 20,000 bills and resolutions were introduced, 20 percent more than in the first session of the previous Congress. The same approach has been in evidence on the state and local levels. The objective seems to be to hold together our fractured moral structure by wrapping it in endless layers of new laws—a kind of LSD trip by legislation. Yet it should be clear by now, even to busy lawmakers, that the great lesson to be learned from our attempts to legislate morality is that it can't be done. For morality must come from the heart and the conscience of each individual." George Champion, "Our Moral Deficit," *The MBA* (October 1968), p. 39.

36. H. L. Johnson, "Can the Businessman Apply Christianity?" *Harvard Business Review* (September-October 1957), pp. 68-76; J. W. Clark, *Religion and the Moral Standards of American Businessmen* (Cincinnati: South-Western, 1966).

37. T. F. McMahon, "Moral Responsibility and Business Management," *Social Forces* (December 1963), pp. 5-17.

38. See *Fortune* editorial in response to Pope Paul's encyclical "On the Development of Peoples" (May 1967), p. 115. The editors argue that the Church's view would hinder growth and harm the underdeveloped nations more than a few unethical companies do.

39. A. Z. Carr, "Is Business Bluffing Ethical?" *Harvard Business Review* (January-February 1968), pp. 143-153. In a similar vein, Levitt argues that advertising is like

art: it is not reality, but illusion and everyone knows it. Therefore, some distortion is acceptable. T. Levitt, "The Morality of Advertising," *Harvard Business Review* (July-August 1970), pp. 84-92.

40. Baumhart, op. cit.

41. On the difficulties of managers who are confronted with accepting questionable conduct of their superiors, see J. J. Fendrock, "Crisis in Conscience at Quasar," *Harvard Business Review* (March-April 1968), pp. 112-120. For reader response to the situation, see J. J. Fendrock, "Sequel to Quasar Stellar," *Harvard Business Review* (September-October 1968), pp. 14-22. Ninety-eight percent said it was wrong to keep quiet, but 64 percent admitted they would be tempted to.

42. K. R. Andrews, "Toward Professionalism in Business Management," *Harvard Business Review* (March-April 1969), pp. 49-60. Some are skeptical about whether business schools really affect the ethics of their graduates. An executive observes, "They tend to get the notion up at Harvard that some things are more important than profits. But that doesn't affect them when they come here: They're not really contaminated. They're typical, intelligent, ambitious, greedy, grafting, ordinary American males." Quoted in S. Klaw, "Harvard's Degree in the Higher Materialism," *Esquire* (October 1965), p. 103. Schein argues that educational institutions tend to accept the values of the enterprises they prepare students for. E. H. Schein, "The Problems of Moral Education for the Business Manager," *Industrial Management Review* (Fall 1966), pp. 3-14.

43. On different career perspectives, see H. O. Prudent, "The Upward Mobile, Indifferent and Ambivalent: Typology of Managers," *Academy of Management Journal* (September 1973), pp. 454-464.

44. Career advice is summarized in E. E. Jennings, *Routes to the Executive Suite* (New York: McGraw-Hill, 1971). See also, R. H. Buskirk, *Your Career: How to Plan It, Manage It, Change It* (Boston: Cahners, 1976). A summary of books on career planning may be found in K. Feingold, "Information Sources on Life Style/Career Planning," *Harvard Business Review* (January-February), 9 p. 144ff.

45. B. M. Bass and L. D. Eldridge, "Accelerated Managers: Objectives in Twelve Countries," *Industrial Relations* (May 1973), pp. 158-170.

Y. K. SHETTY AND
NEWMAN S. PEERY, JR.

Are Top Executives Transferable Across Companies?

The chief executive officer (CEO) plays a crucial role in determining the efficiency of an enterprise. He is responsible for the proper use of company resources—human, technical and material. His decisions, his power and his leadership have vital consequences for the company as a whole.

Management of a total enterprise demands different ways of thinking and the exercise of skills beyond those required for the management of a division or department. Companies are increasingly aware that they must select and develop effective CEOs. As yet, however, clearly established selection criteria that might make top executives transferable across companies and industries do not exist. This article examines the relationship between existing executive transfer patterns and the organizational performance criterion of profitability.

VIEWS ON TRANSFERABILITY

Two basic positions have been advanced about top executive transfers. One holds that all top executives perform the same major functions and use the same basic skills; hence, executives are readily transferable across companies and industries as well as from position to position. Some prominent individuals often cited as examples to

Source: *Business Horizons*, June 1976, pp. 23-28. Copyright © 1976 by the Foundation for the School of Business at Indiana University. Reprinted by permission.

substantiate this viewpoint include Robert McNamara, George Romney, McGeorge Bundy and Arjay Miller.

The second position is that top executives use fairly specialized skills, many of which are uniquely related to the industry and the environment of a specific job. Thus, executives are not readily transferable. Ernest Dale, after many years of management consulting experience, noted that ". . . there has been little transfer of management from one major sphere of administrative activity to another—from say, military organizations to business or vice versa. . . . There is even relatively little transfer of general managers from one industry to another. It is almost impossible to transfer in or out of some industries, or even in or out of some companies, and often for very good reasons. The knowledge required to fill a management position satisfactorily is not only managerial. Familiarity with technical matters, products, personalities and tradition, a type of knowledge that can be acquired only through long and painstaking experience in the actual situation, is also required in most cases."[1]

Many practicing managers express strong reservations about top executives switching industries. They do not think that a manager who lacks a basic knowledge of the firm's product line and markets can still be an effective manager. Furthermore, the experience of conglomerate firms in recent years provides some additional support for the nontransferability position. Generally speaking, conglomerate firms have performed poorly in recent years. It might be argued that this poor performance can be largely attributed to the lack of, or limited, cross-industry transferability of managerial skills. The issue of transferability is of increasing concern to companies seeking yardsticks by which to measure the performance of their top executives, as well as to others seeking guidelines for the selection and development of such executives.

A recent study by Donald L. Helmich found that when executives were selected from outside a former CEO's immediate circle within the firm, the results were more growth in sales, greater product diversification and an increased number of added subsidiaries than when executives were selected from the former CEO's immediate group.[2] Though this suggests that some transferability of skills exists, the question remains whether a CEO selected from outside the organization would also perform well, and the relationship between outside transfers and profitability remains.

The study discussed in this article was designed to answer such questions as: To what degree are CEOs transferable across companies and industries? What is the relationship between chief executive transfer patterns and company performance? Are any dimensions of successful chief executive skills crucial in the transfer process? To what degree do top executive transfers reflect the particular contexts within which an organization functions?

Subjects of the study were 270 chief executives of companies included in *Business Week's* list of 368 large firms. Background information relating to the positions held prior to their current posts was collected for each executive. Mobility patterns were used as indicators of the transferability of their skills. Executives were subsequently classified according to whether they: (1) were associated with the same company for a number of years; (2) came from another company within the same industry, as indicated by identical Standard Industrial Classification (SIC) codes; (3) came from a company in a *similar* industry, as indicated by the two companies having at least the first digit of their SIC codes in common; or (4) came from a company in a completely unrelated industry, as indicated by completely different SIC codes.

Since the performance of a chief executive is closely related to the performance of the company itself, profitability and growth were used as measures of performance. Average return on invested capital for 1970-74 was the basic indicator of profitability. Sales growth for the same period was used as an indicator of growth. Data on return to invested capital, sales, number of employees, and so forth, were obtained from company financial statements and from *Moody's Industrial Manual* and *Standard & Poor's Register of Corporations, Directors and Executives.*

PATTERNS OF EXECUTIVE TRANSFERS

Findings indicate that top executives do not transfer readily across companies and industries (see table 1). For example, of the 270 chief executives in the study, 241 (89%) had previous positions with the same company. Only twenty-nine firms (approximately 10%) had gone outside their organizations to recruit their chief executives. Of these twenty-nine firms, eight stayed within their industry group, seven went to a related industry, and fourteen ventured outside the industry.

Table 1: Chief executive transfer patterns

Sources of Executive Transfer	*Number*	*Percent*
Internal—same company	241	89.3
External—same industry	8	3.0
External—related industry	7	2.5
External—different industry	14	5.2
Total	*270*	*100.0*

A comparatively higher proportion of smaller companies (40,000 employees or less and sales of $3 billion or less) than larger ones recruited their top executive officers from outside the firm. As the size of the firm increases there is a higher percentage of executives who have worked up within the firm. A smaller company may not provide as much opportunity to gain broader experience required at the top level compared to a larger firm. Increasing size is also usually accompanied by a diversification of the company's product market, which in turn provides for broader experience in general management. The nature of the industry and the patterns of executive transfers showed no significant relationship.

EFFECT ON COMPANY PERFORMANCE

The average incumbency for a chief executive officer is approximately six years. Of the 270 CEOs in the original sample, 110 had been appointed prior to 1970. To measure the relationship between transfer patterns and executive performance, data on the operations of those 110 firms between the years 1970-1974 were collected.

Most executives averaged between 5-10% on their rates of return on invested capital regardless of whether they were recruited from within the same organization or not. Although 23% of the firms with inside CEOs achieved a return on invested capital in excess of 10%, only one of the eleven outside CEOs achieved a return on investment in excess of 10% and he was from a related industry. Similarly, only one of the firms with average sales growth in excess of 20% had a chief executive from outside the organization. Thus, given a choice between an inside and outside CEO, an inside seems to increase a firm's chances of high performance.

CASE FOR INTERNAL SELECTION

A number of interrelated reasons contribute to the strong bias in favor of internal selection of a CEO. First, firms seek to maintain a satisfactory level of performance and are likely to avoid unnecessary risks. Our results indicate that satisfactory performance is likely to be achieved by an inside CEO. An outside executive is not likely to significantly improve performance and may simply add another source of uncertainty. Second, most companies pursue systematic internal promotion programs as a matter of organizational policy. A well-planned system of internal promotion is an effective way to maintain a high degree of motivation among executives and create a sense of loyalty to the organization.

Another explanation is that companies may be trying to avoid the potential instability and discontinuities resulting from bringing in an outsider. When a company hires an outside man as chief executive, he generally brings with him his own people to fill top management positions. The result is an executive exodus. Research shows that the outside successor precipitates a greater number of strategic replacements and reassignments than does the inside successor.[3] Bringing in an outsider also means that the inside executives are passed over in the selection process, which may prompt their leaving the company.

An inside successor, by contrast, often has developed commitments to the current management group and is less likely to generate substantial uncertainty and instability. Continuity can be maintained. Coupled with this is the influence of the retiring chief executive in selecting his own successor. Most people think that corporate directors are responsible for selecting the chief executive. In reality, the chief executive most often recommends his successor and the board usually routinely approves the choice. Only when sluggish growth and slowing profits threaten the company are corporate boards likely to develop more interest in picking a new chief executive. When a company is doing well, directors tend to let the incumbent name his own man. In such cases, the top positions are usually filled by internal people.

Another constraint on the transferability of chief executives might be the need for personal information as a central part of the executive's job. A prior study of 190 managers found that they used personal sources of information far more than impersonal sources.[4] More recently, Henry Mintzberg found that executives rely heavily on face-to-face contacts and personal information sources for most decisions.[5] An executive recruited from another company is not likely to have the personal information contacts in the organization and may therefore initially have to rely more on formal reports and official sources than would an executive promoted from within.

CASE FOR EXTERNAL SELECTION

Some writers argue that external executive recruitment might be a source of external contacts who supply environmental information for an organization.[6] This suggests that the selection of an executive from another firm within the same industry could provide important inputs into the policy-making process. However, our data suggest that such inputs would be potentially less disruptive if they occurred at lower executive levels. The skills required at the top executive level may be highly specialized and unique to industries as well as to companies.

THE EXECUTIVE SKILL MIX

Executive skill—an ability to translate knowledge into action—combines distinct areas of expertise.[7] It appears that the three most important skills are technical, organizational and institutional.

Technical skills involve an understanding of, and proficiency in, relevant methods, processes, procedures or techniques.

Organizational skills involve an ability to: structure organizational relationships both physical and interpersonal; work effectively as a group member; coordinate others' activities; and see the organization as a whole.

Institutional skills involve an ability to define the overall goals of the organization by opportunistic surveillance of, and negotiation with, the environment and also insuring legitimization of the organization. It involves the relationship of an individual business to the industry, the community and to the political, social, economic and technical forces of the nation.

The relative importance of these skills varies with the organizational hierarchy. At the lower levels of management, technical skills are most important; at the intermediate levels, organizational skills are as important as technical skills; at the top level, both organizational and institutional skills are required, but the major requirement is for institutional skill.

Organizational skills are primarily concerned with the internal aspects of structure, coordination, mediation and interpersonal relationships, and institutional skills are primarily concerned with creating organizational responses to a changing environment. Exercising institutional skills entails having an understanding of the external environment relevant to the company. Extensive knowledge about the industry in which the company operates is a crucial ingredient. To define realistically the overall goals of his company, a top executive must be continually engaged in opportunistic surveillance of and negotiation with the company's environment, and must strive for legitimization of the organization in its milieu.

Importance of Institutional Skills

Institutional skills are more important today than ever before; the chief executive has increasing responsibility for adjusting the company to its environment. Many top executives claim that besides managing internal affairs, they are more and more frequently called upon to arbitrate conflicting claims of workers, consumers, shareholders, environmentalists and the government. Alonzo L. McDonald, Jr., managing partner of McKinsey and Co., the consulting firm, says, "Just a few years ago the CEO of a big company spent 10% of his time on external matters. Today the figure is generally 40%."[8]

If institutional skills are of primary importance to top executives, infrequent shifts across industries by CEOs and companies may indicate that different industries have particular economic, market, technical and other characteristics, each of which calls for unique managerial strategies and skills. For example, it would be exceedingly difficult for an executive to transfer between an electronic industry and a consumer goods industry. The technology, markets and general industrial environments of these industries differ drastically. Electronic industries put a premium on advancing the state of the art and on new technological achievements, and face an uncertain and variable market environment. In the consumer goods field, there is much less emphasis on research and development and a greater concentration on low-cost mass production operations and on promotional advertising. Each industry requires unique managerial approaches and skills.

Our data suggest that the transferability of top executives is limited even between companies in the same industry. Different companies within the same industry may have somewhat particular environments, each of which demands unique combinations of managerial strategy and skills. This may be due to variations in size, ownership, personalities, traditions and internal functioning characteristics. All of the above factors—emphasis on maintaining internal promotion patterns, minimizing instability, the requirements of personal information, and uniqueness of industry and company environments—may be operating in various combinations to limit transfers of executives across companies and industries.

IMPLICATIONS FOR MANAGEMENT

This study suggests several alternatives for companies to help them create more effective strategies for top executive selection and development. Since internal recruitment of CEOs is more likely to lead to higher performance, planned development of executive talent should receive top priority. Companies should try to perfect meaningful programs that tag high-potential individuals early in their careers so that they may be properly motivated and adequately rewarded to remain with the organization. Then they may be appropriately groomed for responsible top management spots.

Companies looking for catalysts from outside may do well to bring in executives earlier in their careers at lower levels in the organization. Such a strategy would provide an opportunity for the new executive to familiarize himself with the firm. Also, this tactic would combine the benefits of new ideas and familiarity with the company.

Finally, any top executive coming from outside would do well to realize his inherent limitations. Decisions regarding transfer should not be based on an assumption that homogeneity exists within any industry. Organizational factors play a major role in influencing the effectiveness of a top executive, and since these are minimally susceptible to change, the new executive needs to attempt to adapt to the key factors of the new company.

Though the top executive is important to the success of a firm, the most effective source of qualified executives has not been identified. Some have argued that top managers are interchangeable across firms and industries, and that managers can therefore switch jobs and perform effectively irrespective of industry. Others believe that top managers are unlikely to be successful unless they have a thorough understanding of the industry and its environment. This study indicates that there seem to be serious constraints limiting the transferability of executives across companies as well as industries. Of those surveyed, companies recruiting their chief executives internally performed much better than those that recruited from outside. This implies that executives promoted from within are aided by knowing the company, its traditions, personalities and unique ways of functioning. In other words, knowing the "organizational culture" is a crucial factor in defining the effectiveness of a chief executive.

NOTES

1. Ernest Dale, "Management Must be Made Accountable," *Harvard Business Review* (March-April 1960), p. 53.
2. Donald L. Helmich, "Organizational Growth and Succession Patterns," *Academy of Management Journal* (December 1974), pp. 771-775.
3. Donald Helmich and Warren B. Brown, "Successor Type and Organizational Change in the Corporate Enterprise," *Administrative Science Quarterly* (September 1972), pp. 371-381.
4. Francis Joseph Aguiler, *Scanning the Business Environment* (New York: MacMillan Co., 1967).
5. Henry Mintzberg, "A New Look at the Chief Executive's Job," *Organizational Dynamics* (Winter 1973), pp. 20-30.
6. Jeffrey Pfeffer and H. Leblebici, "Executive Recruitment and the Development of Interfirm Organizations," *Administrative Science Quarterly* (December 1973), pp. 449-461.
7. Robert Katz, "Skills of an Effective Adminstrator," *Harvard Business Review* (January-February 1955), pp. 33-42.
8. "Chief Executive Officer," *Business Week* (May 4, 1974), pp. 37-86.

IV | PEOPLE IN ORGANIZATIONS

Central to any organization are the people who comprise it. Establishing policies and practices for handling the human affairs of an organization are crucial managerial decisions. For several decades now there has been a strong current of opinion that set policies had to become more employee centered, that practices had to be developed to tap the natural capabilities and potentialities of organization members. A wide variety of policies and practices intended to do just this has evolved. The intent is not to abandon the basic idea but to pause and examine how well practice compares with promise.

Two widespread practices are participation by lower members of an organization in decision making processes formerly reserved for management, and sensitivity training in the interpersonal skills and awareness through special forms of training. Albrook in his article, "Participative Management: Time for a Second Look," and Lakin in his paper, "Some Ethical Issues in Sensitivity Training" look carefully, though not unfavorably, at these practices. Albrook and Lakin identify matters that need attention if these techniques are to be more useful.

In "Modern Times" Charlie Chaplin skillfully satirized boring industrial jobs. Numerous books and countless articles since have described in great and graphic detail jobs that are intellectually stultifying, emotionally draining and socially demeaning. The need to correct this has long been recognized and frequently attempted. One approach currently receiving wide attention is Job Enrichment, a way of designing work based upon psychological principles rather than engineering principles. Some impressive results using these concepts are described by Robert Ford, in "Job Enrichment Lessons from AT&T."

Leonard Sayles looks at this growing movement and sees problems. As he sees things, job enrichment is drawing attention away from the broader concerns of all aspects of behavior in organizations, and many other matters concerning the effective relations between human beings and organizations, to focus instead on details.

One of the great social decisions of all time has been to make sure that all persons in this country have access to housing, education and jobs, regardless of race, religion or sex. This has meant major changes for all facets of our society, including business firms and other organizations. Silberman's article, "Black Economic Gains—Impressive but Precarious," and a Newsweek article, "Still More Room at the Top," examine some aspects of the movement to eliminate race and sex barriers in management.

ROBERT C. ALBROOK

Participative Management: Time for a Second Look

The management of change has become a central preoccupation of U.S. business. When the directors have approved the record capital budget and congratulated themselves on "progress," when the banquet speaker has used his last superlative to describe the "world of tomorrow," the talk turns, inevitably, to the question: "Who will make it all work?" Some people resist change. Some hold the keys to it. Some admit the need for new ways but don't know how to begin. The question becomes what kind of management can ease the inevitable pains, unlock the talent, energy, and knowledge where they're needed, help valuable men to contribute to and shape change rather than be flattened by it.

The recipe is elusive, and increasingly business has turned to the academic world for help, particularly to the behavioral scientists—the psychologists, sociologists, and anthropologists whose studies have now become the showpieces of the better business schools. A number of major corporations, such as General Electric, Texas Instruments, and Standard Oil (N.J.), have brought social scientists onto their staffs. Some companies collaborate closely with university-based scholars and are contributing importantly to advanced theoretical work, just as industry's physicists, chemists, and engineers have become significant contributors of new knowledge in their respective realms. Hundreds

Source: Reprinted from the May 1967 issue of *Fortune* magazine by special permission; © 1967 Time Inc.

of companies, large and small, have tried one or another formulation of basic behavioral theory, such as the many schemes for sharing cost savings with employees and actively soliciting their ideas for improved efficiency.

For forty years the quantity and quality of academic expertise in this field have been steadily improving, and there has lately been a new burst of ideas which suggest that the researchers in the business schools and other centers of learning are really getting down to cases. The newest concepts already represent a considerable spin-off from the appealingly simple notions on which the behavioral pioneers first concentrated. The essential message these outriders had for business was this: recognize the social needs of employees in their work, as well as their need for money; they will respond with a deeper commitment and better performance, help to shape the organization's changing goals and make them their own. For blue-collar workers this meant such steps as organizing work around tasks large enough to have meaning and inviting workers' ideas; for middle and upper management it meant more participation in decision making, wider sharing of authority and responsibility, more open and more candid communication, up, down, and sideways.

The new work suggests that neither the basic philosophy nor all of the early prescriptions of this management style were scientifically sound or universally workable. The word from the behavioral scientists is becoming more specific and "scientific," less simple and moralistic. At Harvard, M.I.T., the University of Michigan, Chicago, U.C.L.A., Stanford, and elsewhere, they are mounting bigger, longer, and more rigorous studies of the human factors in management than ever before undertaken.

One conclusion is that the "participative" or "group" approach doesn't seem to work with all people and in all situations. Research has shown that satisfied, happy workers are sometimes more productive—and sometimes merely happy. Some managers and workers are able to take only limited responsibility, however much the company tries to give them. Some people will recognize the need to delegate but "can't let go." In a profit squeeze the only way to get costs under control fast enough often seems to be with centralized, "get tough" management.

Few, if any, behaviorists espouse a general return to authoritarian management. Instead, they are seeking a more thorough, systematic way to apply participative principles on a sustained schedule that will give the theory a better chance to work. Others are insisting that management must be tailor-made, suited to the work or the people, rather than packaged in a standard mixture. Some people aren't and never will be suited for "democracy" on the job, according to one viewpoint, while others insist that new kinds of psychological training can fit most executives for the rugged give-and-take of successful group management.

As more variables are brought into their concepts, and as they look increasingly at the specifics of a management situation, the behaviorists are also being drawn toward collaboration with the systems designers and the theorists of data processing. Born in reaction to the cold scientism of the earlier "scientific management" experts with their stopwatches and measuring tapes, the "human relations" or behavioral school of today may be getting ready at last to bury that hatchet in a joint search for a broadly useful "general theory" of management.

WHY EXECUTIVES DON'T PRACTICE WHAT THEY PREACH

Before any general theory can be evolved, a great deal more has to be known about the difficulty of putting theory into practice—i.e., of transforming a simple managerial attitude into an effective managerial style. "There are plenty of executives," observes Stanley Seashore, a social psychologist at the University of Michigan's Institute for Social Research, "who'll decide one morning they're going to be more participative and by the afternoon have concluded it doesn't work."

What's often lacking is an understanding of how deeply and specifically management style affects corporate operations. The executive who seeks a more effective approach needs a map of the whole terrain of management activity. Rensis Likert, director of the Michigan institute, has developed a chart to assist managers in gaining a deeper understanding of the way they operate. A simplified version is presented in Figure 1.[1] By answering the questions in the left-hand column of the chart (e.g., "Are subordinates' ideas sought and used?"), an executive sketches a profile of the way his company is run and whether it leans to the "authoritative" or the "participative." Hundreds of businessmen have used the chart, under Likert's direction, and many have discovered a good deal they didn't realize about the way they were handling people.

Likert leads his subjects in deliberate steps to a conclusion that most of them do not practice what they say they believe. First, the executive is asked to think of the most successful company (or division of a company) he knows intimately. He then checks off on the chart his answers as they apply to that company. When the executive has finished this exercise, he has nearly always traced the profile of a strongly

		SYSTEM 1 Exploitive authoritative	SYSTEM 2 Benevolent authoritative	SYSTEM 3 Consultative	SYSTEM 4 Participative group
LEADERSHIP	How much confidence is shown in subordinates?	None	Condescending	Substantial	Complete
	How free do they feel to talk to superiors about job?	Not at all	Not very	Rather free	Fully free
	Are subordinates' ideas sought and used, if worthy?	Seldom	Sometimes	Usually	Always
MOTIVATION	Is predominant use made of 1 fear, 2 threats, 3 punishment, 4 rewards, 5 involvement?	1,2,3, occasionally 4	4, some 3	4, some 3 and 5	5, 4, based on group set goals
	Where is responsibility felt for achieving organization's goals?	Mostly at top	Top and middle	Fairly general	At all levels
COMMUNICATION	How much communication is aimed at achieving organization's objectives?	Very little	Little	Quite a bit	A great deal
	What is the direction of information flow?	Downward	Mostly downward	Down and up	Down, up, and sideways
	How is downward communication accepted?	With suspicion	Possibly with suspicion	With caution	With an open mind
	How accurate is upward communication?	Often wrong	Censored for the boss	Limited accuracy	Accurate
	How well do superiors know problems faced by subordinates?	Know little	Some knowledge	Quite well	Very well
DECISIONS	At what level are decisions formally made?	Mostly at top	Policy at top, some delegation	Broad policy at top, more delegation	Throughout but well integrated
	What is the origin of technical and professional knowledge used in decision making?	Top management	Upper and middle	To a certain extent, throughout	To a great extent, throughout
	Are subordinates involved in decisions related to their work?	Not at all	Occasionally consulted	Generally consulted	Fully involved
	What does decision-making process contribute to motivation?	Nothing, often weakens it	Relatively little	Some contribution	Substantial contribution
GOALS	How are organizational goals established?	Orders issued	Orders, some comment invited	After discussion, by orders	By group action (except in crisis)
	How much covert resistance to goals is present?	Strong resistance	Moderate resistance	Some resistance at times	Little or none
CONTROL	How concentrated are review and control functions?	Highly at top	Relatively highly at top	Moderate delegation to lower levels	Quite widely shared
	Is there an informal organization resisting the formal one?	Yes	Usually	Sometimes	No—same goals as formal
	What are cost, productivity, and other control data used for?	Policing, punishment	Reward and punishment	Reward, some self-guidance	Self-guidance, problem solving

Figure 1. Diagnose your management[1]

"participative" management system, well to the right on Likert's chart. He is next asked to repeat the procedure for the least successful company (or division) he knows well. Again, the profiles are nearly always the same, but this time they portray a strongly "authoritative" system, far to the left on the chart.

Then comes the point of the exercise. The executive is asked to describe his own company or division. Almost always, the resulting profile is that of a company somewhere in the middle, a blend of the "benevolent authoritative" and the "consultative"—well to the left of what the executive had previously identified as the most successful style. To check out the reliability of this self-analysis, Likert sometimes asks employees in the same company or division to draw its profile, too. They tend to rate it as slightly more "authoritative" than the boss does.

Likert believes that the predominant management style in U.S. industry today falls about in the middle of his chart, even though most managers seem to know from personal observation of other organizations that a more participative approach works better. What accounts for their consistent failure to emulate what they consider successful? Reaching for a general explanation, Likert asks his subjects one final question: "In your experience, what happens when the senior officer becomes concerned about earnings and takes steps to cut costs, increase productivity, and improve profits?" Most reply that the company's management profile shifts left, toward the authoritarian style. General orders to economize—and promptly—often result in quick, across-the-board budget cuts. Some programs with high potential are sacrificed along with obvious losers. Carefully laid, logical plans go down the drain. Some people are laid off—usually the least essential ones. But the best people in the organization sooner or later rebel at arbitrary decisions, and many of them leave.

At the outset, the arbitrary cost cutting produces a fairly prompt improvement in earnings, of course. But there is an unrecognized trade-off in the subsequent loss of human capital, which shows up still later in loss of business. In due course, management has to "swing right" again, rebuilding its human assets at great expense in order to restore good performance. Yet the manager who puts his firm through this dreary cycle, Likert observes, is often rewarded with a bonus at the outset, when things still look good. Indeed, he may be sent off to work his magic in another division!

Likert acknowledges that there are emergencies when sharp and sudden belt-tightening is inescapable. The trouble, he says, is that it is frequently at the expense of human assets and relationships that have taken years to build. Often it would make more sense to sell off inventory or dispose of a plant. But such possibilities are overlooked because human assets do not show up in the traditional balance sheet the way physical assets do. A company can, of course, lose $100,000 worth of talent and look better on its statement than if it sells off $10,000 worth of inventory at half price.

A dollars-and-cents way of listing the value of a good engineering staff, an experienced shop crew, or an executive group with effective, established working relations might indeed steady the hand of a hard-pressed president whose banker is on the phone. Likert believes he is now on the trail of a way to assign such values—values that should be at least as realistic as the often arbitrary and outdated figures given for real estate and plant. It will take some doing to get the notion accepted by bankers and accountants, however sophisticated his method turns out to be. But today's executives are hardly unaware that their long payrolls of expensive scientific and managerial talent represent an asset as well as an expense. Indeed, it is an asset that is often bankable. A merely more regular, explicit recognition of human assets in cost-cutting decisions would help to ensure that human assets get at least an even break with plant and inventory in time of trouble.

Likert and his institute colleagues are negotiating with several corporations to enlist them in a systematic five-year study, in effect a controlled experiment, that should put a firmer footing under tentative conclusions and hypotheses. This study will test Likert's belief that across-the-board participative management, carefully developed, sustained through thick and thin, and supported by a balance sheet that somehow reckons the human factor, will show better long-run results than the cyclical swing between authoritarian and participative styles reflected in the typical middle-ground profile on his chart.

CONVERSION IN A PAJAMA FACTORY

Already there's enough evidence in industry experience to suggest that participative management gets in trouble when it is adopted too fast. In some cases, an authoritarian management has abruptly ordered junior executives or employees to start taking on more responsibility, not recognizing that the directive itself reasserted the fact of continuing centralized control. Sometimes, of course, a hard shove may be necessary, as in the recent experience of Harwood Manufacturing Corp. of Marion, Virginia, which has employed participative practices widely for many years. When it acquired a rival pajama maker, Weldon Manufacturing Co., the latter's long-held authoritarian traditions were hard to crack. With patient but firm prodding by outside consultants, who acknowledge an initial element of "coercion," the switch in style was finally accomplished.

Ideally, in the view of Likert and others, a move of this kind should begin with the patient education of top executives, followed by the development of the needed skills in internal communication, group leadership, and the other requisites of the new system. Given time, this will produce better employee attitudes and begin to harness personal motivation to corporate goals. Still later, there will be improved productivity, less waste, lower turnover and absence rates, fewer grievances and slowdowns, improved product quality, and, finally, better customer relations.

The transformation may take several years. A checkup too early in the game might prove that participative management, even when thoroughly understood and embraced at the top, doesn't produce better results. By the same token, a management that is retreating from the new style in a typical cost squeeze may still be nominally participative, yet may already have thrown away the fruits of the system. Some research findings do indicate that participation isn't producing the hoped-for results. In Likert's view, these were spot checks, made without regard to which way the company was tending and where it was in the cycle of change.

A growing number of behaviorists, however, have begun to question whether the participative style is an ideal toward which all management should strive. If they once believed it was, more as a matter of faith in their long struggle against the "scientific" manager's machine-like view of man than as a finding from any new science of their own, they now are ready to take a second look at the proposition.

It seems plain enough that a research scientist generally benefits from a good deal of freedom and autonomy, and that top executives, confronted every day by new problems that no routine can anticipate, operate better with maximum consultation and uninhibited contributions from every member of the team. If the vice president for finance can't talk candidly with the vice president for production about financing the new plant, a lot of time can be wasted. In sales, group effort—instead of the usual competition—can be highly productive. But in the accounting department, things must go by the book. "Creative accounting" sounds more like a formula for jail than for the old behaviorists' dream of personal self-fulfillment on the job. And so with quality control in the chemical plant. An inspired adjustment here and there isn't welcome, thank you; just follow the specifications.

In the production department, automation has washed out a lot of the old problem of man as a prisoner of the assembly line, the kind of problem that first brought the "human relations" experts into the factories in the 1920's and 1930's. If a shop is full of computer-controlled machine tools busily reproducing themselves, the boy with the broom who sweeps away the shavings may be the only one who can put a personal flourish into his work. The creativity is all upstairs in the engineering and programing departments. But then, so are most of the people.

"Look what's happened in the last twenty years," says Harold J. Leavitt, a social psychologist who recently moved to Stanford after some years at Carnegie Tech. "Originally the concern of the human-relations people was with the blue-collar worker. Then the focus began to shift to foremen and to middle management. Now it's concentrated in special areas like research and development and in top management. Why? Because the 'group' style works best where nobody knows exactly and all the time what they're supposed to be doing, where there's a continuous need to change and adapt."

DEMOCRACY WORKS BETTER IN PLASTICS

One conclusion that has been drawn from this is that management style has to be custom-designed to fit the particular characteristics of each industry. The participative approach will work best in those industries that are in the vanguard of change. A Harvard Business School study has compared high-performance companies in three related, but subtly different, fields: plastics, packaged food, and standard containers. The plastics company faced the greatest uncertainties and change in research, new products, and market developments. The food company's business was somewhat more stable, while the container company encountered little or no requirement for innovation. The three achieved good results using markedly different management styles. The plastics firm provided for wide dispersal of responsibility for major decisions, the food company for moderate decentralization of authority, and the container company operated with fairly centralized control.

Less successful enterprises in each of the three industries were also examined, and their managements were compared with those of the high-performance companies. From this part of the study, Harvard researchers Paul Lawrence and Jay Lorsch drew another conclusion: not only may each industry have its own appropriate management style, but so may the individual operations within the same company. The companies that do best are those which allow for variations among their departments and know how to take these variations into account in coordinating the whole corporate effort.

Both the sales and the research departments in a fast-moving plastics company, for example, may adopt a style that encourages employees to participate actively in departmental decision making. But in special ways the two operations still need to differ. The research worker, for example, thinks in long-range terms, focusing on results expected in two or three years. The sales executive has his sights set on results next week or next month. This different sense of time may make it hard for the two departments to understand each other. But if top management recognizes the reasons and the need for such differences, each department will do its own job better, and they can be better coordinated. On the other hand, if top management ignores the differences and insists, for example, on rigidly uniform budgeting and planning timetables, there will be a loss of effectiveness.

It seems an obvious point that sales must be allowed to operate like sales, accounting like accounting, and production like production. But as Lawrence comments, "The mark of a good idea in this field is that as soon as it is articulated, it does seem obvious. People forget that, five minutes before, it wasn't. One curse of the behavioral scientist is that anything he comes up with is going to seem that way, because anything that's good *is* obvious."

PEOPLE, TOO, HAVE THEIR STYLES

Other behavioral scientists take the view that management style should be determined not so much by the nature of the particular business operation involved, but by the personality traits of the people themselves. There may be some tendency for certain kinds of jobs to attract certain kinds of people. But in nearly any shop or office a wide range of personality types may be observed. There is, for example, the outgoing, socially oriented scientist as well as the supposedly more typical introverted recluse. There are mature, confident managers, and there are those who somehow fill the job despite nagging self-doubt and a consuming need for reassurance.

For a long time, personality tests seemed to offer a way to steer people into the psychologically right kind of work. Whether such testing for placement is worthwhile is now a matter of some dispute. In any case, the whole question of individual differences is often reduced to little more than an office guessing game. Will Sue cooperate with Jane? Can Dorothy stand working for Jim? Will Harry take suggestions?

The participative approach to management may be based upon a greatly oversimplified notion about people, in the view of psychologist Clare Graves of Union College in Schenectady, New York. On the basis of limited samplings, he tentatively concludes that as many as half the people in the northeastern U.S., and a larger proportion nationwide, are not and many never will be the eager-beaver workers on whom the late Douglas McGregor of M.I.T. based his "Theory Y." Only some variation of old-style authoritarian management will meet their psychological needs, Graves contends.

Graves believes he has identified seven fairly distinct personality types, although he acknowledges that many people are not "purebreds" who would fit his abstractions perfectly and that new and higher personality forms may still be evolving. At the bottom of his well-ordered hierarchy he places the childlike "autistic" personality, which requires "close care and nurturing." Next up the scale are the "animistic" type, which must be dealt with by sheer force of enticement; the "ordered" personality that responds best to a moralistic management; and the "materialistic" individual who calls for pragmatic, hard bargaining. None of these are suited for the participative kind of management.

At the top of Grave's personality ladder are the "sociocentric," the "cognitive," and the "apprehending" types of people. They are motivated, respectively, by a need for "belonging," for "information," and for an "understanding" of the total situation in which they are involved. For each of these levels some form of participative management will work. However, those at the very top, the unemotional "apprehending" individuals, must be allowed pretty much to set their own terms for work. Management can trust such people to contribute usefully only according to their own cool perception of what is needed. They will seldom take the trouble to fight authority when they disagree with it, but merely withdraw, do a passable but not excellent job, and wait for management to see things their way. In that sense, these highest-level people are probably not ideal participators.

Graves believes most adults are stuck at one level throughout their lifetimes or move up a single notch, at best. He finds, incidentally, that there can be bright or dull, mature or immature behavior at nearly all levels. The stages simply represent psychological growth toward a larger and larger awareness of the individual's relationship to society.

If a company has a mixture of personality types, as most do, it must somehow sort them out. One way would be to place participative-type managers in charge of some groups, and authoritarian managers in charge of others. Employees would then be encouraged to transfer into sections where the management style best suits them. This would hardly simplify corporate life. But companies pushing the group approach might at least avoid substituting harmful new rigidities—"participate, or else!"—for the old ones.

THE ANTHROPOLOGICAL VIEW

Behaviorists who have been studying management problems from an anthropological viewpoint naturally stress cultural rather than individual differences. Manning Nash, of the University of Chicago's business school, for example, observes that the American emphasis on egalitarianism and performance has always tempered management style in the U.S. "No matter what your role is, if you don't perform, no one in this country will defer to you," he says. "Americans won't act unless they respect you. You couldn't have an American Charge of the Light Brigade." But try to export that attitude to a country with a more autocratic social tradition, and, in the words of Stanley Davis of Harvard, "it won't be bought and may not be workable."

Within the U.S. there are many cultural differences that might provide guides to managerial style if they could be successfully analyzed. Recent research by Lawrence and Arthur N. Turner at the Harvard Business School hints at important differences between blue-collar workers in cities and those in smaller towns, although religious and other factors fog the results. Town workers seem to seek "a relatively large amount of variety, autonomy, interaction, skill and responsibility" in their work, whereas city workers "find more simple tasks less stress-producing and more satisfying."

In managerial areas where democratic techniques *are* likely to work, the problem is how to give managers skill and practice in participation. The National Education Association's National Training Laboratories twenty years ago pioneered a way of doing this called "sensitivity training" (see "Two Weeks in a T-Group," *Fortune*, August, 1961). Small groups of men, commonly drawn from the executive ranks, sit down with a professional trainer but without agenda or rule book and "see what happens." The "vacuum" draws out first one and then another participant, in a way that tends to expose in fairly short order how he comes across to others.

The technique has had many critics, few more vocal than William Gomberg of the University of Pennsylvania's Wharton School. Renewing his assault recently, he called the "training" groups "titillating therapy, management development's most fashionable fad." When people from the same company are in the group, he argues, the whole exercise is an invasion of privacy, an abuse of the therapeutic technique to help the company, not the individual. For top executives in such groups,

Gomberg and others contend, the technique offers mainly a catharsis for their loneliness or insecurity.

"PSYCHING OUT THE BOSS"

Undoubtedly the T-group can be abused, intentionally or otherwise. But today's sensitivity trainers are trying to make sure the experience leads to useful results for both the individual and his firm. They realize that early groups, made up of total strangers gathered at some remote "cultural island," often gave the executive little notion of how to apply his new knowledge back on the job. To bring more realism to the exercise, the National Training Laboratories began ten years ago to make up groups of executives and managers from the same company, but not men who had working relationships with one another. These "cousin labs" have led, in turn, to some training of actual management "families," a boss and his subordinates. At the West Coast headquarters of the T-group movement, the business school at U.C.L.A., some now call such training "task-group therapy."

Many businessmen insist T-groups have helped them. Forty-three presidents and chairmen and hundreds of lesser executives are National Training Laboratories alumni. U.C.L.A. is besieged by applicants, and many are turned away.

Sensitivity training is supposed to help most in business situations where there is a great deal of uncertainty, as there is in the training sessions themselves. In such situations in the corporate setting there is sometimes a tendency for executives to withdraw, to defer action, to play a kind of game with other people in the organization to see who will climb out on a limb first. A chief ploy is "psyching out the boss," which means trying to anticipate the way the winds of ultimate decision will blow and to set course accordingly.

The aim of sensitivity training is to stop all this, to get the executive's nerve up so that he faces facts, or, in the words of U.C.L.A.'s James V. Clark, to "lay bare the stress and strain faster and get a resolution of the problem." In that limited sense, such therapy could well serve any style of management. In Clark's view, this kind of training, early in the game, might save many a company a costly detour on the road to company-wide "democracy." He cites the experience of Non-Linear Systems, Inc., of Del Mar, California, a manufacturer of such electronic gear as digital voltmeters and data-logging equipment and an important supplier to aerospace contractors. The company is headed by Andrew Kay, a leading champion of the participative style. At the lower levels, Kay's application of participative concepts worked well. He gave workers responsibility for "the whole black box," instead of for pieces of his complex finished products. Because it was still a box, with some definite boundaries, the workers seized the new opportunity without fear or hesitation. The psychological magic of meaningful work, as opposed to the hopelessly specialized chore, took hold. Productivity rose.

VICE PRESIDENTS IN MIDAIR

But at the executive level, Kay moved too quickly, failing to prepare his executives for broad and undefined responsibilities—or failing to choose men better suited for the challenge. One vice president was put in charge of "innovation." Suspended in midair, without the support of departments or functional groups and lacking even so much as a job description, most of the V.P.'s became passive and incapable of making decisions. "They lost touch with reality—including the reality of the market," recalls Clark. When the industry suffered a general slump and new competition entered the field, Non-Linear wasn't ready. Sales dropped 16 percent, according to Kay. In time he realized he was surrounded with dependent men, untrained to participate in the fashion he had peremptorily commanded. He trimmed his executive group and expects to set a new sales record this year.

Sheldon Davis of TRW Systems in Redondo Beach, California, blames the behavioral scientists themselves for breakdowns like Non-Linear's. Too often, he argues, "their messages come out sounding soft and easy, as if what we are trying to do is build happy teams of employees who feel 'good' about things, rather than saying we're trying to build effective organizations with groups that function well and that can zero in quickly on their problems and deal with them rationally."

To Davis, participation should mean "tough, open exchange," focused on the problem, not the organizational chart. Old-style managers who simply dictate a solution are wrong, he argues, and so are those new-style managers who think the idea is simply to go along with a subordinate's proposals if they're earnestly offered. Neither approach taps the full potential of the executive group. When problems are faced squarely, Davis believes, the boss—who should remain boss—gets the best solution because all relevant factors are thoroughly considered. And because everyone has contributed to the solution and feels responsible for it, it is also the solution most likely to be carried out.

One of the most useful new developments in the behavioral study of management is a fresh emphasis on collaboration with technology. In the early days of the human-relations movement in industry, technology was often regarded as "the enemy," the source of the personal and social problems that the psychologists were trying to treat. But from the beginning, some social scientists wanted to move right in and help fashion machines and industrial processes so as to reduce or eliminate their supposedly antihuman effects. Today this concept is more than mere talk. The idea is to develop so-called "social-technical" systems that permit man and technology *together* to produce the best performance.

Some early experimentation in the British coal mines, by London's Tavistock Institute, as well as scattered work in this country and in Scandinavia, have already demonstrated practical results from such a collaboration. Tavistock found that an attempt to apply specialized factory-style technology to coal mining had isolated the miners from one another. They missed the sense of group support and self-direction that had helped them cope with uncertainty and danger deep in the coal faces. Productivity suffered. In this case, Tavistock's solution was to redesign the new system so that men could still work in groups.

In the U.S. a manufacturer of small household appliances installed some highly sophisticated new technical processes that put the company well in the front of its field. But the engineers had broken down the jobs to such an extent that workers were getting no satisfaction out of their performance and productivity declined. Costs went up and, in the end, some of the new machinery had to be scrapped.

Some technologists seem more than ready to welcome a partnership with the human-relations expert. Louis Davis, a professor of engineering, has joined the U.C.L.A. business-school faculty to lead a six-man socio-technical research group that includes several behaviorists. Among them is Eric Trist, a highly respected psychologist from the Tavistock Institute. Davis hopes today's collaboration will lead in time to a new breed of experts knowledgeable in both the engineering and the social disciplines.

"IT'S TIME WE STOPPED BUILDING RIVAL DICTIONARIES"

The importance of time, the nature of the task, the differences within a large organization, the nature of the people, the cultural setting, the psychological preparation of management, the relationship to technology—all these and other variables are making the search for effective managerial style more and more complex. But the growing recognition of these complexities has drained the human-relations movement of much of its antagonism toward the "super-rationalism" of management science. Humanists must be more systematic and rational if they are to make some useful sense of the scattered and half-tested concepts they have thus far developed, and put their new theories to a real test.

A number of behaviorists believe it is well past time to bury the hatchet and collaborate in earnest with the mathematicians and economists. Some business schools and commercial consulting groups are already realigning their staffs to encourage such work. It won't be easy. Most "systems" thinkers are preoccupied with bringing all the relevant knowledge to bear on a management problem in a systematic way, seeking the theoretically "best" solution. Most behaviorists have tended to assume that the solution which is *most likely to be carried out* is the best one, hence their focus on involving lots of people in the decision making so that they will follow through. Where the "experts" who shape decisions are also in charge of getting the job done, the two approaches sometimes blend, in practice. But in many organizations, it is a long, long road from a creative and imaginative decision to actual performance. A general theory of management must show how to build systematic expertise into a style that is also well suited to people.

The rapprochement among management theorists has a distinguished herald, Fritz J. Roethlisberger of Harvard Business School, one of the human-relations pioneers who first disclosed the potential of the "small group" in industrial experiments forty years ago. He laughs quickly at any suggestion that a unified approach will come easily. "But after all, we are all looking at the same thing," he says. "It's time we stopped building rival dictionaries and learned to make some sentences that really say something."

NOTES

1. This figure is adapted from a technique developed by Rensis Likert, director of the Institute for Social Research at the University of Michigan, to help businessmen analyze their companies' management style. Anyone—executive or employee—can use it to diagnose his own company or division. Check the appropriate answers, using guide marks to shade your emphasis. After the first question, for example, if your answer is "almost none," put the check in the first or second notch of the "none" box. Regard each answer as a sort of rating on a continuous scale from the left to the right of the chart. When you have answered each question, draw a line from the top to the bottom of the chart through the check marks. The result will be a profile of your management. To determine which way management style has been shifting, repeat the process for the situation as it was three, five, or ten years ago. Finally, sketch the profile you think would help your company or division to improve its performance. Likert has tried the chart on a number of business executives. Most of them rated their own companies about in the middle—embracing features of Systems 2 and 3. But nearly all of them also believe that companies do best when they have profiles well to the right of the chart, and worst with profiles well to the left. (Adapted, with permission, from *The Human Organization: Its Management and Value*, by Rensis Likert, published in April, 1967, by McGraw-Hill.)

MARTIN LAKIN

Some Ethical Issues in Sensitivity Training

Sensitivity training, in its various forms, has evolved over the past two decades. It is a powerful form of experiential learning that includes self, interactional, and organizational understanding. It has its origins in the study of change and conflict resolution through attention to underlying as well as overt interactional processes. It has been widely used to reexamine managerial, pedagogic, and "helping relationships" from the factory to the classroom, from the community to the home. Typically, small groups of participants under the guidance of a "trainer" use the data of their own spontaneous interactions, and reactions to one another. The trainer functions to facilitate communication, to indicate underlying problems of relating, and to model constructive feedback. He keeps the group moving and productively learning about processes and persons and helps to avoid counterproductive conflict or unnecessary damage to participants. With the evolution of mutant forms of training, particularly over the past few years, and their growing popularity, examination of latent ethical questions has become urgent. This article is presented not to censure an obviously significant and often helpful growth in American psychology, but rather to open for discussion and scrutiny elements of it that affect public welfare and reflect on professional standards.

Source: *American Psychologist*, October, 1967, pp. 923-928. Copyright © 1969 by the American Psychological Association. Reprinted by permission.

The number of persons who have experienced some form of training is rapidly growing. However named (training, encounter, human relations), the experience invariably involves emotional confrontations and even an implicit injunction to reconsider if not actually to change personal behavior patterns. Since participants are not self-avowed psychotherapy patients but "normal" persons, and because the trainers are presumably not concerned with reparative but with learning or personal enhancement, it is difficult to draw a firm line between it and other psychotherapeutic forms. Indeed, comparison inevitably forces itself upon us and suggests strongly what many of us realize so well, that a distinction between "normal" and "pathological" behavior is hazy at best. However, the comparison also compels one to consider ethical implications of the differences between the contractual relationships between participant and trainer, on the one hand, and those between patient and therapist, on the other. Concerns about the contractual implications have been only partially met by statements of differences in the goals of training from those of therapy and by the difference in self-definition of a participant from that of a patient, as well as by the avowed educational objectives of trainers. Also, formerly it could be argued that the trainer had little therapeutic responsibility because he initiated little; that interactions of the group were the resultant of collective interchange and give-and-take, and did not occur at his instance: that is, a participant "discloses" intimate details of his life or "changes" behavior patterns as a result of a personal commitment or a collective experience rather than because a trainer directs him to do so. Training groups evolved from a tradition of concern with *democratic* processes and *democratic* change. The generally accepted hypothesis was that the best psychological protection against unwarranted influence was individual and collective awareness that could forestall insidious manipulation by dominant leaders or conformist tyranny by a group.

Many people currently involved in the various forms of training are not as psychologically sophisticated or able to evaluate its processes as were the mainly professional participants of some years ago. The motivation of many present participants is cathartic rather than intellectual (e.g., seeking an emotional experience rather than an understanding). Particularly because training is increasingly used as a vehicle for achieving social change, it is necessary to explore its ethical implications—notwithstanding our as yet incomplete understanding of its special processes. There are ethically relevant problems in setting up a group experience, in conducting the group, and following its termination.

PREGROUP CONCERNS

A psychotherapeutic intention is clear by contrast with the training intention. Sophisticated therapists know that this clarity is not absolute; complex issues of values and commitment to specific procedures cannot really be shared with patients, despite the best intentions of a therapist to be candid. Nevertheless, the therapist's mandate is relatively clear—to provide a corrective experience for someone who presents himself as psychologically impaired. By contrast, participant expectancies and fantasies about training vary much more widely. By comparison with the therapist, the trainer's mandate is relatively ambiguous. For example, some trainers view the group experience primarily as a vehicle to produce increased awareness of interactional processes to be employed in social or organizational settings. However, currently, some others dismiss this goal as trivial in favor of an expressive or "existential" experience. Both approaches are similar in that they require a participant-observer role for the trainee. Yet, the emphasis upon rational and emotional elements differs in these approaches, and this difference makes for divergent experiences. The problem is that there is no way for a participant to know in advance, much less to appraise, intentions of trainers, processes of groups, or their consequences for him. It is not feasible to explain these because training, like psychotherapy, depends upon events that counter the participant's accustomed expectations in order to have maximum impacts. Since it is inimical to training to preprogram participant or process, the nature of the training experience depends more than anything upon the particular translations, intentions, and interventions the trainer makes. This makes it imperative for the trainer to be first of all clear about his own intentions and goals.

Training has begun to attract the participation of more psychologically disturbed persons in recent years—a higher proportion of more frustrated individuals seeking personal release or solutions. Correspondingly, there is a larger supply of inadequately prepared persons who do training. To my knowledge, only the National Training Laboratories—Institute of Applied Behavioral Science has given systematic consideration to the training of leaders, but even its accredited trainers are not all prepared to deal with the range of expectations and pathologies currently exhibited by some participants. Some people who are inadequately prepared are suggesting to other people what they feel, how to express their feelings, and interpreting how others respond to them. Some, equally poorly prepared persons, are engaged in applying training to social action and to institutions. Recently, it has come to my attention that there are inadequately prepared trainers who lead student groups on college campuses without supervision. Several eye-witness accounts of these groups suggest that highest value is placed upon intensity of emotionality and on dramatic confrontations. Screening of participants is virtually unknown and follow-up investigation of the effects of these groups is unheard of. Their leaders are usually individuals who have participated in only one or two experiences themselves. Most disturbing of all, there is no sign that these leaders are aware of or concerned about their professional limitations. I think it must be recognized that it will be difficult to restrain poorly prepared individuals from practicing training in the absence of a clear statement of standards of training, trainer preparation, and the publication of a code of training ethics. (An antiprofessional bias is very popular just now, as we all know, and training fits nicely the image of "participative decision making.") Unfortunately, accredited and competent trainers have done little to deter the belief that training requires little preparation and is universally applicable. I do not exempt the National Training Laboratories from responsibility in this regard.

"Adequate preparation" should be spelled out. One would wish to avoid jurisdictional protectionism, although a degree in a recognized educative or therapeutic discipline is certainly one index of responsible preparation. For work with the public, trainers should have had, in addition to a recognized advanced degree in one of the "helping professions," background preparation in personality dynamics, a knowledge of psychopathology as well as preparation in group dynamics, social psychology, and sociology. They should also have had an internship and extensive supervised experience.

It should be recognized that it is difficult, if not impossible, to do effective screening in order to prevent the participation of persons for whom training is inappropriate. One reason is that it is almost impossible to prevent false assertions about one's mental status on application forms. It is also true that it is difficult to assess the precise effects of training upon a particular individual. It could be argued that short-range discomfort might be followed by long-range benefits. Probably the most important step that could be taken immediately would be the elimination of promotional literature that suggests by implication that training is, indeed, "psychotherapy," and that it can promise immediate results. Why has such a step not been taken until now? I suggest that one reason is that currently many trainers do indeed view training as a form of therapy even though they do not explicitly invite psychologically troubled applicants. They do not wish to screen out those who do seek psychotherapy. But this reluctance to exclude such persons makes it almost certain that psychologically impaired individuals will be attracted in large numbers to training as a therapy.

More serious is the fact that there is little evidence on which to base a therapeutic effectiveness claim. To me it seems indefensible that advertising for training should be as seductive as it is in offering hope for in-depth changes of personality or solutions to marital problems in the light of present inadequate evidence that such changes or solutions do occur. Greater candor is necessary about the needs that are being addressed by the newer training forms. A legitimate case could perhaps be made for the temporary alleviation of loneliness that is unfortunately so widespread in contemporary urban and industrial life, but the training experience as a palliative is neither learning about group processes nor is it profound personal change. Such candor is obviously a first requisite in face of the fact that some training brochures used in promotion literally trumpet claims of various enduring benefits. I suggest that immediate steps need to be taken to investigate these claims, to reconsider the implementation of screening procedures, set up and publicize accreditation standards, and monitor promotional methods in order to safeguard the public's interest and professional integrity.

ETHICAL QUESTIONS RELATED TO THE PROCESSES OF TRAINING GROUPS

Being a trainer is an exciting role and function. Being looked to for leadership of one kind or another and being depended upon for guidance is a very "heady" thing as every psychotherapist knows. On the other hand, training, in its beginnings, was based on the idea that participation and involvement on the part of all the members of the group would lead to the development of a democratic society in which personal autonomy and group responsibility were important goals. The trainer had only to facilitate this evolution. Personal exertion of power and influence, overt or covert, was naturally a significant issue for study and learning in group after group. Evaluation of the trainer's influence attempts was crucial for learning about one's responses to authority. The trainer was indeed an influence, but the generally accepted commitment to objectification of his function made his behavior accessible to inquiry and even to modification. Correspondingly, experienced trainers have almost always been aware that the degree of influence they wield is disproportionately large; therefore they, themselves, tried to help the group understand the need for continual assessment of this factor. Awareness of this "transference" element has stimulated trainers in the past to emphasize group processes that would reveal its operations and effects.

However, with the advent of a more active and directing training function that includes trainer-based pressures upon participants to behave in specific ways, but without provision for monitoring of trainer practices, the "democratic" nature of the group interaction is subverted. More important is the fact that there is less possibility for participants to overtly evaluate the influences exerted upon them by the trainer. In some groups that emphasize emotional expressiveness, some trainers purposefully elicit aggressive and/or affectionate behaviors by modeling them and then by inviting imitation. Some even insist that members engage one another in physically aggressive or affectionate acts. Still others provide music to create an emotional experience. Such leadership intends to create certain emotional effects. It does so, however, without sufficient opportunity to work them through. Moreover, analytic or critical evaluation of such experiences would almost certainly be viewed as subversive of their aims.

It will be argued that participants willingly agree to these practices. The fact that the consumer seeks or agrees to these experiences does not justify them as ethically defensible or psychologically sound. It should be remembered that "the contract" is not between persons who have an equal understanding of the processes involved. It cannot be assumed that the participant really knows what he is letting himself in for. At the request of the trainer, and under pressure of group approval, some aggressive displays (e.g., slappings) or affectional displays (e.g., hugging) have occurred that some participants later came to view as indignities.

The question of group acquiescence involves a related point. A crucial element in the history of training was its stress upon genuine consensus. This emphasis was a deterrent to the domination of any single power figure or to the establishment of arbitrary group norms. Action and "decision" were painstakingly arrived at out of group interaction, consisting of increasingly candid exchanges. Influence could be exerted only under continuing group scrutiny and evaluation. Some trainers who are impelled to elicit expressiveness as a primary goal are also committed to democratic values; however, owing to their primary commitment to the significance of emotional expressiveness, they may employ their sensitivities and skills to achieving it in ways that are relatively subtle or even covert. When the participant is encouraged to experience and express strong emotions, the trainer's function in promoting these is often obscured. What is often *his* decision or initiative is presented as *group* initiative. In his recent book, Kelman (1968) has suggested that a group leader has the responsibility of making group members aware of his own operations and values. I find no fault with that suggestion; however, it is very difficult to accomplish this. It is made even more difficult, if I am correct, because some trainers may even have an interest in the group remaining *unaware* of their particular manipulations because they wish to sustain the illusion that it is the group's rather than their own personal decision that results in a particular emotional process. The intention may not be to deceive consciously. It is difficult for trainers to practice complete candor with their participants and yet to facilitate the processes of training for reasons I suggested above. Nevertheless, in the light of these questions, trainers should reexamine their own activities. It might be that aroused concern will lead established trainers to take the necessary steps to educate aspirants for professional status to a new sensitivity to these issues.

LEARNING AND EXPERIENTIAL FOCUSES

There are genuine differences in point of view and in emphasis between trainers. Some regard the emotional-experiential as the primary value in training. Others uphold a more cognitive emphasis, while recognizing that a high degree of emotional engagement is a vital part of training. For their part, participants are, more often than not, so emotionally involved as to be confused about just what it is that they are doing, feeling, or thinking at a given point in time. We know that participants slide back and forth between cognitive and effective experiencing of training. The participant must partially depend upon external sources for confirmation or disconfirmation. He looks to other members, but most of all to the trainer himself, for clarification. Surely, dependency plays a huge role, but it will not be destroyed by fiat. It is the responsibility of the trainer to make as clear as he can his own activities, his own view of what is significant, and to encourage exchanges of views among participants so that all can have the possibility of differential self-definition and orientation during the training process. This would help prevent a situation where inchoate and inarticulated pressures push individual participants beyond their comprehension.

In training, as in any other society, there are pressures of majority upon minority, of the many upon the one. Scapegoating, where recognized, would be objected to as demeaning whether it occurs as a means of inducing conformity or to build self-esteem. When the focus is upon group processes, it is often brought into the open, discussed, and countered. Where, however, the emphasis is purely on personal expressiveness, the same phenomenon may be used as a pressure rather than exposed. The implicit demand for emotionality and emphasis upon nonverbal communication even makes it more difficult to identify scapegoating when it occurs in such groups.

ETHICAL ISSUES AND EVALUATIONS

Participants sometimes come to training under "threat" of evaluation. The implications of a refusal to participate by an employee, a subordinate, or a student have not been sufficiently studied. I recall one instance where an employee of a highly sensitive security agency was sent for training. His anxious, conflicted, and disturbed response to training norms of "trust" and "openness" were not only understandable but, in retrospect, predictable. True, the commitment to maintain confidentiality was honored; nevertheless, should his participation have been solicited or even permitted? Evaluation as a participant concern is unavoidable, despite protestations and reassurances to the contrary. Training of trainers should emphasize the professional's ethical responsibility in these matters, but it will not obviate these concerns. The increase in unaccredited and marginally prepared trainers must increase them. It is difficult for most people to monitor their own tendencies to gossip or inform. Especially if the trainer is also an evaluator of participants, he cannot really compartmentalize the impressions he gets of behavior in training, from other data that he has about the participants. Perhaps it would help to make everyone aware of this fact. At least the "risk" then becomes explicit from everyone's point of view.

A diminution of risk was thought to be one of the major advantages of "stranger" groups where time-limited contact was thought to encourage a degree of candor and interpersonal experiment that was nominally proscribed. Obviously, this cannot be the case in groups where participants are related, classmates, or involved in the same company or agency. It should be recognized that it is almost impossible to assure confidentiality under such circumstances or to prevent "out of school" reports. Trainers need to be especially sensitive to this in preparing other trainers. For example, where graduate students are involved in training groups and have social or other connections with one another, or with those they observe, numerous possibilities for teaching the importance of professional detachment present themselves. Trainees should learn how important it is to avoid irresponsible behavior in order to maintain the confidence of participants, how vital it is to inhibit a desire for personal contact when they have a professional role to play. Essentially, they have the same problem that faces the fledgling psychotherapist in inhibiting his own curiosity and social impulse in order to fulfill a professional function. The necessary detachment emphasized here is yet another significant and ethically relevant area that emotional expressiveness as an end in itself does not articulate. Responsibility is taught and modeled. It should be as consciously done in training as in any other helping relationship.

POSTTRAINING ETHICAL ISSUES

A strongly positive reaction to training more frequently than not impels the gratified participant to seek further training experiences. Unfortunately, almost as frequently he seeks to do training himself. After all, it appears relatively easy. The apparent power and emotional gratifications of the trainer seem very attractive. If steps in professional preparation in becoming a trainer are not better articulated, and closely wedded to the traditional helping professions, we shall soon have vast numbers of inadequate trainers who practice their newly discovered insights on others, in the naive conviction that they have all but mastered the skills involved in group processes and application to personal and social problems.

A final issue to which I wish to call your attention is that of posttraining contact with the participant. Participants are often dramatically affected by training. In some cases, trainer and group are mutually reluctant to end the group. In a recent case that came to my attention, my view is that the trainer was seduced, as it were, by the group's responsiveness to him. In turn, the participants were delighted by the trainer's continuing interest. Trainers must be aware of the powerful desire to sustain a relationship with them. Therefore, they must be clear at the outset what limits they propose for training. It is as important to be determinate about the termination point of training as about any other aspect of its conduct. Under the conditions of ambiguity and ambivalence of an "indeterminate" relationship, participants appear to be caught, as it were, midstream, uncertain as to the definition or possibilities of a relationship with this presumed expert upon whom they naturally depend for guidance and limit setting.

The questions that I have raised do not admit of a quick solution. They are ethical dilemmas. Steps to eliminate or ameliorate the grossest of them can be taken through awareness and self-monitoring. One practical step that I propose is the immediate creation of a commission by our professional organization to investigate training practices, standards of training preparation, and to recommend a code of ethics for accredited trainers. Research may help, but I doubt that it can come quickly enough to affect the increasing danger of the current and potentially still greater excesses in this area.

Sensitivity training is one of the most compelling and significant psychological experiences and vehicles for learning as well as a promising laboratory for the study of human relationships, dyadic, and group. It may be a superior device for personal and social change, even for amelioration or resolution of social conflict. However, it may also be abused or subverted into an instrument of unwarranted influence and ill-considered, even harmful, practices. The immediate attention of the profession is necessary to maintain its positive potential and correspondingly respectable standards of practice.

REFERENCE

Kelman, H.C. *A time to speak—On human values and social research?* San Francisco: Jossey-Bass, 1968.

ROBERT N. FORD

Job Enrichment Lessons From AT&T

There is a mounting problem in the land, the concern of employed persons with their work life. Blue-collar workers are increasingly expressing unhappiness over the monotony of the production line. White-collar workers want to barter less of their life for bread. More professional groups are unionizing to fight back at somebody.

The annual reports of many companies frequently proclaim, "Our employees are our most important resource." Is this a statement of conviction or is it mere rhetoric? If it represents conviction, then I think it is only fair to conclude that many business organizations are unwittingly squandering their resources.

The enormous economic gains that sprang from the thinking of the scientific management school of the early 1900's—the time-and-motion study analysts, the creators of production lines—may have ended insofar as they depend on utilizing human beings more efficiently. Without discarding these older insights, we need to consider more recent evidence showing that the tasks themselves can be changed to give workers a feeling of accomplishment.

The growing pressure for a four-day work-week is not necessarily evidence that people do not care about their work; they may be rejecting their work in the form that confronts them. To ask employees to repeat one small task all day, at higher and higher rates of speed, is no way to reduce the pressure for a shorter work-week, nor is it any longer a key to rising productivity in America. Work need not be so frequently a betrayal of one's education and ability.

From 1965 to 1968 a group of researchers at AT&T conducted 19 formal field experiments in job enrichment. The success of these studies has led to many company projects since then. From this work and the studies of others, we have learned that the "lifesaving" portion of many jobs can be expanded. Conversely, the boring and unchallenging aspects can be reduced—not to say eliminated.

Furthermore, the "nesting" of related, already enriched jobs—a new concept—may constitute another big step toward better utilization of "our most important resource."

First in this article I shall break down the job enrichment strategy into three steps. Then I shall demonstrate what we at AT&T have been doing for seven years in organizing the work beyond enrichment of individual jobs. In the course of my discussion, I shall use no illustrations that were not clearly successful from the viewpoint of both employees and the company.

While obviously the functions described in the illustrations differ superficially from those in most other companies, they are still similar enough to production and service tasks in other organizations to permit meaningful comparison. It is important to examine the nature of the work itself, rather than the external aspects of the functions.

Moreover, in considering ways to enrich jobs, I am not talking about those elements that serve only to "maintain" employees: wages, fringe benefits, clean restrooms, a pleasant atmosphere, and so on. Any organization must meet the market in these respects or its employees will go elsewhere.

No, employees are saying more than "treat me well." They are also saying "use me well." The former is the maintenance side of the coin; the latter is the work motivation side.

ANATOMY OF ENRICHMENT

In talking about job enrichment, it is necessary to go beyond such high-level concepts as "self-actualization," "need for achievement," and "psychological growth." It is necessary to specify the steps to be taken. The strategy can be broken down into these aspects—improving work through systematic changes in (a) the module of work, (b) control of the module, and (c) the feedback signaling whether something has been accomplished. I shall discuss each of these aspects in turn.

Work Module

Through changing the work modules, Indiana Bell Telephone Company scored a striking success in job enrichment within the space of two years. In Indianapolis, 33 employees, most of them at the lowest clerical wage level, compiled all telephone directories for the state. The processing from clerk to clerk was laid out in 21 steps, many of which were merely for verification. The steps included manuscript reception, manuscript verification, keypunch, keypunch verification, ad copy reception, ad copy verification, and so on—a production line as real as any in Detroit. Each book is issued yearly to the customers named in it, and the printing schedule calls for the appearance of about one different directory per week.

In 1968, the year previous to the start of our study, 28 new hires were required to keep the clerical force at the 33-employee level. Obviously, such turnover had bad consequences. From every operating angle, management was dissatisfied.

In a workshop, the supervisors concluded that the lengthy verification routine, calling for confirmation of one's work by other clerks, was not solving the basic problem, which was employee indifference toward the tasks. Traditional "solutions" were ineffective. They included retraining, supervisor complaints to the employees, and "communicating" with them on the importance to customers of error-free listing of their names and places of business in the directories. As any employee smart enough to be hired knows, an incorrect listing will remain monumentally wrong for a whole year.

The supervisors came up with many ideas for enriching the job. The first step was to identify the most competent employees, and then ask them, one by one, if they felt they could do error-free work, so that having others check the work would be pointless. Would they check their own work if no one else did it?

Yes, they said they could do error-free work. With this simple step the module dropped from 21 slices of clerical work to 14.

Next the supervisory family decided to take a really big step. In the case of the thinner books, they asked certain employees whether they would like to "own" their own books and perform all 14 remaining steps with no verification unless they themselves arranged it with other clerks—as good stenographers do when in doubt about a difficult piece of paperwork. Now the module included every step (except keytape, a minor one).

Then the supervisors turned their attention to a thick book, the Indianapolis directory, which requires many hands and heads. They simply assigned letters of the alphabet to individuals and let them complete all 14 steps for each block of letters.

In the past, new entries to all directories had moved from clerk to clerk; now all paperwork connected with an entry belonging to a clerk stayed with that clerk. For example, the clerk prepared the daily addenda and issued them to the information or directory assistance operators. The system became so efficient that most of the clerks who handled the smaller directories had charge of more than one.

Delimiting the module: In an interview one of the clerks said, "It's a book of my own." That is the way they felt about the books. Although not all modules are physically so distinct, the idea for a good module is usually there. Ideally, it is a slice of work that gives an employee a "thing of my own." At AT&T I have heard good modules described with pride in various ways:

- "A piece of turf" (especially a geographic responsibility).
- "My real estate" (by engineers responsible for a group of central offices).
- "Our cradle-to-grave modem line" (a vastly improved Western Electric switching-device production line).
- "Our mission impossible team" (a framemen's team, Long Lines Department).

The trouble with so much work processing is that no one is clearly responsible for a total unit that fails. In Indianapolis, by contrast, when a name in a directory is misspelled or omitted, the clerk knows where the responsibility lies.

Delimiting the module is not usually difficult when the tasks are in production, or at least physically defined. It is more difficult in service tasks, such as handling a telephone call. But modules make sense here, too, if the employee has been prepared for the work so that nobody else need be involved—in other words, when it is not necessary to say to the caller, "Let me connect you with my supervisor about that, please" or "May I give you our billing department, please?"

It is not always true that any one employee can handle a complete service. But our studies show that we consistently erred in forming the module; we tended to "underwhelm" employees. Eventually we learned that the worker can do more, especially as his or her experience builds. We do not have even one example from our business where job enrichment resulted in a *smaller* slice of work.

In defining modules that give each employee a natural area of responsibility, we try to accumulate horizontal slices of work until we have created (or recreated) one of these three entities for him or her:

1. A customer (usually someone outside the business).

2. A client (usually someone inside the business helping the employee serve the customer).

3. A task (in the manufacturing end of the business, for example, where, ideally, individual employees produce complete items).

Any one of these three can make a meaningful slice of work. (In actuality, they are not separated; obviously, an employee can be working on a task for a customer.) Modules more difficult to differentiate are those in which the "wholeness" of the job is less clear—that is, control is not complete. They include cases where—

- the employee is merely one of many engaged in providing the ultimate service or item;
- the employee's customer is really the boss (or, worse yet, the boss's boss) who tells him what to do;
- the job is to help someone who tells the employee what is to be done.

While jobs like these are harder to enrich, it is worth trying.

Control of the Module

As an employee gains experience, the supervisor should continue to turn over responsibility until the employee is handling the work completely. The reader may infer that supervisors are treating employees unequally. But it is not so; ultimately, they may all have the complete job if they can handle it. In the directory-compilation case cited—which was a typical assembly-line procedure, although the capital investment was low—the supervisors found that they could safely permit the employee to say when sales of advertisements in the yellow pages must stop if the ads were to reach the printer on time.

Employees of South Central Bell Telephone Company, who set their own cutoff dates for the New Orleans, Monroeville, and Shreveport phone books, consistently gave themselves less time than management had previously allowed. As a result, the sale of space in the yellow pages one year continued for three additional weeks, producing more than $100,000 in extra revenue.

But that was only one element in the total module and its control. The directory clerks talked *directly* to salesmen, to the printer, to supervisors in other departments about production problems, to service representatives, and to each other as the books moved through the production stages.

There are obvious risks on the supervisors' side as they give their jobs away, piece by piece, to selected employees. We have been through it enough to advise, "Don't worry." Be assured that supervisors who try it will say, as many in the Bell System have said, "Now, at last, I feel like a manager. Before I was merely chief clerk around here."

In other studies we have made, control has been handed by the supervisor to a person when the employee is given the authority to perform such tasks as these:

- Set credit ratings for customers.
- Ask for, and determine the size of a deposit.
- Cut off service for nonpayment.
- Make his or her own budget, subject to negotiation.
- Perform work other than that on the order sheet after negotiating it with the customer.
- Reject a run or supply of material because of poor quality.
- Make free use of small tools or supplies within a budget negotiated with the supervisor.
- Talk to anyone at any organizational level when the employee's work is concerned.
- Call directly and negotiate for outside repairmen or suppliers (within the budget) to remedy a condition handicapping the employee's performance.

Feedback

Definition of the module and control of it are futile unless the results of the employee's effort are discernible. Moreover, knowledge of the results should go directly to where it will nurture motivation—that is, to the employee. People have a great capacity for mid-flight correction when they know where they stand.

One control responsibility given to excellent employees in AT&T studies is self-monitoring; it lets them record their own "qualities and quantities." For example, one employee who had only a grade-school education was taught to keep a quality control chart in which the two identical parts of a dry-reed switch were not to vary more than .005 from an ideal dimension. She found that for some reason too many switches were failing.

She proved that the trouble occurred when one reed that was off by .005 met another reed that was off by .005. The sum, .010, was too much in the combined component and it failed. On her own initiative, she recommended and saw to it that the machine dies were changed when the reeds being stamped out started to vary by .003 from the ideal. A total variance of .006 would not be too much, she reasoned. Thus the feedback she got showed her she was doing well at her job.

The example shows all three factors at work—the module, its control, and feedback. She and two men, a die maker and a machine operator, had the complete responsibility for producing each day more than 100,000 of these tiny parts, which are not unlike two paper matches, but much smaller. How can one make a life out of this? Well, they did. The six stamping machines and expensive photometric test equipment were "theirs." A forklift truck had been dedicated to them (no waiting for someone else to bring or remove supplies). They ordered rolls of wire for stamping machines when they estimated they would need it. They would ship a roll back when they had difficulty controlling it.

Compared with workers at a plant organized along traditional lines, with batches of the reeds moving from shop to shop, these three employees were producing at a fourfold rate. Such a minigroup, where each person plays a complementary part, is radically different psychologically from the traditional group of workers, where each is doing what the others do.

(In the future, when now undreamed-of computer capacities have been reached, management must improve its techniques of feeding performance results directly to the employee responsible. And preferably it should be done *before* the boss knows about it.)

IMPROVING THE SYSTEM

When a certain job in the Bell System is being enriched, we ask the supervisory family, "Who or what is the customer/client/task in this job?" Also, "How often can the module be improved?" And then, "How often can control or feedback be improved? Can we improve all three at once?"

These are good questions to ask in general. My comments at this stage of our knowledge must be impressionistic.

The modules of most jobs can be improved, we have concluded. Responsibilities or tasks that exist elsewhere in the shop or in some other shop or department need to be combined with the job under review. This horizontal loading is necessary until the base of the job is right. However, I have not yet seen a job whose base was too broad.

At levels higher than entrance grade, and especially in management positions, many responsibilities can be moved to lower grade levels, usually to the advantage of every job involved. This vertical loading is especially important in mature organizations.

In the Indianapolis directory office, 21 piece-meal tasks were combined into a single, meaningful, natural task. There are counterparts in other industries, such as the assembly of an entire dashboard of an automobile by two workers.

We have evidence that two jobs—such as the telephone installer's job and the telephone repairman's job—often can make one excellent "combinationman's" job. But there are some jobs in which the work module is already a good one. One of these is the service representative, the highly trained clerk to whom a customer speaks when he wants to have a telephone installed, moved, or disconnected, or when he questions his telephone bill. This is sometimes a high-turnover job, and when a service representative quits because of work or task dissatisfaction, there goes $3,450 in training. In fact, much of the impetus for job enrichment came through efforts to reduce these costs.

In this instance the slice of work was well enough conceived; nevertheless, we obtained excellent results from the procedures of job enrichment. Improvements in the turnover situation were as great as 50%. Why? Because we could improve the control and feedback.

It should be recognized that moving the work module to a lower level is not the same as moving the control down. If the supervisor decides that a customer's account is too long overdue and tells the service representative what to do, then both the module and the control rest with the supervisor. When, under job enrichment procedures, the service representative makes the decision that a customer must be contacted, but checks it first with the supervisor, control remains in the supervisor's hands. Under full job enrichment, however, the service representative has control.

Exhibit I shows in schematic form the steps to be taken when improving a job. To increase control, responsibility must be obtained from higher levels; I have yet to see an instance where control is moved upward to enrich a job. It must be acknowledged, however, that not every employee is ready to handle more control. That is especially true of new employees.

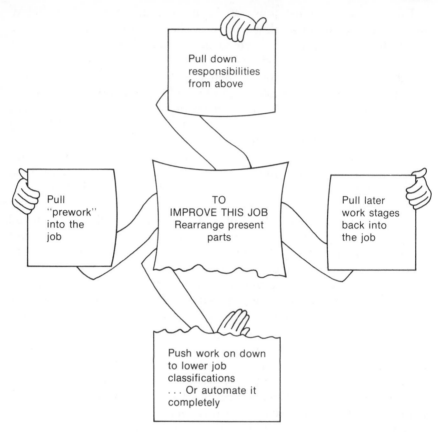

Exhibit I. Steps in improving a job

Moreover, changing the control of a job is more threatening to supervisors than is changing the module. In rejecting a job enrichment proposal, one department head said to us, "When you have this thing proved 100%, let me know and we'll try it."

As far as feedback is concerned, it is usually improvable, but not until the module and control of it are in top condition. If the supervisory family cannot come up with good ways for telling the employee how he or she is doing, the problem lies almost surely in a bad module. That is, the employee's work is submerged in a total unit and he or she has no distinct customer/client/task.

When the module is right, you get feedback "for free"; it comes directly from the customer/client/task. During the learning period, however, the supervisor or teacher should provide the feedback.

When supervisors use the performance of all employees as a goad to individual employees, they thwart the internalization of motivation that job enrichment strives for. An exception is the small group of mutually supporting, complementary workers, but even in this case each individual needs knowledge of his or her own results.

These generalizations cannot be said to be based on an unbiased sample of all jobs in all locations. Usually, the study or project locations were not in deep trouble, nor were they the best operating units. The units in deep trouble cannot stand still long enough to figure out what is wrong, and the top performers need no help. Therefore, the hard-nosed, scientifically trained manager can rightfully say that the jury is still out as to whether job enrichment can help in all work situations. But it has helped repeatedly and consistently on many jobs in the Bell System.

JOB 'NESTING'

Having established to its satisfaction that job enrichment works, management at AT&T is studying ways to go beyond the enriching of individual jobs. A technique that offers great promise is that of "nesting" several jobs to improve morale and upgrade performance.

By way of illustration I shall describe how a family of supervisors of service representatives in a unit of Southwestern Bell Telephone Company improved its service indexes, productivity, collection of overdue bills, and virtually every other index of performance. In two years they moved their Ferguson District (adjacent to St. Louis) from near the bottom to near the top in results among all districts in the St. Louis area.

Before the job enrichment effort started, the service representatives' office was laid out as it appears in *Exhibit II*. The exhibit shows their desks in the standard, in-line arrangement fronted by the desks of their supervisors, who exercised close control of the employees.

As part of the total job enrichment effort, each service rep group was given a geographical locality of its own, with a set of customers to take care of, rather than just "the next customer who calls in" from anywhere in the district. Some service reps—most of them more experienced—were detached to form a unit handling only the businesses in the district.

Then the service representatives and their business office supervisors (BOS) were moved to form a "wagon train" layout. As *Exhibit III* shows, they were gathered into a more-or-less circular shape and were no longer directly facing the desks of the business office supervisors and unit managers. (The office of the district manager was further removed too.)

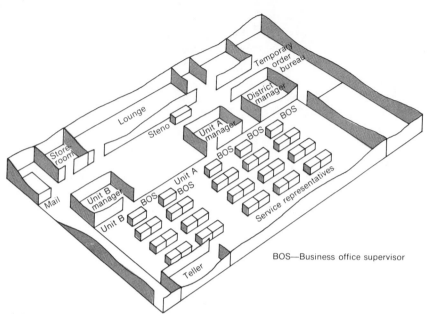

Exhibit II. Ferguson District service representatives' office layout before job enrichment

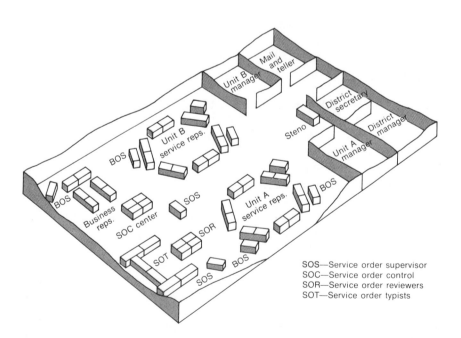

Exhibit III. Service representatives' office layout after job enrichment program was implemented

Now all was going well with the service representatives' job, but another function in the room was in trouble. This was the entry-level job of service order typist. These typists transmit the orders to the telephone installers and the billing and other departments. They and the service order reviewers—a higher-classification job—had been located previously in a separate room that was soundproofed and air-conditioned because the TWX machines they used were noisy and hot. When its equipment was converted to the silent, computer-operated cathode ray tubes (CRTs), the unit was moved to a corner of the service reps' room (see *Exhibit III*).

But six of the eight typists quit in a matter of months after the move. Meanwhile, the percentage of service orders typed "on time" fell below 50%, then below 40%.

The reasons given by the six typists who quit were varied, but all appeared to be rationalizations. The managers who looked at the situation, and at the $25,000 investment in the layout, could see that the feeling of physical isolation and the feeling of having no "thing" of their own were doubtless the real prime factors. As the arrangement existed, any service order typist could be called on to type an order for any service representative. On its face, this seems logical; but we have learned that an employee who belongs to everybody belongs to nobody.

An instantly acceptable idea was broached: assign certain typists to each service rep team serving a locality. "And while we're at it," someone said, "why not move the CRTs right into the group? Let's have a wagon train with the women and kids in the middle." This was done (over the protest of the budget control officer, I should add).

The new layout appears in *Exhibit IV*. Three persons are located in the middle of each unit. The distinction between service order typist and service order reviewer has been abolished, with the former upgraded to the scale of the latter. (Lack of space has precluded arranging the business customer unit in the same wagon-train fashion. But that unit's service order review and typing desks are close to the representatives' desks.)

Before the changes were started, processing a service request involved ten steps—and sometimes as many persons—not counting implementation of the order in the Plant Department. Now the procedure is thought of in terms of people, and only three touch a service order on its way through the office. (*See Exhibit V*.) At this writing, the Ferguson managers hope to eliminate even the service order completion clerk as a specialized position.

Has the new arrangement worked? Just before the typists moved into the wagon train, they were issuing only 27% of the orders on time. Within 30 days after the switch to assigned responsibility, 90% of the

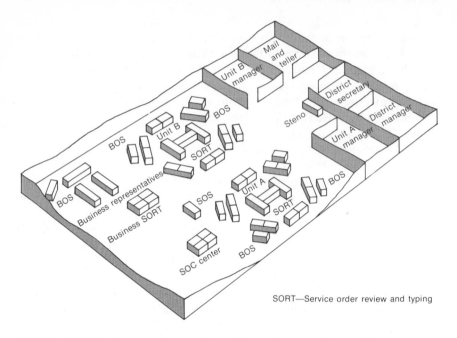

SORT—Service order review and typing

Exhibit IV. Office layout after service order typists were "nested"

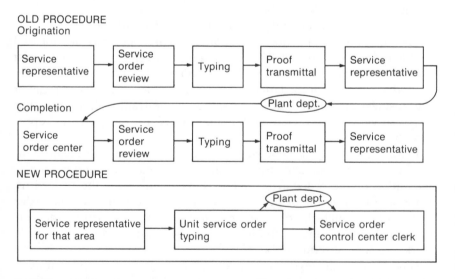

Exhibit V. Old and new processing procedures in request-for-service department

orders were going out on time. Half a year later, in one particular month, the figure even reached 100%.

These results were obtained with a 21% jump in work load—comparing a typical quarter after "nesting" with one before—being performed with a net drop of 22 worker-weeks during the quarter. On a yearly basis it is entirely reasonable to expect the elimination of 88 weeks of unnecessary work (conservatively, 1½ full-time employees). Unneeded messenger service has been dispensed with, and one of two service order supervisor positions has been eliminated. The entire cost has been recovered already.

The service order accuracy measurement, so important in computerization, has already attained the stringent objectives set by the employees themselves, which exceeded the level supervisors would have set. Why are there fewer errors? Because now employees can lean across the area and talk to each other about a service order with a problem or handwriting that is unclear. During the course of a year this will probably eliminate the hand preparation of a thousand "query" slips, with a thousand written replies, in this one district.

And what of the human situation? When on-time order issuance was at its ebb, a supervisor suggested having a picnic for the service representatives and the typists. They did, but not a single typist showed up. Later, when the on-time order rate had climbed over 90%, I remarked, "Now's the time for another picnic." To which the supervisor replied facetiously, "Now we don't need a picnic!"

The turnover among typists for job reasons has virtually ceased. Some are asking now for the job of service representative, which is more demanding, more skilled, and better paid. Now, when the CRTs or the computer is shut down for some reason, or if the service order typist runs out of work, supervisors report that typists voluntarily help the service reps with filing and other matters. They are soaking up information about the higher-rated jobs. These occurrences did not happen when the typists were 100 feet away; then they just sat doing nothing when the work flow ceased. (Because of this two-way flow of information, incidentally, training time for the job of service representative may drop as much as 50%.)

As the state general manager remarked when the results were first reported, "This is a fantastic performance. It's not enough to enrich just one job in a situation. We must learn how to put them together."

Different Configuration

While the Ferguson District supervisory family was making a minigroup out of the service reps and their CRT typists, a strikingly different minigroup was in formation in the Northern Virginia Area of the Chesapeake and Potomac Telephone Company. There the family hit on the idea of funneling to selected order typists only those orders connected with a given central office, such as the Lewinsville frame. Soon the typists and the framemen—those who actually make the changes as a result of service orders—became acquainted. The typists even visited "their" framerooms. Now some questions could be quickly resolved that previously called for formal interdepartmental interrogations through supervisors.

At the end of the first eight months of 1972, these 9 CRT typists were producing service order pages at a rate one-third higher than the 51 service order typists in the comparison group. The absence rate in the experimental unit was 0.6%, compared with 2.5% for the others, and the errors per 100 orders amounted to 2.9 as against 4.6 in the comparison group.

The flow of service orders is from (a) service rep to (b) service order typist to (c) the frameroom. The Ferguson District enjoyed success when it linked (a) and (b), while productivity for the Lewinsville frame improved when (b) and (c) were linked. Obviously, the next step is to link (a), (b), and (c). We are now selecting trial locations to test this larger nesting approach.

LESSONS LEARNED

In summary fashion, at the end of seven years of effort to improve the work itself, it is fair to say that:

- Enriching existing jobs pays off. To give an extreme example, consider the fact that Illinois Bell Telephone Company's directory compilation effort reduced the work force from 120 persons to 74. Enriching the job started a series of moves; it was not the only ingredient, but it was the precipitating one.

- Job enrichment requires a big change in managerial style. It calls for increasing modules, moving control downward, and dreaming up new feedback ideas. There is nothing easy about a successful job enrichment effort.

- The nesting or configuring of related tasks—we call it "work organization"—may be the next big step forward after the enrichment of single jobs in the proper utilization of human beings.

  It seems to produce a multiplier effect rather than merely a simple sum. In the Ferguson District case the job modules were not changed; the service representatives were not asked to type their own orders on the cathode ray tubes, nor were the typists asked to take over the duties of the service representatives. The results came from enriching other aspects (control and feedback) and, more important, from laying out the work area differently to facilitate interaction among responsible people.

- While continuing job enrichment efforts, it is important not to neglect "maintenance" factors. In extending our work with job nesting, for example, we plan to experiment with "office landscaping," so called. The furniture, dividers, planters, and acoustical treatment, all must add to the feeling of work dedication. By this I mean we will dedicate site, equipment, and jobs to the employees, with the expectation that they will find it easier to dedicate themselves to customer/client/task. Especially in new installations, this total work environmental approach seems a good idea for experimentation. We will not be doing it merely to offset pain or boredom in work. The aim is to facilitate work.

- A "pool" of employees with one job (typing pool, reproduction pool, calculating pool, and so on) is at the opposite extreme from the team or "minigroup" which I have described. A minigroup is a set of mutually supporting employees, each of whom has a meaningful module or part in meeting the needs of customer/client/task. What is "meaningful" is, like a love affair, in the eye of the beholder; at this stage, we have difficulty in describing it further.

   A minigroup can have several service representatives or typists; one of each is not basic to the idea. The purpose is to set up a group of employees so that a natural, mutual dependence can grow in providing a service or finishing a task. It marks the end of processing from person to person or group to group, in separate locations or departments and with many different supervisors.

   The minigroup concept, however, still leaves room for specialists. In certain Scandinavian auto plants, for example, one or two specialists fabricate the entire assembly of the exhaust pollution control system or the electrical system. Eventually, a group of workers may turn out a whole engine. In the United States, Chrysler has given similar trial efforts a high priority. The idea is to fix authority at the lowest level possible.

- Experience to date indicates that unions welcome the kind of effort described in our studies. Trouble can be expected, of course, if the economics of increases in productivity are not shared equitably. In the majority of cases, the economics can be handled even under existing contracts, since they usually permit establishment of new jobs and appropriate wage grades between dates of contract negotiation.

   An employee who takes the entire responsibility for preparing a whole telephone directory, for example, ought to be paid more, although a new clerical rating must be established. Job enrichment is not in lieu of cash; good jobs and good maintenance are two sides of the same coin.

- New technology, such as the cathode ray tube, should enable us to break free of old work arrangements. When the Ferguson District service order typists were using the TWX machines, nesting their jobs was impractical because the equipment would have driven everybody to distraction. Installation of the high-technology CRTs gave the planners the opportunity to move together those employees whose modules of work were naturally related. This opportunity was at first overlooked.

Everyone accepts the obvious notion that new technology can and must eliminate dumb-dumb jobs. However, it probably creates more, rather than fewer, fragments of work. Managers should observe the new module and the work organization of the modules. This effort calls for new knowledge and skills, such as laying out work so attractively that the average employee will stay longer and work more effectively than under the previous arrangement.

Moreover, technology tends to make human beings adjuncts of machines. As we move toward computerized production of all listings in the white pages of the phone books, for example, the risk of an employee's losing "his" or "her" own directories is very great indeed. (Two AT&T companies, South Central Bell and Pacific Northwest Bell, are at this stage, and we must be certain the planned changes do not undermine jobs.) Making sure that machines remain the adjunct of human beings is a frontier problem which few managers have yet grappled with.

- Managers in mature organizations are likely to have difficulty convincing another department to make pilot runs of any new kind of work organization, especially one that will cause the department to lose people, budget, or size. Individual job enrichment does not often get into interdepartmental tangles, but the nesting of jobs will almost surely create problems of autonomy. This will call for real leadership.

- When the work is right, employee attitudes are right. That is the job enrichment strategy—get the work right.

LEONARD R. SAYLES

Job Enrichment: Little That's New—and Right for the Wrong Reasons

I shall endeavor to illustrate that the job enrichment movement, and indeed it is a movement, represents an amalgam of ideas, concepts and beliefs. As such it is neither "provable" in any social science sense, nor implementable from a management point of view. This not-so-new organization religion does contain a number of "truths" (most of which are a good deal older than the current crop of proponents are willing to admit). It also contains some questionable assumptions which are also worth examining.

WHAT IS JOB ENRICHMENT?

In reviewing the literature, it appears to me that job enrichment comprises really three quite distinguishable sets of ideas having minimal interrelationship.

1. The first element is the belief that new workers are different from older workers and the 1970's are different from the 1950's. More education, higher aspirations and reduced internal fears of poverty or damnation are presumed to lead to ever more restless workers demanding better jobs.

Source: *Proceedings of the 26th Annual Meeting*, 1973, pp. 201–209. The Industrial Relations Research Association, Madison, Wis. 53706. Copyright © 1973 by Leonard Sayles.

2. The second element concerns the nature of worker motivation or what "releases" employee energies in work directed pursuits.

3. Then there are a number of techniques designed to improve or enrich jobs, presumably consistent with those motivational theories.

THE NEW BREED: THE DEMANDING ONES

We are told with impressive evidence that ours is a new age and older management is likely to find itself out of step with a younger work force. The young of today have greater education, sophistication and much greater expectations, and surely this will cause them to demand more fulfilling work.[1] That youth are more restless, more demanding, and that race can aggravate those feelings, is hardly surprising. What gets debatable is the meaning given to those dissatisfactions.

One can trace such ideas back almost as far as the eye can see. David Riesman excited many of us years ago when he helped us see that cultural myths were related to economic development. Affluent societies shifted "motivations" toward consumption values (living the good life and maintaining social acceptability) and away from "production" values (hard work and economic success).[2]

The implications for the so-called Protestant "work ethic" were and are clear: work, at best, is a means not an end and the employer has the tougher job of convincing employees to work when family and religion no longer do that particular kind of socializing.

However, after accepting all that, I still admit to some skepticism that we are increasing the number of employees seeking demanding jobs. A culture which glories in consumption, deifies hedonism, where there is overriding concern with inner placidity, is more likely to produce employees attracted to 3 day weekends and flex-time than jobs with substantial challenge and responsibility. Employees are legitimately in revolt against the trappings of nineteenth century employer colonialism: piddling and demeaning work rules, time clocks, oppressive, ever watchful supervisors and jobs which imply they are but an extension of the machine. They want to end the unjustifiable distinctions between blue and white collar work.

Obviously auto assembly lines are among the worst offenders where every motion is predetermined, personal time must be scheduled precisely, and job's motions are designed to fill-in for still imperfect automation.

But Lordstown itself is no demand for self-actualization; it is a demand for fair work standards (easier jobs) and humane working conditions as have 30 years of auto industry similar strikes. No one doubts there are achievement oriented workers who want significant

career opportunities that will provide the deeper psychological satisfactions which most managers and professionals enjoy. But are all
workers so motivated?

It is the petty tyrannies of work that are less tolerable to the youth
of today brought up with extraordinary stress on independence, "doing
your own thing" (which rarely means your "work" thing) and the absolute right to challenge their elders. Authority, in all its societal forms,
has lost its momentum to command so that worker discontent is often
focused more against rigid discipline than rigid job procedures.

One cautionary note: perhaps we should not rush to conclusions
about these inter-generational differences. As my colleague James
Kuhn points out, a good deal of the social unrest of the sixties may
have nothing to do with new values so much as with simple population
changes: "In the single decade of the sixties, the youth population aged
14 to 24 increased by over 13 million, growing nearly twice as fast
as it had in the previous fifty years."[3]

While it's tempting (and even reasonable) to believe that the restlessness in U.S. culture, perhaps reflecting the insecurities of any highly
industrialized, mobile society, would show itself in higher turnover,
unambiguous evidence doesn't exist. Correcting for seasonal and cyclical variations, there is no clear trend toward more turnover that might
support the contention that employee dissatisfaction with the intrinsic
nature of their jobs is motivating them to move elsewhere.[4]

To be sure in a relatively full employment economy employees will
seek to avoid oppressive work. The U.S. and England after the war
experienced problems in getting men to go into the coal mines—not
because the jobs lacked autonomy and responsibility (quite the contrary) or were unchallenging, but because they were *dangerous, heavy*
and *dirty*. Similarly, perhaps more in Europe than the U.S., auto plants
have had turnover and recruitment problems because the work was
relatively unappealing in a full employment economy and this surely
has motivated many of the European experiments with job enrichment.[5] (But note the increased demand for U.K. mining jobs after
wages increased in 1974.)

Thus, as far as the "new breed of workers" hypothesis goes, our
conclusion is that workers, particularly insofar as they are more youth-
ful, are less disciplined, in the classic management sense of accepting
of what the boss says is right, more demanding of their rights and
privileges as citizens and human beings, but we are much less sure
about their wanting more demanding, fulfilling work. Even with the
"old breed," it was hard to simply "hire a hand" and management
would be naive to think that the number of challenges to its authority
would decrease with more self-fulfilling work.

What we do know is that employees don't like being glued to one spot, doing one small job, in a precisely prescribed manner for endless (or what must appear like endless) periods of time—whether they are typists or assemblers. And there is not much new in repeating what Walker and Guest found in the late 40's: workers prefer the jobs off the assembly line and those with less mass production characteristics.[6] Or do we learn much when we rediscover what students of fatigue and monotony have been saying for almost half a century: repetition is boring and leads to fatigue.[7] (And is it surprising that some workers trade-off money for working conditions?)

RELEASING WORKER ENERGIES

It would be difficult to find a job enrichment enthusiast who did not trace his ancestry through the Maslow-Herzberg family tree. The genetic material is a good deal less complicated than biological chromosomes. Its nucleus is the now very familiar need hierarchy. The oft-cited conclusions are that motivation is only derived from relatively unsatisfied needs. Thus, the catechism that in our relatively affluent society, only the more subtle "ego" needs are a potential source of motivation at work. The physicals can cause grievances, but only the psychologicals can create motivation.

The criticisms of this dogma are many, and this is not the place to subject the need hierarchy theory to a thorough review, deliciously tempting as that may be. In passing, I will just cite the decade-old criticism of my co-author George Strauss who showed that employees, in fact, continuously make trade-offs among physical, social and ego needs and further that old fashioned monetary incentives are often as much ego as stomach fulfilling.[8] Thus, the basis of motivation does not shift inexorably "upward." A further critique is provided by the work of the psychologist Charles Hulin. He demonstrates the significance of individual differences for who gets motivated by what and when.[9]

My own criticism is one based on parsimony, that one doesn't require the paraphernalia of the "need hierarchy" to cope with much of the phenomenon analyzed by the job enrichment movement. Back in the 1940's Douglas McGregor, seeking to improve the quality of supervision, noted the inevitable industrial tension—and even conflict—produced when managers controlled and manipulated rewards and punishments to obtain worker performance. In his "means control" terminology, which we students of McGregor learned in those heady postwar MIT classrooms, the ideal situations was one in which employees themselves obtained satisfactions from their on-the-job experiences rather than having to have these bestowed by a beneficent boss or threatened by a tyrannical one.[10] The manager's job was to provide the conditions under which this was possible.

McGregor's views on leadership really had two components. Minimize the power differences between the leaders and the led and allow positive reinforcements to "pull" rather than using managerial "pushes." (Of course, the latter also relates to the now famous operant conditioning studies of Skinner and the path-goals type of analysis favored by Professors Porter and Lawlor.)

I don't think there is any need to question the desirability of work becoming its own reward (unless one happens to be married to the professional). But as the economist in George Strauss noted in the above cited article, at what cost and for whom.

JOB ENRICHMENT IS ALL OF ORGANIZATIONAL BEHAVIOR

I have tried to read a number of the experiments and descriptions of company adoptions of job enrichment techniques. One is forced to the conclusion that the term has become a "code word" for most, if not all, of the recommendations and research findings of the organizational behavior field since Western Electric days. In other words, job enrichment in practices does not simply imply broadened job responsibilities that will provide a greater sense of personal worth, challenge, and fulfillment on the job. Instead JE typically also includes:

1. Building smaller, more cohesive work groups, some of which encourage integration by job trading, but all of which have improved inter-worker communication, more clearly defined boundaries and a stable organization.

2. More careful use of feedback mechanisms to insure that employees know not only what is expected of them, but know almost continuously how well they are performing, how close to target. (Obviously at times this feedback is combined with monetary as well as these "ego" incentives of being "successful.")

3. Seeking to make work group boundaries coterminous with unit work flow boundaries so that the group includes all those operations necessary to maintain its own internal regularity and stability—in contrast to the use of functional specialization.[11]

4. Greater use of straw bosses, that is, informal leaders with some management recognized supervisory responsibility and status.

5. Greater managerial attention and recognition given to work areas and jobs which had formerly been ignored or neglected. (This, of course, is often the core of the so-called "Western Electric" effect.)

6. Related to #5 is the increased likelihood that management will be responsive to employee requests, complaints and interests and that employees feel that legitimate concerns they have will be responded to by management rather than being ignored.

7. Changing the balance between initiations to workers and accepting initiations from workers. Often old fashioned increased employee participation in decision making is called job enrichment.

8. Increased recognition that extreme specialization increases coordination costs, particularly the managerial costs of insuring adequate mutual responsiveness among work stations. The JE movement has sensibly caused management to rethink its trade-offs between specialization and coordination. (In the past, too many managers assumed that Adam Smith's pin makers were the ideal standard and they neglected—not only the boredom—but the coordination costs.)

Thus, my quibble is not that these eight elements are wrong, far from it, but that calling them job enrichment adds confusion to fields which already have a number of language and semantic problems. It is not easy to communicate on management and organization problems given the absence of unambiguous, operational terminology. It further inhibits research and training if broad, global terms are used to encompass a number of identifiable, and conceptually discrete structural elements. Note also that none of the eight elements have anything to do with job challenge or breadth or inner satisfactions; rather they all have something to do with relationships: among workers and between workers and managers.

Further most correlational studies that endeavor to demonstrate the impact of job enrichment upon worker satisfaction or performance are flawed seriously by the fact that the research data are confounded by the presence of one or more of these eight elements. While the JE researcher finds it easy to conclude that it is the "enrichment" that has *caused* some improvement in employee reactions, I am just as willing to believe that it is a change in one of these other uncontrolled elements that is responsible. Can one find studies where only the intrinsic nature of the individual job has changed?

On a more anecdotal level, I should just like to refer to the most highly motivated, most productive and perhaps proudest work group I have ever observed. For many years, I have been engaged in organizational field work, and some years ago I studied several hundred work groups in a wide variety of industrial settings.[12] One in particular sticks in my memory because both the workers themselves and their managers confirmed their extraordinary morale and productivity. They were a five man metal bending crew making the frame for folding chairs. Each did a short cycle, repetitive, manual job involving one of the bending and spot welding operations and then passed the part on to a colleague who did a similar, but slightly different bend and weld. The frame was completed in what must have been no more than a minute or two, and to the naked, neophyte eye it looked as though the metal just flowed among these ten hands. They earned more incentive pay and were faster and higher paid than any team in the factory. Everyone knew their reputation and they would work like proverbial greased lightning for perhaps an hour and then take whatever break they felt like because they were always ahead of the standard. They were so independent and so perfect a physical team that they insisted on having a veto over any changes in team membership should there be illness or turnover.

No job interest or complexity or ego challenge here, just a good old fashioned, cohesive work group that had gotten a great piece rate for itself.

CONCLUSIONS

Our review has emphasized that job enrichment is neither a unitary theory nor a homogenous set of recommendations to management for work organization. Rather it is a mishmash of ideas, many good and relevant although hardly logically consistent. Further, this jumble of ideas is hardly new or revolutionary. In fact, what is called job enrichment has a distinguished heritage going back to those early experimental industrial psychologists who first looked at fatigue, monotony and boredom after World War I.

It thus becomes interesting to ask why all the sudden excitement. The temptation is strong to provide an historical explanation of why job enrichment has suddenly come into vogue although many of its varied components have been around for a generation. As should be obvious, I have little patience with cliches, but maybe there is something to the one about ideas whose time has come.

Lordstown and the Arabs' oil blockade may represent a similar phenomenon, and, if this were more a social occasion than an intellectual one, I would ask you to "guess" what they have in common. But rather obviously I am simply saying that both represent shocks which served to identify long standing trends. The Arabs didn't create an energy crisis and the young Turks at Lordstown (to keep this a Middle Eastern analogy) didn't suddenly discover worker aspirations. Management has known, or should have known, for decades that some of the earliest work in scientific management was seriously flawed. Extreme specialization for workers has a number of costs associated with it stemming from the well established observations that human beings are not machines nor do they essentially become extensions of machines. Thus, jobs which require them to do precisely the same simple motions, constantly and endlessly—the typical automobile assembly line, but not the typical industrial job—create boredom and fatigue and even inefficiency. Auto workers have been wildcatting ever since strong unions allowed them the freedom to protest.

But somehow, Lordstown triggered the rediscovery of a great many things social scientists had been saying about work organization. In fact, job enrichment became a new, glamorous "code word" for all of those separate, and even unrelated findings about job design, work group organization, feedback and leadership techniques that we listed earlier.

As we've already noted, while the long assembly line is not the sole or typical form of industrial work organization, it obviously fascinates social critics and social researchers because of its machine-control of human beings and the constraints on autonomy in use of time or motion. Few have doubted for decades that the absence of small work groups, of the opportunity to adapt one's own timing and motions was perceived as undesirable by workers and even injurious of their will to produce. However, breaking up this long line and introducing less rigidity of timing and job has little to do with what most students of job enrichment talk about when they refer to higher other needs.

Additionally, and here the attribution must go to the ecologists and other economists who sought to measure secondary effects, as a society we've begun to explore social costs that the price system may measure only imperfectly.

I fear that too much of the enthusiasm for "job enrichment" is just another of a long line of examples of naive management looking for panaceas: the one big idea that will solve all their personal problems.[13] Further, as we've already said, job enrichment can also represent the temptation to find solutions in the hearts of workers rather than in the minds of managers. Productivity, for the most part, is really not a work motivation problem. Managing people will continue to mean doing a lot of small things involving work organization, leadership and grievance handling and doing them tomorrow again, just as they had to be done today. That's the curse of administration, and there's no Garden of Eden to return to in which contented, mature workers work autonomously. That was the utopian dream of those who first looked at the Relay Assembly Test Room data, too, not unlike my chair benders.

My overall conclusion: the job enrichment movement has performed a major service for the management and industrial relations fields by refocusing our attention on *job design*. However, for my part, I do not accept as a unifying principle their emphasis on self-actualization and worker motivation. Such concepts satisfy our commendable Jeffersonian values, and I am pleased they exist, but I don't think they explain much of organizational behavior.

NOTES

1. An impressive synthesis of materials relating to changing values and business organization is presented in Carl Madden, *Clash of Culture: Management in an Age of Changing Values*, National Planning Association, Washington, D.C., 1972.
2. David Riesman in collaboration with Reuel Denney and Nathan Glazer, *The Lonely Crowd*, Yale University Press, New Haven, Connecticut, 1960.
3. James Kuhn, "The Immense Generation," *The Columbia Forum*, Summer 1973, p. 11.
4. Cf. Harold Wool, "What's Wrong with Work in America—A Review Essay," *Monthly Labor Review*, March 1973, pp. 38–44.
5. One of the best reviews of current European experimentation with job enrichment is provided by the new journal *Organizational Dynamics*. Its editor, William Dowling, did the field work and wrote, "Job Redesign on the Assembly Line: Farewell to Blue Collar Blues?" Vol. 2, No. 2 (Autumn 1973) pp. 51-67.
6. Charles Walker and Robert Guest, *Man on the Assembly Line*, Harper & Row, New York, 1952.
7. S. Wyatt and J. Langdon, *Fatigue and Boredom in Repetitive Work*, Industrial Health Research Council, Report #77, H. M. Stationery Office, London, 1938.
8. George Strauss, "Notes on Power Equalization" in Harold Leavitt, editor, *The Social Science of Organizations*, Prentice-Hall, Englewood Cliffs, New Jersey, 1963, pp. 45–57.
9. Charles Hulin, "Individual Differences and Job Enrichment—The Case Against General Treatments" in John Maher, editor, *New Perspectives in Job Enrichment*, Van Nostrand Reinhold, New York, 1941, pp. 159–191.
10. Douglas McGregor, "Conditions of Effective Leadership in an Industrial Organization," *Journal of Consulting Psychology*, Vol. 8, No. 2 (March 1944) pp. 55–63.
11. We didn't call this job enlargement when we first recommended this as a major criterion for designing the organization structure in 1960: Eliot Chapple and Leonard Sayles, *The Measure of Management*, New York, Macmillan, 1961.
12. Leonard Sayles, *Behavior of Industrial Work Groups*, John Wiley, New York, 1958.
13. For other evidence of this consistent management frailty see my article, "Whatever Happened to Management—or Why the Dull Stepchild?" *Business Horizons* Vol. XIII, No. 2, (April 1970) pp. 25–34.

CHARLES E. SILBERMAN

Black Economic Gains—Impressive But Precarious

Some students of the racial problem argue that only a relative handful of blacks have been able to move into the economic mainstream. Dr. Andrew Brimmer, the first and only black member of the board of governors of the Federal Reserve System, speaks of a "deepening schism between the able and the less able, between the well prepared and those with few skills" and suggests the schism may be widening.

In fact, job barriers have been coming down for all blacks, not only those with a college degree. The number of Negro families earning less than $3,000 a year decreased by one-third between 1960 and 1968, after adjusting for changes in the purchasing power of the dollar, as high-school graduates—and even "dropouts"—have been able to move into jobs from which Negroes traditionally have been barred, or to which they have had little access. Since 1960 the number of Negroes holding clerical jobs has more than doubled, and the number of Negro sales workers has risen 61 percent. In the blue-collar sector, the number of Negro craftsmen and foremen increased by 70 percent, of semiskilled workers by 41 percent. Equally important, a substantial proportion of the increase in semiskilled jobs occurred in comparatively well-paying durable-goods industries such as autos and steel.

Source: Reprinted from the July 1970 issue of *Fortune* magazine by special permission; © 1970 Time Inc.

As more Negroes found better-paying and/or higher-status jobs, their numbers decreased in the kinds of low-paying and low-status jobs to which Negroes traditionally have been confined. Thus the number of Negro domestic household workers dropped 28 percent, the number of nonfarm laborers by 8 percent, and the number of farmers and farm laborers by no less than 56 percent. And while the number of Negro service workers did increase, more of them graduated to more prestigious service jobs, such as firemen, policemen, guards, and watchmen.

The consequence of all this has been a rapid increase in the returns Negroes receive from investment in education, an increase already being reflected in the statistics of Negro income. In sharp contrast to the situation of only a few years ago, the gap between median Negro and white incomes is now smaller for Negroes with a year or more of college than it is for those with no more than a high-school education (and smaller for those with a high-school education than for those with only an elementary-school diploma). Actually, current statistics understate the situation, since they take no account of the fact that a large proportion of better-educated Negroes are men and women who got their schooling recently and are just starting out in life.

The discrepancy between blacks and whites is likely to narrow still more in the near future, since the experience of other ethnic groups who have encountered discrimination indicates that there tends to be a lag of one or two decades between gains in educational attainment and their translation into increased income and occupational status. The same thing appears to be happening now to black Americans. And as the returns from education increase, so does the incentive to stay in school longer. The combination of more education and more job experience in turn is laying the base for a new period of catching up.

But Negroes will not be able to catch up unless the economy returns to a rapid rate of growth. Indeed, a rate of growth fast enough to keep the economy at full employment for an extended period of time is a prerequisite for any Negro progress at all. Full employment is the most effective solvent of discrimination in the labor market, because the alchemy of labor shortage turns people previously classified as unemployable into highly desirable employees. Since 1963, when it began intensive recruiting efforts, Chase Manhattan Bank has hired half of its new employees from minority groups. In part, of course, this reflects management's growing social consciousness, in part its desire to avert racial violence, but the overriding reason is that the bank's traditional supply of white clerical help has largely dried up. As one bank officer explains, "We need people. They're people. It's as simple as that."

MOVING DOWN THE QUEUE

It is not quite as simple as that. But, allowing for some rhetorical exaggeration, the bank officer has provided a concise explanation of what economists call "the queue theory of the labor market." According to this theory, the available supply of labor is arrayed in order of workers' desirability, and employers choose job candidates from as far up the queue as they can. As aggregate demand for labor increases, employers have to move further and further down the line, taking people they previously had found unacceptable.

Since Negroes are heavily concentrated at the bottom of the queue, it takes a sustained period of expansion before employers begin reaching into the black labor pool. In part, this is because Negroes do have poorer qualifications. But only in part. While employers do move down the queue in an orderly sequence, the criteria for rating workers are highly subjective and frequently quite irrational.

A large element of irrationality is introduced by employers' lack of knowledge about the relation between entrance requirements—amount and quality of education, age, score on qualifying tests, etc.—and actual performance on the job. Since personnel men cannot admit their ignorance, still less admit that hiring is arbitrary and irrational, they feel bound to rest their judgments on such so-called "objective" criteria. Yet there is considerable evidence that the correlation between job performance and length of schooling or grades is quite low for a broad range of occupational categories. In some occupations there may even be an inverse correlation between education and job performance: the more education employees have, the higher their rate of turnover and, in some instances, the lower their productivity.

Just how senseless many "objective" standards really are was revealed during the past few years when, under the pressures of an apparent labor shortage, corporate managers took a hard look at their personnel practices. The experience of New York's First National City Bank is typical of a great many corporations, manufacturers as well as financial companies. Robert Feagles, a senior vice president, recalls that, when he was put in charge of personnel in 1965, turnover was abnormally high, with about 500 jobs going begging in a work force of 12,000. More important, supervisors were hanging on to incompetent people for fear that they would be replaced only by even less competent people—or not at all. Feagles' first move, therefore, was to create a personnel-research group, which proceeded to analyze the nature of the work performed in the job categories that accounted for the largest proportion of new hires.

The results were discomforting, to say the least. By and large, the researchers found that the qualifications the bank required for a broad range of jobs bore little relationship to the actual requirements of the job. For example, supervisors all over the bank had been complaining that the young people hired as pages rarely stayed more than three months or thereabouts. The reason, Feagles' researchers found, was that the personnel department, which gave a battery of entry tests, had set a score of 130 on the Wonderlic I.Q. test as the minimum for a job as a page. But youths with that degree of intelligence found they could not stand the monotony for more than a few months.

For most entry jobs a high-school diploma was required, yet the jobs could be performed just as well, and in the case of particularly monotonous routine tasks, perhaps better, by people with substantially less education. A high degree of literacy was essential in other jobs, not because of the intrinsic nature of the work but because of the way it had been structured. By breaking the work down in different ways, dropouts could do the job without difficulty.

The labor shortage, in brief, was the product of the bank's unrealistic requirements. By lowering job requirements to those actually needed to perform the work in question, and by substituting a newly created set of aptitude tests for the old ones, First National City was able to tap a completely new source of supply in the city's predominantly black and Puerto Rican neighborhoods. At first, the flow of applicants was small; on the basis of past experience, many blacks and Puerto Ricans did not bother to apply since they took it for granted that they would not be hired. "We had to make ourselves believable in the labor market," Feagles puts it. To do so, the bank began active recruiting in minority neighborhoods, advertising in Negro and Spanish newspapers, contacting church groups and antipoverty agencies, and visiting high schools. As a result, the minority complement went from 12 percent to 24 percent of the work force in four years; it is now above 30 percent.

WHEN THE "HARD CORE" SOFTENS

Many of the factors corporate managers used to cite as compelling reasons for their inability to find or hire many Negro employees have turned out to be a lot less compelling when the supply of white workers dried up. Many blacks, to be sure, do lack the necessary job skills, but when labor is in short enough supply, it pays employers to incur substantial costs to teach the skills. There is reason to believe, in fact, that a substantial proportion of the "new" jobs which members of the National Alliance of Businessmen claim to have created for the so-called "hard core" unemployed are filled by men the companies would have hired even if there had been no special program.

A prolonged period of full employment softens the hard core in another way. For most jobs the most important kind of intellectual capital is what has been learned on the job rather than what has been learned in school. Negroes have been caught up in a vicious circle; the fact that so many jobs were barred to them in the past left many blacks poorly equipped for the jobs that began to open up in the Sixties. All the more so, since workers need two kinds of knowledge: specific work skills, and social skills—i.e., punctuality, acceptance of discipline and work rules, and so on. Lack of these social skills has constituted the biggest disadvantage of Negroes who previously had been limited to casual labor or other transient jobs. But social skills are learned on the job in much the same way that specific work skills are acquired. Hence the boom of the late Sixties—by providing steady jobs for previously unemployable blacks—equipped them with the social and other skills they need to compete for employment in the future.

THE ZERO-SUM GAME

A further reason why economic growth helps the Negro is that it reduces white resistance to black gains. Some of this resistance stems from deep-rooted racial hatred, but a great deal of it, though cloaked perhaps in anti-Negro rhetoric, grows out of a real conflict of interest. The harsh fact is that if Negroes gain a larger share of the "better" jobs, whites, by definition, will be left with a smaller share. More black foremen will mean proportionately fewer white foremen; more black school principals will mean fewer white principals; more black corporate vice presidents will mean fewer white vice presidents.

What this means is that the struggle to achieve Negro equality is, in the parlance of game theorists, a "zero-sum game," in which one group's gains are offset by another group's losses. Not entirely so; to some degree, whites' losses in terms of jobs and income are offset by less tangible gains—greater social peace (or less social disruption), a sense of satisfaction that justice is being achieved. What a good many civic leaders have sometimes failed to recognize, however—the Urban Coalition is a prime example—is that the people who enjoy the intangible or psychic gains are not necessarily the ones who bear the brunt of the losses, e.g., white blue-collar workers, whose chances of becoming foremen are diminished.

But if job opportunities are growing for everyone, whites are likely to be less resentful of the fact that Negroes are taking a larger share of the better jobs. If the number of foremen, craftsmen, plant managers, corporate executives, and school principals is growing, the absolute *number* of whites holding such jobs can increase even though the white *proportion* declines. Rapid economic growth can reduce white resentment still more, by making it possible for whites to move into other occupations. And if their real income is growing, whites are less likely to object to the fact that their tax dollars are being used, in part, to provide compensatory education and job training for Negroes.

Government has a large role to play, therefore, both in overcoming discrimination and in keeping the economy expanding rapidly. Governmental policy is important, too, as a means of influencing the composition of economic output, since the opportunities for upgrading black occupations and incomes vary widely from industry to industry.

Construction, for example, is a labor-intensive industry with a wage scale well above average, which means that increased employment of Negroes there would have a greater impact on black income than increases in almost any other blue-collar industry. And since the potential demand for construction will grow substantially over the next ten years, the number of blacks employed can be increased without threatening the jobs of whites. The degree to which the industry will be able to meet the projected demand will be strongly influenced by what the government does to stimulate housing and urban renewal. The degree to which that demand leads to greater employment of blacks depends on what government does to break down racial discrimination, which is more intense in construction than in most industries.

While rapid economic growth is a prerequisite for Negro progress, it is not enough; it must be supplemented by a direct attack on all forms of discrimination. The changes of the past five or ten years have reduced and occasionally eliminated some forms of discrimination. As is usually the case, however, solving one set of problems creates another set, or brings old problems into sharper focus. The more that overt discrimination in hiring recedes, the more important other kinds of discrimination become. Eliminating the disparities between blacks and whites is a two-stage process: giving Negroes equal access to initial employment, and giving them an equal crack at advancement.

THE EXECUTIVE AS EDUCATOR

It is not enough for presidents or executive vice presidents to decree an end to discrimination within the company. Such decrees frequently are nullified by what one black executive calls "the not-in-my-department syndrome," whereby department managers express agreement in principle but find all sorts of reasons to explain why the decree cannot be put into practice "in my department." Hence top executives must act as educators, persuading supervisors—plant managers, foremen, etc., down the line—to change their ways.

Executives will be unable to educate their subordinates, however, unless they first educate themselves. There is no particular reason to assume that managers are any freer from racial prejudice than the rest of us; it is virtually impossible to have grown up in the U.S. without having absorbed *some* sense of superiority or distaste toward blacks. But executives have been quicker than most to recognize the high stakes that are involved for business and for the whole society in overcoming prejudice and discrimination. Businessmen made considerable progress in that direction in the Sixties. There is reason to hope that they will find the courage and strength to do what needs to be done in the Seventies.

CHARLES E. SILBERMAN

Still More Room at the Top

When Betsy Prahl graduated from Mount Holyoke College ten years ago with a fine record and a degree in economics, none of the jobs available to her held promise for much advancement. But she wanted to work, so she joined IBM as a trainee in computer systems.

Today, the 31-year-old Mrs. Prahl is manager of an IBM branch in Columbus, Ohio, where she supervises a staff of 70 employees, mostly male. She's blunt about the reasons for her success. "I'm capable," she says. "But it's undeniable that additional support was afforded me as a female."

Mrs. Prahl is only one of a growing number of women suddenly moving up in industry. Prodded by women's groups and by directives from the Federal Equal Employment Opportunity Commission, many corporations are pushing women up the rungs of company management. Women have had the most success in getting lower and middle management positions, such as production supervisor or computer marketing manager. They have also broken into previously all-white, all-male executive preserves such as brokerages and corporate finance. Priscilla Perry, the only female vice president of the Chicago Title and Trust Company, now gets numerous job offers from investment firms who refused even to talk with her a few years ago.

Source: *Newsweek*, April 29, 1974, pp. 74, 79, 80. Copyright © 1974 by Newsweek, Inc. All rights reserved. Reprinted by permission.

But few women feel that there is much to cheer about just yet. Although times are improving for females in business, gains are still small and slow in coming. Of the 3.2 million people listed in the 1970 census as "managers and administrators" earning $10,000 or more a year, only 154,952—or 4.8 per cent—were women. A Fortune magazine study of 1,220 major corporations, with 6,500 top executives earning more than $30,000 apiece, shows that only eleven of those executives are women. Bankers Trust in New York is fairly typical. No women are in command executive posts, and out of 200 vice presidents, only seven are women.

One obvious explanation for this lag is the still prevalent attitude among men that women simply do not belong in business. "The world in which they live is mostly male, and that is the most comfortable and natural way for them," sociologist Cynthia F. Epstein told a "Women In Management" conference at Stanford University's Graduate School of Business last week. Men employers still consider young males better job risks for management-training programs, especially since many women refuse to relocate when the company says to and choose to stay with their families instead. Many firms also say there aren't more women in key positions because the special efforts needed to recruit and train them are costly.

BASICS

The companies are partly justified in this last defense. Until recently, most women simply lacked the specialized business training usually considered a bare minimum for starting the executive climb. But female enrollment in prestigious business schools has shot up dramatically in the past few years. Twenty-one per cent of the business students at Columbia are women, up from 5.1 per cent in 1968, and next year's class may be 30 per cent women. Almost 18 per cent of the 600 enrolled at Stanford Business School are women vs. 1.6 per cent in 1970.

Once they enter executive suites, women face all the traditional problems of novice managers, such as the pressures of increased responsibility and learning how to deal with subordinates. For instance, colleagues of Ramona Bullock, a 53-year-old foreman at Ford Motor Company's Ypsilanti plant, rode her at first to see if she could stand the pressure. "It made me mad," she recalls. "But it made me a better foreman."

Many women adjust and do well. Madelon Talley, the 42-year-old president of Dreyfus Offshore Trust in New York, manages portfolios with more than $60 million, and she says, "I like the responsibility fine. I've got the job I want here, which is running aggressive money."

Phyllis A. Cella, 53, who received the title of second vice president of the John Hancock Mutual Life Insurance Company in Boston after nearly 30 years on the job, is equally happy. "There are a lot of men who work for me, but I haven't seen any problems of acceptance," she says.

PROBLEMS

Yet few women deny that they face special problems as executives. Some who rose into management from secretarial jobs find that they lack self-confidence. Others find they have trouble supervising workers, particularly women, who were once their co-workers and close friends. Almost all women complain that they lack the chance for informal but valuable contact with male superiors at places like men's clubs or restaurants. Ms. Perry of Chicago Title and Trust says that when she first joined her firm she was told that it would be better to take her coffee breaks with the secretaries, rather than male executives.

Even things like company physicals can become embarrassing situations for women. When Marion Howington, creative director of J. Walter Thompson's Chicago office, showed up for her first annual physical as an executive, she was the only woman in the room; there were no provisions for women in the examining rooms—or even in the medical forms. "So here I was," she recalls, "standing in line wrapped in a sheet in a room full of men wrapped in sheets. It was all unsettling, and I thought rather inconsiderate."

Female managers also face put-downs from male clients as well as male colleagues. Jetta Brenner, 47, for example, general manager of the Sheraton-Russell Hotel in New York, recalls receiving a call from a complaining male guest one night. "First he got the female operator and then a female secretary and then me," she says. "By the time he got to me, he said, 'How many women do I have to talk to before I get the manager?' And when I told him it was me, he got flustered and said he didn't want the manager after all."

To help women cope with their changed positions, companies, outside consultants and the women themselves organize management seminars. At some seminars, newly promoted women not only are taught managerial skills, but are encouraged to organize themselves into groups to talk about a woman's special problems on the job.

While all this is heartening, many women feel that most of the company doors open to them right now will start to close unless they and the government apply continuous pressure. American Telephone & Telegraph, for example, agreed to give $38 million in salary increases and back pay to women and other minority employees only after the

EEOC forced it to settle a job-discrimination suit. Other firms such as General Motors and Sears, Roebuck & Co. also began to establish hiring goals and time-tables when charges of job discrimination were brought against them. Women say that as long as men dominate corporations and keep women in a secondary place in business, they will continue to file lawsuits and challenge the companies in court—and so far, at least, the strategy seems to be working.

V | MANAGERS AND SOCIAL ISSUES

We have noted several times already that business managers can no longer operate their organizations as if nothing but their own interests mattered. Increasing numbers of laws, a concerned public and the changing values and consciousness of managers themselves create increasing pressures for managers to operate their organizations in a socially responsible way. The dilemma is, how can this be done?

Petit in his article "The Doctrine of Socially Responsible Management" accepts, as many do, that management should be socially responsible. He points out that there must be a consistent set of values or an ethic to back and guide managers in being socially responsible. He questions whether such an ethic exists, and examines some of the issues which will have to be settled to create one.

As Petit points out, the new social responsibility ethic will supplant the profit ethic that has long been the guiding value system of business. In "What is Wrong With Profit Maximization?" Phillips raises an interesting and troublesome question. If the profit ethic were simply a matter of greed, we could probably dispense with it easily; but as Phillips notes, it is not. Therefore the idea of profit maximization cannot be so easily dismissed.

George Lodge looks at these same matters in his paper, "Business and The Changing Society." He says, in effect, that while these seem like matters of wide and sweeping concern, they are only the tip of the proverbial iceberg, for behind them lie even more basic changes in our world, with implications that will alter the character of all aspects of our lives. Of necessity, they will also alter the fundamental issues with which management deals. Lodge does not claim to see the full extent of the changes we are encountering but insists that we must accept the fact that we are undergoing vast changes before we can even begin to cope with the consequences.

The second section of Part V looks at some first-hand details in two areas where the question of managerial social responsibility has been raised. In "The Corporation and the Community: Realities and Myths," Cassell looks at corporate actions attempted for social rather than business ends. Nehemkis, in "Business Payoffs Abroad: Rhetoric and Reality," looks at some of the problems encountered when firms do business abroad. Often business and social practices may be quite different overseas. The contrast may cause unrest when reported back home in the press or in financial reports. Both writers point out that the issues are very complex. What is to be done is hardly clear. What we need now is to give attention to understanding the issues and options better.

THOMAS A. PETIT

The Doctrine of Socially Responsible Management

Businessmen need an ethical standard to choose between morally right and wrong courses of action. The profit ethic—the idea that business is to maximize profits—once served this purpose. It enabled businessmen to make profit maximizing decisions on moral grounds. Today this ethic cannot be used, however, since there are goals other than profit.

The corporate and managerial revolutions have led to a moral crisis in American business by undermining the profit ethic. Today's large corporation is the prime agency for organizing our social as well as economic life. Managers take into account goals other than profit. Therefore the profit ethic no longer serves as an unequivocal moral guideline for business. But without it how do managers determine which decisions and actions are morally good or bad?

The doctrine of socially responsible management emerges as a possible new business ethic. According to this ethic management takes into account the welfare of all groups in society affected by the corporation in conducting its affairs. We are concerned here with the question of whether this doctrine can take the place of the profit ethic and thus resolve the moral crisis of business.

Source: *Arizona Review*, Vol. 14, No. 2 (December, 1965), pp. 1-4; 22, with permission of the publisher.

YESTERDAY'S POWER-SEEKERS AND TODAY'S BUSINESS MORALISTS

Change in the roles of the corporation and the manager have brought, in turn, change in the motives and personality of men who direct American industry. At the turn of the century the businessman needed power to lead rapidly industrializing society into greater heights of productivity and wealth than ever before. Thus he became a "power-seeker."

Today the power-seeker is being replaced by a new kind of manager who underplays his power—the "business moralist." He knows that he must use power to get his job done, but he fears the consequences of its full exercise for the welfare of the corporation and himself. The business moralist may emerge as our next business hero.

What are the causes of this shift of management motives and personality? Because of his success, the businessman has created new social responsibilities for himself. When the American standard of living was low, the first order of business was to expand the flow of goods and services. The power-seeking businessman led the transformation of a rural farming society into one huge factory. For the majority of American citizens mankind's ancient foe of poverty was defeated.

The modern manager has earned his high place among the leaders of the nation. But his responsibilities have kept pace with his enlarged social role. People want other things besides goods and services from the modern corporation. More and more it is considered the manager's job to see that they get them.

There has been a decline in the broad public support of the power-seeking businessman. When the nation was first industrializing, his approach was in harmony with general ethical standards. After all, power is needed in any period of rapid mobilization of resources to accomplish broad social goals. But once these goals have been accomplished, generally there is a negative reaction to the concentration of power. The public clamors for its dispersal or control by society. During wartime the government takes over power to wage the war, but at the war's end there is a strong urge to disarm and "get back to normalcy." The early drive toward industrialization can be looked upon as a battle against poverty. That battle has been largely won. The American people no longer want managers to openly exult in their power.

Modern professional managers are well aware of this attitude. They recognize they must be careful in the use of their vast power. They no longer defend this power as the divine right of capital. They are fearful that if they do not accept the full social responsibilities which go with the power, they will lose it and probably to someone antagonistic to business management and free enterprise. Business moralists think that the reconstruction of the moral foundation of business is the most urgent problem facing American business today. This is why they are searching for a new precept to replace the old one based entirely on profit maximization. The doctrine of socially responsible management is a result of this search.

DEFINING THE DOCTRINE

According to the doctrine of socially responsible management, the corporation is such a powerful institution in American life that it is socially disastrous to regard it as only a profit making organization. Whether managers like it or not, their function must change. They must accept the full responsibility for the impact of big business on society. If they do not, the corporation may not survive.

From this viewpoint, the proper function of management is to administer the enterprise not only for the welfare of shareholders but other groups as well—employees, customers, suppliers, dealers, the community, government and the like. Managers should arbitrate impersonally among these various interests.

There is evidence of the doctrine of socially responsible management: participation by executives in political affairs; corporate support of educational institutions; various employee welfare measures, community relations programs; and intensified public relations campaigns. These activities are considered essential to safeguard the position of the corporation. Sometimes they are justified on this basis alone. "A prudent regard for all the interests that merge in making the business a going concern now and in the future is, in fact, the only way to protect and to augment shareholder equity."[1]

Social responsibility of management is not merely a public relations gesture to protect the firm's profit position. "Self-conscious dedication to social responsibility may have started as a purely defensive maneuver against strident attacks on big corporations and on the moral efficacy of the profit system. But defense alone no longer explains the motive."[2] There is a sincere desire on the part of responsible executives to win respect of the general public by utilizing their power for the common good. The corporation is regarded as a multi-purpose social institution. The pursuit of profit is secondary in importance to the public interest.

PROBLEMS OF THE DOCTRINE

Now we turn to the second aspect of the moral crisis of business—the inadequacy of the doctrine of socially responsible management. If it were able to give managers moral guidelines in making day-to-day decisions, it could take the place of the profit ethic. But at present the doctrine is more of a philosophical position than an ethical system. It is not widely accepted, largely because of its implications for the status, functions, power and control of the corporation and manager.

Status

Status refers to social position. The status of an organization like the corporation is defined by its relationship to other social structures.

Status of the firm in classical economics is defined by its market relations. The firm is a private organization pursuing the single goal of profit. It buys or hires resources, labor and capital and produces goods and services. Its specialized economic function limits its relations with other social entities. These relations do not go beyond the exchange process in the market.

The doctrine of socially responsible management implies that the status of the corporation transcends the market relationship, but it tells us nothing definite. The corporate revolution has turned a single-purpose economic entity into a multi-purpose social institution. The corporation's relations with government, education, religion and the family cannot be defined by the exchange process alone. But the doctrine does not have a conceptual foundation which clarifies the status of the corporation in modern society.

The same kind of ambiguity surrounds the status of the manager. Separation of ownership and control has given management an autonomy difficult to fit into the concept of private property. Managers no longer seem to feel entirely responsible to stockholders. The doctrine of socially responsible management implies that somehow they are accountable to society at large. But what is the nature of this relationship? How can one occupational group holding power based neither on property ownership nor political election be related to all groups of society under its influence?

Function

Closely related to the problem of status is that of function. In recent years the corporation has expanded in function as well as size. It no longer is just a producer of goods and services. It now performs a number of political, welfare, social and cultural functions as well. Examples of the noneconomic corporate functions are:

1. *Political:* generally considered to be the responsibility of government, such as the diplomatic relations of oil companies with small oil-rich countries in the Middle East.

2. *Welfare:* corporate donations to private colleges and loaning of executives for community, charitable and civic betterment programs.
3. *Social:* meeting needs of society, such as providing social status for workers and managers based on occupation.
4. *Cultural:* influencing beliefs, values and goals of members of society; for example, application of the criteria of success in business to non-business areas of life.

Economists are opposed to noneconomic functions because they interfere with the corporation's traditional economic function. Political scientists have misgivings about corporate functions which have been traditionally the prerogative of the state. They question whether the tendency of the corporation to take on political functions is in keeping with the pluralistic tradition of American social structure and political processes.

Jurists fear that well worked out legal standards are endangered by noneconomic corporate functions and there is nothing to replace them. Cultural objections to the trend stem from a dislike for corporate values and goals becoming the common denominator in all walks of life. Opposition on social grounds is based on the fear that the open society will be destroyed and we will enter a new age of corporate feudalism.

The doctrine of socially responsible management is vague about which functions the corporation ought to perform. Should the socially responsible manager be a "business statesman" who conducts the affairs of the corporation to bring about a better world? If so, there ought to be no limitations placed on the functions performed by the corporation. Few Americans would agree to such a broad interpretation of the manager's social mandate. But if there is anything to the doctrine of socially responsible management, the corporation should perform at least some noneconomic functions. But which ones and on what grounds?

Power

Problems of status and functions would not be significant without problems posed by the great power of the corporation. There are two aspects of this problem: the concentration of corporate power and the legitimacy of management power.

Many economists believe the ideal economy is one composed of purely competitive markets in which many small firms are closely controlled by competition. The market performs the essential social task of economizing by channeling resources into their most efficient use and maintaining a check on production costs. Clearly industries dominated by large corporations cannot have decentralization of economic power. This structural characteristic is the basis of most criticism of big business by economists. They are unwilling to accept the good intentions of responsible managers in place of the rigors of market competition.

Great corporate power is therefore a precondition of the doctrine of socially responsible management. Without such concentrated power, it would not matter whether or not managers were socially responsible. Whatever their intentions, they would be constrained by market forces to behave in ways best for society.

The economists fear power not controlled by the market as irresponsible power. As Carl Kaysen put it, in the absence of market constraints "what management takes into account [in decision-making] is what management decides to take into account." Therefore, corporate power "... is responsible only in terms of the goals, values, and knowledge of management."[3]

The problem of the legitimacy of management power is basically political. The large corporation frequently is criticized as undemocratic. By democracy we mean a political system in which those in authority receive their power from the people and use this power according to the wishes of the majority. An organization is democratic if its leaders acquire their power legitimately and if the power can be taken away for misuse.

A few thousand top managers actively control big business in America. But who selected these men? Of course they selected themselves. Management groups of large corporations are self-perpetuating oligarchies. One of the major tasks of aging top executives is to select and groom their successors. But to whom are they responsible? There is no generally accepted answer. It constitutes the problem of the legitimacy of management power.

Lawyers argue that corporate managers must be responsible to the stockholders. They contend that if the link between owners and managers is ever dissolved management will lose the legal basis for its existence. What real claim will managers have to their positions if they do not own the company or represent the owners' interests? The implication is clear. To the extent that management is not directly responsible to the stockholders, its powers are not legitimate and big business is undemocratic. The doctrine of socially responsible management has no rebuttal to this charge.

Control

Economists are uneasy about the large corporation because it seems to be running without any discernible controls. This is of more concern to them than the idea that large corporations perform poorly in the public interest.

The most sophisticated analysis of how society controls the manager has been made by Adolf A. Berle. He believes the only real control over managers is their philosophy. The source of this philosophy is the "public consensus." "This is the existence of a set of ideas, widely held by the community, and often by the organization itself and the men who direct it, that certain uses of power are 'wrong,' that is, contrary to the established interest and value system of the community."[4] Public consensus furnishes the basis for public opinion. Professors, journalists, politicians and others translate public consensus into public opinion. If managers violate the public consensus they lose prestige and esteem. If this does not produce results desired by the community, more forceful penalties are invoked.

Berle's ideas about how society controls managers have been severely criticized. Economists have no faith in public consensus and question the wisdom of replacing the invisible hand of the competitive market with the heavy hand of powerful corporate management. Lawyers criticize Berle's analysis because it seems to undermine the rule of law. They want something more tangible to limit the wide scope of managerial discretion than the somewhat nebulous concepts of management philosophy and public consensus. Political scientists are critical of Berle's thesis because they have misgivings about any check on power other than power itself.

Edward S. Mason, former President of the American Economic Association, has asked academic proponents of the doctrine of socially responsible management to produce a "managerial apologetic"—an up-to-date explanation of how society controls corporations through managers that can gain general acceptance.[5] Thus far no such explanation has appeared.

CONCLUSION

The doctrine of socially responsible management has been suggested as a logical successor to the profit ethic. It is in tune with the trend of the American economy in the twentieth century. Nonetheless this doctrine presently is inadequate as a business ethic. It lacks a conceptual foundation. It is more a philosophical viewpoint than a moral guide to management action. Before it can receive acceptance as the ethical system of modern business it must be able to cope with the problems of status, function, power and control of the corporation and manager.

NOTES

1. Richard Eells, "Social Responsibility: Can Business Survive the Challenge?" *Business Horizons*, Vol. 2, No. 4 (Winter 1959), p. 41.
2. Theodore Levitt, "The Dangers of Social Responsibility," *Harvard Business Review*, Vol. 36, No. 5 (September-October 1958), p. 41.
3. Carl Kaysen, "The Social Significance of the Modern Corporation," *American Economic Review*, Vol. XLVII, No. 2 (May 1957), p. 316.
4. Adolf A. Berle, Jr., *Power Without Property* (New York: Harcourt, Brace & Co., 1959), p. 90.
5. Edward S. Mason, "The Apologetics of 'Managerialism,'" *Journal of Business*, Vol. XXXI, No. 1 (January 1958), pp. 1-11.

CHARLES F. PHILLIPS, JR.

What is Wrong with Profit Maximization?

Corporate management must face up to a predicament that has crucial economic and social implications. On the one hand, many argue that business must assume social responsibilities, in addition to its historic economic and legal obligations, by becoming involved even more deeply in such activities as corporate giving, support of higher education, political participation, and representation in community affairs. In discussing the changing role of business in our economy, David Rockefeller, President of the Chase Manhattan Bank, argues:

> "In *social* terms, the old concept that the owner of a business had a right to use his property as he pleased to maximize profits has evolved into the belief that ownership carries certain binding social obligations. Today's manager serves as trustee not only for the owners but for the workers and indeed for our entire society. ... Corporations have developed a sensitive awareness of their responsibility for maintaining an equitable balance among the claims of stockholders, employees, customers, and the public at large."[1]

On the other hand, an equally vocal group contends that management should adhere to its traditional economic function of producing

Source: *Business Horizons*, Winter, 1963. Copyright © 1963, by the Foundation for the School of Business at Indiana University. Reprinted by permission.

goods and services at maximum profit. In the words of Milton Friedman, the University of Chicago's well-known economist:

> "Few trends could so thoroughly undermine the very foundations of our free society as the acceptance by corporate officials of a social responsibility other than to make as much money for their stockholders as possible. This is a fundamentally subversive doctrine."[2]

Professor Friedman believes, moreover, that even business contributions to support charitable activities represent "an inappropriate use of corporate funds in a free-enterprise society."

The choice of a course involves far more than mere intellectual exercise. As challenging as that may be, management faces the grave prospect of undergoing a significant modification of its traditional role unless it faces decisively the issues raised by the present controversy. As a result of indecision, a solution may be forced upon management—perhaps against its best interests.

THE THESIS

In the past few years, some businessmen have tended more frequently to soft-pedal profit maximization and to emphasize the modern corporation's growing list of social obligations. But the phrase "social responsibility," rarely defined, remains a hazy concept. Sometimes it implies only a shift in emphasis, perhaps for public relations purposes, without modification of business goals or values. At other times, however, the implication is that corporations should step beyond their traditional economic and legal functions *even at the sacrifice of long-run profit*. This view of social responsibility is, to use Joseph W. McGuire's phrase, "a crude blend of long-run profit making and altruism."[3]

In the writer's opinion, both business and our private enterprise system would suffer if profit maximization were sought irresponsibly, but they would also suffer if uncritical philanthropy were introduced in the guise of social responsibility. Profit maximization must remain as the basic goal of business firms. In turn, the profit maximization approach can guide management in the area of social responsibility. Businessmen must be socially responsible insofar as social responsibility leads to higher profits, but they must possess a fine sense of double-entry bookkeeping! Argues Henry Ford II, Chairman of the Board of the Ford Motor Company:

> "Once 'business is business' meant dog-eat-dog, the devil take the hindmost, the law of the jungle. Today we need the phrase 'business is busi-

ness' just to remind us that business is *not* first and foremost a social institution, a charitable agency, a cultural gathering, a community service, a public spirited citizen. It is an action organization geared to produce economic results in competition with other business."[4]

Why is it felt that management should be responsible to society as a whole rather than to its stockholders? What are the long-run implications of social responsibility? What is a socially responsible enterprise in a market economy? Finally, is the quandary regarding social responsibility and profit maximization real or illusory?

SOCIAL RESPONSIBILITY: ORIGINS

The traditional justification for a private enterprise economy rests on the assumption that rigorous competition will prevail. One of the basic tenets of competitive theory, as developed by Adam Smith and other classical economists, is that business firms will seek to maximize profits. By so doing, business will allocate society's scarce resources in the best possible manner, and serve the best interests of both their stockholders and the general public. A competitive market system thus reconciles private interests with the public good.

In 1932 Adolf A. Berle, Jr. and Gardiner C. Means questioned the relevance of these assumptions for modern capitalism and, in so doing, started a continuing debate over corporate responsibilities.[5] The authors noted that the ownership of corporate stock was becoming dispersed among society's members, while control of corporate capital assets was becoming concentrated in the hands of a relatively few salaried managers. The first trend tends to reduce the effectiveness of stockholder control and the second to increase the economic power of management.

Few today disagree with the conclusions of the Berle and Means study; statistics on the dispersion of ownership and the concentration of control of corporate assets are familiar. More important for present purposes are the problems raised by these developments.

The first arises from the fact that in our modern economy stockholders own property without effective control while management has power without substantial ownership. The classical economists assumed that ownership and management were synonymous; profits were the reward for successfully exercising this ownership-management function. The separation of ownership and control, therefore, raises a question: to whom is management responsible? To use Berle's phrase, the stockholder has become a "passive receptive" who cannot manage and who is thus functionless. But management has no legitimate claim on profits because it lacks ultimate ownership. On the matter of corporate control, Edward S. Mason writes:

> "What Mr. Berle and most of the rest of us are afraid of is that this powerful corporate machine, which so successfully grinds out the goods we want, seems to be running without any discernible controls. The young lad mastering the technique of his bicycle may legitimately shout with pride, 'Look, Ma, no hands,' but is this the appropriate motto for a corporate society?"[6]

The second problem is raised by corporate size. Economists generally believe that competition among large enterprises is different from competition among small decision-making units. This belief is reflected in the popular feeling that competition has declined in the United States and that prices are administered or institutionally determined. Management, the argument goes, has the freedom (within limits) to set prices and to determine the rate of technological change and economic growth. Competition, many feel, is not the strict disciplinarian it was once thought to be and, as a result, the goals of management have changed. Management is far more interested in the corporation as an institution and in its continued existence than in immediate, or even long-run profits.

Because the irresponsible use of this immense power is unthinkable, management must become socially responsible; it has been suggested that management has no choice. The accumulation of power by any group in a democratic society has always been suspect. The tremendous economic power of Big Business, unless used justly, will be further restricted by Big Labor and Big Government. (Both of the latter have also been subjects of debate.) To maintain a private enterprise economy, so the argument goes, business must assume new social responsibilities.

SOCIAL RESPONSIBILITY: ITS IMPLICATION

If social responsibility becomes the dominant force in business decision making, three significant implications should be understood. In the first place, the idea of a corporate conscience assumes that management has the option of being socially responsible or not. While such an assumption may be vehemently denied by business leaders, the fact remains that vigorous competition and social statesmanship are logically incompatible. In the words of Theodore Levitt:

> " . . . only businessmen who are free from the rigid demands of competition are free to practice the prerogatives of business statesmanship. Statesmanship is a luxury of some degree of monopoly. Any business

that habitually practices statesmanship must be presumed to have achieved the felicity of not having to keep its nose continuously to the competitive grindstone. If it can purposely hold prices down or freely raise them, if it can have extravagant employee welfare plans, make handouts to every solicitor for a supposedly good cause, make its headquarters a crystal palace of ankle-deep rugs and solid-gold water coolers—if it can do these, one may begin to question whether the industry is entirely competitive."[7]

Levitt may be pushing the argument to the extreme, but his point is valid; a business firm cannot have the best of two worlds. The first implication of social responsibility, then, is that competition in our economy has become so "imperfect" that the market is a poor regulator of corporate behavior.

In the second place, conscience requires that value judgments be made. Two questions immediately arise: does business know what is good for society and, even if it does, should business force its value judgments on society? One may properly question whether any interest group in the economy knows what society really wants or should want; clearly a consensus does not exist. Argues Ben W. Lewis:

"Economic decisions must be right as society measures right rather than good as benevolent individuals construe goodness. An economy is a mechanism designed to pick up and discharge the wishes of society in the management of its resources; it is not an instrument for the rendering of gracious music by kindly disposed improvisers."[8]

In the third place, the acceptance of social responsibility may make it impossible for business to carry out its major function of economizing, that is, to be efficient in the use of the nation's scarce and limited resources. Responsibility or conscientiousness has nothing to do with economizing. Should society at large come to accept the idea of a corporate conscience, business may find it exceedingly difficult to make sound economic decisions with respect to prices, wages, and investment. Such decisions are often unpleasant—for example, the decision to move a plant from one community to another. Again, Professor Lewis' words are well worth considering:

"Ponder the plight of the management of a giant firm producing a basic commodity, employing thousands of workers at good wages, making splendid profits, and presently facing a crippling strike unless it accedes to a demand for a wage increase. The increase can easily be passed along in higher prices. Workers want higher wages and no interruption in employment; consumers want continued output at an increasing rate and so do stockholders. The public does not want further inflation, and large numbers of small firms do not want further increases in wages. The White House, which wants high production, full employment, healthy wages, abundant profits, and low prices, now admonishes industrial statesmen to recognize their public responsibility and to adopt measures appropriate to the maintenance of equity, full employment, stability, and progress. The management—as allocator, distributor, stabilizer, trustee, conservator, prophet, and chaplain, as well as manager—consults its conscience. The diagnosis of the attending psychiatrist will be 'multiple schizophrenia': The management's personality will not be split. It will be shredded and powdered!'"[9]

One can sympathize with United States Steel's Roger Blough when, in the face of overwhelming governmental displeasure, he attempted to defend his company's 1962 price increase to the nation in terms of profits and investment needs. But it would be difficult to imagine his defense in terms of social responsibility: to maintain equity among the company's interested groups, higher wages were voluntarily granted to workers and increased prices to suppliers, which, in turn, necessitated higher steel prices to provide greater profits for stockholders' dividends and for new investment to satisfy consumer demand (all beneficial to society at large). Or consider the following reply by an executive of one of the country's largest corporations when asked by a stockholder to defend his firm's annual educational gifts: "We in the ... Company believe in being good corporate citizens. We think the principle of corporate giving is well established. It is encouraged by our tax laws; it has been upheld in our courts; and the public has come to expect it of corporations."

Is not this the crux of the issue? Since bigness is frequently suspect and the level of existing profits as well as the need for higher profits questioned, corporate actions are frequently defended in terms of responsibility. But such a defense will subject management's conscience to countless pressures, and the public will come to expect contributions, even when the corporation cannot expect either direct or indirect benefits. "A competitive establishment cannot be selfless in any genuine fashion. Selflessness, however, is what socially responsible behavior implies," writes Levitt.

If these implications are correct, management's attempt to justify both its size and its power in terms of social responsibility may end in gigantic failure. The corporation is an economic institution, not a welfare organization, and its real justification is profit maximization for the benefit of its stockholders. By stepping into the social arena where there are few, if any, acceptable standards of efficiency in the use of society's resources, business may invite restrictions on its freedom.

Social responsibility is a function of government, civic organizations, and business leaders as individuals. Public officials are responsible to the public at large, but "it is highly repugnant that a corporate manager, not publicly elected and hence not subject to popular recall, should have a special responsibility for what the managerialists call the process of government. At least a socialistic government can be defeated at the polls."[10] Benevolent management rule is not, I am confident, the intent of those advocating social responsibility.

THE CASE FOR PROFIT MAXIMIZATION

Eugene V. Rostow has succinctly stated the case for profit maximization:

> "The law books have always said that the board of directors owes a single-minded duty of unswerving loyalty to the stockholders, and only to the stockholders. The economist has demonstrated with all the apparent precision of plane geometry and the calculus that the quest for maximum revenue in a competitive market leads to a system of prices, and an allocation of resources and rewards, superior to any alternative, in its contributions to the economic welfare of the community as a whole. . . . If, as is widely thought, the essence of corporate statesmanship is to seek less than maximum profits, post war experience is eloquent evidence that such statesmanship leads to serious malfunctioning of the economy as a whole."[11]

In short, according to Rostow, social responsibility will "sabotage the market mechanism and systematically distort the allocation of resources," thereby making "the task of monetary and fiscal authority in controlling general fluctuations of trade more expensive and more difficult," and perhaps making "it impossible to sustain high levels of employment save at the cost of considerable price inflation."

In everyday phraseology, profit assumes that management is responsible for running an efficient business organization, that is, performing its economic function. *In so doing, the organization is being socially responsible.* In making a decision, whether that decision concerns prices, investment, plant location, or an educational contribution, some criteria must be used as guides. Profit maximization is a criterion; social responsibility, emphasizing equity, is not.

> "The corporate conscience is irrelevant to the corporate purpose. Conscience is not something you introduce as a piece of organizational decor, performing simply a decorative function. If it is allowed to influence the mechanism of economic decision-making, conscience automat-

ically assumes a central role. Nothing could be worse. The stronger the conscience the harder it will be to make a businesslike decision and get the economic job done."[12]

Further, the primary philosophy adopted by management—whether social responsibility or profit maximization—determines the decisions made. Should Firm X continue to operate in Community Y, where it is the largest employer, or should it move to Community Z where the profit potential is greater? Should corporations sponsor higher quality television programs at the risk of smaller audiences in an attempt to get the industry out of the "vast wasteland," or should program content be aimed at capturing the largest possible audience? Clearly, social responsibility and profit maximization are two entirely different concepts involving different goals and values.

It might be argued that the traditional or orthodox justification for profit maximization is no longer suited to the needs of modern capitalism. One of the basic assumptions of those advocating corporate social responsibility is that the market mechanism no longer functions as effectively as was once thought and that corporations consequently have some degree of market power or choice over such variables as prices and the rate of technological innovation. My own opinion is that competition, whether in the price or nonprice dimension, exists in sufficient strength to limit the long-run area of choice open to the managements of most American corporations.

Let there be no misunderstanding. Competition is far from "perfect" and public policy could and should promote, to achieve maximum efficiency and personal freedom, a stronger procompetitive policy (by eliminating trade barriers and fair trade laws, to name only two examples). Yet in most industries, the existing degree of competition is sufficient (in economic terms "workable") to protect the consumer interest. The danger in accepting the philosophy of social responsibility is that management will forget its economic function and will attempt to assume the functions that have traditionally been assigned to the market mechanism. (Just as dangerous are attempts by either government or labor to assume managerial functions.[13]) Concludes Ford:

"I have deep faith in the stimulating power of competition and in the capacity of the free market to allocate resources and to bring us optimum growth and progress, if we only let it work. And we will let it work if we can bring ourselves to accept a few very simple ideas about business: that business is a tool, and that the sharper its cutting edges are the stronger its motivating power, the better job it will be able to do for all of us."[14]

It has been suggested that a compromise is necessary to solve the issue of social responsibility. Thus, Richard Eells argues that "the root of the conflict over social responsibilities lies in the irreconcilability of two equally untenable theories of the corporation," namely, the "traditional corporation," which intends to maximize profits, and the "metrocorporation," which assumes limitless social obligations. He puts forward the "well-tempered corporation," a compromise between these two extremes, which regards profits as primary but also considers its social obligations in the decision-making process.[15]

The editors of *Fortune* find it difficult to distinguish between the "well-tempered corporation" and the "metrocorporation." In their words:

"... it is impossible to attach a definite meaning to the expression 'profits are secondary' or even to 'profits are primary but coordinate with other functions.' If profits are secondary, then they can *always* be sacrificed for the sake of fulfilling obligations that are primary; but since profits are an indispensible condition of the corporation's existence, this is tantamount to saying that the corporation can sacrifice its existence and at the same time fulfill its obligations to the community. Again, to say that profits are a primary function, coordinate with other functions, amounts to saying that these other functions are also primary and hence of equal importance. So what does the corporation do in the event of a conflict?"[16]

The management of a modern corporation may be a "self-perpetuating oligarchy" (Berle's phrase), but that management making inadequate profits will not survive for long. Moreover, social responsibility is a fair-weather concept; management cannot even think in terms of philanthropy unless profits are adequate.

SOCIAL RESPONSIBILITY IN A MARKET ECONOMY

The basic proposition, as every businessman knows only too well, is that profits are the indispensable element in a successful business enterprise. The role of profits may not be recognized or understood by as many of our citizens as would be desirable, but to duck the issue by hiding behind the cloak of "social responsibility" does not seem to be the answer. Management must operate at maximum economic efficiency to get rid of the evil connotations attached to the word "profit." The corporation that is efficient, that constantly strives to improve old products and introduce new ones, and that seeks to satisfy consumer demand in the most efficient manner and at the lowest possible price is the one with the strongest case for maximum profit.

Yet conscience is an integral part of management's everyday decision making and profit maximization functions. Responsible behavior requires scrupulous adherence to the spirit of the law as well as to its letter, avoidance of any misrepresentative advertising, and bargaining with labor in good faith. This point has been well stated by Frederick R. Kappel, Board Chairman of the American Telephone & Telegraph Company:

> " ... the purpose of business is not simply to provide the opportunity for making a fast buck.... The fast-buck philosophy not only stands in the way of a good job, it also robs the individual of the feeling of accomplishment that he needs in his personal life. I don't mean that one needs to be a 'do-gooder' in the sense in which that phrase is often used. But *the person of character* will approach business life with the idea that he has obligations to fulfill. He will set his ethical sights high and hold himself strictly to account. He will act on the principle that good management, sound business practice, and balanced judgment are ideas well worth his best striving."[17]

Similarly, profit maximization does not imply that business leaders can be indifferent to the country's social system. Management has an interest in trying to maintain and aid the development of a social system in which firms can operate with maximum freedom, profitability, and longevity. However, *business should seek society's good in ways that are also good for business.* Philanthropic acts often have economic justification: gifts to a local school construction program may improve the company's labor force; matching employees' gifts to their universities or other philanthropies may increase both the stability and the effort of its labor force; and community gifts of many kinds may improve community relations in ways that admittedly are difficult to measure. For these reasons, insurance companies conduct safety education, banks employ agricultural specialists, and railroads promote area development.

Therefore, a contribution to a charitable organization should be made because it benefits the corporation and not because it is the thing to do or because it is expected. The executive who was quoted earlier concerning his company's policy of contributing money to educational institutions was asked to defend the policy again a year later. This time, however, his answer was quite different: "When we finally commit ourselves to an expenditure, we feel that within the limits of human fallibility we have done our best to be able to say: 'This expenditure, this investment, will be profitable and remunerative for the company and, through it, for the shareholders.' We devote exactly the same attention to our contributions for philanthropy and education." No longer is the emphasis upon responsibility; it is upon profits.

Would it not be ironic for management to lose the struggle for public recognition of the role of adequate profits, for which it has fought so long, just at a time when it appears that the chances of success may be at hand? It has been a long time since an administration has actively advocated and sought a tax cut to stimulate economic growth. And it has been an even longer time since a Democratic president has publicly argued that increased business profits are one means of achieving this goal. Many obstacles remain before words become deeds, but this hardly seems to be the time for a basic shift in management's philosophy.

What is wrong with profit maximization as management's basic decision making goal? Nothing, if properly understood. The choice between profit maximization and social responsibility is not an either-or proposition. As long as profit maximization is the dominant factor in corporate decision making, guiding management in the area of social responsibility, no problem exists. But if business adopts a dominant philosophy of social responsibility, our free, competitive, private enterprise system cannot survive.

A business firm is not a charitable or philanthropic organization. It is an economizing institution and its basic function is to economize; only by performing its economic function well is a business firm socially responsible. Nor is a business firm an instrument through which its management seeks to replace the functioning of the market with its value judgments as to what is good or bad for society. Business operates within a legal framework and is subject to market control. If the market does not adequately control business decisions, then the public can be expected to demand government control. Market control is the essence of a democratic, private enterprise system.

Many will disagree with the view being expressed. Some, such as McGuire, have termed profit maximization the "traditional" approach, one that does not permit business "to adapt to a changing world." Nothing could be further from the truth; business has changed and will continue to change. Certainly the public expects more from business today than it did fifty years ago and assumes that businessmen will be men of character with a high sense of what is right and wrong. But as executives of corporations, business leaders' major responsibility is to manage as efficiently as possible the allocation of that portion of society's resources that come within the corporation's control. Is this not, after all, the only economic, legal, and social justification for a business enterprise in a free society?

NOTES

1. David Rockefeller, "The Changing Role of Business in Our Society," in an address before the American Philosophical Society, Philadelphia, Nov. 8, 1962.
2. Milton Friedman, *Capitalism and Freedom* (Chicago: The University of Chicago Press, 1962), p. 133.
3. Joseph W. McGuire, *Business and Society* (New York: McGraw-Hill Book Company, Inc., 1963), p. 144.
4. Henry Ford II, "What America Expects of Industry," in an address before the Michigan State Chamber of Commerce, Oct. 2, 1962.
5. Adolf A. Berle, Jr. and Gardiner C. Means, *The Modern Corporation and Private Property* (New York: The Macmillan Co., 1932). See also Adolf A. Berle, Jr., *Power Without Property* (New York: Harcourt, Brace and Company, Inc., 1959).
6. In Edward S. Mason (ed.), *The Corporation in Modern Society* (Cambridge: Harvard University Press, 1959), pp. 3–4.
7. Theodore Levitt, "The Mythological Potency of 'Peoples' Capitalism,'" in *The Corporation: Its Modern Character and Responsibilities* (Columbus: The Ohio State University, 1960), pp. 15–16. See also, by the same author, "The Dangers of Social Responsibility," *Harvard Business Review*, XXXVI (Sept.–Oct., 1958).
8. Ben W. Lewis, "Economics by Admonition," *American Economic Review*, XLIX (May, 1959), p. 395.
9. "Economics by Admonition," p. 396.
10. "Have Corporations a Higher Duty Than Profits?" *Fortune*, LXII (August, 1960), p. 148.
11. Eugene V. Rostow in *The Corporation in Modern Society*, p. 63.
12. "The Mythological Potency of 'Peoples' Capitalism,'" p. 15.
13. Charles F. Phillips, Jr. and Harmon H. Haymes, "'Psychological' Price Control: Meddling or Masterstroke?" *Business Horizons*, V (Summer, 1962), pp. 99–106.
14. Henry Ford, "What America Expects of Industry."
15. Richard Eells, "Social Responsibility: Can Business Survive the Challenge?," *Business Horizons*, II (Winter, 1959), p. 37.
16. "Have Corporations a Higher Duty Than Profits?" p. 109.
17. Frederick R. Kappel in an address at the commencement exercises of Michigan State University, June 9, 1963 (emphasis added).

GEORGE CABOT LODGE

Business and the Changing Society

The United States is in the midst of one of the great transformations of Western civilization. Like many other managers, the chief executive of General Motors feels the quakes:

> "I am concerned about a society that has demonstrably lost confidence in its institutions—in the government, in the press, in the church, in the military—as well as in business."[1]

What is happening is that the old ideas and assumptions, which once made our great institutions legitimate, authoritative, and confident, are fast eroding. They are slipping away in the face of a changing reality and are being replaced by different ideas and different assumptions, which are as yet ill-formed, contradictory, and shocking. The transition is neither good nor bad; there is the possibility of plenty of both. The point is that it is taking place.

It is hard for managers, especially those in large corporations, to operate in an environment in which the old ideas no longer seem to work. If these new ideas were well defined, it would be difficult enough for managers—and for all of us—to cope with them; but since they are still plastic, unfamiliar, and disruptive, we are baffled—and perhaps afraid.

Source: *Harvard Business Review*, March-April 1974, pp. 59-72. Copyright © 1974 by the President and Fellows of Harvard College; all rights reserved.

We need to stand back and look at the whole body of our problems and not merely at the dilemmas and questions each one presents to us individually—we must look at the forest, now, instead of the trees. It behooves managers to clear their heads, to inspect all old assumptions, to identify as precisely as possible what is happening and what new ideas and definitions of values are germinating, and then to look objectively at the choices that remain.

This is not an easy thing to do. The old ideas are hard to let go; they have glorious associations for us, springing as they have from the revolutions against hierarchical medievalism of the sixteenth and seventeenth centuries. It is difficult also because the old ideas are what in many cases have made legitimate the seats of power. They justify the status quo. Nobody likes to look at the weakness beneath him.

But the stakes are high. Some institutions may be able to adapt to the incoming ideology, and survive and prosper. Others may have to look outside the United States for more hospitable surroundings where the old ideas are still acceptable. Still other institutions will be shaken apart, and they are beginning to know it; but they are paralyzed, unwilling or unable to change or move. Why?

OUR INSTITUTIONS ARE SPINNING THEIR WHEELS

As I write this, the nation's economy is at full throttle. Sales, profits, and production have never been greater. But there is an unease, a certain absence of control and direction with which the economists cannot reckon. We have lost confidence in ourselves and the world knows it:

- The decline of the dollar is a measure of our loss.
- Food and fuel are in short supply.
- The malaise on the assembly line continues.
- The trade-off mechanisms through which we balance energy, policy, technology, transportation, economic growth, and ecological integrity are not functioning.
- The structures of government are bloated and inefficient, manipulated by powerful interest groups whose clear-cut ends seem to justify any means.
- Opinion polls confirm Gerstenberg's perception of declining confidence in our political leadership; and each day's newspaper brings to each of us new revelations of illegality by business and government leaders.

Thus an ominous self-doubt prevails, a fear that we are moving inexorably away from old, familiar moorings and sailing off, for all we are worth, into an unknown sea of storms. We need a chart, a plan, to find our way. But whom can we trust to draw the plan and mark the course?

There is a propensity in times like these to blame the devils and praise the angels. Some are even tempted to welcome the ruin and destruction of the old, blindly hoping to find the good and reliable in the purity of the ashes.

But neither praise nor blame nor ruin is the answer. We need new social and political constructs that (a) clearly embrace our economic and technological activities and (b) allow for the development of a new sense of community. But what should these constructs be?

In essence, they must weave together for us a new system of definitions for the ancient values—survival, justice, creativity, self-respect, and the like. All communities everywhere have treasured these values; they are timeless and essentially noncontroversial. It is the definitions of such values that vary from time to time and place to place.

For example, in ancient Egypt, justice and self-respect involved lugging stones to memorialize Pharaoh's transition to the next life. And in modern China, these same values are fulfilled by total service to the community and the nation.

Our own definitions are quite different; but they are also fuzzy and contradictory. The proof of this statement is the fact that we have lost our sense of what "ought to be"—we have lost the sense of direction that would allow us to answer the questions being raised about our society today:

- By what criteria will we measure our progress?
- What is the good community?
- How many people should it have?
- Where should they live?
- What do they need?
- What are their rights?

There are no pragmatic answers to questions such as these. Ad hoc experimentalism of the kind to which we have become addicted constitutes floundering from crisis to crisis.[2] The need for broad conceptions has become essential.

They may come, as they have so often in the past, with cruelty, bloodshed, repression, and waste. They may come humanely, efficiently, and with a maximum of liberty, as they have relatively seldom. If we perceive the nature of our crisis sooner rather then later and do not shrink from its implications, however threatening to existing assumptions and interests those implications may be, the chances will increase that our transition from our old ideology to a new ideology will be relatively benign.

But if we wait, confident of somehow muddling through, we shall lurch from crisis to crisis until large-scale depression and disruption cause us to welcome the orderly relief of dictatorship.

IDEOLOGY AS CONNECTIVE TISSUE . . .

One great difficulty we have in facing up to this problem of ideological transition is that we have always thought of ourselves as a pragmatic people that does what needs to be done to meet the requirements of the time. We have supposed that ideology is something we left behind in Europe with our ancestors—a theoretical bag of confusion that trammeled up socialism and communism and the other "isms," from which hardheaded Americans are happily free.

This, of course, is nonsense. We are just as deeply imbued with ideology as any other community—probably more so. We sometimes call it Americanism. It is the basis of our motivation, our national "collective unconscious." To assert that we are free of it is as absurd as to assert that a true man exists who does not have a subconscious mind.

. . . in the Old Body

Our traditional ideology is not at all hard to identify. It is composed of five great ideas that first came to America in the eighteenth century, having been set down in seventeenth century England as "natural" laws by John Locke, among others. These ideas found a particularly fertile soil in the vast, underpopulated wilderness of America and served us well for a hundred years or so. They are now in an advanced state of erosion.

Individualism This is the atomistic notion that the community is no more than the sum of the individuals in it. It is the idea that fulfillment lies in an essentially lonely struggle in what amounts to a wilderness where the fit survive—and where, if you do not survive, you are somehow unfit. Closely tied to individualism is the idea of *equality*, in the sense implied in the phrase "equal opportunity," and the idea of *contract*, the inviolate device by which individuals are tied together as buyers and sellers. In the political order in this country, individualism evolved into *interest group pluralism*, which became the preferred means of directing society.

Property Rights Traditionally, the best guarantee of individual rights was held to be the sanctity of property rights. By virtue of this concept, the individual was assured freedom from the predatory powers of the sovereign.

Competition Adam Smith most eloquently articulated the idea that the uses of property are best controlled by each individual proprietor competing in an open market to satisfy individual consumer desires.

The Limited State In reaction to the powerful hierarchies of medievalism, the conviction grew that the least government is the best government. We do not mind how big government may get, but we are reluctant to allow it authority or focus. And whatever happens the cry is, "Don't let it plan—particularly down there in Washington. Let it just be responsive to crises and to interest groups. Whoever pays the price can call the tune."

Scientific Specialization and Fragmentation This is the corruption of Newtonian mechanics which says that, if we attend to the parts, as experts and specialists, the whole will take care of itself.

There are a number of powerful American myths associated with these ideas: John Wayne as the frontiersman; rags to riches with Horatio Alger; and, most fundamentally, *the myth of material growth and progress.*

Implicit in individualism is the notion that man has the will to acquire power, that is, to control external events, property, nature, the economy, politics, or whatever. Under the concept of the limited state, the presence of this will in the human psyche meant the guarantee of progress through competition, notably when combined with the Darwinian notion that the inexorable processes of evolution are constantly working to improve on nature.

Scientific specialization has been part of this "progress," fragmenting knowledge and society while straining their adaptability. This splintering has brought us at least one hideous result: an amoral view of progress "under which nuclear ballistic missiles definitely represent progress over gunpowder and cannonballs, which in turn represent progress over bows and arrows."[3] This treacherous myth places no apparent limit on the degree to which man can gain dominion over his environment, nor does it stipulate any other ideological criteria for defining progress.

If we consider the past 6,000 years of human history, we are struck by the extent to which this atomistic, individualistic ideology constitutes a fundamental aberration from the historically typical communitarian norm. It stands as a radical experiment that achieved its most extreme manifestation in America in the nineteenth century. Since that time it has been steadily deteriorating in the face of various challenges—wars, depressions, new economic and political systems, the concentration and growth of populations, and institutional as well as environmental degeneration.

. . . and in the New

Institutions that depended on the traditional ideas for their legitimacy—notably the large corporations—have thus become unmoored. It is now important to determine what new ideas are moving in as "legitimizers" so that more fitting institutional forms and structures can be created. Here are my own impressions.

Individual Fulfillment Occurs Through Participation in an Organic Social Process. The community as conceived today is indeed more than the sum of the individuals in it. It has special and urgent needs, and the survival and the self-respect of the individuals in it depend on the recognition of those needs. There are few who can get their kicks á la John Wayne, although many try. Individual fulfillment for most depends on a place in a community, an identity with a whole, a participation in an organic social process. And further:

- If the community, the factory, or the neighborhood is well designed, its members will have a sense of identity with it. They will be able to make maximum use of their capacities.

- If it is poorly designed, people will be correspondingly alienated and frustrated.

In the complex and highly organized America of today, few can live as Locke had in mind.

Both corporations and unions have played leading roles in the creation of the circumstances which eroded the old idea of individualism and created the new. But invariably they have been ideologically unmindful of what they have done. Therefore, they have tended to linger with the old forms and assumptions even after those have been critically altered:

- A central component of the old notion of individualism is the so-called protestant ethic: hard work, thrift, delayed gratification, and obedience to authority. Business has extolled these virtues on the production side of things even as it has systematically undercut them on the marketing side. Advertising departments spend millions reminding us that the good life entails immediate gratification of our most lurid desires, gratification which we can buy now and pay for later. Leisure and luxury are touted as the hallmark of happiness.[4]

- Similarly, the assembly worker has been led to believe by management, parents, and TV that the old idea of individual fulfillment is valid. But he finds himself constrained in an inescapable work setting dramatically unlike anything that he has been led to expect. He is liable to strike out, perhaps violently. Or he may join the absentee lists, taking Fridays and Mondays off to eke out some spurious individualism via drugs, drink, old movies, or—if he is lucky—a walk in the hills.

- Paradoxically, such behavior puzzles both management and unions. They linger with the traditional individualistic idea of the contract long after the contract has ceased being individualistic and has become "collective," unmindful of the irrelevance of the individual labor contract to the communitarian problems at hand.

- Our former social policy attempted to guarantee that each worker have equal opportunity. The young lawyers enforcing equal employment legislation, however, have taken quite a different tack. In the case of AT&T, for example, they argued that discrimination had become institutionalized; it had become endemic to the AT&T community, and women, for example, had been slotted into certain tasks.

When this kind of argument is being accepted, it is no longer necessary to prove individual discrimination in order to get redress.

The government then moved to change the makeup of the whole of AT&T so as to provide, in effect, for *quality of representation* at all levels. Without any specific charge having been brought, the company in turn agreed to upgrade 50,000 women and 6,600 minority group workers and—perhaps most significantly—to hire 4,000 men to fill traditionally female jobs such as operator and clerk. The company also agreed to pay some $15 million in compensation. Thus the issue became one of *equality of result* not of opportunity; a communitarian idea had superseded an individualistic one.

Given this definition of the issue, the company's task was to redesign itself according to certain overall criteria, in recognition (a) of the fact that individuals are unequal in many important respects and (b) of the dictum that the good organization is one which adapts itself to those inequalities to assure equality of result.

Needless to say, the union at AT&T protested bitterly, since the government's action was a direct threat to the contract which previously had been the device used to resolve inequities in seniority and promotion policies.[5] The company itself has had commensurate difficulty in meshing its old thinking with the specific steps demanded by the representatives of the new ideology. Yet the changes are being forced forward, in one fashion or another, nonetheless.

Rights of Membership Are Overshadowing Property Rights. A most curious thing has happened to private property—it has stopped being very important. After all, what difference does it really make today whether a person *owns* or just *enjoys* property? He may get certain psychic kicks out of owning a jewel or a car or a TV set or a house—but does it really make a difference whether he owns or rents?

Today there is a new right which clearly supersedes property rights in political and social importance. It is the right to survive—to enjoy income, health, and other rights associated with membership in the American community or in some component of that community, including a corporation. As of January 1, 1974, for example, all U.S. citizens who are 65 years old, or blind, or disabled, have had an absolute right to a minimum income of $140 a month. President Nixon's Family Assistance Plan would have guaranteed an income to all. Health legislation guaranteeing medical care to all is likely.

This right derives not from any individualistic action or need; it does not emanate from a contract. It is a communitarian right that public opinion holds to be consistent with a good community. It is a revolutionary departure from the old Lockean conception under which only the fit survive. President Nixon, apparently unaware of what is happening, said once: "If you underwrite everybody's income, you undermine everybody's character." Well, of course, that depends on the definition of self-respect.

The utility of property as a *legitimizing* idea has eroded as well. It is now quite obvious that our large public corporations are not private property at all. The 1,500,000 shareholders of General Motors do not and cannot control, direct, or in any real sense be responsible for "their" company. Furthermore, the vast majority of them have not the slightest desire for such responsibility. They are investors pure and simple, and if they do not get a good return on their investment, they will put their money elsewhere.

Campaign GM and other similar attempts at stockholder agitation represent heroic but naïvely conservative strategies to force shareholders to behave like owners and thus to legitimize corporations as property. But such action is clearly a losing game. And it is a peculiar irony that James Roche, as GM chairman, branded such agitation as radical, as the machinations of "an adversary culture ... antagonistic to our American ideas of private property and individual responsibility." In truth, of course, *GM is the radical;* Nader et alia were acting as conservatives, trying to bring the corporation back into ideological line.

But, the reader may ask, if GM and the hundreds of other large corporations like it are not property, then what are they? The best we can say is that they are some sort of collective, floating in philosophic limbo, dangerously vulnerable to the charge of illegitimacy and to the charge that they are not amenable to community control. Consider how the management of this nonproprietary institution is selected. The myth is that the stockholders select the board of directors which in turn selects the management. This is not true, however. Management selects the board, and the board, generally speaking, blesses management.

Managers thus get to be managers according to some mystical, circular process of questionable legitimacy. Under such circumstances it is not surprising that "management's rights" are fragile and its authority waning. Alfred Sloan warned us of this trend in 1927:

> "There is a point beyond which diffusion of stock ownership must enfeeble the corporation by depriving it of virile interest in management upon the part of some one man or group of men to whom its success is a matter of personal and vital interest. And conversely at the same point the public interest becomes involved when the public can no longer locate some tangible personality within the ownership which it may hold responsible for the corporation's conduct."[6]

We have avoided this profound problem because of the unquestioned effectiveness of the corporate form per se. In the past, when economic growth and progress were synonymous, we preferred that managers be as free as possible from stockholder interference, in the name of efficiency. But today the definition of efficiency, the criteria for and the limitations of growth, and the general context of the corporation are all much less sure. So the myth of corporate property is becoming a vulnerability.

There is no doubt that some means will be found to legitimize the large corporation and to make it responsive to community demands. Several options seem possible:

- Effective shareholder democracy might work in small companies.
- More comprehensive and intelligent regulation by the state might be a possibility, with respect to public utilities.
- Self-management schemes such as those in Europe are being tried by some U.S. companies.
- Federal corporate charters that define corporate purpose, management rights, and community authority might be successful "legitimizers."
- Finally, there is nationalization, perhaps the most brutish and inefficient way to legitimization. If managers do not take leadership in rebuilding

their base of legitimacy, and do it artfully and well, they might as well contemplate the worst of the possibilities.

Community Need to Satisfy Consumer Desires is Replacing Competition as a Means of Controlling the Uses of Property. It was to the notion of community need that ITT appealed in 1971 when it sought to prevent the Justice Department from divesting it of Hartford Fire Insurance. The company lawyers said, in effect: "Don't visit that old idea of competition on us. The public interest requires ITT to be big and strong at home so that it can withstand the blows of Allende in Chile, Castro in Cuba, and the Japanese in general. Before you apply the antitrust laws to us, the Secretary of the Treasury, the Secretary of Commerce, and the Council of Economic Advisers should meet to decide what, in the light of our balance-of-payments problems and domestic economic difficulties, the national interest is."[7]

Note that here again it was the company arguing the ideologically radical case. The suggestion was obvious: ITT is a partner with the government—indeed with the Cabinet—in defining and fulfilling the communitarian needs of the United States. There may be some short-term doubt about who is the senior partner, but partnership it is. This concept is radically different from the traditional idea underlying the antitrust laws—namely, that the public interest emerges *naturally* from free and vigorous competition among numerous aggressive, individualistic, and preferably small companies attempting to satisfy consumer desires.

In the face of the serious pressures from Japanese and European business organizations, which emanate from ideological settings quite different from our own, there will be more and more reason to set aside the old idea of domestic competition in order to organize U.S. business effectively to meet world competition. Managers will probably welcome if not urge such a step; they may, however, be less willing to accept the necessary concomitant: if, in the name of efficiency, of economies of scale, and of the demands of world markets, we allow restraints on the free play of domestic market forces, then other forces will have to be used to define and preserve the public interest. These "other forces" will amount to greater regulation by the political order, in some form or other.

The Role of Government is Inevitably Expanding. It follows that the role of the state is changing radically—it is becoming the setter of our sights and the arbiter of community needs. Inevitably, it will take on unprecedented tasks of coordination, priority setting, and planning in the largest sense. It will need to become far more efficient and authoritative, capable of making the difficult and subtle trade-offs which now confront us—for example, between environmental purity and energy supply.

Government is already big in the United States, probably bigger in proportion to our population than even in those countries which we call "socialist." Some 16% of the labor force now works for one or another governmental agency, and by 1980 it will be more. Increasingly, U.S. institutions live on government largess—subsidies, allowances, and contracts to farmers, corporations, and universities—and individuals benefit from social insurance, medical care, and housing allowances.[8] The pretense of the limited state, however, means that these huge allocations are relatively haphazard, reflecting the crisis of the moment and the power of interest groups rather than any sort of coherent and objective plan.

The web of interrelated factors which together constitute the energy crisis is the direct result of governmental "ad hocism" and the lack of an integrated plan.

Significantly, like Franklin Roosevelt before him, President Nixon cloaks his departures from the limited state in the language of the traditional ideology. Seeking to make his massive and increasing (but uncertain) interventions palatable, he has tried to make his motives appear pragmatic, not ideological. But he, like ITT, is the radical in the case: even as he has regularly called us to loyalty to what he terms cherished values (essentially, the Lockean five), he has deliberately acted to subvert these very notions. This is worse than merely confusing because it delays the time when we will recognize the planning functions of the state for what they are and must be.

If the role of government were more precisely and consciously defined, the government could be smaller in size. To a great extent, the plethora of bureaucracies today is the result of a lack of focus and comprehension, an ironic bit of fallout from the old notion of the limited state.

The greatest significance of Watergate is perhaps that it has set back the inevitable trend toward increased executive power and efficiency at a time when we need strong, sound executive leadership more than ever. It is ironic that at this juncture Sam Ervin, as pure and noble an embodiment of the Lockean faith as one could imagine, is a national hero. There has not been a hero in America since the turn of the century, and there probably will not be again.

Watergate, however, will have served a most useful purpose if it alerts us to the need for strict and explicit statutory limitations on executive power as we go into a time when that power will necessarily grow.

Reality Now Requires Perception of Whole Systems, Not Only the Parts. Finally, and perhaps most fundamentally, the old idea of scientific specialization has given way to a new consciousness of the interrelatedness of all things. Spaceship earth, the limits of growth, the fragility of our life-supporting biosphere have dramatized the ecological and philosophical truth that everything is related to everything else. Harmony between the works of man and the demands of nature is no longer the romantic plea of conservationists. It is an absolute rule of survival, and thus it is of profound ideological significance, subverting in many ways all of the Lockean ideas.

The Dilemma of Protest But introducing cohesive and organic order into our fractionated world is not painless. It is difficult even for those most intimately involved in the process to see clearly what the real problems are. For example, consider the decline in youth protest—many have remarked on it. What really happened?

The so-called counterculture was rooted in an ideological contradiction which it diligently avoided resolving. It voiced a traditional (if extreme) cry for the full promises of the Enlightenment, individualistic and romantic: "Do your own thing, now, no matter what." It was also, however a radical call for new communitarian norms governing income distribution, inheritance, harmony with nature, and a new political order. Young people, not surprisingly, were unable to live with such contradiction.

And educational institutions gave them little help in understanding or coping with it. Academic bureaucracies, based on the old idea of specialization, constitute a series of long dark tunnels called disciplines. The best man in each field is at the end of his tunnel, digging an ever-narrowing trench of new knowledge. "If you are diligent you may find him," the student is told, "and if you are persistent you may get him to raise his head and mumble."

Whatever the ultimate value of academic research may be, the student has come to wonder whether this kind of education is what he needs to understand the world—whether, in fact, what is truly important is not what ties the tunnels together and how they are related to one another. What, for example, are the implications of genetics, biology, or psychology for political science, philosphy, and sociology?

If he tries to find out, there are only a few mavericks to hold his hand. It is no wonder that increasing numbers of college seniors have no conception of where they are going to fit. It is also no wonder that increasing numbers of students are dropping out to seek their own integration through direct experience in the world.

Understandable as this reaction may be, it is woefully inefficient. Realizing this fact, the educational bureaucracies are beginning to budge—but no more than that. And hierarchies of the business world are not doing much better.

An Autopsy on Industry Once General Motors was beautifully harmonious with the community. In 1910, what were to become GM's components were clearly owned by entrepreneurs: Louis Chevrolet and his counterparts at Buick, Oldsmobile, Hyatt Roller Bearings, and so on. Their authority and legitimacy were clear. Young men came out of the hills hungry for work in Detroit; thousands massed outside the hiring gates. Survival was at stake. The rights of property were secure, and the contract which followed from them was authoritative. Mr. Chevrolet offered the terms, and workers took them or left them.

Time passed, and workers demanded more power. They submerged their individualism into an interest group, the United Automobile Workers. Management, acting out of a sense of property rights, resisted. Violence ensued. The UAW finally won, and the contract became collectivized—almost a contradiction in terms, if one thinks of the contract in its pure, individualistic form.

Also, property rights were themselves eroded by becoming a subject for bargaining in an adversary procedure. These rights were further diluted by the emergence of an entirely different type of management, one divorced from ownership. Nevertheless, the structure worked efficiently, and the United States accepted it because of its respect for the automobile and for material growth per se.

Then in the 1960s, the UAW started to splinter, individual locals and individual workers within locals feeling needs which could not be embraced by the already bloated contract. Survival having been assured by the community, the workers began to demand avenues to individual fulfillment in a communitarian setting where it could not be found.

By this time, too, the ownership of GM had become immensely diluted, and today the legitimacy of its function is increasingly suspect. In 1964, Sloan wrote of flying over the countryside, delighting in the "splash of jewel-like color presented by every parking lot."[9] Such a lyrical description falls a bit flat today.

So the legitimacy and power of management, on the one hand, and of the labor contract and thus the union, on the other, have deteriorated. But the hierarchies have barely budged. For a while, company management's answer was to pay workers more for their unhappiness, a recourse suitable to the contractual form. The union hierarchy, on their side, had roughly the same idea—a fatter contract. Absenteeism, sabotage, and lowering productivity have continued, however. Meanwhile, at Toyota, when the night shift goes off duty, it cheers the day shift on to harder and harder work.

This whole syndrome is generic to U.S. industry. Its root is simply that we have outgrown the old ways of doing things. We must now find a new way of doing things, one that accords with present realities and new definitions of values.

THE MANAGER'S MIND

Let me now consider what these five transformations imply for managers—in particular, managers of large, publicly held corporations. In simplest terms, the manager must form a certain attitude of mind, a willingness to confront manifold change openly and with breadth of vision, not with the heels dug in and the old blinders on. More than ever, he must see his task as a general not a specialized one. He is not an expert; he is an integrator, a synthesizer, responsible for the whole and capable of perceiving the whole, within and without; and he had better recognize the fact.

This requires both courage and hope:

- It requires courage, to rinse out the mind and inspect all the assumptions (especially those that underlie his power and legitimize it); to consider the interests of the whole and not merely his own momentary bureaucratic status and prerogatives; to think the unthinkable and discuss it.

- It requires hope, not for "the good old days" to return, nor for more ad hoc solutions, but for the potential value of the future. It requires the hope of those who "see and cherish all forms of new life and are ready at every moment to help the birth of that which is ready to be born."[10]

Once the manager has opened his mind fully, he can consider two sets of problems which the changing ideology raises for the large corporation. The first has to do with the internal organization of the corporation and concerns matters of ownership, accountability, and contract. The second has to do with the relationship between the corporation and the communities which it affects: the neighborhood, the city, the state, the nation, and the world.

Then he can focus on the questions that all these problems raise:

- Which problems should the corporation resolve and which must be decided by the community?

- With respect to community decisions, how are they best made—by government, by consumers, or by interest groups?

- If by interest groups, then *how*—by direct (perhaps radical) action, through legislative and legal pressure, or through leverage on the executive branch, as has ITT?

- To what extent is dispersion of power a desirable thing politically? As the legitimacy of management has declined, the central government has moved in to control increasing segments of corporate operation. Should corporations try to regain what political edge they have lost?

- If dispersion of power is a good thing (which I think it is), how should the corporation encourage the design of more dispersed forms of community legitimization and control, within its own framework and outside it?

This is a valuable exercise, not so much because the manager can always influence the answers directly, but because it helps the manager set out the possibilities for himself. (*Exhibit I* diagrams the context of these questions.)

Directions to Consider Industry has taken some hesitant steps of its own toward resolving its ideological confusions, some of which are oriented toward minimizing or eliminating the labor contract and replacing it with institutionalized consensus. Somewhat like its Japanese and European counterparts, the U.S. corporation is moving away from the adversary-contractual structure toward a consensual, collective form in which, to put it simply, no one feels left out of anything. As this change occurs, alternatives to property rights are emerging as the way to provide legitimacy and thus authority to management. Here are some vignettes of the change.

Food Processing A plant manufacturing pet food in Topeka, Kansas, is organized into self-managed work teams which are given collective responsibility for large parts of the production process. To accommodate the capabilities and needs of individual workers, assignments of individuals to tasks are subject to team consensus. There is a deliberate attempt to break down division of labor and specialization: "Pay increases are geared to an employee mastering an increasing proportion of jobs first in the team and then in the total plant."[11] All signs are that this plant is extremely productive and profitable.

Note the radical implications of this experiment. In a real sense, the legitimacy and thus the authority of the management of the Topeka plant comes from the workers as a whole, not from some outworn conception of property rights. This fact feeds the workers' sense of fulfillment and thus contributes to the high productivity and profits of the operation.

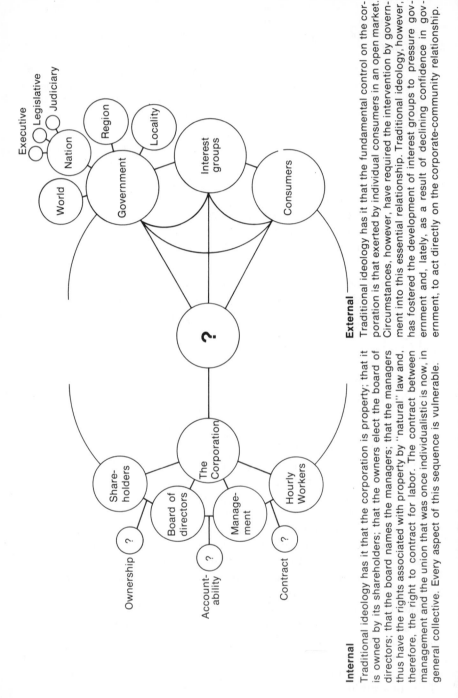

Executive
Legislative
Judiciary

World   Nation   Region   Locality

Government   Interest groups   Consumers

?.

Share-holders   The Corporation   Hourly Workers

Board of directors   Management

Ownership ?   Account-ability ?   Contract ?

Internal

Traditional ideology has it that the corporation is property; that it is owned by its shareholders; that the board of directors; that the owners elect the board of directors; that the board names the managers; that the managers thus have the rights associated with property by "natural" law and, therefore, the right to contract for labor. The contract between management and the union that was once individualistic is now, in general collective. Every aspect of this sequence is vulnerable.

External

Traditional ideology has it that the fundamental control on the corporation is that exerted by individual consumers in an open market. Circumstances, however, have required the intervention by government into this essential relationship. Traditional ideology, however, has fostered the development of interest groups to pressure government and, lately, as a result of declining confidence in government, to act directly on the corporate-community relationship.

Exhibit I. Internal and external questions relating to large public corporations

The top management of the company thus faces some excruciating questions:

- "Do we extend this idea to other plants—maybe to headquarters itself—to increase ROI, even though it will undercut our jobs?"
- "If we do it anyway, what happens to the myth that we are answerable to the board of directors, who represent the shareholders?" (The answer to this one is complicated by the fact that shareholders appear to be getting a better return on their investment from Topeka. Perhaps the management hierarchy, or part of it, *should* be dispensed with.)

It is indeed difficult to open one's eyes to the possibility—the mere possibility—of extinction.

Also, note the threat to the idea of equality when an organization moves to consensus from contract. Each team is responsible for hiring replacements; presumably it selects those who will get along well with the group. If the group objects to certain persons, they will not be hired. Race might be involved. My point is that collectivism can be dehumanizing unless it is controlled by a definite social theory—an ideology.

Moving from contract to consensus obviously threatens unions as well. The Topeka plant is small and new, with an innovative management and no union. To apply the same principles in the automobile or steel or utilities industries, however, raises many problems. All these industries are trying, although in somewhat different ways.

The Auto Industry The automobile industry is introducing job enrichment and organizational development programs. Union leaders have critized these efforts as elitist nonsense, as paternalistic attempts to divide the worker from the union. "The better the wage, the greater the job satisfaction," says William Winpisinger, general vice president of the International Association of Machinists. "There is no better cure for blue-collar blues."[12] Company industrial relations officials join Leonard Woodcock of the UAW in attributing "the alienation problem" to academics who do not know what they are talking about.[13]

It is not surprising that labor relations bureaucrats on both sides eye any threat to the contract anxiously, since it is the idea that supports their bureaucracies. Their resistance testifies both to the ideological nature of the problem and to the difficulty of solving it in situations where rigid hierarchies are unwilling to inspect the assumptions beneath them.

Steel The steel industry appears to be following a somewhat different route to establishing a basis for consensus. Industry labor relations officials and union leaders have worked out a peace agreement involving a no-strike clause and binding arbitration in the face of the common interest—namely, making U.S. goods more competitive against foreign imports.[14] Although neither side is likely to admit it, such an arrangement is a step toward replacing the idea of contract with that of consensus.

This scheme may have more promise than the organizational development and job enrichment schemes of the automobile industry because it protects directly *all* of those whose power is threatened. Its weakness is that, in itself, it does nothing to give a greater sense of participation to workers on the shop floor. But a recent HEW task force notes that this may be a serious shortcoming: "What workers want most, according to more than 100 studies made in the past 20 years, is to become masters of their immediate environments and to feel that their work and they themselves are important—the twin ingredients of self-esteem."[15]

If consensual systems are going to work, it will be necessary to educate young people according to the new ideology rather than the old. It will also be necessary to hire people who want to become part of a certain whole. No matter how consensual a collective may get, there are going to be boring jobs which will not provide the necessary sense of fulfillment to college graduates, for example. Workers will have to be screened for jobs with the idea of weeding out those whose capacities are *more* as well as *less* than the work requires. This prospect raises ominous specters of Orwellianism and deserves careful watching.

Electric Utilities For years, the utility companies have tried—successfully—to keep government regulation diffuse. Government has responded by steadfastly failing both to manage our nation's energy needs and to plan a procedure to fulfill them. The result is that many utilities find themselves in a devil of a mess: rates fixed by state agencies, taxed by the cities, partly regulated by the Federal Power Commission, and affected by the Atomic Energy Commission and a host of other local and national governmental entities.

At the same time, the environmental interest groups are grabbing for the utility companies' throats. The Scenic Hudson Preservation Society, for example, successfully kept Consolidated Edison Company of New York from building its pump storage power station at Cornwall on the Hudson River for ten years, and the battle is not entirely over yet. Like great dinosaurs, many public utilities are being bitten to death in a swamp partly of their own making.

The need for federal intervention to plan the future of electric power seems plain. Regional power production jurisdictions should be planned; research on new technologies needs to be increased; technology and site decisions must be made. The problem is far too big and too national in scope to leave to a scattering of private companies.

But this does not mean that these companies should be nationalized. That will be the inevitable result, however, unless more intelligent steps are taken soon. These companies must realize what government, and *only* government, can and must do: plan the allocation of resources and make the critical judgments of costs and benefits. To do this it must intervene with authority and coherence.

ONE'S OWN RESPONSIBILITY

The viewpoint I have laid out in this article has, I hope, triggered some thoughtful responses in the reader. Even if he argues with the way I diagnose our problems, I do not believe he can deny their omnipresence, their interrelation, and their seriousness.

If he can inspect his own ideological assumptions objectively, he may find himself reasoning out a new personal position of his own, one that accords more closely with the realities of the world we live in today than does the hodge-podge of quasi-official ideological notions we have inherited from our ancestors.

Most importantly, this may enable him to perceive more clearly the nature of the crises which abound. The quick and accurate perception of crisis is crucial because it is through the intelligent use of crisis that change occurs most effectively. The central managerial task of the future may well be the use of minimum crisis to cause maximum change with least waste and violence.

Ideological analysis and contemplation also will allow managers to consider how what is best and dearest in the old ideology may be preserved. One ideology obviously builds on another. The glories of the old—the rights of the individual, his dignity, the beautiful efficiency of competition in many areas, the incentives of enterprise and invention—are all in jeopardy. The best of them can be preserved only if we consciously design them into what is coming.

Broad reading can help to provide an understanding of what paths we might take. I also stress that *no* amount of reading, automatically pursued, will broaden the hidebound. The old preconceptions and prejudices must be washed away first, by a conscious effort of a person's will, before he can appreciate, weigh, and evaluate the myriad alternatives we might pursue—alternatives that are, in fact, often articulated by champions of special causes or of ideologies that are foreign, even hostile, to our own.

Why should managers bother? Because they lead corporations, collectively an immensely powerful force. What managers believe affects the way they lead. The effect of a manager's mind on the corporation he works for may be subtle or obvious, but it is always there, directly and indirectly.

Also, managers, taken as a class, are an important and influential group of citizenry. Perhaps the ultimate question they must consider now is whether or not our current procedures for producing political leadership and a vision of the community are sufficient. Can we rely on the Republican and Democratic parties to call forth the leadership this country needs now and in the future? Or do we need a new political movement—avowedly radical—to address openly and forthrightly the unquestionably radical problems of ideological transformation which we confront and to reestablish the confidence which Mr. Gerstenberg rightly says has been lost?

NOTES

1. Richard C. Gerstenberg, *1973 Report on Progress in Areas of Public Concern*, February 8, 1973, p. 87.
2. See my article, "Top Priority: Renovating Our Ideology," HBR September-October 1970, p. 43.
3. Gunter Stent, *The Coming of the Golden Age: A View of the End of Progress* (Garden City, Natural History Press, 1969), p. 90.
4. See Daniel Bell, "The Cultural Contradictions of Capitalism," *The Public Interest*, Fall 1970, pp. 38-39.
5. See Harvey D. Shapiro, "Women on the Line, Men at the Switchboard," *New York Times Magazine*, May 20, 1973, pp. 26 and 73-91; see also Daniel Bell, "On Meritocracy and Equality," *The Public Interest*, Fall 1972, p. 40.
6. Quoted in Herman E. Drooss and Charles Gilbert, *American Business History* (Englewood Cliffs, Prentice-Hall, 1972), p. 264.
7. See *Hearings Before the Committee on the Judiciary, United States Senate, 92nd Congress, Second Session on Nomination of Richard G. Kleindienst of Arizona to Be Attorney General* (Washington, Government Printing Office, 1972).
8. See Daniel Bell, *The Coming Post-Industrial Society: A Venture in Social Forecasting* (New York, Basic Books, 1973).
9. Alfred P. Sloan, Jr., *My Years With General Motors* (Garden City, Doubleday, 1964).
10. Erich Fromm, *The Revolution of Hope* (New York, Harper & Row, 1968), p. 7.
11. Richard E. Walton, "How to Counter Alienation in the Plant," HBR November-December 1972, p. 75.
12. *Wall Street Journal*, February 26, 1973.
13. *Newsweek*, March 26, 1973, p. 82.
14. *Business Week*, April 7, 1973, p. 64.
15. *Work in America: Report of the Special Task Force to the Secretary of Health, Education and Welfare* (Cambridge, The M.I.T. Press, 1972), p. 13.

FRANK H. CASSELL

The Corporation and Community: Realities and Myths

It is now twenty years since a board member of one of the largest Chicago banks proposed that the bank employ some Negroes. The board chairman, aghast at the suggestion, asked if the director didn't realize that then *they* would be sitting on the same toilet seats. The board turned down the proposal.

At the close of the decade of the 1960s the Chicago banks, including the one involved in that incident, passed the hat for $815,000 to finance a black "think tank," originated and headed by some of the most militant black leaders in Chicago.

That is change. It is change perhaps even broader in its implications than some of the contributing businessmen may yet realize, for it departs radically from the usual "safe" participations of business symbolized by Junior Chamber of Commerce man-of-the-year contests and the Community Fund charities administered by whites for blacks. It would be incorrect to interpret the support of the think tank as reflecting a trend in business in general. But its structure and support does imply that a number of businessmen, among them men considered leaders of the Chicago business community, have had their community stance affected by profound social changes in the city. And it is significant that it is in the historically conservative banking industry that such a change comes into focus.

Source: Reprinted from *MSU Business Topics* (Autumn 1970), pp. 11-20, by permission of the publisher, Division of Research, Graduate School of Business Administration, Michigan State University.

Chicago, like other large American cities, is undergoing a painful metamorphosis. On the one hand, it is engaged in a vast effort to rebuild the central city. Billions of dollars worth of new steel and glass high-rise office and apartment buildings are going up. The banking and insurance industries have been in the forefront of this building boom.

Simultaneously, great changes are taking place in the character of life in the city. Chicago lost population during the 1960s and the rate was speeded in the last half of the decade; its population has decreased to pre-depression levels. A third of the remaining population is black; 56 percent of elementary school pupils and 48 percent of the high school pupils are black, many of them increasingly angry at the system which they see as designed to keep them in second class roles. Black unemployment figures continue to be more than twice as high as white, and far higher than that among the young people. The jobs which the burgeoning black population might fill are fleeing to the suburbs; the metropolitan area outside the city gained 277,000 jobs from 1957 to 1966, but the city of Chicago lost 48,000 jobs. It is difficult or impossible for many blacks to follow the jobs because of housing discrimination in the suburbs and the great costs of commuting long distances.

These economic facts, plus a profound change in the feelings of the black community—growth in black consciousness, search for a black identity, regard for one's heritage, and reaction to white rejection in housing and school patterns—are making for a qualitative difference in the problems of the city. The Kerner Commission warning that we are drifting toward two separate societies, one white and one black, a sort of indigenous apartheid, has not altered the drift. Some say, including both white leaders and black militants, that it is only a matter of time.

Separateness may be much further advanced than many of us are willing to admit. Separateness has gone a long way when a militant black leader in Chicago attempts to roll down the curtain and not permit whites to enter black neighborhoods at night. The suggestion was made by the Rev. C. T. Vivian, Executive Director of "Think Tank," at a moment of deep fury in the black communities over a raid by district attorney's police on a Black Panther apartment, a raid in which two Panther leaders were killed. The Rev. Vivian withdrew his angry proposal for a curfew, but not before the whites got the message.

The political ferment is reflected in the high schools, too, where black students are increasingly strident—and sometimes threatening—about the lack of quality of their schools, about what they call irrelevancy of the traditional school program, and about the shortage of black teachers and administrators who, they believe, can understand the black perspective better than whites. In some areas this has led to demands for community control of schools, through little boards of education responsible to the people of an area rather than to a central hierarchy. In other areas, it has meant turmoil in the schools, particularly at times when community tension is high. In most areas, disillusion with school leads many black young people to drop out (or to be pushed out), which increases the unemployment problem, already a staggering one among poorly trained young blacks. White-managed industries in and near the ghettos feel the effects of this kind of unrest. If they fill their work forces from the area, they find the discontent transplanted into factories; some first line white supervisors leave because they fear for their own safety.

These forces add impetus to the flight of higher income whites from the city. Those who stay behind are more and more determined to preserve their turf and not let the blacks cross over from "the other side"—the other side of the city, or the neighborhood, or the street that has been a traditional dividing line between white homes and black. Where this has occurred in other smaller cities the remaining whites have sought to preserve their political power, giving only token appointments to blacks. This too has heightened political tension. The whites don't see the fact that the vital, pulsating new force of the cities is a rapid increase in determination by blacks to have a say in their own destiny. There is an increase in strong, savvy black leadership, including men of education and experience in coping with both the militants and with recalcitrant white leadership. They want a share of the power, and they are going to get it. The choice as to how they get it is pretty much up to the whites.

AN EXAMPLE OF BUSINESS RESPONSE

It is in this context that Chicago's Strategy Center, the think tank, was born. Basically it provides business support for "the black communities to establish its own priorities," in the words of one of its supporters. At the Center, staff will be all black. It will use the funds for research and training, conducting surveys to establish needs, assisting with budgets, and taking packaged proposals to the city and federal government and to foundations for funding. There seem to be no grandiose ideas about training for the use of power; instead, the focus will be on the economic, educational, and health problems that plague the ghetto. Presumably the Center will not engage in politics, although some of the programs it devises will have to be promoted politically by someone.

The Center is being supported for a variety of motives—some lofty, some not. One of the motives is the hard-headed practical need to face reality. Planners think that by 1980 blacks will have the majority vote in Chicago and that a black mayor may be elected in that year.

Some of the most influential of the white contributors probably clearly perceive the need for an avenue for sharing power with the black community and would like it to be an avenue where they can erect some of the traffic signals. The Center, if it works well, can be a valuable training locale for black leaders. Leadership has been diffuse in the black community; it has been hard to know who to listen to. There is some feeling that the Center can be a black structure for the white power structure to deal with.

Others are perhaps more concerned with safeguarding their investment in the city and are thinking about the business climate of Chicago under a black administration. Business has no intention of abandoning its home base, and there are those new buildings to prove it. Some business supporters of the think tank see their contributions as sort of an insurance policy for all that plate glass.

Those are some of the white views of the Strategy Center, and they are a mixed bag, indeed. The black views may be just as mixed. There is no consensus that the people running the Center really are Chicago's black leaders. Some say the Center people are just being paid off by whites. There is much skepticism about the nature of business support. (One old-line black leader, not involved in the Strategy Center, wondered, for example, if the whites were "doing the right thing for the wrong reasons.") They wonder what will happen when the black-proposed solutions to problems don't coincide with white solutions.

There are, indeed, many pitfalls, and we don't know whether the Strategy Center will ever be able to change any of these facts the banker-supporter was talking about. Among the pitfalls are several financial ones: the Center still has not been given tax exempt status because it is not clear how it can avoid political action entirely, the businessmen have set up "fiscal safeguards for the disbursement of money" although they say they are not policing the programs, and there is no present provision for continued business support of the Center once the initial funds run out. There are other pitfalls, too; it seems inevitable that there will be considerable infighting, a good deal of rhetoric, and the destruction of some false hopes. One big question mark centers around Mayor Daley, without whom nothing much happens in Chicago, but who has taken a "hands off" approach to the Center.

REAL SIGNIFICANCE

But despite the conflicting views about the things that can go wrong, the establishment of the Center has real significance. It is a facing of the reality that blacks do have problems that concern us all and that blacks want a greater share in decision making to solve them. It is a recognition of the need for thinking and planning and understanding that you can't operate a society in change on an ad hoc basis. At the very least, the Center does give status to a point of view, a black perspective which black leaders have always insisted is simply not being heard. If the Center works, it can be a step toward an orderly transference of power to a soon-to-be-realized black majority in the city. If it doesn't work, the inevitable changes will be less orderly. Either way, it is a dramatic departure from the traditional business method of dealing with community problems, one very much out of character for conventional business organization and operation.

TRADITIONAL BUSINESS RESPONSE TO CHANGE

The mechanisms of business, like all authoritarian institutions, are not well suited for coping with basic change outside its product markets. Business has no strong internal mechanism for criticism of its performance in the community. Unlike an institution like Congress, it has no constituency that votes it in or out on the basis of its success in community life. Its organization is designed for stability, for continuity, not for change.

The conventional business policy has been to place the bets on those in power, people like Mayor Daley, because they seem to give the best promise of stability as against the more menacing leaders who want to change the status quo. Where the power structure has had to give way before powerful underlying forces, the strategy has usually consisted of participating in the least risky ventures, minimizing the risk with strings attached to the money contributed in order to control the speed and direction of the advance, and supporting politically only those dissidents who could be counted upon to merge with the establishment. (Martin Luther King was invited by business executives to talk in Winnetka, Illinois, not before Selma and Bull Connor's cattle prods, but after his "I have a dream" sermon at the March on Washington, a march the executives did not make.) However, the conventional business policy for action in the community has led to supporting the forces of reaction, the establishment, the entrenched political forces rather than the forces which accommodate change and prepare the way for new leadership. The Chicago Urban League is an interesting case in point. It is only a few years ago that business supporters of the League could have met in a telephone booth; the League was trying to cause the schools to change. But in 1970, 2,500 business leaders and others attended a luncheon to pay homage to the retiring Urban League director. A very safe event.

The interpretation of this by the underclass could hardly be that the establishment was in their favor. And when company policies began to change, it was to support organizations which, though useful, had themselves sometimes lost touch with the times and the realities and the people. The old line groups working for change got support only when newer, much more radical groups appeared and threatened.

Conventional corporate policy is based essentially upon a stable environment with change occurring only at a rate sufficient to be easily absorbed. Because business mistrusts unorthodoxy, it also mistrusts the "bubble up" theory of participative democracy, of community action programs which have been spawned in the cities under the sponsorship of the Office of Economic Opportunity. (This policy began to be abandoned in the closing months of the Johnson administration and has been buried by the Nixon administration.)

The businessman is a top-down person. That is how he is selected, how he is trained, and how he is developed in an environment which is essentially authoritarian and carefully structured. Important decision making is limited to the few at the top (despite the years of effort by Peter Drucker and Douglas McGregor to change things); and those at the bottom are expected to comply. In some magical way hierarchical position seems to confer wisdom regardless of knowledge or experience; those down the line with less status have less wisdom and competence.

THE CONVENTIONAL STAND

The conventional business stand is in favor of strong top-down government as against grass roots neighborhood decision making because the former is perceived as the most "efficient" way to govern. This concept leads the businessman to work through established organizations which are essentially top-down, such as the charity and settlement house boards. The typical structure of a Community Fund parallels the business organization; in fact, it is often designed by business consultants whose object is efficiency, not necessarily relevancy. Attempts of black people and poor people to participate in the fund allocation process are resisted bitterly, much as some school superintendents resent meddling by "outsiders" in the affairs of the schools. Most important, these money allocations are directed to preserving the structure and the underlying assumptions of those who control it; they are steered away from those in the black or Spanish-speaking community who would use the money to develop political power to challenge the establishment and change the system.

This is similar to the Community Action Organizations which were converted into nodules of political power and were opposed alike by northern big city mayors, southern governors, businessmen, and the established federal bureaucracies. The Community Action Program (CAP) was designed deliberately to skirt the established organizations because they had shown no particular talent or interest in solving the problems of hard core poverty or unemployment. It was thought that those experienced in the condition of poverty might contribute to its solution. No more upsetting measure could have been devised, and before the nodules could grow into power centers they were effectively squelched by the passage of the Green Amendment. And order has been restored with the new (or old) federalism so that poverty funds and other funds for relieving the condition of the poor are channeled through the offices of the governors, from there to the mayors, and from there to the neighborhoods—the trickle down theory.

The distaste of the businessmen for doing business with those outside the established organizations is represented by the virtual failure of the Concentrated Employment Program of the U.S. Department of Labor which began in the latter part of the 1960s. The object of this effort was to link up indigenous leadership of the ghetto with other organizations both public and private to provide a job delivery system including outreach, job readiness training, remedial health care, and job survival skills leading to a job in private enterprise.

It was believed that if those who needed jobs, those who operated the employment market, and those who had the jobs to give, were put under one administrative tent, the whole operation would be more efficient, duplication of functions would be reduced, and understandings would be developed among employers, government, and the poor which would lead to productive and cooperative relationships. Nothing of the kind happened. The Community Action Programs at the grass roots let the employers know in no uncertain terms that they were not liked in the slums; nor did they think private enterprise had much to offer in the line of social improvement. The employer reciprocated. He was not interested in revolutionaries and incompetents; furthermore, he didn't want to get mixed up with government bureaucracy—meaning the federal government.

About the same time the Labor Department developed the idea of contracting out to private enterprises the complete package of training and job development, with the expectation that the community action people would refer unemployed people to the job or training openings. And this didn't really work either. An example serves to illustrate this point. In a large city in Connecticut, a defense contractor received a contract under a Manpower Administration grant from the Labor Department to train ghetto people for employment in the various industries in the town. The defense contractor's office was located at one end of a large building in the slum area. At the other end of the building was the Community Action Program. A door between the two ends of the building was locked, having never been opened during the tenure of the tenants despite the fact that the CAP and the defense contractor were supposed to cooperate in putting people into the training program and to work.

In city after city this is the case. The employer prefers to do the job himself even if he does not have the expertise or the relationship with the slum. This he is doing under the National Alliance of Businessmen. No doubt he is more efficient in organizing to do the job of employment than the people at the bottom of the job scale. This reluctance of the businessman to share authority with others in the community represents a deep desire for order, the need to control his situation (as he has been taught in business schools), and the need to assure the continuity of the firm. It reflects also the public relations man's approach to things to make sure the numbers are counted and the credit goes where it belongs—to the company, as in the case of the National Alliance of Businessmen.

A PHILOSOPHICAL GAP

More importantly the inability of community action people, ghetto militants, and business to work together represents more than the political differences, although this is a factor; more than the businessman's distaste for long hair and blue jeans, more than his resentment of having to share power with people he feels have not earned the honor by hard work. It represents a huge philosophical gulf. In the Connecticut situation the employer said that he did not cooperate with the CAP because the people whom the CAP sent for training did not fit the jobs and that they (the CAP) raised their expectations too high. The CAP people said that the employers did not have jobs which fit their people. Here is a conflict of tradition and of philosophy. The employer expects to reject people who are not qualified according to his standards. The individual, if not qualified, should adjust. This is the expectation of free private enterprise. The CAP people, however, expect the enterprise system to adjust to the people, that is, if they have no qualifications, make a job of some kind or redesign it and train the person to fill it. The enterprise system should help people realize their ambitions, even the lowliest of them. The company should serve people, not vice versa.

If one looks particularly closely at these arguments he will find that the CAP people are challenging the legitimacy of the private enterprise system. How can it be justified solely on the basis of profits? What about the welfare of people and the good of society? Does not business exist at the pleasure of the people? Should it not serve them? Would it not be better if business had a social purpose as its prime goal? Whether or not the businessman has sensed this, he has kept away from these people as much as possible.

A CORPORATE DICHOTOMY

The corporate ethos, regardless of the imperatives of community, is to make profits and not to produce social uplift. Social responsibility must always be an adjunct. Consequently, it is not reasonable to expect community relations to be the firm's specialization. It is equally unreasonable to expect the corporation to take the load of the community on its shoulders, or to expect it to be expert in solving such problems. Furthermore, if the corporation assumes this function it must then expect to live with the criticism which inevitably comes to all who would attempt to lead and influence social change, criticism which may affect it adversely in its product markets.

The realities are that the corporation faces two ways, inward and outward. Its inner core capitalizes upon the specialized skills of its managers and other employees to exploit markets. It is beyond the range of normal expectation that men expert in manufacturing and marketing will be equally expert in the political and social milieu of the outer environment. If the chairman of the firm is skilled in his ability to be persuasive with the commerce commission or relates well to black militants this is a bonus for the firm, but he is paid to make a profit. No matter how successful his community relations, he will not survive too many poor profit years.

Having to face both outward and inward leads to a dichotomizing of management. Over time individuals emerge who develop the characteristics which bring success in the outer environment, including interest in human beings, a capacity to understand political and social complexities, and above all the ability to exist in ambiguous situations. In contrast, those who live on the inside tend to work by plan, are often uneasy with politics, and are uncomfortable with ambiguity. In other words, specialization exerts itself to lead people either toward the inside of the corporation or toward the outside.

As time goes by a gap develops between the external and the internal people, much in the manner of the "growing apart" of the corporate labor relations people and the line operating people. In both cases there develop differences in viewpoint. The corporate labor relations people come to view the politics of elective leadership as they affect corporate collective bargaining strategy. This often places the labor relations people at odds with the internally oriented people whose lack of contact with the outside preserves a parochial view, often times a hard line which ignores the politics of power over which the firm has limited control.

In much the same way the corporation executives who face toward the community inevitably are confronted with the realities of a world which they cannot control. Employees can be fired, but not the community. Such executives often find themselves interpreting the outside to an unsympathetic internal management.

The people inside are often impatient with the tools of diplomacy and the complexities of social and political organization. The results of community activities cannot be chalked up neatly on the blackboard in the manner of so many automobiles produced per hour. The people operating on the inside, accustomed to operating within a structured and controlled environment, as contrasted to the uncontrolled community, have difficulty understanding why this outer world cannot be put in order.

Sufficient time has passed since business and industry have employed labor relations and community relations experts to suggest that these careers are not the roads to the top of the firm. When the promotion decisions are made, it is the person who has attended to the nitty gritty of selling, producing, or financing who gets the job. And this is entirely consistent with the object of the corporation, namely to make profits. As long as the goal of the firm is so perceived, the community relations function is likely to be secondary and correspondingly the level of skill and effort applied to it will lag behind the skill and effort devoted to the operation of the firm. In addition the evidence seems to be that men allocated by the corporation to handle the community relations of the corporation are not "main line" executives and consequently lack the prestige or power within the corporation to materially influence corporate policy. (In the case of companies which have taken on government contracts to train the hard core or to administer the Job Corps camps, the men assigned have not generally been main liners, and furthermore when cutbacks have occurred their reintegration into the main organization has either been accomplished with maximum difficulty or not at all. One large eastern firm which had held large government contracts to improve the skills of the poor was unable to effect the reintegration and tried to convert the government contracts division into an internal human-relations consulting division. It was not a success. The main divisions felt they could get along without internal human relations consultants.)

CALCULATING THE RISKINESS OF COMMUNITY INVOLVEMENT

Although the financing of the black "think tank" may be a portent of things to come insofar as corporate policy toward the community is concerned, business today is not generally geared to engaging in such high risk community relations. The businessman is sophisticated in the things he does well, namely managing financial and entrepreneurial risk. Community risk, however, is another matter. Typically he ranks his risk from high to low in a sort of cost-benefits relationship. At the low risk end of the community activity scale (high prestige) is the Community Fund, the settlement house, or a liaison relationship between his suburban church and a community organization in the city. He has substantial control; the results, being based upon the past, are predictable; the assignment is not overly time consuming; and he is not likely to find his name in the newspaper because of some rash act of the staff. But in today's terms the organization is not likely to be particularly relevant either.

At the high risk end of the scale, he might find himself participating in a privately financed, slum based and led model city-type program which challenges the established political and economic institutions to which the company he represents is linked. This is a situation which exists in Chicago today. A number of firms are supporting a community based program called Towards Responsible Freedom. The program is located in the Kenwood-Oakland section of the city. It is a self-help effort to create community structure and machinery to cope with the problems left untouched by the established political structure and government programs—including preparation for better jobs, improvement of the local schools, elimination of garbage in the streets, better law and order—and justice for the residents, renovation and improvement of housing, and self-developed local businesses. No money was allocated to the area by the federal Model Cities program.

The community organization known as KOCO includes just about everybody in the area including the leaders of the Black P Stone Nation, a street gang. It does not, however, include the local alderman. It does not include the local school people. Many of its leaders have at one time or another been in jail or prison. A chief organizer of KOCO, who is also a leader of the Black P Stone Nation, was charged with murder but later acquitted. KOCO is financed through the Community

Renewal Society from the contributions of foundations, individual givers, and a few corporations—referred to collectively by the Chicago police as soft-headed liberals who are financing revolution. The strings attached are minimal. During the past two years as KOCO has been getting under way, repeated police harassment of the organization generally has not frightened supporters into withholding their funds. But the police efforts have not helped to broaden the financial support either.

It is indeed significant that in the range of risk value, many Chicago corporations seem more willing to finance a "think tank" despite its often violent rhetoric than a community self development and self determination effort. Perhaps community action ranks higher on the risk scale than revolutionary speech, especially when the condition is that the speech must be non-political, in order to get tax deductible corporate contributions. After all, community self development effort may produce fundamental changes in the community.

The basic difference between the community fund and KOCO is that the businessman who supports KOCO does not have strings which he can pull if the neighborhood people get out of line. He has essentially given up his right to control as to how the money will be spent, and who will be employed. This is alien to the prudent businessman or the politician who needs to maintain control.

Whether it is the businessman or the established political structure, or old line unions, this kind of community activity is the ultimate in risk—though it may turn out that this is one of the few ways slum and ghetto people can be aided to enter the main stream of American society through self-government and breaking down of colonialist control.

The evidence so far is that businessmen in general are not yet ready for this kind of long range political planning. Support of rhetoric, yes, as long as it is apolitical—action no. And in this they are joined by practically everybody in the organized structure from the president of the United States on down. The burgeoning black and brown communities, however, will continue to militate for involvement in the action. The "think tank" and the Community Renewal Society efforts in Kenwood-Oakland are among the very few efforts remaining where the underclass can have a say and can develop community experience in leadership.

It seems to be that business efficiency can be brought to bear on solving unemployment, housing, and urban planning programs, as long as it is through the established structure. It can solve problems as long as the people of the slums have no effective say to change the plans, or to obstruct them. This is how the model cities program seems to be proceeding. Without the grass roots, business participation is easier to get. Without the CAP community action activities, the National Alliance of Businessmen is willing to exercise its talents in finding jobs for people.

Their efforts can be brought to bear best upon those things that cannot talk back—such as pollution. Maybe, as Tom Wicker observes rather cynically, Mr. Nixon's State of the Union message was a clever flank movement into the environment and away from the ghetto. Suddenly almost everyone rich and poor and in between is concerned about choking to death. These quite legitimate concerns represent finite challenges which can be met (unlike the ghetto) by energy, technology, and money without challenging the system.

This is the word: finite. Finite, certain, planned, order, continuity, those are the needs of business. And it attempts to shape the environment around it to fill those requirements. It can do that with the physical environment to some extent, it cannot do it with people.

This should be a troublesome concern for the educator, especially business school deans and faculties. How does one train a businessman to cope with a world in profound change where values are shifting, and the environment is quite uncertain? The business school training equips the individual with the tools to take the risk out of taking risks. It teaches him about controls so that he can operate with greater certainty that error will not creep in. He is given knowledge about systems planning so that he can account for every last item in his planning. He is taught supervisory skills which work when the work force is docile, or when it is organized and follows carefully designed procedures to settle differences. But he is not equipped or even selected because he has the capacity to cope with risk and uncertainty and revolutionary forces. There is nothing in the business school which lets him know that his tools will seldom if ever help him solve the problems of the community. It is a peculiar fact of life which also affects the business school that we believe we can manage the most difficult of all endeavors, namely, human affairs, by ear, without training, without knowledge, without experience. Perhaps that is why we do it so badly.

It is human qualities—generosity and selfishness, loving and hating, cooperativeness and perverseness—which make molasses out of the best designed procedures either inside or outside the organization. We teach people to delegate responsibility when they are not psychologically able to relinquish it. We skip over political concepts that have much to do with how people are governed and govern. We say very little about how authoritarian organizations such as business clash with the underlying notions of democracy.

We must ask whether business should be socially responsible. Can it have multiple and even contradictory objectives? Should it exist to serve the society or to make profits; what really is its ultimate objective? Does the man attracted to business have the special talents and the capacity to be a leader in a world of change and uncertainty which is characteristic of the community? Will businesses and businessmen respond constructively to increasingly harsh criticism, or will their response exacerbate the already wide gulf between the corporation and a large portion of the community?

PETER NEHEMKIS

Business Payoffs Abroad: Rhetoric and Reality

An investigation begun in 1974 by the Securities and Exchange Commission into illegal corporate contributions to former President Nixon's 1972 reelection produced a serendipity effect: the revelation that a number of prominent American corporations engage in overseas payoffs.

The disclosure that U.S. corporations operating abroad pay—or are solicited to pay—bribes in order to obtain or engage in business, or to procure favorable tax and other administrative decisions from foreign governments, has opened a Pandora's box of complex and troublesome issues, which affect U.S. foreign relations, national security, and the investment and marketing policies of American international companies.

Since the SEC's inquiry, the Internal Revenue Service and the Departments of State and Defense have launched their own probes—the former to determine whether overseas payoffs were deducted as "business expenses," the latter to ascertain the legitimacy of commissions paid to middlemen in negotiating the sale of military aircraft and hardware. The Senate Foreign Relations subcommittee investigating multinational corporations and other congressional panels were quick to hold public hearings on the leads developed by the SEC.

Source: © 1975 by The Regents of The University of California. Reprinted from *California Management Review*, Vol. 18, No. 2, pp. 7-20, by permission of the Regents.

Also confronted with difficult decisions as a consequence of the SEC's investigations are the outside members of the boards of directors whose managements, without their prior knowledge or approval, may have countenanced overseas payoffs. What is the extent of their fiduciary responsibility, they ask, to have known of this practice in the past or to ascertain whether it now prevails and to disclose it? The SEC believes that directors are accountable for a company's conduct. But the outside directors wonder if the price of their directorial inquisitiveness, ironically, will produce a swarm of stockholders' suits.

Nor are members of the legal profession immune from perplexing dilemmas. Are corporate counsel under a duty to reveal information to which they are privy with respect to bribes? Will this breach the confidential attorney-client relationship? Is it the lawyer's responsibility to discover whether such payments have in fact been made by his client and to report them? To whom? Some lawyers fear that forcing them to perform policing functions in the business world will destroy the confidentiality essential to their primary responsibility—advising the client and representing his interests.

Corporate auditors have long been a target of criticism by successive SEC members and staff for the limited reach of the audit certificate.

They are now feeling the heat of the SEC's censure for continuing to use an audit procedure that is too random to discover the concealed payoff and whose standards of financial "materiality" exclude such transactions.

Whether the customary audit procedures can be extended or expanded raises practical cost/benefit questions. An improved audit can be many times more costly than the actual payoff unearthed. When and if such payments are—or can be—found to exist, is it the auditor's obligation to disclose them to the board of directors (as the SEC believes he should)? Why, the embattled auditor asks, should he be expected to act as a surrogate of corporate morals?

LET THERE BE LIGHT

"Sunlight" is a widely used word among officials of the SEC. It derives from a maxim of Supreme Court Justice Louis D. Brandeis, who wrote, "Publicity is justly commendable as a remedy for social and industrial disease. Sunlight is said to be the best of disinfectants; electric light the most efficient policeman."[1]

A "cleansing effect" can be obtained in the universe of corporate enterprise—so the watchmen of the securities markets believe—by focusing the spotlight of publicity on the corporation's financial transactions. Full disclosure has been the prophylaxis used by the SEC to safeguard the investor against misleading or untruthful information.[2]

To enable investors to reach informed decisions, the SEC has promulgated two pivotal disclosure forms—8-K and 10-K. Form 8-K is used for filing a monthly "current report" in which the registrant is expected to supply information on any new developments pertaining to such matters as changes in the control of the company, acquisition or disposition of assets, significant litigation to which the corporation is a party, and other "material" financial data. The 10-K form is an "annual report" designed to pick up previously unreported legal, business, and financial activities of the registrant—activities which, if disclosed, are presumed to enable an investor to keep informed on what management is doing with his money. Both reports must be filed by corporations subject to the SEC's jurisdiction, that is, those whose stock is traded on the New York Stock Exchange and other registered exchanges. For all practical purposes, every major U.S. corporation is obligated to file these two reports.

But How Much Light?

The gravamen of the SEC's injunctive actions against five—at this writing—corporate offenders is their failure, among other things, to disclose on one of these forms the use of corporate funds to buy the favor of government officials and politicians of ruling and governing parties in exchange for special treatment. Members of the SEC's enforcement division are reported to believe that, when a company receives substantial benefits as a result of a payoff, or if its continued operations are subject to extortion, investors are entitled to know.

Widening the circle of disclosure to encompass under-the-table payments overseas has engendered both approval and criticism. To the increasingly vociferous critics of the multinational corporation, payoffs to foreign officials or political parties strengthens the demand for stringent regulations. Hence the tightening of the screws by the SEC is applauded. On the other hand, a White House aide is reported to see a "revolution" in the SEC's views of what constitutes material information that can influence investment decisions. Others assert that the SEC has embarked on a typical American exercise in ethnocentrism—imposing its own moral judgments on foreign governments and U.S. international corporations.

Actually the commissioners are not united in their stance regarding disclosure of overseas payments. A minority of the members perceive the issue with an uncluttered moral simplicity: transgressors should disclose their sins of omission and commission; in telling the truth, they must bear the consequences. The majority, on the other hand, recognizes that full disclosure, including the names of recipients, their official positions, and the sums paid to them, can be harmful to U.S. foreign relations and jeopardize U.S. investments abroad.

Despite the accusation of its critics—and, indeed, of the moralists within the commission—the majority members do not believe that the SEC has a mandate "to enforce, even indirectly, through compulsory disclosure, all of the world's laws and all of its perceptions of morality and right conduct." As former chairman Ray Garrett said, "some forebearance not only seems implicit in our governing statutes, but also may be essential to enable us to do a competent job of investor protection."[3]

BUYING FAVORS

Bribery is an institutionalized fact of international business life. It is to be sure no more prevalent in other industrialized countries—Italy is an exception—than it is in the United States. Bribery is, however, pervasive throughout virtually the entire Third World of Latin America, the Middle East, Africa, and Asia.[4]

It has also appeared in the Soviet Union (where as a warning to other Soviet trade officials—and to foreign businessmen who deal with them—the former head of the furniture import corporation was recently executed by a firing squad for accepting $150,000 in bribes from a Swiss supplier), and in the Eastern Communist bloc (where, for example, Yugoslav officials doing business with West European firms demanded—and received—bribes, which were deposited in Swiss bank accounts).

In the morass of global palm greasing, a distinction must be made between two types of payoffs: the "lubrication" bribe and the "whitemail" bribe.

THE LUBRICATION BRIBE

The lubrication bribe usually involves payment of relatively small sums of "speed money" to make the wheels of administration turn more rapidly. In the days of the rule of the political boss and the dominance of the political machine in the big American cities, this kind of money transfer was known as "honest" graft. (This is not to suggest that bribes, big and small, are no longer familiar to American cities. Payoffs in New York City, for example, are said to be endemic.)

Third World countries are awash in administrative bribing. Payments are made to the customs official to accelerate his paperwork to allow a shipment of machinery, raw material, or semifinished components to move from dockside to plant. (There is, to be sure, a suspicion that the slowdown is designed to produce a payoff.) The gratuity is used to encourage a clerk in one of the ministries to reshuffle his papers to find an application—on file for months—for a construction permit. An under-the-table payment facilitates issuance of a permit to allow the entry of company personnel—an engineer, a cost accountant, a marketing specialist. A tip helps to obtain the requisite authorization for foreign exchange for needed imports or repatriation of dividends.

The lubrication bribe expedites clearances that ought to be made available to business enterprise as a matter of convenience but that in practice require a "token of appreciation." In the former British West African colonies, for example, the foreign firm that doesn't "dash" the local functionaries will eventually be unable to operate. The West African dash system of payoffs is so widespread that foreign companies treat it as a routine business expense. The ostensible reason for the ouster of the Nigerian regime led by Major General Yakubo Gowan by another army faction was that too many high officials had their fingers in dash. The new military regime has mounted a broad attack— so, too, had its predecessor—against corruption. In an unprecedented step for black Africa, the new military leadership has dismissed hundreds of civil servants and required all high-ranking military officers and civilian officials to disclose their finances.

Kenyan government officials are wont to request "contributions" from foreign business executives for hospitals, churches, and charities. In return, they promise smooth sailing in the establishment of a business or its unhampered continuance. When these requests are granted—not all are—they can sometimes run into six figures.

Elsewhere in East Africa, with the notable exception of Tanzania, bribery is so rampant that the elite class of government officials has earned the derisive Swahili term "Wabenzi." (*Wa* is a prefix that means group of people. *Benzi* is a root word coined from Mercedes Benz cars, the hallmark of virtually all elite Africans.)

Latin America is another world region in which the payoff is pervasive. Venality flourishes because of a symbiotic relationship between business enterprise and government. Businessmen perceive those in the seat of power in statist governments as the dispensers of privileges and exemptions. Most public officials see themselves in the same light.

The bribe—known variously as *mordida* ("the bite") in Mexico; *pajada* ("a piece of the action") in Honduras; *jeitinho* ("the fix") in Brazil— ensures, on the one hand, flexibility in the application of administrative discretion, and on the other hand, the opportunity for business growth in competition with state-owned corporations. In consequence, the private and public sectors are bound to each other by a profitable cash nexus.

The Confucian Tradition

Graft, it should be remembered, has different moral sanctions in different cultures. Corruption in the Far East stems largely from the Confucian tradition, which countenanced the use by the world's first elite civil servants of public office for personal aggrandizement—acceptance of gratuities supplemented low government salaries. In Japan, and other Asian countries that were formerly British-ruled territories, *kumshaw* (literally "thank you"), "tea money," or an actual gift to an official symbolizes the difference in status between the one who does the asking and the one who confers the favor.

In passing, it should also be mentioned that in Malaysia and Singapore civil servants are expressly forbidden to accept gifts or other perquisites of office. The climate of honesty created by Prime Minister Lee Kuan Yew—an authentic Chinese Puritan—in his island city-state causes even a policeman to think twice before accepting a cigarette from the owner of an illegally parked bicycle. Lee has pointedly admonished his Third World colleagues, particularly those from Africa, that "instead of dams and power stations, roads and railways, we have Rolls Royces and executive mansions, not to mention golden bedsteads." But in nearby Indonesia, high-ranking military officers and civilian officials in the government accept gifts in cash or stock in foreign companies as the quid pro quo for helping them "adjust" to the Indonesian business climate.

India is, perhaps, a classic illustration of an environment in which the lubrication bribe is indispensable for the survival of private business enterprise—indigenous and foreign. In India's socialist-oriented society, the civil servant is vested with discretionary power to grant or withhold permits for almost every commercial activity. Hence, at every stage of the administrative process there is scope for bribery. "Not a single file can move if the clerk's palm is not greased," a correspondent for the *Hindustan Times* once wrote—before India's press was muzzled by Madame Gandhi's authoritarian rule.

India's political "democracy" was built on corruption. Payoffs, shakedowns, and gaining access to illegal wealth—known as "black money"—occupies much of the time and energy of the government's ruling Congress Party. Bribery of government officials bought official tolerance of hoarding, adulterating, smuggling, and black-marketing.

The corruption factor has to be taken into account before a management decision is reached on penetrating the Indian market. Once a foreign company is established there, only the corporate Quixote will believe it can remain outside the mainstream of corruption with which Indians have lived for centuries.

The Envelope

Earlier it was suggested that Italy is *sui generis* among the European countries in the use of the lubrication bribe. Italy's colossal bureaucracy makes the employment of *bustarella* (an envelope stuffed with varying amounts of 10,000 lire notes, each worth about $17) mandatory for the Italian business enterprise—and, indeed, for the citizen who can afford it—to overcome the chronic governmental chaos.

In his illuminating book *The Italians*, Luigi Barzini points out that his country's regulatory structure is a "tropical tangle of statutes, rules, norms, regulations, customs, some hundreds of years old, some voted last week by Parliament and signed this very morning by the President."[5]

Within the vast, inchoate Rome bureaucracy no one knows for certain which laws are still valid and what some of them really mean.

This Byzantine web of statutory ambiguities, inconsistencies, and contradictions—all subject to the interpretation of poorly chosen, wretchedly underpaid and badly organized bureaucrats, whose primary loyalties are to the political parties and only secondarily to their government—can only be made to function by means of *bustarella*. In other words, corruption makes an inefficient and chaotic social system work.

THE WHITEMAIL BRIBE

Though there may be official tolerance in Washington for the lubrication bribe, there is a definite reluctance to condone the whitemail variety. The reason is not hard to find. The latter type of payoff generally involves an elaborate system for concealing the use of large sums of corporate cash. These payments are invariably accompanied by false accounting, fictitious bookkeeping entries, and bogus documentation. To generate the cash needed for the big payoff, it is usually necessary to resort to legerdemain transfers of funds between subsidiaries, employment of dubious consultants, and routing money through overseas bank accounts. In a word, the corporation's internal system of financial accountability is distorted by a small number of high-ranking managers, whose actions are cloaked in secrecy.

When viewed in the abstract, such transfers of corporate funds are indefensible. When seen in the context in which they take place, however, there may be a reasonable doubt as to whether to condemn them.

In the discussion that follows, three major SEC prosecutions are analyzed. This will serve to place in perspective the "pressures"— psychological, cultural, and political—which impelled a course of conduct now under criticism.

The Banana Tax: The Case of United Brands

To offset soaring petroleum prices that were bankrupting their economies, the seven banana-producing countries of the Western Hemisphere, under the initiative of Costa Rica's outgoing president, Jose Figueres, and the Marxist-oriented Panamanian dictator, General Omar Torrijos, met in Panama in March 1974. Their objectives were to establish a "banana cartel," modeled after the Organization of Petroleum Exporting Countries (OPEC); raise the export price of bananas, unchanged for about twenty years; and break the control over banana production held by the big three fruit companies—United Brands Company (whose Central American banana division is the old United Fruit Company), Standard Fruit Company (a subsidiary of Castle & Cook, Inc.), and Del Monte Corporation.

Present at the Panama meeting were Colombia, Ecuador, Guatemala, Costa Rica, Honduras, Nicaragua, and their host, Panama. Together, these seven countries account for 80 percent of the world's banana production—250 million of the 350 million crates of bananas exported annually to the consumer markets of the United States, Canada, and Europe.

The "Saudi Arabia" of the banana-producing countries is Ecuador, the world's largest source of supply. Hence, Ecuador's adherence to the proposed price-fixing-production-curtailing pact was crucial. Ecuador refused to join the other producing countries in imposing an export tax of $1 a crate. She agreed, however, to raise her own export tax from 21 cents per crate to 41 cents, but almost immediately made the decision inoperative by announcing that exporters would be compensated by 50 percent of the value of the tax. Moreover, Ecuador declined to meet with the other producing countries at the next scheduled meeting (to be held at the end of March in Bogota, Colombia). Ecuador's refusal to participate with the other banana producers in an OPEC-inspired cartel doomed the idea of a Union of Banana Exporting Countries.

The "banana war"—as it was called in the Central American press—was reduced to individual country skirmishes. Costa Rica, Honduras, and Panama began negotiating their own tax increases—Guatemala, Colombia, and Nicaragua had none in effect at that time—with the big three multinational companies.

In April, Honduras announced an export tax of 50 cents on each forty-pound box of bananas, although it was not to take effect until June.

The proposed tax would have increased United Brands' costs by some $15 million.

The new levy could not have come at a worse time for United Brands:

- The banana market in the U.S. was already oversupplied as a result of the industry's increased shipments during the early months of 1974.

- Hurricane Fifi had swept through Central America during the fall, severely damaging 85 percent of the company's own and associated producer acreage in Honduras. The loss of crops and facilities amounted to $19.5 million.

- The John Morrell meat-packing division of United Brands had sustained a $6 million loss from increased cattle-feeding costs.

- Combined Central American banana export taxes, increased labor costs, and other charges amounted to around $18.8 million.

The company reported an aggregate loss of $43.6 million and was forced to omit dividend payments on its preferred and preference stock. To cover these losses and to provide the company with additional working capital, Eli Black, then chairman, was obliged to sell United Brands' 62 percent interest in Foster Grant, Inc., a sunglasses and plastics producer.

The Bribe. In August 1974, Black wrote to his shareholders that the Panamanian tax of $1 per box, the Costa Rican tax of 25 cents a box, and the Honduran tax of 50 cents "violated and breached the provisions of existing agreements with these countries." He also said that the company realized the need of the banana-producing countries for additional revenue, and he intended to negotiate with them to arrive at a reasonable formula.

Later that same month the company announced that it had reached an understanding with Honduras whereby the export tax would be reduced to 25 cents a crate, with yearly escalations beginning in 1975 depending upon market conditions. The reduction in the impost represented a saving of $7.5 million. The price for the favorable governmental action was the payment to Honduran officials of $2.5 million.

In September the company arranged for the deposit in Swiss banks for the account of designated officials of the Honduran government—understood to be the former president and the minister of economy—the sum of $1.25 million, to be deposited in the spring of 1975. Corporate funds for the initial payoff were obtained from United Brands' subsidiaries. Fictitious entries were made in the company's books to conceal the sources and the use of the funds.[6]

Four months later, early in February 1975, Eli Black jumped to his death from his forty-fourth floor office in mid-Manhattan. The SEC began looking into the operations of the company following the suicide of United Brands' chairman, a routine type of investigation when there is an unusual death of a chief executive. Also looking into the affairs of United Brands Company were several members of the staff of the *Wall Street Journal.* Their story of the payment of the bribe was published on April 25—well before the SEC had completed its investigation.

With the fat thus in the fire, United Brands' board of directors issued a statement that they had belatedly learned of the payoff, which had been authorized by its late chairman, but which they had not approved.

The evidence is conflicting on whether the initiative for the bribe came from the company or from Honduran officials. Several high-ranking executives of the banana division have asserted that they were solicited by the former Honduran minister of economy for a $5-million payoff in return for a tax reduction—a charge that is denied by Abraham Bennaton, the former minister. Another version has the late Eli Black himself meeting with former president Lopez and making the proposal for the bribe—an allegation that is vehemently denied by the Black family.

Such is the bare recital of the events that rocked the company's management and board of directors, induced the suicide of its former chairman, caused a *coup d'etat* in Honduras by junior army officers that ousted President-General Oswaldo Lopez Arellano, and produced a change in the ownership pattern of the company's investment in Honduras and a multiplicity of lawsuits by the federal government and stockholders. (As if the company did not have enough troubles, it has been charged by the European Economic Community with antitrust violations.)

There is an aspect of Greek tragedy in this human drama. Eli Black was a rabbi by training and a businessman by inclination. A sensitive man with a social conscience, Black believed that he could straddle the spiritual and temporal worlds and do justice to both. Events—his own actions—proved him wrong.

Under his leadership, the company sought to eradicate the lingering image of the old United Fruit Company as a swashbuckling corporate pirate. Black sought to promote community development programs for the people of the region in home improvement, nutrition, child care, education, and other fields of social betterment.

For the moralist on the sidelines, the payment of a bribe is a simple issue: it is improper conduct and therefore must be condemned. Yet to the individual at the head of a corporation, under relentless pressure from stockholders and the financial community to increase earnings and his own reputation as a successful professional manager hanging on the outcome, a payoff, though deplorable, may offer a means to buy time while the company recovers from a temporary illness.

The question remains: were United Brands' investors really benefited by telling the world of the payment of a bribe?

Keeping Friends and Influencing People: The Case of the Oil Companies' Political Contributions

Congressional hearings as a rule are not intended to serve as political science seminars. More often they are a legislative version of an American morality play. At the raised dais—now familiar to millions of American television viewers of the Senate Watergate hearings—sit the "tribunes of the people," the forces of "good." Seated below them are the witnesses, who if they are executives of the big oil companies, occupy a place equivalent to that of Satan in medieval times.

Conforming to this stereotype were the public hearings held in the ornate Senate Caucus Room in mid-July 1975 by the Senate subcommittee investigating overseas payoffs by multinational corporations. The substantial contributions to the Italian political parties made by the Italian affiliates of Exxon Corporation and Mobil Oil Corporation were excoriated by the subcommittee's chairman, Senator Frank Church (Democrat, Idaho), as "bribes" for obtaining special favors. Not so, responded Mobil Oil's executive vice president for international operations; his company's political contributions were made "to support the democratic process." In an Italian context, the distinction may have been without a difference, except that in the American news lexicon, "bribe" is a pejoratively loaded word.

Few high-ranking business executives are endowed with the politician's contrived bonhomie and the forensic skills needed for dominating a legislative committee before whom they appear as witnesses— usually reluctant witnesses. Most end their ordeal wearing a dunce cap. Yet the experienced New York or Washington political law firm can usually arrange helpful stage props for its clients.

Instead of acting the part of "culprits"—political contributions by corporations are not forbidden under Italian law—the witnesses from Exxon and Mobil, nudged by leading questions planted with friendly members of the panel, could have used the hearings as a forum for a realistic discussion of the political facts of life in Italy. They could have shown that:

- Nearly all Italian politicians and certainly all the political parties (from the ruling Christian Democrats to the coalition groupings of Social Democrats, Socialists, Republicans, and Neo-Fascists to the Communists) are tied to the *bustarella* system. (Some knowledgeable observers believe that the Communists are indirectly financed by Italian big business through the brokerage fees earned in arranging deals with Communist bloc countries. The Socialists are said to earn similar fees for arranging ventures with Yugoslavia and Communist China).[7]

- Members of Parliament are expected to kick back up to 50 percent of their salaries—about $2,000 per month—to their respective parties. With the galloping inflation, the high cost of living, and large families to support, most of the deputies and senators have to "put the arm" on the one certain source of supplemental income—business enterprise, both domestic and foreign.

- The larger parties run schools and youth centers, publish newspapers and journals, and maintain their own publishing houses for the printing of party books, pamphlets, and tracts. Most, if not all, of these activities operate at a loss. The scale of election spending—by Italian standards—is massive.

- The losses are made up in large part by the private and state-owned corporations—the Fiats, Olivettis, Pirellis, Montedisons, ENI (State Hydrocarbon Corporation—the huge state oil company), IRI (Industrial Reconstruction Institute), *Confindustria* (General Confederation of Italian Industry), and the Italian subsidiaries and affiliates of major international corporations from Western Europe, Japan, and the United States. (In 1974 a law was enacted by the Italian Parliament granting public subsidies of about $75 million annually for all political parties. The 1974 law continues to recognize the legality of contributions made by corporations, but for the first time requires disclosure of the recipients of such contributions. Prior to this—by mutual understanding of donors and donees—it was the practice to conceal the names of the recipients. This led to disguising such payments on the corporate books so that they could not be identified by the prying eyes of the tax inspectors. In a candid letter to his fellow Exxon employees, dated July 14, 1975, the now retired chairman, J. K. Jamieson, acknowledged that adherence to this practice by Exxon's affiliate, Esso Italiana, was a "mistake.")

- Oil is big business in Italy. She has the largest refining capacity in Western Europe. Middle East oil is processed not only for the large Italian market but for the other Common Market countries as well. The Italian affiliates

of the international oil companies are important sources of political contributions to the parties. For example, from 1963 until 1972, Exxon contributed $29 million to the major non-Communist parties, mainly through
party-owned newspapers. Contributions by foreign business enterprises
(such as Esso Italiana claims to have made) to newspapers owned by the
big private or state corporations—*La Stampa* (by Fiat), *Il Giorno* (by ENI),
La Notta and *Il Giornale* (by Pesanti and Italcementi)—also end up in the
coffers of the political parties.

- The Italian business community supports the political parties—even the
  powerful Communist Party as insurance against the not-too-distant day
  when it will share in or take over the Rome government—for the same
  pragmatic reasons as obtain among the other parliamentary democracies
  of Europe and Japan and in the United States: to influence party attitudes
  and to exert leverage over party votes. But in Italy there is also an additional reason for contributing to the parties; the secretaries-general of the
  major parties have more influence with the rank and file of the bureaucracy (who are beholden to the parties for their part-time jobs) than the
  regular government ministries. In consequence, a telephone call from party
  headquarters works a miracle in cutting red tape.

- Political contributions to the major parties provide the leverage for the
  award of lucrative government contracts, public utility franchises, subsidies, protection against import competition, and other favors that a
  friendly government can confer. (Exxon's controller, Archie Monroe, testified that his company's contributions were allocated to "categories relating to business objectives," such as efforts to reduce or defer taxes, obtain
  refinery licenses, win permission to import natural gas and secure favorable locations for service stations.)

- Financing the Italian political parties has helped to keep the political
  damage to private business enterprise within tolerable limits, and through
  the majority ruling party—the Christian Democrats—for thirty years has
  ensured the preservation of the status quo—a condition that the Christian
  Democrats seem less and less able to continue as Italy is increasingly
  racked by civil violence and class warfare.

The moral—and, perhaps, the ultimate irony—of the presentation
would have been the depiction of the plight of the oil companies after
they ceased making any contributions to the political parties last year
in the wake of an investigation of alleged bribery of Italian politicians.

With the goose no longer laying golden eggs, the Italian politicians
applied their own pressure—they refused to grant authorization to the
companies for price increases to reflect increased crude costs. The
consequences were predictable: profit margins were severely crimped;
the affiliates piled up sizable losses; and several of the companies may
be forced out of the Italian market.

The elicitation of these facts would have portrayed Italian politics
as not greatly different from American politics. Special interest groups

in Italy slip cash to politicians in the same way that milk producers in the United States, for instance, finance Democrats and Republicans to fix milk prices, or the unions finance Democrats to see things labor's way.

It is no secret that the subcommittee's chairman, Senator Church, a latter-day populist, attacks the multinational corporation because it is not an instrument of the political sovereignty of the state. For the doctrinaire populist and political moralist, as Professor Peter Drucker observes, "the crime of the multinational corporation is that it is not [also] an instrument of American morality." It eludes the populist critic that the multinational corporation cannot fulfill either of these functions because it operates in a myriad of cultures and under diverse environmental—economic, sociological, political, and governmental—constraints. In consequence, "it must fit itself . . . to the prevailing legal and moral beliefs of the political sovereignty in the country where it operates."[8]

An evangelical fervor that insists on carrying the torch of American moral values, albeit in disarray at home, into every foreign environment in which the U.S. international corporation does business will not everywhere be appreciated. In many countries, a display of American corporate righteousness will be resented as presumptuous. And to the crescendo of grievances, real or fancied, against the multinational corporation there will be added still another: "moral imperialism."

The Shakedown

When does a donation to a political party cease to be a contribution and become extortion? When the individual making the request is the late S. K. Kim, financial chairman of South Korea's Democratic Republican Party. "He happens to be as tough a man as I've ever met. I have never been subjected to that kind of abuse," Bob R. Dorsey, chairman of Gulf Oil Corporation, told the Senate subcommittee on multinational corporations.

An American public that thought it had heard the last word on the rascality of its own politicians was given a behind-the-scenes glimpse of raw, Oriental political power, as Gulf's chairman described how he was strong-armed into making $4 million available to South Korea's ruling and governing party.

Dorsey testified that Kim had extracted the payments under "severe pressure" and under conditions that amounted to "what is basically blackmail." Kim's threats, Dorsey said, "left little to the imagination" as to what would happen to Gulf's $300 million investment, most of it in refining and petrochemicals, if "the company would choose to turn its back on the request."

Gulf gave the party $1 million in 1966, "based upon what I sincerely considered to be in the best interest of the company and its shareholders," Dorsey said. In 1970, Dorsey met personally with Kim, who demanded a payment of $10 million for the 1971 election compaign. "I had heated discussions with officials of the party and flatly rejected both the intensity of the pressure being applied and the amount demanded," he stated. Kim's $10 million was haggled down to $3 million.

Gulf's chairman informed the subcommittee that he was told "that all foreign companies in Korea were expected to contribute" to President Park's election campaign. He added that the political pressures in Korea were even more intense than those to which many American corporations were subjected during the traumatic and scarring 1972 American presidential election.

Foreign companies are particularly vulnerable to political intimidation from the ruling party, as most of them operate in joint ventures with Korean nationals. Many such ventures were begun with extensive government support and continue to obtain much of their business from the government. Moreover, many of the more important and larger enterprises are headed by Koreans who are close friends of President Park and who owe their positions—and affluence—to his patronage. Thus, Park Won-Suk, who heads Gulf's 50-percent-owned Korean Oil Company, is a former deputy director of the Korean central intelligence agency and a former Air Force chief of staff. The late S. K. Kim also owed his good fortune to President Park. Kim headed a group of companies, which included South Korea's largest cement manufacturer, a profitable trading company, and an influential news service, Orient Press. He also was president of the Korea Chamber of Commerce and Industry,

It is said that, when Kim was a businessman on the political "giving end," he himself balked when requested to make an especially heavy contribution. Another Korean businessman tells of the treatment meted out to Kim for his recalcitrance. One of the president's intimate aides took him to the top of Namsan Mountain, the peak that overlooks Seoul, and in that rarified atmosphere, pulled every hair from Kim's greatly prized moustache. Kim and the other members of the Seoul business community got the message.

The ruling Democratic Republican Party used the Korean nationals to exert leverage on the foreign partners in the joint ventures. The Koreans were threatened with economic reprisals, such as tax audits, difficulties in clearing goods into customs, refusal of permits or the repatriation of dividends by the foreign partners and other enumerated harassments, not excluding nationalization.

The Koreans transmitted their fears to their foreign associates. Some of the local foreign managers, exercising their own discretion, refused to comply. They were usually with smaller companies. In some instances, where the Korean partner had control over the purse, the foreign partners learned of the contribution after it had been made. (Thus, the Korean partners of General Motors Korea paid $250,000 to officials of the party, for which General Motors seeks reimbursement on the grounds that it had not authorized the payment.)

Most of the foreign partners, however, concluded that compliance was the better part of valor. Political intimidation produced the cash "donations," "gifts," "contributions" (to one of President Park's favorite projects, a technical high school in his home town), and the "half-compulsory" contributions (in the phrase used by the incumbent party chairman, Park Joon Kyu) for the "national defense fund" used to strengthen the fortifications at the 39th parallel and around Seoul. Over a period of six months, from the end of December 1973 to May 1974, about $40 million was bled from the business community for the national defense fund, according to the defense minister.

Some critics question whether the late Kim wasn't bluffing on the fate awaiting Gulf if its chairman had refused to submit to the political shakedown. Fortified by the judgment of hindsight, they contend that Gulf's shareholders did not receive full value for Dorsey's payoff in view of the Korean company's deteriorated financial position (it lost more than $6 million on its integrated petroleum operations in 1974 and is endeavoring to dispose of its interest in a naphtha cracking plant).

There is a short answer to the self-appointed keepers of the corporate conscience. Unlike Gulf's chairman, they weren't subjected to the late Kim's orchestration of pressures. And, if Kim had made good his threats, it would not have been their responsibility to face a questioning board of directors and a skeptical shareholders' meeting to explain how a $300 million investment was lost because of a loss of nerve.

Unlike the moralists in the media and among dissident church activists, Sister Jane Scully, president of Carlow College in Pittsburgh and a member of Gulf's board of directors, was able to visualize the complexities and dilemmas of applying ethical precepts in an amoral political environment. She aptly observed: "It troubles me that there are no easy answers."

The Intermediary: The Case of Northrop Corporation

Northrop utilized a battalion of political and commercial agents to promote procurement of its military aircraft by foreign governments. In the service of the company were such luminaries as a retired former chief of staff of the French Air Force and vice president of the French National Assembly, a World War II German Luftwaffe combat ace, a former German ambassador to Iran and member of the *bundestag*, a celebrated former CIA station chief with access to the royal monarchs of the Persian Gulf and Arabian Peninsula, and ubiquitous Swiss lawyers who roamed the European corridors of power. In all, according to a report prepared for the board of directors by the international accounting firm of Ernst & Ernst, Northrop employed during the period 1971 to 1973 between 400 and 500 consultants and agents, including a shadowy Swiss-based corporate sales agency.

In an apt and striking phrase, Northrop's president, Thomas V. Jones, described the agent as "the stethoscope on the workings of government." He is able to consummate government sales by promoting, again in Jones's words, "broad and high-level support at political levels that are important to the selection of any major government procurement."

Though the agent is used to influence sales, the concern of the investigators was Northrup's use of payoffs to overseas government officials to obtain its sales. A case in point is Northrop's Saudi Arabian agent, Adnan Khashoggi, who also provides marketing and consulting services for Lockheed, Chrysler, and Raytheon. Northrup documents show that it paid $450,000 to Khashoggi, who claimed that the money was demanded by two Saudi generals during negotiations for a multimillion dollar sale of fighter aircraft. Khashoggi has denied funneling the money to the Saudi officers.

The SEC's investigation into Northrop's domestic political contributions had disclosed that some $30 million in fees had been paid to overseas agents and consultants. The SEC contends that the company did not keep adequate records to "insure that such transfers and disbursements were actually made for the purposes indicated." In other words, Northrup had not identified on its corporate books the recipients of under-the-table payments.

It is blinking at reality to suppose that sophisticated aerospace managements are not aware that some portion of the fees paid to agents is used for payoffs to government officials to secure favorable decisions on government procurement of aircraft and military hardware. Northrop's payment to the two Saudi generals was in the form of non-interest-bearing advances on commissions due Khashoggi. And in a parallel investigation of the use of commissions for payoffs, Lockheed Aircraft Corporation conceded that "of the total commissions and other payments made during the period 1970 through June 29, 1975, at least 15 percent is known or thought to have flowed to foreign officials in a number of countries abroad." In all, Lockheed disbursed nearly $30 million to foreign officials and political parties for help in winning orders valued at more than $2 billion.

Yet for a principal to monitor how his agent uses his commissions—as the SEC believes is necessary—presents both legal and practical difficul-

ties. The courts, for one thing, may be reluctant to require accountability from an agent on the expenditure of his fees because it would
be a departure from the settled rule of common law that a principal
is not responsible for the acts of his agent.

The other difficulty is probably more critical. Asking a successful
agent to make a detailed accounting of his disbursements is apt to
be rebuffed as none of the principal's business. A shrewd guess can
be made of the direction of Adnan Khashoggi's commissions. He has
built his Triad Group of companies into a $400 million multinational
network of financial interests, with land, banking, and other holdings
in the United States alone valued at roughly $100 million. But seeking
similar information from other agents is a guaranteed way to lose their
services. This contingency is immediately relevant for the Middle East
market, probably the fastest growing and potentially the most lucrative
in the world.

The Go-between

The SEC is a domestically oriented institution. Its preoccupation
since its inception forty years ago has been with the U.S. securities
markets. Staff members are not expected to be international business
experts. Yet the investigation into overseas payoffs requires a broader
angle of vision of other cultures and customs than the training and
experience of the lawyers of the enforcement division allow. The
projection of American cultural or moral standards into other environments is intellectually confusing. And a perception of Middle East
business as if it were an extension of American business is bound to
lead to distortions in judgment. This is especially true when the role
of the go-between is misconceived.

Islamic scholar Raphael Patai describes the compelling need for the
services of the intermediary in the Moslem world, still gripped by the
constraints of a traditional society, in order:

> not to be cheated in the marketplace, in locating and acquiring a job,
> in resolving conflict and litigation, in winning a court decision, in speed-
> ing government action, and in establishing and maintaining political
> influence and bureaucratic procedures, in finding a bride and, in fact,
> for the social scientist to locate and convince respondents to give an
> interview.[9]

Culture Bridge

Although many Middle East rulers—and their Western-trained young
technocrats—have superficially adapted their thinking to the concepts
of the West, they are still suspicious of and uneasy with financial and

business transactions undertaken with foreigners. The heads of the emergent Arab conglomerate family enterprises, particularly those with Western affiliations, and the older Maronite Christian Lebanese families, with their network of international banking and commercial connections, play an important role in providing a sense of confidence for the traditional oil-rich sheiks.

In addition, the commercial and banking families are the repositories of economic, financial, and political intelligence with respect to the individual countries, their rulers, and governing political factions. In this respect, the heads of the great Arab clans are equivalent to the West's international banks, local chambers of commerce and trade associations, and the professional groups (lawyers, accountants, and consultants) as information networks.

If the Middle East's intermediaries didn't exist, they would have to be invented. For the Western business executive, the intermediaries:

- Overcome the formidable language barrier.

- Penetrate the orbit of Moslem power. "Foreign firms entering the market," explains Robert E. Bernard, executive vice president of Kaiser Engineers in charge of international operations, "have difficulty getting to the handful of key people who make the decisions."[10] The intermediary, however, knows who among the palace courtiers has the ruler's ear and which ministers truly hold the levers of decision. (It was Adnan Khashoggi who arranged Lockheed's first sale of C-130 Hercules transport aircraft to the Saudi air force in 1965. Since then Lockheed has been awarded multimillion-dollar contracts for the sale of radar and communications systems, Jetstar private aircraft, and most recently four Tristars to the Saudi airline.)

- Sandpaper the typical American business abrasiveness into acceptable Arab diplomatic verbiage—an important consideration in a culture that places a high value on the "spoken" word.

- Provide "thinking time" for the parties to consider all the implications involved in the proposed transaction. By the same token, if, upon reflection, it seems desirable for one of the parties to withdraw from the negotiations the presence of the intermediary allows this to be accomplished without incurring a loss of face.

- Short-circuit the Arab passion for verbosity and lyrical hyperbole.

- Perform the contract haggling—a ritualized form of "horse trading" in the Middle East (and other world regions) with which most U.S. executives are not psychologically attuned.

- Bear the brunt of attending the interminable talk sessions, which are at odds with the Western structured time frame.

- Obtain from each side the concessions that enable the parties to strike a bargain.

- Play down the U.S. businessman's obsession with a written contract, which to the traditional Arab mind is an affront to the honor of a commitment conveyed by a spoken word and sealed with a handclasp. (The typical voluminous contract, drafted by lawyers schooled in the American legal tradition of anticipating every conceivable breach or default and bristling with covenants invoking the right to litigation, is an anomaly in virtually every legal environment save the Soviet Union, which, ironically, shares the American *idee fixe* of a prolix legal instrument.)

In sum, in dealing with Western businessmen, the traditional centers of Arab power and wealth are more comfortable with an intermediary of the same culture, who practices the same religion and shares a mutual pride in the renaissance of Moslem world influence. Where the intermediary has himself been exposed to Western education and influence and is involved in joint business undertaking with foreigners, he serves to unite the West's psychological attitudes and cultural preconceptions with his own appreciation of local customs, negotiating habits, and sociological and political constraints.

Servant of the Ruler

Consider Mehdi al-Tajir, one of the Middle East's leading middlemen.[11] A Bahraini-born Arab of an old and wealthy trading family, al-Tajir, like other well-to-do Bahrainis, was educated in England. His personal wealth is reputed to eclipse Khashoggi's. Al-Tajir is not only a capitalist-entrepreneur in his own right, but he is also an official of Dubai and the United Arab Emirates (a cluster of seven desert sheikdoms on the Persian Gulf-Arabian Peninsula, formerly known as the Trucial States). Al-Tajir acts as financial advisor to his ruler, Rashid bin Said al-Maktoum; he is head of the Office of the Ruler, the administrative office of the government, and is Director of Petroleum Affairs of Dubai. He also acts as the financial advisor to Sheik Zayed, ruler of Abu Dhabi, who is president of the emirates and the real power of the U.A.E. Al-Tajir is the U.A.E.'s ambassador to London—the emirates have had close financial ties with the City and political relations with Whitehall for nearly a century—and he is Ambassador-at-Large to the European Economic Community.

In sum, not only does Mehdi al-Tajir have personal entree to the centers of political and financial power in the Middle East and the West, but he is the link between the oil-rich emirates and the outside world. Al-Tajir is obviously "the man to see" for access to the Middle East's enormous pool of self-generating petrodollars, currently estimated at between $85 and $100 billion.

In the listening posts at the trade and entrepot centers as well as in Beirut, the financial capital of the Middle East (until the Christian-Moslem civil war made a shambles of the city), it is widely believed that al-Tajir was the man Boeing saw for effectuating its recent sale of 747's to Syria and Egypt. The company denies any such connection. Curiously, other U.S. firms that have retained al-Tajir to assist them in establishing a foothold in the area likewise swear they never heard of him. Yet by a strange coincidence, Syria bought over $100 million worth of Boeing's jets, the sale was financed by Dubai, and al-Tajir handled the negotiations. A similar procedure was followed in the May 1975 sale of $60 million in Boeing aircraft to Egyptair.

"I don't know what Mehdi al-Tajir got out of it," says a State Department Foreign Service officer, "but I'd be willing to bet he got something." The word is that he received $22 million, 15 percent of the contract price.

Corporate Baksheesh

The Mehdi al-Tajirs, Adnan Khashoggis, and other major Middle East intermediaries furnish their Western principals with vital supportive services. But they do something more to earn their handsome fees: they supply the magic elixir that makes certain any deal they handle will materialize.

It should be borne in mind that hundreds of years of Ottoman rule have stamped the contemporary Arab world with the dry rot of corruption. The go-between facilitates his—and his principal's—work by the judicious dispensation of *baksheesh*—a fact of cultural life without any of the West's overtones of impropriety.

The funds used for such payments are frequently paid by the consumer to the seller's agent and are included in the purchase price. Or they are paid (as was done by Northrop and Lockheed) to the agent and transferred by him to the recipient of the payoff. In other situations, the local agent inflates the bid price and skims off the difference between the original price and his markup to cover the payment of bribes. In Mexico, for example, the "coyotes"—the sobriquet applied to the lawyer-politicians and other middlemen with government connections—utilize this technique for the payment of *mordida*.

Unlike the officials of the SEC's enforcement division, the ranking civilian officials of the Department of Defense are attuned to diverse overseas environments. It is not surprising, therefore, that in the spring of 1974 an official of the Defense Security Assistance Agency—the arms sales organization of the Pentagon—should address the Electronics Industry Association on the topic, "Agents' Fees in the Middle East."

With a realism born of experience the speaker described how obtaining aircraft contracts involved the use of *baksheesh*—from the payment of substantial amounts of cash to the rent-free use of a villa on the French Riviera to occupancy of a fashionable London flat complete with car, chauffeur, and servants.

Such is the way French and British orders are obtained. The French and British aerospace industries are "masters in dealing through agents," the speaker observed. "They have no compunctions in agreeing to excessive fees, if, in the final analysis the sale is consummated," he said.

Though prominently featured in the headlines, Northrop is in reality only a minor player in the high stakes being played in the Middle East. Arms sales to the area—$8.4 billion for 1974-75—are probably Secretary of State Kissinger's most useful diplomatic currency for the attainment of this nation's strategic objectives in this critical world region. Not only are military sales important in redressing the balance of trade and for paying the cost of imported oil, but they enable the Department of Defense to maintain a technologically advanced arms industry with a minimum of subsidy.

The Northrop case underscores the difficulties involved in coming to grips with overseas payoffs. Not only are they deeply embedded in the Middle East's business and cultural environments, but they are inextricably tied to military sales now used as a legitimate means for the furtherance of competing foreign policies of the Soviet Union, Mainland China, France, Britain, Sweden, and the United States.

POLICY CONSIDERATIONS

Out of the welter of charges, innuendoes, headlines, congressional moral indignation, self-righteous media sermons, and corporate *mea culpa* breast-beating, a number of policy proposals have emerged to deal with overseas payoffs.

Corporate Action

There are, to be sure, companies whose managements have successfully resisted whitemail solicitations by government officials and politicians. Such companies have recognized that payoffs, though temporarily relieving political pressures, may create even bigger problems later. The big payoff is not likely to be a one-time transaction; it is part of a way of life. And the ante is apt to be raised by another ruling group or political party upon discovering the sums paid to its predecessors, as with Gulf Oil and the Democratic Republican Party of South Korea.

A high-technology company with a commanding position in the market—IBM is an example—can turn down a venal official and make its "no" stick. But other, less fortunate firms, which have sought to follow the book of Scriptures, have lost out to competitors—U.S. and foreign—whose punctilio of conduct was not above that of the marketplace.

Companies whose superior technology or engineering capabilities place them in a privileged position to resist extortionate demands for payoffs can let it be known that at home and abroad they compete on product quality, price, delivery, and financing—not in the purchase of politicians. In the business world, as elsewhere, the crowd follows the leader.

But what of the companies—numbered in the thousands—whose size and market position prevent them from adopting a bold moral stance? These companies are impaled on the horns of a dilemma. If they adhere to ethical precepts and decline to pay off or buy their way into a contract, competitors from countries more tolerant of the practice will eliminate them from important markets. The ultimate victims of righteous conduct will be the workers who are laid off and stockholders whose dividends are reduced or eliminated. If these companies pay off in order to remain in an overseas market, they face exposure by the SEC or a congressional committee, or both. The resultant publicity may trigger retaliatory legal action—or even expropriation of an overseas investment.

A resolution of the dilemma might be for managements whose firms risk the loss of markets to tell their stockholders how much of their money is spent on payoffs each year to remain competitive. To be sure, the practice of making under-the-table payments is not thereby eliminated, but neither is it concealed. Guidelines for the partial disclosure of overseas payments now in preparation by the SEC (but not released at this writing) may facilitate such voluntary disclosures to stockholders.

A logical extension of such an approach by management would be for the stockholders, and the company's employees, to express their views on whether the practice of making payoffs should be continued or discontinued. If the practice is to be curtailed, the parties directly affected will have determined that they are willing to suffer the consequences of reduced earnings.

State Department Action

The U.S. international corporation should not have to serve as a milk cow to overseas politicians—augmenting personal incomes, financing election campaigns, and setting up "escape funds," deposited in

Swiss banks, for use in the event of a political disaster. The Department of State can play a decisive role in the eradication of overseas payoffs by making it known that the diplomatic shield of the U.S. government will protect U.S.-based firms that are the targets of extortionate demands.

Even a government riddled with corruption has its *amour propre* touched when an American ambassador can point to a specific official—or officials—who are on the take. For the honest official who needs personal financial assistance or funds to arrange a "safe haven"— examples include Third World chiefs of state, prime ministers, and dictators—U.S. ambassadors rarely decline to help a supplicant.[12]

Legislative Action

Some members of Congress have proposed the enactment of legislation making it a crime for a U.S. corporation to make payoffs to foreign officials or to contribute to overseas political parties. The proponents believe that such legislation will, among other things, help U.S. managers ward off extortion and deter them from initiating bribes.

Restrictive legislation, to be sure, can provide ersatz morality. But the baneful effects of such a law, if enacted, far outweigh its benefits— if any. A law that puts a brake on permissable business conduct abroad can be just as mischievous as a foreign policy that presupposes that it has a monopoly on morality. Each contains the ingredients for becoming quixotic or obnoxious. And for this reason, the Department of State opposes enactment of the proposed legislation.

Enforcement of extraterritorial legislation—and that is precisely what a congressional ban against overseas payoffs would be—has in the recent past involved the United States, and the U.S. overseas subsidiaries and their directors, in unpleasant controversies. The extraterritorial application of American antitrust concepts is not everywhere accepted as sound economic policy or a moral blessing.

A British court refused to enforce an order issued by a U.S. District Court that a British company grant exclusive patent licenses to another British company. Swiss officials objected to an attempt by a U.S. District Court to extend the reach of the Sherman Act to the Swiss watch industry. And a decree issued by a U.S. District Court aroused Canadian resentment because it had ordered the dissolution of a Canadian patent pool, whose participants included General Electric, Westinghouse, and Phillips, while directing the licensing of others.

Enforcement of the Trading with the Enemy Act—directed mainly against trade with Mainland China prior to the Nixon policy of *rap-*

prochement—brought U.S. overseas subsidiaries into conflict during the 1950s and 1960s with the governments of Britain, Belgium, Canada, and France. More recently, the Argentine government let it be known that, if the Argentine subsidiaries of General Motors, Ford, and Chrysler were prevented from exporting cars and trucks to Cuba under the U.S. embargo against trade with the Castro regime, they would be nationalized.

In December 1974, Litton Industries directed its Canadian subsidiary to cancel a contract for the sale of office furniture to the Cuban government, after learning that the proposed transaction was in violation of the United States' embargo policy. Litton's action was denounced by Alistair Gillespie, Canadian Minister of Trade, who said, "I consider this action an intolerable interference and a form of corporate colonialism."

In sum, a restrictive law against overseas payoffs by U.S. companies is not only difficult to enforce, but it is also self-defeating. U.S. companies would be displaced from lucrative markets because foreign competitors were not similarly restrained; the law would be resented as an interference with companies domiciled in host countries and subject to their—not U.S.—national laws; and finally, such extraterritorial legislation would be regarded as a shining example of hypocrisy by the United States, whose own household is scarcely a paragon of moral rectitude.

Agreement With Other Industrialized Nations

A more fruitful approach than unilateral action by the United States is for the State Department to enlist the other industrialized nations to enter into an informal understanding to restrain *all* firms from making payoffs to the officials of foreign governments. A small beginning might be made in the area of military sales.

A precedent for such informal international action (which obviates the impractical treaty or convention approach) exists in the international alignment of export credits granted to the Soviet Union and the Eastern European Communist bloc countries. The *Union D'Assureurs des Credits Internationaux*, headquartered in Berne, consists of some twenty-three governments and private credit insurance organizations from eighteen countries. The rules of the association amount to no more than a loosely drawn gentlemen's agreement, without binding legal force. Yet the "Berne Union," since its establishment in 1934, has provided a reasonably effective forum for the coordination of international credit insurance.

Code of Conduct for Multinational Corporations and Third World Countries

UN Ambassador Daniel Moynihan (who essays the role of a Socratic gadfly to the Third World) might remind his ambassadorial colleagues at the United Nations that just as it takes two to tango, it also takes two to bribe.

As the Third World is the heartland of "grease," he could inquire if the governments of Africa, Asia, and Latin America are agreeable to have included in a UN Code of Conduct for Multinational Corporations a provision that foreign investors should neither make nor be pressured into making payoffs to government officials, or to politicians and their parties.

Though Ambassador Moynihan's masters at the State Department are not likely to permit him to lay such a suggestion—even though made with tongue in cheek—before his UN colleagues, the articulation of the idea would have a salutory effect. It would strip away the rhetorical pretentiousness of Third World diplomats, whose oratorical self-righteousness disguises the blatant corruption of so many of their leaders and elite peers at home.

NOTES

1. Louis D. Brandeis, *Other People's Money* (New York: Frederick A. Stokes, 1914), p. 92.
2. See William O. Douglas, *Go East Young Man* (New York: Random House, 1974), p. 272. Mr. Justice Douglas served as an SEC commissioner and chairman from 1936 to 1939.
3. Ray Garrett, speech before the American Society of Corporate Secretaries, June 27, 1975.
4. See, for example, Ronald Wraith and Edgar Simpkins, *Corruption in Developing Countries* (New York: W. W. Norton, 1964).
5. Luigi Barzini, *The Italians* (New York: Grosset & Dunlap, 1964), pp. 108-109.
6. The facts relating to the bribery of the Honduran officials are based on the complaint (Civil Action No. 75-0509) filed by the SEC in the United States District Court for the District of Columbia, April 9, 1975).
7. Norman Kogan, *The Government of Italy* (New York: Thomas Y. Crowell, 1962), p. 66.
8. Peter Drucker, *Management: Tasks, Responsibilities, Practices* (New York: Harper & Row, 1974), p. 360.
9. Raphael Patai, *The Arab Mind* (New York: Charles Scribner's Sons, 1973), p. 232. See also, Roy Jastram, "The Nakado Negotiator," *California Management Review* (Winter 1974), pp. 88-90. (Professor Jastram describes the importance of the intermediary to the American businessman whose experience in international business is restricted to markets governed by the Anglo-American common law or the civil law system.)
10. *Business Week* (28 May 1975), p. 52.
11. For a vivid account of Mehdi al-Tajir, from which the writer has borrowed, see *Forbes* (15 June 1975); and also Ray Vicker, *The Kingdom of Oil: The Middle East, Its People and Its Power* (New York: Charles Scribner's Sons, 1974).
12. Miles Copeland, *Without Cloak or Dagger* (New York: Simon & Schuster, 1974), p. 217.

VI | MANAGEMENT IN OTHER CULTURES

There are many sets of beliefs about management and business. Some support each other and some contradict. Most are accepted or rejected with little thought; and probably most should be seriously and regularly examined. In this section, we look at three illustrations of the many different ways management and businesses can operate, and they can give us reason to pause and reflect.

Some claim that if the basis of ownership of industry were changed, the nature of business and management would automatically change also. Burck, in "A Socialist Enterprise That Acts Like a Fierce Capitalist Competitor," describes a Yugoslav enterprise owned by the workers which has developed a strong central management, is growing rapidly, and competes successfully both in Yugoslavia and abroad. The firm is beginning to receive some of the same criticism at home that firms receive here. In his article, "I Have Seen China—and They Work," Kraar describes successful firms where every effort is made to keep management to a minimum both in size and power. In Japan Diebold observed firms which were in many ways more capitalistic than firms in this country, yet their employee practices differ sharply from those assumed essential to the economic health and survival of a U.S. firm.

These three articles bring only a small sample, yet they give some hint of the scope and diversity of approaches and responses which exist. As you read these articles, see if your beliefs about management and business are challenged or altered by the information they present.

VI MANAGEMENT IN OTHER CULTURES

GILBERT BURCK

A Socialist Enterprise That Acts Like a Fierce Capitalist Competitor

Most Americans who know anything about Sarajevo think of it as the Balkan town where Archduke Franz Ferdinand's assassination touched off World War I. Few would imagine it as a modern industrial center. But that's what it is. Among other things, Sarajevo is the headquarters city for an industrial enterprise called Energoinvest, which may be described without undue exaggeration as one of the most ambitious, arresting, edifying, and important conglomerates the business world has ever sprouted. Founded twenty-one years ago by an entrepreneurial genius named Emerik Blum, Energoinvest has recently been expanding at more than 20 percent per annum. It now encompasses forty-one units turning out a wide range of products dominated by electrical and processing equipment such as heat exchangers, and it plans to become a major aluminum producer. It employs some 22,000 people, maintains sales offices in thirty-two countries, grosses about $160 million, and spends $5 million to $6 million a year on research, development, and scholarships. As a conglomerate, it is a rare if not unique phenomenon: because its affiliates can always secede from the group if they choose, the company's very existence depends on doing better for each affiliate than the affiliate can do by itself.

This sounds like something out of a capitalist Shangri-La. But Sarajevo is the capital of Bosnia and Herzegovina, which is one of the six repub-

Source: Reprinted from the January 1972 issue of *Fortune* Magazine by special permission; © 1971 Time Inc.

lics of Yugoslavia, a nation that thinks of itself as being in the vanguard of true Communism. Blum himself, as a matter of fact, is an esteemed member of the League of Communists of Yugoslavia, as the party is known there. But Yugoslavia's Communism is nothing if not flexible, and it practices a kind of market socialism that compels "social" enterprises to operate like private enterprises.

Energoinvest certainly does just that. One of the most enterprising of Yugoslav enterprises, it scours the world for ideas, pays stiff fees to American management consultants, and exists not merely to make things but to sell them in competitive markets. Along with some other successful Yugoslav firms, Energoinvest has shown that the best way to make socialism work is to subject it to the discipline of the market and put it under good management. It provides an excellent example of a truth now being grasped throughout the whole industrial world: no matter what the political and social bent of a country, the art and science of producing and distributing goods and services efficiently are governed by essentially the same economic laws. The comrade consumers in the East are just as coy and elusive as the freewheeling buyers in the west. Inflation follows an inordinate expansion of the money supply just as inevitably in a totalitarian state as in representative democracies. Whether socialized or private, production and trade flourish under good management and languish under bad.

THE BIGGER THE PROFITS, THE HIGHER THE WAGE

The key to the Yugoslav economic system is that it recognizes these facts. The system is not as strange and paradoxical as it sounds, nor is it something really new. A brilliant job of improvisation, it resembles very closely the private enterprise system, and it needs good management for the same reason the private system does. The basic difference between the two is that the Yugoslav system is based on so-called self-management *(samoupravljanje)*, which does away with private ownership and invests ownership in "the people," and expects workers and their councils to act as trustees for the people. Self-management is not universal in Yugoslavia; most of the country's farms and hundreds of thousands of small enterprises are privately owned. But the great bulk of the nonagricultural labor force works in "social" enterprises run by worker-elected councils. These workers are the "bosses." Technically they can fire their managers and pull their factories out of a complex like Energoinvest; and they make the final decisions on wages and investment. Their pay depends directly on profits, whereas pay in a private enterprise depends indirectly on them. But the profitability of a Yugoslav firm depends, as it does for enterprises at all times and everywhere, on management.

How the Yugoslavs adopted this mixed system is one of the most instructive stories in all economic history. During World War II their Partisans beat back the Nazis and gained national hegemony with hardly any help at all from the Soviet Union. But the nation's admiration for the Soviet Union remained unbounded, and after the war Yugoslavia set up a Stalinist command economy even more rigid than that of the Soviet Union itself. Planners and administrators in Belgrade ran everything, just as those in Moscow still do. Enterprise managers telephoned Belgrade for orders every evening, and devoted their talents, such as they were, to executing those orders the next day. Since true management consists of making decisions about matters like quantity, quality, costs, markets, prices, and investments, they were not managers, but mere robots.

But Tito broke with Stalin in a row that culminated, in 1948, in Yugoslavia's expulsion from the Moscow-run Cominform, Stalin's denunciation of Tito as a capitalist agent, and a Soviet blockade of the country. Never in history has a nation been confronted so suddenly with the necessity for rethinking the reasons for its existence. In retrospect, eminent Yugoslavs now agree, it was the best thing that ever happened to them. Like Dr. Dodd facing the gallows, they found that the shock concentrated their minds wonderfully. They began, as one of them puts it, to rediscover the laws of economics.

Literally asking one another what was wrong with the Soviet Union, the Yugoslavs came up with a good answer. The Soviet Union, they decided, represented not true socialism but bureaucratic despotism that exploited workers worse than private monopolistic capitalism was supposed to. The Yugoslavs concluded that their own economy had to be decentralized, for true socialism had to be based on motivation, not on command. The obvious way to decentralize without restoring private ownership was to turn to the well-known device of workers' councils—to set up councils in the enterprises and transfer most and eventually perhaps all of the state's economic power to them. But that, of course, meant allowing the enterprises to act freely, subject mainly to the discipline of the market. Without self-government, Yugoslav economists agreed, socialism was impossible. Without free enterprise, by the same token, workers' self-government was impossible.

HIRED HANDS TO BOSS THE BOSSES

The independence of the councils has been intermittently strengthened since 1950, when the era of self-management legally began, and today they are beholden to no one, at least in theory. In every firm with more than five jobs, the workers elect a council by secret ballot. Most councils number anywhere from 15 to 120 members, depending on the size of the enterprise, and they serve for two years. Since the councils generally meet only every month or two, they often choose a managing board, which includes the enterprise's director or chief executive, to keep the councils in frequent touch with the company's affairs. Each plant boasts at least one council, and large companies with several plants or divisions elect a central council that generally handles broad policy matters. Thus each of the forty-one affiliates of Energoinvest elects a council, often supplemented at lower levels by informal discussion groups. And a central council of about a hundred, elected by all the workers, assembles periodically in Sarajevo.

Legally, the director has a very ambiguous job. As chief executive officer, he is the chief hired hand, and implements the council's decisions. Appointed by the council from candidates selected by a committee, he must be re-elected by the council every four years; and the council can sack him if the case against him is strong enough. At the same time, he is charged with seeing to it that the enterprise does nothing contrary to the public interest.

As the Yugoslavs cheerfully explain, they are experimenting and learning from experience. In practice, the original statutes or charters of most enterprises have been rewritten to specify managerial prerogatives and authority. Energoinvest's statute, for instance, has been amended several times. It now empowers the managing director to coordinate the activities of the units or affiliates in the interests of the whole enterprise, to annul decisions made by his executives, to ask the councils to annul acts by their management boards if he considers them unwise, to sign agreements on behalf of the enterprise, and so on. He is also allowed to choose his own collegium or advisory body, composed largely of his chief executives and technical specialists.

At the plant level, the manager can usually mete out discipline for minor offenses and participate in the hiring and firing processes. But he generally cannot overwork even such limited powers. A diligent, stern manager who improves productivity and profitability is obviously doing more for his workers than an easygoing one who overlooks workers' transgressions. But since a diligent, stern man is likely to antagonize workers, the good Yugoslav manager is one who understands how to handle people and is willing to keep on patiently explaining to his bosses how good performance results in higher wages.

POINTS ON THE PAY SCALE

Essentially, wages and salaries are what is left after all fixed expenses (purchases, materials, depreciation, interest, taxes, etc.) are paid, and after appropriate amounts have been set aside in reserves, such as housing and capital funds. Thus wage payments vary from unit to unit and from month to month. Energoinvest, for example, reckons pay by a point system. Each worker, including Blum himself, is rated by points, the number of points depending on education, seniority, and function. At the end of the month the value of each point is determined by the amount left for wages and salaries; the individual's pay is figured simply by multiplying the value of a point that month by the number of points to his credit.

Energoinvest workers earn between 1,000 and 2,000 dinars a month, with the average at about 1,600; a plant manager may earn 3,500; managing director Blum gets around 5,700. Since the dinar exchanges for only 6.6 U.S. cents, this amounts to only $376, which might seem like pretty thin pickings. But mere exchange rates are very misleading. A more relevant criterion is the spread between lowest and highest pay, and when U.S. income is counted after taxes, the Yugoslav spread is not much narrower than in many U.S. companies. By American standards, however, key Yugoslav executives are underpaid; some plant managers make less than engineers or even skilled workers with long seniority. Aside from tempting officials to abuse expense accounts, such salaries tend to kill incentive; and outsiders who have studied the Yugoslav system believe that eventually key people will earn salaries reflecting more accurately their contribution to the company's success.

A REFUGEE FROM BUREAUCRACY

Blum himself, despite perquisites like an apartment and a car and chauffeur, perforce lives very modestly. His job, of course, is its own reward. A slender, balding, bespectacled man of sixty, who in lighter moments adopts a kind of Foxy Grandpa expression, Blum is simple, direct, unaffected, and dignified. He does not slap other people's backs, nor does he encourage anyone to slap his. He simply knows what he is talking about, and is always eager to listen to people who know what they are talking about. He also knows when to stop talking and start acting; on these occasions he can behave a little abruptly, but because he times his abruptness well, he is admired all the more for it. Above all, he keeps his councils informed. He never advances a proposition that has not been fully explored, backed up with facts, and tested in discussions at various levels. "The councils cooperate when they have all the facts," he says laconically.

Blum was born in 1911 in Sarajevo, where his father, a Hungarian Jew, served as a minor official of the then Austro-Hungarian State Railways. Educated in Prague and Vienna, he was jailed more than once as a student radical; but he began his career conventionally

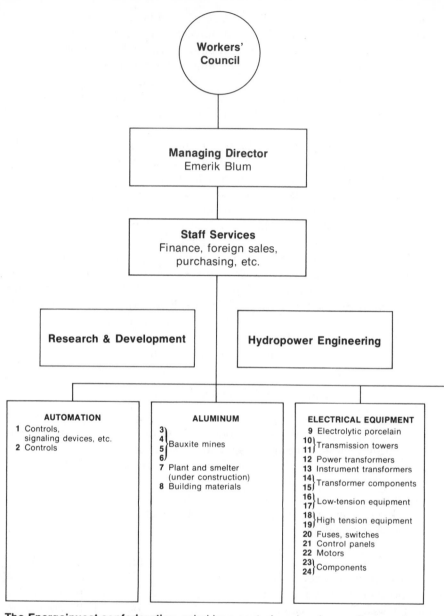

The Energoinvest confederation, ruled by a central workers' council, comprises thirty-five factories and six mines, grouped in six divisions. Each plant or mine is a legally autonomous unit, with its own workers' council. Very soon the roster will include several more units, including a petrochemical operation; Energo-invest plans on more than doubling its business by 1975. The units are guided, integrated, and supplied with financial and other services by the parent

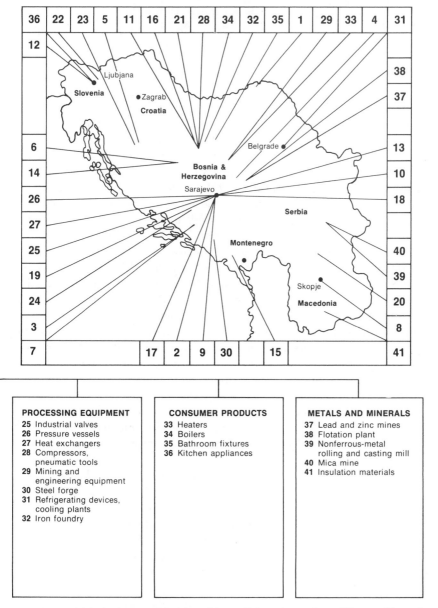

| 36 | 22 | 23 | 5 | 11 | 16 | 21 | 28 | 34 | 32 | 35 | 1 | 29 | 33 | 4 | 31 |

Within the map (clockwise): 12, 38, 37, 6, 13, 14, 10, 26, 18, 27, 25, 40, 19, 39, 24, 20, 3, 8, 7, 17, 2, 9, 30, 15, 41

Map labels: Ljubljana, Slovenia, Zagrab, Croatia, Belgrade, Bosnia & Herzegovina, Sarajevo, Serbia, Montenegro, Skopje, Macedonia

PROCESSING EQUIPMENT
25 Industrial valves
26 Pressure vessels
27 Heat exchangers
28 Compressors, pneumatic tools
29 Mining and engineering equipment
30 Steel forge
31 Refrigerating devices, cooling plants
32 Iron foundry

CONSUMER PRODUCTS
33 Heaters
34 Boilers
35 Bathroom fixtures
36 Kitchen appliances

METALS AND MINERALS
37 Lead and zinc mines
38 Flotation plant
39 Nonferrous-metal rolling and casting mill
40 Mica mine
41 Insulation materials

company, which has no capital but lives off fees from the affiliates. Abroad, Energoinvest has also established three joint ventures: Energomex in Mexico, Energowassir in West Pakistan, and Energolibya in Libya. In addition, it maintains thirty-three foreign sales offices. The one in New York City, called Interenergo, is incorporated as a subsidiary.

enough as a mining engineer in Sarajevo. Before he had time to show his business talent, the Nazis invaded the country, and Blum spent most of the war in concentration camps, from which he finally escaped in time to join the Partisans. During the Stalinist period after the war he held down several responsible jobs in the government-operated power industry, and in 1947 was appointed Deputy Minister of Electricity in Belgrade.

But Blum had no stomach for bureaucracy, particularly the kind then prevailing, and looked around for better opportunities for his talents and vision. In 1951, shortly after the passage of the first decentralization law, which turned over all enterprises to workers' councils, he returned to Sarajevo. Almost any Yugoslav who can raise the money can start an enterprise and then, if he has more than five employees, form a council. Blum persuaded a bank to finance him, got together a small staff, and founded a company he called Elektroprojekt, to design electric power systems and transmission lines. Blum, however, wasn't happy merely designing electric systems. The money and the action were in building them, and he had no trouble in making his council see that this was the thing to do. But it meant getting into manufacturing, a long and expensive process. So he decided to look around for small and medium-sized enterprises with the skills he needed. "There was no sense in creating new competition," he explains. The first company that joined Elektroprojekt was a 400-man outfit called Elektroremont, also in Sarajevo, which specialized in repairing electrical equipment.

Soon Blum again demonstrated his ability to move ahead of events. At that time, most if not all Yugoslav enterprises elected only a single council. When one company merged with another, only one council survived; and trade unions, politicians, and others began to denounce mergers as bad for the self-management system. So Elektroprojekt began to set up separate councils in its plants and offices. The process was nearly completed by 1958, when the company changed its name to Energoinvest. By 1965, when a law was passed compelling all companies to decentralize their councils, Energoinvest had thirty. Each plant was therefore technically autonomous, free to secede from the group at any time.

JOIN US AND MAKE MONEY

Just to keep itself together, therefore, Energoinvest has had to make each affiliate much better off in the federation than it would be on its own. So it built up an organization that offers prospective affiliates advantages they could get nowhere else. As early as the middle 1950's,

Blum decided to develop export markets. The Yugoslav market was too small to allow economies of scale, and was still without a really competitive price structure. Blum realized what the Soviet Union and some other East European countries have still to recognize: modern industrial management in a closed society is a contradiction in terms. The only way to become an economic organization was to fight for business in world markets.

The group's first customers were Czechoslovakia and East Germany. Then, as Yugoslavia developed relations with "non-aligned" countries like itself, the company began to develop markets in the Middle East, the Far East, Africa, Pakistan, and eventually even in Europe and North America. Last year it sold cranes to Krupp and refinery equipment to a U.S. supply house, and, competing against the Japanese, it won a $1,500,000 contract to build a penstock for British Columbia Hydro & Power Authority. Exports in 1970 came to nearly 40 percent of revenues; the company's goal is 50 percent.

Energoinvest has also built up staff service departments unmatched anywhere in its part of the world. It maintains four research-and-development centers, including a new high-voltage laboratory; together these centers cost between $4 million and $5 million a year. Other services are provided by a large modern computer center, five designing departments, central export and purchasing departments, and a central financial department complete with a bank that handles all the group's money and financial transactions. And the company has ensured a steady supply of young executive talent, probably the scarcest industrial resource in Yugoslavia, by financing more than 3,100 scholarships at Sarajevo and a few other universities.

So the company's pitch to prospective affiliates can be summed up this way: "We ask you to adhere to our basic program, and charge you 4 to 6 percent of your gross, depending on the kinds of products you make. We have access to money, support all kinds of expertise, and can help you export in a way that nobody else can. If we cannot boost your profits in a couple of years, you are free to withdraw from our group."

Most affiliations have turned out very well indeed. Back in the early 1960's, for example, the company got interested in a plant at Črnuče, a suburb of Ljubljana, the capital of Slovenia. This factory made some 300 different electrical devices, from insulators to circuit breakers and transformer parts, but its sales were only about $600,000, its payroll totaled about 170, and its profitability and wages were minimal. Precisely because it was so disorganized, Energoinvest's investigators saw possibilities in it.

At that time the local government had to approve all such deals lest they result in monopoly. The authorities at Ljubljana turned the proposal down, not because they smelled monopoly, but they could not understand how those backward Bosnians, who had languished for centuries under the Turks, could possibly help progressive Slovenians, who had known industrialization under the Austrians for a century. After a second look, however, the authorities thought better of the proposal and let it go through. Today the plant at Črnuče, modernized and expanded, specializes in large transformers. It is doing a $7-million business, 60 percent for export, and it employs 420 people. Capacity and production are being increased by 30 percent.

The one Energoinvest affiliation that went wrong was the Obod consumer appliance enterprise at Cetinje, the ancient capital of Montenegro. When Obod joined the group nearly two years ago, Energoinvest rejoiced. The country's second-biggest appliance outfit, Obod was turning out several hundred thousand washing machines, refrigerators, and stoves a year, and it seemed the perfect complement to Energoinvest's consumer-products line. It also had a big export potential. But last summer Obod seceded. Just what happened neither party will say, except that the arrangement was ended by mutual agreement. Insiders' gossip is that Energoinvest is happier about the divorce than Obod.

DON'T EAT UP YOUR FUTURE

Probably the most arresting of Blum's achievements is the way he has handled the workers' council system. That system, it so happens, is now under severe criticism by Yugoslav workers, economists, journalists, and politicians. Much of the carping represents the exuberance of a once totalitarian country now enjoying almost complete freedom of speech and press, but some has a basis in fact. Yugoslav workers and directors often find themselves taking very different views of what is good for the business. Unlike a capitalist enterprise, which tends primarily to maximize the earnings on investment, the self-managed enterprise tends to maximize profit *per worker*. Therefore councils are reluctant to hire people for research market analysis, or other "unproductive" jobs because these outlays reduce, at least temporarily, profits and hence wages per worker. Thus the council tends to take the short-term point of view, while the conscientious director takes the longer view. Blum has estimated that wages could be raised across the board by as much as 15 percent if his "investments" in research and other long-term intangibles were abolished. But this means, as Yugoslavs say, the workers would "eat up their future."

In many enterprises, workers feel the decisions that count are made not by them but by the "technocrats." This may be the fault of the council itself. A council's president, if he is to discharge his job effectively, has to spend practically all his spare time familiarizing himself with the many and often highly complex problems of his company. Frequently he does not or cannot spend the time. Sometimes the fault is with the directors; they and their aides do not pass on enough information to the council chief, or they even go out of their way to confuse him. Occasionally, on the other hand, the councils don't care what management does so long as wages rise. The new director of one company turned its fortunes around in short order, nearly doubling wages per worker. But he also dipped deeply in the company till, built a fine new house, bought a sports car, and made expensive "business" trips abroad. A lot of workers knew what was happening, but nobody gave a damn. It wasn't until the press got hold of the story that the council ousted him.

As a result, there seems to be a movement to let the trade unions play a more important role. Yugoslav trade unions, in the main, dispense broad wisdom to the workers, and adjudicate minor grievances and misunderstandings. Although workers often stage spontaneous sit-downs and walkouts when they get mad at their councils or directors, genuine strikes are rare; you don't strike against yourself. Some party leaders, however, are now arguing that self-management will not work well until the unions are empowered to call a strike. To many Yugoslavs this prospect is dismaying. They have studied the U.S. and European labor unions, and are familiar with featherbedding, make-work rules, monopoly mentality, and the propensity to paralyze a nation's industry at the drop of a hat. Such practices, Yugoslavs observe, reduce both production and productivity; and since labor in the last analysis pays the bill, they are really antilabor.

It is certainly hard to find anyone in Energoinvest even mildly critical about the workers' council system. Alija Alić, president of the company's central trade union, argues that the chief function of the union is to educate workers about the system, and that trouble arises only when they have fallen down on their jobs. Making the unions the sole custodians of workers' rights, he believes, would reduce productivity and wages, and abet alienation. Alić's motto, which he has lettered on banners and hung in appropriate places: *Samoupravljanje—naše, juče, danas i sutra—*"self-management, ours yesterday, today, and tomorrow." Such views seem to prevail in the shops. Buttonholed while working on the floor, Bosko Marković, council president in the thermal-apparatus factory near Sarajevo, said, "There is nothing better in sight."

Blum himself says the current discontent is concentrated in enterprises that are doing badly, often as the result of recent liquidity crises that have left many companies short of cash. Some managers moreover refuse to accept the fact that the councils legally possess close to absolute power, and are forever trying to test that power. "The only way to release creative energy," he says, "is to enable as many people as possible to share in decisions about their work."

What is more, Blum argues that the workers' management system facilitates rather than hinders his job. Speaking before a symposium in Amsterdam two years ago, he declared flatly that it is easier for a Yugoslav director to function efficiently than it is for managers in the West, who face the incessant and arbitrary opposition of trade unions, or managers in the Soviet Union, who are "subject to the assessments and wills of government bureaucrats."

Blum has, of course, seen to it that Energoinvest's efficiency and wages are above average; when a company performs well, its council tends to be agreeable. But what Blum really demonstrates is that there is no substitute for strong, intelligent leadership. Even Karl Marx, in one of his deviations into practicality, wrote that an orchestra composed of great players still needs a director.

YOU CAN'T BE DEMOCRATIC ABOUT TECHNOLOGY

In keeping his councils thoroughly informed about everything, Blum does not dispense soul butter. He lays the facts on the line candidly, and explains why his proposals are best for the company and therefore its workers. "We are living in the world," Blum says, "and the councils must adapt to the world." In February, 1966, when his job was up for election, he pursued this theme with almost startling candor. Much of the talk concerned the effect of new technology on industrial relations. "We must make a determined break with the notion that further development of technology is the job of workers' management," he said. "Technology is not a matter for democratic discussion." To create the right conditions so that "our people can manage technological means," he continued, the right people must be put in the right jobs, and "we should not accept the opinions of people that lead us into egalitarianism . . . People must be paid what they deserve; key executive jobs must be attractive from the standpoint of pay."

Blum went on to discuss the most unpopular proposal he has ever put forward—modernization of the company's working hours. For centuries, people in what is now Yugoslavia have gone to work at 6:00 or 7:00 A.M. and knocked off early in the afternoon. Now that the country is enjoying an abundance of goods, these hours are still popular, for they allow people to moonlight and earn extra money to buy more goods.

But as Blum told his council, "I am certain that this does not make for efficiency. I am not talking through my hat. The whole modern world begins working at 9:00 A.M. This has not been arranged out of spite or for any other silly reasons, but purely and simply for purposes of greater productivity ... Why should we not be the first in our country, or among the first, to change things for the better?" They now are. Energoinvest workers report to work at 9:00 A.M. and go home at 4:30 P.M. Blum was re-elected as managing director without opposition and is now completing the first year of yet another four-year term.

For some time Blum had been aware that Energoinvest needed a great deal of reorganization. The company lacked a marketing strategy; there is incidentally, no word in Serbo-Croatian for marketing. In deciding what to produce, a plant too often used to decide what it *could* produce rather than what the market wanted. So in 1968 Blum appointed an aide to investigate management-consultant firms and find one that could help Energoinvest. Meantime, he addressed his councils on the subject of organization, strategy, and expertise. As the following paraphrase of his talk suggests, he pulled no punches: "We are suffering from the old Yugoslav disease of not being able to implement decisions properly. As good as we are at improvising, our organization is defective. Social relationships in Yugoslavia may be different from those in other countries, but our enterprises must be organized like those in other developed societies. This is a matter of expertise. Since we do not have it, let us be frank, we must buy it, just as we buy licenses to make products patented elsewhere. What is more, we must buy the best. That we can do only in the U.S. Even though it will cost a lot of money, we must take the step if we are to expand our prosperity. Our motto must be the liquidation of amateurism."

A few months later the central council voted to hire McKinsey & Co., even though several other companies would have been cheaper. McKinsey assembled a group headed by a young American named Charles Shaw, who had been born in Zagreb and could speak Serbo-Croatian, and the group fared to Sarajevo to look things over. Blum told them they faced a tougher job than they perhaps realized, and not to underestimate its cost. Presumably they did not. Over the past two years it has cost Energoinvest $300 to $600 a day per consultant, for an average of five men, and the job will probably need the attention of one or two men for two or three more years. Such compensation was unheard of in Yugoslavia, and to many seemed antisocialist. When the news reached Belgrade, there was an uproar. Mladen Korać, a prominent Serbian economist, all but accused Blum of going capitalist.

Most if not all the McKinsey analysis and suggestions have been followed closely, and everybody seems satisfied, not to say enthusiastic, about the results. McKinsey divided the forty-one affiliates into six groups, each with certain staff functions, and each with a general manager, who among other things would assume a lot of responsibilities that hitherto found their way to Blum himself. It clarified and rearranged the general staff functions and sold the service departments on the notion of actively selling *their* services to the affiliates. Since the parent Energoinvest has no capital and its revenues depend on the payments made to it by its affiliates, this would give it additional resources. At all times the McKinsey group stressed the importance of thinking in terms of the market—of emulating the best in the West, developing new ideas and products, practicing better pricing, and investing only in capital goods that turn out products somebody is willing to pay a remunerative price for. Right now McKinsey is helping with long-range divisional marketing strategies.

The group also analyzed the properties plant by plant. Energoinvest's largest factory is the electrical-equipment plant at Lukavica, near Sarajevo. "Before McKinsey," says Hamdja Djuliman, twenty-nine, director of manufacturing at Lukavica, "this plant was divided into ten sections, each a little factory, and there were a lot of duplications. Now there is only one factory, with one part devoted to high-voltage and the other to low-voltage equipment. The new scheme hasn't made us all rich at once, but everything is improved."

One potentially profitable byproduct of the McKinsey operation is that Energoinvest is developing a cadre of what Shaw describes as capable and enthusiastic management specialists. So it may not be long before Energoinvest will be able to set up a management department to peddle expertise to other Yugoslav firms.

THE GREAT WAGE INFLATION

Blum's success with self-management does not dispose of all the criticisms of it. Moscow, describing self-management as "anarchosyndicalism," abhors it and the freedoms that accompany it, just as it abhorred similar freedoms in Czechoslovakia before it snuffed them out in 1968. On its own terms, self-management has many defects, at least as now practiced. For one thing, the system is an even greater inflationary force than U.S. and British labor monopolies, for it tends to drive up wages even faster than they do. Wage rates have been rising two to three times as fast as productivity, which has been rising at around 5 to 7 percent. The National Bank, not wanting to create intolerable unemployment, has on the whole gone along with the increase by printing bales of money. In 1968 it increased the money supply by no less than 22 percent; since then it has heroically held the rate down to a great deal less. But prices are still rising at about

15 percent a year, and unemployment is very high—about 7 percent of the nonfarm labor force.

Late in November, the Yugoslav Government froze all prices temporarily. This, of course, creates an awkward situation for a system based on the idea that democratic socialism can be achieved only by letting the workers' councils do as they will, at least in the economic realm. There is still provocative talk, even in government circles, of providing workers with incentives to forgo higher wages by issuing securities such as variable-interest bonds or even stock. For its part, Energoinvest is beefing up its pension system. Since the money for it comes out of profits, the move may dampen wage pressures from workers who otherwise would want all they can get before they retire.

KEEPING AHEAD OF THE TREND

Reacting to the criticism of the council system, the *Skupstina* or National Parliament in Belgrade last year adopted four new constitutional amendments dealing with self-management. Two of the amendments merely reiterate the rights and sovereignty of the councils. The other two are aimed at narrowing some of the unintentional inequities of the system. A worker in factory A, for example, may make twice as much as one in factory B, even though both have exactly the same job. When this discrepancy is the result of efficiency and hard work, it is all right. But often it is a result of market power, or even a monopoly position, with easy or windfall profits.

How the inequities should be dealt with has not yet been specified, but Blum isn't worrying about that very much. Energoinvest is so well run that all its affiliates, after they have been with the company a couple of years, can pay close to the average group wage. What is more, Blum anticipated the changes in the law and drew up a tentative agreement embodying no fewer than thirty-seven proposals for improving Energoinvest's self-management system. Last month these proposals, along with several others suggested by workers' councils, were approved by 91 percent of all the workers who voted.

In general, the agreement calls for some leveling off of profitability. Units with "unutilized" resources will, through the central organization, advance credits to others that need the money, or form joint ventures with them. And units enjoying high prices and profits will put a certain amount in an equalization fund for special group projects that cannot be expected to be profitable immediately.

The Yugoslav economic press has begun to decry the growing power of "big business" and the banks, which supply nearly all industrial capital, and to profess alarm about the growing concentration of the country's resources. Blum's agreement in effect anticipated more of this kind of talk by clarifying, sometimes in great detail, just how the affiliates retain their autonomy. For example, the central organization will handle all financial matters—raise money, pay it out, establish lines of credit at home and abroad. Each affiliate, however, will make its own decisions, within a broad framework of guidelines, about working capital, investment, and the size and disposition of special funds, such as those for housing.

Thus the great Yugoslav experiment goes on. What will the system be like a decade from now? It is possible, but only remotely possible, that advocates of a centrally planned command economy, with the help of Moscow, will get the upper hand. Barring this, the chances are that more strong industrial leaders like Blum, by demonstrating the close relationship between good management and workers' welfare, will make the system work.

JOHN DIEBOLD

Management Can Learn
From Japan

Rather surprisingly, the Japanese business system is now plainly outper-
forming the American business system in some of the most important
respects. Successful American firms may want to learn variants of
Japanese methods. Without suggesting that we need a Commodore
Perry in reverse, it is time to start a debate about which ones to learn.

The two most distinctive and most-frequently-derided features of the
Japanese system are: lifetime employment (*sushin koyo*) for nearly all
the white-collar and many of the permanent blue-collar workers in
big corporations in Japan, and payment by age and length of service
(*nenki jorestu seido*). It is fashionable and polite to say that the Japanese
are changing the system, but they are changing it much less than many
commentators like to suppose. The status and pride of life of a Japanese
employee, therefore, still usually depend almost wholly on the automatic factor, his length of service. (He is "Mr. Noyamura, a university
graduate who has been an executive with the firm since 1953.") His
status is not tied to his present nominal job as "executive vice-president
in charge of marketing circular widgets in Southeast Asia." As a result,
he is not always fighting mainly for the maximum budget for marketing
circular widgets. And he is not personally insulted if technological
change and market experience signal that sales of circular widgets in
Southeast Asia should be run down.

Source: Reprinted from the September 29, 1973 issue of *Business Week* by special permission, pp. 14, 19. © 1973
by McGraw-Hill, Inc.

Americans have always assumed that this Japanese system would have four main bad results, in mounting order of importance:

- Lifetime employment in Japan, it was assumed, would inhibit firms from efficiently trimming payrolls in times of cyclical recession. This is true, but in a modern industrial country, with problems of labor unions, personnel relations, and redundancy pay, it does not matter. Modern corporations are not going to succeed if they are the sort that expect to have to dismiss workers in large numbers during each small downswing.

- Lifetime employment was supposed to make it likely that Japanese firms whose products became technologically obsolete would hang on to making those products with too large labor forces instead of changing step with the times. This has proved to be the opposite of the truth. In an American corporation, changes are likely at some early or late stage to be delayed because they will cut across the interests of some senior and respected executive who is in charge of producing or marketing existing products in the established way. The Japanese system, making one's status depend on length of service instead of on the continued relative importance of one's present job, puts fewer human barriers in the way of diversification.

- The biggest disadvantage of the Japanese system was supposed to be that payment and status by seniority, instead of by achievement, would rob Japanese executives of the incentive to dare and to take risks and even to work. This fear has certainly proved the opposite of the truth. Nearly all Japanese executives (and an extraordinary number of ordinary Japanese shop-floor workers) plainly feel a massive group urge to see their company emulate and beat all competitors. In part, this is a normal pecuniary urge, because if you work in a successful company you will get bigger group bonuses and better group fringe benefits. But in even larger part, it is because the sense of belonging to a proudly successful company is more fun than in belonging to an unsuccessful one. It is common in America to crack jokes at such spectacles as the Matsushita workers singing each morning their company hymn, "Grow, Matsushita, grow, grow, grow." But a team feeling that hymns advance a corporate entity in this way is likely to lead to dynamism and innovation. By contrast, there are positive stagnationist dangers in the equally mystic, though sometimes unadmitted, feelings that commonly develop in American business: group pride in belonging to some craft that ought to be superseded gradually by technological advance, pride in the traditional products which can become obsolescent, attachment to some outdated way of doing things.

- Americans have always liked to believe that Japanese firms are likely to get nowhere because so much of their decision-making is arrived at by consensus, in fairly large meetings where nobody seems willing to show that he is disagreeing too sharply with anybody else. In fact, however, it has become apparent that, in our more competitively hierarchical business establishments in the West, some American and even more European corporations are now very bad at securing adequate participation by middle and lower management in the decision process. The Japanese system whereby everybody pretends politely that he is agreeing with everybody else, even when he is plainly saying something quite different, has to some degree been turned into a rather sophisticated form of middle management communication and even participation. A bright junior Japanese executive who is very keen on some particular innovative idea may now be able to push it through more easily than a junior executive in an American firm. Nobody above him will be afraid that success in this venture will allow the young man to get ahead of himself in the rat race.

As a result of all this, I now suspect the Japanese business system may outperform the American business system in the following fields: making investment decisions that require long lead times and rather lengthy payback periods (e.g., 20-year periods when no American executive expects to be with the same firm, but most 35-year-old Japanese do); introducing very innovative production methods; introducing very innovative training and retraining methods (including much more scientifically programmed and computer-based instruction, which is going to become very important); taking advantage of some, though not all, of the other opportunities that in the next decades will be produced by the computer revolution.

In addition, the Japanese may enjoy a very general advantage in approaching the increasing number of problems where initiatives, even by single companies, should be multiple instead of stereotyped. The Japanese approach to establishing their equivalent of multinational corporations, for instance, may be successfully eclectic and multi-variantly adapted to political conditions in each host country.

I find this a rather frightening list.

The question is: How can American business adopt some of the advantages which have proved to attach to the Japanese system, but do so in a gentle progression and while retaining the advantages of our own system? My feeling is that the main problems can be identified under three heads:

1. **Pains of change.** Remember the story of the Australian aborigine who was given a new boomerang, and killed himself trying to throw the old one away? We have a hierarchical system in most of our big American corporations now, with elements of rat race built into it instead of the Japanese *nenko* system. This can only be changed gradually, but the crucial need is that corporations should regard it as proper that their initiatives should be multiple, instead of each initiative being regarded as most strictly within Mr. So-and-So's province. It may be increasingly important that organization charts, preferably rather untidy ones, be

drawn with this in mind, that words like "unacceptable intrusion" become forbidden, that the biggest black mark against a departmental head should be when his subordinates are not themselves sponsoring and urging new initiatives (including the airing of some with which he disagrees).

2. **New products and investment.** Japan's real GNP has expanded by 10% to 15% in many years. The annual growth in production by its most successful corporations has often been over 25%. A company on that sort of growth path introduces much of its machinery and many of its products brand-new every year. Big Japanese firms, therefore, have large numbers of people wholly engaged in the task of bringing in new projects, and they are now more practiced at it than anybody else. It is no good saying just that American corporations ought to put more people on to the task of planning innovations. What is needed is some change in our business system so that interest in innovation becomes more lively and diffuse. One way toward this may be to make the executives increasingly into participatory entrepreneurs. When there is some proposed new product which the firm has decided—on a narrow balance of advantage—not to make, it might often be worth asking whether anybody in the firm would like to make it himself as an entrepreneurial venture in partnership with the firm. The corporation, having judged the quality of the employee who is bidding to start the venture, would specify the size of the stake it is itself willing to risk (distribution facilities, office space, research material, and probably a stated willingness to take the executive back into his place in the corporate hierarchy if the venture fails). It will be argued that this is not the Japanese system. It isn't, but it would be an American-style move in the direction of achieving the same results.

3. **Corporate loyalty.** The ordinary Japanese makes most of his friends through his work, he is happiest when he is with them, and this has extraordinary consequences: Many (perhaps most) Japanese foolishly do not take the full annual holiday to which they are entitled, and they admirably feel a sense of enjoyment with each achievement of their firm. Here again, it is not possible to establish this feeling in American corporations simply by organizational restructuring. (Anyway, it is not in all respects desirable to do so.) But, as only one example of paternalism, middle-grade Japanese executives generally regard it as their job to watch out whether any of their employees look lonely or unhappy. While such concern could easily become vulgarly intrusive, it also could be a sophisticated form of personnel relations.

There are many other aspects of the Japanese business system that deserve study and some thought in the West. They include the generally supportive relations between the Japanese bureaucracy and Japanese business. They include the emphasis Japanese trading houses put on understanding the distribution systems employed abroad. They include the capability for constant retraining that springs from the lifetime employment system.

They include many adverse factors as well. Japanese companies are often overstaffed, and they make disgracefully little use of the talents of women; Japan's internal distribution system is most inefficient, and the subcontracting system is sometimes loaded murderously in favor of big business; small Japanese businesses are influenced too much by nepotism; and too many Japanese businessmen engage in very wasteful high living on business expenses. A notable shortcoming is that Japanese decision-making is ineffective in crisis situations—for example, in reacting to the yen problem. But nobody is suggesting America should copy the worst features of the Japanese system. We should just start thinking very carefully about the features that have succeeded, and how we could emulate some of them.

LOUIS KRAAR

I Have Seen China— and They Work

Soon after entering China, a visitor begins to see that its methods of running the economy are different from those of any other nation. Throughout the rest of the world, in both industrialized and underdeveloped countries, the basic thrust of development is to substitute capital for labor. In China, this is a secondary theme. At every level, China mobilizes its abundant resources of labor—from a population that amounts to nearly a quarter of mankind—to compensate for a scarcity of capital.

In the South China countryside I saw farmers wading barefoot through brilliant green rice paddies to toss handfuls of fertilizer. Along roadways, men and women pull carts or pedal trishaws heaped with grain, petroleum drums, or scrap metal. Neighborhood workshops organize every able-bodied person not otherwise employed. One group of housewives in Canton (or Kwangchow as the Chinese call it) takes oily rags that industrial plants have used to wipe machinery, cleans them, and returns both the cloths and the extracted oil for re-use.

BLURRED AUTHORITY

The dedication and discipline required for all this exertion are fostered by a relentless process of indoctrination, which stresses psychic rather than material rewards for individuals. Workers are endlessly

Source: Reprinted from the August 1972 issue of *Fortune* by special permission; Copyright © 1972 Time Inc.

exhorted to show their revolutionary zeal by increasing production. The ubiquitous thoughts of Chairman Mao Tse-tung are supposed to provide the motivating doctrine, and the rigorous programs of Maoist study for the entire work force do appear to give most Chinese a strong sense of purpose. But they try to apply the often vague or ambiguous doctrines in ways that yield practical results. The Pearl River Paper Mill, for instance, follows the Maoist principle of relying on ordinary workers to help devise technical improvements, but one of the managers emphasizes: "Only the rational ideas are accepted. Before adopting anything, we first make experiments."

Management, the Chinese claim, is in the hands of the "broad masses." Every factory and farm is nominally controlled by a "revolutionary committee" of workers, party members, and Army personnel. Administrators and engineers now work closely with those on the assembly line. And while China operates its economy according to a state plan, central controls are sufficiently loose to allow each factory's committee considerable autonomy in setting its own targets for producing goods, raising capital, and building production equipment. Some Chinese are more equal than others, of course, but the system of participatory management seems to give everyone at least the sense of helping to shape basic decisions. It also provides a typically Asian forum for smoothing over conflicts and disagreements through lengthy discussions.

The blurring of formal structures of authority is facilitated by a pervasive egalitarianism. Official titles and other status symbols are avoided. In this ostentatiously classless society, a boss wears the same drab, baggy garb as laborers, and is officially ranked only as a "responsible person." There is also a remarkable degree of equality in consumption. The Chinese share a lean, but gradually improving, standard of living. Austere housing and nearly free medical care are generally available. Workers do not own automobiles, but neither do factory directors.

Within this egalitarian atmosphere, the system often demands hard toil and seems to evoke remarkable diligence. I watched some 1,500 young men and women "volunteers" from Shunte County's agricultural communes patiently wielding little steel hammers mounted on long, thin bamboo staves to break up stones for a new power and irrigation project. The workers are repeatedly told they are "the masters of the country," and loudspeakers set up around the torrid work site blare out strains of Chinese revolutionary symphonies to inspire sweaty efforts. "The people cannot wait for machines, so we use our own hands and indigenous tools," explains a ranking "responsible person" attired in plain cotton work clothes. Although the project was begun only last year, it was able to draw as many as 5,000 peasants during slack periods in farm work and now is well on the way to completion.

In keeping with a national policy to rely on local factories, ten generators for the power project have been built and installed by the county's own small electrical-machinery workshop. At the factory I found a dark, hot, noisy, Dickensian atmosphere. Two men wearing ordinary work fatigues, cloth gloves, and gauze masks hand-carry a bucket of molten steel clear across the shop to pour into sand molds. Women patiently wind each electric coil. The workers proudly show production machines they pieced together from scrap and castoffs of larger plants.

A network of these small, local industries supplements major factories and helps provide jobs for the endless tide of young people entering the labor force. In Canton's Bao Gong neighborhood, I visited a group of residents who have set up a household facility for assembling semiconductor diodes used in electric meters. Two people were trained at a large state-run factory and then instructed others. Bao Gong operates thirteen other simple cooperatives that serve as the Maoist equivalents of subcontractors to larger plants. Also, small rural factories make a variety of products for their own communities. This dispersal of industry is in keeping with Maoist doctrine, but it also serves important practical purposes. It eases burdens on China's weak transportation system, and it restrains the flow of peasants into urban centers.

EXTRA EFFORTS FOR THE REVOLUTION

Throughout the Chinese economic system, a great deal of rationality is mingled with the abstract thoughts of Chairman Mao. Managers make use of such practical concepts as cost and even profit. I particularly noticed this at the Kwangchow Bicycle Plant, where workers in a series of converted old machine shops are increasingly mechanizing the production process. Kuo Chiang-swea, vice chairman of the factory's revolutionary committee, explained the moves in terms that any capitalist counterpart could appreciate: "Our Kapok brand twenty-eight-inch model is now very popular in the countryside, but our production cost is still higher than other factories." To expand output and reduce unit cost, the plant has designed its own equipment for electroplating and spray-painting parts. (Young women workers, however, still must put ball bearings into the wheel assemblies by hand.) The improvements have shaved production costs by 6 percent to about $32 per bike; consumers pay a standard state-fixed price of about $47.

Vice Chairman Kuo and his comrades receive no extra financial reward for extra efforts. Salaries are set by government on an industry-wide basis, and since the recent Cultural Revolution, bonuses and overtime pay have been eliminated. "We do not improve efficiency for the purpose of increasing our own wages, but consider it more of a contribution to the socialist revolution," Kuo maintains.

Careful accounting is made of costs and receipts at the bicycle plant. It must pay "fraternal factories" for tires and a few other parts the plant cannot produce. "Yes, we make a profit," the vice chairman reported with undisguised satisfaction. Last year the plant earned about $3 million. It was not clear whether the concept of profit took account of depreciation or simply represented income minus outgo. In any event, higher authorities allowed the plant to keep $120,000 for investment in new equipment. The rest of the profit was turned over to the state. China (unlike even the Soviet Union) levies no personal or corporate income taxes, and earnings of industries constitute a major source of government revenue.

The workings of the Chinese economic system are visible on a larger scale at the Kwangchow Heavy Machine Tool Plant. At the entrance a billboard proclaims in bold red letters, "Unite to win even greater victories." Within the huge, fenced compound, 5,000 employees work in three shifts turning out equipment for mining, petroleum refineries, chemical plants, and sugar mills. Along with keeping industrial production going around the clock, the factory maintains agricultural plots for raising pigs and growing vegetables, dormitories for unmarried workers, eating facilities, and an array of anti-aircraft guns discreetly shrouded in canvas. And it serves as a center for subtle group dynamics and political action—directed toward motivating workers to increase output.

Members of the factory's revolutionary committee greeted me at the doorway of a hulking, grayish brick administration building and led the way down its gloomy corridors, past roomfuls of clerks clicking off accounts on abacuses. In a conference room, portraits of Marx, Engels, Lenin, Stalin, and Mao looked down sternly from the white plaster walls. Two young women in pigtails quickly padded over the concrete floor to pour tea. They were factory workers and they sat down and joined the discussion.

Chang Chow-kwong, a member of the committee, explained the fundamental management philosophy. "Before the Cultural Revolution," he said, "directors and engineers managed production. Now we rely on the broad masses of the people—the workers, who are masters of the country." Politics, he went on, plays a commanding part in motivating the workers. "We use Mao Tse-tung's thoughts to educate the workers and staff members to grasp revolution and promote production."

ENGINEERS AGAINST THE MASSES

Behind these incessantly repeated stock phrases lies a complex system that does allow a lot of worker participation in management. All important decisions for the plant are made by the factory's revolutionary committee, a supposedly representative "leading body" of twenty-one workers, eight party members, and two Army men. Administrators and engineers, including all committee members, are expected to spend a full day each week performing manual labor. "In this way, they're more closely linked with the masses," claims an administrator. In less doctrinaire terms, the practice thrusts managers into continuing contact with the realities of the production process.

Workers, moreover, fully discuss every management problem with representatives of the revolutionary committee before any decision is reached—a procedure that helps laborers identify with the broader aims of the plant and quietly smothers disagreements. Ordinary workers also participate in other managerial duties, such as helping to supervise financial operations and quality-control measures. Some even serve alongside engineers in the development of new production machinery and techniques. The so-called "technical innovation teams" help the plant to make the most of its meager resources. One workshop, for instance, assembled a metal-planing machine from scrap steel and spare parts, including the gears of an old truck. "We have a shortage of big equipment and our mechanical level is still not high," a technician said, "so we combined modern and indigenous methods."

The machine-tool plant adopted cooperative management after a siege of political action during the Great Proletarian Cultural Revolution, the disruptive ideological rumble that went on from 1966 to 1969. As factory officials recall, the plant plunged into an intense period of "struggle and mass revolutionary criticism" in 1967. Taking their cue from the nationwide movement, workers held countless meetings, wrote polemical articles, and plastered workshops with posters—all to denounce "the revisionist line that depends on a few experts to run the factory."

The antirevisionists concentrated bitter attacks on the five engineers who until then had solely managed all production processes. "They would not accept the rational suggestions of the workers," says a staff member who participated in the upheaval. "The initiative and creativeness of the broad masses of workers could not be brought into play."

Management responsibility shifted to the revolutionary committee in March, 1968. One incident that workers now like to recount is how they rebelled against rules the engineers established in the stainless-steel workshop—rules that forbade casting operations without the presence of technicians, at night, or on windy or rainy days. Once those restrictions were dropped, the plant found it could easily increase output of stainless steel because casting could be done at any time.

During the radical reform drive, which Mao instigated to shake up China's bureaucratic elite, many party officials and engineers were removed from managerial positions to spend six months to a year as ordinary laborers in the plant. Since this "re-education" they have returned to management—but with new obligations. "Every week I spend one day in the workshop," explains the former vice director, Hwang Siang. "Before the Cultural Revolution, we were supposed to do manual labor, but frankly I did not do it as often as now. Since the establishment of the revolutionary committee, we adhere to this as a system."

Hwang, who has worked in the machine-tool factory for twenty-two of his fifty-seven years, is now vice chairman of its management committee. Although back in a top executive slot, he wears gray cotton work clothes and sandals without socks. He pointedly refers to his "worker orgin." As he recalls the turmoil of 1967, counterrevolutionary elements "instigated people to stop production." Management found a remedy: "These people were deceived, so we carried on education to raise their consciousness."

The Army's presence undoubtedly helped the learning process too. When the Cultural Revolution got out of hand, Mao ordered the People's Liberation Army to move into every enterprise and restore order. Though inconspicuous, the military men still exercise widespread authority—at the Kwangchow machine-tool plant, among other places. The "most responsible person" at the plant, and its chairman, is an Army representative whom I was never able to meet. Confronted with this apparent contradiction in the principle of management by the masses, a member of the committee blandly says: "We can learn what we don't know through practice. After the chairman came to the factory, he integrated himself with the broad masses."

IN MEMORY OF MAO

The broad masses as well as the integrated chairman participate in the factory's most crucial decision, the setting of the annual production target. This process involves a combination of participatory democracy and Communist political manipulation. In the third quarter of the year the municipal revolutionary committee that governs Canton proposes a tentative draft target for the machine-tool plant. This initial plan allows ample leeway for the factory to gain status by enlarging the production goal. In 1970, for instance, the municipal committee recommended a 30 percent increase in output over the previous year. Through a series of discussions in the workshops, employees at the machine-tool plant realized that improved equipment could enable them to expand output 100 percent. The revolutionary committee surveyed the shops to make sure the goal was realistic and then accepted it. The plant overfulfilled the higher target. That, anyway, is how people there tell the story now.

Once the production goal is officially set, the factory committee mounts a relentless effort that draws together national pride, Maoist ideology, and practical production advice to mobilize the work force. "We take measures to guarantee fullfillment of the targets," says Lu Yuan-mei, the slight, articulate woman who is No. 2 in the administrative department. She wears the same loose-fitting trousers and jacket as male colleagues—and seems a bit more self-confident than most of them. "Every month," she says, "we give the production targets to workers in different shops. Simultaneously, we let them know the significance of fulfilling the targets. We explain that it's not only to build up our own country, but that they have an international duty to support revolution." Each production line also gets specific guidance on its part of the production process.

In practice, this approach appears to prod the work force into giving its utmost effort. In the plant's No. 1 Workshop—which Chairman Mao personally inspected sixteen years ago—a team was recently ordered to develop a new vertical lathe for production of mining equipment. The workers were fed elaborate explanations of how important their tasks would be in supporting the vital growth of China's iron and steel industry. Higher-ups endowed the lathe with special significance by proclaiming it a factory monument to mark the anniversary of Mao's visit. A few model workers, it is said, became so fired up with the mission that they stayed on the job for twenty hours at a stretch.

"THE SWEETNESS OF TODAY"

Political manipulation to inspire worker effort is a pervasive and insistent aspect of life in China. Even the songs I heard children singing in the factory kindergarten promote the ideals of unselfish devotion to the state and the satisfaction of hard work. Upon joining the machine-tool plant at sixteen, new workers divide their first month equally between workshop duties and special classes. The young people are drilled in Maoist principles and given down-to-earth lectures by older workers who recall their own personal hardships in pre-Communist China. "These young people know nothing of past sufferings," maintains Comrade Lu. "Veteran workers let them know the sweetness of today through comparisons with life before liberation."

Workers who reveal inadequate "class-consciousness" by showing up late at the factory or performing jobs poorly are singled out for special treatment. Older workers visit their homes to provide what is called "patient ideological education." In practice, this amounts to a fierce form of political and social pressure that never lets up until the errant employee falls into line. Committee members profess to find it beyond belief that boredom and apathy are a problem in some American factories.

Psychological prodding is also built into the routine of every production team. Members of a team work together in the shop forty-eight hours a week and spend the compulsory four and a half hours a week studying together. The study sessions review Maoist works, discuss current events, and devise specific means for meeting production targets. Leaders try to relate all of this to the tasks at hand. Peking's admission to the United Nations, for example, served as a rallying point for urging the factory toward greater efforts to show that China was a nation worthy of the support it received. The factory's well-staffed political department guides the study groups in party policies and provides topical material. Every worker seemed completely conversant with details of the Shanghai communiqué issued at the end of President Nixon's visit to China. The political department also seeks out examples of model workers and glorifies their accomplishments—both as a reward to the individuals and as an example for others to emulate.

With all these vigorous nonmaterial incentives acting upon the Chinese, material incentives are decidedly modest. As part of a national wage raise gradually extending to all factories, the average pay at Kwangchow Machine Tool recently rose by $1.20 a month, to $26.80. On that income a worker subsists on a level that cannot by any means be considered dire poverty. For one thing, he pays no income taxes or major medical expenses. What's more, the Chinese pricing system (along with rationing of essential foods and cotton cloth) assures that salaries readily cover necessities and leave a surplus for saving to buy relatively expensive consumer durables, such as a bicycle or radio. The average worker with a family pays about $2 monthly rent, including water and electricity, about $6 for food, and the simple people's costume that almost everyone wears costs only a few dollars. Shops are well stocked with textiles and basic household goods at low prices that have largely remained steady for a decade. A sewing machine or bicycle, on the other hand, costs slightly under two months' wages. Even so, the spread of consumer goods is clearly visible—village homes with sewing machines, teen-agers taking snapshots with Chinese-made cameras, workers with shiny new Shanghai brand wristwatches.

Despite the egalitarian tone, there are significant inequalities in pay. At the machine-tool plant, new employees start at $16 per month, an experienced hand gets about $39, and Vice Chairman Hwang $59.60. He seemed perfectly willing to tell me his salary in a room filled with lower-paid workers. Factory managers say that the long-term goal is to make the pay scale more nearly equal.

There is an even greater disparity of incomes between industrial workers and peasants, who constitute 85 percent of the population. The collective farms pay members according to their contribution and some intangible measure of ideological development; cash incomes sometimes run as low as one-sixth of factory wages, but peasants supplement earnings by raising much of their own food and gaining extra "work points" through participation in other commune efforts. On a larger scale, Peking's currently moderate economic strategy is to provide agriculture with larger amounts of fertilizer and farm machinery. State prices on these items were slashed last year, while farmers received more for peanuts, sugar cane, and other cash crops. Eventually, the Chinese figure, bigger inputs of modern farm technology will raise peasant incomes. And the government is banking heavily on small rural industries to make the means more readily available.

LEAP FORWARD TRACTORS

In Shunte County, a lush farming area in the Pearl River Delta of Kwangtung Province, a network of small manufacturing plants turn out much of the equipment used on the agricultural communes. "We're carrying out the revolutionary spirit of self-reliance," asserts Chiu Tan, an official in the county's industrial department. These county manufacturing units are helping to modernize agriculture by closely gearing operations to the particular needs of the locality.

One plant has mobilized 520 workers—nearly half of them women—to make water pumps, crop sprayers (described as "artificial rain makers"), and other farm equipment. The factory has just started assembling ten-horsepower Leap Forward brand "walking tractors." They are so called because farmers walk the machines through fields for plowing. The ten people's communes in the county provide a captive market for the plant's machinery. But the Chinese have their own form of consumerism. Under a policy launched during the Cultural Revolution, local plants must make certain their products are completely acceptable to commune customers. "At first, our tractors were not up to the standard," acknowledges a county official. The first batch drew complaints from peasants that the plowing-depth controls tended to stick; the factory recalled the tractors to work out the kinks and is now finally ready to assemble a hundred units this year.

Although the local factories use fairly primitive methods (such as hand-forging metal parts), they obviously help spread the use of modern equipment throughout the countryside. Farm machinery, electric generators, and water-control equipment can be seen in wide use at the county's communes. At Lo Lui People's Commune, most of the 17,000 households have electricity, its leaders claim, and a day's observations around the 12,000-acre spread indicate that this is probably true.

The commune—once pushed as a giant basic production unit—is now mainly an administrative center with a market and small processing facilities. Lo Lui, for instance, cultivates silkworms and sends cocoons to a county factory for processing into thread. Actual farming is performed by "production teams" in each village, where peasants cultivate collectively held land as well as tend their smaller privately owned plots. At lunch in the cottage of one peasant family, my host noted that much of the food came from his private plot, and the commune even lends initial capital to households that want to raise their own animals. These deviations from the strict collective system were found to be necessary to increase food production. Communal mess halls and backyard steel furnaces, pushed by Peking during its disastrous and ill-managed Great Leap Forward phase of 1958-60, are no longer part of commune routines.

LIKE A BIG FAMILY

But discipline and sacrifice of personal aspirations to state goals are still very much in evidence, as I discovered in long discussions with several peasant families. Wu Chen-chu, a twenty-seven-year-old peasant in the No. 6 Production Team of the commune's Lu Nan Production Brigade, shares with his sister an austere but immaculately clean three-room brick cottage. Sitting in his whitewashed bedroom, which doubles as the living room, he maintains, "Our lives have been getting better and better." But Wu's daily routine is still far from easy. Each morning he rises at six and works in collective fields for four and a half hours. He returns home for a lunch of fish, rice, vegetables, and eggs, and is free to cultivate his own crops for a while. In midafternoon he returns to collective duties for several more hours. His sister works in the commune's silkworm-cultivation center.

Their combined annual cash earnings come to about $440, which is supplemented by fruits, vegetables, chickens, and pigs raised on the land around their home. Questioned about personal ambitions, Wu professed none beyond service to the state. "I'm a farmer and a commune member. Without the country, which is like a big family, what am I?"

This is a characteristic voice of the new China. It is a voice so remote from traditional American values that a visitor from the U.S. cannot fully grasp the Maoist system, much less judge it. The Chinese dedication to rigorous toil to build up their country certainly seems admirable—all the more so because in the U.S. affluence has so widely eroded the will to work and pride in manual labor. It's clear, however, that most Chinese have no alternative but to respond to the constant pressures for arduous effort.

Despite deep differences in values and economic systems, the Chinese are making a determined effort to carry out the directive of Premier Chou En-lai that China and the U.S. should "learn from each other." Everyone from party leaders down to young factory workers and peasants has thoroughly studied the joint communiqué issued at the close of President Nixon's visit. Individual Chinese are groping toward trying to learn from the U.S. even though their knowledge of it is even more hazy than Americans' knowledge of China. At the Kwangchow Heavy Machine Tool Plant, a revolutionary committee member told me apologetically: "I'm very sorry now that we still don't understand each other well, so it's hard to say what we should learn from you." And it's hard for an American visitor to say what we should learn from China.

VII | LOOKING AHEAD

In this last section we do not look ahead in the sense of making predictions or forecasts. Even the most casual reading of the material in the preceding sections would reveal the folly of attempting to predict management in the future. Rather, in this section, we look at longer range issues, matters of continuing importance which have not been fully focused upon.

In "New Needs and New Approaches" Drucker begins by noting that change and adaptation are continuing, never-ending organizational processes. New forms of organization supersede older ones; new forms of management supplant established ones. Looking at this progression, he highlights some basic things which can be learned from the experience and also uncovers some things which he claims need to be unlearned.

But is there all that much change? Perrow, in his article "Is Business Really Changing?" seriously questions this. Basically, he asks whether some of the things we observe really are evidence for the changes we think are occurring. Perrow does not say that change is not occurring, but rather that we may be misunderstanding it.

One point in Perrow's critique is that we may presume connections between an organization and its environment, or between parts of an organization, that do not exist. A central connection assumed and described by managers, if we are to believe what they say, is that performance should be linked with pay. Murthy and Salter point out that there is not much of a relationship between what chief executives earn and the financial performance of their companies. This finding raises a host of questions: If not on financial performance of the company, what *is* the basis for rewarding chief executives? Or perhaps more pointedly: What *should be* the basis for rewarding executives and managers?

Questions about compensation, social responsibility, and many other issues mean that the role of managers, particularly those at the top of organizations, is becoming increasingly demanding and difficult. Carl Burgen points out, in "Scenario for Tomorrow's Chief Executive," that all this may give future generations of managers reason to question whether or not they want to cope with it all.

For some managers, the answer is no, at least unless they receive more support and protection than they are currently getting. For these and other reasons, Ross-Skinner reports that managers in Europe are doing the unthinkable: forming unions. Some of the reasons he notes grow from conditions special to Europe, but not all. Will forces and changes such as those noted in this book make the work of management so unattractive that people turn to unions to make the work more tolerable, not only in Europe but elsewhere?

We end this collection with an article that looks ahead in an entirely different way, by looking at some of the newer knowledge and ideas about how our minds work. Leavitt, in the second part of his article "Beyond the Analytical Manager," takes us on an imaginative, eclectic tour through some of the new material about thinking, consciousness and creativity, and asks us to examine for a minute what connection this could have with the way managers go about their work. At first you may think that some of what he covers seems far fetched; but try the ideas out anyhow. As Drucker points out in the article beginning this section, management is characterized by adapting and making changes. Of necessity, this means coming up with new ways of looking at things which may at first seem strange. Change, adaptation, and flexibility are, in the long run, what the best management in a changing world is all about.

PETER DRUCKER

New Needs and New Approaches

"Of the making of organization studies there is no end"; this might well be the plaint of a modern Psalmist. For organization studies leading to reorganizing companies, divisions, and functions has been one of the more spectacular "growth industries" of the last few decades. Everybody, whether government department or armed service, research laboratory, Catholic diocese, university administration, or hospital—in addition to countless businesses—seems forever to be engaged in reorganizing and being reorganized. Management consultants, thirty or forty years ago, concerned themselves mainly with work study, production flow, and sales training. In the sixties they got the bulk of their assignments and revenues from organization studies, especially of large companies and government departments.

Even the Bank of England, which had admitted no outsiders through its doors for almost three hundred years, was finally reorganized by one of the large American consulting firms; and to add insult to injury, it was a Labour government that, violating the privacy of the "Old Lady of Threadneedle Street," forced an organization study on it.

There are reasons for this interest in organization and for the underlying conviction that inherited organization structures or structures that "just grew" are unlikely to be appropriate to the needs of the enterprise.

Source: "New Needs and New Approaches" (pp. 518-528) from *Management: Tasks, Responsibilities, Practices* by Peter F. Drucker. Copyright © 1973, 1974 by Peter F. Drucker. Reprinted by permission of Harper & Row, Publishers, Inc.

Above all, we have learned the danger of the wrong organization structure. The best structure will not guarantee results and performance. But the wrong structure is a guarantee of nonperformance. All it produces are friction and frustration. The wrong organization puts the spotlight on the wrong issues, aggravates irrelevant disputes, and makes a mountain out of trivia. It accents weaknesses and defects instead of strengths. The right organization structure is thus a prerequisite of performance.

The small enterprise needs right structure just as badly as the big one—and may find it more difficult to work it out.

Only a few short decades ago, such interest as there was in organization was to be found only in very large businesses. The earlier examples, e.g., the example of Alfred P. Sloan's organization structure for General Motors in the early twenties, were all examples of large businesses.

Today, we know that organization becomes critical, above all, when a small business grows into a medium-sized one, and a simple business into a complicated one. The small business that wants to grow, even into only a medium-sized business, therefore has to think through and work out the right organization which enables it at one and the same time to function as a small business and to be able to grow into something bigger. Similarly, the simple one-product, one-market business faces crucial organization problems the moment it adds even a little diversity or complexity.

As recently as the early or middle fifties, managers still had to be convinced that they need to pay attention to the organization of work and the design of organization structure.

The most stubborn opposition to the reorganization of the General Electric Company in the early fifties did not come from those who objected to the seemingly radical proposals. It came from GE managers who did not see the need for doing anything about organization. They admitted that the inherited structure was a crazy, shapeless jumble which the business had long outgrown. "But why waste time on organization?" they asked. "We make and sell turbines, so why bother about who does what?" Ten years later this was still the reaction of many managers when Paul Chambers, as new chief executive of England's Imperial Chemical Industries, tackled the organization structure of another giant that had "just grown."

Today one often needs, on the contrary, to convince managements not to rush into organization studies and not to become enamored of reorganization as an end in itself—or as a substitute for strategic planning and business decisions.

YESTERDAY'S FINAL ANSWERS

But while we have accepted that organization and management structure are crucial, we are outgrowing yesterday's "final answers."

Twice in the short history of management did we have the "final answer" to organization. The first time was around 1910 after Henri Fayol, the French industrialist, had thought through what, to this day, are the functions of a manufacturing company. At that time the manufacturing business was, of course, the truly important organizational problem.

A generation later one could again say that we "knew." Fayol had given "the answer" for the single-product manufacturing business. Alfred P. Sloan, Jr., in organizing General Motors in the early twenties, made the next step. He found "the answer" for organizing the complex and large manufacturing company.* The Sloan approach, which used Fayol's functional organization for the subunits, the individual "divisions," but organized the business itself on the basis of "federal decentralization," that is, on the basis of decentralized authority and centralized control, became after World War II the organization model worldwide, especially for larger organizations.

Another generation later, that is, by the early seventies, it had become clear that the General Motors model was no more adequate to the realities, or at least to the most important challenges in organization, than Fayol's model was adequate to the realities of a very big business which Alfred P. Sloan, Jr., faced when he tackled the task of making General Motors manageable and managed.

Where they fit the realities that confront designer and architect of organization structure, Fayol's and Sloan's models are still unsurpassed. Fayol's functional organization is still the best way to structure a small business, especially a small manufacturing business. Sloan's federal decentralization is still the best structure for the big multiproduct company. Indeed none of the new design structures that have emerged in the decades since World War II are nearly as close to fulfilling the design specifications of organization structure as are functional organization and federal decentralization *if and when they fit.* But more and more of the institutional reality that has to be structured and organized does not fit. Indeed, the very assumptions that underlay Sloan's work—and that of Fayol—are not applicable to major organization needs and challenges.

*Sloan drew heavily on Pierre du Pont's slightly earlier work at the Du Pont Company. On this see the two books by Alfred D. Chandler listed in the Bibliography.

TRADITIONAL ASSUMPTIONS AND CURRENT NEEDS

The best way, perhaps, to bring out the current needs of organization structure is to contrast the basic characteristics of the General Motors Company which Sloan so successfully structured with current needs and realities of organization and structure.

1. General Motors is a manufacturing business, producing and selling highly engineered goods. And Fayol too was concerned with a business producing physical goods; his model was a fair-sized coal-mining company. Today we face the challenge of organizing the large business that is not exclusively or even primarily a manufacturing business. There are not only the large financial institutions and the large retailers. There are worldwide transportation companies, communications companies, companies which, while they manufacture, have their center of gravity in customer service (such as most computer businesses). Then there are, of course, all the nonbusiness service institutions with which Chapters 11 through 14 dealt. These nonmanufacturing institutions are increasingly the true center of gravity of any developed economy. They employ the most people. They both contribute and take the largest share of gross national product. They are the fundamental organization problems today.

2. General Motors is essentially a single-product, single-technology, single-market business. More than four-fifths of its sales are automotive. The cars which General Motors sells differ in details, such as size, horsepower, and price, but they are essentially one and the same product. Indeed, most U.S. "made by GM" cars, regardless of nameplate, are now assembled in the same plants and under one assembly manager. A man who came up the line in, say, the Pontiac Division, will hardly find Chevrolet totally alien—and even Opel in Germany will not hold a great many surprises for him.

By contrast, the typical businesses of today are multiproduct, multi-technology, and multimarket businesses. They may not be "conglomerates." But they are "diversified." And their central problem is a problem General Motors did not have: the organization of complexity and diversity.

3. General Motors is still primarily a U. S. company. It looms very large on the international automobile market. But the foreign markets do not loom very large for GM (though perhaps they should). In America General Motors dominates the automobile industry. But only in Australia—a secondary market—does General Motors dominate any non-U. S. market. In Europe it is at best number four. Organizationally the world outside the United States is still, for GM, "separate" and "outside." Organizationally GM is still an American company, and its

top management is primarily concerned with the American market, the American economy, the American labor movement, the American government, and so on.

By contrast, the most rapid growth in the last twenty-five years has been the multinational company, that is, the company for which a great many countries and a great many markets are of equal importance, or at least are of major importance.

4. Because GM is a one-product and one-country company, information is not a major organizational problem and need not be a major organizational concern. Everyone in GM speaks the same language, whether by that we mean the language of the automotive industry or American English. Everyone fully understands what the other one is doing or should be doing, if only because, in all likelihood, he has done a similar job himself. GM can therefore be organized according to the logic of the marketplace, and the logic of authority and decision. It need not, in its organization, concern itself a great deal with the logic and the flow of information.

By contrast, multiproduct, multitechnology, and multinational companies will have to concern themselves in their organizational design and structure with organization according to the flow of information. At the very least they will have to make sure that their organization structure does not violate the logic of information. And for this GM offers no guidance—GM did not have to tackle the problem.

5. Four out of every five GM employees are production workers, either manual workers or clerks on routine tasks. GM, in other words, employs yesterday's, rather than today's, labor force.

But the basic organization problem today is knowledge work and knowledge workers. They are the fastest-growing element in every business. In the service institutions, they are the core employment.

6. Finally, General Motors has been a "managerial" rather than an "entrepreneurial" business. The strength of Sloan's approach lay in its ability to manage, and manage superbly, what was already there and known. General Motors has not been innovative—altogether the automobile industry has not been innovative since the days before World War I. (There was innovation at General Motors. But it was essentially the contribution of one man, Charles Kettering, who was indeed an innovative genius of the first order. But GM itself did not have to organize for entrepreneurship and innovation.)

But the challenge is going increasingly to be entrepreneurship and innovation. What we need is the innovative organization—in addition to the managerial one. And for this, the General Motors model offers no guidance.

The need for new approaches is therefore again as great in the field of organization as it was when Fayol and Sloan each did his pioneering work. The period when federal decentralization could be considered the universal model—as it largely was in the quarter century of the management boom—is at an end.

But of course we have learned a great deal in the three-quarters of a century since Fayol's generation first tackled organization. We know what the job is. We know the major approaches. We know what comes first. We know what will not work—though not always what will. We know what organization structure aims at and therefore what the test of successful organization design is.

WHAT WE HAVE LEARNED

1. The first thing we have learned is that Fayol and Sloan were right: organization structure will not just "evolve." The only things that evolve in an organization are disorder, friction, malperformance. Nor is the right—or even the livable—structure "intuitive"—any more than Greek temples or Gothic cathedrals were. Traditions may indicate where the problems and malfunctions are but are no help in finding solutions to them. *Organization design and structure require thinking, analysis, and a systematic approach.*

2. We have learned that the first step is not designing an organization structure; that is the last step. The first step is to identify and organize the *building blocks* of organization, that is, the activities which have to be encompassed in the final structure and which, in turn, carry the "structural load" of the final edifice.

This is, of course, what Fayol did in his functions. But the trouble is not only that these functions fit only a manufacturing company. Above all, Fayol tried to design his functions according to *the work* they did.

We now know that building blocks are determined by the kind of *contribution* they make. And we know that the traditional classification of the contributions—e.g., the "staff and line" concept of conventional American organization theory—is more of a hindrance to understanding than a help.

Designing the building blocks is, so to speak, the "engineering phase" of organization design. It provides the basic "materials." And like all materials, these building blocks have their specific characteristics. They belong in different places and fit together in different ways.

3. *"Structure follows strategy."* Organization is not mechanical. It is not "assembly." It cannot be "prefabricated." Organization is organic

and unique to each individual business or institution. For we now know that structure, to be effective and sound, must follow strategy.*

Structure is a means for attaining the objectives and goals of an institution. Any work on structure must therefore start with objectives and strategy. This is perhaps the most fruitful new insight we have in the field of organization. It may sound obvious, and it is. But some of the worst mistakes in organization building have been made by imposing a mechanistic model of an "ideal" or "universal" organization on a living business.

Strategy, i.e., the answers to the questions "What is our business, what should it be, what will it be?", determines the purpose of structure. It thereby determines what the key activities are in a given business or service institution. Effective structure is the design that makes these key activities capable of functioning and of performance. And in turn the key activities are the "load-bearing elements" of a functioning structure. Organization design is, or should be, primarily concerned with the key activities; the rest are secondary.

THE THREE KINDS OF WORK

It was a misunderstanding to define the building blocks as different kinds of work. But there are different kinds of work in every organization, however small and simple.

There is, first, operating work, that is, the work of managing what is already in existence and known, building it, exploiting its potential, taking care of its problems.

There is always top-management work. And it is different work, with its own tasks and requirements.

Finally, there is innovative work—and it too is different work, requiring different things with respect to both operations and top management.

No one of the available design principles can be used for organizing all three different kinds of work. Yet they need to be organized. They need to be integrated into one overall organization.

WHAT WE NEED TO UNLEARN

There are also a few things we need to unlearn. Some of the noisiest and most time-consuming battles in organization theory and practice

---

*The fundamental work on this was done by Alfred D. Chandler in his book, *Strategy and Structure* (M.I.T. Press, 1962), a depth study of the design of modern organization in pioneering American companies, such as Du Pont, General Motors, and Sears.

are pure sham. They pose an "either/or"; yet the right answer is "both—in varying proportions."

1. The first of these sham battles which better be forgotten fast is that between task-focus and person-focus in job design and organization structure. To repeat what has been said already, *structure* and *job design* have to be task-focused. But *assignments* have to fit both the person and the needs of the situation. There is no point in confusing the two as the old and tiresome discussion of the nonproblem insists on doing. Work, to say it once more, is objective and impersonal; the job itself is done by a person.

2. Somewhat connected with this old controversy is the discussion of hierarchical versus free-form organization.

Traditional organization theory knows only one kind of structure applicable alike to building blocks and whole buildings: the so-called scalar organization, that is, the hierarchical pyramid of superior and subordinates. Traditional organization theory considers this structure suitable for all tasks.

Today another—equally doctrinaire—organization theory is becoming fashionable. It maintains that shape and structure are what we want them to be—they are, or should be, "free-form." Everything—shape, size, and apparently tasks—derive from interpersonal relations. Indeed the purpose of the structure is to make it possible for each person to "do his thing."

The first thing to say about this controversy is that it is simply not true that one of these forms is regimentation and the other freedom. The amount of discipline required in both is the same; they only distribute it differently.

A hierarchy does not, as the critics allege, make the superior more powerful. On the contrary, the first effect of hierarchical organization is the protection of the subordinate against arbitrary authority from above. A scalar or hierarchical organization does this by defining carefully the sphere within which the subordinate has the authority, the sphere within which the superior cannot interfere. It protects the subordinate by making it possible for him to say, "This is *my* assigned job." Protection of the subordinate underlies also the scalar principle's insistence that a man have only one superior. Otherwise the subordinate is likely to find himself caught between conflicting demands, conflicting commands, and conflicts of interest as well as of loyalty. "Better one bad master than two good ones," says an old peasant proverb.

The first organization structure of the modern West was laid down in the canon law of the Catholic Church eight hundred years ago. It set up a strictly scalar organization. But most of the provisions in the canon law that deal with the structure and organization of the Catholic

Church define those things which *only* the parish priest, i.e., the bottom man in the pyramid, can do in his parish. The bishop appoints him; and, within clear procedural limits, the bishop can remove him. But within his parish only the parish priest can discharge the parish priest's canonical functions, e.g., dispense the sacraments of baptism and matrimony or hear confession. Even the Pope has to be formally invited by the individual priest before he can officiate in a priest's parish.

At the same time, the hierarchical organization gives the most *individual* freedom. As long as the incumbent does whatever the assigned duties of his position are, he has done his job. He has no responsibility beyond it.

There is much talk these days about the individual's "doing his thing." But the only organization structure in which this is remotely possible is a hierarchical one. It makes the *least* demands on the individual to subordinate himself to the goals of the organization or to gear his activities into the needs and demands of others. Altogether, the more clearly a structure defines work, authority, and relationships, the fewer demands does it make on the individual for self-discipline and self-subordination.

Free-form organization is, of course, a misnomer. What is meant is organization designed for specific tasks rather than for supposedly "eternal" purposes. In particular, what is meant is organization of work in small groups and teams.

This demands, above all, very great self-discipline from each member of the team. Everybody has to do "the team's thing." Everybody has to take responsibility for the work of the entire team and for its performance. Indeed, Abraham Maslow's criticism of Theory Y as making inhuman demands on that large proportion of people who are weak, vulnerable, timid, impaired, applies with even greater force to free-form organization. The more flexible an organization is, the stronger do the individual members have to be and the more of the load do they have to carry.

But also, hierarchy is needed in any structure by both individual members and the entire organization. There has to be someone who can make a decision; or else the organization deteriorates into a never-ending bull session. The knowledge organization in particular needs extreme clarity with respect to decision authority and specific, designated "channels." Every organization will find itself in a situation of common peril once in a while. And then all perish unless there is clear, unambiguous, designated *command* authority vested in one person.

The hierarchy versus free-form argument is simply another version of the oldest and stalest argument in political theory: the argument between the constitutional lawyer who—rightly—insists that there have to be good and clear laws, and the educator who—equally rightly—insists that the best constitution fails unless there are upright rulers.

And just as statesmen learned long ago that both good laws and good rulers are needed, so organization builders (and even organization theorists) will have to learn that sound organization structure needs *both* a hierarchical structure of authority, decision-making, and pyramid, and the capacity to organize task forces, teams, and individuals for work both on a permanent and a temporary basis.

Both the advocates of hierarchical and those of free-form organization assume, if only unconsciously, that an organization must have one axis. It must be either hierarchical or "free-form." But this is a mechanistic assumption—and organization is a social phenomenon.

The classical organization structure was, indeed, presumed to have only one axis: that of formal authority downward and "reporting" upward. But the first studies of actual organization in the early work of the "human relations school" in the twenties* brought out immediately a second structure present in every work group studied. The human relations people called it—misleadingly—"informal" organization ("unwritten" organization would have been better; there is nothing informal about an informal organization which, being based on custom rather than explicit rules, tends to be more formal and, above all, to be far less flexible than the written rules of the formal organization chart). Still, the belief persists that organization structure should be "single-axis" structure.

But every system higher than the simplest mechanical assemblage of inanimate matter is a "multi-axis" system. An animal body such as that of man has a skeletal-muscular system, a number of nervous systems, an ingestive-digestive-eliminating system, a respiratory system, sense organs each a system, a procreative system, and so on. Each is autonomous. Yet all interact. Each is an "axis of organization."

No business could or should be as complex as a biological organism. Yet the organizations we need to design and to structure—the organizations of business enterprise and public-service institution—have a number of axes: decision-authority but also information; the logic of the task but also the dynamics of knowledge. That individual jobs have to be designed and positioned in contemplation of a number of axes—task and assignments; decision-responsibility: information and relations—has been discussed earlier.

The same applies to organization design and structure.

3. At bottom these sham battles—between task focus and person-focus and between scalar and free-form organization—reflect the belief

*Especially by Elton Mayo.

of traditional organization theory that there must be "one best principle" which alone is "right" but which is also always "right." There must be *one final answer.*

Perhaps; but if so, we do not know it.

Instead of the "one right" principle, *three* new major design principles have emerged in the twenty-five years since World War II ended, to join Fayol's functions and Sloan's federal decentralization. These three—the team, simulated decentralization, and systems management—do not supersede the older designs. None of them could lay claim to being a "universal" principle; indeed, all three have both serious structural weaknesses and limited applicability. But they are the best answers available for certain kinds of work, the best structures available for certain tasks, the best approaches to such major organization problems as top management, innovation, the structure of comparison in the materials, transportation and financial industries or the multinational corporation.

The final tradition we will have to unlearn therefore is that "there must be one final answer." The right answer is whatever structure enables people to perform and to contribute. For liberation and mobilization of human energies—rather than symmetry or harmony—is the purpose of organization. Human performance is its goal and its test.

CHARLES PERROW

Is Business
Really Changing?

Organizational theory has gradually developed a rather comprehensive paradigm for handling the impact of technological and environmental change upon organizations, which I have represented in Figure 1. Inventions and innovations in techniques and in goods and services have stimulated the growth of the "knowledge industry," and been stimulated by it. As a consequence, the environment of organizations has shown rapid and turbulent change and has led to new forms of competition. This, in turn, has stimulated both education and research, and resulted in still more innovations and inventions. The consequence for organizations, limited here to economic organizations, has been a change in the character of the workforce: more professionalization and higher skill levels; more rapid change in technologies and products; and more decentralization of authority, as those on the firing line have to make more decisions on their own and can do so because they possess the requisite skills. This creates greater instability in the environment, more innovations, and more growth in the knowledge industry. It is characteristic of our systems model that all the arrows are double-headed.

This model has been with us for several years now; it is celebrated in the works of almost all management theorists and popular authors, and is at least implicit in the work of most organizational theorists.

Source: Reprinted by permission of the publisher from *Organizational Dynamics*, (Vol. 3, No. 1: Summer 1974) © (1974) by AMACOM, a division of American Management Associations.

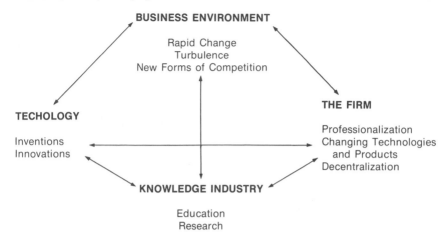

Figure 1. Organizational theory paradigm

Such widespread acceptance suggests there is a great deal in it, but I am no longer so sure, and what I want to do here is try to convince the reader that he should not be so sure, either. I am not certain that the dominant perspective is wrong, but I think it is greatly exaggerated. It takes as given many things that should be considered quite problematical. To create the necessary skepticism about it, I shall go to the other extreme and argue against it at every point.

In contrast to this view, and frankly in a spirit of controversy, I shall emphasize the stability of the system in Figure 1 and the glacial rate of change. Let me start with the symbol of futurology that appears in the charts of Buckminster Fuller or Alvin Toffler and that pervades the writings of people like Daniel Bell and Zbigniew Brzezinski. Take the curve represented in Figure 2. Almost any behavior the futurologists are interested in can be plotted in this form. Nothing much happened for a long time, but then the increase in the behavior became exponential. The dates that one would enter at points A, B, C, et cetera would vary with the phenomenon, but the number of scientists that have been produced has increased at the rate suggested by the curve, as has the speed at which new innovations in industry can be made operational or new products marketed, the tons of metal or whatever that can be produced per hour, the velocity at which man gets about, and so on. We walked for thousands upon thousands of years on the plateau from point A to B, took horses and carriages around point B, steam engines and automobiles at C, aeroplanes and jet planes at D, and space capsules at point E, roughly 1969.

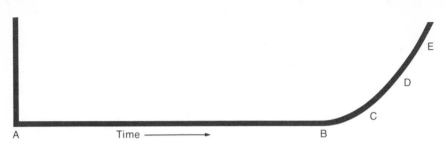

Figure 2. Future shock

The fallacy is the evaporation of the denominator. The futurologists talk of mankind, but they ignore the world population of billions when they talk about how much faster the 10-or-so percent of Americans who use commercial flights get around today. Were they to put that small number in the numerator over the huge denominator of "mankind," the rate of change would be glacial indeed. In fact, most people in the world today don't even ride horses, let alone fly. And of course, the number who have orbited the earth is truly insignificant.

Only a tiny fraction of men are scientists. Regardless of whether this figure doubles or trebles in a few decades, the vast majority of men know nothing about what these scientists are doing, nor are their lives changed significantly by the scientists' actions, except in the case of radioactive fallout, pesticide poisonings, and so on.

The output statistics of steel for a few industrialized countries should be compared with the figures of the many nonindustrialized countries. The same is true of our organizations. When you take them all into account, rather than the few exotic ones we read about in the business journals or the exotic parts of large corporations, the overwhelming conclusion is one of stability or very slow rates of change.

PROFESSIONALIZATION

Turning now to the paradigm for organization and environment, let us start with one crucial item in Figure 1, the professionalization of the workforce, which has resulted from the knowledge explosion and education and training associated with it. It is a well-known fact that in industrialized countries the number of white-collar employees comes to exceed the number of blue-collar employees (if you count service workers as white-collar, although many are not). It happened several years ago in the United States. What is less well known is that this would not be true if females were excluded. They swell the ranks of the low-status white-collar positions and hardly are there by virtue of technological breakthroughs. In 1970, 41 percent of the females in the labor force were in clerical or sales positions. Of those classified as "professional, technical, and kindred" by the Census Bureau in 1960, 43 percent were teachers. Women are in the workforce for a shorter time than men and change jobs almost twice as often as men. All this suggests that they are marginal to industry in several respects—found mostly in low-status, low-skilled, high-turnover positions.

So let's leave them out of account and look only at males. If technological change and professionalization have had a significant effect, we should expect a considerable decline in the proportion of males in the blue-collar category. Professionals, technical specialists, engineers, and the like should be manning organizations, while blue-collar workers evaporated rapidly, dried up by automation and the rapid spread of higher education.

However, over the 70-year period from 1900 to 1969, from C to E in Figure 2—a period of massive technological and organizational change—we find that the percentage of the male workforce engaged in blue-collar and service activities declined by only 13 percent. It went from 70 percent in 1900 to 57 percent in 1969, and even in the 20-year period from 1950 to 1969, the period of postwar boom and knowledge explosion, it declined by only 5 percent. Indeed, if we exclude the service workers and deal only with male manual employees, the proportion of manual workers has actually been increasing slightly in the last decade.

The proportion of professional, technical, and kindred workers, the heart of the technological revolution, is indeed up; for males, it doubled from 7 percent in 1950 to 14 percent in 1969. But 14 percent is still a small percentage of the workforce; moreover, this category appears to be heavily concentrated in two areas: aerospace and "defense" industries (for example, 19 percent of the category are engineers), and the service sector, where technological change is scarcely rampant (for example, 14 percent are teachers). To make a rough estimate, about 30 percent of this group of males are in the high-technology sector of industry, while 35 percent are in the service sector. This suggests that most of industry is not greatly affected by the doubling of the professional and technical category. Most of industry is at level C in Figure 2. To point out that TRW or a nuclear engineering firm has a large proportion of scientists or engineers is like saying the Air Force has a large proportion of people who travel at very high rates of speed. Most of industry still plods along, and plods profitably.

DECENTRALIZATION

Nevertheless, you might say there has been an obvious increase in highly trained personnel in most firms, and it should lead to more decentralization in firms. This is because the market changes are more rapid, the technology more complicated, and the skills outdated sooner, so power must be delegated to those on the firing line with the latest skills and the latest information on the environment. Furthermore, there has been a management revolution, and there are all the T-groupers, sensitivity trainers, 9,9 Grid® men, matrix managers, and the integraters. Decisions have been shoved down to lower levels. Firms are becoming more decentralized.

A rigorous definition of decentralization is impossible at present; the closer one looks, the more it looks like a meaningless term. Sometimes we seem to associate it with what some have called "organizational hygiene." I suppose that most organizations today are concerned that there be less smell, safer devices, more choices as to size or color or method, less roughness, irritation, and rudeness, and less secretiveness. The social sciences have marketed a lot of products to ease human interaction and make effort more benign. I think most will agree, however, that better working conditions and more humane supervision have little to do with the decentralization of power or decision making.

The term participative management goes a bit further. It includes the hygienic sprays that are supposed to reduce alienation, but it also deals with feelings of powerlessness. The lower orders are consulted on decisions and encouraged to make their own in some areas, subject to the veto of superiors. The veto is important; it is like saying we have a democratic system of government in which people elect their leaders, but subject to the veto of the incumbent leaders. Workers and managers can have their say, make suggestions, and present arguments, and there is no doubt this is extremely desirable. It presumably results in the superior's making better decisions—but they are still his decisions.

We seem to have lost sight of something important in our packaging of pacifiers, namely, that good managements have *always* found it in their interests to utilize the skills, information, experience, and knowledge of people under them. These people know more about some things than management does, and failure to consult them not only is an affront to them, but also means that management must do much more work on its own to get the information. If it doesn't have the time or resources to do so, it makes inferior decisions. Max Weber, the much-maligned theorist of bureaucracy, was explicit about this some 60 years ago. He saw that a man has a set of skills, expertise, or experience and a sense of career with the firm. The skills, expertise, and experience can be developed, and he expects to utilize them—indeed, he wants to. It is wise, then, as we now see, to allow him the freedom to exercise these skills and to use his discretion, for that is why we employ experts and experienced people. However, he should exercise his skills in the service of organizational goals that are set for him. He is not expected, or encouraged, to inquire into the legitimacy of these goals.

Even if we move toward a more psychological model, such as the self-actualization one of Chris Argyris and others, it seems clear that self-actualization by the employee has to be on organizational terms. I don't think they would include the following as proper examples of self-actualization: organizing employees for better working conditions; exposing the cover-up of unjustified expenses in government contracts; opposing the development of chemical warfare techniques in a university research laboratory; advocating mass-transit subsidies as opposed to subsidies for highways while working for an automobile manufacturer; opposing price-fixing techniques or illegal campaign contributions at any number of large corporations; or calling for better testing of drugs and more accurate advertising in a pharmaceutical firm.

It is extremely difficult to get data demonstrating such restrictions, but one minor, though revealing, example was reported in *Look* magazine: At a stormy meeting concerning the activities of the Stanford Research Institute, a young physicist heard the president of SRI argue that no researcher was forced to undertake any project he found morally objectionable. The physicist contradicted him, saying that he had been pressured into doing chemical warfare research. The physicist was fired. As the executive vice-president of SRI put it, according to the article, "People like that have a decision to make—do they want to support the organization or not?"

Were actions such as these possible without penalty, I would agree that we would have decentralized firms. But as long as the superior can define the problem employees work on, he need not fear discussions of possible solutions. The fact that subordinates are using their expertise and skills more fully, and even with more enthusiasm, does not necessarily mean that authority or even decisions have been decentralized; it may merely mean a more effective organization (though I should add that careful critiques of research in the human relations area have as yet been unable to firmly support even that conclusion).

We hear today that large organizations have become more democratic, in that subordinates are encouraged to set their own production goals, control methods, make up their own work teams, and so on.

Dog food, pacemakers, television sets, even cars are being produced by "autonomous groups." Just as no one in his right mind would instruct the maintenance staff how many sweeps of the broom were to be taken for any 6' x 6' area of floor, no superior should dictate how an experienced work group should go about meeting the production (and quality and scrap) standards, unless the superior really has much more expertise or experience in the matter. The good supervisor-coordinator gets the resources and monitors outputs; he doesn't give orders about task sequences if his men are competent. But the standards are still there, and nonperformance brings sanctions. And the supervisors who set the standards are still there; the men cannot vote them out of office. The ideological confusion attending the gummy word democratic is well represented by Chester Barnard, who quoted with approval an army officer in World War I who remarked that the army is the greatest of all democracies, because when the order to move forward is given, each man decides on his own whether to obey or not.

No serious organizational theorists in the United States, to my knowledge, have advocated the form of decentralization of authority that democracy seeks to provide. That is, there are no calls for workers to elect management and to have the contenders for managerial positions run on platforms such as no speed-up, better washrooms, no defense contracts, no gifts to universities, or no price fixing, let alone less pay for managers and more for workers. In Europe, especially eastern Europe, where there seems to be more progressive management in this respect, the experiment with that most anemic form of democracy, workers' councils, has had only a slight impact on organizations.

TEMPORARY ORGANIZATIONS

A more serious usage of the term decentralization occurs in connection with the appearance of temporary work groups or matrix structures, associated mostly with the name of Warren Bennis. (Dr. Bennis has lost his vision on the way to an organizational presidency, but he had many followers in this Buck Rogers school of theory who still embrace the model with which I opened this article.) Proponents of his view argue that because of rapid environmental and technological changes, those with the most relevant skills and information are in the lower reaches of the hierarchy, and they also suggest that rapid changes call for task groups that have no fixed membership. The groups form and reform, depending on the problem at hand. One is a leader at one time and a subordinate at another. The organization, then, is made up of little cells or work groups that appear and disappear according to the cycle of innovation and implementation. Upper management merely provides the resources and offers what guidance it can.

Once again, I think that the ability of top management to formulate the problem other managers are assigned so limits the range of available solutions that we find very little decentralization of authority. But even if this were not true, I think that all we have here is a slight expansion of the size of the goal-setting unit. A few elite teams are added to the goal-setting unit, while the bulk of management personnel still remains outside of it. Granted, this would constitute a form of decentralization, but I suspect that the examples given in the literature are very special and deal with very special aspects of our large firms. They will cover only a tiny minority of corporations and only a tiny minority of the employees in them. Again, I should like to refer to Figure 2; because a few men have orbited the earth, does that mean that mankind is moving any faster?

There is another important consideration. Those who argue for the reality of organic structure and its expansion write as if innovations were the only things that corporations produce. (Roy Ash some time ago took this position, pointing to pop-top disposable cans and the SST.) But after the innovations and the design, production, and marketing decisions have been made by these elite teams, an army of personnel must carry them out on a volume basis. High-volume production, with masses of workers, clerks, technicians, and personnel men doing largely routine jobs, characterizes industry, not the floating, dissolving teams of innovators and troubleshooters. To suggest otherwise is to succumb to a myth about economic organizations.

DIVISIONALIZATION

Finally, let me come to the most interesting argument of all for decentralization, found in the literature on divisionalization of large corporations. There are a number of books about divisionalization that equate it with decentralization, and some of them are very scholarly and admirable books indeed. All of them deal, at least in part, with General Motors. The first was by Peter Drucker; then came Ernest Dale; then the very influential book *Strategy and Structure*, by Alfred Du Pont Chandler, Jr., and then one by Alfred Sloan himself on his years at General Motors. The evidence given in these books supports a quite different conclusion than the one that their authors put forth (though Chandler is more circumspect about actual decentralization than the rest). The evidence strongly suggests that General Motors was quite decentralized when it was run by William C. Durant—in fact, it was the very model of a present-day conglomerate or holding company, with the main office doing little more than allocate capital among the divisions.

When Sloan came in, he radically and continously centralized the organization. He introduced inventory-control and production-control devices and internal pricing, allotted markets to the various units, controlled capital outlays, centralized advertising and personnel, standardized parts, and routinized innovation. At every step the divisions lost autonomy. At present there is hardly an area of policy- or goal-setting that is not controlled by the very large central headquarters, and in addition, it controls an enormous number of detailed decisions, including minute aspects of styling. The functionalized exception to divisionalization at General Motors has always been the Fisher Body plant, serving all divisions. That principle is now being extended to include multidivision assembly plants, further reducing the power of the division manager.

Sloan himself takes a characteristically ambiguous position about decentralization. His book opens with praise for decentralization in General Motors; a bit later, though, he criticizes Durant, his predecessor, for allowing General Motors to be too decentralized; and still later he calls for a happy medium between centralization and decentralization. Harold Wolff, in a perceptive discussion of the General Motors structure some years ago, concluded that reading the General Motors experience as an example of decentralization was an error: "If any *one* word is needed to describe the management *structure* of General Motors as it was recast by Sloan and the brilliant group around him, then that word is not decentralization, but *centralization.*" He goes on to say that it is difficult to label the process, as distinct from the structure, but it is clear, he says, that it is not one of decentralization.

The usual way out of this labeling dilemma is to say the policy is centralized and the execution decentralized. But I contend that if policy is centralized, so is execution; the choice is execution through wasteful (and unpleasant) close supervision and direction, or execution through controlling the premises of decisions—through sharply delimiting the options available. Wolff captures it well: "The decentralized operating executives were left with smaller responsibilities than they had before. But the responsibility they did retain was total and sharply defined. They had the right to do only those things which would make the precise plans and policies of the top management work." This hardly fits the pattern of decentralized organizations that has lower-level people responding fully and freely to the turbulent environment.

There is another matter that clouds our perception of the realities of control in industry and organizations in general—the matter of scale, or volume of output, or number of things done. The head of an automotive division at General Motors is no puppet; he makes many decisions that have a great deal of impact on his division and on the corporation as a whole. But the facts that the divisions of General Motors are large and involved in very complex operations and that the division manager and his staff have a great deal to do and a great deal of responsibility do not mean that the controls exercised over them with regard to either means or ends are not great. There are simply more things to do in a large and complex organization such as a General Motors division.

The division manager is not, I understand, free to change legroom lengths, control auto frame production, formulate his own labor policies, raise capital, change the price range of his cars, engage in any significant research and development, or set up his own accounting system—let alone decide that General Motors should change its goals and policies with regard to pollution, highway sprawl, mass transit, product safety, or product warranties. Both his means and his ends are closely monitored and controlled by headquarters. There is nothing inconsistent with being both more closely controlled and having more decisions to make. As James March and Herbert Simon pointed out some time ago in their book *Organizations,* to shape the premises of decision is the key to control; it is unnecessary for members of the superior unit to make the decision themselves.

UNTANGLING THE ISSUES

I think we are only beginning to unravel some of the threads in the cloth we have woven for ourselves concerning the issues of control, delegation of authority, and decision making. I find it instructive that we can so readily assume, to use the words of Zbigniew Brzezinski, that "the increased flow of information and more efficient techniques of coordination need not necessarily prompt greater concentration of power," but can make possible a "greater devolution of authority and responsibility to the lower levels of government and society." Brzezinski's example of this summary of the model is as instructive as it is terrifying: "It is noteworthy that the U.S. Army has so developed its control systems that it is not uncommon for sergeants to call in and coordinate massive air strikes and artillery fire—a responsibility of colonels during World War II."

What Brzezinski does not note is that the ability of the U.S. Army to destroy more living things today than in World War II has increased. There are more decisions to make. The sergeant of today makes more decisions than the colonel of World War II because the lethal output of the system is so much higher. I doubt that the colonel feels robbed of authority and I doubt that he has lost any in the process. Perhaps we should begin to pull apart these two strands in our cloth—control over the premises of decision, which makes the sergeant so ready to call in massive air strikes and artillery fire, and delegation of the authority that might have given him the ability to say it is just not worth all that destruction.

The way we're conducting our research suggests, however, that we are not likely to disentangle these threads. The work of Peter Blau and his associates and of the Aston Group in England has concluded, to use Aston's terms, that the more structured the activities of an organization (that is, the greater the degree of bureaucracy), the greater the degree of decentralization of decision making or authority. But what has been measured when they speak of decentralization of authority?

I suspect that they have found that in large firms, with all their economies of scale and specialization and expert personnel, there has been an absolute increase in the output of the system. In consequence, lower managements have to make more important decisions than they do in weaker systems, but this also means that top managements have increased the importance and scope of their decisions, including those that shape the premises of lower management. It need not be a zero-sum game. Blau and Aston (and I, among many others) have not measured these kinds of decisions by top management because we are not privy to them, and, perhaps more important, not conceptually alert to them.

To say that lower management is more expert or experienced is to say that management will view the situation in the proper light and make the sensible decision in conformance with the interests of the organizational elites who control the organizations. The less the expertise, the more direct the surveillance and the more obtrusive or formal the controls; the more the expertise, the more unobtrusive the controls. The best situation of all is to hire professionals (though they do not come cheap), for someone else has socialized them and even unobtrusive controls are hardly needed. The professional, the prima donna of organizational theory, is really the ultimate eunuch, capable of doing everything well in that harem except what he should not do—and in this case that is to mess around with the goals of the organization or the assumptions that determine to what ends he will use his professional skills.

FLAWS IN THE ARGUMENT

I am quite aware that this argument has many weaknesses, and I will mention two of them. First, it is always possible to deny empirical generalizations, such as those by Blau and the Aston Group, on the grounds that the variables were not measured adequately. This is rightly called cheap criticism, but in an area as important as the centralization of authority I think it is worth raising the point quite strenuously. We should not measure decentralization by the level at which people may hire, fire, or spend a few thousand dollars without proper authorization. We must also measure the unobtrusive controls.

A more serious problem with my position is that it is difficult to know what would be a decentralized organization. Centralization seems to be inevitable, and variations in the degree are quite minor. Let me elaborate. I have argued that what we take to mean decentralization of authority generally means: (1) a larger, or more complex, or more busy organization, as there is more for people in the lower levels to do; (2) more effective bureaucratization, so that the virtues of experience, training, and expertise are more fully realized throughout the organization; (3) more effective control from the top, so that unobtrusive control has a wider scope—and this can include more effective control of the environment; and (4) better organizational hygiene, so that people are not treated so badly. This, I realize, tends to equate effective organizations with the centralization of organizations, and makes it difficult for me to be proved wrong.

This point bothers me. So let me remind you that my purpose is not to prove that the rosy new view of firms emerging from the model of our social scientists is wrong, but merely to ask for a critical pause before we continue to rush headlong into that model. My extended remarks on centralization are meant to open up the debate a bit, in the face of an ever-enlarging consensus.

I have concerned myself mainly with decentralization, but the environment and technology itself require some brief remarks to put that part of the pattern into a critical perspective, since they are important aspects of the general consensus.

ENVIRONMENT

Is the environment really turbulent? The most important fact, but one we seem to ignore systematically, is that the environment of organizations is primarily made up of other organizations that have similar interests. The shared interests are much greater than the competitive ones. Mobil Oil and Exxon may compete furiously at the intersection of two streets in any American town, but neither of them is really threatened by this marginal competition. They work very closely together in the important matter of oil depletion allowances, our foreign policy about the Mideast, federal tax policies, the pollution issues, and private transit-versus-mass transit. In fact, they cooperate quite well with large organizations in other industries that share their interests, such as the automobile industry. And the automobile industry cooperates with, and has a stake in, the steel industry, and so on. Where, then, is the furious rate of competition? At the lower levels in the organization—the levels of the regional manager who moves prices up and down a fraction and the station manager who washes the windshields and cleans the rest rooms. Who sets the parameters of their behavior and judges them in terms of their performance? Top management. Coping with the environment, then, not only is consistent with centralized control but requires centralized control if the turbulence is going to be minor and limited to the lower echelons.

A little reflection on some obvious behavior will illustrate the stability of large firms and their ability to do three things: select the environment they wish to deal with, create new environments if necessary, and change those that threaten to produce instability. Few firms move from the top 200 in the *Fortune* listing to the next 300; few drop out of the top 500 altogether except by merger, which is, of course, a device for increasing stability and gaining control over environments. Corporations resist technological change when it suits them, and quite successfully. After inventing the transistor, AT&T declined to use it, for it would have required scrapping too much existing equipment, even though the company asked the public to put up with increasingly poor service.

The techniques for managing the environment are so well known I would hesitate to mention them, were it not for the fact that the literature on organization-environment relations and on organizational change largely ignores them. Some obvious ones are administered pricing, government subsidies, price fixing, padded cost figures, planned obsolescence, tariffs, cartels, political payoffs, special governmental aid, takeovers and mergers, and, or course, monopsony, oligopoly, monopoly, and advertising.

In the United States there is overwhelming evidence that industries are able to regulate the regulatory agencies; that the vast majority of top officials in government have come from, and will return to, private business or the law firms that service business; that despite a briefly mobilized citizenry, the heat is off the pollution area, as the main polluters control the programs and advertise their dedication—and so on and so on. There are exceptions, I readily admit—industries where the competition extends to the very top of each firm and affects large areas of policy. But, surprisingly enough, these are generally not the professionalized, technologically advanced firms, but those in the backward industries of food production, food distribution, auto parts and service, furniture, clothing, and the like. Their environments are relatively unstable because they lack size, standardization, centralized control, and mass production and mass marketing. They are 19th century industries, not 21st century industries.

TECHNOLOGICAL CHANGE

One might finally say in exasperation: "The evidence of technological change is overwhelming. Whether environments are controlled or not, surely there has been a great deal of technological change, and as a consequence, more influence on the part of technicians, engineers, scientists, and recently trained managers."

But just as the decline of the proportion of blue-collar workers in the workforce has been very slow and relatively even over the last 60 to 70 years, so has the rise in output per manhour. There have been fluctuations in this figure due to the depression of the 1930s, the war boom of the early 1940s, and more wars and recessions along the way right up to the present. Overall, though, the increase in productivity has not fluctuated greatly even from one environmental disturbance to the next. The impression is one of slow and stable change.

The reason seems to be that while most firms have routine technologies, they are only *somewhat* routine. Most are unable to automate extensively. In the large majority, new technologies have simply not created the condition for the decentralized, responsive, adaptive organization that organizational theorists seem to dream of.

I can only argue from examples here, and I shall give three of them. First, the automatic factory that was heralded as a possibility in the late 1940s and accepted as a reality by the mid-1960s is, as far as I know, still not with us. In 1965, a reporter for *Fortune*, Charles Silberman, tracked down the various references to startling examples of automation that had been served up by journalists and by social scientists. The results were very disappointing. Case after case turned out to be grossly overstated or simply not true. He could find, for example, no automated chemical complexes that had discharged their employees in droves. Most had experienced either no reduction in personnel or even some increase, and none were fully automated. After careful research, Silberman concluded that "no fully automated process exists for any major product in any industry in the U.S." Since we cannot seem to get social scientists to do this kind of work, I hope that *Fortune* magazine will send another crew out in 1975 to see if things have changed much since 1965. I don't think they will have.

The second example concerns the prima donna of technological change, computers. Again, it was *Fortune* that did the investigative work, rather than the social scientists. Tom Alexander, writing in the October 1969 issue of that magazine, concluded: "It turns out that computers have rarely reduced the cost of operations, even in routine clerical work. What they have accomplished is mainly to enable companies to speed up operations and thereby provide better service or handle larger volumes." He reported a survey by the Research Institute of America of some 2,500 companies that found that only half of those with in-house computers were certain that they were paying off—that heady enthusiasm about computers' providing total management information control systems had dissipated greatly.

Perhaps there is always waste with the adaptation of new technologies, but if so, we have been misled about its degree in this age of scientific and technological sophistication. When we look at developments like powdered metallurgy or numerically controlled machines, the story is the same. Fantastic progress is predicted but not realized, because we refuse to recognize the limits of routinization and the ability to control environments so that technological change is not required.

One last example is the Vega automobile produced by General Motors. It planned and built a completely new car and built a new plant to produce it. If automation could ever strike, it should strike here, in this key and wealthy company. (It turns out, incidentally, that the planning was completely centralized in the headquarters of General Motors and not handled by the division.) The computers in this supposedly computerized installation are limited to balancing production (though they were used in designing and making templates), and there are a few automatic welders on the production line. But as far as I can gather, there is nothing more radical in terms of technological change than this.

What allowed the company to use about 20 percent less direct labor in producing the cars was not the technology of the 1960s but that of the 1920s. First, there was the speed-up of the line, which could account for much of the labor-saving. Since it was achieved by having men work harder, we can hardly call it automation. (The line has since been slowed down as a result of high absenteeism, turnover, and wildcat strikes). Second, because there are many more interchangeable parts for all models, the number of parts was reduced and thus the complexity, allowing for longer production runs for parts. Third, the increased number of subassemblies simplified the assembly line. Fourth, there are streamlined assemblies, including the very important simplification of a one-piece roof. Finally, there is a basic model life of five years, rather than three. All of these innovations were made by the first Henry Ford, back in the 1920s. Yet the business press heralded the new plant as "the model of automation."

These examples suggest that technological change is not so widespread, continuous, and rapid as we tend to believe (as well as more wasteful of resources than we had been led to believe). I do not dispute the change that has occurred in, say, electronics, process firms, and even manufacturing, with its roller bearings and engine blocks. I am saying only that the striking examples are few, and that productivity has not taken the great leaps to be expected if these were the norm.

It is also quite possible that technological change is not impelled by market forces and scientific advancement so much as it is by government and corporate political strategy. Surely, the huge concentration of technical and scientific manpower in the defense, space, and atomic power industries is the result of political decisions. There is no free market for these products.

CONCLUSION

In conclusion, then, I have argued that there has been no rapid and drastic change in the workforce, except for the increasing employment of women in low-level, white-collar jobs in the service industry; that firms are more complex and larger, but not necessarily more decentralized, since we have been measuring only part of the control system; that the environment is not unstable and turbulent for the progressive and technologically advanced firms, but very stable, because it is controlled by the companies and managed in their common interests; and that technological change has been quite selective—far less extensive than is usually believed, resisted when it pleases firms, and well-controlled when it exists. At each point I have contradicted what I see as the dominant viewpoint on these matters in organizational theory.

Let me finally add a note to extend my contention to social and political theory. The evidence from our social and political systems also signifies overwhelming stability. The social structure of the United States has not changed much in a hundred years. There has been very little income redistribution; the class system is still quite intact; our political structures and mechanisms remain much as they were at the beginning of the century. It depends upon one's necromancy, but one interpretation of this similarity of the dominant economic, social, and political institutions is that if economic institutions do not change, we can't expect a change in the political and social ones.

SELECTED BIBLIOGRAPHY

Some of the issues raised in this paper are discussed in my recent book, *Complex Organizations: A Critical Essay* (Scott Foresman, 1972). That book deals with the concept of unobtrusive controls derived from the seminal work of James March and Herbert Simon, *Organizations* (John Wiley, 1958), the participative management school, professionalization, and the issue of environments. The statistics on the labor force are all from the usual government publications. See a more extended discussion in Richard Hamilton, *Class and Politics in the United States* (John Wiley, 1972). The main books on General Motors are Alfred P. Sloan, *My Years with General Motors* (MacFadden-Bartell Co., 1965); Peter Drucker, *The Concept of Corporation* (Beacon Press, 1946); and Alfred Du Pont Chandler, *Strategy and Structure* (M.I.T. Press, 1962). Harold Wolff's essay appeared in the *Harvard Business Review*(September-October 1964). The Zbigniew Brzezinski quotations come from "The American Transition," *New Republic* (September 23, 1967).

For a look at the recent literature on how bureaucracy is associated with decentralization, one has to dig into some technical, scholarly articles and books, written for academic peers rather than practitioners. The first and most accessible are Peter Blau *et al*, "The Structure of Small Bureaucracies," in the *American Sociological Review* (April 1966), and Marshall Meyer, "The Two Authority Structures of Bureaucratic Organization," in *Administrative Science Quarterly* (September 1968). See also Peter Blau, "The Hierarchy of Authority in Organization," in *American Journal of Sociology* (January 1968), and the massive tome by Blau and Richard Schoenherr, *The Structure of Organizations* (Basic Books, 1971). The English studies of the Aston Group are well summarized in John Child, "Predicting and Understanding Organization Structure," in *Administrative Science Quarterly* (June 1973).

For a debunking view of technological change that echoes my own position in part, see Victor C. Ferkiss, *Technological Man* (New American Library, 1969).

K. R. SRINIVASA MURTHY AND

MALCOLM S. SALTER

Should CEO Pay
Be Linked to Results?

When we read that the chief executive of a major U.S. corporation has received a substantial increase in total compensation, how easy it is to assume that this munificence reflects an increase in his company's profit performance. Since our business traditions and folklore accent the importance of the bottom line, we naturally expect that year-to-year variability in the compensation of top-level decision-makers should be closely related to changes in the profit performance of the businesses they manage.

However, the validity of this assumption must be questioned. It does not seem to be supported by the published data on the compensation of top executives of major U.S. companies. Consider, for example, the following results of a survey on the compensation of 53 chief executives who were, with one exception, in office for six or more years during the period 1960–1974:

- As *Exhibit I* shows, for 66% of the executives studied there was no statistically significant relationship between changes in their compensation (salary plus bonus, whether deferred or current) and changes in their company's return on equity.

- For 40% of the executives there was no significant relationship between changes in compensation and earnings per share.

Exhibit I. Relationship between changes in top executive compensation and measures of corporate performance

	Return on equity		Earnings per share	
Nature of relationship	Number of companies	Percent of companies	Number of companies	Percent of companies
Significant and positive relationship	18	34%	32	60%
No significant relationship	35	66	21	40
Total	**53**	**100%**	**53**	**100%**

Why was there no significant relationship between financial performance and top executive compensation for such a large proportion of the companies surveyed? Do the statistics reflect a lack of systematic procedures in compensating a large segment of chief executives? Or do they hide the fact that companies following certain organizational strategies consistently and systematically choose to uncouple chief executive compensation from current measures of financial performance?

A FRESH LOOK AT THE DATA

In pursuit of answers to these questions, we looked more carefully at the compensation of the 53 executives and at the characteristics of their companies. We decided to test the relationship between compensation of selected top executives for an average of nine consecutive years. In addition, we classified our sample of companies into three strategy categories in ascending order of product-market diversity:

1. Companies with revenue coming largely from a single business (for example, U.S. Steel, Alcoa, and International Paper). Characteristically, they have an integrated sequence of manufacturing operations with a variety of end products. Hereinafter, these companies will be referred to as *dominant-business companies.*

2. Companies with businesses that tend to be related through technological, marketing, or other skills (for example, RCA and Procter & Gamble). The largest single business accounts for less than 70% of total revenues, but the related group of businesses accounts for more than 70% of total revenues. These companies will be referred to as *related-business companies.*

3. Companies with a portfolio of old and new businesses that bear little relationship to one another (for example, ITT, Textron, and FMC). Less than 70% of total revenues comes from any single group of similar businesses. These companies will be referred to as *unrelated-business companies.*

The compensation characteristics of each company were compared with those of others in its class to derive patterns of practice associated with that class. These patterns were then contrasted with those of other classes to determine how much corporate strategy influenced the characteristics of top executive compensation. We also wanted to discover how differences in the level of corporate profit performance affected compensation characteristics. To do this we divided each strategic class into high- and low-performing companies.

Exhibit II shows the companies included in each strategy class and the period for which compensation data were collected.

PATTERNS AND TENDENCIES

While we found that corporate pay practices vary widely, these patterns stand out in importance:

- *The total compensation of the top executive varies from year to year more in unrelated-business than in dominant-business organizations. Exhibit III* summarizes our supporting data. It shows that if only high-performing organizations are considered, the percentage with medium or high variability in total compensation increases from 55% among dominant-business to 77% among related-business and to 100% among unrelated-business organizations.

  In addition, *Exhibit III* shows that variability in top executive compensation depends partly on profit performance, at least in the unrelated-business class. Note that the percentages in *Exhibit III* indicate the proportions of companies *in the column* that have low or medium-to-high variability.

- *Changes in top executive compensation are linked to changes in the financial measures of performance, especially earnings per share, more commonly among the high-performing related- and unrelated-business companies than among the dominant-business ones.* As *Exhibit IV* shows, the proportion of companies with a significantly close and positive tie between compensation and earnings per share is 27% for high-performing companies in the dominant class, 92% in the related class, and 100% in the unrelated class. The contrast between high-performing and low-performing companies stands out in the unrelated class.

Exhibit II. Strategy classification and time period of companies studied

Dominant-business companies		Related-business companies cont'd	
Alcoa	1964-1972	Dow Chemical	1964-1970
American Smelting		Eastman Kodak	1962-1969
and Refining	1963-1969	Georgia-Pacific	1960-1971
Anaconda	1960-1966	Johnson & Johnson	1964-1971
B.F. Goodrich	1960-1971	Mead	1960-1968
Crown Zellerbach	1960-1967	Merck & Co.	1965-1972
Diamond International	1960-1969	Miles Laboratories	1965-1970
Fibreboard	1964-1972	Minnesota Mining & Mfg.	1963-1970
Firestone	1960-1971	Monsanto	1961-1968
Goodyear	1964-1972	Pfizer	1965-1971
Great Northern Nekoosa	1962-1971	Procter & Gamble	1960-1970
Hammermill Paper	1960-1966	RCA	1960-1970
International Paper	1960-1965	Smith Kline	
Kimberly-Clark	1960-1966	& French Laboratories	1960-1965
Republic Steel	1960-1970	Sterling Drug	1960-1971
Reynolds Industries	1961-1972	Upjohn	1963-1971
Scott Paper	1962-1971	Warner-Lambert	1960-1966
St. Regis Paper	1960-1971		
Union Camp	1960-1971	**Unrelated-business companies**	
U.S. Steel	1960-1968	Airco	1965-1972
Westvaco	1962-1971	American Standard	1960-1966
		Avco	1961-1971
Related-business companies		FMC	1961-1969
Abbott Laboratories	1960-1971	W.R. Grace	1961-1974
American Cyanamid	1960-1966	ITT	1960-1972
American Home		Martin Marietta	1961-1971
Products	1961-1971	Olin	1960-1963
Borg-Warner	1960-1971	Textron	1963-1971
Bristol-Myers	1960-1966	TRW	1960-1969
Corning Glass Works	1962-1972	USM	1963-1972

- *The emphasis on stock options as a means of long-term income greatly increases as product-market diversity increases. Exhibit V shows that the proportion of companies placing a medium or high emphasis on stock options increases from 26% in the dominant class to 58% in the related class and to 73% in the unrelated class. Also, this exhibit suggests, as might be expected, that stock option gains for top executives in the high-performing*

Exhibit III. Variability in total compensation of the top executive

	Dominant-business		Related-business		Unrelated-business	
	Performance		Performance		Performance	
	High	Low	High	Low	High	Low
Variability:						
Low (less than 15%)	45%	56%	23%	22%	0%	57%
Medium or high	55	44	77	78	100	43
Number of companies	**11**	**9**	**12**	**9**	**4**	**7**

Exhibit IV. Percentage of companies in which top executive compensation is closely related to financial performance

	Dominant-business		Related-business		Unrelated-business		All classes	
	Performance		Performance		Performance		Performance	
	High	Low	High	Low	High	Low	High	Low
Measure of performance:								
Profitability	9%	22%	31%	33%	75%	43%	29%	32%
Return on equity	18	33	31	44	50	43	29	40
Earnings per share	27	44	92	67	100	43	68	52
Any one of above measures	36	36	92	78	100	43	71	56
Number of companies	**11**	**9**	**13**	**9**	**4**	**7**	**28**	**25**

companies are generally higher than for those in the low-performing ones in each strategy class.

- *Companies in the unrelated class tend to have a steeper compensation differential between the top two executives than do related-business or dominant-business companies.* As *Exhibit VI* shows, the proportion of corporations with a differential of 25% or less between the second level and the top executive level decreases from 50% among dominant-business companies and 45% among related-business companies to 18% among unrelated business corporations. When stock option compensation is considered, the differential is again greatest among companies with unrelated businesses.

Summing up, our data show that the compensation of chief executives is not totally idiosyncratic to each organization and that several dimensions of top executive compensation can be related to different organizational strategies. There is a plausible explanation for this, which we shall summarize in the next section. However, *Exhibit IV*

Exhibit V. Companies emphasizing stock options for top executives

	Dominant-business Performance			Related-business Performance			Unrelated-business Performance		
	High	Low	All	High	Low	All	High	Low	All
Degree of emphasis:									
Low (less than 20% of total compensation)	70%	78%	74%	25%	71%	42%	0%	43%	27%
Medium or high (more than 20%)	30	22	26	75	29	58	100	57	73
Number of companies	10	9	19	12	7	19	4	7	11

Note: This exhibit is based on data for 49 companies: 4 companies were excluded from the sample because of incomplete information. The degree of emphasis was determined by calculating the percentage of an executive's total compensation represented by his options when exercised. Both the gains from the options and total regular compensation were aggregated for as long a period as was possible.

Exhibit VI. Second-level executive's total compensation expressed as a percentage of top executive's compensation (excluding stock options)

	Dominant-business Performance			Related-business Performance			Unrelated-business Performance		
	High	Low	All	High	Low	All	High	Low	All
Differential:									
High (less than 60%)	18%	11%	15%	0%	0%	0%	50%	29%	36%
Medium (60%-74%)	46	22	35	69	33	55	25	57	45
Low (75% or more)	36	67	50	31	67	45	25	14	18
Number of companies	11	9	20	13	9	22	4	7	11

shows that for the vast majority of all dominant-business companies and a large number of low-performing unrelated-business companies, there is neither a significant nor positive relationship between top executive compensation and any of three traditional measures of corporate performance. The issues raised by this finding will also be addressed in the remainder of this article.

JUSTIFYING THE LACK OF LINKAGE

The key to the varying patterns of compensation could be the role of the chief executive, given his corporate strategy, the functions of the corporate office, and the nature of corporate-divisional relationships. As the degree of a company's product-market diversity increases, and as the role of the corporate office shifts away from the details of managing individual businesses toward allocation of financial resources to them, it is logical to expect financial measures of performance of the separate businesses or divisions to become the basis for evaluating investment opportunities and rewarding excutive personnel. Furthermore, as executives at the corporate level start evaluating operating divisions according to traditional financial measures of performance, it is a logical next step to evaluate the top corporate officers on a similar basis. In fact, the rules of fairness may require it.

As a result, the compensation of the chief executive of a widely diversified company tends to vary in some relation to total corporate performance, just as a division general manager's compensation varies with divisional performance. Recognizing the necessarily short-run orientation of financial measures of performance, the widely diversified company also emphasizes stock options or other long-term reward instruments. Finally, the greater pay differentials for the more diversified company can be explained on the ground that they reflect the status differentials inherent in an organization where the CEO has the task of allocating corporate funds to different businesses, each of which is strenuously competing for these funds.

Varying Rationale

But when companies do not link top executive compensation to corporate performance, how do they justify their behavior? *Exhibit IV* indicates that quite a few low-performing unrelated companies fail to make this connection. There are at least two possible explanations for their practices:

1. The directors of low-performing widely diversified companies may have been forced to adopt more long-run, qualitative measures of performance for their chief executives than were adopted by the directors of high-performing companies in the same class.

2. They may simply have had to offer attractive employment terms (such as stable compensation or guaranteed increases in pay) to attract and retain chief executives recruited from the performance leaders.

But what about the dominant-business companies, where the performance-compensation relationship was the weakest of all across the board? *Exhibit IV* shows that in only 36% of the cases is there a close relationship between top executive compensation and any one of three measures of corporate performance. What can be the logic of this state of affairs?

For low-performing companies in the dominant-business class, explanations similar to those just given for unrelated-business companies may be offered. In addition, it is argued that the highly qualitative, judgmental systems for measuring top executive performance are reflected in the compensation of the chief executive. It may be pointed out that in vertically integrated dominant-business companies the administrative functions and subunits are linked together in a complex web of interdependencies. This reality, it is argued, reduces the value of simple quantitative measures of the performance of a function of division.

A further argument stresses that the relationship between executive action and corporate performance, which is a complex chain in almost any type of large company, is most complex in the case of dominant-business companies operating in cyclical, oligopolistic industries. Such companies must pay careful attention to goals like market share and capacity utilization, giving less emphasis to financial accounting measures. As opposed to the more diversified organization, which depends less on one product line and market and has a greater ability to enter and exit from any one market, the dominant-business company may find it strategically unwise and quite difficult to maximize current profitability or earnings per share.

Conflicting Evidence

The arguments outlined in the foregoing discussion suggest that it is possible to rationalize both the linkages and lack of linkages between top executive compensation and corporate performance. All considered, however, it seems to us that the rationales fall short. The practices of companies that do not relate top executive compensation clearly and positively to corporate performance are wide open to challenges by skeptics. The most serious challenge comes from within the business community.

Myles Mace, who has been studying boards of directors for over 25 years and who recently interviewed several hundred directors, concludes:

> "Boards of directors of most companies do not do an effective job in evaluating, appraising, and measuring the company president until the financial and other results are so dismal that some remedial action is forced upon the board. Any board has a difficult job in measuring the performance of a president. Criteria are rarely defined for his evaluation. The president's instinct is to attribute poor results to factors over which he has no control. The inclination of friendly directors is to go along

with these apparently plausible explanations. Control of the data made available to the board which provides a basis for evaluation of the president is in the president's own hands, and board members rarely have sufficient interest and time to really understand the critical elements in the operations of the company. Only when the company's results deteriorate almost to a fatal point does the board step in and face the unpleasant task of asking the president to resign."[1]

Mace's conclusion implies a quite different rationale from the ones presented herein for the lack of linkage between compensation and performance. Judging from his observations, there are few companies where the chief executive's compensation and performance are systematically correlated. Mace believes that the needs of chief executives are informally ascertained and invariably complied with, and that only if the requests are unconscionable are changes made. Friendly boards, usually chosen by the chief executives, and interlocking board memberships make the compensation process a congenial give-and-take affair.

This is not to say that all chief executives act without restraint, responsibility, or peer pressures. Certainly, some of them are critical evaluators. Nor can anyone doubt that some directors decide on top executive compensation in an objective, critical manner. However, from an institutional point of view, Mace's data suggest that there is a tremendous amount of ambiguity surrounding the compensation of chief executives.

RISKS OF AMBIGUITY

In our opinion, the modern corporation runs some risks in perpetuating this ambiguity. Where executives see their top-level officers "playing by different rules of the game" than others are asked to do, a morale problem is likely to lurk in the background. Most executives prefer to have their pay tied to performance, and they expect to be treated on the same basis as their colleagues and peers.[2] When these preferences and expectations are denied, the psychological contact between an executive and his organization is substantially weakened. In addition, a lack of perceived consistency in matters of pay dulls the power of incentive compensation systems to influence executives below the top level.

Paralleling this internal risk is an external one. Shareholders and the public have more than a passing interest in this matter. On the one hand, the shareholder wants to be assured that management is accountable to the directors he elects. Where top executive pay is not linked in some apparent way to traditional measures of corporate performance, it is difficult to communicate such assurances of accountability to the shareholders. On the other hand, the public is becoming increasingly concerned about the social role of the modern corporation. If the corporation is perceived as distributing income inequitably to managers and other employees, then it is only natural for skeptics to gain confidence in their doubts about the corporate role in society.

Relating Pay to Performance

We believe that the risks of this ambiguity are increasing. Until changes in a top executive's compensation can be related meaningfully to financial measures of performance, directors will have an increasingly difficult time justifying pay levels to employees, unions, stockholders, and the general public.

Every chief executive's compensation, therefore, should be at least partially related to corporate performance. Where that relationship is loose, clear explanations of compensation policy should be given to employees and shareholders. Current theories of executive compensation alone are not sufficient to justify the decisions made. The theories say, in effect, that management should pay some measure of the executive's market value and follow industry practices. While market constraints are important and cannot long be ignored, our study suggests that corporate strategy also should be taken into account.

This step would give a company plenty of leeway to individualize its compensation policy. Companies in the same industry can and do follow different strategies. Also, they tend to emphasize different goals at different times—expansion and market share during some periods, growth through diversification or acquisitions during others, and profitability during others. Given such differences, attempts to relate top executive compensation to strategy, particularly to the role of the corporate office and the nature of the desired corporate-divisional relationships, may be more satisfactory from an administrative standpoint than simply following industry practices.[3]

Top executives are often the most ardent supporters of the notion that compensation systems reinforce the company's communication system, signaling the types and amount of individual effort that management values. So why not compensate the chief executive in a way that emphasizes links between performance and rewards, minimizes the risks of hurting morale in the company, and heads off suspicious inquiries from the outside? Judging from our research, such a policy is practical and realistic.

NOTES

1. Myles L. Mace, *Directors: Myth and Reality* (Boston, Division of Research, Harvard Business School, 1971), p. 41.
2. See I. R. Andrews and Mildred M. Henry, "Management Attitudes Toward Pay," *Industrial Relations*, October 1963, p. 29; Edward E. Lawler, III, "Managers' Attitudes Toward How Their Pay Is and Should be Determined," *Journal of Applied Psychology*, August 1966, p. 273; and J. Stacy Adams, "Toward an Understanding of Inequity," *Journal of Abnormal and Social Psychology*, Vol. 67, No. 5, 1963, p. 422.
3. For a detailed discussion of one such approach, see Malcolm S. Salter, "Tailor Incentive Compensation to Strategy," HBR March-April 1973, p. 94.

CARL G. BURGEN

The Scenario for Tomorrow's Executive

It is axiomatic that soldiers are trained to fight the last war. Much the same point can be made about the men who run the nation's corporations.

The typical CEO has been trained to manage a corporation far smaller and less complex than the one he finds himself running, and has been conditioned to think of himself as merely the manager of a business in an age that is demanding that he play a far broader role.

The chief executive may not like it very much, but America's corporations and the men who manage them are obliged to play a more public role than ever before, and are being criticized as never before when they do not play it to the public's satisfaction. A nation that is increasingly concerned about the power of big government and big business is demanding that someone be held personally accountable for how that power is being used.

Corporations do not practice representative democracy. Shareholders really have nothing at all to say about the day-to-day running of the business and very little to say about the setting of longer-range goals. In very few companies today does the board of directors play more than a subsidiary role in management. It is the chief executive who has the power, and the demand for personal accountability falls most heavily on his shoulders.

Source: Reprinted from the May 4, 1974 issue of *Business Week* by special permission, pp. 85-86. © 1974 by McGraw-Hill, Inc.

The CEO must continue to manage his business at a profit because that is what the shareholders are paying him to do. But he must also deal with all of the diverse groups that in one way or another now fall within the corporate orbit: workers, consumers, environmentalists, minorities, bankers, investors, the press, Congress, government agencies, and often foreign governments.

He can expect to be judged not merely on how well his company performs in the marketplace by also on how successfully he deals with these groups—not merely satisfying their demands but in some cases anticipating them. Even the chief executive's salary has become part of the public record, and so become a subject of public debate.

AN UNFAMILIAR LANDSCAPE

No chief executive could be oblivious to the economic and social turmoil of the past decade and to the impact it has had on his job. If the typical CEO has been slow to respond, it is because there was next to nothing in his training or conditioning to tell him how to respond. Besides, given the incredible amounts of time required just to manage today's huge, diverse, far-flung companies, few CEOs have found time enough to formulate a suitable response.

There is an obvious hesitancy on the part of most managers to move on to what is seen as unfamiliar ground—into politics, for instance, or the handling of the demands of minority groups. To many CEOs, the serious trouble that some corporate executives got into for illegal contributions to President Nixon's 1972 campaign is seen as an indication of what can happen to a man when he ventures into areas removed from running a business.

There are still some very serious philosophical questions about the proper role that a corporation and its chief executive should play in the world outside. Neil Chamberlain, professor of economics at Columbia University's Business School, warns that while the chief executive must be sensitive to social and political issues, "he doesn't have to be out ahead of the pack. I don't see him as a white knight."

For all these reasons and more, few corporations have yet tried to formulate a reasoned, strategic response to the demands being made of business, and very few chief executives have gotten deeply involved yet in the formulation process.

Business, says Dean Harold M. Williams of the UCLA Graduate School of Management, has typically responded only to those groups with enough power and backing to threaten the company. And the chief executive in most companies is likely to get involved only when things reach a crisis point; otherwise, things are taken care of at a lower echelon.

Yet as corporations lag in this business of redefining their role in 1974 America, events are being taken out of their hands.

PUBLIC AND PRIVATE

Government and business have both grown big and complex, and it becomes harder and harder to determine where one ends and the other begins. How much of a major defense contractor is in the private sector and how much in the public sector? New York State will help bail out financially distressed Consolidated Edison. Multinational companies are often bigger in terms of wealth than the country in which they operate. Where is the line between what is public and what is private to be drawn?

The corporation could once be seen as simply the organizer of capital and labor to produce goods and services. That is still true today, of course, but that notion underplays the impact that the modern-day corporation has upon society. The corporation hires and fires and can bring about a sociological revolution if it begins hiring and promoting more blacks and more women. It can stay in a community and keep it prosperous or move out and leave it destitute. It can pollute the environment or it can help clean it up. The corporation is an absolutely integral part of society today—more so than ever before because it is bigger and richer than ever before—and if it is difficult for the average CEO to see it in that light, it is true just the same.

No big corporation can escape this redefinition of its role in the world, and no chief executive can ignore the extent to which his role within the corporation has changed. The pressures on both the corporation and the chief executive to adapt to this "new reality" are strong and they will certainly get stronger in years to come.

CEOs are already burdened with outside interests, some of which have relatively little to do with the day-to-day running of a company. But as a number of the CEOs interviewed in this Special Issue have come to realize, it is a role that cannot be dodged. When the chips were down, it fell to President Harry Bridges of Shell Oil Co. to defend his company before Senator Jackson's subcommittee on investigations.

In the end, of course, it will fall to the CEO to move his own company because only he has the power to do so. And that is not an easy job. The CEO is, in most cases, only a hired professional and not the owner of the business. Some companies have gotten into trouble because the CEO stayed on the job too long, but the more common practice today is to give the man the job for just a few years—too short a time, in many cases, to make substantial changes.

GROUNDWORK FOR CHANGE

A big corporation is like any other big institution in that it resists change. "In very large companies there is always a quality of the institution molding the manager—always," says Professor Richard Eells of Columbia's Graduate School of Business. "But," he adds, "occasionally you have men with the strength to turn a company around to something completely different. The corporate chief executive, after all, often has longer than the President of the U.S. to develop and implement long-range plans."

The groundwork for change is already visible. It is highly questionable whether the big corporation of today can be run by one man, and it will probably prove all but impossible for any one man to run what surely will be the still bigger corporations of tomorrow.

This will become a shared responsibility in more and more companies, with the chief executive picking other people to make all but the most critical decisions. Collective management is coming back into style, with an "office of the chief executive" that includes several men rather than just a single corporate leader.

The corporation of the future will also need a new type of CEO, trained and motivated in a different way than today's CEO. The man will be less of a doer and more of a planner, and his training will put more stress on the humanities and less on nuts-and-bolts business courses. Appearance will count for more because the CEO of tomorrow will be more of a public figure.

The typical CEO will be fairly young—most chief executives think 45 to 50 is the ideal age to enter the job—but his tenure will be limited. "Five years is ample time to build a management team better than the one you inherited," says James B. Farley, president of Booz, Allen, & Hamilton, the consulting firm. But a CEO can overstay his welcome, too. "After 10 years there's a tendency to become a defender of your own achievements," says management philosopher Peter Drucker.

THE ROLE AND THE STYLE

The CEO of tomorrow will come under heavy pressure to build a stronger and more representative board of directors. Boards have been opened to blacks and women, but the newcomers have had virtually no impact on business—because few CEOs pay more than passing attention to their boards. The Investor Responsibility Research Center, a Washington-based public interest group, surveyed a group of chief executives recently and found that few wanted the broad selection process opened to greater shareholder participation. Similarly, there was little interest in opening the board to constituency representatives.

Few CEOs, the Washington group concluded, are doing much to change the basic balance of power between top management and the board.

The biggest change of all, though, will probably be in how the CEO sees his own function, not only within the corporation but also within society.

Frank A. Armstrong recalls in his new book, *Memos to Management*, that "the so-called 'Organization Man' was reconciled to his role of serving big companies. He wasn't particularly concerned with preserving his individuality. He had no interest in changing corporate life or corporate goals, and he almost never doubted the worth of these goals nor the worth and importance of his role."

Today a strong commitment still is needed—but not an unquestioning one. To Alonzo L. McDonald, Jr., managing partner of McKinsey & Co., the top management job now carries such enormous responsibility that the man accepting it must consciously commit himself to the good of the organization and its various constituencies as well. Personal aims will have to be sacrificed, but not for some blind faith in the corporation. "Every ounce of status and power must be balanced by a corresponding level of moral responsibility toward the organization and its constituents," says McDonald.

RECONCILING CONFLICTS

In the final analysis, it is an evolutionary thing. It took one sort of chief executive to create the companies in the first place—Rockefellers and Carnegies and Harrimans—and quite another sort to take what was created and turn it into the diversified multinational corporation of today. Still another sort of chief executive—schooled and motivated differently from his predecessors—is needed to mesh today's corporation into the broader framework of society. It will take a man skilled at reconciling what now often seem irreconcilable conflicts between the interests of shareholders and those of all the other constituencies that the corporation serves.

If corporations cannot make the adjustment themselves, then they risk having it forced upon them. No less important, failure to adjust risks turning off the generation that should provide the top executives 20 and 30 years from now.

"The present generation," says McDonald of McKinsey, "does it because they were taught to reach for the brass ring. I think future generations increasingly will ask: Is it really worthwhile?"

JEAN ROSS-SKINNER

European Executives: 'Union Now'

They might have been agents *provocateurs* bent on foreign intrigue. Actually, though, the two men who met one dark rainy night last March near the waterfront of the ancient Netherlands town of Dordrecht were a couple of Dutch business executives. One was Jan van Leeuwen, a sales manager at giant Unilever; the other a senior engineer with E.I. du Pont's Dutch subsidiary. Over steins of pale golden lager in an old raftered pub, they talked long and animatedly, taking copious notes and poring over documents. Several hours later, the two men nodded agreement, shook hands and walked out into the rain-drenched streets of Dordrecht.

What the intent negotiators accomplished that night would have been considered a European impossibility only a scant few years ago—the creation of a new union of middle-management executives in Dutch industry. For on top of his Unilever sales job, van Leeuwen is a vice president of the Netherland Central Union for Higher Personnel (NCHP) and his moonlighting mission is to establish company-based unions of executives throughout Holland. As a result of that clandestine conference, he told Dun's last month, "We formally established the du Pont de Nemours (Nederland) Association of Higher Personnel. Out of a potential 300 members, we already have 125 signed up."

Unlike American middle managers, who talk a lot about job disenchantment ("The Revolt of the Middle Managers—Phase Two," *March 1973*), Europe's second-echelon executives are doing something about

Source: Reprinted with the special permission of *Dun's Review*, April 1974. Copyright 1974, Dun & Bradstreet Publications Corporation.

their grievances as they flock to join rapidly expanding middle-management unions. In effect, they are European industry's new militants, rushing to the business barricades in double-breasted suits.

Executive unions have been part of European industry since the Forties. But only in the past few years of increased militancy has the middle-management labor movement become sufficiently broad to cause waves of apprehension in executive suites from Stockholm to Rome.

The unions are strongest in Sweden, where about one-half of all middle managers are unionized, and in Holland, where some 40% are dues-paying members. In France and Germany, the unions have signed up about one out of ten middle managers, while in Britain, which has enough trouble trying to mollify miners let alone executives, the movement has only recently sprung to life.

Following the common market concept, moreover, the middle-management unions are finding strength in bigness. Most national unions have grouped together in the International Confederation of Executive Staffs (ICES), which serves as a combination listening post and lobby for its several hundred thousand members across the Continent. With offices and full-time staffs in Paris, Geneva and Brussels, ICES acts as a clearing house for information on executive benefits and pressures European governments and the EEC Commission for legislation favorable to middle managers.

At first glance, perhaps, it would seem that the European cry of "Union Now" is being heard in the wrong place. Most European middle managers may earn less and pay higher taxes than their American counterparts, but they enjoy considerably greater security and are cushioned by their companies against a variety of future shocks. Pensions are vested early and are often as high as 75%-80% of final salary, compared with the U.S. norm of around 50%. In a number of countries, executives are entitled by law to immediate 100% vesting in their pension rights, which are even inflation-proofed by being tied to cost-of-living indexes. When a retired European executive dies, his widow can expect to receive 50% to 70% of her husband's pension; in the U.S. she would get only a modest lump sum. And in Belgium and Italy, the executive who is laid off after fifteen years of service is assuaged with severance pay amounting to three years' salary, a lot more than his opposite number in the U.S. could expect.

ODD MAN OUT?

Why, then, the urge to unionize? Basically, the European middle manager, like his American counterpart, worries that he is fast becoming industry's odd man out, squeezed from the top by management's cost-cutting limitations on his salary growth and from below by the growing demands of increasingly militant blue-collar trade unions. The European middle manager fears that the once poles-apart difference between his salary and that of rank-and-file company employees is narrowing to the point that his very status and prestige are at stake. At the same time, of course, inflation has slowed the growth of his purchasing power. "In West Germany," says Jeurgen Borgwardt, general secretary of the Union der Leitenden Angestellten (ULA), the German executives' union, "some managers have actually suffered a fall in their real purchasing power."

But money is by no means the only issue. The discontent of the middle managers cuts much deeper than that. Demanding a voice in the way their companies are run, they see unionism as a base from which they can insist on dialogue with top management. Declares Louis Bouan, president of France's executive union Centre National des Jeunes Cadres, and a consultant with the Metra group in Paris: "French middle managers carry out company policy, but they have no say in the framing of it. Their frustration is pushing them to unionism."

German executives are particularly vociferous in demanding a bigger say in company affairs. They see themselves as an emerging third force powerful enough to play a major independent role in shaping corporate policy. Just recently, for example, they won a limited right to representation on the supervisory boards that appoint the top managers of all large German companies. Explains Jeurgen Borgwardt, "Sometimes employers make short-sighted decisions with short-term profits in mind. Or they ignore the company's impact on the public. At the other extreme, the workers have been pushing for excessively high wage demands. We believe our interests are most closely aligned with the long-term health of the company itself. And," adds Borgwardt determinedly, "we want a say in how it is run."

Nevertheless, executive unionism is growing fastest in those countries where changing company fortunes and policies appear to threaten the status of middle managers. Across Europe, in fact, executive unionists consider their first goal to be the improvement of job security and direct aid to those middle managers who, through no fault of their own, are marked "redundant" (a European synonym for "expendable"). In Sweden, for instance, the brisk surge in membership in SACO, the union that represents most of the 50% of Swedish executives who have organized, closely parallels the recent climb in managerial redundancies.

To lighten the burden of the laid-off executive, SACO and the Swedish Employers' Confederation set up a joint fund three years ago that finances a nationwide executive placement agency and provides free retraining to executives over forty. And SACO itself has a special fund that pays luckless managers who are separated from bankrupt companies without severance pay about 80% of their former salaries for up to 300 working days.

When multiple redundancies threaten, SACO negotiators move in and negotiate with management, often winning reprieves for many a middle manager who could not survive alone. Says an official of the Swedish Association of Graduate Engineers, a SACO affiliate representing executives with economic and engineering backgrounds: "When a company tells us it must dismiss, say, 150 executives, we often find that we can cut the number of dismissals to seventy or less by persuading the company to move men into other divisions and to retrain others."

In Britain, the Staff Association of Britain's Cadbury Schweppes was little more than a cozy company club until the chocolate maker and beverage bottler merged in 1969 and began furloughing middle executives as a fillip to efficiency. Now more than 500 of Cadbury Schweppes' 750 middle managers belong to the company's executive union. "Even senior managers, who had been pretty complacent, have joined," reports union chief Gilbert Drake, a controller in the confectionery division. "They saw the virtue of having an organization the company would listen to."

Similarly, the house executive union at giant Imperial Chemical Industries was launched in 1971 as a defensive move against a new cost-cutting program designed to whittle down the work force. Says a key organizer for the ICI Staff Association: "We did not dispute the fact that the company was overmanned. But we felt that because executives were unorganized, they were bearing the brunt of the cutbacks."

Even at the Common Market level, the International Confederation of Executive Staffs, the federation representing most European executive unions, pushes for special assistance from the EEC Social Fund for executives thrown out of work by shutdowns and mergers in depressed areas. Explains Martinus Vermeer, an insurance executive who is a vice president of Holland's NCHP: "Because of their specialization, these men have difficulty finding new jobs. We think the Social Fund should help by providing them with free retraining and paying older redundant executives a percentage of their pay on a reducing scale."

FLACK FROM LABOR

As might be expected when two salesmen work the same territory, the rise of executive unionism in Europe has led to bitter acrimony between middle-management organizers and the established labor unions. The labor unions maintain that they should be the representatives of executives, who are, after all, company employees. They also charge that house executive unions are the creatures of top management and are designed only to preserve differentials between base pay and other benefits—a barb that in many cases is not far from the mark.

In some cases, the conflict with labor has also helped swell executive-union ranks. In Holland, for instance, membership in the NCHP doubled last year. The increase was directly fueled by an agreement between government, industry and the workers' unions to clamp a ceiling on the total cost of wage agreements. When the blue-collar unions lobbied to increase their share of pay increases and diminish that of managers, Dutch executives saw red and rushed to join the union. Says President Henk van der Schalie of the NCHP, a onetime senior economist at Philips Lamp: "A lot of senior managers who thought they were too important to organize suddenly realized they did not count for anything and needed better protection."

A growing force in Dutch industry, the NCHP's structure, its methods and many of its goals are broadly similar to those of other executive unions throughout Europe. A federation that offers common ground to all executives up to—but excluding—board level, the NCHP membership roster includes 3,500 individual executives, associations of managers in such industries as banking and textiles, and 75 company-based unions. The NCHP has organized at such big Dutch names as Philips Lamp, Unilever, KLM, Fokker, DAF and Hoogovens Steel, and at important U.S. subsidiaries like those of General Electric, Mobil Oil, Cincinnati Milacron, Merck, Sharp and Dohme and now, thanks to Jan van Leeuwen's mission to Dordrecht, du Pont.

With member managers paying annual dues of $30 a head, last year's 100% increase in membership has enabled the burgeoning NCHP to move into a twelve-room modern office suite in downtown Utrecht and staff it with fifteen full-time employees. Under President van der Schalie and Manager Paul Labohm, another former Philips executive who turned to executive unionism because of frustrations on the job, the NCHP has succeeded in getting the managements of most Dutch companies to sit down and discuss their differences. Even on that informal basis, considerable progress has been made in middle management's impact on long-term planning. For one thing, the unions have persuaded a number of companies to project their executive needs ahead five years and more, a trend that will help guide undergraduates into the most needed skills.

But the NCHP is after a lot more than that. "We want knowledge," says Labohm. "We want to know what executives are being paid in all companies. And we want a role in deciding salary levels and differentials. The federation's goal is nothing less than collective-bargaining agreements with companies throughout Dutch industry, and with contracts binding on both sides."

What's more, van der Schalie sees success at hand. "Within the next few weeks," he predicts, "the first companies will give in, starting with AKZO [the big Dutch textile manufacturer]."

To achieve its aims, the NCHP trots out all the tools of traditional labor unions. It pressures individual companies, industry groups and the national employer's federation, prods the Ministry of Social Affairs and lobbies politicians of all parties. One thing the executive union has going for it that the trade unions do not is an alumni of highly placed Dutch business executives who have graduated out of middle-management ranks and are highly sympathetic to NCHP aims.

Even the ultimate weapon of labor—the strike—is kept fully primed. "We would be reluctant to use it," allows courtly Martinus Vermeer, "and there are better methods. But if, for example, industry gave in to the workers' unions and executive salaries actually fell, then we would certainly strike."

At the moment, a rise in real executive income does not seem to be in the cards. "We are fighting more to preserve what we have," Vermeer admits. "Our backs are to the wall." But the federation is campaigning to improve the middle manager's lot in a number of ways.

Among the current demands on van der Schalie's list: "time for time" (extra time off for executives who work overly long hours); protection of the rights of senior staff people who develop patents; compulsory pension funds for all sizable companies plus the executives' right to appoint half the pension fund trustees; and the creation of a new state-run job agency geared to placing redundant executives. The NCHP recently scored a breakthrough in another goal: salary adjustments for all executives to offset the eroding effects of inflation. It persuaded one reluctant U.S. subsidiary to introduce the plan, not just for junior staff members, but for senior executives as well.

MANAGEMENT HOSTILITY

But the permissive attitude of Dutch companies toward executive unions is far from universal. Corporate attitudes range from wary neutrality to outright hostility. Possibly because blue-collar unions have been putting on the pressure, Britain's Imperial Chemical Industries, for example, has steadfastly refused to recognize the ICI Staff Association as a negotiating body. Yet even that may come if, as seems likely, the executive union wins official standing under Britain's Industrial Relations Act.

According to Belgian Jean Defer, joint secretary general of ICES, the big European federation, U.S. subsidiaries are among the least receptive to executive unions, at least at first. While "many soon grasp the advantages of a continuing dialogue with their executive ranks," Defer allows, he says that others remain staunchly opposed to a concept that could have dangerous repercussions back in the U.S.

Particularly in Germany, says ULA organizer Jeurgen Borgwardt, "many U.S. companies are very shortsighted and fight our organization. They think their executives are only interested in higher remuneration and won't talk to them. They should wake up and recognize the social realities in Germany."

Ford of Europe, for one, rejects any suggestion that the company is anti-union, but questions whether corporate executives ought to engage in collective bargaining. While Ford regularly deals with white-collar unions that include lower echelon managers, it steadfastly refuses to have any truck with organized senior executives. Declares Vice President Walter Haynes: "It is our view that above a certain level our executives are members of management, and to be a member of a union as well is a contradiction in terms. We are not willing to discuss this type of union."

That attitude certainly reflects the views of American parent companies back home, where, despite rumblings of middle-management discontent, no groundswell for executive unions has yet developed. But in Europe, the idea has not only come, but seems here to stay. Conceivably, an economic boom in the late 1970s could alleviate middle-management fears of redundancy, take the pressure off mounting demands for more pay and perks and stem the growth of executive union membership. But most of the managers who are signing up with unions today for purely defensive reasons see a much wider potential for their organized strength in the future.

"There is a spirit among middle managers now," says Holland's Henk van der Schalie, "a realization that we should continue to increase our power. For example, when we approached the executives at AKZO a short time ago, we found that those men had not really thought about organizing before. But when they heard what we were doing, 92% of them favored organizing. Their immediate reaction was, 'Yes, that's right. That's what we want.' "

HAROLD J. LEAVITT

Beyond the Analytic Manager: Part II

PART II: SOME SEEDLINGS OF ALTERNATIVES AND SUPPLEMENTS TO ANALYTIC METHODS

Part I of this essay argued that the criticism of management analysts, currently widespread both in management and in society at large, signals more than empty antagonism. The contemporary world of ideas seems alight with a whole variety of more positive experiments into alternative styles of thought. The ideas can be found in many stages of development and in extremely diverse intellectual regions, among physicists, philosophers of science, neurologists, social scientists, religionists, engineers, and artists. Some are only sparks of relatively undirected search; some are enlarging at a rapid rate and promise to bear upon the practice of management within a relatively short time. Many look crazy, and probably are.

My particular perspective in Part II will be based in the tripartite model of problem solving mentioned previously, a model that breaks the larger problem-solving process into three aspects, problem finding, problem solving, and problem (solution) implementing. These steps by no means need to occur in that order, or even serially. And in this section my emphasis will, of course, be primarily on the problem-finding part of the process, because it appears that these alternative styles

Source: © 1975 by the Regents of the University of California. Reprinted from *California Management Review*, Vol. 17, No. 4, pp. 11-21, by permission of the Regents.

of thought are mostly relevant to that aspect of the broader problem-solving issue.

I would like to be able to say that the remainder of this article will constitute a review and mapping of these diverse signals, but it would take a far wider competence than mine to cover all the relevant realms. So I shall try only to reach as far out in as many directions as I can, simply pointing to potentially relevant ideas that seem to be out there. Then, as we come back in closer to the more traditional realms of management and social science, I perhaps can build a more detailed map.

It is not modesty that leads to these disclaimers; it is the nature of the terrain. The problem is to examine alternative ways of thinking while using only one way of thinking, which may be a little like a fish trying to understand the nature of a ship sailing above him. In any case, treating management as the center of the world, let's begin by looking rather far out.

Some Far-out Signals: Zen and Meditation and the Human Brain

"Far-out" means both far out from the current practice of management and also far-out relative to prevalent analytic and rational rules of thought. One justification for looking far out in the first sense is just historical hindsight. Much of the commonplace in management today was far-out and unrelated yesterday—cybernetics and information theory, for example, or the techniques and theory derived from psychoanalysis. It is harder to offer managers an easy justification for searching far out in the second sense, that is, outside our traditional framework of rationality. So let me simply ask the reader to go along for a while, to relax his usual evaluation rules long enough to consider some notions that most of us have heretofore treated as too distant from our accepted ways of thinking to be worth much attention.

There is, out there, the whole world of *consciousness raising*,[1] ranging from Zen to transcendental meditation to the teachings of Don Juan as transmitted through Carlos Casteneda.[2] Analytically speaking, all of those are far-out, so far-out that it is simply difficult to comprehend what those people are talking about. They all seem to be concerned with alternative routes to peace of mind, or to "understanding," with alternative ways of thinking about the self and the world. Right now, they are even receiving peripheral respectability in universities, although usually more at the behest of students than of faculty. All of them seem to share, to some degree, a search for other ways of using the mind. Some appear to be not only nonanalytic but *anti-analytic*.[3] Their techniques include laborious training in how *not* to think analytically, how *not* to respond to the usual stimuli in the usual way. Most of these approaches, that is, seem to treat traditional rationality as interference—noise that blocks the learning of what they have to offer.

Thus, briefly and amateurishly, Zen (out of mainland Asia via Japan) tries to teach new levels of understanding, initially by clearing away traditional habits of rationality. One technique is to require students to "solve" problems that cannot be solved analytically, such as, "What is the sound of one hand clapping?" The hypothetical student is likely, apparently, to return again and again to "solutions" that are the products of active analytic thought. Only when he has finally given up these self-conscious analytic habits is "understanding" to be achieved. The role of the master seems to be a nondirective one, of gently returning the acolyte to the drawing boards, until the student has finally seen his own light.

The intent of Zen is not usually withdrawal from the real world. It seems rather to be heightened concentration and attention to the world. What is to be turned off is the intervening noise and interference of "normal" adult mental activity. In his introduction to Herrigel's *Zen and the Art of Archery*, Suzuki describes the nature of Zen this way: "Zen is the 'everyday mind.' This 'everyday mind' is not more than 'sleeping when tired, eating when hungry.' As soon as we reflect, deliberate, and conceptualize, the original consciousness is lost and a thought interferes. We no longer eat while eating, we no longer sleep while sleeping. . . . Man is a thinking reed but his great works are done when he is not calculating and thinking. 'Childlikeness' has to be restored with long years of training in the art of self-forgetfulness. When this is attained, man thinks yet he does not think."[4]

Transcendental meditation (TM) is a more recent input out of India, a form of yoga. From my extremely limited perspective, it seems somewhat more simple than Zen. TM, like Zen, seeks concentration, but apparently in the interests of self-control, of gaining psychological distance from the tribulations of everyday life. The freeing-up theme, the shaking loose from rational habits, appears here as well. Thus, "While practice in most activities implies the development of habits and the establishment of conditioning, the practice of meditation can be better understood as quite the opposite: a persistent effort to detect and become free from all conditioning, compulsive functioning of mind and body, habitual emotional responses that may contaminate the utterly simple situation required by the participant."[5] The technique of TM apparently is very simple. It apparently can be learned quickly and requires only brief daily periods thereafter. Indeed some promoters of TM (and there are many) seem essentially to argue that one big advantage of TM over its competitors is that its techniques for relaxation are so cheap and easy to acquire.

From Mexico, the teachings of Don Juan, as translated through the writings of anthropologist Casteneda, have much of the same flavor. Thus, Ornstein quotes Casteneda conversing with his teacher:

> " 'For years I have truly tried to live in accordance with your teachings,' I said. 'Obviously I have not done well. How can I do better now?'
>
> 'You think and talk too much. You must stop talking to yourself.'
>
> 'What do you mean?'
>
> 'You talk to yourself too much. You're not unique in that. Everyone of us does that. We carry on an internal talk. Think about it. Whenever you are alone, what do you do?'
>
> 'I talk to myself.'
>
> 'What do you talk to yourself about?'
>
> 'I don't know; anything, I suppose.'
>
> 'I'll tell you what we talk to ourselves about. We talk about our world. In fact we maintain our world with our internal talk.'
>
> 'How do we do that?'
>
> 'Whenever we finish talking to ourselves the world is always as it should be. We renew it, we kindle it with life, we uphold it with our internal talk. Not only that, but we also choose our paths as we talk to ourselves. Thus we repeat the same choices over and over until the day we die, because we keep on repeating the same internal talk over and over until the day we die.' "[6]

These unorthodox, rather far-out ways of thinking have not, for me at least, seemed relevant enough to worry much about as they and I have stood until now. But my analytic heritage snaps to attention upon learning that there may be interesting neurological correlates to some of them. Electroencephalographic patterns of alpha waves during Zen and some other types of meditation, for example, are found to be faster than during normal thought.[6] That kind of empirical finding suggests that things may really be going on in those people's heads that are not going on in mine.

In the same vein, recent work on patients in whom the connections between left and right cerebral lobes have been surgically separated looks extremely exciting.[6-8] It appears that the left hemisphere (controlling the right side of the body) may be where most of us do most of our logical analytic thinking and where symbolic (verbal and numeric) languages of thought reside. But the right hemisphere, while illiterate and verbally almost mute, seems to be more holistic, visual, spatial, and more impulsive and intuitive. So a patient may be able verbally to describe objects and deal with numbers if they are presented to the left brain while he is almost entirely unable to perform those activities when they are presented to the right. But a patient can put together a two-dimensional puzzle with his left hand (right brain) but not with his right hand; or he can recognize complex visual patterns (faces) when presented to the right brain but not to the left. And he can respond emotionally to, say, embarrassing photographs presented to the right brain without being able to say what he is seeing. It has been proposed that Western training and education have tended to emphasize and indeed train left-brain functions to the neglect of right, and that perhaps some Eastern orientations such as Zen may serve to exercise and train the right brain. It seems interesting to speculate about such matters as Zen and other forms of meditation from that perspective. I, at least, can handle such speculations much more comfortably having been reassured by the presence of these neurological correlates.

But one can properly ask: suppose we do get a better grasp on Zen and meditation and brain functions. What possible implications might there be, say in a couple decades, for the practice of management? Certainly no one can now give a very useful answer to that question. But at the speculative level, let me return to an argument raised in Part I of this article. I proposed that one of the weaknesses of "pure" analysis on the management scene lay in identifying the problems to be solved. Analysis seems an excellent tool for specifying and evaluating alternatives to problems already given but not very good for deciding what problems are the important ones, for helping us to set our own or our organization's long-term goals, or for being very creative about what kinds of possibilities lie out there. Which is to say, the kind of ideas we have just been talking about, if they turn out to be useful at all, will do so by bearing upon the questions of managerial values and organizational goals, questions that will surely loom larger in the years ahead.

Of course there are some potential negative consequences. One may be a propensity for some managers to return to just what our analytic methods have helped us to escape from: dependency on the counsel of astrologers or seers or physiognomists, this time in the cloaks of Zen monks or mediators (instead of the counsel of contemporary management scientists!); a return, that is, to nonsystematic, nonrefereed, nonanalytic decision making. But is a return to other superstitions the only alternative to analysis?

The World of Encounter Groups

At the outer edges of clinical and social psychology, beyond the now almost old-fashioned methods of group therapy and sensitivity training, lies the diverse and multi-formed world of the encounter group.[9] The visitor into this terrain will soon encounter primal screams, Laing-type therapy, body awareness, the Esalen Institute, and a great collection of other intermediate shapes and sounds. They are intermediate only in the sense that they seem to occupy a space somewhat closer-in to Western thought than Eastern mysticism or Don Juan, and somewhat farther out than T-group training or some other areas of humanistic psychology. The encounter world can serve as a bridge. Many members of the various facets of that movement are at the same time into mysticism and the farther reaches, and at the other end, into sensitivity training, organizational development, and various forms of more conventional management practice.

The encounter group seems to have grown up roughly like this: first, sensitivity and T-group trainers, and some other humanistic individuals and groups in psychology in the fifties, took a then fairly radical position in proposing that empathy and sensitivity, as well as understanding of group dynamics, could be taught and learned. They saw sensitivity (personal and interpersonal) as a kind of supplement to and enabler of rationality. They proposed that people might work together more effectively if they learned to communicate with one another empathetically, trying better to understand one another's feelings. In doing so, many of them rejected what was called "intellectualizing," that is, *talking* (analytically) about one's feelings instead of directly expressing or reacting to them. The method of the T-group was aimed at getting people to sense and express their here-and-now feelings toward one another. The words used to express those feelings were to serve only as an instrument of communication, and not as a means of abstracting from the "feelings level" to the "intellectual level." It was (and is) believed that this general method helps people to feel themselves as others feel them, to "loosen" people, and to make their interpersonal relations more comfortable.

By thus clearing away the unexpressed but operant emotional barriers, the method is presumed secondarily to enable people to solve problems better (more creatively and more imaginatively), particularly in interpersonal situations. Beyond this enabling notion, there was not much concern in the T-group movement with the *nature* of thinking processes. One idea (akin to Zen, but at the interpersonal level) was to eliminate tensions and discomforts that constituted barriers to creativity and imagination for people working in groups.[10] A second idea, and the one pushed hardest in organizational settings, was that people, in groups, would "support the ideas they helped to create." Most early applied group work (and even most contemporary organizational-development work) seems concerned mostly with this second issue, that is, with improving the implementation of problem solutions by bringing the problem-solving (decision making, alternative generating) and problem-implementing phases of the larger problem-solving process closer together. It was to gain commitment that planning and doing were to be brought together through group techniques.

The more recent encounter-group movement (much of which is an outgrowth of the T-group movement) represents yet another step away from the traditional rational analytic models. While T-groupers were content to talk to one another about their feelings, encounter groupers have preferred more direct, less verbal methods, encouraging people to act out their feelings toward one another physically as well as with words. Hence the emphasis on "touchies and feelies," on body awareness and physical control of the body (as in yoga), and in other expressive, nonverbal activities such as finger painting or dancing. Hence, too, an even greater tendency to reject the "restrictiveness" of rational analytic rules.

Many of these farther reaches of humanistic psychology have been actively antianalytic,[9] rejecting the mores and the paraphernalia of the analytic method almost altogether. It is not quite fair to say that they have argued against analysis, because for the most part they have refused to argue, on the grounds that argument itself is one of the rules of the old game.[11] They seem to feel that full exploration of this new territory of the senses is disallowed by the old rules. If they worship at any intellectual altar, it is probably the altar of existentialism.

In Part I, I suggested that many analysts are such true believers in "The Method" that they seem blind to other perspectives. The same criticism, of course, can be leveled in spades at many humanistic-behaviorist types. They are often blindly antianalytic and extraordinarily in-groupy, valuing—rather unquestioningly—an image of "natural" man, childlike, uninhibited, pure; and suspicious of the "distorting" and "inhibiting" effects of almost any formal education or formal organizational structures.

To the analytic mind, these more radical manifestations may look not just irrelevant, but silly, at least until one can find some kind of theoretical structure to account from them. But such structures now seem to be turning up. Thus, the left-brain-right-brain research, mentioned previously, might be brought to bear. The emphasis on feelings and emotions and on direct sensing can tentatively be seen as an effort to build up the right-brain functions.

There is also a second kind of structure that makes sense to me.[10] Developmental psychologists (for example, Bruner and associates[12]), in studying the development of children, describe three gross phases of "thinking" that most children seem to go through. The initial one of very early childhood is largely kinesthetic or "enactive," that is, the meaning of things is found through manipulating them or dealing with them with the body, touching them, feeling them, and so on. A little later, at about age four or five, children become more "ikonic," understanding the world by generating pictures. These pictures may be visual or they may be representations in any other sensory mode. And finally, particularly as an effect of education, children begin to think "symbolically," meaning, in this case, in words and numbers. Thus, post facto, one might argue that the sensitivity and encounter movements are working backward through this developmental model.

Indeed, much of what encounter groupers write and say seems consonant with this view. They, like some Zen people, are enamored of the "naturalness" of the child, a naturalness of which he has been robbed by his socialization and toward which he should return. So one way to think somewhat analytically about sensitivity training is to treat it as an effort to increase human vocabulary in the ikonic realm; and one way to think of encounter groups is as an effort to increase human vocabulary in the enactive realm. Although neither sensitivity trainers nor encounter groupers talk very much about the nature of human thinking, one can reasonably argue that if one learns to be more ikonically or enactively perceptive, one is also learning new languages of thinking. Perhaps we can learn something more by this route about how to formulate problems in nonsymbolic forms and how better to understand issues that are not easily convertible into words or numbers. For example, rational analytic thought as we know it is not sufficient for learning to swim, to play musical instruments, or to assess paintings. If we develop better "vocabularies" at the enactive and ikonic levels (whether we do it through sensitivity and encounter or some other means), perhaps new ways of working on problems like those may emerge.

Earlier I labelled this area as middle ground, although to many readers it may seem rather far-out. Certainly it is middle ground in relation to management, if not in relation to traditional rational thought. Sensitivity training is something that many managers are aware of and have utilized in their organizations. And one of its offshoots, organizational development (OD), is now widely practiced in American companies and widely taught in American business schools.[13] But OD has not been centrally concerned with thinking, either. It has been more concerned with gaining commitment, developing a kind of interpersonal "glue" in the organization, and building and maintaining strong and trusting relationships among people, especially small groups of people within the organization. Its concern with thinking has been secondary, again largely in an enabling way. If we have a good, open, trusting set of human relationships in this organization, the OD argument goes, people will not only feel more committed and work harder, they will also become freer to think more creatively and solve problems better. OD has also impinged on the broad issue of organizational problem solving in two other ways: first, by raising the question of the relationship between the personal values and needs of organizational members and organizational goal setting; and second, by continuing a longstanding effort to improve implementation of problem solutions through participative means. That is to say that OD has been concerned a little with problem finding, a lot with solution implementation, and minimally with problem solving.

There have been important bridging individuals who have carried some of the initially far-out ideas of sensitivity and encounter closer to management and closer to more traditional social science. Thus, Abraham Maslow,[14] a positive, optimistic, humanistic psychologist, while wedded to the analytic method throughout his life, also rejected narrow, tight-lipped interpretations of the analytic method, just as he rejected weirdly undisciplined and antianalytic touchies and feelies. He argued for a broader interpretation of man, with more input doors and wider boundaries for "legitimate" research into the ways that humans understand their world. And his message reached both groups; Maslow's influence on contemporary managerial thinking has been considerable. Many managers have been significantly influenced by his conception of the hierarchy of human needs and particularly by the concept of self-actualization. And so have many encounter groupers. My own view is that Maslow's major influence on managers has been to reinforce their tendency to search for the "right," the "satisfying," the "challenging" things to try to do; that is, the major influence has been toward encouraging managers to use *internal* criteria in selecting problems to work on, influence, that is, toward looking more closely into the problem-finding process.

The World of ESP

Much as many of us would like to avoid it, it doesn't seem possible to consider ideas about alternative ways of thinking without considering extrasensory perception (ESP). I once had an acquaintance who was an eminent statistician. He had been charged with assessing the evidence for and against the existence of ESP. He concluded that there were two possibilities: one was that ESP is real; the other that ESP'ers have consistently fudged their data. He himself chose the second alternative, he said, because he simply could not accept the first explanation. It generated too much dissonance.

ESP is an especially tough one for most analysts because much ESP research has taken place within the analytic ballpark, using analytic rules and analytic referees. But since there is no satisfactory analytical-theoretical basis for ESP, positive findings tend to paralyze many analysts. Most of us seem to escape the conflict by staying away from that part of the world altogether. All I am willing to do at this point is put a small pebble into the water. From my point of view there appears to be moderate analytic evidence for the presence of something like extrasensory perception in some people, but that evidence makes me feel so uncomfortable that I don't want to discuss it further.

Some Closer-In Signals

Even within the analytic camp itself a great many signal fires seem to be burning. Thus, *Time* magazine's review of some of these issues points out that among physicists, mathematicians, and philosophers of science, there is considerable disaffection with the limitations imposed by traditional rational thought.[15]

One can also hear continuing but small noises from the world of the arts. When artists do verbalize their attitudes and beliefs about thinking at all, they tend to reject the impersonal rigidities of the technically dominated world in favor of much more individualistic and intuitive rules in which every person does his own thing in his own way. But artists are not likely to have much influence in a world dominated by analysts, even though some of their ideas may be correct ones.

Perhaps the most powerful intellectual pressures on traditional analysis, as related to organizations, are emerging from a slightly deviant minority within the academic research establishment. One source is research into the nature of human thinking, much of it made possible by the development of information theory and the computer. Thus, Simon's conception—originally and self-consciously descriptive—of *satisficing* as opposed to *optimizing* suggested that most of us did not solve problems according to the textbook analytic models we had been taught.[16] We do not assemble all possible alternatives from which to choose the best, but search for any likely looking alternative. If it works, we use that one. Simon's observations suggested that even sophisticated men were locally, not broadly rational, solving problems with the aid of simple heuristic rules rather than more elaborate formal analytic schemes. "Heuristics" do not seem too different from "intuitions." In any case, Simon's description of problem-solving behavior was not intended to apply only to muddle-headed problem solvers, but to scientists, good chess players, and even management analysts.

Simon tried mostly to describe and model behavior. He did not propose that people *should* approach problems heuristically, satisficingly, locally. But he almost did, for he pointed out that the costs of satisficing were usually much lower than the costs of rigid applications of optimizing methods. Over the last few years, there has been a tendency, as has so often been the case, gradually to convert what was originally descriptive into a more normative form—to suggest that the halfway rationality of satisficing may be *better* in many instances than the full-scale analytic rationality of optimizing. A somewhat similar view, but more unabashedly normative, has been offered by the political scientist Lindblom,[17] who defends the strategy of "muddling through" as an effective, albeit a non-beautiful strategy.

From a somewhat different perspective, one of the strongest cases for reconsideration of the analytic method has been made from within the fortress of management science and systems analysis itself. The management scientist-philosopher West Churchman, in his *A Challenge to Reason*, examines the limitations of analysis thoughtfully and fully. He attacks rationality, but also defends it, arguing that a critical self-appraisal of reason surely will not destroy it.[18]

Research on creativity has also generated some consideration of possible alternatives and supplements to the analytic method. The work on thinking already mentioned has cast some light on the nature of creativity, but not full light. Analysts have been able to count creativity, perhaps even partially to understand it, but not to generate or manage it in organizations. It has, in my view, been the less analytic, more imaginative researchers who have come up with the most useful ideas to date for the management of creativity. If you want to know how to get creativity into your organization, you are better off looking to brainstormers and exponents of "lateral thinking"[19] than to more classical analytic researchers.

Certainly until recently, if you wanted to find out about creativity, you did not go to most engineers (who are the predecessors of the new analysts). They not only didn't know much about creativity, they weren't creative. At least there is some analytic evidence[20, 21] developed in studies of engineering students that shows a decline in imaginativeness-creativity (as measured by standard tests) over the period of undergraduate engineering education, while over the same period undergraduate students in fine arts show higher and higher levels of imaginativeness, but at the cost of analytic skills. That is to say, the two sets of students diverge: the engineers become more analytic (left-brain dominant?) and less imaginative, the fine arts students becoming more imaginative (right-brain dominant?) and less analytic. Moreover, given certain analytic-type problems, engineers solved them most of the time, but they did less well at discovering the most elegant solution than did fine arts students. Fine arts students often failed to solve the problem at all; but when they did, they were apt to do so through the discovery of a better way than the engineers had discovered.

At any rate, it appears that certain kinds of professional training may increase analytic skills at the cost of imaginative skills. This tendency seems to be particularly true of engineering education, but some of my unpublished data suggest it may also be directionally true of graduate education in management science. Indeed, these divergent processes probably start much earlier than the undergraduate years.[22]

The work on styles of thinking associated with particular professions has obvious implications for management. If analytic education drives out imagination, and we want "imaginative" problem finding, problem solving, and problem implementing, then we had better be careful about overcrowding our organization with analysts and about maintaining an organizational climate dominated by the analytic tradition.

A strong intellectual case for nonanalytic supplements to analytic thinking is now also being made at the organizational level. Cohen and March, for example, have put forward the notion of "organized anarchy."[23] They argue, in effect, that many organizations delude themselves into believing that they analytically set their goals. Although executives may believe that they "control" their organizations and steer them toward those goals, March proposes that they in fact exert relatively little influence on the directions in which their organizations move.[24] He proposes further that organizations do not really set their goals in an analytic sense; rather, they tend to find out where they are going by looking at where they have been. And he goes on to suggest that exaggerated insistence upon consistency and other rules of rationality may often be dysfunctional.

We can turn, for a moment, from the analytic method to its mother, rationality. One area, much closer in to conventional analytic thought, from which new proposals relevant to the nature of rationality itself are beginning to emerge is in work on the "externalities" problem, or what Platt has called "social traps."[25] One problem is simply that there are many cases in which "rationality" in an individual sense may generate irrationality in a group sense. It may be to my personal advantage, for instance, to use clean public lake water, pollute it, and send it back into the river to kill the fish. If only I pollute, the water will stay clean enough for my use. While that may be rational behavior in the sense that it maximizes my self-interest, it may, of course, become irrational in another sense. If many users should pollute simultaneously, the water may become unusable for all of them. Platt cites a host of such dilemmas and he and his group propose some ways out. In the same vein, Rubenstein, using data from a pollution game, raises a distinction between "rational individualism" and "rational groupism."[26] Thus, if all individuals in a group deny their individual self-interest in favor of the group's interest, they are rational as a group, but it may be argued that their behavior is irrational as individuals.

It may be that these issues do not raise questions of the analytic method itself or of alternatives to rationality, but only of alternative forms of rationality. So be it. But some widely held and rather simplistic conceptions of rationality are being examined nonetheless, and in a realm in which there are strong implications for important managerial problems: competitive behavior, social responsibility, long-range planning.

As suggested in Part I, still another potentially rich direction may lie in exploration of the thinking and problem-solving styles of salient minorities in our society (or in other societies), some of whom seem to use nonanalytic methods rather effectively. Thus far, as organizations have incorporated more blacks and Chicanos and women into their managerial ranks, they have also tried to socialize them into behaving like WASP, male managers. The slow rise of members of minority groups and women into key managerial positions may not be entirely the result of traditional racial or sexual prejudices, but also prejudices about "good" managerial thinking. Some of the soulful and perhaps impulsive thinking that is stereotypically associated with blacks, or the intuitive thinking associated with women, might turn out to be more useful for managing than it seemed a decade ago. It may be time to bring minorities and women into the organization, not to be socialized into prevailing white male managerial styles, but to socialize male managers into alternative styles.

Much less radical but directionally similar changes have been creeping into management education. Almost all schools of management now include a set of behavioral courses. That was not true twenty years ago. This entry of psychology and sociology occurred concurrently with the growth of quantitative analysis and, not surprisingly, it generated some problems. In some schools behavioral courses were approved only if they met the dominant analytic criteria. In those schools behavioral science has been taught as hard science—empirically, analytically. Many business students didn't find that very useful. In some other schools, a softer form of behavioral science was developing, preferred by students, less by the analytic faculty. Human-relations courses, sensitivity training, and other more empathetic approaches grew up. Those, helped by growing student interest in their own souls and their own skills, gradually and unevenly gained ascendancy both in MBA and in-company curriculums. But the process has been costly and painful, especially for the academic careers of young, nonanalytic faculty members. Predominantly analytic faculties have remained suspicious and often hostile.

As new generations of students enter business schools, including an increasing percentage of women and minorities, further pressures should build up in the same direction. If we return to our tripartite model of problem finding, problem solving and problem implementing, we should see more experimental efforts to teach implementation skills, because that is reasonably palatable to analysts. Managers, after all, are like physicians. They realize that they need skillful bedside manners. The strong analytic thrust of the last couple of decades has left an "implementation gap," noticeable even to analysts. Behavioral people offering courses designed to build up the analytic student's influencing skills, his muddling-through skills, and his human relations skills, do not seem very dangerous or very stupid. Offering "creativity" courses in most business schools is still a little far off, though such courses are turning up in engineering curriculums.

The same trend seems even more apparent within business organizations. Further efforts toward new ways of problem finding (such as brainstorming)—to free people up, to reduce cognitive rigidities—seem to be more frequent. The growing interest in executive sabbaticals[27] and three-day bull sessions in the mountains is part of the picture. Can they not be interpreted as searches for (or forms of) alternatives to the analytic method? And among a subgroup of organizational theorists at least, the notion of *organizational playfulness* is being seriously discussed.[23, 28] They suggest that organizations might usefully (and temporarily) abrogate normal organizational rules and constraints for certain of their members so that those members can "play," and by playing perhaps discover not only new ways of approaching old problems, but new goals, new interests, and new objectives.

At least two aspects of the problem-finding issue are distinguishable in all this. One is a pragmatic issue, the issue of building more creativity and innovativeness into the organization. How do we make ourselves more imaginative to help us create new products or new services or new ways of organizing? The other is a value issue, a concern with some underlying questions about what it's all for; what's the meaning of things; what are the "really" important things the organization might try to do.

The two issues are probably not independent. My own guess is that we will see much more managerial interest and many more "experiments" into both of these issues in the next few years. Some of the efforts will be extensions of techniques that have been around for a good while—brainstorming, managerial retreats, and the like. Most of those efforts have thus far been justified pragmatically as means to greater innovativeness in the organization. I think, however, that in the future a larger proportion of them will be aimed at the deeper moral and value issues, as a response to our society's increasing pressures on the organization to reexamine its traditional behavior.

Summary

Part I of this article proposed that analytic thinking and analytic thinkers, recent heroes of U.S. management and of U.S. society, have run into trouble. Broad social changes toward humanism have included strongly antianalytic components. And within management itself there seems to be a growing disillusion with what had appeared to be the almost limitless potential of the management scientist.

The analytic method, in its computer-assisted form, has been accused of missing unmeasurable subtleties, of redefining the real problems into forms that fit the method but miss the point, and of naivete and arrogance in its dealings with human problems of input and implementation.

I have proposed that if we broaden our usual conception of problem solving into at least a tripartite model—problem finding, problem solving, and problem implementing—some of the issues surrounding the analyst in management may be clarified. Improving analytic training and analytic skill have contributed enormously to the problem-solving segment of that three-step process. The softer, applied parts of the behavioral sciences have contributed little to that aspect of the process, but they are making a modest contribution to the implementation segment.

It appears, however, that neither quantitative analytic people nor conventional behavioral scientists have contributed much, or even worried very much about, problem finding. Attention now does seem to be focusing more on that issue, both in management and in other fields.

But useful alternatives and supplements to the analytic method have been few and poorly integrated into management. Perhaps that is because the assumptions underlying most of the alternatives are radically different from those assumptions about rationality underlying the analytic method.

The analytic method has tried to understand the world by taking it apart, by identifying the pieces and their relationships with one another. In effect, the analytic method has tried to improve upon raw natural man by inventing particular new ways of dealing with problems and then training men to use them. The analytic way, grossly speaking, involves working any problem backward into subparts and their interconnections, and then putting the pieces back together. In contrast, most of the alternatives we have considered here seem to fall into a broadly different category. They are what might be called *fertilizer approaches* to problems, as distinct from the *analytic approaches*. The fertilizer approaches do not try to analyze the insides of the problem so much as they try to manage the conditions under which man thinks about the problem. So, for example, they try to understand creativity not by analyzing the inner nature of the creative process, but by discovering the situational conditions under which humans will become more creative.

They treat the inner man as a rather mysterious and marvelous black box, capable of all sorts of things—if the conditions are right. Hence, the alternative methods tend toward heuristics more than algorithms and toward higher variance in the results generated (since each black box is a little different). They require implicit trust in the capacity of man, and hence tend to look more humanistic and less evaluative. And they search continuously for other conditions and situations that might fertilize new kinds of growth.

To a considerable extent, the fertilizer way is an old way of doing things, perhaps even a preanalytic way. But given what we have learned from the analytic method, we may now be able to use that old way more effectively. If it will make analysts more comfortable, they can think of the fertilizer methods as temporary, to be used only until analytic methods become even more encompassing in the realms that analysis does not yet encompass well enough.

And although more analytic work is surely ahead of us, movement in the other directions seems certain too—not just more deeply (and more distantly) into finding analytic means for coping with everything, but rather into integrating wisdom and feeling with analysis. There are good social and psychological reasons why such integration will prove difficult. Training in the analytic style tends to drive out intuitive and empathetic styles. Socialization into one style causes suspicion and hostility toward others. But some individual analysts do seem capable of such integration. Those individuals are worth a great deal. And occasionally, within an organization, one encounters a group of persons of differing styles who seem to be able to communicate and work well together. Perhaps we can generate educational and organizational changes that will speed up such integration both within and among individuals.

NOTES

1. C. T. Tart, ed., *Altered States of Consciousness* (New York: John Wiley & Sons, 1969).
2. C. Casteneda, *Voyage to Ixtlan* (New York: Simon & Schuster, 1972).
3. See, for example, Frankel's defense of rationality against the attacks of the hostile "irrationalists": C. Frankel, "The Nature and Sources of Irrationalism," *Science* (June 1973), pp. 927-993.
4. E. Herrigel, *Zen and the Art of Archery* (London: Pantheon, 1953), p. 11.
5. C. Naranjo and R. Ornstein, *On the Psychology of Meditation* (New York: Viking, 1971; an Esalen book), p. 9.
6. R. E. Ornstein, *The Psychology of Consciousness* (San Francisco: W. H. Freeman, 1972), pp. 156-157.
7. R. W. Sperry, "A Modified Concept of Consciousness," *Psychological Review*, Vol. 76 (1969), pp. 532-536.
8. M. S. Gazanniga, *Bisected Brain* (New York: Appleton, 1970).
9. K. W. Back, *Beyond Words* (Baltimore: Penguin Books, 1973).
10. H. J. Leavitt and R. Doktor, "Personal Growth, Laboratory Training, Science and All That: A Shot at a Cognitive Clarification," *Journal of Applied Behavioral Science* Vol. 6 (1967), pp. 173-179.
11. Two exceptions are R. D. Laing, *The Politics of Experience* (Baltimore: Penguin, 1967) and W. E. Schutz, *Joy* (New York: Grove Press, 1967).
12. J. Bruner, et al., *Studies in Cognitive Growth* (New York: John Wiley & Sons, 1966).
13. W. G. Bennis, *Organizational Development: Its Nature, Origins and Prospects* (Reading, Mass.: Addison-Wesley, 1969; part of Addison-Wesley series in Organization Development).
14. A. Maslow, *The Farther Reaches of Human Nature* (New York: Viking, 1971).
15. "Second Thoughts About Man—IV: 'Reaching Beyond the Rational,' " *Time*, 23 April 1973.
16. H. Simon, *Models of Man* (New York: Harper & Row, 1960).
17. C. E. Lindblom, "The Science of Muddling Through," *Public Administrative Review*, XXIX (1959), pp. 78-88.
18. C. W. Churchman, *A Challenge to Reason* (New York: McGraw Hill, 1968).
19. E. deBono, *Lateral Thinking: Creativity Step by Step* (New York: Harper & Row, 1970).
20. R. Altemeyer, "Education in the Arts and Sciences: Divergent Paths" (Doctoral dissertation, Carnegie Institute of Technology, 1966).
21. R. Doktor, "The Development and Mapping of Certain Cognitive Styles of Problem Solving" (Doctoral dissertation, Graduate School of Business, Stanford University, 1970).
22. L. Hudson, *Contrary Imaginations: A Psychological Study of the Young Student* (New York: Schocken Books, 1966).
23. M. D. Cohen and J. G. March, *Leadership and Ambiguity* (New York: McGraw Hill, 1974).
24. J. March, "The Technology of Foolishness," in H. J. Leavitt et al., eds., *Organization-Environment Relations in the Future* (New York: Praeger, forthcoming).
25. J. Platt, "Social Traps," *American Psychologist* (August 1973).
26. F. Rubenstein, "A Behavioral Study of Pollution: The Role of Perceived Instrumentality in an Externality Situation," doctoral dissertation, Graduate School of Business, Stanford University, 1971.
27. E. Goldston, "Executive Sabbaticals: About to Take Off?" *Harvard Business Review* (September-October 1973).
28. H. J. Leavitt, L. T. Pinfield, and E. J. Webb, *Organization-Environment Relations in the Future* (New York: Praeger, 1974).

INDEX

Albrook, Robert C., 265
Al-Tajir, Mehdi, 404–05
American Telephone & Telegraph
    Co., 265, 292–308, 357–58, 470
Ardrey, Robert, 194, 196
Argyris, Chris, 35–36, 97, 101, 106, 463

Bennis, Warren G., 36, 120, 464
Berle, Adolf A., 31, 337, 341–42, 347
Black, Eli, 393–95
Blacks. See Negroes
Blake, Robert R., 115
Blau, Peter, 468
Blauner, Robert, 100–01
Brzezinski, Zbigniew, 459, 467
Burck, Gilbert, 411
Bureaucracy. See Organizations,
    bureaucratic forms of
Burgen, Carl, 446
Burns, Thomas S., 129

Carlisle, Arthur Elliott, 129
Carmichael, Steve, 228
Cassell, Frank H., 330
Chandler, Alfred Du Pont, Jr., 453,
    465
Chief executive officers (CEO):
    compensation of, 444–45, 475–84,
        487;
    external selection of, 261;
    internal selection of, 260–61, 263;
    transferability of, 257–64.
    See also Management; Managers
Churchman, C. West, 180, 189–90, 508
Clark, James V., 278–79
Community Action Program (CAP),
    377–79, 383
Corporations:
    community relations of, 364–65,
        371–84, 486–87 (see also
        Management, social
        responsibility of);
    ethics in, 245–49, 329–30, 332;
    foreign payoffs by, 385–410;
    optimum size of, 203–06;
    optimum size of groups in, 201–03;
    organization of, 445, 447–57, 462–69
        (see also Organizations);
    role of, in eroding individualism,
        56, 356–57, 363;
    size of, affecting competition, 342,
        469–70;
    size of, affecting managers'
        attitudes, 63–78, 234, 468;
    size of, affecting
        personality-organization conflict,
        100;
    status hierarchy in, 196–99;
    territorial defense in, 199
Crick, Francis, 195–96
Cyert, RIchard M., 91–92

Dale, Ernest, 258, 465
Davis, Louis, 280
Davis, Sheldon, 279
Dawes, Robyn M., 186, 188
DeButts, John, 229
De Tocqueville, Alexis, 22, 109, 119
Diebold, John, 411
Dorsey, Bob R., 398–400
Drucker, Peter, 115, 123–24, 162, 190, 192, 376, 398, 445–46, 465, 489
Dubin, Robert, 102–03

Eells, Richard, 347, 489
Ellul, Jacques, 125
Energoinvest, 413–28
Exxon Corporation, 395–97

Fayol, Henri, 449–50, 452, 457
First National City Bank (N.Y.), 320–21
Follett, Mary Parker, 123
Ford, Henry II, 340–41, 346
Ford, Robert, 265
Friedman, Milton, 340

Gardell, Bertil, 84–85
Geneen, Harold, 163–70
General Electric Co., 45–49, 448
General Motors Corp., 358–59, 363, 449–51, 465–67, 472
Gerstenberg, Richard C., 351, 352, 370
Goldthorpe, John, 87
Gomberg, William, 277–78
Graves, Clare, 276
Grayson, C. Jackson, 130, 183
Gross, Ernest, 94
Gulf Oil Corp., 398–400, 406

Halberstam, David, 210, 217
Hart, David K., 1, 18, 24
Hellriegel, Don, 130
Helmich, Robert, 258
Herzberg, Frederick, 85, 97, 107, 312

International Confederation of Executive Staffs (ICES), 492, 494
International Telephone & Telegraph Corp., 163–70, 360, 361

Jay, Antony, 130
Job enrichment, 88–90, 95–96, 143, 265, 292–308, 309–17;
    correlated with job satisfaction, 88–90;
    elements of, 313–14
Job "nesting", 293, 301–06
Job satisfaction:
    correlated with company size, 64–65;
    correlated with job enrichment, 88–90;
    correlated with job level, 66, 85, 86–87;
    correlated with job specialization, 85;
    correlated with self-actualization, 83–84
Jung, Carl, 221–22, 223, 231;
    personality theory of, 221–26, 231

Kahneman, Daniel, 184–85, 186, 188, 189
Kappel, Frederick R., 348
Kay, Andrew, 278–79
Khashoggi, Adnan, 401–02, 403, 405
Kim, S. K., 398–400
Kraar, Louis, 411

Labor unions:
    role of, in eroding individualism, 356–58, 363–64
Lakin, Martin, 265
Lawrence, Paul, 274–75, 277
Lazarus, Ralph, 129
Leavitt, Harold J., 100, 104, 130, 274, 446
Levitt, Theodore, 342–43, 344
Lewis, Ben W., 343–44
Likert, Rensis, 105, 113, 269–72, 273, 281
Lilienthal, David, 1
Lockheed Aircraft Corp., 403, 405
Lodge, George Cabot, 329–30
Lorenz, Konrad, 193, 194, 196
Lorsch, Jay, 274

Mace, Myles, 482–83
Management information systems, 92, 188

Management:
  accountability of, 334, 336, 341–42,
    358–59, 483–84, 486, 489–90;
  in China, 434–44;
  in Japan, 429–33;
  in Yugoslavia, 414–28;
  profit maximization by, 271–72,
    329, 331, 333, 339–49, 379, 380,
    487;
  selection of, 336, 359;
  social responsibility of, 1, 7, 11–14,
    329, 331–37, 339–49, 371–84,
    486–88, 490 (see also
    Corporations, community
    relations of);
  unionization of, 491–97.
  See also Chief executive officers;
  Managers
Management, line, 77, 162–66, 172,
    204, 209, 380
Management, staff, 57, 77, 162–66,
    204, 209
Management science, 129–30, 171–82,
    183, 187–92, 207;
  compared with management,
    171–82, 187, 188, 189–92
Management styles:
  analytic, 191–92, 207–18, 236, 239,
    503–13;
  authoritative, 268–72;
  centralized, 162–63, 466–67;
  collective, 489;
  decentralized, 162, 449, 462–64,
    465–66, 468, 469;
  determined by business type,
    274–75;
  determined by personalities,
    275–76;
  intuitive, 191–92;
  nonanalytic, 498–513;
  open ("astronaut"), 149, 150–51,
    152–53;
  participative, 99, 105–06, 133–34,
    145, 265, 267–81, 462;
  persuasive, 159–60;
  structured ("homesteader"),
    148–49, 150, 152
Managers:
  compared with management
    scientists, 172–82, 187–88, 189–92;
  early career problems of, 233–52;
  function of, 3, 8, 10–11, 146–47, 364;
  historical role of, 3–7;
  level of, 75, 77;
  personalities of, 58–60, 71–72,
    222–26.
  See also Chief executive officers;
  Management
March, James, 91–92, 467, 509
Maslow, A. H., 72–73, 96, 97, 98, 312,
    455, 506. See also Needs,
    hierarchy of
Mason, Edward S., 337, 342
McDonald, Alonzo L., Jr., 490
McGregor, Douglas, 97, 113, 276,
    312–13, 376
McGuire, Joseph W., 340, 349
McNamara, Robert, 91, 209, 210–11,
    258
McNeill, W. H., 4–5
Means, Gardiner C., 31, 341
Miewald, Robert D., 36
Milgram, Stanley, 23, 32
Mintzberg, Henry, 146, 261
Mobile Oil Corporation, 395–97
Mommsen, Wolfgang, 126
Morris, Desmond, 194, 196
Mott, Stewart Rawlings, 226–28
Multinational corporations, 398, 451
Murthy, K. R. Srinivasa, 445

Nash, Manning, 277
National Alliance of Businessmen,
    378, 383
National Training Laboratories, 277,
    278, 284, 285
Needs, hierarchy of, 72–73, 97–98,
    506. See also Maslow, A. H.
Negroes, employment of, 11, 318–24,
    372–73, 488
Nehemkis, Peter, 330
Nixon, Richard M., 358, 361, 383, 385,
    487
Northrop Corp., 400–01, 405, 406

Organizational development, 505–06
Organizational imperative, 15–34
Organizations:
  administrative norms of, 18–22;
  bureaucratic forms of, 109–19,
    120–26;

Organizations *(cont.)*
  future structures of, 118–19, 445;
  impact of technological change on,
    458–73;
  influence of, on cultural values,
    22–32;
  influence of, on individual
    behavior, 35–36, 54–61, 76–78,
    79–96, 98–107;
  needs of, 15–34;
  structure of, 454–57.
  See also Corporations, organization
    of
Oskamp, S., 188

Patai, Raphael, 402
Peery, Newman S., Jr., 131
Perrow, Charles, 90–91, 445
Personality and organization theory,
  79–80, 91, 93, 94. *See also*
  Corporations;
  Organizations
Petit, Thomas A., 329
Phillips, Charles F., Jr., 329
Porter, Lyman, 35
Power equalization. *See* Management
  styles, participative
Presidential Personnel Interchange
  Program, 180
Price Commission, 130, 171–73,
  176–78
Problem finding, 214–15, 498, 502, 513
Problem solving, 17–18, 214, 498,
  512–13;
  styles of, 191, 220–31
Profit maximization. *See*
  Management, profit
  maximization by
Protestant ethic, 21, 39, 40, 58, 63, 310,
  356

Rabbie, Jaap, 115
Riesman, David, 71, 310
Rockefeller, David, 339
Roethlisberger, Fritz J., 281
Ross-Skinner, Jean, 446
Rostow, Eugene V., 345

Salter, Malcolm S., 445
Sayles, Leonard, 266

Scott, William G., 1, 18, 24
Securities and Exchange
  Commission, 385–388, 392, 394,
  401–02, 405, 407
Self-actualization, 95, 100, 101–02,
  293, 463, 506;
  correlated with job satisfaction,
    83–84
Sensitivity training, 265, 277–78,
  282–91, 502–03, 505
Shapiro, Irving, 230
Shetty, Y. K., 131
Silberman, Charles E., 266, 471
Simon, Herbert, 91, 93–94, 97, 106,
  467, 507–08
Sloan, Alfred P., Jr., 359, 363, 448–50,
  451, 452, 457, 465–66
Slocum, John W., Jr., 130
Slovic, Paul, 186–87
Social responsibility. *See*
  Management, social
  responsibility of
Solution implementing, 156–61, 214,
  498, 512
Strategy Center, 373–75
Strauss, George, 36, 312–13

Taylor, Frederick W., 81, 90
Torgerson, W. S., 187
Training programs, 37–40, 50–51;
  Ford Motor Company, 51–52;
  General Electric Company, 45–49;
  Vick Chemical Company, 40–45
Turner, Arthur N., 277
Tversky, Amos, 184–85, 186, 188, 189

United Auto Workers, 363–64, 367
United Brands Company, 392–95

Webber, Ross, 130
Weber, Max, 81, 120–23, 462–63
Wertheimer, Michael, 208
Western Electric Company, 313
Whyte, William H., Jr., 20–21, 35,
  63–64, 74
Wicker, Allan, 85–86
Wilensky, Harold, 86
Wilson, Charles R., 129

Wolff, Harold, 466
Women, employment of, as
    managers, 325–28, 488
Worthy, James, 65

Yntema, D. B., 187

Zeleny, Milan, 130